Provided in Memory
of

Stanton Watts Pickens
1906–1968

Captain, Medical Administrative Corp, U. S. Army
38th Evacuation Hospital
1942–1945

38TH EVAC

THE STORY OF THE MEN AND WOMEN WHO SERVED IN WORLD WA

38ᵀᴴ EVAC

H THE 38th EVACUATION HOSPITAL IN NORTH AFRICA AND ITALY

JEL 38TH EVACUATION HOSPITAL FORT BRAGG, N.C.
JULY 26, 1942

By LeGETTE BLYTHE

Books by LeGette Blythe

MARSHAL NEY: A DUAL LIFE
ALEXANDRIANA
SHOUT FREEDOM!
BOLD GALILEAN
WILLIAM HENRY BELK: MERCHANT OF THE SOUTH
A TEAR FOR JUDAS
MIRACLE IN THE HILLS (with Mary Martin Sloop, M.D.)
VOICE IN THE WILDERNESS
JAMES W. DAVIS: NORTH CAROLINA SURGEON
THE CROWN TREE
YES, MA'AM, MISS GEE (with Mary Wilson Gee)
GIFT FROM THE HILLS (with Lucy Morgan)
CALL DOWN THE STORM
THOMAS WOLFE AND HIS FAMILY (with Mabel Wolfe Wheaton)
HEAR ME, PILATE!
HORNETS' NEST: THE STORY OF CHARLOTTE AND MECKLENBURG COUNTY
    (with Charles R. Brockmann)
ECHO IN MY SOUL (with Septima Clark)
MOUNTAIN DOCTOR
MAN ON FIRE
ROBERT LEE STOWE: PIONEER IN TEXTILES
38TH EVAC

Copyright © 1966 by LeGette Blythe
Manufactured in the United States of America
Heritage Printers, Inc.   Charlotte, N. C.

TO THE MEN AND WOMEN OF THE 38th WHO YET SERVE
AND IN GRATEFUL REMEMBRANCE OF THOSE OTHERS
WHOSE TERMS OF ENLISTMENT HAVE BEEN COMPLETED

FOREWORD

By General Mark W. Clark, U.S.A., Retired

In combat art, in conversation among high ranking officers, and in minds of Army Medical Service personnel, our medics were the unsung heroes of World War II. A better gauge of the place of medics in history, however, is the attitude of the doughboy, and in his mind the medic is invariably a heroic figure of the first magnitude. I agree with the doughboy's image of the medic because my observation of the invaluable role played by the medical service in North Africa, in Italy, and in Korea convinces me that no nobler achievements were attained in those theaters than the selfless accomplishments of medical personnel.

Since I was keenly aware of the practical value of effective medical service, including the morale factor associated with their work, I continually inspected medical units and installations and constantly evaluated the quality of their performance. In the process of these assessments, I came to realize that there was no finer medical unit than the 750-bed 38th Evacuation Hospital. I watched it mature as it gained Tunisian experience and I saw the payoff on the beaches of Salerno and Anzio and through the long familiar list of areas in Italy where this unit performed its near miraculous "healing ministry" throughout the Italian campaign.

My respect for this unit gave me special affection for the men who led it and for those who comprised its ranks. The friendships I formed with many of its personnel have lasted through the years, and I still number among my closest friends several veterans of this splendid organization.

I know the good that the men of the 38th Evacuation Hospital accomplished with the almost countless casualties they treated on the battlefields did not terminate there. Instead, many of the medical lessons learned in the performance of their awesome wartime duties have been passed on to our present-day society and have contributed in a material way to the saving of lives in peace time and to the fantastic upward trend in the life span of our people.

Nothing could please me more than for the spirit of the 38th to be preserved in a history such as this. I am delighted that it has been undertaken, and honored that I was asked to write this foreword to a publication that records for posterity the attainments and trials of such a magnificent military unit.

CALENDAR

Unit activated at Fort Bragg, North Carolina
15 April 1942

Fort Bragg, North Carolina
15 April 1942 to 31 July 1942

Indiantown Gap, Pa.
1 August 1942 to 5 August 1942

New York City, New York
6 August 1942

ENGLAND

Liverpool, England
17 August 1942

Huyten Park Camp, Liverpool, England
18 August 1942 to 20 August 1942

Tidworth Park Camp, England
20 August 1942 to 10 September 1942

Musgrove Park Military Hospital, Taunton, England
10 September 1942 to 5 October 1942

Norton Manor Camp, Somerset, England
5 October 1942 to 25 October 1942

Bristol, England
23 October 1942

Gourdek, Scotland
24 October 1942 (at sea)

NORTH AFRICA

Arzew, Algeria, Africa
8 November 1942 to 9 November 1942

St. Cloud, Algeria, Africa
10 November 1942 to 2 March 1943

Oran, Algeria
2 March 1943

El Guerrah, Africa
4 March 1943 to 9 March 1943

Telergma, Africa
9 March 1943 to 2 May 1943

Beja, Africa
2 May 1943 to 21 June 1943

CALENDAR

Tunis, Tunisia, Africa
21 June 1943 to 3 September 1943

Oran, Algeria, Africa
7 September 1943 to 15 September 1943

ITALY

Blue Beach, 25 miles south of Salerno, Italy
21 September 1943

Paestum, Italy
21 September 1943 to 16 October 1943

Caserta, Italy
16 October 1943 to 7 November 1943

Vairano, Italy
7 November 1943 to 26 March 1944

Carinola, Italy
26 March 1944 to 8 April 1944

Anzio Beachhead, Italy
9 April 1944

Nettuno, Italy
9 April 1944 to 8 June 1944

Doria Pamphilli, Rome, Italy
9 June 1944 to 30 June 1944

Massa Marittima, Italy
1 July 1944 to 17 July 1944

St. Luce, Italy
18 July 1944 to 13 September 1944

Pisa, Italy
14 September 1944 to 9 November 1944

Montecatini, Italy
10 November 1944 to 21 April 1945

Marzabotto, Italy
22 April 1945 to 29 April 1945

Fidenza, Italy
30 April 1945 to 26 May 1945

Salsomaggiore, Italy
26 May 1945 to 3 July 1945

Florence Redeployment Training Area, Florence, Italy
3 July 1945

1

American military historians, seeking perhaps years from now to discover the time and place of birth of Charlotte's famed World War II Evacuation Hospital Unit, might be expected to search the records of the various Charlotte hospitals.

But they won't find the vital statistics there. The 38th was not born in a hospital.

Officially organization of the unit was approved at the War Department in Washington early in January of 1941. Actually the 38th was born three months earlier at a lawn party in Charlotte on October 12, 1940. The birth was precipitated by a football game played earlier that afternoon in Charlotte's American Legion Memorial Stadium.

The circumstances of the 38th's birth provide an intriguing story.

In the early fall of 1940, General George C. Marshall, Chief of Staff of the United States Army, tired after many months of directing the nation's defense preparations in a world situation that daily was growing more alarming, had accepted the invitation of his Charlotte brother-in-law E. P. Coles to spend a few days resting at the Coles home. The planned visit would also give the General an opportunity to see the football team of his alma mater, Virginia Military Institute, play the eleven from Davidson College.

But a few days after the Marshalls had accepted the invitation to come to Charlotte, Secretary of War Henry L. Stimson and Mrs. Stimson announced that they were giving a reception for members of the General Staff. General Marshall felt that he and Mrs. Marshall should cancel their plans for the Charlotte visit and instead attend the Stimsons' reception.

Mrs. Marshall, however, thought that the Charlotte trip would provide her husband a few days of needed relaxation, and she spoke to the Secretary of War about it.

Mr. Stimson agreed with Mrs. Marshall. But how, he asked her, could he tell the General not to come to his reception but to go to Charlotte.

"Give him an official order," the General's lady suggested.

So the next morning Secretary Stimson with a wry grin handed the Chief of Staff an order. The General read:

The President of the United States directs that General George C. Marshall during the period between Friday, October 11th, and Monday, October 14th, shall visit the city of Charlotte, North Carolina, for the purpose of making a report upon the comparative skill and valor of the football teams of Davidson and Virginia Military Institute.

During said period he shall be under the exclusive control and direction of Mrs. Marshall and shall be protected against all interruptions, particularly by members of the War Department and of the Congress.

During said period the War Department shall be relegated to the tender mercies of the Secretary of War, the Assistant Secretary of War, and the Deputy Chief of Staff, General Bryden.

(Signed) Henry L. Stimson

The Marshalls went to Charlotte. In further pursuance of the order given him by Secretary Stimson, he sat in the stands on Saturday afternoon, October 12, and watched his school's team in a warmly fought game defeat the Davidson Wildcats 13 to 7. And as a result of his compliance with the happily-contrived order to attend the football game, Charlotte's soon to be widely heralded hospital unit was proposed and soon afterward organized.

It was after the football game, however, at a party on the lawn of the Martin L. Cannon home that General Marshall in chatting with Dr. Paul W. Sanger, a Charlotte surgeon, first considered the possibility of the organization by Charlotte medical men of a military hospital unit. Charlotte, Dr. Sanger told the General, as one of the South's most important medical centers was the home of numerous specialists of national reputation in various fields as well as scores of skilled general practitioners. These men, said Dr. Sanger, were anxious to make their contributions to the rapidly developing effort to prepare the nation's defenses to withstand any assault that might be made upon them.

The staff of Charlotte Memorial Hospital on the night of April 8, 1942, honored the commissioned officers of the newly formed 38th Evacuation Hospital unit at a dinner party at the Myers Park Club. One week later the unit was activated at Fort Bragg, North Carolina. Shown, left to right, are the following: seated, R. S. Dickson, chairman of Memorial Hospital's executive committee; Dr. Raymond Thompson, chairman of dinner arrangements committee; and Major Richard Z. Query; standing, Major George T. Wood, Major Paul W. Sanger, Lieutenant-Colonel T. Preston White, and Captain H. Stokes Munroe. (Charlotte Observer staff photo.)

General Marshall was impressed. He promised Dr. Sanger that he would give the proposal careful consideration. There was one serious obstacle, however, in the way of the organization by Charlotte physicians of a military hospital unit. The War Department by a long established policy required such units to be organized under the sponsorship of medical schools. And Charlotte had no such institution.

Since the medical staff of Charlotte Memorial Hospital was such a highly qualified group, however, and so recognized, it was hoped that the War Department's policy might be relaxed to permit the hospital to sponsor the organization of a military hospital unit. On December 1, some six weeks after General Marshall's visit to Charlotte, Dr. Brodie C. Nalle, the hospital's chief of staff, in a telegram to the Surgeon General of the Army, asked if the hospital could sponsor such a unit.

On December 13 in a letter written December 2 by Lieutenant Colonel Francis M. Fitts, Medical Corps Assistant, Dr. Nalle received the answer to his inquiry:

My dear Dr. Nalle:

The Surgeon General has directed me to acknowledge your telegram of December 1st, and to inform you that he is pleased to be able to extend to the Charlotte Memorial Hospital an invitation to organize a military Evacuation Hospital as an affiliated unit of the Medical Department of the United States Army.

I am inclosing a compilation of the War Department directives governing such units, together with copies of Table of Organization and of Training Regulations No. 405-960. I feel that careful perusal of those will present rather adequately the proposal and the conditions of affiliation. Should the hospital authorities decide to make a formal request to the Adjutant General for authorization to organize an Evacuation Hospital, the application should be forwarded through the Commanding General, 4th Corps Area, Atlanta, Ga.

When approved, I will send the necessary blank forms to accomplish the appointment in the Officers' Reserve Corps of those individuals recommended for assignment to the unit. If eligible individuals now in the Officers' Reserve Corps are desired for assignment in their existing grades, only the names need be submitted. If desired for a higher grade, application for a new appointment should be forwarded together with report of physical examination.

It is not contemplated that affiliated units will be mobilized in connection with the present limited emergency, nor are those who are appointed in the Officers' Reserve Corps for assignment to affiliated units eligible for extended active duty. Others, however, now in the Officers' Reserve Corps, assigned to these units in existing grade, are eligible for duty and may be selected for twelve months' service by the Corps Area Commander prior to transfer to the jurisdiction of the Surgeon General; the War Department will issue orders in the cases of those who have so been transferred.

Very truly yours,
Francis M. Fitts
Lt. Colonel, Medical
Corps Assistant

Dr. Nalle's response was immediate. The next day, December 14, 1940, he wrote to the Commanding General of the 4th Corps Area, Atlanta:

Dear Sir:

As per letter from war department, office of Surgeon General 326.01-1, FMF-mw.

In reply to letter of above, we wish to make a formal application to organize an Evacuation Hospital, Charlotte Memorial Hospital of Charlotte, North Carolina, and wish to apply for the necessary blanks to be sent to us from the 4th Corps Area.

Very truly yours,
Brodie C. Nalle,
Chief of Staff, Charlotte
Memorial Hospital
Charlotte, North Carolina

On January 9, 1941, Major General E. S. Adams, the Adjutant General, in a letter to Dr. Nalle, announced action upon the application:

Your proposal for the sponsorship of an Evacuation Hospital Unit by the Charlotte Memorial Hospital has been approved by the Secretary of War. This hospital will be organized as the 38th Evacuation Hospital. The Commanding General, Fourth Corps Area, and The Surgeon General have been advised of this action.

The infant now had a home and a name.

Upon receiving from General Adams official notice of the approval by the Secretary of War of Charlotte Memorial Hospital's application to serve as sponsor in the organization of a military medical unit, Dr. Nalle as the hospital's chief of staff appointed Dr. Paul W. Sanger as chairman of a committee from the hospital's staff to proceed with the organization of the unit. The other members of the committee were Dr. Thomas W. Baker and Dr. Thomas D. Sparrow.

On February 8 the committee sent to the members of the staff of Charlotte Memorial Hospital notices of the contemplated organization of the unit and asked the doctors who wished to affiliate with the unit to notify the committee within the next one week.

The letter to the hospital's staff members said:

As you know, Charlotte has received special recognition in the field of medicine by our Government in its national defense program. So far as we are able to determine, the Charlotte Memorial Hospital is the first hospital in the country not associated with a medical school to be granted the privilege of organizing its own hospital unit. This unit will be designated as Evacuation Hospital #38, and the hospital has been instructed to perfect its own organization.

This group will function as a unit and will be called only as a unit in some dire national emergency. The following is a verbatim quotation:

"Prior to the declaration of a national emergency *by Congress*, individual Reserve officers required for extended active duty may be called upon to perform such active duty on a volunteer basis *only*."

Those who are best acquainted with the medical angles of the present military situation are strongly advising physicians, particularly those of the draft age, to affiliate with some hospital unit if possible, and secure the proper commission before being called by the draft, or by a separate draft of physicians which may be in the offing. The advantage of being affiliated with a local unit are obvious to you.

The number of physicians to be included in this hospital unit is only *31*, with two dentists. The number of applications which have been received is almost sufficient to complete the unit, but several of the applicants are from neighboring communities. Your Committee, which was elected by a recent call meeting, deems it only fair that Charlotte doctors should be given preference and hence this letter offering you the opportunity.

All applications must be in the hands of the committee by February 15, 1941. This is the date on which commissions will probably be assigned and the organization perfected. Since we realize that it may take several days for you to complete your physical examinations, etc., we are asking you, if interested, to return the enclosed card immediately.

Response to the committee's notice was immediate and enthusiastic. A large group from the hospital staff tentatively enrolled in the unit being formed and these doctors and the committee members during the next several months proceeded with the procurement of a commissioned personnel and initiated the necessary

3

Lieutenant Bessie V. Fullbright and Lieutenant Lela O. Russell pose in their dress uniforms soon after they were commissioned as officers in the newly formed 38th Evacuation Hospital unit.

steps toward obtaining reserve commissions for those doctors who had definitely decided to enroll in the unit.

During this period, too, the doctors were successful in interesting several young Charlotte businessmen in joining the unit's administrative corps section. Five were selected and procedures were started to obtain commissions for them.

But during these early months in 1941 an unforeseen problem arose. Because of the response of the Memorial Hospital's staff members, it was discovered, the hospital's staff would be dangerously depleted if all those considering joining the hospital's new military unit should be called into Army service.

So in order to enroll a full complement of doctors without materially decreasing the hospital's staff, the committee presented the situation to the Mecklenburg County Medical Society. Several members who were not on the Memorial's staff volunteered to enroll in the new unit being formed. Several other volunteers were enrolled by Dr. Sanger from among his friends in surgery in various communities in the Southeast. And since the Surgeon General required that all doctors enrolling in the 38th Evacuation Hospital Unit be members of the staff of Charlotte Memorial Hospital, these doctors not on the staff were given courtesy appointments to it. Three dentists were also enrolled to serve in the unit should it be called to duty.

Among the Charlotte physicians who joined the unit during these early months of its existence was a veteran of World War I, Dr. T. Preston White. He was commissioned a lieutenant colonel in the medical section and thereby became the ranking officer in the unit. Dr. Sanger was commissioned major in the Medical Reserve

Corps. Because of his seniority, Colonel White took charge of further organizational procedures and with the aid of Major Sanger and the other enrolled doctors began to recruit additional commissioned personnel, nurses, and enlisted men.

And then, eleven months after formation of the unit was approved by the Secretary of War, on a day—December 7, 1941—termed by President Franklin D. Roosevelt infamous in history, the Japanese struck Pearl Harbor.

The war was on.

When would Charlotte's 38th Evacuation Hospital Unit be called to active duty? Everybody remotely concerned was asking the question. And no one knew the answer.

But the procurement of officer personnel was speeded. And in February, with the unit's complement of officers nearly filled, Colonel White and Major Sanger went to Washington to report to the Personnel Section of the Surgeon General's office the status of the Charlotte unit.

Three and a half months after the attack upon Pearl Harbor the 38th Evacuation Hospital was ordered into active service.

The orders, dated March 21, 1942, came from the War Department, the Adjutant General's office, and were addressed to the commanding generals of the Fourth Corps Area and the Medical Replacement Centers at Camp Grant, Illinois, Camp Lee, Virginia, and Camp Barkeley, Texas.

The first paragraph of the orders provided that:

The 38th Evacuation Hospital, Charlotte, North Carolina, is ordered into active military service of the United States at Fort Bragg, North Carolina, as directed by the Commanding General, Fourth Corps Area, at the earliest practicable date and will be organized in accordance with the Table of Organization 8-232. Concurrently therewith, the personnel of the 41st Evacuation Hospital, Fort Bragg, less a small cadre, will be transferred to the 38th Evacuation Hospital. Additional personnel required will be requisitioned on this office and furnished from Medical Replacement Centers.

The order, which contained four other paragraphs of instructions, was signed by General Otto Johnson, the Adjutant General.

Five days later, on March 26, telegrams similar to the following one addressed to Captain Henry Stokes Munroe, Jr., were received by officers of the 38th:

Contemplate ordering you Fort Bragg, N. C. effective April fifteenth. Await orders.

Clapham, Adjutant General

These preliminary orders provoked a furor of excitement and activity. Each of the officers began immediately to arrange plans for the care of his family while he was away on duty. The businessmen in the administrative section made arrangements for the conduct of their businesses or for closing them temporarily. The doctors began preparations for the future care of their patients. The case histories of their patients were made available to other doctors who durin g the absence of the regular physicians might be called upon to treat them. Some doctors closed their offices, others decided to continue to rent theirs in order that the offices would be quickly available to them on their return from the war. Innumerable details of preparation had to be made, and made quickly. Now that the time had almost arrived for the actual departure, some of the 38th's members were depressed and others were elated as they awaited orders to report.

They were not long arriving. Five days after the preliminary telegrams came from Washington, the fateful order reached Charlotte. This one, dated March 31, 1942, was signed "Ulio, Washington, D. C.":

You will proceed on April fifteenth to Fort Bragg, N. C. reporting to commanding officer thirty-eighth Evacuation Hospital for duty.

Two weeks remained for finishing the job of getting ready to go to war.

To command the Charlotte unit a veteran of the Regular Army's Medical Corps, Colonel Raymond W. Whittier, had been transferred from Camp Grant, Illinois, to Fort Bragg in an order dated March 26. He reported for duty on April 5 and one of his first duties was to select an area in the vast Fort Bragg reservation to serve as the training home of the 38th. Colonel Whittier chose a location on the shore of Spring Lake.

Seventeen buildings, including the headquarters building, kitchen, day rooms, barracks buildings, and storerooms were assigned by the Fort Bragg commanding officer to the Charlotte unit. During this early period also 108 men were selected from the enlisted personnel of the 41st Evacuation Hospital. Their transfer to the 38th left but a small cadre as a nucleus for building up that unit. Two officers, Captain Willard F. Angen, M.C., and First Lieutenant Alfred Yankauer, Jr., Medical Reserve, were also transferred from the 41st.

All buildings were placed in readiness for occupancy by April 15, 1942. The nurses of the unit were not to arrive until about two weeks later and awaiting their arrival the buildings that were to house them were being put in condition. Forty nurses to serve the unit were ordered to active duty in a letter from the Fourth Corps Area headquarters at Atlanta, dated April 24.

On arrival at Fort Bragg, however, the nurses were placed on temporary duty at the station hospital pending movement of the 38th.

Three days after Colonel Whittier's arrival at Fort Bragg the medical staff of Charlotte Memorial Hospital honored the commissioned officers of the unit at a dinner party at the Myers Park Country Club in Charlotte. The party was held on the evening of April 8, one week before they were to report to Fort Bragg to begin training.

More than 150 persons, including the doctors and nurses in the unit, Colonel C. E. Dunbar, Medical Corps, commanding officer of Camp Sutton hospital at nearby Monroe, Major J. Kingsley MacDonald, M.C., officer in charge of the substation in Charlotte, and several of the Army doctors and nurses stationed at Charlotte's Morris Field, attended the dinner party.

Speakers included Dr. Addison Brenizer, who organized and led a similar unit in World War I, Dr. John Q. Myers, Colonel Waldrop of Morris Field, Colonel Dunbar, R. S. Dickson, chairman of Memorial Hospital's executive board, Dr. O. L. Miller, Dr. Allan Tuggle, acting administrator of Memorial Hospital, Lieutenant Colonel White and Major Sanger. A special entertainment program had been arranged by a committee from the hospital composed of Dr. Raymond Thompson, chairman, Dr. Robert Moore, Dr. B. C. Nalle, Dr. W. M. Summerville, and Dr. O. L. Miller.

It was revealed that when the unit was fully organized it would have more than 400 members. The roster, incomplete, was announced on April 8. It listed:

Medical officers: Lieutenant Colonel T. Preston White of Charlotte, internal medicine; Major Paul W. Sanger of Charlotte, chief of surgical service; Major Laurence E. Fleming of Charlotte, surgery; Major George Thomas Wood of High Point, surgery; Major William H. Pennington of Lexington, Kentucky, internal medicine; Major Richard Z. Query of Charlotte, internal medicine; Captain Glenn Perry of High Point, surgery; Captain Duncan G. Calder of Concord, surgery; Captain George Aubrey Hawes of Charlotte, urologist; Captain Otis Hunter Jones of Charlotte, medicine; Captain William T. Cavanaugh of Cooleemee, internal medicine; Captain John C. Montgomery of Charlotte, anesthetist; Captain Henry Stokes Munroe, Jr., of Charlotte, surgery; Captain McChord Williams of Charlotte, surgery; Captain Robert B. Stith of Florence, South Carolina, surgery; Captain William P. Leonard, formerly of Charlotte, then in the armed service, surgery; First Lieutenant Robert E. McCall of Charlotte, nose and throat specialist; First Lieutenant William C. Matthews of Davidson, internal medicine; First Lieutenant Robert H. Schirmer of Jacksonville, internal medicine; First Lieutenant George A. Sotirion of Gastonia, surgery; First Lieutenant Claud Walter

With Colonel Raymond W. Whittier, right, commanding officer, is Major George T. Wood, executive officer. Major Wood would later command the unit.

Perry, Jr., of Louisville, Kentucky, surgery; First Lieutenant Charles Bryant Porter of Calhoun, Kentucky, surgery; First Lieutenant George Rowe of Atlanta, surgery; First Lieutenant Colin Munroe of Charlotte, surgery; First Lieutenant Robert Miller of Lincolnton, surgery.

Dental officers: Major Vaiden B. Kendrick, Captain Bernard N. Walker, and First Lieutenant Milo Johnson Hoffman, all of Charlotte.

Administrative officers: Captain Stanton W. Pickens and Captain George C. Snyder of Charlotte and Second Lieutenant James R. Felts of Concord.

Enlisted personnel: Sidney H. Murray of Charlotte, X-ray technician; Alfred G. Chiswell of Durham, X-ray technician; W. G. Calhoun of Mooresville, laboratory technician; Joseph Walton Neal of Shelby, pharmacist; Randall K. Davis of Huntersville, laboratory technician; Clarence O. Kuester, Jr., of Charlotte, general clerk; and William F. Masten, Jr., of Charlotte, chief clerk.

Nurses, all second lieutenants: Hallie E. Almond, Ida Pauline Bell, Mary I. Boggs, Violet O. B. Burgess,

Mary Louise Cashatt, Evelyn Kohler Eggler, Martha G. Fliedner, Lucille Frye, Bessie Viola Fullbright, Josephine Lee Harmon, Bertha Elizabeth Hough, Ruby Elnora McCain, Ruby G. McElwee, Angeline Neil, Hazel Ann Simmons, Mary Lahome Thompson, and Elva Earle Wells.

The week following the party for the unit was one of strenuous activity as members of the 38th completed arrangements at home and set out for Fort Bragg and the unique experiences they looked forward to with activation of the new hospital.

Among the doctors reporting one would have the unusual experience of finding that another doctor with the same name had reported ahead of him. He was Dr. John C. Montgomery, Charlotte anesthetist. Fortunately for the recording of the story of the 38th, Dr. Montgomery would keep a diary throughout his service, beginning with his first day at Fort Bragg. On April 15, 1942, he wrote:

Left Charlotte around 9 A.M. Arrived Raeford and had lunch. Duncan Calder and Jimmie Felts drove up & ate also at the hotel. Arrived Fort Bragg at 2:30 P.M.

6

At Post Headquarters I learned that a Capt. John C. Montgomery had already entered active duty with the 38th Evacuation Hospital. Since my orders have never been received I was in a mess. Went over to the Spring Lake area where the unit was located. Col. Whittier suggested that I stay around until my orders came.

Five days later Dr. Montgomery made another notation:

April 20th. No orders yet. John Crowson Montgomery nice fellow. Will go home soon unless they arrive.

On April 28 he wrote in the little brown diary:

In Charlotte. Wired Washington again for orders. Found that my physical was on CO's desk at Morris Field all the time.

The next day he noted:

Received radiogram today to report at Fort Bragg May 1st.

And on May 1 his ordeal of getting into the service was ended. He wrote:

Reported for duty with the correct orders.

The next day, May 2, the other Dr. John C. Montgomery, a Texan, left Fort Bragg. He, like Charlotte's Dr. Montgomery, had been in a quandary because of the mixup in orders. The Charlotte men were reluctant to lose him; in the two weeks at Fort Bragg they had come to like him.

But it was quickly discovered that the unit had two other captains with the same names. One was Charlotte's Dr. Otis Hunter Jones, an obstetrician; the other was Chaplain Otis Jones, a Baptist minister from Bude, Mississippi. Chaplain Jones would remain with the unit until May 22, 1943; Dr. Jones would not leave until February 5, 1945.

2

Hardly a month after their arrival at Fort Bragg to begin their training, Captain Stanton Pickens in a letter to his wife spoke of the early results of the training. Though it was not intended that it be preserved, the letter fortunately survives to provide an interesting observation on the situation in which the members of the 38th found themselves four weeks after they had been called into active service.

The letter, dated May 12, 1942, revealed:

"The exercise and the drill continue and gradually I am getting a little harder and my stomach is moving upwards and my chest is taking its rightful place. I don't think I have lost any weight but my pants feel free around the middle.

"We took a turn thru the gas chamber the other day to make sure our masks were in good shape. The chamber was loaded with tear gas only but it showed some weakness in our preparation and some of the men cried all the way back home. I, for once, was lucky in that my mask fit exactly and I suffered no ill effects. We were all interested in Mr. Churchill's warning to the Germans about the use of gas. However, our attitude is that when a rat gets cornered he will bite you, so you had better be prepared for the worst.

"Arrangements have been made for me to attend the Officers' Cooking and Baking school when it opens again. I am anxious to find the difference between a carbohydrate and a protein. It might teach me to slow up on the potatoes that come almost each meal in the Army. Next week I have an assignment to talk to the Officers in our unit on Mess. If I don't get better prepared than I am now, the title will be most apt.

"I brought my projector down last week and some of the men were interested in the fishing pictures. We had taken some pictures of our drill and these proved funny at times as well as instructive. This is a picture taking crowd so we should have a good record of our early training. It is our understanding that no cameras will go overseas with us.

"Just before I left home I tried my first colored still pictures and the results were surprisingly good. I recommend this to you.

"This note will be short because I must get back to my class. We are studying map reading at present. When I get thru I am sure not to be lost, if I have a map."

In these early days at Fort Bragg the doctors would discover quickly how little they knew about the routines in the life of the military, particularly the rules of military courtesy. For instance, two decades after the ending of the war several of them recall what Dr.

One of the routines of the Fort Bragg training was the gas mask drill. Captain Alfred Yankauer, Jr., is the officer on right adjusting the mask. Left to right, Kendrick, Rowe, Colin Munroe, Hoffman, Snyder, Calder, Yankauer.

O. Hunter Jones describes, from the vantage of almost a quarter century later, as "one of the funniest things that happened while we were at Fort Bragg." He tells the story:

"We had been at Fort Bragg but a short while and we didn't know much about this business of military courtesy—respecting rank and authority. One day several of us were sitting around talking, when this general came up. He was inspector-general at Bragg, and he was really a big shot. I remember Paul Sanger was lounging in an easy chair and three or four others were sitting on the railing, and no one got up to greet the general and no one saluted. In fact, few of us knew how to salute properly anyway. But as the general approached us, two or three nodded to him and said, 'How do you do?' 'How are you?'—something like that, pretty casually. About that time the general saw Paul Sanger lying back in his chair. 'Get up out of that

chair and stand at attention!' he shouted. 'Don't you know any better, Major, than to sit there like that?' Paul was a major then, not yet a colonel, and Major Sanger jumped up and saluted. 'Yes, sir, General!' So that day we got a pretty sound lesson in military courtesy."

Dr. Montgomery recalls a somewhat similar lesson learned at Fort Bragg:

"We had the same thing to happen one day when Preston White and I went in to see Colonel Whittier. Preston sat down on the corner of the Colonel's desk. Colonel Whittier was a small man, and he seemed to swell out like a frog. And he was regular Army, too. He glared at Preston.

" 'Colonel White, how long have you been in the Army?' he demanded.

" 'Well,' Preston answered, 'I just came.'

" 'Well, stand up!' he commanded. 'Don't sit on my

8

desk!' So we got some sharp lessons those first days at Fort Bragg. It didn't take us long to find out we weren't practicing medicine in Charlotte. And though some of us were learning it the hard way, we soon discovered that we were really in the Army and really in a war."

The 38th's Fort Bragg training period was given further elaboration by Captain Pickens in a letter one week later. On May 19, 1942, he wrote Mrs. Pickens:

"Here I sit on a hot summer day at 6:15 P.M. having finished dinner an hour ago. This cot is not the most conducive spot for typing and this letter table, 14″ by 14″, is not too steady for the machine. These buildings, having been put up in a hurry, have warped considerably and nothing is level. However, I will do the best I can under the circumstances. The original of this letter looks all right but I can't promise about the four copies.

"My mailing list has all responded with the exception of the Washington correspondent and I know he is too busy running and winning the war to be bothered about the morale of the line officers. I want to thank those I have heard from for the news and keeping me in touch with what goes on in the outside world. You have no idea how time slips by without keeping up.

"Things are beginning to tighten up around our unit. It appears that the first phase of our training is over and the Commanding Officer is beginning to be tough and strict. I cannot argue about the need of it since I am associated with a group of medical men who, without a doubt, are the largest bunch of prima donnas on record and they need some teaching on teamwork and cooperation. The chances are that we will not take part in the maneuvers scheduled for July and August since we will very likely be on our way to some foreign port. I think we will be ready when the time comes. Next week we move out on a problem but will bivouac not far from our base since we have only three trucks. It would take more transportation, as you can see, to move 150 men and their equipment and keep them fed. In addition, we have been cut on gasoline we are allowed. Incidentally, I was given a B3 rating on gas, personally, which will let me get to Charlotte on my turn.

"Today I gave a lecture to our group on Mess Management. I have learned a lot about calories and vitamins and the difference between proteins and carbohydrates, but the success of the session came when my baker served some cookies and coffee made before the meeting.

"The calisthenics go inexorably along and the waist line tightens. The muscles get stronger. I feel fine but tired when the day finishes. Let me hear from you when you get time to write."

Members of the 38th had been at Fort Bragg six weeks when Charlotte relatives and friends sponsored a benefit performance for the unit. It was staged at the Carolina Theatre on the night of May 27, and was a complete sellout. The show grossed $3,108, and the money was given to Lieutenant Colonel Preston White to be placed to the credit of the unit as a contingency fund from which money would be available for the use principally of nurses and enlisted personnel in emergency situations.

Bob Hope, who had already started on a career of entertaining service personnel at home and abroad that in succeeding years would send him many times around the world to give his inimitable shows before hundreds of thousands of men and women in the various branches of the armed forces, headed a cast that included the mustachioed Jerry Colonna, Frances Langford, and Salisbury's Skinnay Ennis and his orchestra. Sixteen men from the 38th, led by Captain Lewis Burwell, who would later be transferred to the Air Corps, came to Charlotte to participate in the program in a series of songs staged around an improvised campfire.

The Bob Hope show, for those members able to obtain leaves to attend it, was one of the unit's most pleasant short interludes in the training at Fort Bragg. And that the training was daily growing more rigorous was emphasized in many letters written home, some of which would survive to add coloring details to the official reports.

The next letter received from Captain Pickens to be preserved, dated June 9, 1942, describes interestingly and in considerable detail the 38th's bivouac he had anticipated in the letter of May 19:

"So far I have been able to send one note a week but missed last week because our outfit was out in the field on bivouac, or what might commonly be called eating and sleeping with the bugs and the flies.

"We moved out with full equipment and each officer had to put up his own tent, so they said, for the practice. Not having been a sturdy Boy Scout in my youth, I had some trouble with my installation. In addition to getting my own person cared for, I had to supervise the erection of all kitchen equipment. This was not so difficult since there were enlisted men along who had had experience during maneuvers last fall and they did most of the work. What was a job for me, however, was the preparation necessary before we ever left the area. We had only 100 men in all but the job of getting food for the crowd and making preparations for refrigeration in the field and getting all the supplies required for giving them palatable dishes kept me busy for a week. Every time I read about an army moving anywhere away from their base I marvel at the ability of someone that made the plans and preparations.

Bob Hope, shown with Colonel Raymond W. Whittier, the 38th's commanding officer, gave a benefit show, sponsored by the Charlotte Variety Club, at the Carolina Theatre June 6, 1942, at which more than $3,000 was raised to provide an emergency fund for the newly activated unit.

10

However, we arrived at our spot and finished the time allotted and I found that the only piece of equipment we had forgotten was a potato masher. This was not too great a handicap since we gave them potatoes fried, boiled and baked and left off the mashed dish. For our refrigeration we had plenty of ice and we dug a hole in the ground, built a box and put (left out) in it, and packed ice around it. It was covered with a tarpaulin and it kept our dry food well below 50 degrees for the three days we were out. In addition we used a couple of GI cans for the other things we could wet, including Coca-Cola for the crowd.

"Our main purpose was to see how the hospital could function. It was set up and received simulated patients who moved through the various departments and were either evacuated to the rear or sent to the front. We had one or two deaths (simulated, of course) and the Chaplain and the Quartermaster representatives had their practice also.

"We were situated on the edge of a beautiful little lake named Lake McArthur, named, as I found out later, for General McArthur's father, who was a noted army man also. In the late evening, when all my work was thru, I went out and tried to attract some of my finny friends. I had smuggled my tackle in my bedding roll before we took off. I caught one nice bass.

"My main difficulty during the whole procedure was eating out of the well known army mess kit. This is an aluminum can which holds all of your food and when it all runs together, it looks so predigested. Of course, it holds the heat somewhat but it is actually hotter on the outside than the food is inside. This is also true of the canteen cup that is part of the equipment which cares for your coffee. The knife, fork and spoon which goes with this outfit each has a hole in the handle and when you are thru eating you fasten the whole business together and dip it into cans full of boiling water to clean. One of my jobs was to keep one man busy keeping a fire under these cans all of the time. Of course, the guards kept the fire going during the night. The flies in the area were as ferocious and tenacious as the General for which the place was named, combined with his illustrious son. We had no hopes after the first day of gaining a victory. We just held on.

"The most attractive thing about living close to nature is the grand, hot shower you get when you get back among civilized people. To get dirt and grime and the smelling clothes off is worth the whole experience. Soap and hot water are wonderful creations.

"Mary came down to Fayetteville on the day I got back and stayed two days. That really made me feel like I was arriving in civilization. It was good to see her. I went back to Charlotte with her on Saturday.

"So far we are still here. There is no news of our moving. However, I have been spending considerable time working on plans for moving. These plans are for short trips like moving to Fort Dix and for long trips to the west coast. This work is against the time when we do take off and should make the work at that time easier.

"This letter has been written under trying circumstances. Sitting on this cot and balancing this typewriter is not so hard but trying to think while forty men are playing radios, shining shoes, fixing new air mattresses, telling funny stories, complaining about all phases of army life, cleaning gas masks and doing all manner of other things makes it almost impossible. Excuse the parts that don't seem to make sense and interpret those that sound unintelligible."

Exactly two weeks later, on June 23, 1942, Captain Pickens reported much change during the past fortnight in the 38th's Fort Bragg routine of training, but revealed that the unit had received no definite information relative to when or where it might be sent next.

"There have been so many changes in our setup in the last few days that I have been unable to get time to sit down and get off one of these group letters. In the first place we were taken away from the 1st Army Corps but still remain with the Second Army. This was a help, since the Columbia group was not the most cooperative. However, we have been snowed under with the battle of inspections and papers. So far, we are standing up under the constant barrage but are in no humor for any counter-attacks. We thought that getting away from the 1st Army Corps would relieve us from going on maneuvers but now it appears that there is some doubt. We had hopes that we might get out and be on our way to foreign parts, but now there is no telling. It appears that we will get the remaining part of our enlisted men about the 18th of July, so we will sit here until then, I presume, and possibly for some time thereafter. This will give us our full complement of enlisted strength and lacking only some ten nurses and four officers.

"All of this, coupled with the finishing of our basic training and getting into our jobs in full force, has kept me busy. Up to now I have been Mess Officer in name only, not actually doing a great deal of the work. Now I am catching it on all sides and loving it. When there is a job to be done and I get some inkling of how to do it, I enjoy it more than just sitting. The main trouble I find in the Army is the fact that no one is quite sure of how to do a job because of the many regulations and their constantly changing qualities. So far, I am just barging ahead somewhat like the bull in the china shop and when the mistakes turn up I will just have to take the consequences. At least I am working. When the change was made I was relieved of drill, which I miss. The medical officers continue and their marches get longer each day. They are now moving about four miles on each march. Some of the doctors, when they first came in and lay on their backs, looked like igloos, but now they have lost their protuberance in their middles. They protest but the Army moves inexorably along.

"In talking with one of the enlisted men the other day I got a fair description of a pup tent. That is the little tent that they use for shelter when in the field. He said they normally accommodate two men, provided neither of them walked in his sleep. If three are to use the tent, at least two of them must be midgets or children in arms. Cooks must never sleep two in a tent because of their tendency towards plumpness. You could appreciate this more if you have seen the little igloos.

"The Mess Officer's job in the Army has been revised today. I have just completed ordering curtains for the nurses' barracks, and in addition, have picked out an ironing board with proper trimmings. If this keeps up, I am going to cut off a little of the tie-back frills from one of the ecru curtains and paste on my drawers. However, I think the job will be temporary and my status should not be affected too much.

"I must leave, you know, and get back to the job of directing a group cleaning some stoves. The group is made up of X-ray and laboratory technicians, two graduates from the University of Pittsburgh in pharmacy and some other well qualified stove cleaners. The Army is funny."

When the hospital unit was ordered to active duty on April 15, 1942, it was assigned to the command of the commanding officer of Fort Bragg and Fourth Corps Area headquarters. On May 11 it was attached to First Army Corps, Second Army, for all purposes. On June 17 the hospital was detached from the First Army Corps and assigned to Headquarters, Second Army, for all purposes. On June 25, eight days later, First Headquarters and Headquarters Detachment, Special Troops, Second Army, was activated at Fort Bragg for the purpose of supervising the training of units assigned to that headquarters. The commanding officer, First Headquarters and Headquarters Detachment, Special Troops, Second Army, also assumed jurisdiction over certain administrative matters. The 38th Evacuation Hospital was assigned to First Headquarters and Headquarters Detachment, Special Troops, Second Army, as one of the component commands, pursuant to general orders No. 61, Headquarters Second Army, June 23, 1942.

The Charlotte men's Fort Bragg training had hardly started before they began to learn from experience of the Army's traditional practice of involving even its slightest operations in a maze of red tape.

Ten weeks after the 38th started training at the sprawling great base in the North Carolina sandhills Captain Pickens wrote on June 29, 1942, humorously but nevertheless accurately, of his own experiences, which were perhaps typical:

"To date I am agreeing with the common description often heard about the Army, 'pass the buck,' 'sling the bull,' and make six copies. If any of those reading these erudite pages from the civilian angle think that they have trouble with priorities, regulations and red tape, they are just amateurs compared with those left in the army. I have been working for two weeks trying to get two wire brushes with which to clean up my kitchen stoves. I have spent the government's time and the liberal pay they hand me for what I am worth now. I have hounded everyone I have run across that might know how to get the brushes. I have filled out requisitions in more than six copies. I have sworn that the brushes were absolutely necessary for the health and welfare of the troops. I have secured similar affidavits from Medical Inspectors. I have done almost everything except write my congressman. I haven't found the brushes. I know they are here in Fort Bragg, but so far I have been unable to get my hands on them. That is just a small example of a hundred experiences I am enjoying. Getting things done. But I am learning and the further I go the more I get done."

Captain Pickens wasn't long discovering another Army tradition and the determination of old line Army officers to uphold it inviolately. He tells about it in this same letter:

"The other day my Colonel stated that he had requisitioned some plates, cups and saucers, etc., to take care of some thirty nurses that were coming to join us. He wanted me to get these supplies. Where he had sent the request he was not sure and where the supplies were located he did not know—that was my job. So I got a truck and a driver (an officer cannot drive a truck; it's beneath his station altho I have spent many a day in civilian life doing just that and it didn't hurt my standing) and started out to find the source. I spent half a day tracking down the requisition and the other half finding the supplies. When I found them I made the frightful error of packing the dishes in a barrel myself and loading the barrel on the truck while my driver watched. When I returned to my area, little Napoleon was waiting for me and asked how I had managed to get the work done so swiftly. When I replied that I had done the work myself, he set in on me and dressed me down to his size and let me know that an officer should never be caught doing any such things so long as I could 'pass the buck', or better still, pass to the buck private. But it's all in the day's work, I suppose."

In this letter of June 29, Captain Pickens told of the arrival of the unit's contingent of nurses. He reported:

"The nurses have moved in next door, or rather the next barracks. I have looked them over and I know Powers or Ziegfeld would never have picked them out. They wear a blue denim outfit similar to the enlisted men's fatigue uniform or more like what a Negro would plow in. That doesn't help their rather forlorn appearance either. But with their coming came special orders that we must keep our shades down and not be caught out without a shirt on and a lot more other items with the admonition that if we disobeyed, 'disciplinary measures' would have to be taken. From now on I will have to watch myself lest I wander out without a shirt or fail to pull down the shades. Of course, having lived in the little house in Charlotte so close to my neighbors, I am still in good practice."

"From the nurses," he added, "I learn they have been working in one of the station hospitals, that patients are split into two classes: (1) those who have athlete's foot, and (2) those who have colds. If you have athlete's foot you get your feet swabbed with iodine. If you have a cold, you get your throat swabbed with iodine. Anyone who claims he has neither athlete's foot nor a cold is sent to the guard house for impersonating an officer."

His next letter, written July 8, 1942, began with a continuation of his discussion of the unit's newly arrived nurses:

"After the arrival of the nurses things quieted down for a few days in our part of the Army," he disclosed. "But it was not for long. The commanding officer of the Second Army, representative of General Lear, the head man, came to pay us a visit. He came for an inspection. It's a funny thing to me that they always give you ample warning before they come and you work like fury to get everything in shape and then they casually check over and pass on. On this particular day I was taking time to see what a K.P. did during the day. I put on some old coveralls and peeled potatoes, shucked corn, mopped the floor and washed dishes. I did just what the men do. It so happens that the inspector did not catch me at it, so I did not get bawled out for conduct unbecoming an officer, nor praised for leading my men."

His letter went on to reveal the chaplain's description of an American soldier:

"Our Chaplain added this thought for us the other day. He said that the American soldier was not to be known as Johnny Doughboy any longer. He had changed it to Johnny Dogface, since the soldier wore a dog tag, sat on his behind all day and growled and stayed up all night and howled. I am sure I am not in this category because I have not yet received my dog tag and altho I do my part of the growling during the day, I am too tired to do any howling at night."

He spoke of the enlisted personnel who had been slated to join the unit:

"The names of the men who *were* to have come would make the Fordham football team look like they belonged to the Baptist church. I never saw so many consonants in all of my life. We, of course, don't know where they are from originally but it's a draw between Flatbush in Brooklyn and one of the coal mining districts in Pennsylvania. From the names they are still on the bottom of the melting pot. We were in hopes that we would draw some men who speak English, since the crowd we now have are poor at it, but it looks like we are licked again. It has been said somewhere that they put in the Selective Service System in order that the Southern boys wouldn't fill up the Army entirely."

Captain Pickens still was unable to report any news of the probable date of the unit's transfer from Fort Bragg. But a short time before he wrote, he disclosed, the 38th "had word that 77 additional men were coming from Virginia to join our outfit. They were due here on Thursday. I had to open another dining room and get all the equipment necessary to start cooking. Then I got food in the house and was all set when word came thru that the order was cancelled. I wish they would make up their collective minds on what they really mean to do."

A week later, when he wrote again, he had no news of the unit's being ordered out. But he reported that in an official communique issued the Monday before from headquarters of the Second Army, General Ben Lear had warned "that our soldiers were not strong enough physically, that we did not have the stamina that matched the Germans or the Japs and he wanted us to toughen up."

To toughen the men the General prescribed that each man in the Medical and Quartermaster Corps run two miles each day.

So, reported Captain Pickens, "on Monday of this week we started out and did the two miles. The temperature was slightly over 100. This morning we had the test run with stop watches at each turn and General Lear's representative checking our time. We started at 10 A.M. and ran the course just 45 seconds short of regulation. Only one officer of the 40 in our outfit dropped out. . . . Some four of our enlisted men out of 128 dropped by the wayside. The temperature was only 90 at the time of the test. Now this little hard-

OFFICERS AND NURS
COLONEL R. W. WH

This photograph of the officers and nurses of the 38th Evacuation Hospital was made as the unit was completing its

ening is in addition to our half-hour of calisthenics in the morning before breakfast, and an hour's drill in the afternoon. At the same time, I try to carry on my regular job of getting enough food and getting it prepared and served three times a day to approximately 200 people, and, of course, getting the places cleaned up before and after each meal. In addition, I teach two classes each week on Mess Management and Kitchen Police duties. . . .

"In addition to the above dissertation, I might add that I am sitting here in Fort Bragg waiting to get to the theatre of operations."

That same afternoon, July 15, 1942, said Captain Pickens, they were meeting the train "to receive 30 additional men into our outfit. This brings our total up to 158 enlisted personnel while our Table of Organization calls for 318. We received two additional Medical Officers today, making the total 44 of the 47 necessary. We have 33 nurses of the 52. We lost two by marriage last week which was no help in the Army effort. We are moving along and will probably be ready with the full complement when the Navy gets our transportation ready.

"While I am still breathing hard from all my running," he added, "I might say that the other groups belonging to the Second Army that are stationed at Bragg, the Airborne Infantry, Tank Destroyer units, Engineers, Infantry, and Parachute Troops and Tank units all had to run four miles each day. Our two look big to me but those boys are really getting tough."

To illustrate how his 38th members were losing whatever flabbiness they may have had when they started their training exactly three months before, he revealed his own physical transformation:

"My waistline was 38 when I came here and it now measures 34—honest measurement. My weight was 196 when I reported for my last physical examination and it tips the scales at 182 now. I think we will be ready, physically."

Captain Pickens spoke, too, of another problem that all his fellows at Fort Bragg were having, as well as the rest of the citizens throughout the nation:

"The gasoline situation has me worried at present. I have been able to get to Charlotte every weekend so far, but now it looks like I may miss a time or two. We have not yet worked out our supplemental request on the combination traveling together."

Dr. Aubrey Hawes had gone to college at The Citadel in Charleston, South Carolina. So he was given the assignment to train the nurses in military drilling.

EVACUATION HOSPITAL FORT BRAGG, N.C.
C COMDG   7-26-42.

months of training at Fort Bragg. The officer on the front row is Colonel Raymond W. Whittier, commanding.

"And Aubrey had quite a problem," Dr. Montgomery recalls. "When he yelled out 'Forward, march!' they were supposed, of course, to step off on the left foot. But it appeared that few of them could remember which was their left foot. So Aubrey hit on the plan of giving each nurse a rock to hold in her left hand, so she could step off on the foot on the side that had the rock."

But his companions of the 38th like to tell another story of those training days at Fort Bragg involving Aubrey Hawes. Dr. Jones relates their version of what happened:

"While we were at Bragg they had a rule that the company officers had to go out every day and take certain exercises, such as going on hikes, running obstacle courses, and doing such things to harden themselves, like walking half a mile and then trotting half a mile and then walking, and so on. The field officers didn't have to do it, just the company officers. Well, the story is, Aubrey said he just wasn't going to do all that running and walking, he was going to fall out into the bushes alongside the road and they wouldn't miss him. So the time came for the final exam or test—you had to do the course in a certain time, I believe—and the story goes, we insist, that Aubrey ducked out at

the right time and hid in the bushes until the test was about over. And got by with it!"

As July of 1942 moved monotonously for the 38th into the sultry days of midsummer the feeling began to grow that something would soon be happening. Yet no one knew positively what lay ahead for the unit. Rumors were circulating, but they remained rumors. Nobody could say even why everybody seemed to be sensing that the unit would soon be on the move.

The daily routine of training continued unchanged. Each day the training schedule was posted and followed. The schedules varied little from day to day, except they were lighter on Wednesdays and Saturdays. The day's program for officers, nurses, and enlisted personnel began at 7 o'clock each weekday morning with brisk calisthenics that lasted twenty minutes and generally ended with an orientation period from four to five o'clock. Some days the nurses had a somewhat shorter training schedule.

On Monday, July 20, the schedule for officers, prepared on July 11, provided:

From 7 to 7:20, calisthenics, drill field, Captain Calder, instructor; from 8 to 12, professional duties,

15

Officers of the 38th spent many hours drilling during their training period at Fort Bragg, beginning with the activation of the unit April 15, 1942.

station hospital, Colonel Cook, instructor; from 1 to 2:30, public speaking, Lieut.-Col. White, instructor; from 2:30 to 4, close-order drill and march, drill field, Lieut.-Col. White, instructor; from 4 to 5, orientation lecture, Captain Tyson, instructor.

The schedule that day for nurses was:

From 7 to 7:20, calisthenics, drill field, Captain Yankauer, instructor; from 8 to 9:30, close-order drill, road march, drill field, Captain Hawes, instructor; 10 to 11, registrar records conference, Major Query, instructor; 11 to 12, respiratory diseases lecture, Captain Stith, instructor; 1 to 2, clinical pathology lecture, Captain Gay, instructor; 2 to 3, orientation lecture, Major Kendrick, instructor.

The schedule for that day posted for Company A, Group I, provided:

From 7 to 7:20, calisthenics, athletic field, Captain Snyder, instructor; from 8 to 10, drill and march, drill field, Captain Calder, instructor; from 10 to 12, organization and function of medical corps, Captain Yankauer, instructor; 1 to 2, kitchen police duties, Captain

Pickens, instructor; 2 to 3, defense against chemical attack, Captain Kavanagh, instructor; 3 to 4, military courtesy and discipline, Captain Calder, instructor; 4 to 5, interior guard duty, Captain Snyder, instructor.

The following Sunday, July 26, Captain Pickens recorded in his letter home what happened the Tuesday before, July 21:

"I don't know how many more letters I will be able to write from this address, since this unit has been on the 'alert' since last Tuesday afternoon. The notice came in the most casual manner. We had all piled into our trucks, all the officers, I mean, to go over into another section of the camp to hear a speech by our Commanding General, Ben Lear. The time was approximately 3:15 P.M. The speech was to be made, according to the schedule, at 3:30. While we were sitting in the trucks waiting for the Commanding Officer of our unit to get started, he came out of headquarters and walked to the rear of each truck and calmly stated that 'this unit is on the alert as of this time.' Nothing followed. There was complete silence. Then after about five

16

minutes the trucks began to move and there was the usual nervous laughter and small talk that would naturally emanate from such a situation. We all took it in stride until the General, who was supposed to speak at 3:30, got to the theatre at 5:15. And with his lateness came a speech that might have appeared in the morning paper under the National Whirligig which he had not read before coming on the stage. No, I am a little harsh in my indictment; it was not that bad. Part of it gave you an inspiration which was what was needed at that time."

The letter went on to relate the commotion that was caused by the alert notice:

"Since the original alarm, we have been working like beavers getting ready to take off in all directions. There is no telling when the deadline will be or in what direction we will head, but from all appearances, that is the real thing and within a short time we'll be off on a trip. I am quite philosophical about the whole matter. I am not going to be stampeded and so long as the dirty work has to be done I am going to try to get the most out of it as well as do the most for it."

Upon the giving of the alert notice to the unit, Colonel Whittier granted leaves for members of the unit to return for short stays with their families. Captain Pickens wrote further:

"My Colonel was quite decent about letting most of us get away for a day and I went to Charlotte and saw all of my family there and brought Mary back with me. She is staying in Fayetteville and gets out to the Post every day for a visit. Today being Sunday, we went to church at one of the Post chapels. I am Officer of the Day and cannot leave the area until tomorrow afternoon. Mary had dinner with me and supper and is sitting here watching me type this note. She will be back in Fayetteville about 10 or 10:30 to-night with some of the other wives. Most of the wives managed to get down for a final visit. She will stay on until something definite happens."

Though the 38th's members did not know it, something definite had already happened.

The day before the Pickens letter was written—Saturday, July 25—orders from the commanding general of the Second Army were received at Fort Bragg "requesting Commanding General, Fort Bragg, N. C., to issue necessary movement orders." Pursuant to these instructions, Fort Bragg's commander on Monday, July 27, ordered the 38th, along with other military outfits stationed there, to "proceed by rail from stations indicated to the New York Port of Embarkation in the manner indicated below." The strength of the 38th was given in the orders as 47 officers, 53 nurses and 318 enlisted men. Instructions included the provision that

"Personnel will move so as to arrive at Indiantown Gap Military Reservation on August 2, 1942."

The instructions added that "This is a permanent change of station. Vaccinate with typhus vaccine."

The orders specified further:

"Take from present station:

"a. Clothing (winter only) (less helmets, steel) and individual equipment as prescribed in T/BA No. 21, June 20, 1942 (mobilization column) including the following items:

"Caps, winter (one per individual)

"Overshoes, arctic (one pair per individual)

"In addition, one uniform, cotton, khaki, may be taken per individual for comfort during the journey to the Port of Embarkation and during the stay in the staging area."

The 38th, the orders specified, would not take organization equipment, "except motor vehicles which will be taken."

Additional items to be taken were:

"Covers, mattress (two per individual)

"Blankets, wool, OD (two extra per individual, making a total of four)."

The orders, highly confidential, particularly relating to the unit's destination, left the members of the 38th in a mood of lively speculation. The instructions prescribing winter caps, arctic overshoes, winter clothing and woolen blankets indicated surely that the 38th was on its way to the European theater rather than to the South Pacific, and the report was soon in wide circulation that the unit would board ship at Brooklyn for one of the ports in Europe. The fact that few inoculations against yellow fever were given, the late Dr. Henry Stokes Munroe, captain and operating surgeon of the unit's General Surgery Team No. 1, relates in notes he recorded of his experiences, eliminated the Pacific theater as the 38th's destination.

"We wondered why we were to carry woolen uniforms, and we knew that eventually we were to go to Brooklyn, New York, to board ship, and that is all we knew," Dr. Munroe recorded. "We knew that soon our location would be A.P.O. instead of a name. After having fingerprints and photographs made, dog tags issued, blood typed, and innumerable vaccinations and inoculations done, and only a few were inoculated against yellow fever, we had already closed our speculating on the Pacific."

In the final week of July at Fort Bragg the various assignments were completed and the unit was ready for activation of the orders of transferal. The 38th's strength on July 31, 1942, including officers, nurses, and enlisted personnel, totaled 395.

The training period of three and a half months and

the departure from Fort Bragg were treated tersely in a summary by the unit's commanding officer issued the following January under the subject, "Medical History --Year Ending 31 December 1942." This section of the summary recorded:

"TRAINING:

"During the period 15 April 1942 to 31 July 1942, such training as could be given was instituted. This training consisted chiefly of physical exercises and didactic instructions. No organizational equipment was provided and no opportunity was afforded to participate in any field exercises of maneuvers. During this period the nurses were placed on duty in the Station Hospitals at Fort Bragg.

"MOVEMENT OVERSEAS:

"On 27 July 1942 the unit was ordered to duty overseas. Prior to departure, the unit was brought to T/O strength by the transfer of 169 enlisted men from the 134th Medical Regiment, and by the assignment of additional officers. At 2000 hours 31 July 1942 the unit entrained at Fort Bragg, enroute to its staging area at Indiantown Gap, Pennsylvania. . . ."

But Captain Munroe's reminiscences of the departure from Fort Bragg was more graphic:

"During the late afternoon we boarded hot, stuffy coaches on a Fort Bragg railway siding with our usual ignorance of the Army's plans for our destination. The rigid secrecy of troop movements being introduced to us never ceased to plague the unit during our wartime duty. Although Army secrecy was recognized as a necessity, it was very trying to be always in the dark as to when and where our next move would be. Sandwiches and fruit for two meals were ordered and prepared. Enroute many of the recognizable North Carolina and Virginia towns kept us informed of our northerly direction. It was a hot, uncomfortable ride that was spent in speculation, bridge games, poker games, group singing, reading, and attempted sleep. For hours one short-statured, spirited member of the unit, while hanging on a smoking room hook by his shirt, came forth with outstretched arms and 'Praise the Lord' each time he swung forward with the train's motions around the many track curves."

The 38th's commanding officer during the organization period, Lieutenant-Colonel T. Preston White, left, is shown here with Major Paul W. Sanger, chief of the surgical service.

18

During the last week of the unit's stay at Fort Bragg the following assignments of officers were made:

Whittier, Raymond W.	Colonel, M.C.	Commanding Officer
Wood, George T.	Major, M.C.	Executive Officer
Yankauer, Alfred, Jr.	Captain, M.C.	Adjutant
Query, Richard Z., Jr.	Major, M.C.	Registrar and CO Det. Patients
Felts, James R., Jr.	2nd Lt., M.A.C.	Unit Personnel Officer
Snyder, George C.	Captain, M.A.C.	Detachment Commander, M.D.
Jones, Otis	Captain, Chap.	Chaplain
Pickens, Stanton W.	Captain, M.A.C.	Mess Officer
Medearis, William P.	Captain, M.A.C.	Supply and Utilities Officer
Dunn, James W.	1st Lt., Q.M.C.	Ass't Supply and Utilities Officer
Kavanagh, Wm. P.	Captain, M.C.	Receiving Officer
Jones, Otis H.	Captain, M.C.	Ass't Receiving Officer
Rowe, George C.	1st Lt., M.C.	Evacuation Officer
Nowacki, Stanley M.	1st Lt., M.C.	Ass't Evacuation Officer
White, Thomas P.	Lt. Col., M.C.	Chief, Medical Service
Powers, John S., Jr.	1st Lt., M.C.	Ass't, Medical Service
Schirmer, Robert H.	1st Lt., M.C.	Ass't, Medical Service
Matthews, William C.	1st Lt., M.C.	Ass't, Medical Service
Pugh, George E.	1st Lt., M.C.	Ass't, Medical Service
McGrath, Frank S.	1st Lt., M.C.	Ass't, Medical Service
Sanger, Paul W.	Major, M.C.	Chief, Surgical Service
Munroe, Henry S.	Captain, M.C.	Operating Surgeon, Gen. Surg. Team No. 1
Perry, Glenn G.	Captain, M.C.	Ass't Operating Surgeon, Gen. Surg. Team No. 1
Perryman, Olin C.	1st Lt., M.C.	Anesthetist, Gen. Surg. Team No. 1
Fleming, Laurence E.	Major, M.C.	Operating Surgeon, Gen. Surg. Team No. 3
Calder, Duncan G., Jr.	Captain, M.C.	Ass't Operating Surgeon, Gen. Surg. Team No. 3
Porter, Charles B.	1st Lt., M.C.	Anesthetist, Gen. Surg. Team No. 3
Pennington, William H.	Major, M.C.	Operating Surgeon, Gen. Surg. Team 2, (Ex. Of. Surg. Serv.)
Hawes, George A.	Captain, M.C.	Ass't Operating Surgeon, Gen. Surg. Team No. 2, (G. U. Surg.)
Perry, Claud W.	1st Lt., M.C.	Anesthetist, Gen. Surg. Team No. 2
Sotirion, George A.	1st Lt., M.C.	Splint Team, Orthopedist, Orth. Team No. 2
Augustine, Robert W.	Captain, M.C.	Splint Team, Orthopedist, Orth. Team No. 1
Imes, Pat R.	Major, M.C.	Plastic Surgeon, Maxillo-facial Team
Kendrick, Vaiden B.	Major, D.C.	Dental Oral Surgeon, Maxillo-facial Team
Pitts, William R.	Major, M.C.	Neuro-Surgeon, Neuro-surgical Team
Williams, McChord	Captain, M.C.	Ass't Surgeon, Neuro-surgical Team
Miller, Robert P.	1st Lt., M.C.	Anesthetist, Neuro-surgical Team
Leonard, William P., Jr.	Captain, M.C.	Thoracic surgery, Thoracic-surgical Team
McCall, Robert E., Jr.	Captain, M.C.	Ass't Surgeon, Thoracic-surgical Team (ENT Surgeon)
Montgomery, John C.	Captain, M.C.	Anesthetist, Thoracic-surgical Team (Chief Anesthesia Serv.)
Stith, Robert B.	Captain, M.C.	Shock Team, Surgeon, Shock Team No. 1
Evans, William, Jr.	Captain, M.C.	Shock Team, Ass't Surgeon, Shock Team No. 2
Gay, Charles H., Sr.	Captain, M.C.	Chief, Laboratory Service
Tyson, Thomas D.	Captain, M.C.	Chief, X-ray Service
Munroe, Colin A.	1st Lt., M.C.	X-ray Service Ass't
Walker, Bernard	Captain, D.C.	Chief, Dental Service
Hoffman, Milo J.	1st Lt., D.C.	Ass't Dental Officer

3

When the sun rose Saturday morning, August 1, 1942, the 38th Evacuation Hospital unit's members were nearing Philadelphia, and soon they were doing what they and countless others of the nation's military forces would do throughout the duration of the war, calling for coffee. Fortunately, the railway's representative on the train had wired ahead and when the train reached Philadelphia several large milk cans of steaming coffee were awaiting its arrival.

"These were loaded on the train after considerable discussion over the return or salvage of the cans," Dr. Munroe recalled. "The hot drink, sandwiches and cold fruit revived our spirits before our arrival at what appeared to us to be a most dismal place, Indiantown Gap, Pennsylvania, a dull spot, but nestled between beautiful hills."

Upon arriving at the staging area the members of the hospital unit were taken in Army trucks to barracks in Section 13 of the reservation, where they were soon busy completing their supplies and equipment and practicing the order in which they were to board ship. And during the nights at Indiantown Gap the men were awakened in the late hours for inspection, inoculations, and vaccinations.

Movement orders, providing detailed instructions for embarking, were issued August 3 from the New York Port of Embarkation.

"Units of the above shipments named in the attached 'Transportation and Embarkation Table' will move August 5, 1942, as scheduled therein, from their present stations to the designated points of embarkation, by means of the transportation specified," one section of the orders provided.

The 38th Evacuation Hospital unit was one of the units named.

Captain Munroe vividly recalled the departure from the Indiantown Gap staging area:

"At two A.M. on the morning of August 6 we were given coffee containing salt, by mistake, we hoped, and were loaded into a train, still not completely knowing where we were going. By daylight we were in New Jersey, finally disembarking at Jersey City. Ferries took us across to the 59th Street Pier and after a series of long marches and waits we boarded the fabulous 33,000-ton British passenger ship, the H.M.S. *Andes*. During our shiploading we first saw a line of nurses and were delighted to learn that they were joining forces with the 38th Evacuation Hospital Unit after leaving the nurses' pool stationed near New York City. In too short a number of hours we were giving the Statue of Liberty farewell waves. We moved out in broad daylight, in violation of all known security rules, past the Narrows, past quarantine, and with a Navy blimp hovering overhead, we put out to sea."

When they awakened the next morning, the ship had dropped anchor.

"We soon discovered that we were in the harbor of Halifax, Nova Scotia," Captain Munroe's reminiscences continue. "Late that afternoon we put to sea again and quickly moved to our ship position in a gigantic convoy, the biggest convoy up to that period of war. The next morning we spotted numerous destroyers, two very formidable looking heavy cruisers and a battleship, which we afterward learned was the *Arkansas*.

"Fortunately, the crossing was uneventful. None of us knew at the time that during our crossing enemy submarine activity in the Atlantic was at its wartime peak. We zigged and zagged from cold climate to hot, and on August 17, having left part of the convoy, our ship moved up the River Mersey to Liverpool, England. For the first time we saw active evidence of war. Mile after mile, docks and warehouses lay in total ruins and sunken ships with only their masts showing were our beacons as we approached the old historical city.

"The *Andes* was too large a ship to be docked at Liverpool, so we anchored in the river. After the usual hurry and then waits we boarded tenders or ferries with all our belongings and were taken ashore. Here for the first time we witnessed a complete blackout. Make-believe preparations of war were things of the past and at last we knew that we were faced with a reality of which we were woefully but blessedly ignorant. In the long months to come, crowded with difficult adjustments and stark realities, the American mind clung tenaciously to its blind belief that only in its homeland was there such a thing as reality. War was

Eleven of the 38th's nurses are shown here in their dress uniforms soon after the unit's arrival in England. On settee, left to right, Bertha Hough, Beatrice Johnson and Hazel Simmons. Rear, left to right, Martha Pegram, Nellie Shields, Mary Blandford, Christine Wills, Clementine Mills, Winnie Martin, Elva Wells, and Sara Moran. The picture was made in a Red Cross club for service women in London.

pure unreality, a belief which denoted one of the basic differences between the European and the American way of thinking."

But though to Captain Munroe and others of the officers and nurses contingent of the 38th the Atlantic crossing had been uneventful, it had indeed been memorable to one of the unit's most popular and experienced nurses.

"She was Miss Lela Russell, who two decades after the war's ending is still at the Presbyterian Hospital in Charlotte," Dr. O. Hunter Jones reveals in recalling those days aboard the *Andes* on the way to England. "Miss Russell, a wonderful person and one of our finest nurses, had been in excellent health during the training period, but she had been seasick almost from the moment she went aboard the *Andes*. She had been put in the infirmary and was terribly sick, not dangerously ill, of course, but so nauseated she couldn't retain a bite of food. She was pitiful, and we were all distressed about her.

"So one night a bunch of us—I remember there were Buck Medearis, Stan Pickens, the chaplain, and I, and maybe another one or two—were talking about Miss Russell and what a tough time she was having. We decided we might be able to do something for her. 'We'll get Miss Russell down here before dinner and give her something to drink,' one of the fellows suggested. 'We'll get some English schnapps and some saltines and we'll get her to take that, and pretty soon she'll be feeling better, and able to eat a meal.' She just hadn't been able to retain a thing. Well, the chaplain— he was pretty strait-laced on the subject of liquor, the one we had then—and he said he'd better be going. He wouldn't have any part in what we were planning. But I was all for it. 'Well, if you can do it,' I said, 'the more power to you.' I doubt if Miss Russell had ever had a drink before in her whole life, and I wondered how we'd come out with her.

"But about five o'clock one of the fellows goes for her and brings her in. We tell her what we are planning

21

to do, and she doesn't much want to try it, but she knows she needs something. So Stan and Buck fix her a drink of some kind. 'Now, Miss Russell,' one of them says, 'this is mostly carbonated water.'

"So she took the drink. And then they gave her another. And pretty soon she was feeling better; she was no longer nauseated. And in a little while we took her down to dinner. And was that crowd down there surprised. Here they were expecting to see us reprobates coming in together and feeling pretty good and we walk in with Miss Lela Russell, their pride and joy, and she seems to be feeling fine. And she was. She ate a good dinner, and if I remember correctly, she wasn't nauseated any more. I don't think she had any trouble the rest of the trip over."

On their arrival in England, the nurses boarded a train and after a long all-night ride arrived at the First Medical Laboratory in Salisbury. The officers and men traveled in double-deck trains to Huyton, about ten miles from Liverpool. In the nighttime they scrambled about to find sleeping quarters, and after getting settled they were soon aroused and told to report to the officers' mess for a briefing in the facts of war in Britain.

"The following morning Colonel Whittier called a formation of the enlisted personnel to give them the same information," Captain Munroe's account of that eventful early period in England continues. "While he was talking, standing on top of an air raid shelter, our first air raid warning was heard. In the twinkling of an eye three hundred men disappeared, no one knew where. The formation and briefing were never completed."

After a three-day stay at Huyton, the 38th marched the mile and a half to the Huyton railway station and boarded a train. After being shuttled back and forth across England—they thought, at any rate—the officers and enlisted men of the unit found themselves in what they afterward learned was Tidworth Park staging area at Tidworth, Wilts County.

From the train they marched for what seemed miles in complete darkness and then, still in darkness, were told that they had arrived at the staging area. Then after they had been led in chain fashion by one of the British officers they found quarters in tents that the next morning they found were wigwam-shaped. The mattresses, strawfilled and uncomfortable, were triangular in shape, they discovered, with tapering apexes for the feet. That morning, to add to the general gloom, brought rain that continued almost without interruption throughout their stay at Tidworth Park.

"At that time England seemed a dark, dismal country. Many tents leaked, and the bedding was constantly wet and cold," Captain Munroe's account goes on. "The only living creature that seemed happy over our Eng-

lish food seemed to be the English bee. . . . The tasteless English sausages, being almost ninety per cent meal, provided us a protein intake consisting in the main of those inadvertently eaten bees in that dark, damp mess tent. Our stomachs most probably contained many painless bee welts during that stay. Being low in spirit and feeling that we were so useless, we sought to interrupt our training as often as we could by getting leaves to visit London and other English spots in the hope of finding warmth, a bed, edible food and a homelike bath. In addition to being introduced to the English queues that lined up for everything, we were being introduced to England and English ways.

"It is hardly fair to relate our impression of wartorn England when with jaundiced eyes we were seeing a country still being ravaged by war. There was a scarcity of food and all needed items. Our country never knew such rationing as these people had endured so cheerfully and patriotically during the years before we had entered the war. And so many things seemed so expensively out of reach. I remember, for instance, that a peach sold for two dollars. The expense of an evening in London's blackout would make a New York evening seem like a bargain basement in contrast."

But even in the starkness of life during its battle for survival this war-ravaged England had for the newly arrived Americans a charm and quaintness they would never forget, Captain Munroe's reminiscences confess.

"The English countryside with its rolling hills and well tended farms seemingly divided into squares by hedges, the narrow, winding highways lined by vine-covered and flowered embankments that scraped the buses, the quaint neat little villages with their many small flower-fronted nestling houses that seemed to appear around each curve, the pubs where the off-duty late afternoon crowd gathers to leisurely sip their beer while talking of family, war trends, politics and things in general, the tiny British cabs and automobiles, the tea shops and the ever-present tobacco shops—all these," observes Captain Munroe in this flow of descriptive prose, "add to the beauty and quaintness of England."

With these delights of pastoral England he contrasts less desirable aspects of English life:

"We don't enjoy our thoughts of the disagreeable weather, the poorly heated houses with their inferior plumbing, the absence of our spic and span kitchens, the absolute blackouts every evening, those inevitable sausages that were at least ninety per cent meal and ten per cent meat, the difficulty in getting transportation on the overcrowded trains and buses, the strict rationing, the electric current that was too strong for our electric gadgets, the shops opening too late, staying closed for lunch and tea time, and then closing too early in the evening, the British officers driving American

Captain George Snyder, left, and Captain Stanton W. Pickens, shortly after the 38th reached England, discuss their day's duties.

jeeps while American soldiers were thumbing rides, the many unglamorous British girls with bad teeth and legs splotched from open fireplaces (dermatitis ab igne), the men in their never pressed English tweeds, the London cabs always occupied, the hotels always crowded, *et al.* London during wartime was much different from what many remembered it to be."

For example:

"When walking at night in total blackout, and while bumping into unseen pedestrians in the midst of the fog-dampened voices of the unseen, the small, specially built headlights of the little London cabs gave an eerie appearance of subdued lightening bugs. The monotony of the voices with the occasional 'beep' of the cab horns was occasionally interrupted by air raid warnings, but everyone and everything seemed to go uninterrupted. Upon finally finding a night spot or our hotel and after going through several screens of blackout, the suddenness of the bright lights was blinding until visual accommodation returned. For some reason, we'd never ceased feeling that an English pound note was not akin to an American dollar bill until later we began finding that our resources were just about depleted. Most of us were having our military pay sent to families at home and directly to insurance companies, which left little for us overseas. We soon found that a London visit was not 'chicken feed,' and again we were back to the straw mattress and wigwam of Tidworth Park."

Further impressions of wartime England during the first few weeks of the 38th's stay in that embattled island were thus recorded by Dr. Munroe:

"Everywhere in England one saw the tremendous barrage balloons so placed to prevent German planes from low flying for more accuracy in target hitting. The often heard expression that the purpose of the balloon was to prevent the British island from submerging into the sea seemed very apt to us on many occasions. Strangely enough, unless one looked carefully, it was difficult to see the damage of Hitler's bombs in London, for the British quickly repaired such marks. Here and there pock marks were discernible on the buildings and the more recently patched spots on the street nearby could be found. Behind St. Paul's Cathedral with its prominent skyline dome could be found block after block of complete destruction of what was London's poorest section. We were never able to understand why this erstwhile poorest area of London received the brunt of German bombs unless the dome of St. Paul's Cathedral was the air mark of Goering's men. There was only small damage at one end of the Cathedral. The Houses of Parliament and London Bridge, both outstanding targets, were practically unscarred."

It was during the unit's stay at Tidworth Park that Captain Montgomery had his first memorable lesson in war-time letter-writing home.

"One morning while we were at Tidworth Park they had an officers' group meeting," he recalls. "They hadn't been amounting to much, anyway, and I decided not to go; I figured I'd stay in bed a while longer. But pretty soon one of the officers came in and said, 'Colonel Whittier wants to see you right now.' So I got up and dressed and went down. When I walked in, he was holding up a letter for me to see. It was one I had written home and I saw that the censor had cut it all to pieces. It was full of holes where words and sentences and paragraphs had been cut out.

" 'Captain Montgomery, I have your letter here; the censors sent it to me. Captain, this letter's a disgrace! You should know better than to write a letter like this, with all this information you have revealed.' He looked me in the eyes. 'Captain, what if this letter had fallen into the hands of the enemy!'

"I looked at the mutilated letter he was fluttering at me. 'Colonel,' I said, 'I think it did.' "

The unit had arrived at Tidworth Park staging area on August 20. Three weeks later, on September 10, the 38th left Tidworth Park and that same day arrived at Musgrove Military Park Hospital at Taunton, Somerset, England, where it took charge of the Musgrove Park hospital facility, a newly constructed and until then unused British hospital turned over to the 38th for the use of American troops. Facilities were available for the care of relatively few patients, it was found, and the time the unit was based there—from September 10 to October 5—was spent largely in the training of enlisted men in the care of the ill and in outfitting the new hospital.

The 38th's nurses rejoined the unit at Musgrove Park. One of the first and few casualties treated at Musgrove Hospital, Captain Munroe recalled, was an enlisted man who in cleaning his rifle inadvertently pulled the trigger with the result that a bullet went through his toe.

The three weeks at Musgrove had compensations but also presented problems, the Munroe reminiscences reveal:

"We were indoors where we enjoyed our small but new private rooms and again partook of American food. Many bought English bicycles with special gears for uphill riding, which was one step ahead of walking. The want of transportation was ever present with the members of our unit and we did enough walking during our overseas stay to last a lifetime. Our future hospital medical equipment had never been seen and the supply officers were going back and forth to Bristol to check on our table of equipment for an evacuation hospital unit."

News from home was always welcome. Here seven of the 38th's officers in England have been having a look at a copy of *The Charlotte News*, held by Captain Pickens. The others, left to right, are Medearis, Stith, Walker, Kendrick, Calder, and Snyder.

The move on October 5, 1942, was a transfer to Norton Manor Camp staging area, where the process of calisthenics, drilling and lectures was revived. Ten days after the 38th's arrival at Norton Manor Camp staging area it had a new commanding officer, Lieutenant Colonel Rollin L. Bauchspies, M.C., Regular Army. Colonel Raymond W. Whittier, who had taken command of the unit at Fort Bragg, was relieved because of ill health. He died soon afterward of heart disease.

During the 38th's stay at the Norton Camp Staging Area in England, from October 5 to October 23, 1942, the following assignment of the unit's nurses was made:

First Lieutenant Bessie V. Fullbright, chief nurse.

All the other members of the corps were second lieutenants. They were:

Hallie E. Almond, assistant chief nurse; Elva E. Wells and Ruth O. Logan, receiving section assistants;

Katherine Contourso and Mildred Hustac, evacuation section assistants; Rosamond S. Shipp, surgical service operating room supervisor; Lela O. Russell, mess section dietitian; Lola J. LaChance, maxillo-facial team anesthetist; Clementine A. Mills, surgical service neuro-surgical team; Elizabeth E. Killeen, surgical service maxillo-facial team; Hazel A. Simmons, surgical service orth-team No. 1; Mary A. Culley, surgical service orth-team No. 2; Bertha E. Hough, surgical service shock team No. 1; Martha Pegram, surgical service shock team No. 2; Ruth I. Barbee, Helen A. Gaynor, and Sara M. Moran, surgical service general surgical team No. 1; Mary F. Blandford, Helen J. Camenisch, and Ruby E. McCain, surgical service general surgical team No. 2; Violet O. Burgess, Martha G. Fliedner, and Cathaleen V. Radigan, surgical service general surgical team No. 3; Winnie R. Martin, surgical service thoracic-surgical team.

Others assigned to the surgical service of the unit were:

Lorraine M. Benante, Nina V. Brice, Marion J. Cox, Deborah R. Doskow, Josephine L. Harman, Rosalie D. Hirtz, Beatrice E. Johnson, Margaret B. Mizelle, Vera M. Neely, Gladys P. Pilger, Pauline P. Pisinsky, Frances L. Robbins, and Charlotte J. Webber.

Nurses assigned to the medical service were:

Margaret P. Bachoka, Ida P. Bell, Audrey J. Burnham, Bernice Carroll, Vera H. Dexheimer, Edith E. Guyett, Carolyn T. Haltiwanger, Annette M. Heaton, Claire S. Myers, Nellie C. Shields, Christine Wills, and Barbara L. Wingo.

The summary of the unit's service during the year 1942, as prepared by Colonel Bauchspies under the title "Medical History—Year Ending 31 December 1942," summarizes the experience of the 38th in England under "Duty in England." There is a slight divergence in dates between this account and other records, due perhaps to the date of orders to move from one area to another being different from the actual time of removal.

The Bauchspies summary:

"DUTY IN ENGLAND: Upon arrival in Liverpool, the nurses were sent by train to the American Hospital at Salisbury, Wilts. The Officers and Enlisted Men bivouaced at Transit Camp No. 3, Huyton, near Liverpool, until 20 August when they entrained for Tidworth, Wilts, and there bivouaced in a tent camp in Tidworth Park. On 10 September 1942, all personnel were moved to Taunton, Somerset, for the purpose of operating the Musgrove Military Hospital at that place. On 7 October 1942 the unit moved from the Musgrove Hospital to Norton-Manor Camp, about five miles northwest of Taunton. On 15 October Colonel Raymond W. Whittier was relieved from command, per instructions contained in Letter, Headquarters II Corps, October 14, 1942, and was succeeded by Lt. Col. Rollin L. Bauchspies, M.C. At 0500 hours 23 October 1942, the unit entrained at Taunton for Avonmouth where it boarded the 'D.S.S. Nieuw Zeeland' (P-2) the same day. . . ."

The terse history of the unit's movement from one staging area and assignment to another, however, tells little of the lively and unforgettable experience of the various members of the 38th during this short stay in England. Fortunately, the surviving letters of Captain Pickens, the reminiscences of Captain Munroe and others in the 38th provide a wealth of details in recording their experiences, the impressions so vividly received and remembered, and particularly, their sharing with the indomitable British people the desperate dangers under which they were living.

Pertinent paragraphs from letters to relatives and friends at home provide color and feeling and atmosphere, as well as factual information, that formal histories can never provide.

From England's Tidworth Park area a week before the unit left it to move to Musgrove Park Military Hospital, for example, Captain Pickens wrote on September 3, 1942:

". . . So far I have been doing well although there is plenty of rain in England and I am learning to eat beef and cabbage and cheese. . . . Find Coca-Cola available for the troops and you can search it out in London and Edinburgh. We have plenty of American cigarettes. The British have been unusually cordial and friendly. I'm getting so I can drink tea any time."

Ten days later he wrote from "Somewhere in England," though actually by this time the 38th had been for three days at Musgrove Park.

". . . I had a hurried trip to Edinburgh some weeks ago. Had time to get some first-hand information of John Knox—saw the cathedral where he preached, St. Giles, saw his house. Sometime again I might possibly get to stay longer. It appears that we can get seven days leave every three months, so I will try to get around as much as that time allows with the small bit of money I get. I was paid yesterday and drew 31 £ 16s 9 pence. The pound is worth almost $4, and the shilling is 20¢ and the pence is 2¢. I got $128. The rest of my salary goes to Mary. My laundry and cleaning is fairly expensive and slow and I have had to buy some additional clothes, plus my travel costs; however, I have never been flat broke since I've been here.

"I try to get to church every Sunday. Most of the time I go to the English church, which is quite high church. Have not found but one Methodist church."

By October 1, when his next letter was written, also from "Somewhere in England," which was Musgrove Park Military Hospital, Taunton, Somerset, Captain Pickens and others of the 38th had been able to obtain leaves to visit London and other places in England. The letter relating some of these experiences gives a more detailed view of their activities as the fall of 1942 saw the 38th in its last weeks in England:

"The mail has really been coming in and I have been getting my share. Upon my return from London on September 30 I found letters from Mary, Marshall, Jane, Stowe Moody, Vinton, and a cable from Mary. It appears that all the mail finally caught up with me. It was grand to get all the news and hear all is well. I might suggest that in the future when you write you put specific dates down instead of saying that last Thursday I went to so and so. When the mail finally catches me the time doesn't fit because some of the letters are older than others that I have received. I have borrowed this typewriter for a little while and am extremely out of practice, so overlook the mistakes.

"I was sent up to London to do some work, but found time to get about the city a little on my own. I went up with Col. Whittier, Preston White, Paul Sanger, Bill Pitts, and Buck Medearis. Preston White and I took a room together at the Cumberland Hotel where Bob is staying." (Robert Pickens, his brother, was in the service and stationed at that time in England.) "I was particularly glad to stay where Bob was in order to see him as much as possible, although he was extremely busy during my short visit. It is impossible to describe his work to you with the restrictions in vogue, but rest assured that it is important and he is doing it well. I think that I went into some detail about it in one of my letters to Father. It may have been cut out. He reports he writes regularly to his family and doesn't understand why the letters don't come thru. It has happened to others, so if you don't get the mail it is no fault of his."

He turns from the frustrations of censorship to tell of the Charlotte men's experiences in London:

"While in London I got time to get to the theatre twice. Preston and I saw 'The Doctor's Dilemma.' Vivien Leigh played the leading role. You remember her as the heroine in 'Gone With the Wind.' I also saw 'Blithe Spirit,' Noel Coward's fool play. As you probably know, the theatre starts at 6.30 P.M. in order to get thru early. Even though they start early, it is dark as pitch when you get out and unless you carry your own 'torch' you will break your neck. Bob took an awful spill when he first got here and had a bad leg from it for a long time. He is now fully recovered. The shows starting so early, you must eat afterwards. One night we went to Maison Prunier's and had the second steak I have seen in England. The other night we went to the Savoy and really put on the spread. I had lobster thermidor with all the trimmings. However, with all the talk the food is still limited but we get plenty. Bob could not join me either of the evenings. One night he was in his office and the other he had dinner with Stanley Richardson, head of the National Broadcasting here. It was funny about Richardson. Buck Medearis joined us for dinner and Bob brought Stanley by our table after eating and it turned out that Stanley was from Winston-Salem and had grown up with Buck. . . .

"Again on this trip I made the rounds of Parliament, Westminster Abbey, St. Martin-in-the-Fields, the National Gallery, St. James Palace, Buckingham, Wallace Collection, Threadneedle Street and the Bank of England, the British Museum, St. Paul's, Tower of London and London Bridge, and Preston and I even went to

Hyde Park and listened to many soap box orators. They are still here and as violent and vitriolic as ever. The hecklers are still numerous and make the show worth while."

Of transportation and other travel conditions in England during the period of the 38th's stay there he observed:

"Our hotel, as you probably remember, is just opposite the Marble Arch, put up, I think, to commemorate one of Victoria's birthdays or anniversaries. All it does now is hinder traffic, which is not too heavy these times. It is difficult to get a taxi during the day and almost an impossibility at night. The subways still run on time. The trains coming into London also run right on the dot—such an improvement over our system. I came into Waterloo Station and on another to Paddington, always on the exact time we were due. The trains are crowded and very often you must stand for the majority of the trip. Your fellow travelers, the English, will join you in conversation, if you start it yourself. They are still very reserved but cordial enough if you make the first move. Back to the hotel—it is modern, fireproof and the service is good, considering the constant crowds. You have to reserve your space at least a week in advance. Of course, we enjoyed having breakfast in bed. I like the custom and am only sorry that the Army can't get around to it. When I get home, after sleeping for six months, I want to wake up and have breakfast in bed, with good coffee and plenty of sugar and eggs that come out of shells."

He spoke of his relatives and friends at home having written him to ask what things they might send him. "My needs are slight," he told them in this same letter. "I have plenty of clothes and toilet articles, plenty of food, and since we have to travel often and light, I have little room for carrying a supply. I think the one thing that you might start on the way is some more paper like this I am writing on and some more of air mail envelopes. I still have a supply but it is gradually dwindling down and may run out before your shipment catches me. However, I still anticipate the box Miss Mary is sending from Atlanta and the one Marshall has on the way from Charlotte."

He went on to tell more of London under war conditions. "At the National Gallery and the Wallace Collection there is little to be seen. Practically all of the old masters have been stored. It is really of little use to visit them except for displays of some modern things showing the war and some of its results and this I see enough of without looking at oil paintings. The changing of the guard at Buckingham is not the show it used to be. The color is lacking."

A day's routine during the 38th's stay in Britain is

A group of the 38th's officers, off duty in England, do a little experimenting with English bicycles. Left to right, Kendrick, Pickens, Medearis, Felts, Stith, Snyder, Walker, Calder, and Matthews.

tersely revealed in the last paragraph of the October 1, 1942, letter:

"Today has been a fairly trying one for me. I got to calisthenics at 7 A.M. and then to breakfast where the Col. assigned me to take some of our officers who had been slightly late for the exercise, on a five-mile march. These officers were Fleming, Perry, Gay, Schirmer, Powers and Rowe. At nine we started out with full pack and got into the country. We studied camouflage and defilade, marched with our gas masks on for a time, practiced dispersing and other things, then ran for a short half mile. When I got back I was tired, but after lunch I had to do some tent pitching with my men and then exercise again at five with supper at six. Now I am ready for bed, with tired muscles, twisted back and falling arches. Tomorrow I shall be back in shape and on the job, but now I will end this bit of a letter. Let me hear from all of you when you get time to write. Nothing cheers a man up more than mail from home."

On the day that Captain Pickens was writing this letter home, General Mark Clark through Lieutenant Colonel F. W. Zies, the assistant adjutant general, was issuing an order for the 38th Evacuation Hospital to "move from Musgrove Hospital, Taunton, to Norton Manor, Taunton, on or about October 3, 1942."

The order provided:

"a. Movement will be made by organic motor transportation.

"b. Exact time and details of movement will be coordinated with local SOS and British authorities.

"2. Arrangements will be made to continue in telephonic communication with this headquarters."

The unit departed from Musgrove Park Military Hospital at Taunton, Somerset, on October 5 and arrived the same day at Norton Manor Camp staging area. It remained there only eighteen days and on October 23 left that staging area and arrived the same day at Bristol, from which after a few hours it sailed aboard H.M.S. *Malta* in a convoy destined for overseas duty.

From Norton Manor Camp on October 21, two days before the 38th left that staging area for Bristol and embarkation at Bristol, Captain Pickens wrote his last

28

letter from England. It, too, was datelined "Somewhere in England." The letter, he said at the beginning, was being written with varying emotions. It provides a further intimate look at England and the British people with whom for more than two months the members of the 38th had been living and at the same time another close-up of this group of professional men suddenly and intricately involved in the rigors and dangers of a world war.

"I had the idea I might try to review the slightly over two months that I have been in England, but with the various restrictions that control our descriptions, it seems like an impossible job to accomplish. I know that my letters to you, whether individually written or where I have used this carbon copy method, have appeared stupid in the main and certainly not up to the standard I made in the states nor the standards set by my writing brothers. But the difference is there where even the typewriter might have ears and looking a smart enemy in the eye directly is no time for careless words. But in spite of the pent-up feeling at present, I am going to set forth as far as possible.

"Just yesterday I was in London again for the day. I was able to get a 24-hour pass, beginning at midnight and ending at midnight, so I set forth at 2 A.M. on one of England's cold trains and rode into Paddington station and wandered out into the night at about 5:30 A.M. After considerable maneuvering around, I hailed a taxi, one of the almost extinct animals in England, and got to the Cumberland Hotel. There the sleepy clerk told me they had no room so I went into Bob's room and waked him up long enough to get two blankets and stretched out on the floor. When the maid came at 7:15 to bring Bob's breakfast, she almost fell out of the room when she discovered me there. Anything that appears out of the ordinary routine just scares these English out of their wits. Everything must be done just like it has been done for so many centuries in the past. I managed to get an hour's sleep after Bob went to work. Then he phoned me that he had General Davis for the day of sightseeing and did I want to go along. Of course I did. General Davis is our only colored General. Bob and I chuckled over two Carolina men carrying one of our colored friends around and watching our Ps and Qs at every turn. When the question of the photographers came up I reported that I had a small amount of work to do and slipped out on Bob for an hour. They picked me up later and we looked at more tombstones in Westminster and horticulture in Kew Gardens than I had ever seen before and more than I want to witness again for some time. All in all, it was a pleasant tour but I failed to have any time with Bob alone during the whole day. I caught the same cold train at 6:30 P.M. and was back in my station at 11:00 P.M. It was worth it even under the circumstances to see Bob one more time. We made a date to march down Fifth Ave. together when this mess is finished."

He turned to a discussion of the English people:

"These people over here have gone 'all out' to make us welcome. Where they won't start a conversation among themselves in a railway carriage, they will talk to the Yanks. They are anxious for us to like them and they are really interested in how the average person lives in America. They have judged us so far by the movies, so I have had a grand time getting those I have talked with back in line. One of the most impressive things that I got here is how much they are doing and have done to win this war. By this I mean people like us who have had a fairly easy time in the last few years. The comparable people here now have no servants, do all of their own work in the house and in the gardens, pedal on their bikes if they want to get to town, carry their rationed groceries home in a basket, have their spare rooms filled with evacuated children or have some branch of the Army or the female Army billeted on them and then have time to work in the canteens cheering the soldiers that pass thru on the trains. They do all of their canning and act as air raid wardens so many nights a month and take their turns with the Red Cross when there is a raid either in their town or neighboring towns around them. They know how to dress a wound, put out an incendiary bomb, dig a ditch, pump a water hose, wash their own clothes and when the day is over, feel like they have really had a part in winning this war. The evidences of their sacrifices are manifest on every face. They have no time for beauty parlors, as a matter of fact, those institutions are nearly as extinct as the taxicabs. Their hands show that they have been used for something besides playing bridge. Don't misunderstand me; I'm not trying to paint a picture that might drive you to foolish acts when they are entirely unnecessary in your case. But too much has been said about the British not doing their part. I know different now and what I say goes for the whole blessed little island. They know how to take it and how to dish it out. There isn't any indication of weakness that I can see among the average people over here. They are slow and know nothing about mass production but what they turn out is usually very thorough. And they are plenty mad about this war and plenty grateful for anything we are doing to help the situation. Even the kids are doing their share, as I see where ours are doing. Only today they called up the toy soldiers for the Toy Town Salvage Corps. They are to give up their toys for waste metal to be made into tanks and guns. It will be somewhat of a heartache to dump that red-coated drum-major and kilted bagpiper into the salvage can, but these children will take to it and do it."

The 38th's encampment at Tidworth Park, England, near Salisbury. The arrow doubtless points to the tent occupied by the now unknown photographer.

He digressed for a long paragraph to discuss the ways of the British barber as compared with those of the American and to outline other personal experiences representative of those of the 38th's members on brief leave in London. They further reveal even better than more formal histories of the period the ordinary day-to-day activities of a nation whose very existence is being threatened by a powerful and relentless enemy almost at its borders.

"Today I got into town for a bit of shopping," Captain Pickens' letter continues. "I had my hair cut at the 'Gentlemen's Hairdressing' place up over the haberdashery. The barber finished in the time it takes the average American barber to get all the towels and clothes arranged around the neck. It is the one thing they do quicker than we. There are no fancy chairs that can be pumped up to the right height. You just sit down in the ordinary chair with a small mirror in front of you and he starts to work. There is no conversation, just a haircut.

"From there I went to purchase a can opener, a tin opener, as they call it. It cost me ten pence or about 20¢ in our money. From there I went to Lloyd's Bank to get some travelers checks. I had about 25 £

which I transferred into checks. It is easier to carry money that way and less chance of losing it. This was done at about four o'clock in the afternoon. They were slow about it and I am sure they took time to have a cup of tea while I waited, but at least the bank was open for even slow business at 4 PM. From the bank I purchased some maps that I had been wanting to get covering the war fronts all over the world. In addition, I picked up a consolidated history of Europe. I find that I need to brush up on what has been going on over here for the past three or four centuries. It will help me understand why certain things are done or not done."

Captain Pickens in the closing paragraph of this letter gives a vague hint that a change in the 38th's location is imminent:

"It will probably be some time before I will get another chance to write you. Don't worry if you do not hear from me. Worry is an enemy. We've got enough without adding that to the list. Worry clouds the vision so that we become blind to the beauty around us, the goodness of human nature and the hopeful factors in any situation. The cure for worry is faith. I've got my share. You keep yours."

4

On October 23, 1942, six months and a week after the 38th began training at Fort Bragg, the unit went aboard H.M.S. *Malta* in the harbor at Bristol, at the head of Bristol Channel on England's western coast about a hundred miles from London.

When the 38th sailed from the harbor it was headed for the battle lines.

Captain H. Stokes Munroe in his reminiscences takes up the story of the 38th as the unit was leaving Bristol:

"On departing Norton Manor on October 23, 1942, the organization entrained for Bristol, where we embarked on H.M.S. *Malta* (New Zealand) at Port of Embarkation. Several of the officers had been ordered to Greenock, Scotland, a few days before to become ship surgeons on convoy ships. This group consisted of Lt. Colin A. Munroe, Lt. Olin Perryman, Capt. William Kavanagh, Capt. William Evans, Capt. Glen Perry, Lt. Claud Perry.

"We had no idea of our destination and you can imagine what bizarre speculation took place—India, Spain, Gold Coast of Africa, etc. We first sailed out of Bristol Channel, up the Irish Sea, to the Firth of Clyde. The Firth was a large bay that seemed completely enclosed by arms of Scottish land. We were anchored in this bay off Greenock. The view was of bleak cold country, the ocean winds wet and penetrating and the bay always choppy. Many small motor craft hurried to and from the many ships in the bay. One fast motor craft delivered Captain William P. Kavanagh to the welcoming arms of the unit. He was one of our officers who had gone to Scotland to become ship surgeon on one of the many American supply ships. He had gone, however, only on verbal orders. His intended ship had left the bay, leaving him stranded in the cold Scottish town without written orders and with a very thin wallet. After being told time and again that our ship was not in the harbor, he was joyous over finding us himself. He spent his last shilling on a 'bit of Scotch mist' to share toast with us over his joy in returning and our happiness in having him back."

Captain Munroe continues with interesting detail his narration of the unit's further travels on its way to its first action assignment:

"The large convoy formed at open sea where nothing of great consequence happened during the early portion of our sea travel. No one knew where we were or where we were going. Again speculation was rife. We joined another huge convoy in mid-ocean at a point that we later learned was near the Azores. Although we did not know it at the time, the convoy had come directly from the United States. For a while we were in the largest single ocean convoy in all history. The large convoy that formed near the Azores consisted of the Western Task Force, which sailed directly from the United States to strike at Casablanca, French Morocco. Our convoy consisted of the Center Task Force (II Corps) to which we were assigned, and was to strike at Oran, Algeria. The Eastern Task Force, largely British, was to storm the Port of Algiers. Unknown to us, the history of the Fifth Army was soon to be in the making. The many cruisers, battleships, liberty ships, and other types of ships zigzagged continuously. During the foggy, dark night in complete blackout, nothing could be seen and only the occasional fog horns were heard. There was no radio communication for fear that enemy submarines would locate us. It will always seem a mystery, even with radar, how so many ships zigged and zagged constantly during dark nights without mishap.

"Some of the convoy broke up just before we reached the Straits of Gibraltar, which our convoy portion entered. Here the Western Task Force convoy left us. For the first time since leaving the States we saw the bright lights of a city, those of the city of Tangiers, Spanish Morocco. The Rock of Gibraltar was recognizable, but there were only scattered lights in the village at its base during those late night and early morning hours. We were in the Mediterranean Sea, but we still did not know of our destination until the officers were called in conference by Colonel Bauchspies. It was then that we first learned that we were a part of II Corps, Center Task Force, and were to land at Arzew, North Africa. We were briefed regarding the unknown amount of French hostility that was to be met, and could hope that only token resistance would be encountered.

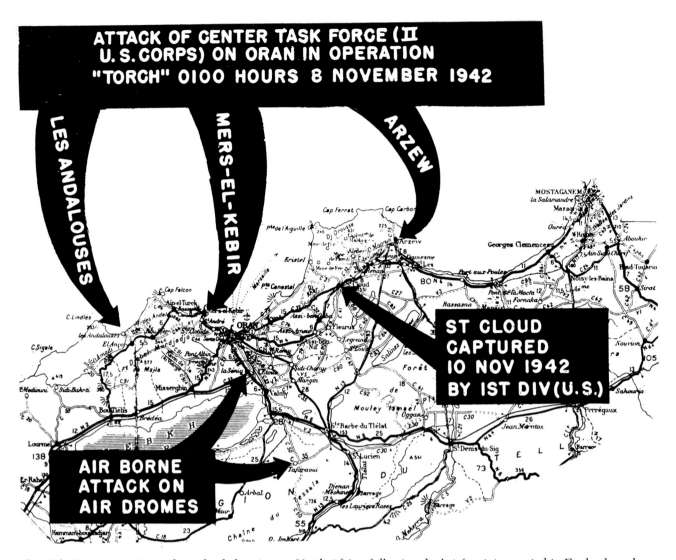

The 38th Evacuation Hospital unit landed at Arzew, North Africa, following the brief training period in England, as shown in this drawing revealing the targets at the Center Task Force's attack upon Oran on November 8, 1942.

"There were many unknown quantities," the captain's account of this period in the unit's history points out. "It was hoped that the increased activity about Gibraltar would lead the German and French forces to believe that an ambitious attempt toward reinforcement of Malta was in the process. In addition to the amount of resistance that might be expected from French troops, there was fear that Spain and its troops in Spanish Morocco might decide to declare war on Allied troops. The fear that German submarine activity and airplane activity might be alerted to await our arrival due to some break in secrecy plans was present. We were briefed in these uncertainties, and in such a state neared our destination."

As Captain Munroe's account nears the 38th's appointed landing date it becomes more exciting:

"During the night of November 7, 1942, we were given orders to remain dressed and to be prepared for immediate ship departure.

"Many of us remained on deck, and when the motion of the ship ceased, nothing was discernible in the blackness of the night—no other ship and no land. In the unseeing dark, Center Task Force had imperceptibly peeled off from the remaining convoy while the Eastern Task Force portion of the main convoy continued eastward. For many hours we knew that our ship had reduced speed.

"In the early morning hours, precisely at 0100 hours, the flash and noise of battleship cannon suddenly disturbed the quiet of the silent night and these were soon answered by the guns of the French shore installations. Shortly thereafter the landing task force went into action on the shore that was softened by the heavy artillery of our ship. During the heavy ship firing L.S.T.s were already enroute to strike the shore installations. Three groups of landing forces of Center Task Force (II U.S. Corps) took part in the Oran area in operation 'TORCH' at 0100 hours, 8 Nov., 1942. One group that we followed landed at Mers-El-Kebir close by the Oran harbor, and the other group landed farther west at Les Andalouses, while the Airborne Rangers parachuted to the more inland French airdromes to the south of the area, La Senig and Tafaraoui, Algeria. These Rangers were our friends and protectors during our Arzew stay. Soon dawn came and everything seemed quiet at the Port of Arzew, Algeria. Everything seemed to happen so quickly and it was comforting to see the fellowship about us. A French passenger liner and its French passengers, captured while departing North Africa for its trip to a French port, lay anchored in the bay.

"During the mid portion of the day we disembarked. The enlisted personnel and some of the officers climbed down the netted ladder; most of the officers and nurses descended the unsteady appearing steps that were let down the ship's side into the landing ship craft of the choppy sea. It was a problem to judge the jump into the small craft that was constantly bobbing up and down, especially after seeing some in full pack and helmet meet the impacts of the upjumping craft in their midair leap.

"The good but foreign soil felt fine. It was North Africa. We felt the unrevealing stares of the strange inhabitants as we marched through the village of Arzew into the fenced, recently deserted French military garrison. In the distance the white stuccoed houses of North Africa appeared so neat and clean in the sun; it never ceased to be disappointments when they were neared and the obvious uncleanliness met the eye, and sometimes the nostrils. But the French garrison was to be our temporary home, even though we hoped that it would not be for long. It was the filthiest place imaginable. We immediately burned all fixtures, including the beds and other furniture. After the floors were cleansed as thoroughly as possible the concrete floor became our beds. Our bedding rolls were not available and we didn't know where they were. We spent cold, fireless nights at the garrison without blankets, bedding, and without any feeling of security."

The 38th, even more than it had during its stay in heavily besieged Britain, was beginning to realize that it was indeed in a war. Captain Munroe reveals further:

"The evenings were punctuated by the strange outside noise of the Arab sniper rifles, followed by the more familiar sound of the few scattered American Rangers' Tommy guns. We were constantly under sniper fire, and only felt security in the thickness of the walls of the buildings and in the knowledge that the Rangers were somewhere about the village.

"Our hospital equipment was unloaded and placed in a large field of the garrison, and several of us were checking the equipment when suddenly we were in-

terrupted. Dirt kicked up all about us as the pings of Arab rifles continued. Paul Sanger beat me to a narrow space between two large crates, but their depth permitted our double-decked sense of more security. We were shortly peeping behind crated equipment at the church steeple, and were happy to see the Rangers soon put an end to the Arab rifles. At that time we were at an unarmed Army unit and we cherished our Ranger protectors.

"During our last night at the garrison we were awakened by a blood-curdling scream from somewhere amongst our midst. Several of us jumped off the floor and upon rounding the corner of our barracks toward the direction of the scream, we suddenly met a gun and were challenged. The Ranger, by the grace of God, had good control of his gun finger, so we all went out to investigate. Thinking of Arab and knives together, and since the scream sounded like a woman in terror, we felt that some Arab had climbed the fence and had knifed one of our nurses. The nurses were soon accounted for, however, and we were in ignorance of the cause of the disturbance until several days later, when we learned that one of the enlisted men of another unit had gone stark mad and had hidden during the night. He died several days later."

Major W. H. Pennington, writing to Mrs. Pennington in Lexington, Kentucky, from North Africa, also summarized the 38th's experiences upon landing in Africa:

"We slept in our clothes on the concrete floor. It was very cold at night and we had no covers except our trench coats. We had eaten canned meat and beans

On a short leave in Oran, North Africa, December 8, 1942, Lieutenants Elva Wells, left, and Charlotte Jean Webber get a respite from their coveralls by donning harem regalias.

for supper. The water supply was very limited. We arose at 5:30 a.m. after a miserable night, following which we were cold and stiff. Beans and meat for breakfast. Heated a cup of water over a bonfire and made coffee out of powdered stuff. No water to wash and shave.

"After our equipment had been set up, snipers in the hills and in various buildings in the town began shooting at us. We dropped flat on the ground and bullets would kick up dust around us.

"American soldiers who had been patrolling the town came advancing across the fields with tommy guns. More firing by both sides. One of the soldiers got down beside the truck I was lying under and began picking off snipers in the hills. I was afraid to stay beside him and also afraid to move. I thought every minute might be my last one. After a while, we got used to the shooting and would watch the soldiers go into some of the hillside homes and bring out natives at point of gun.

"The shooting stopped and we went back to work. Every fifteen or twenty minutes it would break out again and we would dive for cover. We began stacking mattresses, bales and towels around so we would have some protection.

"All through the day the sniping continued and we were kept busy dropping on our bellies and burying our heads. I looked like I'd been dragged in the dirt and no water to wash.

"Everybody very jittery and the firing continuing . . . there was a double ring of guards around the enclosure . . . I saw about 500 prisoners . . . they were quartered in a building just outside the wires . . .

"Two German planes over here just now. At 8:30 a.m. they strafed the beach. Our guns brought one down . . ."

Three days after arriving at the bivouac area at Arzew, Algeria, the 38th received new orders sending them on November 12, 1942, to a station a mile and a half southeast of St. Cloud, Algeria.

Sometimes, though not often or for a long time, members of the 38th were able to do a little sun-bathing. Left to right, Dick Query, Paul Sanger, Pat Imes, Bill Pennington.

Captain Munroe, happily, recorded in considerable detail the moving to St. Cloud and interesting and revealing details of the unit's setting up its field hospital. He wrote:

"With the further eastward move of the fighting line, we received orders to move to a new location. Feeling that the next place would be better, we climbed aboard Army trucks on November 12, 1942, to our new hospital site, a large oat field of approximately 1,000 yards square that was about one and a half miles southeast of St. Cloud, Algeria, and about ten miles northeast of Oran, Algeria. St. Cloud was captured by the First Division (U.S.) on November 10, 1942. On the previous day a detachment of officers and enlisted men surveyed the field and planned a set-up of our 200-tent hospital. We reached the area in the late afternoon of November 12 and several of the essential tents were up, but not completely or securely pegged down. Unsuspectingly, we bedded in our new quarters for a sleepless night, for our first education of what a tent can and cannot withstand soon presented itself. We had hardly fallen asleep when all hell broke loose in the face of the powerful North African wind. Practically all tents were down while we were frantically striving to save tents and personal belongings. Dawn found us still driving tent pegs, while Colonel Bauchspies was still raising cain and profaning the entire unit because of the seeming disaster. Fortunately, the rain was light enough to spare our personal belongings. On the following day, November 13, eight patients were admitted during the course of our setting up and uncrating of unseen hospital equipment."

Dr. Munroe continues his narration with a recital of the hospital's treating of the unit's first battle casualties:

"During the first week of operations 300 patients were admitted, and admissions rapidly increased so that on the twentieth day the capacity of the hospital was exceeded. All types of patients, including American, French, and British personnel, as well as native Arab and French casualties, were admitted. The hospital facilities were enlarged by the addition of further tents until at midnight of December 31, 1942, patient census was 617."

He describes the hospital layout and its operation during these early days at St. Cloud:

"Each ward tent contained 20 beds (cots) and was under control of an officer, a nurse, and corpsmen. They were all arranged in a symmetrical manner down to each tent pole and each tent pin. The nurses did a grand job on readying the hospital ward tents and the operating room tents for the care of the patients. It requires an abundance of sterile supplies for the ward tents and innumerable and repeated sterilization of the operating room equipment. Much ingenuity was in full sway in the sterile management of operating equipment in such a way that this material was always in readiness during the almost constant care and preparations of instruments for further and repeated use. Miss Rosamond Shipp and her assisting nurses deserve much praise for their truly remarkable ingenuity and capability in their enterprise, their first running of an operating room tent. The many nurses who supervised their ward tents, and who were aided by the corpsmen, did a memorable job."

Captain Munroe's account of the St. Cloud hospital further describes the physical layout:

"The roadways between the tents were all named: The Parade, Carolina Avenue, New York Avenue, Pennsylvania Avenue, Kentucky Avenue, Indiana Avenue, First Street, Second Street, etc. The name of each street or avenue was expertly painted on a white spick-and-span sign post by one of our recuperating patients who was a sign painter in civilian life. The U-shaped driveway into the receiving section, situated at the hospital front, was lined with whitewashed stones, which also lined the other hospital thoroughfares. The officers and nurses were quartered on one side of the hospital area, the officers on one side and the nurses on the other side of Carolina Avenue. Each of the tents had a number. These officer and nurse personnel tents, so-called wall tents, although not large, comfortably accommodated two persons. There were fifty of these tents along Carolina Avenue. Then just beyond were 160 shelter half tents (pup tents) which quartered the enlisted personnel. There was a line between the officers' area and the enlisted men's area, made of whitewashed stone and labeled the Mason-Dixon line by the enlisted men. Since nearly all of the officers were southerners and nearly all the enlisted personnel were northerners, it was quite appropriate, although in good fun. In addition to this, we had several large kitchens and mess halls for officers and nurses, enlisted personnel, and patients. We also constructed latrines of the family size, minus the air-conditioned unit of the previous French garrison latrine.

"These things came by degrees and hard work. At last we were getting our meals served on enamel plates and at tables, which was quite a jump from C rations. Our food for days in North Africa came in small rationed tin cans of two types: one contained hard biscuits, hard blocks of sugar, some powdered coffee, and four small pieces of hard candy; the other contained a conglomeration of meat and vegetables. All were eaten cold and out of cans, except during our bizarre methods of heating hot water in one of the cans with matches or cigarette lighters for coffee. We were limited to about one pint of chemically treated water a day for drinking and washing purposes for some time, but soon graduated to water luxury. For a while all water for our new tent hospital was transported from a water point in Arzew, 22 kilometers distance. Canvas reservoirs were erected in the hospital area, and the Engineer Corps assisted in the transportation of the water and its chemical treatment. A detachment of one officer and 30 enlisted men from the 708th Sanitary Company and an Engineering detachment of one officer and twelve enlisted men aided materially in the construction of the utilities for the hospital. It was the rainy season and many adverse conditions due to the water were encountered. The mud was at times almost unsurmountable and everything, as well as everybody, was mud covered. However, the operation of the hospital was not interrupted and the physical welfare and the morale of the personnel continued to be excellent. We were proud of our hospital, we knew that it was a show place, and we felt good. We had graduated from our previous Army feeling of uselessness and now we were doing things."

Progress in developing the hospital had been rapid,

The enlisted personnel's tents were sometimes all above ground, sometimes dug in for protection against bombing.

Preparing for—or just finished with—a bath, Major George Snyder is caught at Paestum by camera between Captain William Evans and Captain Frank (Shorty) McGrath.

35

Captain Munroe's narrative of these early days in North Africa discloses:

"In the beginning we had only one flashlight, advanced to kerosene lamp, then began generating our own electricity with small gasoline engines. Finally the Engineering Corps was bringing electricity from a nearby power line. From the water paucity stage of the hospital the Engineer Corps was soon pumping us water from a not too distant uncontaminated well. Soon there were available showers for the more hardy to graduate from the helmet bath stage. After one experience in the cold water shower, that offered small protection from the cold North African wind, many went back to the helmet stage. We can still visualize Aubrey Hawes' daily trips to that torture tent shower. Few seemed to feel that much in need of a shower."

He speaks of other methods they devised to obtain baths:

"The water was hard and defied the lathering of soap. Many of us, by hook or crook, availed ourselves of Arab stoves, which burned either kerosene or gasoline through a needlepoint valve that was constantly on the blink. We always felt that it took two men and several small boys, with a blend of profanity and patience added, to run the small Arab stove, but it was better than nothing. It was our only method of getting hot water for helmet bathing, and it also partially took some of the chill from the air. We either hovered over the small stove or immediately removed our shoes or boots and climbed into our million-dollar sleeping bags. As so many others had, we had always pictured Africa as hot desert desolation that immediately ran into hot jungles, but we soon learned that North Africa, in the Oran, Algeria, area, was an undeveloped strip of land in which trees, except for the occasional date palms and olive trees, refused to thrive in the face of such filth and such horribly cold wintry and rainy weather.

"There seemed to be no trees for lumber or burning, as practically all wood for burning consisted of roots from burnt out grape orchards. Those first cold dreary nights were a reality of desolation. Our operating room tents and ward tents contained pot-bellied stoves, but due to the coal shortage, the coal was rationed severely. When not at work we all jumped into our sleeping bags and lay in darkness for warmth's sake. When electric lights and reading material came into being for our living quarters, we felt that we were getting up in the world.

"The most interesting part of it all," Captain Munroe concludes his summary of the early experience of the 38th in North Africa, "the organization and running of our hospital inspired us constantly and always gave some surcease from our many discomforts."

5

On November 16, 1942, four days after the 38th left Arzew and arrived at St. Cloud, Captain Pickens wrote the folk at home a long letter in which he sought to tell of his feelings in leaving England three weeks before and of the subsequent experiences of the unit as it began its tour of duty in northwest Africa.

"There was a definite feeling of poignancy upon leaving England. The time spent in the British Isles made a profound impression upon me. As most of my letters expressed, I liked the British people. They were exceedingly good to the Americans in their midst. I like the countryside. It is very pretty."

He had reflected upon his stay in England, he revealed, as he was leaving the beleaguered little island. "Riding along the other night in the back end of a truck, I had time to reflect about some of the things I had seen in England," he wrote. And then he went on to relate details of their leaving and the thoughts that had come to him as they drove toward the embarkation point:

"We had been awakened in the middle of the night, literally, and were being trucked off to the nearest railway station. We were packed in like the proverbial sardines, but I got in last and had a seat on the rear where I could see. The moon was up and the many chimneys, of which England has plenty, made long shadows. England has been good to me and I was grateful. I began to think about some of the little things I could remember. The hedge-lined fields and the lanes and the country roads; we had practiced running for cover along these hedge-lines and had studied camouflage and reflections along them. The friendly public

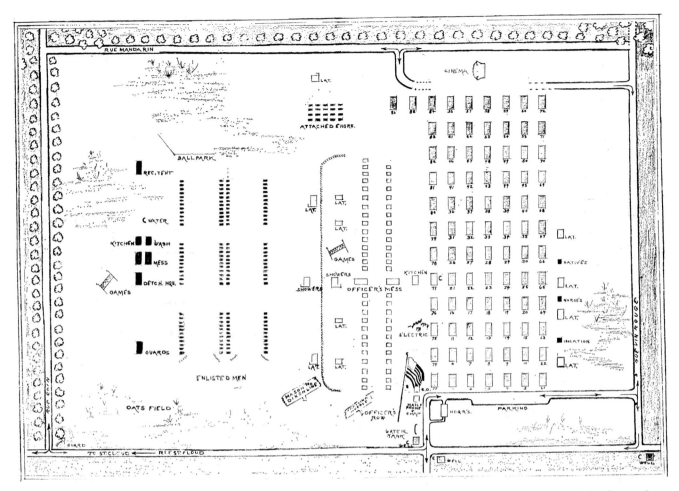

This drawing, made at St. Cloud by Clarence O. Kuester, Jr., of the 38th personnel, shows the layout of the hospital in that North African sector. The "Mason and Dixon Line," center, divides the "southern" officers' area from the "Yankee" enlisted men's quarters.

house with its ever-present dart game. The grazing cattle and sheep, and we had our share of mutton while on British rations. The trains running on time; they never missed a minute on any of the trips I made. The everlasting stop in mid-morning and mid-afternoon for tea and the accompanying bread and jam or the cookies that went with it. The daily rainfall and the accompanying fog, and it can really get damp in England. The lack of sugar in the quantities to which we were accustomed, but you soon get used to it. The left-hand drive on the streets and the thousands of bicycles, and the bicycles having the right of way. There was the everlasting blackout with its feeling of being lost and the sudden jerk when you step off the curb and didn't expect it. The poor teeth possessed by the majority of the population I saw. The many book shops in every town regardless of the size of the town and the complete choice of books on the shelves. They inspired me to some reading which I had gotten away from in these latter years. There was good music on the radio with a lack of commercial announcements. The harbored rivalry between the English and the Scotch is con-

siderably more pronounced than that left between our most rabid Yankees and Rebels. The thousands of crows or rooks or whatever they are called that infest every field and how they could attack a freshly cut field of barley. The handsome cathedral in nearly every town with the tombstones inside instead of out. The lack of heat on the cold days; they are used to it but I don't think I ever will get accustomed to freezing slowly. The hot tea helped to save me. The beep-beep of the nearly extinct taxi in London and the cry in the blackout at night 'Taxi!' to every passing vehicle. The raucous sound of the full-blooded Welshman talking his native tongue. Parliament had just passed a law that the Welsh may plead their cases in the common courts in their own language. The fierce pride all Britishers have in their Navy and RAF and rightfully so. The Navy has kept them in food and the RAF has been striking back at the enemy wherever possible. Every housewife apparently has a perambulator whether she has a baby to push or just uses it to get the groceries. They clutter the streets in every small town. The lack of slang in the King's English; they

37

have picked up a few of our expressions but on the whole you never hear our slang. They judge us by the movies they see and then get mad if we say their newspapers express their public opinions. The people still feeding the pigeons at Trafalgar Square and the queue lines waiting for the buses. Everyone gets in line in England."

So much for embattled brave little England.

"But now I am away from England and turn my attention to other parts of the world. We sailed from the British Isles and the first day was rough and the majority felt the roll. I was fortunate and got by without being confined and I make no claim to being a good sailor. Many of our group stayed in their cabins for two days and came out slowly. We are headed for Northwest Africa and my feeling is not as keen about it as was Stanley's and Livingstone's.

"We have been coached as to our procedure with reference to the natives. We have been immunized against everything from dandruff to falling arches. We know what to do in case the sun gets too hot. We have been weaned from drinking water. This was done in Britain. We learned how to swat flies in the States and this should stand us in good stead. Because of my knock-knees, I have not taken to the short pants and, besides, the longer ones may keep off some of the mosquitoes.

"We have learned something about the Moslem religion and the customs that go with it. We know not to cut bread but to break it and to always eat with our right hand. I am wondering what Bob will do when he gets down here, if he ever does, since he is a southpaw. We have learned that if we are invited out to dinner and are required to sit on the floor to always cross our legs and never eat everything on the plate. What's left goes to the women and children. We know

Colonel Bauchspies, right, is about to—for the photographer, at any rate—begin giving Major Sanger a haircut. It was during the period the 38th was at St. Cloud.

to shake hands upon meeting and leaving. We must always inquire of their health. As a matter of fact, this experience with the people will teach us some good manners, since it is apparent that we will run into them on all sides."

He returned for a moment to refer to the boat trip with the observation that there was "little to be said . . . that would pass the censor and I am not interested in trying to outwit him. I am concerned as much with my own safety as he is." But he did describe briefly their quarters. "I have three roommates, Stokes Munroe, Jack Montgomery, and Buck Medearis. We were assigned in alphabetical order, so they had no choice as to their fourth man. We are in a cabin that measures 6 feet by 12 feet. If you stop and figure that out you can see that we are not overrun with room. We have no chair but we do have two wash basins which are useful only for thirty minutes three times daily when fresh water is available. My bunk is exactly six feet long and I stretch a little over six feet two inches, so I sleep in jack-knife style, up one side and down the other . . . The others are more fortunate since they are not so tall. We get along together in fine fashion. I was able to bring on board two tins of soda crackers and a No. 10 can of peanut butter, so we have a spread every evening before folding into our niches. There is some advantage in being a mess officer.

"Many of our group," Captain Pickens' letter continues, "have taken to my favorite game of chess. Stokes Munroe, Jack Montgomery, Paul Sanger, Bernard Walker, George Wood, Milo Hoffman, George Rowe, Vaiden Kendrick, and George Snyder all have had lessons and now the majority of them can lick me in a game. We have decided that at the old soldiers' reunion all that would be necessary for its success will be to have three or four chess games available. When we have not been practicing boat drill and so forth, the game has helped pass the time. Bridge has also attracted some but I have taken little time off to help my game. Darts are also available but they are difficult on board ship, as are the ping-pong games."

His letter speaks of other entertainment aboard the ship taking them to North Africa:

"We have had a number of amateur shows on the boat put on by talent that turned up or was unearthed. One evening the enlisted men put on a good show with a variety of acts. They turned up with guitars and mandolins and did some songs and a blackface skit and a novelty dance. The dance was to a tune written by one of the men entitled 'G.I. Shoes.' It was really clever. One evening some of the officers did their job. One of the men has a violin with him so we had a solo from him and then some piano selections and then the old glee club which performed with Bob Hope and

The 38th's encampment at St. Cloud had a tall flagpole from which the Red Cross ensign flew just beneath the Stars and Stripes.

Frances Langford in Charlotte came on and did its part. It sounded pretty good to me. After each performance refreshments were served in the dining room. These consisted of cookies, Dutch style, and some punch made from canned fruit salad and carbonated water. But it was good. Under the circumstances I think the whole plan helped to keep up morale and those who participated had a good time working on it."

The voyage and his letter neared their ends together.

"We sighted the African coast last night," he wrote. "I had always heard of Africa as the dark continent, but believe it or not, the first city we passed had the lights on as bright as day, more lights than we have seen since we left the states. To me it looked like Times Square on a clear night. Of course, we were moving along in the blackout and that emphasized the lights we saw. However, it was somewhat of a relief to see land again.

"During the long nights in the dark I have spent much time studying the stars again. It has been a long time since Father gave me my first knowledge of the constellations and Wiley helped by telling stories about them. I was reminded of Tennyson's *Locksley Hall* where he said 'Many a night from yonder casement, ere I went to rest, I watched beautiful Orion, sloping slowly to the west.' I can't quote the rest of the verse, but there was something about the Pleiades and the Hyades. You remember it. Running the eye around the heavens and picking out the stars and planets helped during my tour of duty as officer of the day. Our shifts

Four 38th buddies are caught on a day off in Rome—Jack Macario, Wilbur Knopp, Norman S. Reynolds and Helke McCaughon.

start at 3 AM and go to 3 PM. I always caught the 3 AM starting time so I had several hours on deck to meditate. . . ."

A wealth of details provided in a letter written exactly two weeks later, on December 1, 1942, by Captain Pickens supplements the reminiscences of Captain Munroe and adds both information and descriptive narration to help record the story of the 38th's African experience.

The letter was being written, Captain Pickens said, during the "first opportunity to sit down and really try to write a letter to all the folks at home." Since arriving in Africa everyone had been busily engaged. He began to enumerate some of the tasks:

"For the first few days we lived like the proverbial Indians from hand to mouth, but since the dust has settled we have been hard at work. Our hospital was the first of its kind to be set up in the field and we had a job getting it fixed. Our experience in the states with our meager training was not enough to let us know exactly what we were going to run into, so we had to learn the hard way. This we did in a fairly creditable manner according to the visiting generals we had.

"At present we have more patients in our hospital than all of the hospitals in Charlotte. However, they don't pay as well. They are a cheerful lot on the whole and appreciate the fresh air and sunshine and good food we dish out to them. I am limited in what I can say about our operating here because of the censorship, since we are in the combat zone, but I may come back to it a little later and enlarge as much as possible."

He explained that it was going to be hard for him to describe his experiences, but he promised that he would "just ramble along as I did on the boat coming down." He wondered if that letter had reached them. "But," said he, "here goes on northwest Africa," from where the letter was being written.

"First, the money is on this rate: A dollar is worth 75 francs. We are paid in American currency printed almost the same as your money but with enough variation to make it legal tender only where the government allows. This, I take it, keeps the money we spend from eventually getting into Axis hands and being used against us. Of course, anything we buy is paid for with our money and gladly accepted by the merchants in this area, but in change we receive a lot of Algerian or French notes. These are usually dirty and torn and are not as good as our bank notes. They are larger than ours, as you probably remember, and a few five and ten and twenty-franc notes can fill your pockets. I am always afraid that I will throw some of it away inadvertently or use it the wrong way. Actually there is little to buy, since the Germans apparently have cleaned this part of the world out of all merchandise that could be used and food that could be consumed at home. The local population is almost destitute except for a few fairly well to do planters who had saved enough for the rainy day. Their principal crops are grapes, from which they make the most atrocious wines and brandies. I suppose the Germans took this output in order to get the alcohol from it to use in their war machines. They have some grain and some vegetables. These have to be irrigated. They have wells and irrigating ditches all thru the country. They have a rainy season during the winter and during the spring and summer the place is as dry as Volstead could possibly make it. Of course, we *would* get here at the beginning of the rainy season and have the questionable privilege of wading around in the mud too often for comfort. The grapevines are small and beautifully planted and well trimmed. They take the cuttings or refuse and burn it for fuel or make coke from it to run their trucks. Of course, they have had no gasoline since the war started. There are few trees and no forests and no coal, so the question of fuel is acute at times. It is fortunate that the native Arabs eat no meat, since the vegetable diet requires less cooking and hence less fuel.

"Speaking of Arabs eating no meat," Captain Pickens' letter continues, "reminds me of the experience we had on Thanksgiving. The Commanding General sent out a manifesto that all troops were to divide up their day's rations from one-third to one-half and dish it out to the native population. Of course, we planned to try to execute the order. We didn't know about the Arabs not eating meat. I thought they just didn't eat pork, so after we had planned our party we had to change it and hurriedly give all the meat to the French and the poor Arabs got only hardtack, candy, and English tea and coffee and a little canned fruit and puddings. Of course, the vegetables were canned with the meat. The French were quite orderly in getting their part but when our Moslem friends started down our dole line they just

War has its lighter moments, judging by the demeanor of this quintet from the 38th's personnel relaxing in Rome.

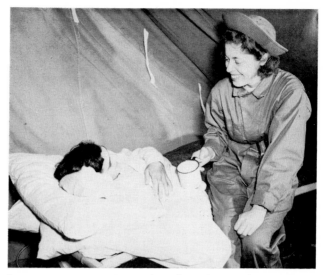

Lieutenant Annette Heaton's wide smile is as therapeutic as her proffered medicine, or is it coffee?

broke the traces and started to mob us. They had never had anything given to them before and they just couldn't stand it. Even their chief could not control them. We finally got thru with the job without anyone being hurt, but we missed only by a hair. Everyone was most appreciative. I had two men in my department, one who spoke French very well and one who spoke Arabic and they were delegated to tell the local populace what Thanksgiving meant to us and why we were sharing with them and why we could not do more. Those two soldiers had a grand time. All in all, I think we had a successful time of it and I know we made more friends than enemies."

Other observations of Africa and Africans in the St. Cloud area, perhaps representative of those shared by the members of the 38th generally, were offered by Captain Pickens in this first long letter written from Africa.

For example:

"There are lots of small donkeys in view. We call them one-fourth horsepower transports. When they are harnessed they pull a two-wheeled cart and with the driver and the load the donkey is about one-tenth the size of the weight he is required to pull. They are strong animals and trudge along with considerable less prodding than our familiar mules. Sometimes you can see a man on one of the little beasts sitting on the side rather than straddle. . . . I have been tempted to try a ride on one that way . . . I hesitate to take advantage of the little critter, however. . . .

"The Arabic dress is funny to me. The men wear baggy, droopy, oversized diapers for pants. Of course, the women are completely covered, including their faces. Occasionally one of them allows her face to be seen and there is always the familiar tattoo of her tribe marked across her face. The same signs are placed on her feet also.

"Everyone shakes hands with you when you meet and as you part. I feel like running home and washing my hands immediately. Of course, this is limited by the amount of water we have or can haul from our water sources, so I am getting used to being dirty and feeling dirty and just not caring. For a while I grew a beard that began to take on the look of the Arabs, but when it got too dirty for me I shaved it off.

"The children all give you the V-sign when you pass in the truck. That is their method of greeting. They cry for bonbons and are overjoyed when we are able to pass out a little of our candy supply. They get a great kick out of our chewing gum of which we get a limited supply. The men really appreciate our American cigarettes."

His letter provides an additional glimpse of the North African climate, scenery, products, people:

"The sunrise here is the most beautiful I have ever seen. Of course, you will say that I had not seen so many before getting into the Army. But the color here is for the painters. After a rain, when the dust has settled, you can see for miles and mountains in the background just make the setting complete. Of course, brushing my teeth with moonbeams in the cold morn-

The most important soldiers in the Army! The Army moves on its stomach, it has long been said, and the cooks move it. This photo was made in North Africa. Roy Morrison is facing the camera. Sergeant Joseph Gleba is the other man.

42

ing is not so pleasant, but it has its compensations when the sun starts up. The sunsets are equally colorful and beautiful. It is cold at night, it must get down to about 40 some nights, but the days are warm and balmy and you can go without a jacket quite comfortably. Under my tent it is good and warm, but the flies interrupt my siesta at midday.

"Along every road there is a line of olive trees on both sides. They line all the fields, but so far as I have been able to see, there are no complete groves. The natives have been busy with long poles knocking the olives down these last few days. I have not tried to eat any of the olives because everyone says they are rancid and bitter, that they need to be pickled first. That I can't say because my experience with olives has been out of bottles so far. They grow like cherries on the trees, and the trees are the only sizable foliage that you see with the exception of an occasional palm with dates. We have had plenty of oranges and tangerines but I have not seen where they were grown. The oranges are large navel types and are delicious. The tangerines are small and tasty. We were glad to get them since we had been without citrus fruit all the time we were in England and the lack of Vitamin C was becoming apparent in our personnel. All of the citrus must grow somewhat to the south of us, not in the desert."

Of the costs of employing an Arab to do his laundry:

"Yesterday I gave some laundry to one of the natives who works near here among the vineyards. The manager of the plantation said he would do my wash for me. I gave him two field jackets and plenty of linen and a complete wool uniform and the sheets out of my sleeping bag. They came back the next day just as white as any laundry could do them, altho not ironed, and the cost was only 50 francs. If I stay at this point long, I will be delighted with this help because I have not had time to do my washing. On the deal with the Arab I had to furnish the soap."

He wrote a paragraph about a famous visitor the hospital had had:

". . . Gen. Theodore Roosevelt, Jr., came by to see the hospital the other day. It was the first time I had met him. I met Mrs. Roosevelt in London. She was doing Red Cross work near where I was stationed and doing a good job of it. I had a pleasant visit with the General and he promised when he wrote Mrs. Roosevelt that he would tell her to see Bob and tell him where I was. . . ."

Captain Pickens adds his account of the setting up of the 38th's hospital. It supplements the report made by Captain Munroe:

"Now back to setting up a hospital of our size. We moved into the area one day and a hundred patients moved in the next. In the meantime we did a lot of moving, and I don't mean maybe. It was hectic for a while but we came thru. On the second night a strong wind started blowing and one tent came down. It housed some twelve nurses and some of them were covered with canvas for a while but were not hurt. It was about three in the morning when the blow started and with it came rain. Everyone was roused out of bed and there was much running around tightening tent pins and ropes. We lived thru it. At first, our latrines were the old-fashioned straddle trench type. After a few days this gave way to well-built boxes, so now we feel quite fancy. Chic Sales never had anything on us. The kitchens and mess halls are the show places, however, since I spend most of my time there. We feed around a thousand people a day and they all appear to get plenty to eat. No S and W can rival our menus. We now have steak, ham, fish, wieners, hamburgers, eggs (dehydrated), bacon, peas, carrots, potatoes, onions, also dry, canned fruit and juices, sardines, cheese, jam, coffee, tea and cocoa. We have corn fritters, hot cakes, butterscotch pudding, chocolate pudding, and canned pineapple. The menu sometimes calls for corn beef or Irish stew. There is nothing we can't get except bread and ice cream. We still eat crackers or hardtack."

Captain Pickens turns his attention from his own specialized duties to write a few lines about the doctors and the nurses:

"The surgeons are prepared to give any sort of operation required, and the medical men are busy going around prescribing for their patients and looking after their general welfare. The nurses add a bit of color and I can see now why the Army likes to have them along. They give a touch that the men can't give. A skirt going by the cot just makes the hospital seem different. And they can write home for the patients better than the men can, and they know what to say. I have seen two nurses teaching lip reading to a man who had lost his hearing. I spent one Sunday afternoon reading Edward Everett Hale's 'A Man Without a Country' to a group of patients. They appeared to enjoy the story, and it helped pass the time for them and me. Of course, I got a kick out of it."

Closing this long letter, he explains how it is being written:

"This letter has been written under the most trying circumstances, with numerous interruptions, so I am sure it won't make much sense to you. I started it yesterday and am just getting it finished. This typewriter is sitting on a hastily constructed box and I am sitting on a small box in front of it. Neither of the boxes is too sturdy, but I do hope you get some idea of what goes on in Northwest Africa with a small part of the American forces.

"So far I have had no mail from the states since arriving in Africa," he concludes the letter. "I don't worry about it. About Christmas I have the feeling that there will be bundles of it for me to peruse. You have probably been in the same boat and I hope you have not been too concerned. I am in good health, as the enclosed picture will indicate."

A quick look at their new African base of operations is provided also in a short note written about that time by Lieutenant Charlotte Jean Webber of the 38th's nurses group to her family in Cynthiana, Kentucky:

"We live in tents somewhere in Northwest Africa and love it. Only we don't take baths, wash our hair, shave or wash clothes—just one big, dirty, happy family. It's cold at night. I sleep on an Army cot in my sleeping bag with my wool robe on and four Army blankets over me and my fur coat in my little field hospital. Worked like blazes to get it set up these first few trying days—and now we have something to be proud of.

"We've named all our little streets in the field—my ward tent is on the corner of Kentucky Ave. and 2nd St. Our mess tent's called "New York Hotel" and my tent is named "My Old Kentucky Home."

"I certainly have a time trying to talk French with these French people. Those two years I had in French in Cynthiana High do come in handy. When I was in

Jacob Groff appears undisturbed by his duties involving the autopsy bucket.

Famed war correspondent Ernie Pyle visited and wrote frequently of the 38th. Here he is shown during a visit to St. Cloud talking with two patients, Private Raymond Astrackon, left, and Sergeant Ralph Gower. The nurse is Lieutenant Annette Heaton, supervisor of the medical service ward.

town I went into a shop to buy some pins; the French shopkeepers kept jabbering to us and we couldn't understand a thing they said. Finally I gathered they wanted us to go with them for a drink of wine. Well, they left their shop wide open and took us down to their house, sat us down and brought out three bottles and finally F.D.R.'s picture and we all drank a toast to Roosevelt."

On December 2, 1942, three weeks after their landing in Africa, the men and women of the 38th Evacuation Hospital had a distinguished visitor who would become perhaps the best known and most widely read correspondent of World War II. Ernie Pyle was the fourth man to sign the 38th's guests register. In his straight up and down distinctive handwriting he wrote:

Dec. 2, '42
Ernie Pyle
Correspondent
Scripps-Howard Newspapers

Ernie Pyle came to be a good friend and great admirer of the hospital's officers, nurses, and enlisted personnel, and he would write a series of syndicated columns about the 38th that would tell its story to his readers throughout the United States.

In his first column mentioning it he said he had planned earlier to write of the nation's preparations for treating war casualties, but had been reluctant to do so because to him the thought of so many men's soon becoming war cripples was positively shocking.

When he did write on the subject the 38th was in Africa and he datelined his column from that sector:

WITH AMERICAN FORCES IN ALGERIA—Back in England last summer, I spent some time with the Army's Medical Corps, intending to write about our preparations for wartime wounded.

But I never wrote the columns. The sight of surgeons being taught to operate at the front, of huge warehouses filled to the roofs with bandages, of scores of hospitals built for men then healthy who would inevitably soon be cripples—it was shocking and too morbid, and I couldn't write about it.

But now that preparation is being put into effect. Our doctors and nurses and medical aides have had their first battle experience. The hospitals are going full blast. And it doesn't seem morbid in actuality as it did in contemplation.

In the Oran area, where our heaviest casualties were, the wounded are in five big hospitals. Three are French hospitals taken over by the Army. One is an abandoned French barracks turned into a hospital. And one is a huge tent hospital out in an oat field. It is the most amazing thing I have seen, and I'll write much about it later.

The hospital in the oat field which he considered amazing was Charlotte's 38th. And, indeed, he did

write of it often and with lavish praise of its accomplishments. But his column continues:

So far the doctors can be, and are, proud of their work. The nurses have already covered themselves with glory. The wounded have only praise for those who pulled them through.

Our only deaths were those killed outright and those so badly wounded nothing could save them. In other words, we have lost almost nobody from infection, or from the hurly-burly of battlefield medical shortcomings.

You've already read of the miracles wrought by sulfanilamide in the first battles of Africa. Doctors and men both still talk about it constantly, almost with awe. Doctors knew it was practically a miracle drug, but they hadn't realized quite how miraculous.

Every soldier was issued a sulfanilamide packet before he left England, some even before they left America. It consisted of 12 tablets for swallowing, and a small sack of the same stuff in powdered form for sprinkling on wounds.

The soldiers used it as instructed, and the result was an almost complete lack of infection. Hundreds are alive today who would have been dead without it. Men lay out for 24 hours and more before they could be taken in, and the sulfanilamide saved them.

It's amusing to hear the soldiers talk about it. Sulfanilamide is a pretty big word for most of them. They call it everything from "snuffalide" to "sulphermillanoid."

There's one interesting little sidelight about it. Some of the wounded soldiers didn't have any sulfanilamide left, because they had surreptitiously taken it all to cure venereal diseases. They say you knock out a venereal case in four or five days with it, and thus don't have to report in sick.

The doctors told me that most American wounds were in the legs, while most of the French were in the head. The explanation seems to be that we were advancing and thus out in the open, while the French were behind barricades with just their heads showing.

Both sides treated the wounded of the other side all during the battle. Our soldiers are full of gratitude the way

While the 38th was at St. Cloud, officers and enlisted men sometimes were able to arrange short rest leaves. Here three young women go for a fast ride, North African style. The two 38th nurses are Lee Rodstein, Elva Wells, and next to driver, Jean Webber. They are at Caserta.

The hospital at St. Cloud sat in a level field bordered by trees, and white stones edged the walkways and roads through the tented encampment.

they were treated in the French hospitals. They say the French nurses would even steal cigarettes for them.

It is fantastic the mixup of French emotions that showed itself during the fighting. One French motor launch went about Oran harbor firing with a machine gun at wounded Americans, while other Frenchmen in rowboats were facing the bullets trying to rescue them.

I know of one landing party sent ashore with the special mission of capturing four merchant ships. They took them all without firing a shot. The captain of one ship greeted the party with "What was the matter? We expected you last night." And the skipper of another met the party at the gangway with a bottle of gin.

There was much fraternization. In one town where fighting was heavy, the bodies of five men were found in a burned truck. Three were Americans and two were French.

Morphine was a great life-saver. Pure shock is the cause of many deaths; but if morphine can be given to deaden the pain, shock cases often pull through. Many officers carried morphine and gave injections right on the field. My friend Lt. Col. Louis Plain of the Marine Corps, who had never given an injection in his life, gave six on the beach at Arzew.

Many of our wounded men already have returned to duty. Those permanently disabled will be sent home as soon as they are able. Those still recovering are anxious to return to their outfits. I've inquired especially among the wounded soldiers about this, and it's a fact that they are busting to get back into the fray again. Morale was never higher than now.

In a subsequent column to his newspapers Ernie Pyle wrote of the 38th's activities. It was one of his favorite military units, as the column, carried by *The Charlotte Observer* on Wednesday, January 13, 1943, reveals. This column with others about the 38th, edited and condensed, was included in his book, *Here Is Your War*, published in 1943 by Henry Holt and Company. Pyle wrote:

WITH THE AMERICAN FORCES IN ALGERIA—When a soldier is in perilous predicament or especially aggravated with the rough-and-tumble life of the battlefront,

This view of the 38th's layout at St. Cloud shows the hospital tents. There were seven rows, a dozen tents to the row. On right are various service tents. The living quarters were to the left of picture.

he usually pacifies himself by thinking, "If the folks at home could only see me now!"

And if the folks of Charlotte, N. C., could only peep down out of the African sky and see their family doctors and nurses in their new kind of life—what a surprise they'd have!

For a bunch of men and women from Charlotte are operating the only American tent hospital so far set up in North Africa, and they're doing a dramatically beautiful job. They're really like something out of Hollywood, and I've visited them time after time just out of fascination.

They are far from any town, set in the middle of a big oats field, out on the rolling plains. They began setting up the day after troops had battled their way over that very ground. They took in their first patients the next morning.

Now the hospital has more than 700 patients, it takes 400 people to run it, and there are more than 300 tents covering 80 acres of oats stubble. The stubblefield was picked so the mud and dust wouldn't be so bad—but they are anyway.

Everything is in tents, from operating rooms to toilets. Everything was set up in three days. They can knock down

and be on the move again in another three days, and they expect it to happen at any moment. They are like a giant medical Ringling Brothers.

◦　◦　◦

They are known as the—evacuation hospital. They were taken into active service last April, practically denuding the Charlotte Memorial Hospital of doctors and nurses.

They arrived in England in mid-August. They stood off the North African coast with the great overwhelming convoy that brought our occupying troops. They came ashore in assault boats the morning after the occupation. They jumped immediately to work.

There are 50 Charlotte men in the unit—mostly doctors and surgeons, but a few businessmen who do the non-medical part of running a hospital. There are 50 nurses too. None had ever lived any closer to nature than an occasional hunting trip. Today they have become nomads of the desert, living on the ground and under the sky, and they love it.

Their commanding officer is a regular Army man—Lieut. Col. Rollin Bauchspies, who only recently joined them. He's

47

a tough, hoarse, friendly guy who cusses continuously and drinks hard likker and drives his own jeep and says to hell with regulations, dying people can't wait. He's a Pennsylvanian and says he could lick the whole damn Dixie tribe if he had to, but you see he doesn't have to because the whole outfit vibrates with accomplishment and they're all proud together.

◦　◦　◦

Pyle tells of the unit's arrival in Africa as inexperienced at living in the open but of their ability quickly to adapt themselves to the new routine:

When they arrived in Africa, they were neophytes at living in the field, for that part of their training had been overlooked. Lieutenant Colonel Bauchspies had taken over command while they were on the boat coming from England, and he'd had no time to give them the neglected field training.

So they arrived in the middle of an African oatfield with three hundred tents to set up, and not a soul knew how to put up a shelter-half or drive a tent-peg properly. But they soon learned. Colonel Bauchspies, who did know how, being a Regular Army man, got out and drove ten pegs himself. Everybody worked like a slave. Doctors helped dig ditches. Nurses helped unload trucks.

One amateur electrician among the enlisted men started wiring the office tents for lights. A couple of carpenters-by-trade made themselves known, and went to work. A professional sign painter turned up among the first patients, and painted the street signs that helped to give the hospital a civilized touch.

In a few days the veterans had taught the tenderfeet how to make themselves comfortable living in the rough. The tents of officers and nurses were touchingly homelike. There was canvas on the floor, mosquito nets over the cots and framed pictures of wives and children standing on the wooden tables. The Charlotte doctors and nurses were wise enough to bring air mattresses and sleeping bags, and they had never slept more comfortably.

Of course, getting up in the cold before daylight and washing in cold water out of a canvas washpan took some getting used to. And yet it grew on them.

Major Paul Sanger was chief surgeon of the hospital. He had been chief surgeon back in Charlotte. He was a highly skilled, well-to-do professional man. He told me, "I never go into town. I feel better out here than I've ever felt in my life. We were all prima donnas back home. We had every comfort that money could buy. We would have been shocked at the idea of living like this. But we love it. We all do. I suppose we'll be making our families live in tents when we get home."

Pyle revealed that Lieutenant Colonel Preston White, the unit's chief medical officer, whom he described as "enthusiastic as a child" over the whole hospital setup, had become "an addict to outdoor living." He quoted Colonel White:

"We have only a quart of water a day to wash, shave and wash clothes in, so we don't take many baths. Maybe we don't smell so good, but when we're all in the same boat we don't notice it. And it sure feels good living out like this."

Pyle continued his description of the 38th in a part of a column he used also in *Here Is Your War*:

The hospital was already spreading a fame for its food. Anybody in the Army knows that a field hospital is the best place to eat. One night we had big juicy steaks for dinner. "Where did these come from?" I asked Colonel Bauchspies.

"Hell, I wouldn't dare ask," he said. "I suppose Stan stole them."

Stan was Captain Stanton Pickens, who had gone along as mess officer. His brother, Lieutenant Colonel Bob Pickens, was a friend of mine in London. Stan set such a good table that the trucks bringing patients from outlying camps always managed to arrive just at lunchtime. And another indication—Stan made arrangements with a local Arab to collect their garbage, for which he was to give the hospital a crate of oranges every three days. But it seems everybody cleaned his plate, and the Arab was getting so little garbage he wanted to give oranges only every four days now.

Ernie Pyle named others in the Charlotte unit's administrative group:

The hospital's supply officer was Captain William F. Medearis. He was a Charlotte bigwig. They said he owned all of Main Street, plus half the real estate and all the laundries. He was national secretary-treasurer of the Laundry Association. He turned down a lieutenant-colonelcy in Washington in order to go to Africa with his friends.

Captain George C. Snyder, who commanded the non-medical detachment of enlisted men at the hospital, shared the Coca-Cola honors with Captain Pickens. Between them they had a special gold mine sewed up in Charlotte. But they had nary a bottle of it in Africa.

He mentioned the two Captain Joneses:

In the outfit there were two named Captain Otis Jones. They were no relation and had never heard of each other until they joined the Army. One was the chaplain, and he was from Bude, Mississippi. The other was a Charlotte obstetrician. Since none of the soldiers was given to having babies, Dr. Jones was registrar for the hospital. So they wisecracked that he "delivered papers" over there.

Pyle's report continues with a return to his describing the physical arrangements of the tented hospital city:

Seen from the mud road leading across a field, the hospital looked like a dark-green sea of tents. It blended so well with the fields and against the low rolling mountains in the distance that a person could hardly pick it out half a mile away.

Even the first tent had a "going concern" air about it—there was a tidy, painted sign on a stake saying "Headquarters," and a little dirt walk lined with whitewashed rocks led up to it. Inside that ten men worked at crude tables with folding legs. Before them were file cases that folded up into small portable trunks. Field telephones rested in their leather cases. It was the same equipment I had seen in all the camps in England and Ireland, and there in Africa its quickly movable character was being genuinely put to work.

Back of headquarters the tents spread out and formed a city, with streets between the rows. The whole place was laid out just as it had been planned on paper in Washington years before. But the little touches—the street signs, the whitewashed rock borders all over the place—they were additional, and were the volunteer work of the enlisted men.

The officers and nurses live two in a tent on two sides of a company street—nurses on one side, officers on the other. The street has a neat sign at the end on which is painted "Carolina Avenue." Some Yankee has painted under this "Rebel Street."

The 300 men who do the non-medical work live in their little shelter tents just on beyond. They're mostly from New England. They've built a little wall of whitewashed rocks between the two areas, and put up a sign saying "Mason-Dixon Line."

The chief nurse is First Lieut. Bessie Fullbright. In true Southern style everybody calls her "Miss Bessie." They've even got a small detachment of Negro Engineer troops, just to make everybody feel at home.

The nurses wear khaki overalls because of the mud and dust. Doctors go around tieless and with knit brown caps on their heads. Pink female panties fly from a line among the brown warlike tents. On the flagpole is a Red Cross flag, made from a bed sheet and a French soldier's red sash.

Your operating room has a dirt floor, and the canvas walls blow in and out. Diseased Arabs, seeking relief, wander timidly in toward the tent marked "Native Surgery."

You wash outdoors in cold water and go to a Chic Sale with a canvas wall around it. You eat and read by lantern light. You almost never take a bath. You seldom drive the 20 miles into town because you get to like it out here, and you feel so healthy.

Planes bound for destruction of the Axis roar tent-high over your weird city of canvas. At night a trillion stars shower down out of the clear African night. You sleep on a folding cot under mosquito bars, with the tent flaps open.

Pyle reported that the Charlotte folk "were up in the darkness of 6:30 A.M.—boy, was it cold! At first, they sometimes even put off washing their faces till later in the day." Yet, he reasoned, their "whole crude existence was built around the call of those thousands of men whose lives depended on them—and they realized they were happier than they had been in a long time.

"Yes," he ended this particular column, "if the folks back in Charlotte could only have seen them!"

The routine of the 38th's reason for existence, the treatment of the battle casualties, was related in highlights by the famous war correspondent in a subsequent report from North Africa:

At the receiving tent, trucks and ambulances arrived with wounded men transferred from other hospitals, with sick men from incoming ships, with ill and injured from our dozens of camps around the countryside, with airmen stricken at high altitudes.

Those able to walk went down a long line of desks, where their history was taken for the files. In the next tent they turned in all their belongings. That tent was stacked high with barracks bags. Rifles and mud-covered bayonets stuck out of bags. Attendants gingerly accepted hand grenades and gave the owner a receipt.

In the next tent the patient turned in his clothes and got a tag in return. He was given a pair of flannel pajamas and

a red corduroy bathrobe. He had to keep his own shoes, for the hospital had no house slippers. Then he went to whatever ward tent his type of illness indicated. His belongings were taken by truck to the opposite end of the hospital a quarter mile away, to await his exit.

The surgical and laboratory tents were in the middle of the big compound. There were three fully equipped surgeries, and they were astonishingly modern. All equipment was brand-new. It was like the newest hospital in New York, except that the floor was canvas-covered dirt, the walls canvas, and the street outside a deeply rutted bog-hole of red clay.

When an operation was going on, a triple flap was pulled over the tent entrance, and a heavy mosquito bar dropped over that. Inside, the air became stiflingly hot even then; by summer it would be cruel. Patients were brought up the muddy street on a field stretcher running on bicycle wheels. Surgeons wore white robes, white masks, rubber gloves. Everything was white, and I was struck with the vast amount of sheeting, swabs, bandages and towels—all white —around a desert operating table.

The light above the surgeons was fiery bright. The hospital tapped a nearby high-tension line for its operating-room current. If that failed, there was a whole progression downward for emergency—a generator run by a gas engine, a portable battery set, then powerful flashlights, then lanterns, then candles, and finally just matches if it ever came to that.

There was an X-ray room, and a fluoroscope. The darkroom was a tent within a tent. All the new equipment shone and sparkled, sitting incongruously on its dirt floor.

There were more than forty tents of wards. Each tent held twenty men, on folding camp cots. The floor was stubble. It sounds makeshift, but the patients were thoroughly comfortable.

There was also the dentist's office, in one end of a surgical tent. The chair was just a hard green metal one, tilted back. There were no arms to hold to when it hurt. The drill was run by the dentist pumping on an old-fashioned treadle. Yet the dentist, Major Vaiden Kendrick, said he could do anything he did back home in Charlotte. He offered to make me a plate just to prove it, but I gnashed my original teeth at him and fled.

One tent housed a laboratory, filled with basins and test tubes and burners. Another was a drugstore, where thousands of prescriptions were filled from endless bottles on shelves. And all this, mind you, every bit of it from tents to kitchen stoves to anesthetics, had come to Africa on a single boat.

In another of his columns to the newspapers at home Ernie Pyle's report of certain incidents involving Arabs in the vicinity of the 38th's hospital serves to supplement stories told about the Arabs by members of the unit.

"There were a lot of things that Charlotte doctors and nurses hadn't visualized before they set up their big tent hospital there in the field," this column began. Then he proceeded to enumerate some of these unforeseen problems:

The natives, for instance. Arabs in their long gowns came wandering across the plains hoping the miraculous Americans could cure their ailments. So the hospital had to set up a separate tent for them. They had local people in there

49

wounded by shrapnel in the first battle. There was one old woman of eigthy-one whose arm had been blown off. There were several patients on whom they had done normal operations.

One Arab woman had been shot through the stomach. Her condition was grave, but on the second morning her husband arrived, said he had to go to work and there wasn't anybody to take care of the kids, and for her to get the hell home where she belonged. So she got up and walked out. The doctors didn't think she could have lived through the day. But you know how it is with us Arabs—we don't like our women gadding about when there's work at home.

While I was there a ragged Arab with a long stick came in with his ten-year-old boy. The child had a hideous rash over his neck and face. Through the interpreter, the Arab said he had been praying and praying for the Americans to come, so they could do something for his boy. His belief in us was touching, but the doctors feared the scourge was beyond their ken.

The Army's Arabic interpreters, incidentally, were completely accidental. They weren't assigned to the hospital unit by design or anything. It just happened.

One was Private Israel Tabi, of 245 Broome Street, New York City. He was born in Yemen, and had settled in America when he was twenty. He was thirty-five when I met him, and a house painter by profession. So far as he knew his parents were still in Arabia, and who could tell, he might see them some day. He said the Arabic spoken around these parts was quite similar to what he knew. I mentioned that he was performing a very valuable service. Private Tabi was volubly patriotic. He said, "I will do anything for my country. Whatever they ask me to do, I will do. I will work day and night. I love my country. I will do anything for it."

The other interpreter was an Egyptian—Private Abraham Casper Leon Saide (pronounced Sadie). He lived at 343½ Seneca Street, Buffalo, New York. He was a watch repairer by trade. He had been born in Alexandria, Egypt, was thirty-four, and had migrated to America in 1921. He spoke Turkish, Greek, Egyptian and all those exotic languages. It looked as if Private Saide might have a very useful career ahead of him in the army.

The hospital already had handled more than 1,000 patients and hadn't lost a one. The doctors ran to the nearest stake and knocked on wood when they said it. The surgeons had performed more than 125 operations.

There was no red tape about whether a patient was legally entitled to enter the hospital or not. They took anybody who came along—soldier, civilian, Arab, Frenchman, anybody. The way they ignored formalities when emergency arose was one of the things that made me feel so warmly toward this battle-front hospital. One day we were looking at the round-bellied iron stoves half buried in the ground in each tent.

"What do you burn in them?" I asked Lieutenant Colonel Bauchspies.

"Wood," he said.

"Where do you get the wood?" I asked.

"Steal it," he said.

When you were saving lives you didn't requisition and wait; you foraged and borrowed and even stole if necessary. And nobody stood on rank. Once Major General Fredendall made an inspection tour through the hospital. Colonel Bauchspies croaked hoarsely like a frog.

"How did you lose your voice?" asked the general.

"I lost it driving tent pegs," said the colonel.

"Your guard looks nice," said the general. "Where did they get those new rifles?"

"I daren't tell you, sir," said the colonel. The general smiled. And nodded.

One of Ernie Pyle's most interesting and revealing columns was devoted to the nurses of the 38th:

The American nurses—and there were lots of them—turned out just as you would expect: wonderfully. Army doctors, and patients, too, were unanimous in their praise of them. Doctors told me that in that first rush of casualties they were calmer than the men.

One hospital unit had a nurse they were afraid of. She had seemed neurotic and hysterical on the way down. The head doctor detailed another nurse just to watch her all through the hectic first hours of tending the wounded. But he needn't have. He admitted afterward that she was the calmest of the lot.

The head of one hospital, a full colonel who was a soldier in the last war, worked in the improvised hospitals set up at Arzew to tend the freshly wounded. He said they worked thirty-six hours without sleep, with wounded men lying around knee-deep, waiting. He said not a soul in the outfit cracked up or got flustered.

"We were so busy we didn't think about its being horrible," he said. "We weren't ourselves. Actually we seemed to become different people. And after it was over, we were thrilled by it. Gosh, I hope I'm not stuck in a base hospital. I want to get on to the front."

Then Pyle wrote of the 38th unit's nurses:

The Carolina nurses, too, took it like soldiers. For the first ten days they had to live like animals, even using open ditches for toilets, but they never complained.

One nurse was always on duty in each tentful of twenty men. She had medical orderlies to help her. Most of the time the nurses wore army coveralls, but Colonel Bauchspies wanted them to put on dresses once in a while, for he said the effect on the men was astounding. The touch of femininity, the knowledge that a woman was around, gave the wounded man courage and confidence and a feeling of security. And the more feminine she looked, the better.

Only about one hundred of the hospital's seven hundred patients were wounded men. The others were just sick with ordinary things such as flu, appendicitis, sprains. They had a whole tentful of mumps, and a few cases of malaria and dysentery.

At the far end of the hospital, behind an evil-looking barricade of barbed wire, was what Colonel Bauchspies called "Casanova Park." Back there were a hundred and fifty soldiers with venereal disease.

"What's the barbed wire for?" I asked. "They wouldn't try to get out anyhow."

"It's just to make them feel like heels," the colonel said. "There's no damned excuse for a soldier getting caught nowadays unless he just doesn't care. When he gets a venereal he's no good to his country and somebody else has to do his work. So I want him to feel ashamed, even though at the same time he does get the finest medical treatment."

Many of the wounded soldiers were then able to be on their feet. On warm days they went out in their bathrobes and sat for hours in the sun, out in the stubble field. Most of them were getting a good tan. At night they played

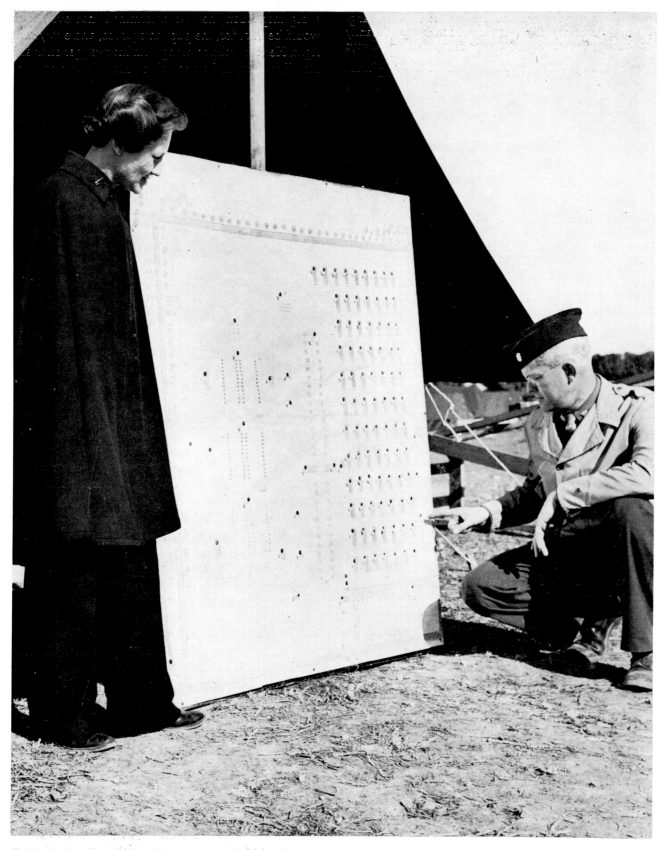

Lieutenant Bessie Fullbright and Lieutenant-Colonel George T. Wood at St. Cloud, North Africa, check over hospital encampment plans.

cards on their bunks, by the light of the lanterns hanging from the ridgepoles. The usual bunkhouse profanity was strangely absent from those tents, for there was always a nurse around.

The boys liked to talk about their experiences. I spent much time with a tentful of men wounded in the harbor battle at Oran, and they recounted the fight by the hour.

More than two decades after they last saw Private Saide of whom Ernie Pyle wrote many veterans of the 38th Evacuation Hospital remember him. Shortly after they arrived at St. Cloud, Joe W. Neil, who was pharmacist of the unit, recalls, Saide brought a pregnant native woman to the hospital and Dr. Hunter Jones delivered her baby. "We hadn't been there but a few days, as I remember," Mr. Neil says of the incident, "when Saide brings in this pregnant Arab woman for Dr. Jones to deliver her. I don't know how he happened upon her; he'd probably been around St. Cloud and had made some connections, since he could speak the language. But that was Saide. He was always doing something unusual."

Mr. Neil supports Ernie Pyle in the columnist's description of Saide as a watch repairer. "One day in Tunis—Saide was working on my watch—I went down to his tent and asked him about my watch. He was working on another one at the time and he had on this magnifying eyepiece that jewelers wear and he put it down for a moment to see about something, and when he did I picked it up and looked through it. Then I stuck my finger through it. He didn't even have any glass in it.

"'Don't tell on me,' he said, and I told him I wouldn't. And I didn't, for a long time. But that really tickled me. I guess he was trying to look very professional. But that Saide was a character."

Joe Neil remembers another incident in which Saide was a participant. It also happened during the 38th's stay at St. Cloud. "Saide had the job of burning the garbage. This particular day the Colonel was pulling

a big inspection; he was determined that everything would be in order, the pup tents just so, and everything right. He was walking along with his swagger stick and his officers walking along behind him. He was pointing out this and pointing out that, and he got down around the kitchen area, where old Saide had all the garbage piled up and saturated with gasoline and ready to burn it. And about the time the Colonel got up pretty close to the garbage, old Saide struck a match and threw it into the pile, and WHOOOM! The Colonel about-faced in a hurry and got away; he didn't say a thing to Saide. He just got away from there.

"Some of us wondered whether Saide didn't pick that time to throw the match. I doubt it though. It was just time for him to burn the garbage; he was ready and he just didn't give a rap whether the Colonel happened to be there at that time or not."

Some time later, said Joe Neil, they gave Saide a job overseeing war prisoners working. "I remember one day going by a group of prisoners who were moving a big pile of dirt, and old Saide was sitting there with his arms folded, bossing the prisoners."

One of the functions of the hospital's pharmacist that helped establish his popularity in the unit was that of custodian of alcohol. It was the custom, Joe Neil recalls, to give two ounces of whiskey to the donor of 500 cc's of blood. "Some of them would try to get back in line after having given the pint in order to get another two ounces of whiskey. Two ounces was about a good double drink and 500 cc's of blood was about a pint," he remembers. "Most of it was cut. I'd pour out half the liquor in other bottles and proof it back with grain alcohol and water, and burn sugar and make caramel to put the color back, and we'd save whiskey that way. But the drinks they got had plenty of alcohol."

"Joe was the most amazing guy to get good liquor I ever saw," declares Randall K. Davis, his war-time buddy who was the hospital's X-ray technician. "He'd head out with his little bag and he'd come back late that afternoon, and that bag would have about five bottles of Scotch in it."

"I had contacts over in the British Eighth Army," Neil explains. "That's where I was getting it. I had two lords from Scotland, brothers, and they'd fix me up. The first time, I got a case. I even got on their ration list. I was getting a quart a week, I believe it was, while we were down there in Africa, and still I could buy it for $1.74. You see, in this ack-ack outfit the way the setup was, all the British soldiers had a ration of whiskey, and a lot of them wouldn't buy it; that's what I was getting; I'd buy that."

He goes on:

"The first time I made contact I got a case; it was

The big boss arrives to visit the 38th at St. Luce. General Mark Clark is being greeted.

52

marked 'For Export Only.' I didn't open it then. Sergeant Baker and I got it up at Cape Bon. That was the time Dr. Query let me have the truck. I went up with Dr. Query and Dr. Pitts and went swimming. I told Baker I was going to look around and see if I could find some of that good English or Scotch whiskey. I ran into a soldier and asked him about whiskey. He said 'Yes, if you get transportation, I can get you some.' So I went over on the beach and I asked Dr. Pitts and Dr. Query if I could have the truck a little while. Dr. Pitts said no, but Dr. Query said, 'Aw, Bill, let the boys have it.' So Sergeant Baker and I went down to this place, the English camp, and walked in, and met this fellow's sergeant, and these brothers, majors, I think, and asked them about the whiskey. They said, 'Yes. How much you want?' I said, 'Well, any amount.' They said, 'You want a case?' Boy, I almost dropped dead! I said, 'Yes.' So they came out with it. I paid them for it, and it figured up $1.74 a bottle for the twelve bottles.

"So we got back, and picked up the officers. I had it under the seat, and it was the first thing Dr. Pitts saw when he got in the truck. He said, 'Joe, what you got in that box?' 'Oh,' I said, 'I've been finagling around a little with those English soldiers, trading with them a little bit.' Dr. Query said, 'Bill, that's Joe's stuff; you leave it alone.'

"So we got home with it, and I got that case under my arm and took off to my tent. And when it got dark, old Baker came down and we opened it up. I didn't know but what we'd bought a pig in a poke. But sure enough there were twelve bottles of Black and White Scotch. So I'd made contact; from then on it was a matter of getting over there. I'd sit around with these two English officers, and we'd have a big time. I kept in contact with them a long time; sometimes we'd be fifty miles apart, sometimes seventy-five. They moved up to Tunis when we did, and were close to us."

His friend Davis recalls, too, the 300-gallon cask of wine presented to the hospital the night it encamped at St. Cloud.

"The first night we got set up there some fellows who ran a winery nearby got a cart pulled by a burro and brought us a big hogshead of wine—it was a 300-gallon barrel, they said—and they set it out in a field and just turned us loose on it. Well, none of us was used to drinking wine; we didn't know how to drink the stuff. That night the whole outfit was drunk. So from that night on they stationed somebody at that big keg and allotted each fellow so much; I think it was half a canteen cup full each night before we ate our supper. That barrel sat out there for two weeks and we finally drank it up. It was cold and good, regular old dago red wine."

Three days before Ernie Pyle signed the 38th's visitors register, Captain Stokes Munroe in a letter dated "North Africa, November 29th," to his Charlotte friend T. D. Kemp, Jr., gave further illuminating details of the operation of the tent hospital at St. Cloud, although he could not at that time reveal where the unit was based.

Captain Munroe's letter is particularly interesting in its revelation of the situation as observed through the eyes of one of the unit's surgeons. His long letter began:

"We are now living under tents, which is a real blessing compared to conditions under which we existed when we first landed. I do wish that I could tell you all the details, but until this war ends, it is not permitted. . . ."

He continues, after a part of the letter appears to have been deleted:

"Then, with a very limited water supply we attempted to make the place as habitable as possible. That attempt, however, was far from being wholly satisfactory. We did not have any of our bedding or baggage so we slept for several nights on the cold concrete floor. We only had a pint of water a day for both drinking and washing and even that had to be first chemically treated. We did not remove any of our clothing for seven days. We were indeed a filthy lot. It would have shocked any of you back home to see us. And we are still far from being just out of the band box. Still everybody was of good cheer and all laughed at our poor state of affairs.

"Our food for days was all in two types of cans: one contained biscuits, three blocks of sugar, some powdered coffee, and four small pieces of hard candy; the other contained a conglomeration of meat and vegetables. All was eaten cold and out of the cans. . . . These African flies aren't like good old American flies. They refuse to move unless you build a fire under them or actually bite them.

"While at the garrison we were constantly sniped at

Off duty for the moment, Captains Duncan G. Calder, Jr., left, and Robert B. Stith, get shot—by a camera.

53

by unfriendly natives in the surrounding houses or from a nearby hilltop. I do wish that I could give you details of these experiences but the censor will not permit. We finally moved out, however, into an enormous open field and there we began setting up our hospital."

Then Captain Munroe proceeded to give a comprehensive view of the 38th's African home in the oats field:

"We are all really very proud of this country hospital. We have over fifty large tents, each of which contains beds for twenty patients. They are all arranged in a symmetrical fashion, down to each tent pole and each stake. The roadways between the tents are all named: The Parade, New York Avenue, Pennsylvania Avenue, Kentucky Avenue, Indiana Avenue, First Street, Second Street, etc. Each name is painted on a white spick-and-span signpost painted by one of our recuperating patients who used to be a sign painter.

"The U-shaped driveway into the receiving section, which is the front of the hospital, is lined with whitewashed stones as are the other streets. The officers and nurses are quartered on one side of the hospital area, the officers being on one side of Carolina Avenue and the nurses on the other. Each tent has a neat number just like the number of your house. The tents are quite large and comfortably accommodate two persons. There are fifty of these tents along Carolina Avenue. Then, just beyond us, are over 160 smaller tents where live the enlisted men. . . . In addition to all this we have several large kitchens and mess halls for officers, enlisted men, nurses, and patients. We also have constructed latrines of the family size. Now all these things have come by degrees and hard work. At last we are getting our meals served on enamel plates and at the table.

"We had only our own flashlights when we arrived. Later we had kerosene lanterns. Now we are generating our own electricity with gasoline engines and soon the Army Engineers will bring us electricity from a nearby power line."

The water supply, too, he revealed, had improved and they were expecting further improvement soon. They still hadn't had baths, however, except for those obtained with wet bath cloths, in more than a month. Things that a few months before they had taken for granted had now become for the 38th's members luxuries they dreamed about. His letter continued:

"Now I come to the most interesting part of all, the organization and running of our hospital. We have an operating tent for clean cases, another for infected cases, and one for minor surgery. Each contains three operating tables with all the necessary equipment so that it is possible for nine operations to proceed simul-

taneously if necessary. The tent floors consist of thick canvas. The surgical instruments as well as all the equipment is of the very highest grade. It is really amazing to see what wonderful equipment the U.S. Army has for every single type of arm and service.

"One entire tent is taken up with X-ray and the X-ray material is the latest and finest. We have a pharmacy and a laboratory that would put many of those at home to shame. Actual numbers are not permitted, but I can say that our hospital here has more than half the patients in the whole area in which we are now operating. With such a large number of men, subject not only to the diseases that they might have at home but also to the results of war, you can well imagine how busy such a hospital will be. Nevertheless, we are all quite happy, as that is exactly what we are here for."

Captain Munroe's letter went on to tell further of the work of the doctors and surgeons:

"The greater part of our surgery closely simulates surgery that one encounters in civilian practice except there is more of it. Since hostilities in this immediate area are now under control, this is now even more true than at first, although we still have some reconstructive cases because of battle injuries. All the services, including surgery, medicine, orthopedics, urology, eye, ear, nose and throat, dentistry, X-ray, and to some extent obstetrics and pediatrics (among the natives) have been busy. I have been doing as much surgery here as at home—and soon will be doing a lot more."

Captain Munroe told of a recent appendectomy he had performed:

"It is really surprising under what fine conditions I can operate. While doing an appendectomy the other day it was amazing to realize that the whole setup was about the same as if I had been at home. My assistant was Lieutenant Miller, who was surgical intern at Duke Hospital and at the Charlotte Memorial Hospital. My scrub-nurse was Miss Martin, who used to be one of the scrub-nurses at Charlotte Memorial. My anesthetist was able Capt. Jack Montgomery. The supervisor was Miss Shipp, who was operating room supervisor at Charlotte Memorial. I have worked with all these very same people many times in Charlotte and it seemed almost incredible to be working with all of them in far-away Africa. I remarked about it and we all had a little laugh."

He spoke of the variety of cases the 38th's surgery and medical services were treating:

"We have an unusual variety of cases and quite a collection of each variety. We could put on clinics on some conditions, with the patients to show, that would surely shame many of the large medical centers back in the States. We are all mighty proud of this outfit. I don't mean to be bragging, but I must tell you how

54

thoroughly the War Department planned this thing and what amazing things can be done, in so short a time, on a bare field simply by a lot of hard work and under an able commanding officer that knows what it's all about. It has surprised me to the n-th degree. Any type of surgery can be done here and there has not been even one infection.

"Thus far I have left the hospital area only one time. I went into the nearby town . . . for about four hours day before yesterday. As far as I'm concerned they can give this country back to the Arabs when this war ends. Here you find mostly Arabs, French, and Spanish, and all three of these languages are spoken. We have interpreters with the unit but I do wish I could understand and speak the languages.

"Well, I'm informed that the General is on the way to look over the hospital, so must close."

6

More details of the 38th's day-to-day existence in the St. Cloud area as seen through the eyes of its mess officer are revealed in the letter begun on December 13, 1942, described by Captain Pickens as "the second of my more lengthy letters to the folks."

It was written, he explained, during the spare moments he was able to find between duties of seeing to the feeding of the unit. That same day, he added, the unit's second mail since its arrival in Africa was received "and my only luck was three copies of the *Charlotte Observer* dated Sept. 16-18 and a copy of the *Charlotte News* dated the same time, which Marshall sent me. The *News* contained some pictures which were made in England about which I had heard from home but had not received a copy. It looks like the mail service is beginning to pick up, so it should not be long before I get some word from someone at home. We got word that one boat containing a great deal of Christmas stuff was lost."

He began the letter with what he termed "a fair description of my Saturday bath," which must have been hardly representative of the baths that even a certain favored few members of the unit were being able at that time to obtain at St. Cloud. "I can remember when every Saturday it was customary for the Pickens household to get some hot water from the kitchen stove and settle down for the weekly bath. My experience here is reminiscent of those days. There are few advantages in being responsible for a mess section in an army," he declared, "but among the few is the opportunity to get hot water. On Saturday, every Saturday, I use my prerogative and call by the main kitchen and get a full gallon of steaming hot water. At the same time I pick up a very large dish pan, of which the Army has

too few. These I carry carefully to my tent, usually going the most out-of-the-way path in order that my advantage not be discovered by the remaining officer personnel. My tent is approximately 7 x 10 feet, in which there are two cots, two large bedding rolls, gas masks, eating equipment, canteens, musette bags, valapaks, a couple of boxes, a lantern, raincoats, trench coats, two sleeping bags which stay on the cots, helmets, toilet articles, a basket of oranges, a violin and some music, extra shoes and galoshes, rubber boots, sterno and accoutrements for heating a little shaving water and a few other odds and ends.

"Into this I carry my dishpan and hot water. Then, after carefully closing the tent in order to have a modicum of privacy, I strip off for my weekly ablution. Into the pan goes Mrs. Pickens' favorite son and off comes a small part of the accumulation of African soil and Mr. Roosevelt's sweat. Boy! does it make you feel good. The only trouble is that the soap sticks to you and you can't get it all off, but that matters little in these times and in this particular place on this socalled green planet. After this rather vicarious procedure and providing there have been no interruptions, I leisurely powder and dress with socalled clean clothes. Thus the Saturday night custom is revived and Sunday's sun finds me sweet-smelling and ready for another week's labor in the interest of Uncle Sam's honor."

The next long paragraph of the letter, he expresses it, is "devoted to the can-opening department of this branch of the Army. I can't imagine how Hannibal crossed the Alps or how Napoleon rushed to Moscow without the aid of the lowly can, the tin can," he begins this particular revelation of the living habits of the 38th in Africa. "Practically everything we get comes in

A group of patients moves along chow line at St. Cloud. Serving, in fatigue hats, are left, William E. Vaughn; center, Jack D. McKenzie, extreme right, Louis F. Cologgi.

cans; I can understand why there would be a shortage of the precious metal at home. It's all over here. And the famous brass hats in Washington (and I say this advisedly) send us out without a can opener. Ain't we got fun? I'm not kidding when I say we got here without a can opener. It's true. Nine-tenths of all our food comes in tin cans—eggs, onions, potatoes, tomatoes, applesauce, jams, coffee, tea, corn beef, crackers, hard tack, butter, cheese, cocoa, all vegetables, chicken, spices, pickles, macaroni, sardines, salmon, codfish, and possibly a hundred other items. Some are packed in No. 2 cans and some in No. 10. You girls who go to the grocery stores know what it is to try and imagine opening enough cans of green peas No. 2 size to feed 1,000 hungry wolves that are dressed like United States soldiers. Well, we get it done, but we had to set up a line that would rival anything General Motors ever devised. The first man uncrates, the second sorts and types, the

third starts with a small axe about the size of a hatchet, the fourth finishes the opening, and then the last two dump the contents into the cooking utensils. It's remarkable what can be done when men get hungry. Our peak day was some time ago when we decided to have one meal cold with the exception of the cocoa. This was a sort of Sunday night pick up job. We had sardines in those flat little cans you are familiar with and added to that was cold corn beef and cheese. Of course, we had crackers and jam and butter and peanut butter, all packed in tin cans. On that day we opened slightly over 4,000 cans and all without a can opener. Necessity is truly the mother of invention. Graduate cooks who know how to season food with the touch of Oscar of the Waldorf now spend their valuable time opening cans without the aid of a can opener. Truly, it is a terrible oversight, but we do very well in spite of it."

56

From the problem of opening thousands of tin cans without a can opener Captain Pickens turned to the problem of purchasing a violin and sheet music in nearby Oran with the aid of an interpreter who was not familiar with musical terms.

"The other day I went into the neighboring city of Oran with the sole purpose of purchasing a violin," he began his account of this adventure. "Stupid idea, I agree, but sitting out here on the edge of nowhere, I thought it might be a way to pass a little spare time pleasantly. Pleasantly for me only, since my neighbors up and down our tent street protest vigorously every time I tune up. But in this I am selfish. Going to town, I took my interpreter along, since my French doesn't extend to musical circles. My interpreter comes from Van Buren, Maine, just fifteen miles from Presque Isle, Bob Whatley's home town. Either his father or his mother was a French Canadian and he spoke French, but I failed to consider that he was not familiar with musical instruments and sheet music. The time I spent trying to tell him what a violin bow was and how the horsehair was used on it and what an opera was and what part the aria takes, I could have spent trying to tell the French what I wanted. But I didn't think about that before I started, so we spent the better part of my afternoon off making the purchase. I had fun at it and that's what matters over here when you have time away from the kitchen knaves and kitchen grease. I bought the violin complete with an extra set of strings and the bow and a dilapidated case for slightly less than 2,000 francs, a matter of about $27. Then I had to get some music. You know that I can't do much by ear, nor much better with the music, but I like it. Getting the sheet music was almost the last straw, but I finally picked up a few selections arranged in a simple manner. Since then I have been having some fun, altho the neighbors must hurt to the quick. It's funny what men in the Army assigned to foreign duty will do for amusement."

An interesting look at a formal ceremony that did not proceed according to the Army's plan is provided in this letter of December 13, 1942:

"One of our generals came in the other day and said that he wanted to return at the proper time and distribute the Purple Heart medals to his men who had been wounded in battle. Our commanding officer told him to return the following day in the afternoon and the stage would be properly set for the ceremony. On the following day the General and part of his staff came in. They rushed up with much fanfare and motorcycle escort. We had arranged for the patients who were to receive the decorations to be put front near our flagpole with all the proper settings. The General stepped from his Ford and took his position before his men and started his discourse about the history of the Purple Heart, how it was started by George Washington and was revived during the last war. Then came the climax. When he approached the first man to award the signal honor, he discovered that he did not have the medal. He turned to his aide and asked for the medal. The aide said he did not have them and turned to the next of rank and requested the medals. The next of rank said he did not have them and turned to the next, and so on down the line practically to the MPs who had escorted them out, but no medals. Then the General got slightly irritated and ordered one of his men to return to his headquarters, some twenty miles away, and get the medals. He told him to go pronto. Then we all waited for his return. Everyone tried to assuage the General, but he was not to be eased from his irritation. So we finally awaited the return of the courier in silence. The patients were the only people to really enjoy the show, and that was as it should have been, since it was staged for their benefit. Finally the messenger returned and again the General stepped up to the first man to bestow on him the honor. He opened the medal box and made his little speech and when he reached for the medal it had dropped to the ground behind him. He had failed to see this and when he discovered it was not in the box he blew off again. It was finally recovered and pinned on the man. And so down the list until the last

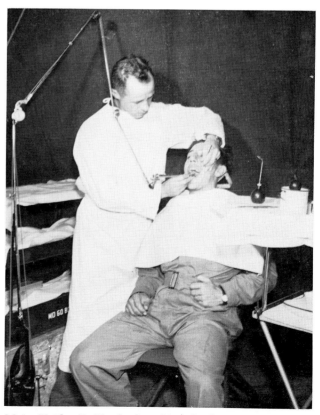

Major Vaiden B. Kendrick, judging by his patient's expression, had a light touch.

57

A company street in the St. Cloud encampment. The top sign on the post at left says "Carolina Ave." The bottom one says "Rebel St."

two men stood awaiting their turn, and then it developed that the courier had failed to bring enough medals to go around. The last two men had to wait for a later delivery.

"All in all, it was a good show," Captain Pickens summarizes the afternoon ceremony, "and the General's parting remark was that 'it was like trying to have a funeral without a body.'"

On December 12, the day before he began writing this letter, Captain Pickens was asked by the Colonel to ride with him on a short trip to visit two friends, a Swiss architect and his American wife. The account of the trip provides another interesting look at that region of Africa and some of its residents as well as the African countryside.

"Into his jeep I clambered with my usual misgivings because he drives like a wild man," Captain Pickens wrote. "Of course, he does other things like a wild man, but in these other things he does not endanger human lives, so they can be properly discounted at the proper times.

"We drove a matter of ten miles up and over one of the nearby mountains. At the top we had a beautiful view of the Mediterranean. There we stopped at a typical hacienda of this section, surrounded by olive trees, cactus, rose bushes, date palms, turkeys, guineas, and dirty Arabs. Here lived a Swiss architect who had married an American woman from Colorado. They had this place as a refuge to which they came during the grape season. But they got caught here and although the man had returned for his service time in the Swiss Army, they were stranded here. Plenty of money but nothing to buy. They actually did not have leather with which to resole their shoes. They were rationed one kilo of bread per week for their whole household. That's about two pounds. And the bread is almost black. Our

58

trip up was to get the wife and take her to our dental department. She had not seen a dentist in three years."

The letter went on to recount more of the visit as seen by the two officers in Charlotte's 38th:

"After many years in Switzerland she had forgotten a great deal of her English but she could still express her gratitude over the coming of the Americans. The Colonel had taken her some beef the day before and some other commodities. She was overjoyed. On this trip we discovered that they had no pepper with which to season their food. Of course, they had hogs and you know what hog-killing time is without some seasoning. Incidentally, they had learned when they killed their goats to cure the skins and use it for leather. It was at their house I had my first olives from this section of the world. They know how to treat them. I told Mrs. Denison that I would trade her some black pepper for some of her olive crop.

"On coming down the mountain we learned the jackals were working havoc on their goats. She pointed out their holes and we saw a small one. They are about the size of a full grown shepherd dog with a nose that is pointed like a fox. They wait for one of the goats to get away from the herd and then they fall on him and that is the end of any goat milk or leather. We made arrangements to come back with some rifles and do a little hunting for them. As a matter of fact, the Colonel got out of the jeep and took several shots at the one we saw, but his revolver was bent in some way and did not harm the scavenger. Mrs. Denison also reported the presence of panthers in the section, but we decided to leave this hunting to Mrs. Denison or whoever wants to bring 'em back alive or dead. Mrs. Denison got her teeth fixed. Major Kendrick did the work. They stayed and had lunch with us and then the Colonel took them home. It was an interesting experience."

This letter, like others he had written home, had been compiled, he explained, over a period of several days. And the day he was finishing it, the 38th had an exciting and most pleasurable experience. Captain Pickens reported it:

"Today the first paragraph is out of date, since mail has come, and it is manna from heaven! Everyone is overjoyed with the news. I had two letters from Mary, two from Marshall, a card from the Holdings of Hempstead Court, a card from Vinton, a letter from Mother, and one from Father.

"Several copies of the *Observer* came also, still September news. Clarence Kuester got an air mail copy of the *News* showing where we had landed in Africa, so now you know just where we are and what we are doing. I got two packages from Davison's containing candy and orange juice. Oh! You will never know what it has meant to the morale of this outfit to get word

Lieutenant Colonel William H. Pennington is caught for snapshot while off duty between operating assignments.

from home, and I am no exception. No longer will I threaten to go out and eat worms and feel sorry for myself. Now I can eat candy instead and feast on what goes on in God's country in these letters. More about them to you individually later."

The *Charlotte News* story to which the letter referred was carried in the Saturday, November 28, 1942, issue under a front-page large banner headline "CHARLOTTE HOSPITAL UNIT IN AFRICA," with subheadlines "Unit Makes History in Operation" and "Story Comes from Oran":

When those Yank troops piled ashore in North Africa, Charlotte's Evacuation Hospital Unit, formed here last year, dragged its gear up on the beaches, set up tents, and started caring for the wounded men. It was the first time in the history of the U.S. Army that a field hospital had been set up in a landing operation, and brought a signal distinction to the unit composed largely of doctors, nurses, and civilians from the Carolinas.

The information was contained in a story by Foreign Correspondent H. R. Knickerbocker, printed in *The Chicago Sun.* His dispatch, datelined Oran, was dated Nov. 19, but was delayed. He had visited the hospital with Generals Terry Allen and Theodore Roosevelt.

It was at the hospital's tent station that 200 American soldiers wounded during the first skirmishes were decorated with the Purple Heart, oldest decoration of the American Army, by their commanding field generals.

Knickerbocker wrote:

"The neatest and most competently organized field hospital the generals had seen in their 30 years of military experience was the evacuation hospital with 200 tents and 300 patients. The outfit arrived four days ago. Today its camp is a model.

"Lieut-Col. Rollin L. Bauchspies of Mauch Chunk, Pa., is the commandant responsible for the organization. Major

Paul Sanger of Charlotte, N. C., founded the outfit composed almost entirely of medical men and civilians from the Carolinas." Knickerbocker described Colonel Bauchspies as "nearly speechless from a sore throat brought about by shouting orders" and quoted the commanding officer as telling him that "This is the first time in history that a field hospital has been set up in a landing operation. My men were so tired this morning that I had to fire my automatic pistol to get them awake. I used a pistol instead of a bugle."

"The quality of our hospital service has never been equaled in the history of any army. The organization of this expedition's medical service provides one of the best illustrations of the vast and competent planning that led to its brilliant success. The expedition carried everything from food to a power plant.

"At Arzew the first two nights operations were performed by flashlight. The Americans now generate their own electricity and purify their own water. And for the first time in the history of North Africa, hospitals are clean.

"This one base has 50 fully qualified medical officers, 60 nurses with the rank of second lieutenant, and 275 medical orderlies headed by a colonel.

"At the peak they cared for 350 patients; now there are only 200. Surgeons said the remarkable good health among the wounded was due to a great extent to the fact that each soldier carried a packet of sulfanilamide to pour on an open wound."

The *News* story added that local confirmation of the unit's arrival in North Africa was contained in a letter received that day by Clarence O. Kuester, Charlotte Chamber of Commerce executive, from his son, Sergeant Clarence O. Kuester, Jr., of the 38th.

Members of the 38th happily experienced a deluge of Christmas mail, if the letters and cards received by Captain Pickens were representative, according to his next letter home, written three days after Christmas. "The mail has been pouring in and it is almost impossible to acknowledge all of the letters," he wrote, and he listed cards and letters from relatives and friends, one of which had been mailed from San Francisco on August 25, had gone to Fort Bragg, then to Fort Sill, Oklahoma, then to England, and after several other delays, had finally reached him in Africa.

"Christmas was quiet with us," he reported of the unit's first Christmas on active duty. "I tried to find some decorations for our tent and for our tables but none were available, not even some colored paper. George and I did take the wrappings off the packages we got and spread this around our tent. We took the string and ribbon and made a simulated wreath. It helped, but frankly, we were homesick for our families and friends. However, we vied up and down our tent street on the first 'Christmas Gift!' The night before Christmas we got together and sang carols around the ward tents for our patients. The heavy rain dampened this somewhat. Some of our enlisted men were invited for dinner at some of the French homes nearby. We distributed a part of our food to the poor in the nearby town. The day before Christmas we took care of the Arabs, since they had practically nothing to eat. It was nearly a mob again, but we finally got the food spread around. Paul Sanger went with me. Of course, we came back to the hospital and washed ourselves immediately. The French on Christmas Day were more orderly and all appeared to appreciate the food we had. Of course, what we had was not so good, since some of the menu advertised for our Christmas dinner was not filled. We missed out on the turkey, but it came in today, so after we get it thawed out we will enjoy a belated feast."

He referred to the earlier letter home in which he had described his Saturday baths. "We now have cold showers available, and I do mean cold. The engineers have tapped a nearby well with all their ingenuity and brought forth some cold brackish water. This they piped down a slight incline and thru the shower connections. We surrounded those connections with some canvas and put in a sort of floor. Now if we are brave enough to face the damp rain and mud and the cold water, we get a shower. Even with this handicap I have stepped up my weekly washing to twice a week."

Further innovations boasted of "in addition to the modern convenience of showers" were the addition of electric lights to the tents. "Now we can sit and look at the dirt in our tents at night as well as in the day time." The electric current had another advantage. "George brought one of his electric razors with him and by borrowing a connection from Bill Leonard next door we can shave with some comfort. It helps. In addition, if you can contort yourself into a position similar to one of those figures over the New York Public Library, you can read in bed. I have not been able to do it yet."

He reported another problem that has plagued soldiers through the centuries:

"It has been raining here since the first of December and it doesn't let up. We wander around in a sea of mud. I can understand how General Mud has so much to do with the movement of armies. We slip and slide and occasionally fall in. After you get your uniform nice and slick with mud you just don't care, and go on. It is a cold, driving rain like we have at home during the winter and it just keeps coming down. We dress with wool uniforms and I keep a sleeveless sweater on and a heavy field jacket and a raincoat and galoshes. It keeps me dry enough and I knock on wood when I say that I have escaped all appearances of being sick. Some of our group have developed colds and have been confined for a day or two. Wading around in the mud gets funny after a while and it's a game to see if you can get thru the day without falling."

Lieutenant Lela O. Russell, the 38th's dietitian, at St. Cloud, is discussing day's duties with one of her chief aides, Sergeant William J. Pricskett.

The terse "Medical History—Year Ending 31 December 1942," a report to the Surgeon General in Washington signed by Colonel Bauchspies, continues from its summary of the unit's duty in England to record the North African tour of duty through the end of the year. This part of the account begins with the unit's boarding the D.S.S. *Nieuw Zeeland* at Avonmouth on October 23:

"On 25 October, 1942, the unit arrived in Gourock, Firth of Clyde, Scotland, where it joined the convoy of the Center Task Force and left Gourock, as part of the convoy, on 27 October. After an interesting, but uneventful voyage, the unit arrived, as part of the 'D' Day convoy, in the Gulf d'Arzew, Algeria, on 8 November 1942 at 0630 hours.

DUTY IN NORTHWEST AFRICA:

At 1000 hours 8 November 1942, all personnel of the unit debarked from the *Nieuw Zeeland* and were transported to the beaches of Arzew on landing craft. The unit moved to the French barracks, where it bivouaced until 12 November. From the time of landing, the personnel of this unit assisted in the care of casualties in this area, and also furnished surgical teams to the hospitals in Oran. On 12 November the unit moved to a site, previously reconnoitered, 3 kilometers south of Saint Cloud, where it went into bivouac and immediately set up facilities for an Evacuation Hospital. Battle casualties were received within twenty-four hours after arrival at this site.

During the first week of operations 300 patients were admitted, and admissions rapidly increased so that on the 20th day the capacity of the hospital was exceeded, for on 3 December the hospital census was 757. All types of patients were admitted, and included American, French and British military personnel, and native French and Arab casualties. The hospital continues to be in operation, using all facilities available. The census as of midnight, 31 December: 617.

All personnel of the hospital were housed under canvas, the officers and nurses in small wall tents and the enlisted personnel under shelter-halves. All patients, utilities, and mess facilities were housed under large ward tents. All water used in the hospital was transported from a water point in Arzew, 22 kilometers away. Canvas reservoirs were erected in the hospital area, and the Engineer Corps assisted in the transportation of the water. A detachment of 1 officer and 30 enlisted men from the 708th Sanitary Company, and an Engineering detachment of 1 officer and 12 enlisted men aided materially in the construction of the utilities for the hospital. It being the rainy season, many adverse conditions due to the weather have been encountered. However, the operation of the hospital was not interrupted, and the physical welfare and morale of the personnel has continued to be excellent.

Captain John C. Montgomery, the unit's chief of anesthesia service, summarizes this same period in the life of the 38th in less than a score of short entries in his diary.

Beginning with the October 15 entry recording that "Lt. Col. Rollin Bauchspies replaced Col. R. W. Whittier as C.O.," he wrote:

Oct. 23rd. Left Norton Manor 3:00 A.M. by train. Arrived Avonmouth and boarded the New Zeeland. Sailed at 7:00 P.M.

Oct. 25th. Arrived Greenock, Scotland, on the River Clyde, where the convoy was assembled.

Oct. 27th. Left Greenock 7:00 P.M. in the world's largest convoy.

Nov. 6th. At 10:00 P.M. entered the Strait of Gibraltar. I was very ill from atabrine and did not see the rock.

Nov. 8th. Sunday, 1 A.M. D day-H hr. In Med. Sea 50 miles north of Oran. Dropped anchor in Arzew harbor at 7 A.M. Many other ships present. Heard on radio that Oran & Algiers had surrendered. Sound of cannon and machine gun fire could be heard all day. French ship Jamaique captured by destroyers in Arzew harbor.

Nov. 9th. Conflicting news about the success of our troops at Oran and Algiers. Went ashore in landing barges. Dick Query almost broke his neck getting in, also Bill Leonard. Bill Pitts lost his flashlight in ocean. One soldier fell in but fortunately was not crushed by barge. Arabs everywhere. We went to a barracks evacuated only 6 hours before by the French. Much personal litter about. Began cleaning the place. 48th Surgical took over.

Nov. 10th. Went to docks for supplies. On returning, sniping started. Spent much time under jeep. Sniping continued all day.

Nov. 11th. Sniping today. This P.M. Rangers cleaned out the town. At 11 PM went to Oran to work in Military Hospital.

Nov. 12th. Arrived in Oran 1:00 AM. Listened to CO rave for 2 hrs. Then went to Military Hospital. Many casualties. Worked until 9 PM when the 77th took over. Went to Civil. hospital where had a nice bed.

Nov. 13th. Spent the day in Oran. A nice town. Bought some perfume for Mildred. Came by bus after dark to St. Cloud where the 38th had moved and had begun setting up as a hospital. Bob Stith and I have tent together.

Nov. 14th. Received 8 patients today.

Nov. 17th. First operation. Acute appendix by Major Pennington.

Nov. 30th. First mail since Oct. 20th.

Dec. 5th. Hospital full. 750 patients.

Many other members of the 38th hospital spent off-duty days in Oran while the unit was encamped at St. Cloud.

Sergeant Davis, the 38th's X-ray technician, still recalls one memorable night in that North African city:

"That's the town where I turned myself in one night to the MP's. I had ridden over to Oran in one of our trucks and had gone to a movie, where I went to sleep. When I woke up one of the ushers was shaking me to tell me that the show was over. I headed out in a hurry. But the truck I came in had either gone or I couldn't find it.

"I knew I could catch a ride once I got to the edge of the city, but I wasn't about to try hitching out of Oran. No, sir, not through those narrow, twisting streets and especially at that time of night. So I just stood there in the square and when some MP's came along, I told them what had happened.

"'Well, you'd better turn yourself in to the curfew club,' they said. So that's what I did. It turned out that the curfew club, as they called it, wasn't anything but a jail, though it wasn't a regular jail but a great big building with marble floors and marble walls and not a chair to sit on.

"And it was cold, and I didn't have an overcoat. I just sat on the floor until daylight, and I almost froze to death; and to make it worse, I ran out of cigarettes. When a sergeant came on duty and took off his overcoat, I asked him to let me borrow it a while, but he wouldn't let me have it. I asked him for a cigarette and he refused me. So just before he went off duty I said to him, 'Sergeant, I'm in the X-ray department in a hospital. I hope I see the day that you come in there for treatment. If you do, I'll turn that machine loose on you and, brother, you won't be any good from then on, I'll promise you that.' But I never saw that sergeant again."

When another soldier came on duty, however, he lent the freezing Sergeant Davis his overcoat.

"And in the morning they took me to MP headquarters and questioned me a little and then they called the hospital. George Snyder was detachment commander at that time, and he told them he would have a truck pick me up. When I got back I told him the story. 'I just wasn't coming out of Oran in the night,' I said. 'I was sure that if I tried it those Arabs would have stuck a knife in me.' And I still figure they would have. I suppose Captain Snyder did too; at any rate, he didn't do anything about it and I went back to my job."

7

As the year 1943 began, the 38th was still encamped at St. Cloud, though letters home from members of the unit still carried the less identifying address of Northwest Africa. Many of these letters, along with snatches of diaries kept, usually with little regularity, by personnel of the 38th, provide interesting close looks at the routine daily life of an Army field hospital that none of the official records can reveal. They often disclose, too, how well or poorly the soldier on foreign duty is able to keep in communication with family and friends at home. Examples of these letters are five that Captain Pickens wrote to relatives and friends in the states. These letters, as were many others written by the men and women of the 38th—and, unfortunately, most of them have been lost or destroyed—reveal what the soldiers are doing, seeing, thinking, aside from their grim duties related directly to the war. They speak of the places and the people and of the soldiers' reactions to them, and since they are so intimately related to people, they are of the essence of historical documentation. They provide the flesh and clothing for the factual frame of events and thereby give life and warmth and color and movement to what without them would be little more than a recital of places and dates and cold statistics that for many persons makes the study of history somewhat forbidding.

Yet these letters often between the lines reveal also that the unit's business was going on at a pace that would continue to gain the approval and admiration of the professional military men and the war correspondents as a highly efficient hospital providing a tremendous service to the nation's military effort. Perhaps the fact that the people of the 38th writing home were not permitted to say much of the unit's war activities caused them to write of the small, intimate, personal happenings and impressions. At any rate, the letters contribute happily to the recording of the 38th's lively and important story.

"I was over in the neighboring town the other day and went to see Ensign Henry Belk for a short visit," Captain Pickens disclosed in his letter of January 4, 1943. "He had called me a few days before and said he had tracked the 38th down and wanted to see a Charlotte face again. He had left the states only a few days before and had the latest news. He had seen Mr. Matthews in New York and had brought news to Stokes Munroe from his father-in-law. Henry was in good health and after a short stay on this side of the world appeared to like it. He had not been here long enough to get fed up on the sorry wine and see plenty of the hunger and filth that is scattered about the countryside. . . .

"George (Snyder) came in the other day with some Coca-Cola syrup from the plant. We have been busy trying to find some carbonated water but so far unsuccessfully. No 'Vichy' water available in the town.

Casanova Park was the unflattering but highly descriptive name given by Colonel Bauchspies to this area at St. Cloud in which patients with venereal disease were treated—behind barbed wire.

Charlie Gay is trying to figure out some way of manufacturing some in his laboratory. So far we have been forced to drink with just plain water, highly decorated. It still tastes good and I remember old man Candler used to take his that way. We are reverting to type. We did not think about catching some rainwater until it stopped. We have had two days of clear weather and it was a relief after a month of mud.

"Paul (Sanger) has just come into my tent, which is a supply tent, and is now stealing some tangerines. We were thrilled about his promotion, and also about George Woods'. Bill Leonard was promoted to major, since he had the longest record in the Army. That is one thing I won't have to worry about, since it is impossible for any of the MACs to move any further."

Captain Pickens began his next letter—of January 12, 1943—with the explanation that he had little he could write about, because of the watchful eyes of the censor

and also because "there has developed a monotonous calm over our place and no one seems to be inspired to do anything." He hinted at an impending moving of the hospital: "We are gradually letting our patients run out in preparation for closing and with nothing building up here there is no inspiration to do anything. Then there is so little to write about when you are afraid that the information might be of value to the enemy or strike the censor wrong. I am not interested in building up a good story to have some bright faced young chap cut it to pieces."

But, said he, he had two principal reasons for writing this particular letter. "Col. White had taken some pictures the other day and I got hold of the two negatives and had a set made with enlargements. I am preparing to send them on to you as soon as I get suitable mailing gear. They are mostly of Col. White, but there are enough of the others to give you some idea about our

64

way of life in the mud. You will also get to see Miss Russell, the dietitian, who works for me and does a lot of my work. She is from Presbyterian Hospital and if you get by there some time, you might show her picture to any of the group left there who are interested. She has done a good job for me and for the Army. . . . There is one picture of Paul cleaning out his tent after a particularly heavy rain. . . . The others are just ordinary scenes and folks around the camp with no military secrets being shown. . . ."

He went on to say what his second reason was for writing: "Today a lot of mail came in and with it some packages for me. The one with the blue Kodak and the films came in and I will try to give you back some real scenes when we get a dry day. . . . Then another package came with some additional outing pajamas and set of boot shoes from Mellon's. The shoes are the thing. George got some a few days ago and has bragged about them so much that I am doubly happy about mine. They fit. They are worn under the galoshes and make working and walking so much easier. It gets tiresome dragging the old G.I. shoes around under heavy galoshes with about ten pounds of mud on the outside."

Another package recently received, said he, was "light paper and some air mail envelopes which I was beginning to need. We get from two to four stamps a week and sometimes when I make copies of my letters and send them all over the country it takes more stamps and envelopes than it appears on the surface. Many thanks. . . . I will try to repay with good letters and some good pictures. Until we do some moving around I will not be able to get much description in what I say. . . ."

He thanked relatives and friends for other presents— a razor, an electric heater, and other gifts especially useful. "It so happens that my socalled office is a common meeting place for the whole camp. In the morning we have an extra pot of coffee on the stove here and most of the boys will stop by some time during the morning for an extra cup. Even Paul has developed into a coffee drinker and sits for an hour sometimes while it cools for him. Stokes usually gets by as well as Jack Montgomery, Preston, Bill Pennington and Bubber Fleming. It's a steady stream for most of the morning and interrupts the working in a most pleasant way, but it also keeps me from having any privacy. . . .

". . . George and I have plenty of food, nic-nacs, candy, and we are overrun with cigarettes and pipe tobacco. Of course, it has all bunched up on us, including packages direct from home and those that went to England and then came down here. It appears that most of our things are coming thru in spite of the enemy claims about sinking our ships. But there I get off on the wrong subject. We are not supposed to talk about any of the maneuvers of the war or to have any ideas on how to run it. Of course, we hear the radio from England every morning and at night a short wave broadcast from Boston and Pittsburgh. I guess we keep up fairly well. The *Charlotte Observers* have been pouring in. I got about ten yesterday and more today, so now I am reading about what we did when we came in, as well as many of the letters written by our folks that were published. I have even read my letter to you which the *Observer* printed. Many of the people have commented on it to me here. They seem to think that it was conservative enough and a fairly good picture of our experience without giving away any military information. . . ."

Heavy rains and high winds of early January added to the discomforts and problems of the 38th in its encampment at St. Cloud. In a long letter written January 15 Captain Pickens pictures the period just before he sat down to record life in the 38th:

"The rain has left for a few days and the wind has been taking its place. When I say wind, I mean real wind, not a gentle breeze. Did you ever try to get four pieces of thin paper and three pieces of carbon paper together in a flimsy tent in a high wind? Well, it's no easy job and if a part of this letter seems to run sidewise of the copy, blame it on the African wind.

"As I said, the rain has let up for a few days but for a while it looked as if we had arrived in the wrong service; we thought we should have been in the Navy. We literally swam and waded around the camp. Now if this wind keeps up we will wade around in dust a mile deep. However, you get used to all things in the Army and dust and mud make little difference."

Although he pointed out the difficulty of trying to tell much about the 38th's position because of the rules of censorship, he did manage to give an interesting and revealing report of the hospital's routine from the viewpoint of the mess officer.

"I have a set place to be most of the day and some parts of the night," he began this section of the letter. "It is a tent, called a ward tent, about 15 x 40 in size. It is set up right next to the main kitchen tent and two-thirds of it is taken up with the storage of foodstuffs. There are cans and boxes packed in as high as the tent will stand. In the rear is a large wooden ice refrigerator, which contains the various types of fruit juices. In the front is my socalled office. I have a small stove which sits directly in the dirt with the pipe running out the top of the tent. It will put out plenty of heat if you can find the fuel. We have had some coal in limited quantities, and we sometimes resort to burning our crating when it gets very cold and damp. Of course, there are no forests anywhere in this part of Africa. But, back to the office, I have a large table built from our crates, with a stool for a chair. Next to me sits my dietitian, one of the older nurses in our organization. She does most of the work, since I have little knowledge of the difference between a soft, liquid, high-caloric, and bland diets. That is, she looks after the patients' food, but that still leaves me fifty officers, fifty nurses and over 300 men to feed. They keep me busy. We have a telephone sitting on the tent pole which connects with the rest of the hospital and the outside world. I could call Charlotte or Washington or Atlanta from my desk if I had the proper pull and the proper luck.

"The day starts officially at 8 AM, or, as the Army puts it, 0800 hours. It ends officially at 5.30 PM or 1730 hours. I find that I spend about three nights a week here at my socalled desk. At 0900 hours I have a meeting each day with my sergeants, of which I have three. We go over the menus for the next day, plan the meals and assign the cooks and cook's helpers for each kitchen. Then I see my corporal, who has the responsibility for getting the food in bulk into the camp. We get out requisitions for the number of people we expect to feed two days hence. All of this takes probably an hour and then the working boys get out and the doctors descend on our little office. I keep a pot of coffee on the stove (as he related in his previous letter) and a few cups, sugar and canned cream handy. They drop by for a cup whenever they have time in the morning. At the same time they talk diets of patients, location of wards, and other things that might come up. We combine business with pleasure. It takes the place of Coca-Cola time at home, and frankly, during the height of the rainy season, I welcomed it. Something hot when everything around was cold and wet was very comforting. I will never develop into the coffee drinker that mother is, since it tastes differently each time. By the way, I see in the papers that you are rationed on coffee now. . . .

"When the others have cleared out, then come the special diet slips that have to be filled out. There are some patients with jaundice who have to eat six and eight times a day and all of them different types of food with lots of candy and sweets thrown in for good measure."

And so, the mess officer's recital reveals, his morning's routine is completed. But this general schedule, he adds, "develops during the afternoon and with this the bulk food comes in by truck and has to be checked and stored. During the day we check food out to the various kitchens also. At one time we operated four separate kitchens. Now we have only three. With each kitchen there is a dishwashing problem and a department to take care of it. This causes more trouble than all of the rest of the work put together, since we have

the problem of water, getting it hot, and not the least of the problems is that of keeping men at work washing dishes. I can't fuss much at them myself when they complain, since I hate the job as much as they do.

"During the afternoon I make an inspection of all mess properties and personnel. That is a real job, keeping everything running smoothly. And when the day is thru and there has been only a minimum amount of complaint, I have the pleasant prospect of doing the same thing all over the next day. Truly, the mess officer's job is never done. I have stayed awake at night and thought of the times I have complained with Mary about how the coffee tastes or about the types of food she has had or say to her, 'if it were on a menu, I wouldn't order it.' Each time I think of my complaints to her, I turn over and try to kick myself in the pants. I pray that I may be forgiven for all that has passed and promise that it will never happen again. I also pray that I may never have to go near a kitchen again or think of a menu or listen to a complaint. Forgive the raving of a kitchen knave who smells of kitchen grease!"

Recent letters from the states, Captain Pickens observed, had revealed that to the coffee rationing had been added gasoline rationing. "I also learn that your gas rationing is getting to brass tacks. When I piece together the fragments from everyone and get the true picture, I have to laugh about your hardships," he added. "I laugh more heartily when I start from my tent to go to the latrine at night and wander around with a flashlight and think about the comforts of home in the same situation."

He returned to expressing how delightful to a member of the 38th would be the experience of a hot bath in the shower or tub at home:

"We had showers for a while with good, honest cold water, but the water gave out in spite of the rains, so now I resort to my old method of Saturday night bathing in my tent. When I think about hot and cold running water in a nice tile bathroom, well heated, I laugh again about your hardships in doing without gasoline and a little less coffee. When I stumble thru the mud or try to get the dust out of my hair I think about the paved streets and electric lights you have to put up with. When the planes pass overhead I think of the casual attention you pay to the same passing there. . . . When I think about being able to change clothes each day and the convenient laundries and dry cleaning service and the choice of colors to wear even down to the tie, I still laugh. When I think about the news being delivered to your door each morning and the radios without any interference and to your knowledge of what goes on all over the world, I smile, at least. Don't misunderstand me, I am not complaining; I am just laughing, and that is the way you must learn to do. Oh, we do our share of griping and fussing. I don't take all these things lying down. I complain loud and hard but I come up laughing. We are getting the gasoline here and we have plenty of coffee, but I'll exchange all of my day's supply for one good bath and a change of clothes."

Captain Pickens closed this long mid-January, 1943, letter with a further description of the natives and the geography of the St. Cloud area, which he was still referring to simply as Northwest Africa.

"I have wanted to write something of the impressions in the city I get to visit occasionally. I think Ernie Pyle has stolen my thunder on this, since I see where his articles are appearing in the *Charlotte Observer*, and then he gets better pay for his writings. I think I told you he was here at our hospital for several visits. He had a good story on it that never has appeared as far as I know. . . . But back to the city. The French women are better dressed and better groomed than the English. They go in for more makeup and wild-colored hair. They can really look like chorus girls when they get all their to-do on. This is true of the classes from the low to the high. The men are no more conservative. They go in for loud colors both in dress and hair dye. Most of them wear the familiar tam-o'-shanter instead of a regular hat."

His experiences in trying to communicate with the folk in the St. Cloud area and to understand better the people and their homeland were doubtless shared by the others, officers, nurses, and enlisted personnel of the Charlotte unit. Some of his experiences and impressions he reveals:

"They rattle their French at you entirely too fast for comfort. I arm myself with a few phrases that should get me along and then I run into trouble. I do better when I stick to American, as they say. However, I still try, and think it is best to practice, altho they must laugh at me as much as I would at a Greek cafe operator who had been in America for ten days.

"The shops are almost empty. They have had little merchandise since the war started. The stores have unusual designs on their windows with the tape that protects them from air raids. The English never thought about that, but these folks make the place look attractive. They go in for plenty of photographs, since there are usually two or three places in each block where you can get your picture made. In these same shops they will fit your glasses. The opticians and the photographers are the same people. There are the same sidewalk cafes as you see in France, but there is little food. I have eaten one meal in town. I had a sort of salad to start with, consisting of a small tomato and some green stuff that resembled lettuce, and not much of either. Then came the main course, fish that was like Mobile Bay catfish, and a pot of spaghetti. No bread or butter and nothing to drink if you didn't like their very poor wine, vin rose or vin rouge; after that a small tangerine. That was all. Now you know why I seldom eat any-

Dress for chow line in North Africa is informal—and varied.

It ended bloodlessly. T. D. Tyson and Colin Munroe get more sunshine than bruises.

Nurses Barbara Wingo and Elva Wells relaxing at Santa Lucia, Africa.

where but in my own backyard out of good American tin cans.

"The hotels have been taken over by the Americans. They must have opened them when they came, since they look as if they had not been cleaned up since the war started. The streetcars run two together like they do in Boston, with the last car open. The people pack in worse than a New York subway, with little Arabs hanging on everywhere. There is little indication of anyone working except the people mending the streets and those helping unload American vessels in the harbor.

"There are a good many French soldiers in sight now and they appear to be a determined lot. They make a better military appearance than we do, but I guess we will take care of our share of the load. Every little Arab has a shoeshine box. I forget them when I said there were few people working. They will shine your shoes at every corner for two francs or one cigarette or one stick of gum. They really get in the way. . . . The Arabs have an open air market where they trade horses and donkeys. There are few good horses in sight. It sounds like an American tobacco auction. . . ."

Enclosed in his next letter, written January 24, 1943, were pictures of members of the 38th made by Captain Pickens with the blue Kodak that he had received from home. This letter serves further to reveal the African people of that area and the feelings of the Americans toward them.

"The reason or inspiration for this letter is the enclosed group of pictures," he began. "You will see that Paul, George Wood, Bob Miller, Tom Tyson and I were off together. Bob Miller had had a letter from Mrs. Davison, wife of the Dean of the Medical School at Duke, stating that she had a friend over there, a classmate from Bryn Mawr, and she wanted Bob to try and see her."

So the group set out in search.

"We went to a neighboring town to the east and some thirty to fifty kilometers and tracked the good lady down. On the way over we had lunch on the beach, which you can see from the pictures. These are the first pictures from the blue Kodak and are much better in the negatives but the developing over here now is very poor—shortage of developing paper. However, you can see us and see that we are being fed well and that we are happy and healthy.

"The trip was taken last Sunday, January 17th. We had a time finding the lady but she finally turned up as the wife of a French colonel in charge of the garrison in that particular town. . . . The visit with her was most instructive, since she gave us the viewpoint of the French about our coming here in November. Her husband was up at the front with the French troops which are helping our men and the English. We had a typical Sunday afternoon tea; she said she was able to get a supply of tea but very little else. We had some cheese and white bread left from our picnic lunch and Miller had some fruit cake left over, so we contributed our share to the tea party. Her oldest daughter, age 17 or 19, was there and had a good time talking English with us. The mother said she went back to Cincinnati about once in every ten years. She married after the last war in Germany while her husband was in the army of occupation and has been in Syria and France and North Africa ever since. She was in the class of 1916 at college. . . . They went for the cheese, just plain old Kraft's rat cheese, and the white bread, which they had not seen for three years. Of course, the fruit cake was the piece de resistance. If we get another chance to go back I will take her a little sugar, bread, and some corn beef and spam. We have plenty of the latter and can spare it."

One of the pictures they had made showed Dr. Sanger with a herd of goats and sheep. "We tried to catch a small lamb and have him hold it for the picture, but were unable to get it done," Captain Pickens wrote. "The Arabs minding the flock did not understand French and I think thought we either wanted to buy the lamb or shoot it and put up a great deal of interference with our plan for proving to Mary Ann that she was not the only one that could have a lamb. You would have laughed to see us trying to corner enough of the flock to get the picture. Paul was running with the animals, Tyson was trying to get behind them and shoo them toward me and I was trying to stay in front of them in order to snap at the proper time. Miller stayed in the jeep and George Wood was driving along behind us enjoying the show.

"The other pictures are of George Snyder near our tent, and to finish the roll and get it developed in a hurry I caught one of our nurses shining her shoes back of her tent. I hope you will be able to add these to the collection of pictures in the album. I have given all of the boys copies so they can send them to their wives if they wish. As a matter of fact, they very likely have already sent copies along, since they seem to have more time than I do for such things."

The final paragraph in the letter was revealing:

"You have indicated an interest in our new CO and have said that no one had written about him. There is little that can be said except that he is better in many respects than the old one and not so good in others. His personal conduct is better and he gets the work done, although we don't always agree with his methods. He is very profane, which always indicates a lack of vocabulary and consequently poor education or poor thought. He is good natured almost to a fault; he wants to be liked and respected and admired and doesn't know exactly how to get it across. He is moody, either up in the clouds or down in the dumps. You can never tell just which way he will get out of bed, but all in all I think we gained in the trade. I wonder if all CO are selfish, conceited, egotistical, and consider their troops as being a bunch of dumbbells."

The preoccupation through the years of American service men and women on duty in foreign lands, particularly those in the field, with the idea of surviving long enough to obtain somewhere a hot bath with soap is revealed in countless letters home. During World War I American fighting men holed up in the trenches in France dreamed of escaping some day into the steaming warmth of a hot shower bath and after that into the clean sheets of a real bed.

In World War II in Africa, members of Charlotte's 38th Evacuation Hospital unit, sloshing through the mud and perspiring in the dust of Algiers as they labored to keep the hospital operating at peak efficiency, were likewise soon obsessed with one consuming desire. Everybody was hoping and dreaming and figuring and scheming how to get a hot bath. In their bunks they dreamed of oceans of hot water and clouds of foaming soap suds.

And one day—it was January 30, 1943—a group of the officers and nurses decided to fashion their fantasies into realities. They decided to drive southward, though it meant a trip of many miles, to get baths.

Captain Pickens describes in considerable detail this unusual journey. The letter was written the next day:

"Never did I think I would ride 140 miles for a hot bath, but that is exactly what I did yesterday. 65 miles down to the spot and 75 miles back on a small truck with ten other people is the story's beginning."

Then he tells the story:

"Our commanding officer had made arrangements for us to make the trip. One half of our officers and one half of the nursing staff were to go. One half of the reason for the trip was to get a hot bath and the other half was to see the scenery. The bath outweighed the scenes in my estimation, but that is beside the point now. I will try to give you a picture of the trip.

"Lt. Col. White, Major Pitts, Capt. Medearis, Capt. Snyder, Lt. Schirmer and four of the nurses were on the truck with me. It is what the Army calls a weapons carrier and normally would accommodate about eight people comfortably. We were after a hot bath, so we put up with the inconvenience of being packed in. There were two other large trucks in the movement filled equally as well. I had made arrangements for us to stop along the way and have some sandwiches and some fruit juice for lunch.

"The spa to which we were headed is almost due south of our station. It was one of the Trans-Atlantic hotels built to take care of the tourists for a day or two off the boats making Mediterranean cruises. The water comes from the earth at an even temperature of 150 degrees, summer and winter. The place has been used as a watering spot since the days of the Romans. . . .

"The roads down and back are surprisingly good. They are well paved and cover some rough and hazardous territory. We were on our way to the desert and passed over the northern part of the Atlas mountains. Of course, the desert is far to the south, but the vegetation gets more sparse as you go south. The roads are well marked. On the way we passed thru two very fertile valleys. There were many orange groves and olive groves, the first I had seen. There were few, if any, grapefruit trees and few lemons, but plenty of tangerines in sight. Also seen for the first time in Africa were two large cotton fields with a little cotton still left on the stalks. I did not get a chance to see if it was long or short staple, but I would guess that it was long. There is plenty of grain growing and there was some grazing land with sheep and goats in sight. Where there was a little water there were truck farms with tomatoes, artichokes, cauliflower, turnips, carrots, and cabbage. These items were being harvested. As a matter of fact, we have recently had an issue of fresh cauliflower and cabbage for our mess.

"We saw large numbers of quail that looked more like English grouse. They were large and healthy looking, but of course we could not take a shot at them. The flowers were beautiful—roses that looked like sunflowers in size, bougainvillea, hibiscus that reminds me of Florida. The children in the towns and along the roads, whether Arabic or French, have a chant which is either 'shooing gum' or 'OK Americano.' Some of them venture a 'shocolot' or 'cigarette' occasionally. Capt. Snyder had a good time throwing chewing gum and candy to them as we passed. He said that possibly someone might do the same for his children sometime. We had to keep riding when this was done; otherwise we would have had a mob around us in ten seconds. I think the people are beginning to like us a little better since they have gotten used to the American ways.

"But back to the trip," his letter continues. "On almost every mountain top there is a small mosque with its white dome shining in the sun. It is said that the Moslems make a trip to these places of worship once a year. They are so inaccessible that this is well understood. I would hate to make the trip up one of those barren peaks even once in a lifetime to say my prayers in public.

"There were plenty of Arabs in view, along with the inevitable donkey, the man usually riding and the woman walking and carrying the burdens. We stopped for lunch in a sort of canyon overlooking a small stream far below. Before we had been there ten minutes there were at least six Arabs peeking at us from around the rocks, children mostly. They grew bolder as time went on and came out into full view. One little girl had so little with which to clothe herself that our chief nurse finally broke down and gave her scarf to the waif to help her keep warm and decent. Of course, they fell upon the food we did not eat and made for the empty tin cans. When we prepared to leave they disappeared as quickly as they came and there was no indication of where they had gone. They were beautifully camouflaged, since they look like the dirt that surrounds them and usually have a great deal of it on them.

"But back to the bath, since we had begun to look somewhat like them. We arrived at the spa, which had been taken over by one of our general hospitals. They had some 300 patients. They were cordial to us, since they, too, had seen some life in the mud and dust before being set up here. There were many baths available, almost one for each of our entire party. We had a choice of shower, tub, or one of those walkdown petit swimming pools. I took the latter, then finished with a cold shower. The water was just right for a good lather. It was a little hard but not bad enough to interfere. I actually took two while I was there, since during one washing I thought about the last time I had had a real bath. Discounting the saltwater baths on the boat coming down, it was back in October in England when I last stepped under a hot shower. I was afraid that another delay might be my part again and I tried to prepare for it. I washed my head as well and discovered that I was more gray-haired than I thought. But it was worth it. There was singing all along the line while the water poured on, the first I had heard from any of our group since our days in England. The women had armed themselves with lemons, vinegar and all sorts of bath salts and had equally as good a time.

"We were rosy when we came out of the hotel. Some of us could have passed for broiled lobsters, we soaked so long. On the outside we looked around the place for a while, ate some oranges, took some pictures, and then started back. It was a grand trip, this 140 miles for a bath."

While the unit was still at St. Cloud the work of the hospital began to gain the attention of not only the war correspondents and visiting generals but also of Army officialdom in Washington.

In his letter of January 31, 1942, Captain Pickens referred to the letter received some days before by Major Pennington from Brigadier General Fred W. Rankin, a member of the Surgeon General's staff. General Rankin was a first cousin of Charlotte's well known Dr. W. S. Rankin, pioneer leader in North Carolina

public health service, and before entering the Army had achieved a national reputation as an authority in the treatment of cancer. His home was in Lexington, Kentucky, but he was a native North Carolinian.

"I think I can quote from a letter received by Major Pennington written by Brigadier General Rankin about our unit," the Charlotte officer wrote. "General Rankin is on the staff of the Surgeon General. He is writing about what the Surgeon General said about us after a trip to Africa. Here is a part of the letter: 'I was very much pleased and delighted to receive a message from the Surgeon General's own hand from you, Paul Sanger, George Wood, Pat Imes and the other officers of the 38th Evacuation Hospital. I was even more pleased at the praise the General showered upon your outfit for the manner in which you are carrying on in that theatre of war. He not only told me how beautifully your hospital is being run and what splendid work is being done, but he told the assembled staff here in the Surgeon General's office. In fact, the only other hospital he mentioned by name was Staige Blackford's Evacuation Hospital from the University of Virginia. He obviously was impressed with the manner in which you people are doing business, and I was delighted, of course, since I feel I am closely associated with you. His description of your location and your difficulties and your spirit flattered you very much and would have pleased you, I am sure, had you heard him.'"

In the last weeks of the 38th's stay at St. Cloud they initiated the practice of having movies twice a week. Since no tent was large enough to accommodate the personnel of the unit, the movies were shown outdoors and even though at that time of the year it was rather cold, the shows were well attended. Although Captain Pickens considered himself no movie fan, he attended regularly the screen showings at St. Cloud. "It helps get your mind off the worries of the day or thinking too much of getting home," he reasoned. "Of course, the latter is uppermost in all of our minds all of the time."

The Post Exchange at St. Cloud was opened once a week for the issuance free of such items as soap, razor blades, candy, writing paper and envelopes. Other things that were available but only for purchase included powder, cigarettes, cigars, and after-shaving lotions. The Quartermaster had opened a place, too, where additional uniform equipment might be purchased.

The 38th's personnel was beginning, too, to understand better and appreciate the Arabs around the hospital encampment, particularly the children who frequently came on various pretexts to visit the encampment. One youngster was a ten-year-old boy named Abduk, who came regularly to collect and deliver laundry. Captain Pickens was one of the youth's regular customers. In a letter to the homefolk he spoke appreciatively of Abduk:

"I think I told you some time ago I was having most of my laundry done by a neighboring Arabic family. They have a young son named Abduk, aged 10, who comes to collect and deliver. He has made friends with all of the unit and has developed a real business. He has learned English in the weeks we have been here and has an amazing conception of what it is all about. He has the brightest face you can imagine and breaks into a quick smile which shows his white teeth. He now knows the value of the dollar with respect to the franc and keeps up with his accounts in good order. He has been at this so long now he can tell whose clothes belong to whom. He is rank conscious and looks after the higher ranks first, altho he says the lower ranks are nicer to him. He is not particularly interested in the money and is now tired of eating candy and chewing gum. He much prefers to come and visit and talk and get a lesson in 'Americano,' as he calls our language. He wants to know the why of everything, why wear leggings, why your insignia is at a certain spot, why so much saluting (here I wonder, too, since according to the regulations we are not supposed to salute in a war theatre, but 'orders is orders'), why we wash so much, why so much laundry, why we have so much soap, and so on. I get a great kick out of spending some time with him and telling him. He will never forget his experience with the American troops. His father works for the planter on whose property we are encamped. He makes 37 francs per day, the father does; that's about 50 cents. There are at least six in the family. They seem to do all right. Abduk is being well fed now and some of the nurses are working on some clothes for him. He has for the time being developed into the mascot of the 38th."

8

Early on a morning in mid-November of 1942 Louie Dennison, the Swiss architect, and his Colorado-born wife heard the disturbing sounds of gunfire from the direction of the nearby Algerian town of St. Cloud.

"I wonder what the commotion over there is about," he said to his wife. "I think I'll ride over and see."

"Well, be careful," she cautioned. "And remember your liver."

He got on his horse and rode into St. Cloud. After some hours he was home again.

"What was the commotion about?" Mrs. Dennison asked him.

"The Americans are coming," he told her.

"Now, Louie, I told you to remember your liver. Drinking this early in the morning doesn't help it. You should have stayed away from those cafes."

"But the Americans are coming," he insisted. "In fact, they're already here. That's what the shooting was about."

"Oh, Louie, your liver. You should think of your liver."

But a few minutes later, when she saw along the road a group of refugees streaming out of St. Cloud, she believed her husband. And she was overjoyed to realize that at last her fellow Americans—though now she was a naturalized Swiss citizen—had arrived to challenge the Nazis.

This was the story Mrs. Dennison herself told to four of the officers of the 38th Evacuation Hospital unit some two months later as the four were guests at dinner in the Dennison home. The four American officers were enjoying an interlude in the hospital routine. Captain Pickens, who had referred in an earlier letter home to a visit he and Colonel Bauchspies had made to the Dennisons, relates the story in a long letter dated "Northwest Africa, Feb. 5-6, 1943."

"Lt. Col. Paul Sanger, Lt. Col. George Wood, Major Vaiden Kendrick and I had been invited to come up on the mountain to the Dennison home for dinner. It was a change and we had heard from Col. Bauchspies what sumptuous meals they could prepare and serve, so we looked forward to the visit. We were not disappointed. The house is comfortable, with tile floors and pleasant furniture on the modern manner," he continued his narration of the visit away from the unit's encampment. "The servants are all Arabic. Rosalie, a middle-aged Arab, is a marvelous cook, with just the right touch for proper seasoning. We had in times past given Mrs.

Dennison some condiments. On this trip I took along some salad oil. They don't have any of that sort of thing now. The others took cigarettes, chewing gum and candy.

"We were invited for 1 p.m. and sat down to eat at 1:30 and finished at 4. We didn't waste much time during that period, nor was there any wasted food." He went on to tell of the African meal, one that was quite a change from the American tinned meats and vegetables of the hospital's mess. "After a peculiar tasting appetizer made from bananas, we set forth on a salad made of deviled eggs, fresh eggs, and they were very good. With salad we had stuffed olives, both ripe and green, a good supply of green lettuce and mayonnaise. That was a meal in itself.

"Then came the piece de resistance, roasted guinea, and I mean roasted to the king's taste. Rosalie brought all of them in on a platter and Mrs. Dennison explained to us that she wanted us to admire them before she took them back for carving. To Rosalie, who speaks excellent French, our reply was 'L'appetit est le meilleur condiment,' 'C'est bon,' 'L'appetit vient en mangeant,' 'La bon cuisiniere,' 'Tres bon.' To these we added all the other expressions we knew. Rosalie beamed and hurried off for the carving. I never saw white meat in a guinea before. This was white and good. We stuffed. With the fowl we had small fresh potatoes, and another salad of lettuce.

"After this was cleared away we went to work on a dish of custard made of goat's milk. The white of eggs had been toasted into a meringue over which was poured the yolk and the cream. It was good. Of course, with each course we had the proper wine and at the finish we enjoyed a choice of Benedictine or Cointreau. I could hardly get up when we finished. It was four o'clock and we were full. During the meal we heard about Louie going to town. During the latter months Mrs. Dennison said he had complained about his liver hurting. After being shot at a few times on that important day," she had added, "he has never mentioned his liver again and has no hurts to speak of."

It was on this visit that the four officers of the 38th had a further first hand view of the Arabic manner of living. It was the first time, Captain Pickens related, that he and his companions had been given an opportunity, as he expressed it, "to get the truth about the ways and habits" of the Arabs in this region of Africa. Later during the visit to the Dennisons, they visited one of the Arab houses on the farm and saw first-hand the way the people lived. "It's primitive, to say the least," he described it. "I think their custom of marriage might interest you. . . . The oldest brother always arranges the marriage of the sisters. Of course, we asked about the chance of having no brothers, but apparently

there is little chance, since they are a prolific race. The brother picks out the groom and makes all the arrangements for the wedding. The bride and groom never see each other until they are married. The groom must give as his part of the dowry one pair of ear rings, one sheet or cover they use to hide their whole body, including their faces, 100 kilos of wheat and 100 kilos of either barley, oats, or rye, one goat, or one sheep. A kilo is about two pounds. The brother usually gets the grain and the animal and the bride gets the ear rings and sheet. She, on the other hand, must furnish one sheet and one pair of ear rings and all the linen for the house. When all arrangements are made by the brother, then the girl has her hand painted with henna and begins to cover her face whenever she goes outside the house. She is not allowed to go out except for very unusual occasions like a funeral for her parents and the like. This hand-painted stage is known as the little marriage, like our engagement time.

"The bride and groom have not yet met. They meet at the wedding. The best man plays the main part at the wedding. He manages everything and has been picked by the brother. He is a witness of the final consummation of the marriage at the wedding bed and when the bride has proven that she was virtuous, he comes out to announce it and the feasting and celebration begin for those attending. If she is found otherwise, she is dismissed immediately and the marriage is off and she and her family are in disgrace and no one ever speaks to them again.

"After the wedding the bride must stay almost within the courtyard of the house until she gets to be thirty years old or approximately that," the captain's account of the Arabic wedding customs continues. "After thirty she can move around the streets of the nearby towns but always with her face covered. They are usually married between the ages of twelve and fifteen. The marriage is performed by the maribout, pronounced maribo. He is a combination lawyer, priest, minister, justice of the peace, judge and jury. His word is law and he is considered perfect. He gets a fee for all of his work so you can see he is usually well to do. He can also grant a divorce. In this case, if the girl wants to marry again, there is no feast or celebration allowed. The arrangements are made as usual by the brother and he gets his cut. It appears to me that he is always trying to marry his sisters off. However, divorce is rare. All of this information came from Mrs. Dennison during our dinner."

At the end of the dinner the American officers asked their hosts if they might visit one of the farm houses. The house was in the nearby hills. This is how Captain Pickens described it:

"The house was built of stone and stucco. There were

three rooms and three generations. I counted twelve people who were supposed to live there; some may have come from other houses. One room was used for storage and some cooking. It was there that they made coffee for us, using the fireplace and the metal pot. They used a bellows to whip the flames; it was made of goat skin and wood. It worked so well that we asked them to get three for us to send home. I don't know whether we will ever get them or whether you will get one, but at least we tried.

"Vaiden Kendrick speaks good Spanish, which these people understand better than French, and he made arrangements for us.

"The other two rooms are for living, cooking and sleeping purposes. George Wood spent most of the time we were there trying to find some sanitary facilities. He reported there were none. It was just every man for himself. George thought he was going to get out of drinking the coffee, but Mrs. Dennison explained that we had to drink it or otherwise they would feel insulted and we would never be welcome again. It was a bitter dose but we all made it. The coffee was made from barley, wheat, and a little coffee ground together. It was hot and that may have saved us. It had been ground in a metal container with an iron muddler. It looked like an oversized gadget used by a pharmacist.

"Then we sat on the floor or in some cases on simple boxes. They, of course, sit on the floor to eat. They had a small, round, wooden table about two feet high and about two feet in diameter from which they serve and eat. They had few dishes. We drank from cups like our cups but without handles. The dishes were arrayed in a sort of cupboard on the wall made from driftwood they had gathered along the coast. They card, spin, and weave their own wool. Their clothes they sew themselves and I must say they do a good job of it. They have heavy wollen comforts and goat skins for their bedding. They cure the skins for this purpose and for the sandals they wear and harness for the donkey. The donkey hauls all the water and supplies with this harness and usually one or two people riding in addition. He is truly a sturdy little animal. He may be an ass to some people, but he's really horsepower to me.

"They have a system of drying their goat meat quickly after the kill and preserving it somewhat like our chipped beef."

He turned aside from food to reveal again the 38th members' preoccupation during these months in Africa with the thoughts of bathing:

"Once each week on their day off from work they go to the neighborhood town of St. Cloud for a Turkish bath. This was the first time I had heard of their taking a bath but it seems to be a fact, and they do it regularly."

Then he returned to his narration about food:

"The oven for the baking of the bread was interesting to me. It is made of mud in the shape of a small igloo about two feet high. Into this they put the charcoal made from the discarded vines from the vineyards. They whip it up and get the place almost white hot and then put the dough in to bake. Mrs. Dennison said it made very good bread, all whole wheat, of course. This all depended upon their getting some wheat. As I told you once before, the Germans and Italians had cleaned out all this part of the country of grain of any sort. They have another crop coming now and should be eating better by June."

He revealed how the Arab families grind their grain:

"They have two stones, one with a short handle and a small hole in the middle. Into the hole goes the whole grain and out the sides between the rocks comes the flour. I will try to get a picture of that operation."

His letter further describes the Arabic household:

"They have a lean-to attached to the house which houses the two donkeys the family owns. They all appear to live happily together. The grandfather suffers from diabetes and since the war started has been unable to get insulin. He is in a bad way now. Paul said he thought he had some in his luggage and would bring it back to the old man. For all the fun and knowledge we had there, that will be real lend-lease if it makes the old man enjoy his latter years. He appeared to be about 85 years old.

"There were four children in sight. They pounced on the candy and chewing gum we happened to have left in our pockets. When I go out away from camp I always carry a generous supply with me. It always makes some child happy and I hope leaves an impression that will last in their minds that the Americans are friendly and believe in peace on earth, good will toward men. The children were healthy and animated. Two of them were positively pretty, with good looking teeth and winsome smiles."

Captain Pickens wrote that they were still at the encampment where they had been for the past months, although the APO number had been changed. The government, too, he reported, had changed the value of money. On February 8 the dollar would be worth fifty frances rather than seventy-five. "Our pay for January was on the old rate, so we had a material increase in the value on our money if we send it home. If we spend it here we get less for it. . . . There is no way to spend money except for haircuts, laundry, photographs, and a few items at the post exchange. . . . The perfumes have gone and there are no semi-precious stones to be found as yet. . . ."

He wrote of plans for a party the officers and nurses of the 38th were planning for the next evening. "The mess section has been called on to have some refreshments. The chief cook asked me to find some fresh eggs. Those are to be used in making some cakes, some mayonnaise for the sandwiches, and some deviled eggs. All our eggs come in dry, dehydrated. I got a jeep and my little Arabic friend Abduk and started to forage around and find the eggs. They are quite rare in these parts, since there are few chickens because of the lack of grain. We went thru the French section and picked up about three dozen and then into the Arabic section and found about three dozen more. I bought them one, two, three, five or ten at a time. The price was five francs per egg. On the rate of exchange that meant I paid ten cents per egg, $1.20 per dozen. Of course, our mess fund, which we had accumulated at Bragg, was tapped for the payment. That was what it had been carried around for and it has come in handy at various times. I think we will have the proper things for the party."

Captain Jack Montgomery's first entry in his diary in 1943 was dated March 1. He wrote:

Left St. Cloud 7:30 P.M. by truck to Oran. Finally got on train by 10:00. 8 to a compartment—Hoffman, Perry, Kavanagh, Query, Stokes, Aubrey, Vaiden & I. Slept on the floor.

His next entry was less informative:

March 2nd. Left at 6:30 A.M.

He next wrote of the arrival at El Guerrah three days later:

March 5th. Arrived El Guerrah after a very unusual trip. Slept on floor. C rations only, only little water. Bought eggs from natives. Arrived here filthy. Everyone in bad humor. A hot breakfast at 61st station hospital helped everyone. Set up temporarily in field 5 miles from El Guerrah. In tent were Sanger, Pennington, Medearis, Query, Pitts, White, & Stith.

His next entry:

March 9th. Moved to Telergma. A nice location along a creek. Trees and grass. A spring gives water for washing. We are not far from Constantine. Bob & I still together.

Two days later, he wrote, the hospital was functioning:

March 11th. Received first patients—23.

The next entry:

March 12th. First operation. Very cold here at night. No lights, heat, or much food. Much grumbling.

A considerably more detailed story of the 38th's routine in these early days of 1943, however, is provided in the narrative that Dr. Stokes Munroe was preparing before it was cut short by his death. His account begins

as far back as January 2, when in preparation for moving to a base nearer the battle lines the hospital stopped receiving new patients.

"No patients, other than from command, were admitted after 2 January 1943," he recorded. "Patients remaining in the hospital were evacuated to duty and to other hospitals as speedily as possible. The last patient was discharged from the hospital at 1800 hours 6 February 1943, and the hospital was officially closed per verbal orders from the Surgeon General, Mediterranean Base Section. During the period from 13 November 1942 to 6 February 1943, a total of 2,027 patients were hospitalized, including 98 battle casualties. After closing the hospital, the ward and necessary tents were struck, and with the equipment of the hospital were packed and stored in readiness for movement to our next location. An intensive training program was instituted and carried out for the remainder of the time spent in bivouac near St. Cloud, Algeria. On 11 January 1943, this organization was relieved from attachment to the II Corps, assigned to the Fifth Army and attached to the Mediterranean Base Section, in accordance with General Order No. 3, Headquarters Fifth Army, dated 11 January 1943."

His account continues:

"On 1 March 1943, the unit started movement to a new location, in accordance with instructions contained in letter from Headquarters, Mediterranean Base Section, subject: Movement Orders, dated 1 March 1943. The movement was accomplished in four echelons: the first echelon departed from Oran on 1 March, via rail, arriving in El Guerrah, Algeria, on 4 March; the second echelon departed form Oran, via rail, on 2 March, arriving in El Guerrah on 4 March; the third echelon departed from Oran, via rail, on 3 March, arriving in El Guerrah on 6 March; the fourth echelon departed from St. Cloud via motor convoy, on 4 March, arriving in El Guerrah on 6 March. The unit established a temporary bivouac area approximately six miles south of El Guerrah, Algeria, awaiting final selection of a site for erection of the hospital.

"On 9 March 1943, the unit moved to the new hospital site, approximately 1 1/2 miles north of Telergma, Algeria, and proceeded to erect the hospital. On 10 March 1943, the hospital was placed in operation, the first patients being received at 1445 hours. Upon arrival at El Guerrah, Algeria, the 38th Evacuation Hospital was relieved from assignment to Fifth Army and attached to Mediterranean Base Section, and assigned to the Eastern Base Section and attached to L of C for maintenance and supply, in accordance with letter, AFHQ, Subject: Troop Assignment, dated 2 March 1943. On 29 April five (5) nurses from the 3rd Auxiliary

Surgical Group were attached for quarters, rations, and duty. No patients were admitted to the hospital after 29 April 1943. 448 patients remaining in the hospital were evacuated to duty and to other hospitals on 29 April 1943. During the period 10 March 1943 to 29 April 1943 a total of 2,995 patients were handled, including 1,136 battle casualties. After the closing of the hospital, the ward and accessory tents were struck and put in readiness for a quick move to a new location."

Captain Montgomery's terse diary speaks briefly of this period:

March 23rd. Went to Constantine. It is a beautiful city.
April 1st. 918 patients.
April 4th. Received my back pay following having my orders changed to April 15th, 1942.
April 11th. Col. Churchill visited hospital.
April 15th. In Army one year today. Eight & half months foreign duty. 5 months 1 week in Africa.
April 30th. All patients were evacuated last night. Today spent in packing and striking ward tents. I cleaned clothes, blouse, pinks & trench coat with gas today. Hope it does well.

Publication of the 38th's Daily Bulletin was temporarily suspended on February 27, 1943. The unit's A.P.O. was then 700.

Daily publication was resumed, following the removal of the hospital to its new base, on Wednesday, March 10. The A.P.O. was 509. On that date, the Daily Bulletin reveals, Lieutenant Felts was the administrative officer of the day and Lieutenant Hoffman was alternate; Captain Gay was medical officer of the day and Lieutenant McGrath alternate; surgical officer of the day was Major Leonard, with Captain Hawes alternate; Major Kendrick was dental officer of the day and Lieutenant Hoffman alternate; and Lieutenant Bachoka was nurse officer of the day and Lieutenant Barbee was alternate.

The Bulletin carried one notice:

The Hospital was set up and ready for operation, including seven wards comprising 146 beds. At 1445 hours, the first patients were received, 23 by transfer from the 77th Evacuation Hospital and 3 from command.

The next day, March 11, the Bulletin prescribed the limits of the camp.

The following limits of the camp are established: on the East by a stone wall running along farm yard; on the North, the creek running along the Camp Area from West to East; on the West by the road running thru ford; on the South, along the mill run. The Officers' and Nurses' Area will include the eastern end of Camp and will be separated from the hospital proper by a barbed-wire fence. The Enlisted Men's Area will be included in the triangle from the bridge over the mill run at the south-eastern section of the Camp directly across to the creek and ending at the road leading into the ford at the western end of Camp.

No personnel will leave the Camp Area except on official business. All messes and supply will be out of bounds to all personnel except those on duty therein. Supplies will be obtained by informal requisitions thru the Chiefs of Services.

The Bulletin showed the following status of the hospital:

Number of patients	26
Admissions	26
Dispositions	0
Vacant beds	120
Wards in operation	7

Fortunately, the recorded story of these months of the 38th in Africa is not limited to the brief notations in Captain Montgomery's diary and the statistical information provided in the Daily Bulletin. Letters survive which provide a wealth of details to give color and drama to the account of the 38th's service during these early months of 1943.

On July of that year, for example, Lieutenant Charlotte Jean Webber in a long letter to her sister, Mrs. Ben C. Fritz of Lexington, Kentucky, summarized the eight-month tour of duty since the 38th's arrival in Africa. The greater part of Lieutenant Webber's letter is devoted to a narration of experiences upon leaving the St. Cloud area.

But even more details are provided in a series of long letters to relatives and friends at home written by Captain Pickens that by good fortune were saved. These letters clothe the frame of the 38th's service during the first half of 1943 with the warm flesh and sinews of day by day existence in this strategic sector of the fighting. He wrote two such letters in March, three in April, and three in May, and though they were not designed, when he was writing them, to be preserved as an informal history of the 38th's experiences during that period, they have survived to afford a close-up, authentic, and interesting picture of those lively and desperate days.

Lieutenant Webber's letter begins with the 38th's arrival in Africa:

"On Nov. 9 we landed at the port of Arzew near Oran—down the side of the ship we came on landing nets and came ashore in barges. I had the toothache, darn it, and felt pretty miserable. We had sneaked into the harbor the night of the seventh and could hear and see the artillery fire ashore and anti-aircraft on the ships around us. We formed first aid teams and prepared to receive the wounded but most of the casualties were ashore. We sat in the ship all day the eighth waiting until our boys had cleared a way for us to land—then around noon on the ninth we landed.

"Arzew is a very small village, about the size of

Paris, Ky. We marched through the village, nothing happened; the French and Arabs peered out at us from their huts apparently very glad to see us. We conversed with some of them. As soon as we reached our destination (a French barracks turned into an American hospital) and got inside the gates, they started shooting at us—snipers, sharpshooters from the rooftops, church steeples and the hills around. Surprised? Golly Moses! We were dumbfounded. We realized then that the town hadn't been taken and that the natives were not on our side. But we gave them bullet for bullet and in a day or two things were quiet. I'll never forget when the bullets started whizzing down through the hills and we all flopped off flat on our faces. . . . We hung around those barracks a few days, slept on concrete floors on anything we could find. I swiped a few old French army overcoats and lay on buttons all night.

"One day around noon the chief nurse and I got tired of eating old cold C rations out of a can (meat and vegetable hash I wouldn't feed to a dog, meat and beans, hardtack and condensed coffee), so we built a fire and dumped it all in a pot of boiling water to make a stew. Well, all the girls came out to watch. Pretty soon everything got quiet and she and I looked around. Not a soul was in sight except an occasional guard ducking around buildings with his gun—everybody else had scrammed inside and locked the doors. Judas Priest! There we were, 'ketched' again, two helpless women. We both got 'kinda' nervous and everybody was screaming for us to come inside, but we couldn't get in. Well anyway, we finally climbed in a window and fell down on our tummies—it seems the snipers got a little closer.

"Well, we left the place in a few days and set up the hospital in the middle of an oats stubble field, lived in tents. We've been in tents ever since we've been in Africa. But I 'kinda' like 'em even though it is 'kinda' hot in this heat—tropical heat, too. Well, we stayed near Oran three and a half months.

"We left there and went on a train ride to a place near Constantine. But I'm getting ahead of myself. We were darn glad to leave that muddy field. It rained three-fourths of the time we were there and the other fourth the windstorms were terrific—dust blew everywhere. Back at those French barracks we took over at Arzew, the Arabs would come up to the gates to sell us eggs and souvenirs, all dressed up in their long multi-colored robes, apparently very harmless. Then when we got up to them they would pull out long knives and guns and start shooting at us. Oh, boy, they were tricky. They'd take big coffins up in the hills to bury their dead (we thought), but the coffins held nothing but ammunition for them to fire down on us.

"We left that little place by the sea and rode four days and five nights on a train, and what a train! The windows were blown out. We had no cushions in our compartment, in fact, we happened to end up in a baggage car. We were allowed only one canteen of water a day. . . . We ate nothing but C rations. Once in a while, during our many stops, we bought eggs from the Arabs but had no way of cooking them. Finally we ran on to some who had them already cooked. I guess we must have paid 10 or 15 cents each for eggs; they sure were expensive eatin's. Then we bought oranges, tangerines, dates and figs. We certainly did crave some home cooked food.

"I remember one night as we pulled out of some town, the Jerries started bombing it, so we had to scramble around in the darkness for hours. None of us slept much—I had my fur coat with me and wrapped up in it on the floor. We wore coveralls which saved our slacks, etc. We were dead tired when we finally got to our grassy little valley. Gee, I loved that place. The Air Corps was only a mile down the road and did we have fun. We worked hard there, too. But we were still many miles from the front and were itching to get there. We had our wish.

"But first, I'll tell you about Constantine. I went there twice. Gee, I wanted to buy jewelry and oriental rugs and everything because I had plenty of francs. Just as we were driving out of the city that night the Jerries came over and dropped a few eggs. We drove on to a safe distance and stopped to look back. It was beautiful. The moon was shining bright as day, which gave Jerry a break, of course. The city fairly shone in the moonlight—white marble buildings, arched bridges. They just glistened. Constantine is the most beautiful city I have seen in Africa. One can see it for miles away.

"We had a long truck ride up here at our present home. I was rather glad to get out of Algeria. I like Tunisia much better. The climate is much drier. . . . It took us a day and night to make it, but we had so much fun. That was a few days before Tunis fell. At one time on the road we were only 10 miles from the actual fighting. Boy, the things we could hear and see! When we got here we set up and worked like mad, for we were badly needed—casualties were pouring in by the hundreds. Germans, Italians, Arabs and French as well as our own Yanks. We are now only a few miles from Tunis. I've been to Tunis once and, darn it, I went one day early, for the big Allied Nations Parade was the next day. Anyway I had my picture taken countless times by English Highlanders, boys who had just come in from long months in the desert and hadn't seen a white woman for so long.

"Tunis is a nice city, not messed up so much downtown but the docks are blown to ————. Our boys did some good work there. We didn't realize what they were doing when they left us every day to go out on

In this posed photograph Lieutenant John S. Powers, left, and Sergeant Paul White and Private Walter Rex are "receiving" a new "casualty," Private Ian (Scotty) MacLean. The smudge on his cheek is mud, not blood.

a mission back there in our little valley. They never talked much about it. But we all stood out and waved to them when they came flying back to us and knew they had accomplished their purpose.

"I've been swimming in the blue Mediterranean. I've been twenty miles behind the fighting lines and I've seen more action the past few weeks than all my days in Africa. I've talked with German boys, Italians, French and Arabs. I've seen all kinds and every kind of defense machine. I think I've seen it all, but they tell me I haven't. I've seen all of North Africa now and I'm ready to leave it all. Where to from here I don't know, but I hope it isn't home. That sounds mighty funny . . . when I come home I want it all to be over with.

"I have a different outlook on this war now. At first I thought it was going to be more of a lark. I realize now that we've all accomplished what we came over here to accomplish and it's serious. . . . The hardships

which seemed big to us at first are small now. I'm used to C rations and men's clothes and dirt and hard work. . . . We're all still one big happy family. Haven't lost anyone except a few who were transferred out to some other unit where they were needed more."

In his last letter home, written early in February, Captain Pickens had noted the change in the unit's A.P.O. number but in it had seen no significance. His next surviving letter, however, would not be written until the hospital had been moved to its new base and was in operation. It was dated March 14, 1943. He speaks first of his feelings on leaving the base that for months had been their home:

"Again the move was made with a feeling of poignancy. At St. C. we had become attached to the oat field with its mud and mice. Of course, as always we moved at night and in the rain. I hated to move; I suppose I am getting older and a little further away from the spirit of the parsonage in that we were always ready for the next place. Thinking back, I recall some of the experiences of our first stand, little things, but things that I will remember. Here are a few of them:

"The original password reminding me of Merita bread and the Lone Ranger; I suppose it is too old now to be used again; my first walk up the street of our original city and seeing the Arabs and the unsanitary conditions they created; the running of jeeps thru the water to land them; the hoisting of guns and tanks from the ships in a hurry; the first night spent on the concrete floor of a hastily emptied building; the scampering for cover when the snipers cut loose on us, and Paul Sanger beating an enlisted man to a hole he had dug for himself; the hurried setting up of the first hospital in the field in North Africa; the consistent rain throughout the entire winter; the heavy winds that always came at night and always made us think our tents would blow down, but they never did; the mud; the mice that eventually came and lived under our improvised floors; I killed five when we broke up housekeeping and tore up our floors; the trips into the neighboring city; watching American soldiers buying cheap jewelry and getting pictures taken—I got mine, too, and sent some copies to you; getting dressed to go into town; we always had to wear our blouses when we were on pass and it seemed so stupid living out there in the mud and then trying to appear to be a stuffed shirt when country came to town."

Once again he refers to that most pleasing of experiences, getting a bath:

"My first bath in Africa was a real event; the movies we had, shown in a tent about 17' by 48' where over a hundred people crowded in to see, but it was something to do, and different; the tour of duty as Officer of the Day and checking the guard after midnight in the rain and mud and slipping down in the mud in the dark; the washing in the morning in the dark and cold;

Pharmacist Joe Neil stands before his improvised shelves. When the hospital moved, he packed his drugs in the boxes below the counter.

the inability to please everyone with the food I was able to get; the comfort of my sleeping bag on my cot; the many oranges we were able to get; the installation of electric lights in the tents (I am now writing with the aid of a lantern); the American flag always blowing in the wind in front of our camp and the installation of the rather inspiring ritual of retreat at five in the afternoon when the flag was lowered; the French and the Arabs who came to look at us on Sunday afternoon and who stole our soap if we left it at the back of our tents; they came literally by the hundreds and just looked and stared as if the circus had just come to town; the remarkable interest in the church services with Chappie doing the best he could to inspire us; the jackals howling at night; the trucks filling the lister bags with water; the exciting time when rumors spread that mail had arrived and how everyone flocked to the recreation tent to see what his luck had been; the nurses in G.I. shoes and coveralls; the playing of volleyball when the weather permitted and the constant chess game that was always in progress in the recreation tent; the difference between pay day in Africa and the same in England; here we had more money than we could use; there we did not have enough to get through the month; the Christmas packages that arrived from so many places with so many useful articles; they were such a surprise and such a pleasure; the collection of pictures of some of the scenes and personnel in the hospital, copies of which I have sent on home; the buying of the violin and the music and the enjoyment I have had with it; seeing Lt. Col. Roy Norton with fresh word from London that Bob was doing all right; the same message from General Lee, which I wrote you about; meeting and visiting with General Roosevelt; the sad feeling among the officers and nurses when the colored troops left us, those men from North and South Carolina who helped build our sanitary section and in addition waited on the tables of the officers' mess; the outdoor band concerts for the patients; the first and only ice cream we were able to get and how welcome it was by the officers and the nurses; the hurried extra ditching done around the tents after a particularly hard rain; the long road marches after the hospital closed, and my first blister; the brackish water we had to drink with all the chlorine added; the plane trip to Algiers which I never got to describe, since there was more business in it than pleasure; the general excitement when Ernie Pyle's articles began to come back to us and we saw ourselves as others saw us (there was a semblance of truth in parts of what he said); the trip down to the hot water spa and the excellent bath; the jeep trip with George Wood and George Snyder over a hazardous trail across the mountain overlooking Oran; my roommate, George Snyder, keeping onions in his mess kit with vinegar and salt and pepper added and our joking about whether that combination or my violin playing smelled the worse; my growth of beard during the first few weeks we were in Africa; my first swim in the Mediterranean on Valentine's Day. I could go on for a day about these simple things that come to my mind now that I have left the place, but I know you are not interested."

Then he brought the letter to date:

"Now we are set up in another section and I will try to give you a picture of the moving, paying particular attention not to give away any military secrets and pass on any information that might be of aid to the enemy.

"As I said before, we always move at night and in the rain. This was exceptional only in that it was mud instead of rain. We boarded a French train with compartments similar to the British trains. . . . There were eight of us to a compartment. The first day I drew for partners Calder, Chappie Jones, Hunter Jones, Bill Evans, Bill Leonard, McChord Williams and Shorty McGrath. After the first night we found some additional room and we had to divide up. We drew lots to see who would move and I lost or won, I'm not sure which, since I had to move. My second group included Bernard Walker, George Snyder, Ed McCall, Bill Matthews and Jimmie Felts. Six to a compartment may have helped some but I couldn't see much advantage. I moved out in the aisle at night and spread my trench coat out and fortunately had brought a blanket along by hand. That kept me reasonably warm but not too comfortable. With me out of the compartment that left a little more room for the others to stretch out. Truthfully, however, we did not do so much sleeping.

"Our water supply was limited to about one quart a day. We carried some five-gallon cans along and found two spots along the way where we could refill with good American treated water. I learned to brush my teeth without water, and, honestly, it is not bad at all. You should try it. One of our dental men said it was actually better for you. Twice during the trip I slipped up to the engine and got the engineer to give me a cup of water from the engine, with which to shave.

"That reminds me of the trip up when we stopped at one place and a freight train pulled in beside us going in the opposite direction. The engineer got off and came back thru our train looking for Capt. Snyder or Capt. Pickens. He was from Charlotte and had pulled a train the day before with some of our advance group unit and found out that little Charlotte was on the way. His name was Clanton and he once ran a small restaurant at the corner of Graham and Sixth in Charlotte. He had bought many a case of Coca-Cola from George and me. He was in a railroad battalion and had gained his railroading experience with the Seaboard. His great big No. 500 American locomotive looked good to me

with a big 'Queen Charlotte' written on it in chalk. It was like old home week. We were sorry that he wasn't pulling our train. He was the one who told me how to get the hot water from the engine for shaving purposes."

He told of meeting a Charlottean for whom some months before he had done a good turn:

"On the way up we ran into Fred Brackett from Charlotte again. He and his gang were on the way back after a harassing experience. He looked healthy and well. For the cot and food I had given him some months back he had his crowd give us some hot coffee from his kitchen car. They were traveling in the old 40 and 8 cars while we were more deluxe without passenger cars (still 6 and 8 to a compartment) but we were not allowed to set up a kitchen car and have hot food and coffee. However, Bernard Walker had a small alcohol burner with him, so we heated water enough for the powdered coffee that comes with our food. We also were able to heat the cans with the ham in them. It made the eating a little more pleasant.

"We also purchased eggs en route from the Arabs whenever the train stopped. These we were able to boil; from time to time we would beg some salt and pepper from some group that was passing. All in all, we fared very well. We were able to buy oranges and tangerines along the way also and had a lot of fun wrangling with the Arabs about the prices. George and I bought a large supply for his men with the help of McChord Williams, who did the interpreting for us. Our living for the three or four days turned out not so badly. The first day we all snapped at each other because we were so crowded, but after that we settled down and made the most of a rather funny situation. The nurses were in a car to themselves and, I think, made the trip very well, if you can imagine 52 women in the same railroad car. I think there were 78 in all in our car. We gave away some of our room for the men."

Colonel Bauchspies, Captain Pickens related, had brought a record player and was able to provide "some good and bad music. He had several of the old canned recordings of radio programs. . . . It helped pass the time. We also had Jack Benny and Bob Hope in their programs. Duncan Calder rigged up our portable battery radio so we could hear from time to time the news from 'This Is London Calling.' "

On their arrival at their destination, he further reported, they "for the first time moved during the daylight. We sat for two days in a temporary location and then moved to this place," which in his letter he had date-lined "Northcentral Africa, March 14, 1943." He went on to describe the new location:

"Here we are in a green valley, plenty of grass and

big trees, one of the few such places I have seen in Africa. For our purpose it is ideal except for the water supply. There is plenty of water but it must be boiled and highly chlorinated. That takes time and few people want to wait. Of course, for washing it is all right.

"Our tents blend with the color scheme and we are fairly well hidden. However, we are painting a large Red Cross in the center of the area. It is reported that the enemy has left the hospital installation alone. The lack of mud is refreshing and the green grass is easy on the eyes. The altitude here is slightly over 775 metres and if I remember correctly a metre is slightly over 39 inches, which would make us up about 2,500 feet. It is cold at night, with a heavy frost every night and freezing almost every night. There is a slight amount of ice on my wash water every morning and we have no heat except what the lanterns put out. It gets warm during the day; just as soon as the sun gets down the cold comes, and does it penetrate! I say we have no heat, but I was wrong in one respect; I got some hot water yesterday, Saturday, for my first bath since February 28th and I got that from the kitchen. I was able to get hold of an empty oil drum and got a man to cut it in half and in that I clambered and took that much needed bath. So far as my clothes are concerned, I have done nothing about washing them. They are piled over here in one corner of my tent awaiting my next move. I have been so much on the go these last few days that there has been no time for laundry. I'll get to it though, in time, no doubt."

He told of having met another Charlottean who was stationed not far from the new base. He was Albert Whisnant. "He has been a great help to me in getting supplies and I appreciate it. I was able in turn to help him today. He came down and said his stoves had quit working and he needed some parts for them. Among his other duties he also looks after the mess with his outfit. We were able to furnish him with the parts he needed. I traded two pounds of yeast and three pounds of baking powder yesterday to a soldier for a 100-pound sack of flour and some repair work on some of my stoves. He had the tools and the flour and could do the work. I had the yeast and the baking powder without any flour. It worked to our mutual advantage. Now he will have hot biscuits and we will have hot cakes. . . .

"I had packed my violin in a box for shipment along with another fiddle owned by Stanley Nowacki and a trumpet and cornet owned by Bob Miller from Lincolnton. All of the musical instruments came thru in good shape but I have been a little slow in playing much here because of the cold at night. Stiff fingers are not conducive to good music and mine is not so good even under the most favorable circumstances. We have

had one session together and no one threw rocks at us, so we may try again when the weather gets a little warmer. Nowacki really knows how to play and is most willing to put up with me. We enjoy it and it helps when things get dull."

In the moving to a new base he had lost his St. Cloud roommate:

". . . Capt. Snyder has been moved down to be nearer the men, since all of his work is with them. I have missed him sorely already. We fussed with each other and enjoyed it and griped in about the same vein about the inefficiency of the Army. I will continue to miss him. It has been the unfortunate fate of Capt. Medearis to be quartered with me. He and I see eye to eye on almost everything so we will hit it off in great shape. . . ."

The first patients were received at 2:45 o'clock on the afternoon of March 10 at the newly established base at Telergma. The next day the hospital had 26 patients. March 12 twenty-eight were listed. But the following day the list increased by five times to 138. On March 14 the list had grown to 160. And five days after the first patients came in the total had jumped to 230. March 16 the patients numbered 319, and the next day, one week after opening for duty, the 38th's Daily Bulletin showed the status of the hospital:

Number of patients	353
Admissions	49
Dispositions	15
Vacant beds	161
Wards in operation	25
Operations performed yesterday:	
Herniotomy	1
Vein ligations	2
Hemorrhoidectomies	3
Miscellaneous	10

The Bulletin also announced that with the present setup of the hospital, it was contemplated that 830 beds would be available for patients. It added that it would be "necessary to use all Government Property such as blankets, lanterns, buckets, basins, towels, etc., now in the hands of the personnel. In the event that anyone has such property, which is not needed for immediate use, it is requested that the same be turned in to either Quartermaster or Medical Supply. If the need becomes more urgent an inspection will be made of all quarters, and all Government Property taken up. It is not desired to cause any personal hardship on any member of the command, however the needs of the patients have priority."

The number of patients being admitted continued to mount as March advanced and the Bulletin two days later—Friday, March 19—showed 448. On March 24 the number had advanced beyond five hundred—to 504, and the next day the patient total jumped to 582. On March 30 the total was 642. As April began the hospital had attained a total of 819 patients. Operations performed that day totaled twenty, including five listed as "excisions for foreign bodies." On April 4 the patients, the Daily Bulletin reported, numbered 856 and there were 21 operations; on April 12 a total of 868 was reported and the next day the number was 880. The

Bulletin for April 30 read, strangely, no patients, one admission, 448 dispositions, no vacant beds, no wards in operations. "The hospital was officially closed 1830 hours 29 April 1943," the Bulletin explained.

Again, the 38th was preparing to change location that would bring it nearer to the fighting.

9

But before the 38th moved from Telergma, Captain Pickens in letters written late in March and during April, told in considerable detail of the stay there—the routine of battlefield hospital administration, the characters, both natives and invading military, encountered there and in nearby communities visited, the day by day happenings that had interested him.

"Fundamentally . . . we think of living in the rough," he wrote on March 27, 1943, "as the quest for food, clothing, and shelter. The refinements follow. Food comes first. . . . Every ambulance coming into this hospital is loaded with sick men and they all report that they are hungry first and sick second. Before they are relegated to their proper stations they are in the chow line crying for food. Of course, food has been refined by the art of cooking. . . . We try to cook the food the Quartermaster is kind enough to give us after he, incidentally, has taken the choice bit for himself. Someone once said they had never seen a thin Army cook and that two Army cooks could never sleep in the same puptent. I'll go a step farther and say no detachment of QM troops ever went hungry.

"Our cooking is done on field ranges, the proper use of which is fully outlined in certain field manuals which we try to follow to the letter. These ranges are operated on gasoline. They were designed to use what is commonly known as white gas, that cheap gas containing little or no lead, that stuff you bought back in the good old days from what might be termed second-rate pumps. But of course only the best for the Army, so all of our gas is leaded, containing tetra-ethyl. This makes the trucks and tanks and planes go zip, but it just stops up the lowly field range. So we just have to take the creation apart after each meal and clean out the lead and carbon. This causes wear and tear on the parts and since the IQ in the Mess Section isn't very high, the care of the parts is correspondingly low. I say the IQ

in the Mess Section is low, advisedly, since if it were otherwise, all of us would have sense enough to be somewhere else."

When the parts wear out, he continued his letter, "the job starts—try and find replacements. It's a game only the stalwarts can play. . . . Inspired by the thought of those sick and wounded and hungry men, we buck the pass-the-buck line in search of parts. We go to the nearest depot and gather rumor that the parts might be found in the second. To the second we go and they never heard of parts being shipped over and so we hurry home to put out a meal and then get to the third source. There they say at the fourth we might find them, since it has been said that parts are there and frozen except for medical units. . . . We take a little hope and go again. Incidentally, the depots are miles apart—good thing, since Jerry likes to find them bunched. With meager hopes we approach the fourth. Voila! Here we find the parts, but none will be issued since they will send a trained man around to visit all units to repair all breaks, and he will carry the parts. . . ." And so, he said, the grand run-around continued.

"The other branches of our unit are also tracking down needed replacements. My good friend Bernard Walker says his dental work must stop if he fails to get certain items, maybe false teeth, I don't know, and the X-ray group is out searching for film. However, I still claim priority, since they all get hungry and it's a funny thing how that hunger comes at about the same time each day. The game is still on and when the final whistle blows we will turn up with the much needed parts."

At this point in the letter he changed his reporting to tell the story related by one of the 38th's patients back from the front:

"He and some of his comrades had captured some Italian prisoners. They say they are not so difficult to take. I don't know. They had picked up some 21 of them and brought them into their side of the line, which was some thirty miles from the main part of the enemy. Just after supper they were strafed and one of the prisoners did not turn up after it was over. They never had to guard them too carefully because the Italians never seemed interested in escaping. But this fellow did get away. The Americans didn't bother much about it, just knew he had gone. The next morning at breakfast he turned up. He had walked all the way back to his own line and brought his brother back with him during the night."

He reported that one of the 38th's officers—he didn't give his name—who enjoyed hearing the complaints of the men back from the front and encouraged them to suggest what was needed most on the fighting line, "got a good answer today. He had stopped at one cot and asked this particular chap what he thought was needed most at the front. The soldier replied that he could tell him in few words. 'What we need most up there,' he said, 'are more Americans and fewer Germans.'"

Captain Pickens told another story:

"A Negro had reported back to one of the hospitals. He was found by an officer lying on a stretcher covered with blankets. His clothes were missing. The officer asked him what was the matter with him and the fellow said nothing was the matter, he was just having his clothes deloused. The officer said no, that he was really sick and he would take care of him if he would only tell him what was the matter. The Negro said nothing was wrong, he was just waiting to get his clothes back so he could return to the front. No, the officer insisted, he had something wrong, and he made arrangements to have him evacuated to the rear. The next thing the

He's engrossed in Nurse Mary Blandford's story. Others, Elva Wells, left, and Ruby McCain.

Negro soldier knew he was in a hospital 500 miles to the rear and still asking for his clothes. C'est la guerre!"

After serving in the administration of the hospital, said Captain Pickens, although a layman, he was beginning to get a rather definite opinion about the doctors and the practice of medicine:

"I always thought that a doctor was a doctor and when you were sick you called for him. But now," said he, "I find I'm all wrong. Oh, I knew that some of them sort of specialized on some things, but I always thought any of them could do anything from giving you pills to taking out your ingrowing toenails. But, no, that is not the case. There are two groups as I see it now. . . . On one side you find the medical man, whom I deem to call the medicine man, and on the other you find the surgeons, whom I call the saw boys. The medicine men try to keep you from getting too close to the saw boys and the saw boys say the only real cure comes from cutting. Then the saw boys divide up into smaller groups. Some of them work on your eyes, ears, nose and throat. They claim to cure back pains by taking out your tonsils. Then there is the group that cuts on the middle part of your poor frame. Don't get near them with a slight old-fashioned stomach ache or they will have your appendix out in nothing flat. Then there is another set called the orthopeds. They can break your bones and set you up in white plaster casts. There are other subdivisions but I haven't gone that far with my study.

"In the medicine man group they deal more with what they choose to call diagnosis and some lean to mental cures. This crowd borders closely on Mary Baker Eddy's setup. This bunch has to know your family history back at least four generations and all of your actions up to the last time you brushed your teeth. From this they can tell you whether you are really sick or just think you are sick. It's all very interesting to me and the more I see of it the more determined I am to stay well and healthy. . . . I almost got sick this week from my second round of typhoid shots. I think Charlie Gay, who gave me the shot, tried to give me the disease instead of immunizing me. I recovered after the first day when I was forced to retreat to my tent for an hour. Of course, the Colonel came around during that particular hour and wanted to raise sand about something. That is always the way."

Three weeks before the 38th's base was moved from Telergma, five members of the unit took a four-hour ride in a Jeep to visit an ancient city built by the Caesars. It was a cold day, with the thermometer hovering around freezing, and the traveling was uncomfortable, but the letter Captain Pickens wrote on their return that evening provides an interesting description

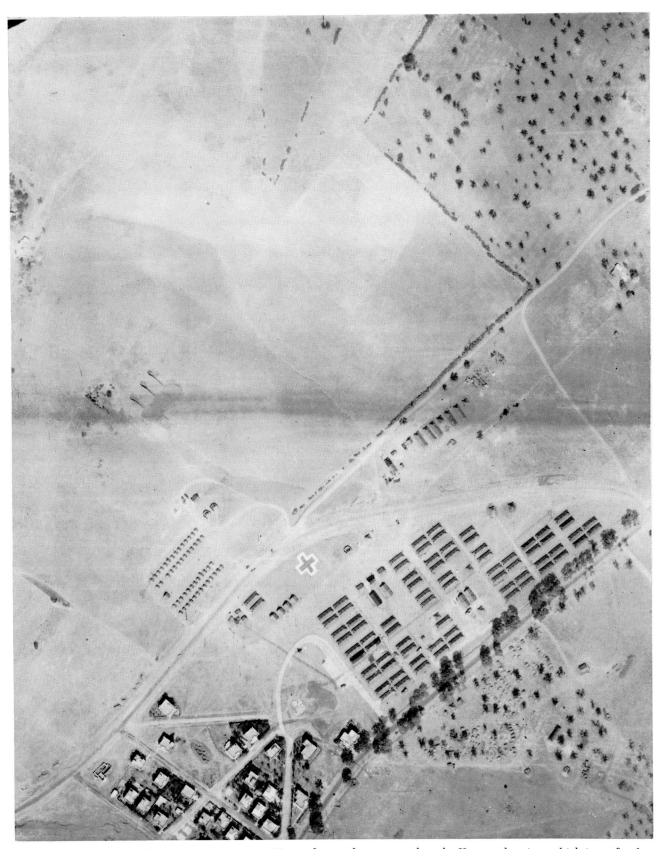

This aerial photograph of the encampment near Tunis shows a larger area than the Kuester drawing, which is confined to the portion shown in the lower right section.

of a surviving Roman city in the area in which the Charlotte hospital personnel served during its first months in north Africa.

The place they visited was Timgad, a city "left over from an ancient era, to which we sacrificed an entire day's leave." The letter was written April 10. "Five of us—Kavanagh, Bob Miller, Bob Schirmer and I, along with a driver named Elmer Neinhouser, spent the day getting to and from and visiting Timgad. Five of us in a jeep that isn't comfortable for one, and the weather just touching 32 degrees. . . . I myself had wrapped in 'long johns,' the common name for G.I. woolen underwear, my normal woolen uniform, a field jacket, another heavier field jacket, a sweater, a heavy woolen scarf, woolen gloves, G.I. shoes with galoshes, and two heavy woolen blankets. The others were dressed likewise. But it was to no avail, as we all froze slowly but surely. . . ."

But they went on, despite the cold and the other discomforts. And on their return that night, Captain Pickens described Timgad:

"There you see what's left of the outpost of old Roman civilization. There the followers of the Caesars had built a city out of stone back in the second century. At least, that was when they started it. Here was a city built out on the plains, miles from the surrounding mountains, snow-capped mountains, without the sign of any rock anywhere. It is said their slaves hauled the rock from Constantine in chariots, a small matter of about a hundred miles. When I say a city, I mean a city whose population was reputed to have been over 50,000 in its heyday. It was built there as an outpost for their military garrison at first, to protect their coastline from the Berbers who lived in the mountains and had a habit of swooping down on their civilized brothers at unpredictable moments. From this humble beginning, Timgad grew. The surrounding valleys are rich and I suspect the Romans were not different from our large landholders before the Civil War and they made good use of their slaves on the land. They were black slaves in those days, too. Where they came from I was unable to find out.

"And so the city grew. It spread and sprawled over the hills. The stonepaved streets are still there with the signs of the chariot tracks plainly visible. The streets are laid out like any modern city. . . . At each intersection there is a manhole made of stone and underneath are the unmistakable signs of a city sewer system, cut in stone. Each street has a sidewalk and each sidewalk shows signs of having been covered overhead with stone. The houses are clearly outlined with the remaining stones in place. They were built right on the sidewalk, with a patio in the rear. The rooms were average size and had small window openings toward

the ceiling. Some of the windows had stone bars in them simulating our window frames or panes. Each house had a sewage system with baths and toilets, all built of stone. The baths were built so they could be heated. In those days the soldiers on the outpost of civilization had hot baths, but not in these modern times. I didn't look for the kitchens; I was spending the day trying to get away from them."

He continued his recital of what the five 38th members on leave for a day saw in Timgad:

"At the top of a hill at the end of what appeared to be the principal street was the forum, clearly outlined with many of the pillars still standing. . . . Here I suppose the population could come and listen to the politicians of that day, or possibly could speak his own mind. I stood there and wondered what had been said over a thousand years ago by the politicians and whether it was any different from what we hear today.

"A little farther on was the theatre, almost intact. The stone seats rose abruptly up the hill, with the white tie and tails area clearly marked. The orchestra pit cut out of very large stones and the stage worn smooth with much dancing, comedy, and tragedy, were marked unmistakably. The footlight setup was there in stone. One of the boys sat on the back row, the goober gallery, and listened while the other three of us sang the parody on the quartet from Rigoletto. The listener said the accoustics were good and the music terrible."

From the forum the visiting soldiers went to the Christian church called St. George's. "I couldn't find the reason for the name," Captain Pickens wrote. "We had no guide but an old Arab who spoke very little French and no English. He walked around with us and we gathered from him that no work had been done on the ruins for the last twenty years. We saw the baptismal font. It was an immersion proposition with beautiful mosaics. The Baptists had a start way back there."

They went next to the market place, "where the various vendors advertised their wares with carved plaques on the stone over the stalls. The vegetable man had a cabbage carved over his place. The bread man showed his product with sheaves of grain cut in the stone. The wine merchant had clusters of grapes on one side and smiling Bacchus on the other. . . . The butcher had his space showing where he cut his meat and allowed the drippings to run into the public drain. All of these shops were located around a circle, indicating that the housewife got in that habit back in those days and nowadays goes in an ever shortening circle with the influx of rationing and rationing cards and the point system."

Timgad had boasted "a small museum on the edge of the forgotten city. Here the mosaics had been pieced together. Caesar was shown as a young man and then

84

Private Israel Tabi, second from left, with hand pointing, a native of North Africa, is interpreting for Lieutenant Colonel T. Preston White, left, as he talks with a native and his two sons. The man's wife is being treated in the native patients section of the hospital during its stay at St. Cloud.

when he was older. Neptune rode a great chariot pulled by four mermaids. Bacchus was there also, always smiling. There were many busts of male and female Romans. There were stones dovetailed as well as any modern carpenters could fit wood. Among other things so far excavated were iron locks and keys, large and cumbersome; coins of many denominations and sizes; crude forks and knives; jewelry after a fashion and even socalled hatpins for the ladies. . . .

"We turned to look at the great arch. Apparently all cities that amount to anything have an arch. . . . And Timgad had an arch built of mammoth pieces of stone and still standing almost intact. I couldn't discover any reason for this one. It was just like the rest, looked good, but caused a traffic jam, made another bottleneck. The one interesting thing about Timgad's arch was the size of the stones. They weighed six tons each, 12,000

pounds for those poor slaves to push that 100 miles. I don't think it was worth it."

The preoccupation of the members of the 38th with the thought of finding somewhere an adequate supply of clean water that would permit them regular baths is further revealed in the group's interest in learning of ancient Timgad's water system:

"Our attention was next drawn to the question of water supply. All cities have to have one, even our tent city of over a thousand population here. We just tap the mill race that runs by our camp and treat the water with calcium hypochloride and run it thru alum and some other chemicals. Ours tastes all right and I think it is clean. The Romans built a long viaduct from the mountains. It was hollowed stone and apparently stretched for miles. I could find no storage tanks, but I suppose they had one. I don't doubt but what typhoid was prevalent, but they had doctors in those days, too, as was indicated on the stones where he had his home." Then the 38th's mess officer made a sly gibe at his medical associates of the 38th: "He was probably a very busy man and his fees must have been sizeable, since he lived in a larger house than the majority and had two bathrooms."

Captain Pickens referred to the fact that the "Germans in their propaganda broadcasts to the American troops in North Africa said in their earlier broadcasts that we were just here on a sightseeing tour. Our five tried to carry out that idea," he admitted. But, said he, "while we were doing that, some of our brethren were impressing the Boche that we could do some fighting at the same time. They never suspect that we are such a versatile group and can sometimes combine business with pleasure. However, I must say in all honesty that I am yet to figure out the pleasure of freezing to death to look at a lot of bones."

He concluded his description of what the five men of the 38th had seen that April day in the ancient ruined city of the Romans:

"So much for Timgad, except this: an earthquake came along in the seventh century and razed the place. Twenty years ago the French got tired of digging it out again, and today I am tired of the whole blooming thing."

10

April 15, 1943, at Telergma marked the first anniversary of the 38th Evacuation Hospital unit's activation into the service at Fort Bragg. The year, more than likely, had been the busiest and surely the most exciting in the lives of the men and women who composed the organization.

Of the twelve months since their beginning training at the great, sprawling North Carolina military base, almost exactly four had been spent in preliminary training at Bragg and sailing for overseas duty; almost exactly the next three were devoted to further training and organizing in England and embarking and sailing for duty in Africa; and the remaining five months had seen the hospital fulfilling in northern Africa the assignment for which it had been organized as the fruition of a dream eighteen months before of certain Charlotte medical men.

For Captain Jack Montgomery the day marked one year in the service, as he noted in his diary, of which, he wrote, "5 m. 1 week in Africa."

The next day, after datelining his letter "16 April 1943 Northwest Africa," Captain Pickens would type out a long message to pay tribute to the work of the Red Cross as he had observed it. Whether his opinion of the organization was generally shared by the officers, nurses, and men of the 38th, he did not venture to suggest. Many returning service men, in fact, were critical of the Red Cross and some were even abusive, and for that reason the 38th's mess officer's observations, particularly if they were representative of the 38th's attitude, are interesting.

After saying that many things had happened during his months in the service that he would prefer to forget, he added quickly that "there is one thing I would like to give you that has proven worthwhile. The clear-cut work of the Red Cross, as I see it every day in our little part in this job of cleaning up North Africa in order to give it back to the French, is a part important."

He proceeded at once to elaborate:

"In our hospital where we first set up, there was no provision for Red Cross and what they do. It seems that this work, being purely civilian, has to be requested by the Army. So, at the request of the commanding officer of this theatre, we have two Red Cross representatives who are stationed with us. They are Mrs. Wright and Mrs. Brooke, the first from Philadelphia and the latter from Englewood, New Jersey. They are both women who obviously had other means of support, refined, well trained, able. One of them reminds me so much of Vinton that it isn't funny. They volunteer, and after a thorough orientation course, are placed in a pool in the States. From there they are drawn to fill in wherever the Army requests them. Here they set up their little pyramidal tent and have gone to work. I will try to give you a little picture of what they do in order that you can appreciate the Red Cross a little more."

He proceeds with his picture:

"First, they handle the home service problem of the patients. This involves so much that I hesitate in going into it. Suffice it to say, they can find out if Grandpa had to give up the farm when the mortgage came due on up to when the last child was born at home, and they can do it faster than any Army postal service. They pick up where the neuro-surgeon and the expert medical men and the chaplain leave off and carry on from there. This sort of work takes time, but they barge in where angels fear to tread.

"Then, they handle most of the patients' outgoing mail. They furnish the stationery which you paid for. After all, a soldier coming back from the front doesn't carry a secretary and a portfolio full of paper, first and copy and carbon. Often, where the soldier is severely wounded, they write his letters for him. They also get all the incoming mail for the patients and see that it is distributed. Sometimes they have to track down a letter that went to the wrong hospital. They seem to be a tenacious lot when they get started, but volunteer workers are that way, I have found from my experience with the Junior League. However, don't let me leave the impression that these people are not paid; they draw what I guess to be about $125 a month. Out of this the Army bills them for their room and board.

"In that little pyramidal tent here they have set up a sort of store. Nothing is for sale, everything is free. Here they keep such items as sewing kits, wash cloths, combs, soap, soap dishes, towels, playing cards, cigarettes, candy, chewing gum, Kleenex, books and stationery. The Red Cross furnishes half and the Army the other half of these items. They have one radio, which is loaned around to the various wards. This is one item they could use more of if it were available. The method of distribution of these things is as follows: one patient or ward man comes from each ward with a list of the needed things and is checked in and out. You must keep in mind that there is a constant turnover in patients. This makes a busy time in the morning for the Red Cross representative. I almost forgot two of

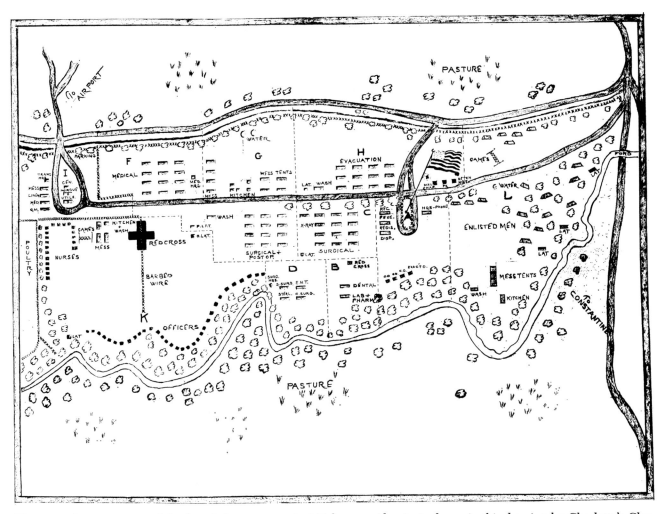

The general arrangement of the hospital encampment at Telergma, Algeria, is shown in this drawing by Charlotte's Clarence O. Kuester, Jr., done in color on the back of a map of that area in North Africa.

the most important things they keep for the men: shaving equipment and tooth brushing equipment. The sick and wounded always turn up without these articles. So they get these things spread around where they are most needed. One thing they said they never had enough of were 'ditty bags.' These are little bags that the soldier can put his toilet articles or any other small articles in for easy carrying. They are sewed in the many Red Cross rooms across the country there. They are made of duck or canvas. You may have seen them; I never have.

"After the distribution of these things," his letter went on, "they work on the mail problem and then to the home service problems which take them into the wards with the men. I have seen them stop and talk over many questions. Sometimes they take the time to tell fortunes with the cards."

In the evenings, his report continued, the Red Cross workers go thru the wards with candy, cigarettes, and any little snacks that may make the time more pleasant for the men. A ward, he points out again, is a tent about seventeen feet by forty feet containing about twenty cots, a small stove in the center, and three small lights overhead. The Red Cross workers, he added, were particularly anxious not to be classed with the nurses and had no nurse or first-aid training. Their work was separate and apart from that of the nursing service. "All in all," he summarized his discussion of the Red Cross workers, "I think they fill a definite need and do a good piece of work."

He wrote, too, of the use of blood plasma—not as a medical man, he emphasized, but as "I have seen it here," though its primary use had been further forward at the battlefront.

"It has been used extensively up there, from all reports, and has saved many lives, ranking possibly second only to the sulfa drugs. Our use has been secondary most of the time and merely supporting. However, we

Lieutenant Elva Wells, center, with Lieutenant Charlotte Jean Webber, appears to be little interested at the moment in the book before her. But he is her husband.

have had a great deal in the case of burns. It seems that a burn immediately takes away the protein and plasma can almost as quickly put it back into the body. It does not have to worry about blood types; it is either combined or it is not necessary, since the red corpuscles are not concerned. It comes in bottles in combination of two, one which holds the plasma and also contains a section that is a vacuum; the other contains the sterile water. It is a simple and swift operation to move the water into the vacuum and the mixture is complete and ready for transfusion. The average transfusion here takes about two pints. Other than for burns, its use here is routine, as you would find it in any hospital where dry plasma is available. This seems to me to be a poor picture of what is an interesting and new treatment of shock, but not being a medical man, I am unable to give it the proper shadings. Suffice it to say, it has proved its worth in many ways many times over."

Their first spring overseas was beginning to arrive in North Africa about the time the members of the 38th were making preparations for moving their hospital base farther eastward from Telergma.

In the last letter written before they moved to the new base, dated April 21, 1943, Captain Pickens devoted a long closing paragraph to describing the place they were about to leave and the climate at that time of the year:

"Spring is beginning to come to North Africa. In this location we have grass and trees, large old beech trees. The green is beginning to show. Our stream that runs by the camp is slowing down. The spring where we have been drawing our wash water is almost dry. The days are starting to be hot. At midday we have off all of our jackets and sweaters and galoshes. At about two o'clock the heat is at its peak. This is the time I would like to take my siesta, but in the Army that doesn't fit in properly. At about four o'clock the sun begins to get away and it gets cold again and back on goes the extra clothing. We sleep under from one to three blankets every night. It is not as bad at night as it was a month ago. Now we can go to an outdoor movie and live thru it. I have seen two this week, *Santa Fe Trail* and *Gentleman Jim Corbett*. The flowers are coming out and there are myriads of wild ones. Whole fields of poppies wave in the wind, blotches of red outlined by the green fields of grain. White iris seem to grow wild and there are a number of rambling rose bushes to be seen. To add to this show, we have at the neighboring farmhouse a number of peacocks, and when papa begins to spread he makes a pretty picture, and can he strut! The almond trees are coming out and soon should be in full bloom. Spring is coming and with it we retire to our mosquito nets and begin the swallowing of atabrine. That, as you know, is the German substitute for quinine. It is said to do the work better, with less harmful effects. We are getting malaria-conscious and are running from the virile, African type. Apparently the Arabs are somewhat like our low country Negroes, immune from the worst of it, but able to pass it along to the puny visitors from across the sea. We are busy running around turning over tin cans and spreading oil on the not too troubled waters. I hope we get by without too much of the dreaded disease. Incidentally, disease causes much more trouble to an Army than guns, dive-bombers, and mines operated by the enemy."

11

In the same concise manner in which he had reported the movement of the 38th's Hospital from St. Cloud to Telergma, Dr. Stokes Munroe in his account of the North African experience wrote of the transfer of the hospital from Telergma in Algeria to Beja in Tunisia and then after a stay of about two weeks there on eastward to a new site near Tunis:

"Preparations to move to the Tunisian battle front were completed and on the 2nd of May 1943, the unit started a movement to a new location in accordance with instructions contained in Letter, Headquarters, Eastern Base Section, Subject: Movement of Troops, dated 5 May 1943, confirming verbal orders. The movement was accomplished in five echelons: the first echelon departed from Telergma, Algeria, on 2 May 1943 via motor convoy, arriving at new location, 4 miles SW of Beja, Tunisia, 3 May 1943 and 4 May 1943. The second echelon departed from Telergma, Algeria, on 4 May 1943, via motor convoy, arriving at new hospital location 5 May 1943. The third echelon departed from Telergma, Algeria, on 5 May 1943, via motor convoy, arriving at new hospital location 6 May 1943. The fourth echelon departed from Telergma, Algeria, on 6 May 1943, via motor convoy, arriving at new hospital location 7 May 1943. The fifth echelon departed from Telergma, Algeria, on 7 May 1943, via motor convoy, arriving at new hospital location the same day. Due to the capture of a number of German hospitals, a considerable number of German prisoner patients were received. A detachment of military police of five enlisted men and one officer was attached to this organization for the purpose of guarding the prisoners. Fifteen additional nurses from the 3rd Auxiliary Surgical Group were attached for quarters, duty and rations.

"On the 19th of June the unit started a movement to a new hospital location 1 1/2 KM north of Tunis, Tunisia, in accordance with instructions contained in Letter, Headquarters, Eastern Base Section, Subject: Movement of Troops, File AG 370.5, dated 19 June 1943. The hospital at Beja, Tunisia, was officially closed at 0930 hours 20 June 1943 with the transfer of 35 remaining patients to the 3rd Provisional Hospital. The total number of patients was 3357, including 842 battle casualties and 760 prisoners of war."

Telergma, as an airplane would fly it, was some twenty-five miles south and west of Constantine, and Bone on the Mediterranean coast almost at the border of Tunisia was about seventy-five miles from Constantine on a straight line. The city of Tunis lay eastward from Bone perhaps twice the distance from Bone back to Constantine. And Beja in Tunisia, the base to which the 38th was moving, was sixty miles nearer Telergma than Tunis.

Captain Jack Montgomery in his usual brief recording in his diary on May 2, 1943, covered the journey from Telergma to Beja in exactly eleven lines. In green ink he wrote:

May 2nd

Left Telergma at 1300 hrs. by truck convoy—about 2 or 3 miles in length. Went over the mountains to Bone. Then east to Morris, arriving about 2230 at the 77th Evac. Hosp. Bob & I pitched our pup tent alongside of the truck. Many mosquitoes—then put up the mosquito netting. May 3rd. Left Morris at 0730—Tabarka—Beja. Hospital set on side of hill—no trees.

Two days later, on May 4, Captain Montgomery made another brief entry:

Tents rapidly going up. Mess tents, OR, X-ray and many wards are up. We have our small wall tents up. This morning officers dug latrines.

First operation tonight in this location. GSW leg and abd. wall.

The next day, Wednesday, May 5, the Daily Bulletin, which had suspended publication on the Saturday before to make the move to Beja, came out. It listed for that day 45 patients, 45 admissions, no dispositions, 267 vacant beds, and 18 wards in operation.

Captain Montgomery noted in his diary for May 6:

A steady stream of casualties the past 24 hrs. Four tables going at a time night & day.

The Daily Bulletin for that day confirms Captain Montgomery's entry. Under Status of the Hospital it listed 125 patients, 80 admissions, no dispositions, 187 vacant beds and 18 wards in operation.

The next day the patient load had increased by an even 200 to 325. Again there were no dispositions. Wards in operation had increased to 31.

On Saturday, March 8, the captain wrote in his diary the two-word observation:

Casualties continue.

And once again the Daily Bulletin's report confirmed his short statement.

Two hundred and forty patients had been admitted to bring the total that day to 513 and ten more wards were being used. But the report showed, too, that 52 cases had been disposed of by the hospital.

Sunday, May 9, was Mothers' Day, and it was the busiest day since the hospital had been set up in the new location. The hospital that day had a total of 673 patients, of whom 256 had been admitted within the 24-hour period, and 48 wards were in use. The surgeons were unusually busy, too. The operations performed were listed:

Craniotomies	2
Thoracotomies	2
Gen. Arthrotomy	1
Amputations	3
Removal shrapnel	4
Reduction fractures	4
Debridement of wounds	27
Minor procedures	10

The Daily Bulletin also carried this message concerning Mothers' Day:

Today is traditionally designated by our President for the purpose of honoring our Mothers. This is part of our American way of living. All of us have had mothers, some of us are still fortunate to have our Mothers back home patiently awaiting our return. It is the earnest desire of the Commanding Officer to have every member of his command write a special letter to Mother or some loved one back home. All persons are enjoined to assist our patients in getting this letter written and posted.

The Bulletin that day was signed by order of Colonel Bauchspies by Captain A. J. Guenther, the adjutant.

Captain George Snyder was administrative officer of the day the following day, Monday, May 10, and Captain Pickens was his alternate. Captain Tyson was medical officer of the day; his alternate was Lieutenant Schirmer. Captain Williams was surgical officer of the day, and Major Fleming alternate. The dental officer of the day was Lieutenant Milo Hoffman and Captain Walker was alternate. The nurse officer of the day was Lieutenant Niemeyer and Lieutenant Trainor was alternate.

It was a busy day. The patients totaled 686, including 261 admissions, and the dispositions numbered 248. Forty-nine wards were in use. The surgeons had a strenuous day. Operations totaled 59, classified as follows:

Debridements of wounds	16
Amputations	1
Reduction of fractures	5
Removal shrapnel	2
Applications of casts	20
Minor procedures	15

That was the day, too, for the hospital to have four distinguished guests, including the Surgeon General, Major General Norman T. Kirk. The other three were Major General Fred W. Blesse, Colonel Joseph I. Martin, Surgeon of the 5th Army, and Colonel Richard T. Arnest, II Corps. In the Daily Bulletin of the next day, Tuesday, May 11, Colonel Bauchspies would issue a memorandum, addressed to all personnel, concerning the visit of the four men. It was one of the longest and doubtless the most effusively complimentary the 38th's commanding officer would issue:

It was a genuine pleasure for your Commanding Officer to have as visitors our newly appointed Surgeon General of the Army, Brigadier General Norman T. Kirk; NATO-USA Surgeon Brigadier General Fred W. Blesse; II Corps Surgeon, Colonel Richard T. Arnest; and Fifth Army Surgeon, Colonel Joseph I. Martin. These officers are personal friends of mine. Brigadier General Blesse and Colonel Martin were my instructors during my first years in the Army. It afforded me great pride and personal satisfaction to conduct them through the hospital, where they inspected the latrines, the messes, the utilities, the quarters, as well as the departments of the hospital itself. It is always my intention to do my job to the best of my ability, but in this particular instance, I wished to show our visitors what their former people had achieved, and that their efforts years ago in training me for the field had not been all in vain. Naturally, as in every effort, success cannot be achieved unless every individual who has a part to do, does his particular job to the best of his ability. This has been true, and was conspicuously evident during the past week when this hospital was erected. The only part I had in the erection of the hospital here was choosing the site, conducting the personnel and equipment to the site, and planning the erection of the hospital. The hard work was done by you. For the first time since taking command of this organization, the personnel of this unit functioned as they should. Officers, nurses, and enlisted men all joined in doing whatever they could to speed the erection of the hospital. You all know why this is so necessary—you are all aware of the kinds and types of patients which have passed through our hospital. This tremendous effort could not have been accomplished if one quality had been missing—the willingness of every individual in the organization to go to work until the job was done, and done to my personal satisfaction. The hospital stands as a monument to your efforts, and it serves the purpose adequately for which it was erected. All of us can have equal shares of personal satisfaction of a job well done.

The campaign in Africa is rapidly drawing to a close. I believe your training days are over. I am convinced now that the 38th Evacuation Hospital can be erected and function in any Theatre of Operations. You have passed your board examination and are now ready to practice. Colonel Martin, the Fifth Army Surgeon, has assured me that this organization will play a prominent part in the next phase of this campaign. I told him we are ready, and yesterday he had the opportunity of seeing an example of what this organization could do.

We are all tired physically, but we must remain on the alert. Discipline must and will be maintained. You all have done an excellent job. I am justly proud of you. I wish to take this means of expressing my thanks to every member of this command, both assigned and attached.

> Rollin L. Bauchspies,
> Colonel, Medical Corps,
> Commanding.

The next day, May 12, 1943, the Daily Bulletin carried a somewhat naively worded notice perhaps even more appreciated than the Colonel's commendation:

An Officers' and Nurses' bath tent has been erected between the Officers' and Nurses' latrines. This utility has been made available for the purpose of providing a place for bathing. Officers and nurses using this facility must remember and *constantly* bear in mind that all water must be carted into this area and the storage space for water in the bath tent is limited. With proper consideration for each other the bath tent can prove of great usefulness to all concerned. Only sufficient water should be drawn for the purpose involved. The hours for use are as follows:

OFFICERS: 0800-1000 hours   1600-1800 hours
NURSES: 1000-1200 hours   1400-1600 hours

On Sunday, May 9, Mothers' Day, Captain Montgomery had written in his diary, in the same green ink, the two-line notation:

Hear today that Tunis & Beserte had been entered.

The next day, the same day that the four distinguished visitors, including the Surgeon General of the Army, were guests of the 38th Hospital, Captain Pickens in a long letter to the homefolk confirmed the accuracy of the report recorded by Captain Montgomery.

"The news has been good these last few days, showing that we have taken both Tunis and Bizerte and are now in the midst of cleaning up the rest of the Tunisian area," he revealed. "This will be old when you read this letter, but now it has provoked everyone into doing even better work than usual. We, of course, follow the trend of the battle and have seen it from

not too far away. At night we could see the flares of the artillery or the dropping of flares. For a short time we heard the sound of the big guns as both the British and the Americans pushed on. There was a determination about the sound and the movement that passes us on the way up that precluded the final result. But the Americans and the British didn't do it all. Our ally, the French, came in for a large part. Among the French troops is a group called the 'Gouams,' pronounced Gooms, and that brings on a tale which has brought us plenty of laughter. They are a cross between the Berbers, Arabs, some of the lost tribes, a few Ethiopians and some European strains. They dress in colorful blue uniforms with those baggy pants that make you think you are looking at a Shriners' parade. They have a blue or red fez on their heads. They carry old-fashioned rifles, relics of the last war, the long bayonets. These rifles they don't use very much on account of the way they are paid. It seems that they draw their clothes and food and a regular ration of wine. No money is involved in their pay envelopes until they run into the enemy. Then they get a bonus of two francs for each German ear they bring into camp. This apparently stimulates them to go out and cut off ears and they really do. An American officer coming back from the front tells of an assignment his group had to take a certain hill position. They were encamped just a few miles forward of a group of Gouams. Their job was to begin at dawn the next day. During the night, the story goes, the Gouams got through their lines without the slightest indication of detection and the next day when the Americans were to storm the hill, they got up there to find no live Germans but a lot of dead ones, sans ears. The Gouams had gotten there ahead of them. Another story about these ferocious soldiers was one told by an ambulance driver bringing some German prisoners back to our hospital. He was stopped on the way back from the front by a few of these strange

Hurry up to stand in line—or hang around—and wait, they say that was the Army—even the 38th. This was after church services at Anzio.

One of the diversions of the personnel of the 38th, both in North Africa and Italy, was watching the American planes come over. Here soldiers and patients at St. Cloud watch transport planes flying fairly low over the encampment.

people and asked if he had any German patients. When he replied that he had, they offered him a hundred francs for them, but he turned the offer down. They not only want their ears but they want their lives as well.

"... These Gouams are interesting and I come back to them again. I have just watched some of them pray. They are all Mohammedans but they add a little ritual that I have never seen before. Before they pray, and praying means anything from falling flat on the ground to kneeling in a dignified manner beside a cot, they have to wash their feet. This has put a rather serious strain on our usually limited water supply. I have seen them out behind our 3,000 gallon canvas water tank just running our good chlorinated water freely washing what in a few minutes are just two dirty feet. They all prefer to go barefoot. Some of the better class have simple sandals, but the majority wander around our

camp in the dust without anything on their feet. Those who are too sick are a problem for our ward men and nurses. They have a feet washing problem the answer to which is not found in any Field Manual put out by the Army. I would like to see what some armchair surgeon in Washington would write in Army regulations, say, AR 250-305 paragraph 16, on the methods to be used in washing Gouams' feet in North Africa. I'll bet it would be a masterpiece."

The letter of May 10 is of primary value, however, in its recording of a description of the new hospital site in Tunisia and of the detailed operations of setting it up. It is one of the most detailed of the close-up views afforded of the 38th's experiences in North Africa.

Captain Pickens went on to tell of their new base:

"But back to this oat field in Tunisia. We sit on the side of a field that has just been cut. The poor Frenchman didn't have time to rack the grain before we moved in. I have often wondered if the Army asked permission to use this and other pieces of land to run a war on, but of course, I know this is a stupid thought. We probably just moved in and the fast talking little Frenchman with his beret bobbing in the breeze just had to say that the Americans are always welcome. He really got upset when we told him we had to have a funeral.

"'Not here,' he said, almost in tears, 'not on my property.' We told him we would move it to the neighboring town and he was greatly relieved.

"But we took over the hillside and pitched a big hospital about as fast as Ringling Brothers could set up their five rings and all the side shows. I have fully decided that I will never attend another circus; it will remind me of some of these Army days with tents flapping and straw on the ground and ants crawling up my legs. I want all the comforts that a modern after-the-war can afford.

"We moved in one day and a couple of hundred patients moved in the next. The surgeons had a field day, the orthopeds just fixed more bones and made more plaster casts and the nurses and ward men did more bandage work. The mess section busied itself as usual feeding a lot of hungry soldiers. It was all routine with us except we had to hurry the first day to get fixed up. We put on the refinements a little later. Everyone worked. Even the officers dug their own latrine, and when you get manual labor out of a group of specialists, that's something for the books. We pitched our own tents; Buck and I struggled with ours, but his long association with the Boy Scouts helped us no end. It was dark when we started but when morning came and we came out to survey our handiwork, we both said it was the best job we had done since entering the armed forces of our nation. We kept on our steel helmets, since everyone up this way seemed to be doing the same thing. They are heavy and bundlesome and more useful for washing in than wearing, but we wore them and felt some comfort with the added protection. We hurriedly put up a large Red Cross. Paul Sanger did some real manual labor on this. He took the burlap that Buck had probably stolen and ran it through some red paint Buck had also brought along and at the end of a long day turned out a creditable looking cross. I went out yesterday to find some lime to mark out the outer line in white. I also took my interpreter from up in Van Buren, Maine. We had to get in the next town and buy the lime thru the black market, Noire Marche, the biggest business setup in the town, incidentally.

"The town itself did not look so healthy. Both sides of this war had argued about its possession and the results were sad indeed. In addition, there were signs posted saying that typhus was prevalent. But we had to have the lime, so a marketing we did go and came back with about 80 or 90 pounds of questionable grade, but it served the purpose. The little Frenchman begged to visit the town hall and post office. It appears that he hasn't been allowed to go into town for some time and from the looks of the place I think he was wise in waiting. He wanted to visit the townfolk and talk the situation over. He also had to get a singletree for one of his carts. This we helped him to do in return for his aid in getting the lime. When we got back to his house he insisted that we come in and have a glass of wine with him. I settled for some fresh eggs and made a deal with him to furnish us with eggs in return for our garbage. He has plenty of hogs and from the looks of them some good American garbage would help them no end. He also gave me some roses. Now what does a soldier out in the middle of North Africa, living in a hurriedly erected tent, do with a bunch of roses from a fast talking French farmer? I just took them back to camp and put them in an empty can filled with cold water and set them on a box I use for a desk. I stopped by the neighboring field and picked some poppies, red as blood, to go with the yellow and white roses. The poppies, as I have said before to you, just grow wild and cover field after field. I wore one yesterday for Mother's Day."

Then he returned, as he invariably did in his letters home, to provide news of the hospital itself:

"We have a number of casualties that are prisoners. I have forgotten what the rule is about mentioning them in mail home. They get the same care that our troops get. The only difference, they have an armed guard that keeps watch over them. They have been so appreciative of getting some good food. They have almost done handsprings over the coffee and cocoa and the white bread. The Italians say they would be satisfied with just the bread alone, even if we gave them nothing else. The Germans say they have an ersatz coffee made from barley and some other mixture which they couldn't describe, but nothing like what we gave them.

"I don't know whether they have been coached about their behavior if captured or not, but almost to a man they say they didn't want the war and would be glad when it is over and they can return to their homes. The Italians were surprised that we had so many with our unit who could speak their language and who had relatives in the old country. They acted like they were back among friends. As a matter of fact, I have a man in my section who fought in the Italian army when Il Duce invaded Ethiopia. He's much better pleased with his treatment and pay in our Army. I have been trying to practice my German on these poor devils but I find that I am now getting German mixed with the little French I have picked up. The result is a grand mess. They all like our cigarettes as much as the British do.

"We are neighbors of the British now and some of them are always dropping in to visit. It is flattering that they always come as near our meal time as is diplomatically possible. The men particularly like to come and eat with our men. It helps us since they are so appreciative of anything they get to eat. They always ask for tea but never fail to take coffee, cocoa, or lemonade, whichever we happen to have at that particular meal. Our men having been in England for a time make it more pleasant for them because they can discuss the advantages of London over the Midlands or vice versa."

In this letter also, as in most of his previously written ones, he turned his attention to the subject of bathing. "I always seem to get back to that subject somehow," he interjected. He went on:

"Our host told me yesterday that he had some hot springs on his land and we could get a shower bath. Tomorrow I hope to get the time to go with him and see what the possibilities are. My last trip into Constantine I went with Bob Miller and Bob Schirmer and Kavanaugh to a hot springs swimming pool. We had a good swim and then in one of the showers I washed the G.I. underwear I had used for the bathing trunks."

At this point in his letter his writing was interrupted. When he resumed writing it he had investigated the hot springs, and he reported:

"Since starting this letter I have had an opportunity look over the bath situation. There are some natural hot springs nearby with sulphur water gushing out of the ground at a rapid rate. The locals have built a house with some basins. We will clean the place and make use of it. The water is very hot, making it possible to put in only one foot at a time, easing it in and gradually working on in. It is going to be a treat when we get the place fixed up, and we will have to make a free use of creosote, lime and soap in order to have the place up to hospital standards. The sulphur water will be of little use in washing clothes, but to get the dirt off the personnel will be worth much. As a matter of fact, there will be many colds when we get one or two layers off some of this crowd."

Soon after they set up the hospital in Tunisia the members of the 38th were visited by an old friend. This time he wrote particularly about the nurses:

With Ernie Pyle in North Africa

IN TUNISIA—American tent hospitals in the battle area seem to be favorite hangouts for correspondents. The presence of American nurses is alleged to have nothing to do with it.

At one hospital three correspondents just moved in and made it their headquarters for a couple of weeks. They'd roam the country in their jeeps during the day, then return to the hospital at night just as though it were a hotel.

There are two favorite hospitals where I drop in now and then for a meal or a night. One is an evacuation hospital—the same one where the other boys stay—which is always kept some 80 miles or more back of the fighting. This is the one staffed largely from Roosevelt hospital in New York.

The other is a mobile surgical hospital, which is usually only about an hour's drive back of the fighting. This is the hospital that landed at Arzew on the day of the North African occupation, and whose nurses were the first ashore in North Africa.

They Keep Moving

This gang is kept pretty much on the move. They don't dare to be too close to the lines, and yet they can't be very far away. So as the war swings back and forth they swing with it. The nurses of this outfit are the most veteran of any in Africa.

There are nearly 60 of them, and they are living just like the soldiers at the front. They have run out of nearly everything feminine. They wear heavy issue shoes, and even men's G.I. underwear. Most of the time they wear Army coveralls instead of dresses.

I asked them what to put in the column that they'd like sent from home, and here is what they want—cleansing creams and tissues, fountain pens, shampoos and underwear. That's all they ask. They don't want slips, for they don't wear them.

These girls can really take it. They eat out of mess kits when they're on the move. They do their own washing. They stand regular duty hours all the time, and in emergencies they work without thought of the hours.

During battles they are swamped. Then between battles they have little to do, for a front-line hospital must always be kept pretty free of patients to make room for a sudden influx. A surgical hospital seldom keeps a patient more than three days.

During these lax periods the nurses fill in their time by rolling bandages, sewing sheets and generally getting everything ready for the next storm.

Social Life Non-Existent

They lead a miserably blank social life. There is absolutely no town life in Central Tunisia, even if they could get to a town. Occasionally an officer will take them for a jeep ride, but usually they're not even permitted to walk up and down the road. They just work, and sleep, and sit, and write letters. War is no fun for them.

They make $186 a month, and pay $21 of it for mess. There's nothing to buy over here, so nearly all of them send money home.

Like the soldiers, they have learned what a valuable implement the steel helmet is. They use it as a foot bath, as a wastebasket, as a dirty-clothes hamper, to carry water in, as a candle-holder, as a rain-hat, and—er, ah—yes, even as an emergency toilet on cold nights!

Being nurses and used to physical misery, they have not been shocked or upset by the badly wounded men they care for. The thing that has impressed them most is the way the wounded men act. They say they've worked with wounded men lying knee-deep outside the operating rooms, and never does one whimper or complain. They say it's remarkable.

94

The girls sleep on cots, under Army blankets. Very few have sleeping bags. They use outdoor toilets. At one place they've rigged up canvas walls for taking sun baths.

Mary Ann Sullivan, of Boston, whom I wrote about last winter, is in this outfit. Some of the other girls I know are Mildred Keelin, of Louisville, Ky.; Amy Nichols, of Blythe, Ga.; Mary Francis, of Waynesville, N. C.; Eva Sacks, of Philadelphia; and Kate Rodgers, of Houston, Texas.

Like the soldiers, they think and talk constantly of home, and would like to be home. Yet it's just as Amy Nichols says—she wouldn't go home if they told her she could. All the others feel the same way, practically 100 per cent.

They're terrifically proud of having been the first nurses to land in Africa, and of being continually the closest ones to the fighting lines, and they intend to stay. They are actually in little danger, except from deliberate or accidental bombing. They haven't had any yet.

On May 13, 1943, Captain Montgomery added another notation in his diary. It, too, was terse:

Hostilities closed in Africa today.

Four days later Captain Pickens in another long letter home would provide embellishing details. It was particularly interesting and of documentary importance in its revelation of the 38th's involvement with German prisoners and their attitude toward the war and especially toward the American soldier.

"The African campaign has been brought to a temporary close," he wrote on May 17. "The fighting has ceased and so far as I know the enemy has not sent a single plane over since the end of the combat. The enormous number of prisoners has been passing for days going back to the prisoner of war camps. During three days I would guess that some 40,000 passed our camp. They came in every kind of vehicle and in most cases they drove them themselves without any visible guards. I may have written this to you before but it struck me as being rather funny that we guard our prisoner patients with much care and the majority of them couldn't walk if they wanted to and yet 40,000 able-bodied men pass here driving their own trucks without a guard ratio of more than one per hundred. We had one truck load of Italians stop and ask us if our place was the prisoner of war camp. I suppose it looked like it with the barbed wire we keep up to keep the Arabs from stealing our shirts and to protect our fair womanhood. We directed him on down the road and he left with his group in a hurry, saying that he had to get along and get there before supper. They sang as they went by and once we asked them why they seemed so happy. A man replied that they were on their way to America and we were the ones that had to go to Italy and Germany. I guess they had a right to laugh."

He told of his conversations with various prisoners:

"I have been visiting with some of our prisoners, mostly Germans. I try to avoid talking politics with them. It always settles nothing and they are so rabid on the subject of Hitler. I said to one of them the other day that I had the privilege of saying in America that I did not like the President, but that he had no such right in Germany to criticize the Fuehrer. He answered that this was true, but that Hitler was so good that no one needed the privilege to criticize him. They have an answer for everything. They rationalize every act that has been perpetrated. They blame the English for starting the war and when asked why they went into Poland they just say they asked a road to run thru the corridor and when the fool Jews refused them they had to take the roadway. In the case of Russia, they say it was to get the Russians before the Soviets got them. They are mortally afraid of the Russians, say they have no feeling, that they know of their own men who have committed suicide rather than be taken prisoner. The Russians apparently have not been as easy on them as we have been. It appears that they all wanted to surrender to the Americans. They fear the French and the English, but seem to think they will get fair treatment from the Americans.

"But in case this leaves you with the feeling that they are not afraid of the Americans I will tell you one man's description of the three armies they met in Tunisia. This man said the French yell and holler at the top of their lungs when they go into battle. They come in with all the noise they can muster and he said it was terrifying at best. The English, he said, come in singing with a grim sort of determination but still singing some regimental ditty. The Americans, he said, just keep coming; they don't say anything, they don't act as if they are mad; it is like they were playing some sort of game and want to get it over, but they just keep coming. He said there was no way of stopping them because they just kept coming. Several of our high ranking men have said that our boys took a licking down on the southern side during the early spring because they lacked equipment and numbers and experience, but

Lieutenants Robert Miller, left, and Colin Munroe pose with two of their North African friends.

95

The Munroe brothers, standing, Colin, left, and Stokes, with Kavanagh, right, pose on the walk outside tent at St. Cloud.

that now with sufficient numbers and enough supplies and the experience gained during this campaign, they were the best soldiers in the world, simply because they won't quit and don't know how to give up. It is not an American's makeup to think of losing once the battle has started. These Germans have a healthy respect for American soldiers."

Captain Pickens talked frequently with German prisoners, most of them youths, and obtained a good cross-section of their views concerning the war and its probable outcome. His letter of May 17 continued:

"Many of these prisoners have said to me that when Russia is licked, they will end the war, since they have nothing to fight us about. They say the English will join us in stopping it. When I tell them that we only stop with 'unconditional surrender,' they laugh and say that we will never get to Europe. They were told, some of them, before they came to Africa that they were just coming over to hold all of North Africa and were surprised when they ran into the hornets' nest in Tunisia. Most of them have been in Africa only a few weeks. One chap I talked with, who had lost his leg from a bomb fragment, aged 19, said he had come over by transport plane in April and was driving a truck for a food depot at Bizerte. He said the bombs just dropped all of the time and he felt lucky that he had gotten out with just the loss of one leg. Most of the Germans are young, none of them over 23 or 24, and most of them say they have been in Russia and some have been in France, Norway and Greece. They all, almost to a man, swear by Hitler and think they will win the war. Some are sullen about it; the officers are arrogant and gener-

ally disdainful. However, they all like our food and are surprised that we are still able to get it. One man asked what the sinkings were for March and April and when I told him he said that was not true, that they had been told that we lost over 2,000,000 tons each month for those two months. I told him that what he said might be true, but I doubted it and the only thing I could go by was the fact that we finished up the campaign in Tunisia with plenty to spare and had been eating every day since and he was not going hungry, so some ships had been coming thru. He thought it was incredible that it could happen to his Germany. It appears to me that this loyalty to Hitler has been hammered into them so long, and that during those years they were growing up, that it really took hold. It will be a hard job to get it out during this generation. One Austrian said he liked the Hitler government because it had given him and many Austrians jobs. He said that before the advent of the Nazis they were hungry and after they had taken over the government jobs were plentiful and his people lived better. He thought that was reason enough to back it. He had not thought that the employment he got was for the purpose of making war. Hitler had given him a job and that was enough. The rest of the demagoguery made no difference."

He reported the condition of the captured Germans' equipment:

"Many of the Germans have shoes made with a little leather around the foot and the remaining part of the shoes made of canvas. Some of them have wooden soles. Their equipment otherwise appears to be good. Their gas mask is more convenient to wear than ours but not as easy to carry while waiting for gas to come. Their chlorinating tablets, which every soldier carries in Africa, are about the same as ours. Their insignias are more fancy than ours and more on the order of the British. You know, the British have all sorts of gadgets on their uniforms and caps showing the Cold Stream Guards or the Royal Rensselaers or the Highland Blackwatch or any number of others. The Germans go in for the same sort of junk. All of the insignias carry the swastika somewhere on them. Many of these men wore arm bands reading AFRICA KORPS. This was woven with some fabric like rayon.

"These men are interested in our currency and its value with reference to the mark. They ask questions about our mail and are surprised when we (bragging just a little) say we get mail from the United States in about three or four weeks. They say it has taken that long for them to get mail from Germany and they are a lot closer home than we are. Possibly I shouldn't kick about our service, but it is the American privilege. They ask if they will be sent to America. Of course I don't know, but I know that it would be stupid to try and keep 175,000 of them here and try to haul enough food over here to feed them and there is not enough food from the land here to take care of them. So I tell them that they will probably be sent over and will be put to work. They are afraid to be sent to Canada. They say that is English and the English will put them in chains. I told them they could do better work without chains and that the idea was a mistake. But, they say, that is what they have been told by the Fuehrer and he never tells anything but the truth. The German officers are afraid of having to go to work. . . .

"Every morning when I go thru and give them the radio news about the bombing of some town in Germany or the work of the Russians, they say that what we get is only propaganda. I appreciate their feeling sorry for my not getting the truth, but I have the privilege of walking around without a guard and can send my mail home thru the Post Office rather than the Red Cross. We are going to have a real job curing the festering sore that Hitler has planted in these poor souls. I am wondering if we will ever do the job satisfactorily and avoid a similar conflict in the future. They are so positive they are superior. They treat the poor Italians with utter disdain. I think they might deign to wipe their feet on the Americans but not much more."

He closed the letter with the observation that it had presented "a worm's eye picture of the enemy as I have seen him. I hope I give you a fair picture. The minister's son is getting in practice again."

12

What the war-ravaged country between the 38th's base at Beja and the coastal city of Tunis, as well as Tunis itself, looked like in the closing days of May 1943 is revealed in a letter written by Captain Pickens on May 20, three days after he had provided what he described as his worm's eye picture of the German prisoners he had been observing and with whom he had been talking.

Two days after he wrote the letter about the prisoners he was off duty and rode into Tunis, about a hundred miles eastward and a little to the north. His letter the next day gives an authentic picture of the North African region in northern Tunisia after fighting armies had swept across it.

"Yesterday was my day off duty and since transportation was available," he wrote, "I took the time to ride into Tunis and look the situation over. The route carried me thru Medjez-el-Bab and across the highly disputed Long Stop Hill. I find these places described in the April *Observers*, so I don't think I will be giving away any secrets if I mention them and tell a little of what I saw.

"I have learned one thing since being in the Army about where a war must be fought and that is, it must be fought on a road. The control of towns is important only if they are the centers of roads or important as ports. If they are the centers of networks of roads, they will contain supplies and men, but the roads are the main things. In this country from where I live you move only on roads. The ground is too rough otherwise. From Long Stop Hill on to Tunis the hills disappear and the open plains are before you. But the road must be occupied up to that point before you can fan out. Medjez is a road junction, and so important; otherwise there is little to the town except the fairly good-sized stream that divides it. The argument over the possession of it left its mark. The ruins are there and we crossed the river over an improvised bridge. The road from there on to Long Stop is pockmarked with shell holes and you can see signs of tank barriers of everything from broken two-wheeled carts to railroad ties and concrete slabs. To the top of the hill it is quite a climb and I can understand how it was a job to get the Bosche moved off. After you get over the hill and move along the plain into the city there are wrecked tanks scattered all over the rolling country. Trucks that have been burned dot the road. The area from about twenty feet away from sides of the road on out is marked unsafe. There are mines still planted. Some of these days some Arab will be pushing his six oxen along to turn the soil and will wake up with Mohammed. I feel sorry for him in advance, since he had no part in the making.

"Between Beja and Medjez we passed a prisoner of war camp with several thousand Germans behind the barbed wire. On the way home we saw them cooking their evening meal around their individual tents. They had evidently been issued some of our individual C rations and were heating the meat and vegetable stew or heating water for their coffee. Across the hills you could see a hundred little fires smoking. In the background, on one hill, was a church with great gaping holes in it, one big hole in the steeple not quite big enough to make it topple over. I don't know which side did the damage, but the Germans now have it as a part of their scenery to study. A lot of the German material was stacked near the camp with rows and rows of captured trucks, half trucks and munitions. Some of the trucks, like the English lorries, were painted a dust color indicating their use in the desert crossing. Their tires do not look as good as ours, but they have probably been used a lot more and they may be made of synthetic rubber."

He turned his attention for a moment to report on attempts to procure souvenirs:

"Some of our folks have been trying to collect some souvenirs of various sorts. My only attempt has been to get an Iron Cross from one of our patients at the cost of five packages of cigarettes. Their medals are cheaply made and in this case, the trader said, if he ever got back to Germany, he could buy a dozen at half the price he got from me. I have no interest in collecting guns, but if I run across a good camera, I think I might withhold it from my government or keep a good pair of German field glasses."

An American soldier's view of an ancient African city is revealed in his report on that May day in the capital of Tunisia:

"Entering the town of Tunis, you are just one truck load out of hundreds. The British have taken the town. The road is packed with moving traffic and the dust is thick. On the edge of town we passed under a great Roman viaduct that carried water from one section to another back many centuries ago. It's a mammoth thing and stretches clear across the city. Then we passed the first gate, reminding me of the gates into Jerusalem. We stayed on the outside of the walled city, since this is confined to the Arabs now and that section is 'out of bounds' to the troops. Around this walled city within a city runs a stone wall some thirty feet high and three or four feet thick. There are many gates leading into the restricted area with names such as Porte de France, Porte de Bab-el-Kadra and Bab-Saddoun. I bought some postcards of them and will mail them to some of my friends. In the city proper it looks like most of the others. There is little difference between the appearance of Oran, Algiers, Constantine, and Tunis. In Tunis there are less Arabs in sight and not every ten steps does an Arab boy try to shine your shoes. There are fewer beggars, less indication of mal-

nutrition. This may be because we have controlled the city for too short a time. There are great numbers of Italians living in the city. The people are better dressed, cleaner looking than in any of the other cities in North Africa. The whole town looks more modern with the possible exception of Algiers. Street cars are running when they buck the traffic line of British lorries and American jeeps. The jeeps are driven by Americans, British and French. You see the yellow color of the desert 8th Army and the Crusaders' Cross of the First Army and the olive drab of the Americans. The French officers still wear the snappy uniforms of the Allies and drive our jeeps with the tricolor painted on the hood. The tallest soldiers and the blackest are the Senegalese and they are meaner looking than even the Gouams. They are all meeting in Tunis and moving in an ever running stream up and down the streets.

"The Germans pretty well cleaned out the town," he recalled. "They bought nearly all the merchandise of any value with their Bank of France notes. These notes they must have printed by the thousands and paid their soldiers well. Now only the Bank of Algiers notes are negotiable. The storekeepers will try to give you France bank notes in change if you don't watch closely. They now know they are hooked with them and are trying to reduce their losses. The Germans bought all of the perfumes that were any good, paying as high as 2,500 francs for an ounce of Chanel's or Guerlain's best. On our exchange that would be $50 for an ounce, right high price to smell good for such a short time, it seems to me. They also cleaned out the cognac and wine markets, too. And before they left, it is said they smashed the telephone exchange and the radio stations, but left the power plant running and the water supply untouched. They obviously left in a hurry."

Of clothing, kodaks and other items, he reported:

"This is the first town we have been in where clothing could be purchased without coupons. I saw a fancy looking sports coat made of good wool that I could have bought for about 3,000 francs, but somehow it looked a little out of place with the rest of my dusty uniform, so I didn't buy it. In one shop I found a kodak exactly like my little blue one. I paid 98 cents for mine ten years ago and have carried it many a mile since. The duplicate in Tunis was 800 francs—$16. I laughed at the shopkeeper and asked if he had any film to go with it and when he said no, I just laughed some more. The old law of supply and demand at work. I didn't find anything worth buying except the post cards. As you know, I seldom buy anything anyway and unless I see something I can't live without, it can stay on the shelves. I did search for some leather covers for telephone directories but none were in sight. There were plenty of those things back in Algiers, but I don't know

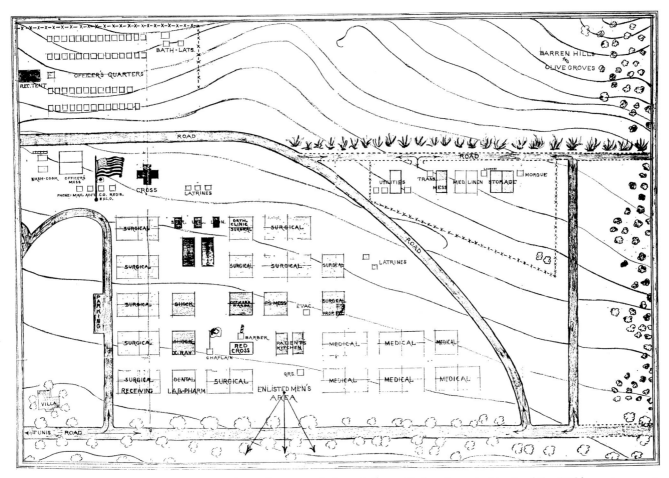

This layout by Clarence O. Kuester, Jr., shows the general plan of the medical and surgical tents of the 38th's encampment near Tunis, Tunisia, North Africa. The road at the bottom of the drawing leads toward Tunis, left.

when I will have a chance to see them again. If I find any I will get a bunch and send them to you."

The city of Tunis, he reported, had been left in good shape as far as bombing was involved. "I saw only about five places," said he, "where the bombs intended for the docks area missed fire. There were five holes with the sides of the buildings glaring at you. The rubbish had been cleaned up. The docks, however, had not fared so well. I think the American Air Force had done that job and they made a systematic destruction of the whole area. It was complete and I don't see how it will ever be used again. Someone suggested that the Germans might be put to mending it, but it will take a long time. The airport was treated in somewhat the same way. The German planes are lined up but useless. I don't know whether we did that or whether the Germans destroyed them before running to the hills on Cape Bone. In either case, they are fit subjects for the junk man."

He didn't have the time to have a look at ancient Carthage. It was "just five or six miles away," said he, "but we did not have the time to buck the traffic and

get over there. If I ever get another chance I will try to see what is left of the ancient city. People tell me that there is little to see, but I still would like to pass over the ground and think about the glorious days when Carthage and Troy were the great cities of the world."

On their way home that day from Tunis, said he, the water supply ran short and the dust and heat were enervating. "We stopped at a British camp and asked for water. They offered us a spot of tea, but we compromised for water. From three to five in the afternoon in any English camp you can get a cup of tea. They will never let a war interfere with their afternoon tea."

Captain Pickens did get a chance to go back to Tunis, and much earlier than he had hoped he might. Three weeks after writing of the first visit to the coastal capital, he wrote again. And this time he got into Carthage. The letter, dated June 10, affords a further close view of the old city, its people, its hodgepodge of merchandise available for purchasing, and even a bit of its history in the days of the Roman conquest of Carthage and that region of Africa.

"The day before yesterday," he began the letter of June 10, "I had an opportunity to visit Tunis and the neighboring city of Carthage. I say Carthage the city, but what I saw were the remains of the city plus the museum and the cathedral. The White Fathers, Les Peres Blancs, run an elaborate establishment there and have collected a lot of things to show the tourists. But I am getting ahead of my story.

"We had no transportation, so Bob Miller, from Lincolnton, and I started out the other morning at about 6:30 to see if we could 'thumb' our way to Tunis. It is supposed to be beneath the dignity of an American officer to stoop to such a level for travel, but I was determined to see that section come 'hell and high water.' We cornered an American ambulance driven by a French lieutenant who was off to Tunis in a cloud of dust. He had to get there in a hurry and several times I wished I had stayed in the oat field at home.

"He talked a little English, said his mother was born in Brooklyn. I don't know why it is that so many of these folks over here claim some kin to Brooklyn, even the German prisoners say they have relatives in Brooklyn. Flatbush fame has spread with the skill of the Dodgers. Our driver also spoke German very fluently, having himself been born in Alsace. Our conversation would have made you laugh if you could take your eyes off the road long enough to listen. It was a real mixture, but we managed to get our mutual stories across.

"We had to stop in Medjez-el-Bab to get some pictures and to build a sort of ford across the river, but still made record time in getting to Tunis. There our host insisted on our stopping at the French Officers' Club for a spot of coffee. It was then over 100 degrees in the shade and coffee was the last thing I wanted. He had coffee and we had a glass of vermouth with some ice added. It was the first time we had seen ice since we left our last station. It was welcome. Then our host said, after he had made a telephone call, that he would accompany us to Souks, the Arabic bazaars or markets. He was anxious that we not get stuck in trading with our Semitic friends. He didn't know it, but I didn't have enough money with me to get hurt. We tried the first gate into the section marked 'out of bounds' for American and British troops and the Tommy MP turned us back but said if we would go down the street for two blocks and turn right we could get into the markets without the interference of the military police. I don't know why that section was forbidden unless for typhus or the threat of Italian snipers, neither of which we were afraid of, since we have been inoculated so many times against typhus and the accuracy of the Italian marksmanship has been discredited too much of late. So in we went to a great maze of little streets with hundreds of holes-in-the-wall shops manned by all types of Arabs, from dignified, well dressed men to moth-eaten, vitamin-lacking, unwashed sons of Abraham's handmaiden. They worked with silver, tin, copper, brass, and empty 88- and 105-millimeter shells. They made shoes from goatskins and rugs from camels' hair. They had perfumes they claimed were the best from the island of the lotus eaters. They would sell you rayon scarfs evidently shipped over here for good will to the locals at a price of only 300 francs ($6.00), all handmade, they said, any one of which could be bought in Grant's or Woolworth's at home for a mere 49 cents.

"All who could speak English had displayed their prize wares at the Sesqui-Centennial at Philadelphia in 1926 and had awards to prove it. They wanted to please the Americans, but of course the Germans had been there and had run the prices up because they had lots of money, Bank of France printed notes. They had not as yet discovered this currency had no value now. The descendants of the trading Phoenicians were aiding and abetting inflation, but they could arouse little interest from me. I saw nothing I would be proud to own. I did make one purchase, a palm leaf fan which has since come in handy in combating the heat of this tropical section. It cost me fifteen francs after an original price set at thirty francs. Either I have a Jewish strain somewhere in my background or the training as the son of a Methodist minister in making a little go a long way makes me wait when trading with these Shylocks. At that, the fan would probably sell to anyone in the know for ten francs. Our Frenchman appeared well pleased with our bargaining ability, altho Bob almost slipped once or twice on some socalled brass vases which would probably gather dust in Betty's attic as well as anything he could have sent home. I am sorry that I can't get steamed up on this business of sending you a lot of souvenirs. I did price a leather cover for the telephone directory, but at 800 francs ($16.00) I thought we could put up with the frayed edge until the telephone company would come thru with a new edition."

After their session with the Arab traders they walked to the officers' mess for lunch, where they had a meal, Captain Pickens reported, that was not as good as the one they would have had had they been back at the 38th's mess tent. After lunch they retired to the French Officers' Club "to sit under the broad canopy in front of the street and snooze a little and awake occasionally to watch the passing crowds. The British still outnumber us, but we saw the Gouams, Senegalese, French, the marines and sailors go by. We watched the Arabs with all of their clothes waving in the breeze, apparently not minding the intense heat, and the beggars as usual came by for their alms. We laughed at two French naval officers who sat near us and jabbered along at a great rate and then when they got ready to leave, one of them dropped a bottle of champagne from his cloak and it spread nicely over the tile floor. I don't know any profanity in French, but I am sure there must have been some small amount of it spoken along with all of the gestures and tears."

It was while they were sitting in front of the French Officers' Club that an American officer came by and greeted them. He had crossed with the 38th from the States a year before as a member of a tank outfit. He asked them if they would like to visit Carthage, and when they replied that they would but that they would then have no way back to the hospital, he promised them that he would take them back, since he was stationed only forty miles from them. So they set out for Carthage some five miles away.

Captain Pickens tells about it:

"I had always connected Carthage with Hannibal and with his invasion of Europe thru Spain and across the Alps. I found that he was mixed up with the finish of Carthage. It seems that during the Second Punic War, about 202 B.C., he had carried the argument with the Romans over the possession of part of Italy and Sicily on into Italy with his elephants. While he was doing so well in Italy, with the help of the Gauls who were easy to persuade, some of the Romans had the bright idea of moving a fleet into Marseilles and they cut poor Hannibal's supply line and his connections with Spain. This made him hurry back to Carthage because he couldn't stand a siege, and when he got home he found Carthage capitulated. They asked for Hannibal's head, but he escaped into Asia and finally committed suicide in order to escape his relentless enemies. Then some fifty years later, when the Phoenicians felt a little stronger, the Romans jumped on her again on slight pretext and this time besieged the city and fought it out in the streets, and when the fighting was over, the population of something over 250,000 was reduced to less than 30,000.

"Then the Romans decided to finish the job and level the city. They sent the remaining population into slavery. Then to further finish the job, they burned the city and the blackened ruins were ploughed and the ground was sown with grain as a sort of 'ceremonial effacement.' Thus was the once principal city of the world, the pride of all Phoenicians, the crossroads of trade, the mecca of Semites, the outpost of civilization, left once more for the growing of grain or the pasture land of the nomads of this section."

Captain Pickens turned from the ancient history of the destroyed city to tell of what they found that day in June of 1943:

"Little is to be found today of that city. What we

Major Paul Sanger, chief of surgical service, and Captain William P. Medearis, supply and utilities officer, brave for a moment the hot North African sunshine.

saw while wandering over this ground was what the White Fathers of the Catholic order had uncovered of the Roman work during the latter years. Apparently the Romans did a thorough job of not leaving a trace of their enemy. The Aryans won that struggle, but left traces which are still being argued on the battlefields today. The site of the city is there, but nothing else. The Romans rebuilt a little to the south in what is now Tunis and the Arabs built a little to the east in what is now Sidi-Bou-Said.

"On the way to Carthage we passed a principal airport where the stepchildren of Scipio Africanus the Elder left some of their wreckage after this last struggle during the twentieth century. Either they left in a hurry and destroyed many planes themselves or our air forces had done a good job, because none of these planes will ever take to the air again. Contrasting these modern engines with the five banks of oars and the huge rams on the galleys of old emphasizes the fact that the superior numbers will eventually prevail."

The visitors from the 38th spent some time in the museum at Carthage and then went across the hill to Sidi-Bou-Said, another holy city of the Arabs. And then they rode along the sea through La Goulette to Tunis in the late afternoon "and partook of another ice-cold vermouth before starting back thru Medjez-el-Bab and Beja over bombed-marked roads. We had enjoyed a busy day with some relief from the duties of war," he concluded the letter, "but we were tired."

101

13

The 38th Evacuation Hospital had been settled at Beja in Tunisia hardly a month when another distinguished newspaper correspondent visited it and wrote of his impressions of the hospital's operations and particularly of the treatment of German prisoners, who by that time were swarming back from the battlefronts where they were suffering one defeat after another.

This correspondent, Thomas R. Henry, reporting his observations by way of the North American Newspaper Alliance, expressed his amazement at the consideration the American doctors and nurses were giving the German prisoners who but a few hours before their arrival at the hospital had been shooting at the Americans.

Mr. Henry's report, coupled with the observations of Captain Pickens in his letters home during that period, offers an on-the-scene commentary on the work of the 38th in treating scores of wounded enemy prisoners.

The correspondent thought the way the prisoners were being treated by the American medical men and nurses "one of the strangest spectacles in the history of warfare," and he emphasized the fact that these prisoners had the freedom of the base even though many of them had shown that they were what he described as "bad customers."

The Henry report was carried widely by American newspapers. From Tunisia he had written:

TUNISIAN FRONT, June 1 (1943)—The night after the big surrender a front line evacuation hospital here afforded one of the strangest spectacles in the history of warfare—German and American patients in the same wards. A German playing popular American tunes on a violin, the prisoners having complete freedom of the grounds.

It was altogether too idealistic for common sense and hospital authorities had to put their feet down on the babying of men who, only a few hours before, had been killing American soldiers. Moreover, some of them gave every evidence of being bad customers—however ingratiating their ways when they had something to gain by them.

The strange scene continued for at least one night, not altogether to the liking of some of the U.S. Medical Corps soldiers who found themselves with wards full of complaining prisoners. Three-fourths of the patients were Germans, taken from a nearby prison bivouac. A few hours before they themselves had occupied the hospital, an old French institution they had taken over. It had been evacuated in the path of the American advance but in a very short time the patients found themselves in their old beds again with what appeared to be much better treatment than they had received from their own medical officers and orderlies.

They soon learned, or thought they had learned, that Americans are "soft" and men who really were only slightly hurt began calling piteously for the nurses and demanding all sorts of little attentions. The soft-hearted girls were gullible enough and waited on the moaning "Jungen" at first with the solicitude of little mothers.

* * *

In one of the wards around midnight all was peaceful except for the loud snores of some of the Germans and the groans of one man. By that time a thoroughly disgusted U.S. Medical Corps corporal was on duty there and let the Nazi moan. The patient, he explained, was one of the Afrika Korps' outstanding "heroes," a sergeant who was credited with knocking out 14 American tanks single-handed. He was loaded with bobbins and medals. His only injury was a broken arm which had been cared for by one of America's best orthopedic surgeons. It is highly doubtful that he was in any pain at all.

"It just shows how yellow these fellows are," said the corporal, "when they are not winning. I might feel different about it if I hadn't seen a bunch of British, strafed on a ship, brought in here a few hours ago. All of them were badly hurt and it was commendable how they took it compared to this fellow."

One man was glad to be taken prisoner because he expects to be taken to the United States, be released there at the end of the war, and settle down. He had been trying to get there before the war but never could get a visa.

"You don't suppose there will be any trouble about it?" he asked. "You don't think Americans might be mad at us Germans?" He was so confident that it was a pity to shatter his illusions. . . .

* * *

The extreme consideration for prisoners during the first few hours can only be explained by the novelty of the situation in which American nurses and soldiers found themselves. They had never dealt with prisoners before and had open ears for tear-jerking stories. The picture was changed as soon as the hospital commandant learned what was going on.

Treatment of the prisoner patients and medical corps soldiers was quite a problem from the first to the Red Cross workers at the hospital. Throughout the campaign they had stayed closer to the front than any other Red Cross girls. Once, last February, they had been evacuated into the mountains with all their belongings in musette bags, barely in time to escape, and had at once set to work organizing what facilities they had to receive the first wave of American wounded. After that they had no particular fancy for the whining Germans.

But soon they were leaning over backwards not to show any obvious partiality against the late enemies. Among the girls were Barbara Brandon of Indianapolis, first Red Cross girl in an evacuation hospital in North Africa, and Edith Taake of St. Louis, a former Missouri school teacher.

* * *

When the Americans took over the hospital they found it fairly well equipped. The Germans had left so hurriedly they did not have time even to clean up the bloody bandages in the wards.

After the hospital authorities tightened up on the Germans they still got as good care as any American wounded and the Red Cross workers handed over with objective impartiality tooth brushes, tooth paste and "klingen," or razor blades when the prisoners asked for them. The Germans are masters at adopting ingratiating ways. The worst faux pas occurred when a major entered the dining room, giving the Nazi salute. He dropped his arm at once, however, when he realized what he had done and never repeated the offense.

On the same day that Correspondent Henry datelined his story, the 38th's Daily Bulletin of June 1, 1943, devoted all but a few lines to three congratulatory messages to the Allied Forces.

The first was from President Franklin D. Roosevelt:

"My warm personal congratulations to you on the great success of the recent operations in North Africa. The power and coordination with which the Allied Forces are crushing our enemies in Tunisia is a tribute to your leadership, the unprecedented degree of Allied cooperation which makes a pattern for the ultimate defeat of the Axis.

"Convey to General Alexander my appreciation of the splendid manner in which he directed the groups of Armies of three nations in a series of devastating blows against the enemy; my congratulations to Air Marshal Tedder on his overwhelming air victory; to Admiral Cunningham on the destruction of Axis shipping by his naval craft; to General Montgomery on the culmination of his odyssey and to General Anderson for his perfect team play."

The second message was from King George VI. The Daily Bulletin styled it the "congratulatory message

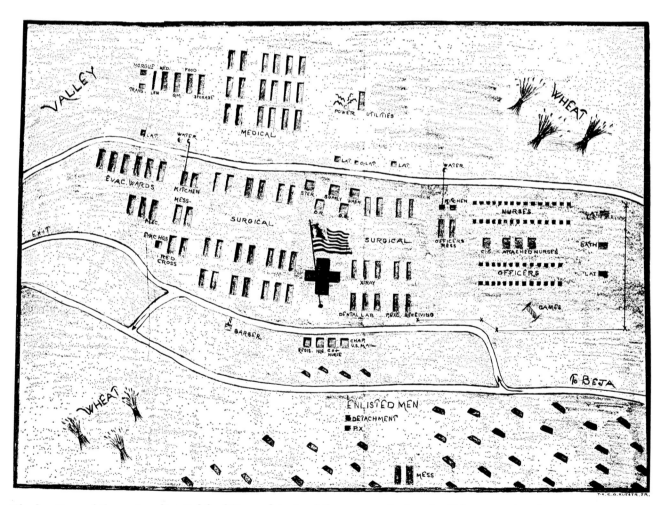

The locations of the various hospital facilities and tents of the personnel when the 38th was stationed near Beja in Tunisia, North Africa, are revealed in this drawing by Clarence O. Kuester, Jr. Beja was off to the right.

from His Majesty The King of England to the Commanding General, Allied Forces." The King's message:

"Throughout the six months during which you have been in command of the Allied Forces in North Africa, I have watched with admiration the progress of operations on land, on sea, and in the air. Under your leadership, forces diverse in nationality and race have been knit into one united and successful whole. Their task has not been easy and the resistance of the enemy has been determined and desperate. But now, with the capture of Tunis and Bizerta, your campaign is almost concluded; the last enemy forces in Africa are being captured or destroyed and the debt of Dunkirk repaid. On behalf of all my peoples I express to you, as supreme Commander of Allied Forces, and to all ranks under your command our heartfelt congratulations on your victory."

The final message, "to all individuals in the United States Army in NATOUSA, from the Commanding General, Allied Forces," said:

"With the virtual destruction of all Axis troops in North Africa, I want to express my sincere thanks to all those portions of the Allied Forces whose work has kept them along lines of communication and in vital ports and bases instead of on the actual battleline. No Allied success in this region could have been possible except as our supply and maintenance problems have been met and conquered. Every tactical commander— Air, Ground and Naval—is keenly aware of the debt he owes to the officers and enlisted men of the Allied service forces who have so loyally and efficiently provided the means needed at the front. I should like every one of the men to know that I thank him personally for his part in the great victory that the Allies have won."

The message was signed: "Dwight D. Eisenhower, Commander-in-Chief."

On that first day of June, 1943, the 38th Evacuation

Five Charlotte officers enjoy leave to North African beach. Left to right, Snyder, Tyson, Colin Munroe, McChord Williams, McGrath.

104

Hospital listed 14 patients, 12 admissions, 16 dispositions, 40 vacant beds and three wards in operation.

The next day the work load had increased considerably, with 44 patients under treatment, 31 admissions, only one disposition, 58 vacant beds and six wards in operation.

Even busier was the hospital on June 3. Fifty-seven patients were listed, 27 were admitted, fourteen disposed of. Forty-five beds were vacant, six wards in use.

The bulletin that day announced, more happily, the award by the commanding officer of the Good Conduct Medal "for exemplary behaviour, efficiency and fidelity in the performance of their duties as members of this unit" to:

> Master Sergeant Frank B. Pedrick
> First Sergeant Herbert L. Johnson
> Staff Sergeant Amelio R. Fenocchi
> Staff Sergeant Howard S. Simpson
> Sergeant David E. Fluck
> Sergeant William F. McDonough
> Sergeant Edward F. Schmidt
> Sergeant William E. Smith
> Sergeant William E. Vaughn
> Tech. 3rd Gr. Alex Baker
> Tech. 4th Gr. Randall K. Davis
> Tech. 5th Gr. Paul H. Kugler

A less cheerful announcement was carried in the Daily Bulletin of June 15:

"On the basis of information received from the Monastery at Thibar, the winery there is placed *out of bounds* to *all* members of this command. Individual purchases thereat are no longer authorized. The Quartermaster Supply Officer should be contacted for information relative to this restriction on purchases by officers."

Its impact, however, was softened somewhat by the note immediately following it:

"Enlisted Men will sign the June payroll between 0900 and 1200 hours, tomorrow, June 16 1943, in the Enlisted Men's Mess Tent."

A more serious prohibition than the out of bounds of the monastery's winery was announced in the Daily Bulletin of June 18. It ordered:

"All personnel of the Army of the United States, North African Theater of Operations, will refrain from eating lettuce or other types of fresh salads. Fresh vegetables and fruits which can be satisfactorily washed and peeled may be consumed except in the Fes-Meknes area where amoebic dysentery is hyperendemic. Vegetables and fruits which are to be consumed will be repeatedly washed in fresh running water and will be peeled before they are served. The dipping of vegetables, fruits, etc., in solutions of permanganate of potash or chlorine is not recommended because such procedure gives a false sense of security not warranted by experience."

The order further provided:

"Examination and analysis of water samples taken from the stream flowing under the bridge on the Mateur-Ain Rhelal Road and other streams in North Africa indicates heavy fecal contamination. Streams throughout Tunisia and Algeria are infested with cercariae which burrow through the skin and cause liver trouble." So, the order continued:

"In view of the facts stated in Paragraph 1, above, all military personnel are prohibited from swimming in any streams in Tunisia and Algeria. Commanding officers will insure strict compliance with this order."

A further lugubrious note in that Daily Bulletin announced that the next evening the subject of the lecture at the officers' and nurses' training session would be "Malaria."

Malaria, in fact, in the terrific heat of Tunis in summer was one of the problems that gave the 38th much concern and a heavy burden of work. Dr. Query still recalls the efforts of the hospital to combat the scourge:

"That period in Tunis—the summer of 1943—was one of the roughest we had, certainly from the standpoint of the temperature. It seemed to stay up around 115 to 120 degrees, and to make matters worse, we had no ice. All we had was water in Lister bags. They would bring these boys in with high fever, temperatures 104 and 105 degrees, and the temperature outside would be 110 and higher. We'd stand under a big bag of water and let the water run down on us, clothes and all, and when we were wringing wet without a stitch of dry thread on us we'd go back to work for fifteen or twenty minutes and then we'd get thoroughly soaked again and work again. We'd do that again and again; we couldn't work more than fifteen minutes or so without stopping and getting wet."

Sometimes the temperature went up as high as 130 degrees, the Charlotte doctors recall, and bits of metal in their tents would be so hot they couldn't touch them. In their attempts to get the patients' fever down the doctors would put wet towels over them. The towels would dry quickly and they would wet them again.

"No shade, no ice," Dr. Query summarizes that experience. "Just hot, hot, hot. And when the sirocco blew in from the desert, man, it was HOT!"

Often during the day they would wrap up in wet blankets and the wind blowing on them would enable them to endure the daylight hours. In the same way they attempted to cool themselves, they would cool their food. George Snyder recalls the procedure: "We'd put cans, like beans, down into a sack, wet the sack, and the wind blowing on it would cool the cans a little."

"Stokes Munroe and Paul Sanger got access to this villa down there in Tunis," Dr. Query remembers also, "and when we had half a day off or a few hours or so, we'd go down there and stretch out on a bed to rest, and then the bedbugs would start coming out and biting us so that we couldn't sleep."

On the same day that the officers' and nurses' training session was devoted to the subject of malaria, June 18, Captain Montgomery recorded, appropriately:

Just out of the hospital following a week's illness—chills and fever with little diarrhea.

Two days later Captain Montgomery recorded:

Moved out of Beja today at 0845 by truck. Arrived Tunis 1145. Hospital being set up in surburb called Beau Site. We are on a small hill from which we can see the Bay of Tunis & ancient Carthage.

And two days after making that entry he wrote, on June 22:

Hospital officially opened at 0800 today although we had an acute appendix last night. Today is my birthday, also my day off. Had a nice day in Tunis. Had lunch & dinner at Tunisian Palace Hotel. Went swimming at La Massa.

The work at the hospital that day, the Bulletin discloses, was light. Seven patients were enrolled. No dispositions were made and 29 beds were vacant. Only one ward was in use.

The next day, June 23, a total of 28 patients admitted brought the number to 35, and thereafter, through the first week in July, the patient list increased steadily: June 24, 54; June 26, 127; June 27, 162; June 28, 206; June 29, 244; June 30, 286; July 1, 330; July 2, 365; July 3, 403; July 4, 436; July 5, 446. For the remainder of July and most of August the patient list ran from about 250 to above 400 a day.

The hospital had been in operation a week at its new location near Tunis when on June 28 Captain Pickens wrote a long letter home. He identified the new position only as "Still North Africa." But from what he wrote it could be clearly reasoned that the 38th Evacuation Hospital was not many miles removed from the action.

"'They are coming in' was the cry all thru the camp," he began. "Everyone moved out of their tents to watch the returning bombers. Bob Miller and I had gone to a nearby airfield to spend the day with a mutual friend. We had seen the takeoff of a mission earlier in the morning and now they were on the way back. It is an exciting time when the bombers come back. We were the guests of the squadron leader. He did not make the trip with his squadron in order to have the day with us. He was anxious to see that they all returned safely. We stood outside his pyramidal tent and counted as the groups of six planes 'buzzed' the field. That buzzing was a privilege that the boys had to show they were on the way home. Some of them tried to see how close they could come to the ground and the prop-wash almost took the tent off its mooring. After the buzzing they peel off in groups of three and land three abreast just a few seconds apart. Finally the major, our host, said with a distinct sigh of relief, 'They are all back.'

"We went back into his tent to talk some more about his work. At present they are leveling off Sicily and Sardinia and parts of southern Italy. They had just finished their part in bringing Pantelleria into the fold. He travels with them on most of the trips, sometimes as pilot, co-pilot, or navigator, sometimes as rear gunner and sometimes just as an observer and photographer. He showed us some pictures of some of the precision bombing they had been doing in Sardinia. From several thousand feet above, the boats in the harbor look like small specks, but the bombs were seen as dropping squarely on the objectives. It is almost incredible to see the accuracy. Occasionally a bomb will go off the course, but that is caused by a faulty fin or the fact that the bomb opening does not coordinate properly. It looks so simple in the pictures taken during the raids, but the main thing is the bomb sight and that is guarded with a vengeance. I did not see the inside parts of one."

He told what happened after the flyers landed:

"The boys from the mission came filing into lunch at a nearby tent. We went over to eat and listen to the major's questions about the trip. One chap had a nice hole in his right wing, he said, and later we went out to look at it. He said they had run into some opposition near their target, but the P-38s had been coaxed up to take care of them. On the way back they passed over an enemy destroyer escorting a freight vessel and the destroyer had opened up on them; hence the hole in one wing. It just missed the control wires, so there was no trouble in getting home. Otherwise, there was no excitement—just a routine job. The boys were in good spirits and bragging on the performance of their ships. The major said they had a top sergeant who was the best mechanic in all Africa and if they ever lost him, they would have to be grounded. The sergeant enjoyed none of the glory of the Air Force, but he appeared to be responsible for this unit's success. The boys give him full credit. The pilots and gunners and radio-navigators are just a bunch of kids, happy-go-lucky, but proud of their part in this war. The major said they had a lot of criticism from the ground forces during the heavy fighting here. The Infantry wanted to know where the Air Force was, but the bombers were always behind the lines of the enemy, working on his supplies and his reserve manpower. He said they could not get too close to the fighting, since they would be fired on by both sides. When a plane came too close, everyone opened up on it and only the fast flying straf-

ing planes could outrun the flak, so the bombers stayed behind. I asked the group why, if they had any additional bombs, they did not start to work on the destroyer and the freighter they had met on the way home. The reply was, 'You go to your target, finish that job, and get home as quickly as possible.' They do not try to do anything else; they used to try that and found the cost too heavy. Do one job and do it well. Of course, they reported the presence of the enemy boats and their position, and they said some other group probably had been assigned that job before they had landed.'

After lunch they stretched out for a siesta, but before they could get to sleep a sudden whirlwind swept down and blew the tent to the ground atop them. Little damage was done, however, and since it was too hot to sleep anyway, their host arranged for them to take a flight on one of the B-25s. It might be cooler, he suggested, at ten thousand feet. Captain Pickens goes on with the account:

"We picked up our pilot and co-pilot and soon found ourselves in the air. I took the seat of the rear gunner, up on a little bicycle seat in a sort of glassed-in igloo toward the back of the plane. It was a tight fit for me and I can see why most of the gunners are fairly small men. I was shown how to manipulate the buttons for the firing of the guns and how to turn the turret around in any direction. I was given a set of earphones and shown where I could grab a parachute if it became necessary. Then I was fastened in in this isolated section of the plane. I had a good time whirling around in the little turret which worked automatically on the pressing of a button, but then I turned cold when I thought about the possibility of running into an enemy plane. Well, I examined the gunsight and gave a couple of practice shots to see if the guns were opened, and then sat there and waited to become the first Medical Administrative officer to bring down an ME 109 in this war. I could picture myself a real hero except when I thought about what would happen if I missed and he happened to hit. Fortunately, no enemy planes appeared while we covered a great deal of Tunisia. I had a good time trying to locate our hospital and its big Red Cross. I looked at Roman ruins the best way they should be seen, from ten thousand feet in a cool plane. Once during the trip the pilot decided to give us a little experience in barrel-rolling in a plane and when he finished, my stomach felt like I had been too long on a stormy sea. At another time during our trip we practiced the much talked of dive-bombing, dropping several thousand feet in a few short seconds. Again I thought I would never make a good sailor. All in all, however, I thought it was a pleasant trip. At least I got some idea of the type thing a medium bomber does."

But they were to receive a greater shock when they

The 38th's encampment near Telergma, Algeria shown distinctly in this high altitude, aerial photograph, was strung out along a straight road, center. Always a huge red cross near the center of each of the encampments warned potential enemy planes that the facility was a hospital.

landed and talked again with their host, the squadron leader. Stan Pickens tells of it:

"When we returned to the base, the major said he was glad we had gone. We not only had a good trip, but, he said, we'd done him a distinct favor. Curious to see how we could have done him a favor, we asked why. He told us then that the chap who had taken us up had not flown for over a month. Once in England he had made a forced landing after losing his landing gear on a trip over occupied Holland. This had shaken the lad considerably. Then just a month before our trip with him, he again had lost his landing apparatus in a sortie over Italy and had been forced down on the beach near Tunis within the German lines. He had lost his plane, but had escaped and made his way back to his outfit. Then he told the major that he was afraid to fly again. His nerve was gone, he said. The major told him he needn't fly until he was back in shape. He was a good man and the major didn't want to lose him. Our trip was the first one he had made.

"The major had told him that two officers from the nearby hospital wanted to fly with him particularly and that he had to get in there and fly, and he wanted us back safely as well as the pilot. The boy had no other choice but try and we acted as guinea pigs. We did not know this before we started, otherwise we might not have been so keen on the trip. I noticed when we landed that the pilot was very interested in what we thought of the trip and particularly of the landing. I told him that I had done considerable traveling by air in civilian life but that I had never been set down easier than with him. I told him he handled a plane perfectly so far as I was concerned. I learned later from the major that I had said exactly the right thing without any exaggeration, and that the boy was very happy about it all. Possibly we did some good in getting the lad's nerve back for him. I hope so."

But the most interesting happening on that trip, the captain would reveal in his letter, would come toward evening when he talked with them about his experiences as one of the pilots who had flown with General Doolittle on the famous flight over Tokyo from a carrier in the Pacific. His letter provided information about the flight months before the details of the sensational assault upon Japan were released. He writes of the major, their host that day:

"He was one of the men with General Doolittle on that much talked of raid. He was a first lieutenant then and was a co-pilot on the trip. I suppose you have heard more about that trip now than I have. I see a good deal in the papers about it and I understand that the Book-of-the-Month will be on that subject in the near future. But in spite of the former buildup I will give you the picture I got from the major.

"They trained for the trip for several months at one of the naval seaplane bases. They took their planes off a wooden or metal runway the same size as carriers they were to use. The only thing they failed to do in the training period was to take off a ship in a heavy sea. But when they left the Pacific coast on their way west, the plan was to have the sixteenth plane hop off the carrier after they had been underway for two days and fly back to the United States. Then they would know it was possible to get off in some kind of weather. But before the first day was over, the pilot and his helpers of this spare plane had persuaded then Lt. Col. Doolittle that they should be allowed to make the raid with the group. They all worked on him on this. They scouted around among their remaining crews and some from the ships to get enough gunners and radio men and whatnot to fully man the sixteenth ship. So they still did not know for sure that the big B-25s could get off a carrier. But, as the major said, none of the men who went on the raid expected to get back alive. It was a real suicide crew and the gayest one you can imagine. All the way across the Pacific they studied maps and pictures of Japan and the neighboring coast of China and the available landing fields in nearby Russia. It seems that our subs had moved along the coast and taken photographs of the targets, so that when our men actually arrived over their targets they knew exactly what they were after.

"Just before they were to arrive at their rendezvous, one of the ships ran into a Jap fishing smack and they were afraid the Jap had radioed their coming back to the mainland. They did away with the fisherman in short order, but it was decided to get off then and not wait the remaining 12 or 24 hours as originally planned. So off they went in the middle of the night and instead of arriving over Tokyo at dawn they got there at high noon. They came in so low they could see the faces of the little yellow men scurrying around the streets. They had to get altitude in order to release their bombs, which they did with deadly accuracy. Every target was hit squarely, according to reports of the men surviving and returning to China. They were only military targets, the major said. He passed right over the top of the Palace and he said he and his crew could have leveled it off in no time, but they had their orders and were then on their way to China.

"There was very little flak. Apparently the Japs thought no such expedition possible and were not prepared. Of course, we are probably in the same state of mind in America. I'm telling you it can come, and, boy, it is sudden and swift. No fighters to speak of came up to protest the visit. So off our friends went to find a spot in old China. They crossed the Sea of Japan and then on across the Yellow Sea just as it was getting dark again. Their gasoline supply was getting low and they were battling a mean storm. The ceiling was exactly zero. They could not see the ground at any level. The major said they knew about the mountains they were to cross, with some rising to an altitude of 10,000 feet, but that they set their altitude at about 6,000 and decided to take their chances on bumping squarely into one.

"They missed. But before they arrived over the field where they were to have their second rendezvous, the gasoline ran out and they had to bail out. The major said he had never been out in a parachute before, but that he wasn't bothered about the chute not opening as much as how he was going to land and where. His commanding officer allowed him to tie his musette bag on his arm before he went out. The major said he took his maps, cigarettes and matches (dry), pistol, a small package of concentrated food and a pint of whiskey and took off in the rain at 6,000 feet. The plane had been set on the automatic pilot. His commanding officer was the last to leave the plane. He stepped out in the rain and it was coming down in sheets. After his chute opened he felt around for his flashlight and turned it on to see if he could spot the ground under him, but to no avail. It was just plain black down there and the rain increased as he moved down. Finally he plumped on the earth in the middle of China in the pitch black dark with the rain beating heavy tattoos on all sides. When he hit, he lost his flashlight, so he wrestled getting out of his harness in the dark after he had stayed on the ground for about three minutes. The sudden stop had knocked the breath out of him. After smoking a cigarette and figuring he was on the side of a hill, he decided to work up to the top of the hill to see if any sign of life could be spotted.

"The major said at that juncture, 'Don't ever go up a blind hill in the dark. It's not hard to get up, but the coming back is bad.' He found nothing from the top and forgot where the sudden drops were coming back, so he finally stopped and lay in the rain and waited for morning. The whiskey helped in passing the time and in keeping warm.

"When morning came he got down the hill and found a railroad line and started walking in the direction of the base where they were all to meet. About ten-thirty that morning he came across his C.O. on his way in the same direction. They had been taught one sentence in Chinese, which said, 'I am an American.' The major said none of the Chinese could understand them when they said that, but that all of them had heard about the raid over Tokyo and brought out pictures of American soldiers and pictures of Mr. Roosevelt. They were always welcome.

"Finally they secured a handcar which they pumped

Captain William P. Kavanagh gets some African sun on a graveled walk at St. Cloud.

on down the railroad to the town where they were to meet, a matter of some sixty miles. That was the hardest part of the trip outside of the taxiing the planes on the carrier in a strong wind. That process was done by inching the plane up two or three feet with a scotch in front and behind. The men on the front scotch always took their lives in their hands. One sailor was caught when one plane got away for a minute and he was pinned quickly against a side wall. He lost his arm in the deal but not his life. The Air Corps boys took up a collection for him before they set sail and left him over $3,000. Many of them thought they had no need for money where they were going anyway.

"Pumping down the tracks brought them to their town and there they were met by a Chinese, a graduate of Harvard, who controlled the transportation of the town. He gave them a car to use and they settled down to wait for the arrival of the others. News came in later in the day about the other planes. One had landed in Russia and the crew had been interned. One had landed in Japan, probably with engine trouble, and the others were in China. No one was lost, so far as they knew. During the next ten days they came in from all sections. The plane that landed in Russia was piloted by a young fellow who had helped train some Russian and Polish pilots in the United States and knew how to speak Russian. The major didn't say it, but I gathered they all thought he had gone in that direction, not only because it was closer, but that he knew a grand reception awaited him. I hope that is true."

109

Their host that day continued with his story of the sensational Doolittle flight over Tokyo by revealing what had happened to the American flyers after their assault upon the Japanese capital and their landing in China and Russia. Captain Pickens relayed the information the major had given them:

"Before the whole gang had gathered they were shipped off to Chungking and then sent to Calcutta to await orders. They traveled in a DC-3, the same type of plane used by Eastern Air Lines. At Calcutta they just waited. They were comfortably housed and the Indians were cordial enough. One day, after lounging around for two weeks, word came thru that all ferry pilots were needed immediately to help evacuate personnel from Burma. So, off to Mandalay the major went to help get the folks out ahead of the Japanese. They just went back and forth between Mandalay and Calcutta for several days. When this experience had run out they sat for another week or ten days and then orders came to start for the Middle East. The major said he had a hard time getting rid of his DC-3, but finally got someone to sign for it, and then boarded a plane for Cairo. After some delay there he was sent back to Miami. Back in the States, he was put in charge of a squadron to train. After three months training in

maneuvering and attack, off they went on their way to England. They were snowed in for two days at Presque Isle and two weeks in Iceland, but finally wound up to start working on the Germans from an east England base. They came down to Africa in December and have been here ever since.

"I think it is quite a saga, this round the world cruise. They celebrated their year's anniversary of the trip over Tokyo last month near us. General Doolittle came down and joined in with the boys that are left. It was a gay party, they report, and I think they are entitled to one gay evening a year for that job. They all, says the major, want to go again when this job is finished over here. They like to see the little yellow rats run for cover."

After hearing the major's story of the Tokyo raid and the lively events that followed it, says Captain Pickens, it seemed to them that their own jobs of helping operate an Army base hospital were rather routine assignments.

"Bob and I finished a pleasant day with the Air Corps and hurried back to the mundane job of helping run a hospital," he concludes his letter. "Our part is just another cog in the big machine organized to lick the enemy of our way of living."

14

Captain Jack Montgomery's next entry in his diary was again characteristic of few words. He wrote on July 10:

Sicily invaded at 0300 hours. We expect casualties from these tomorrow.

Eight days later, on July 18, he added another two lines:

Casualties have been very light. Hospital never as much as half-filled.

The Status of the Hospital report in the Daily Bulletin during that period bears out Captain Montgomery's observation:

On July 9 the number of patients was 344, with 466 vacant beds; July 10, the number was 322, with 488 beds; the next day, 275 and 787; July 12, 229 patients and 833 vacant beds; July 13, 227 patients, 871 vacant beds; July 14, 287 and 811; July 15, 253 and 845; July

16, 254 patients, 844 beds vacant; July 17, patients totaled 284 and 814 beds were vacant; and Sunday, July 18, the day he made his entry in his diary, 363 patients and 735 vacant beds.

The Daily Bulletin reveals in its July 17 issue that "The Commanding Officer had the honor yesterday of presenting to Private Marvin D. Regan, formerly of Company K, 26th Infantry, now a member of this organization, the Award of the Purple Heart for wounds received in action."

With much pride Colonel Bauchspies had inserted in the Daily Bulletin of July 21 two letters just received at the 38th's headquarters. Colonel Bauchspies introduced them with a brief note:

The following letters have been received from Brigadier General F. A. Blesse, Surgeon, NATOUSA, and W. G. MacKay, Lt. Col., RA, British Service. Lt. Col. MacKay was a patient in this hospital while we were stationed at Beja.

110

He expressed his appreciation for treatment he received while a patient in this hospital to the Surgeon, NATOUSA. The letters are as follows:

HEADQUARTERS
NORTH AFRICAN THEATER OF OPERATIONS
Office of the Surgeon
APO 534

17 July 1943

MEMO TO: The Commanding Officer, 38th Evacuation Hospital

1. The attached letter is forwarded for your information.
2. I wish to also express my appreciation of the superior manner in which the 38th Evacuation Hospital has accomplished every task which has been assigned them. I feel that you, and every member of your unit, may be justly proud of their splendid record of highly efficient service and devotion to duty.

/s/ F. A. Blesse
Brig. General, AUS,
Surgeon

The letter enclosed said:

HQ No 1 Regt RA
R.A.T.D., BNAF
5th July 1943

TO: The Senior Medical Officer, United States Army.

Dear Sir,

I would like to express to you my thanks and gratitude for the kindness and most efficient treatment I had from the American Medical and Nursing staffs while I was in your hands.

Except for the great trouble taken both by the doctors and nurses I might easily have been a cripple for the rest of my life. As it is I am now in a little over two months as sound as I have ever been in my life.

I got blown up on an anti-tank mine on the 1st of May, with the result that I got an eye wound, deaf in both ears. My left foot two broken bones. Right foot four broken bones, right heel fractured in four places. (os calcus). I hope that is how it is spelt.

I landed in 38 Evacuation Hospital near Beja. Within two hours I was put to bed in real sheets, examined by a Doctor, given a meal, X-Rayed, on the operating table and in plaster casts and comfortable tucked up in bed. Next day an ear specialist came two hundred miles to see me. I remained in 38 Evacuation unit until sent down to Algiers and sent to the British 95 General Hospital.

I would in particular express my gratitude to Capt. Augustine for not only his expert treatment but for his unfailing patience (I never was a good patient, I am too restless for that). To all those nurses who were always so willing to help and who did so much to relieve pain.

I am indeed Sir most grateful.

Yours sincerely
W. G. MACKAY
(Lt Col RA)
British Service

On the same day that the Daily Bulletin carried Colonel Mackay's letter Captain Montgomery added a three-line diary entry confirming the two-line entry he had made the day before. The July 20 observation had been:

Tonight at the movie we heard that Col. Bauchspies had been relieved.

The confirming entry added:

Col. Bauchspies announced at the Surgical group that he was leaving. Corps VI. Everyone pleased.

July 29 his entry, another three lines, reported:

Col. Bauchspies left this morning by plane for Casa Blanca. Lt. Col. White assumed command of unit temporarily.

The Daily Bulletin of that day made the same announcement:

NOTICE TO ALL PERSONNEL

Members of this command are grateful for the excellent leadership and training given by Colonel Rollin L. Bauchspies, and extend to him heartiest congratulations on his promotion to Surgeon, VI Corps.

As Senior Officer present for duty, Lt. Col. T. P. White assumes temporary command of this organization.

All orders and regulations published by this Headquarters will remain in force until further notice.

During Colonel Bauchspies' final week as commander of the 38th Evacuation Hospital the number of patients had varied day to day from 338 to 365. On his last day, when Charlotte's Dr. White took command of the unit, there were 356 patients, 742 vacant beds, and 38 wards in operation.

One of the last duties of Colonel Bauchspies as commander of the 38th was to award nineteen Good Conduct medals to enlisted members of the unit. The Daily Bulletin of Sunday, July 25, 1943, records the awards:

The Commanding Officer has awarded the Good Conduct Medal on Letter of Award Number 14 to the following members of this command for exemplary behaviour, efficiency and fidelity in the performance of their duties as members of this unit:

Technical Sergeant William J. Pricskett
Technical Sergeant Robert E. Laubengayer
Tech. 3rd Grade Charles L. Purdy
Sergeant Vincent J. Elliott
Sergeant John A. Boulier
Tech. 4th Grade Clarence O. Kuester, Jr.
Tech. 4th Grade Leonard (NMN) Weinheimer
Tech. 4th Grade Louise J. Bakelaar
Tech. 4th Grade Joseph W. Neil
Tech. 4th Grade Myer A. Freedberg
Tech. 4th Grade Louis A. Fink
Tech. 4th Grade Joseph B. Lucy
Tech. 4th Grade Frank C. Link
Tech. 4th Grade Kenneth M. Dale
Tech. 4th Grade Gwynfryn T. Jones
Corporal Virgil H. Cox
Corporal Kenneth R. Sears
Tech. 5th Grade Edward A. Jackson
Pvt. 1cl Richard (NMN) Duerr

The week after Colonel White assumed command of the 38th with the transfer of Colonel Bauchspies the unit marked the first anniversary of its sailing from New York for overseas service. Nine months of this year had been spent in North Africa. And now in the last weeks of the summer the heat had become for the American soldiers almost unbearably oppressive.

Captain Pickens tells in a letter written the day before Colonel White took over command of the unit that the thermometer's readings ranged from about 110 degrees to 120 degrees.

"As Damon Runyon says," he wrote, "it has been hotter here than somewhat. The thermometers we have register only in Centigrade, but by hard arithmetic we figure out the heat according to our own measure. Seldom does the mercury get under 110 during the day and more often it hangs around 120. Even with your heat wave during June you will have to admit that we have first claim, since it is no wave but a pretty steady stream and there is no relief in sight."

The heat, he went on to report, naturally caused them to think of ice cream, and ice cream they were determined to have. But how would the mess officer provide ice cream in North Africa with temperatures well above a hundred? He tells what they were able to arrange:

"Being located near a city enabled me to work out a solution to a problem that came with the hot weather. . . . We found some Italian Jews running an ice cream manufacturing place. Of course, they had no ingredients but they had equipment and occasionally the current was on in the city. I gathered together the ingredients, including sugar which I borrowed from the Air Corps with no intention of ever paying it back. They always have everything and will never miss what crumbs drop to the poor medicos. I also put in a large quantity of dehydrated eggs; that's one way of getting soldiers to eat the awful stuff; you have to camouflage it.

With all the trimmings down to the parlor, we went and asked the price of manufacture. It was 15 francs per litre or about 30 cents a quart, quite high when we were furnishing all the parts; but you can depend on the sons of Abraham to make the most of a war. We had no money in our funds and the commanding officer had forbidden us to make an assessment, so I was stymied as to how to get the stuff paid for."

How he managed to arrange payment is an interesting story:

"Just at this time the old man told me of his son who was ill and he wanted to know if we could cure him. I took one look at his son, a lad of about 23 or 24, and made a hurried diagnosis. He had an ulcerated varicose vein which looked as if we could take care of. I told the old man that I would have to have the specialists at the hospital take a look at it, but that we had the best surgeons in America with us and I knew we could cure the lad. He agreed, and I hurried out with the boy and warned Bill Pitts and Pat Imes about the case. They went over him and said that they could do the work and that it would be successful. Of course, they said, we have no right in this hospital to do any elective surgery on troops and much less on civilians. But when I told them my plight about getting the ice cream paid for, they said to bring him on in and they would do the work.

"Back I went to Papa and told him that we could fix his son up but that it was a very delicate operation and in the United States it was a very expensive one. The average cost for such surgery at home is about $75, but since they had started out to beat me so badly, I thought I would get even. I told Papa that we would do the operation for him in exchange for eight freezings of ice cream for the hospital. One freezing would have cost us 2,250 francs or about $45, so eight would amount to about $350.

"The boy had to come for several treatments before the operation, so we have not yet fulfilled our part of the bargain, but the docs assure me it will be successful. In the meantime we have been getting ice cream once every week at no cost other than the ingredients. I am just waiting for the Air Corps to kick about my excessive borrowing, but so long as they are moving along so blithely, I am not going to worry and in the meantime we beat the heat partially."

On another day the mess officer found himself in a desperate attempt to procure for the nurses of the 38th a supply of as simple and ordinarily commonplace a commodity as sewing machine needles. He relates in the same letter that unmilitary though effective procedure:

"Another experience I had recently threw me with the local French. As you know, Tunisia is a protectorate, not a department of France. They are neutral and apparently don't care to have a war fought in their backyard. For this I can't blame them, but neither do I like to do my part of it this far from home. The war has created a shortage of many things in this section and then an abundance of others.

"One of the things they are apparently short of is sewing machine needles. We picked up a sewing machine back in Oran in the early days. The nurses use it in making operating room sheets and gowns and bandages, etc. They needed some needles or at least one needle. It was like looking for it in the proverbial haystack when we tried to get it away from the local French. Our first trip, of course, was to the local Singer agency. They are as numerous here as they are all over

This photograph of a group of officers was made during the encampment at Tunis, Tunisia, North Africa, from June 21, 1943, to the next September 3.

the world. Between Singer and Eastman, Standard Oil and Coca-Cola, it is hard to forget America wherever you may be on this globe.

"Singer said they had no needles; they hadn't had any for almost two years. They also said they had no machines and from what I could see in their shop, there was little reason for their being open for business. They did tell me where I might find some needles, down at the corner of Rue Es Sadikia and Avenue Jules Ferry. Down we went to a sort of woman's dress shop where there were more jabbering French women all talking at one time and looking daggers at a couple of American soldiers. That didn't bother me since my experience at Macy's in the millinery department. I did feel more comfortable when those without too many clothes on got behind the screens. I asked for needles and they said they had some which they would sell me, but first I must get the approval slip from the Comité du Textile which was over on the second floor of a building on Rue d'Algers. One lady, who spoke very good English, said there would be no difficulty,

but she had to have the slip before she could sell to me, a sort of coupon on needles, I guess. Over to the textile office I went and ran into another snag. There the only person who could understand my French or English was an Arab in a long white robe. He said before he could get the approval I wanted I had to go to the office of the Affaires de Ration and get their approval. It was hot and I was getting a little bit bored at this run-around, but I walked the eight or ten blocks to the building and broke into the first room I came to. While I waited for someone there to get me an interpreter, another one enjoyed one of my cigarettes. They enjoy our cigarettes and take them quickly when offered.

"The interpreter came finally and after hearing my story about going to Singer and then on to the dress shop and then to the Comité Textile and then here, he finally said that they could not give me the approval I was determined to get, but that I would have to go and see the American Consul, whose office was back about where I had come from. By this time I was weary

113

of the whole affair and thought we could do without the darn needles or I would just go and take them away from the source and let the diplomatic department settle the whole thing after the war. I was tired of being shuttled around.

"The day had passed, so the next day I went to see the Consul. This time I went on the offensive and barged in to see Mr. Doolittle, our local representative. I told my story and when he began to think up some other hoops for me to jump thru, I just told him I was tired of running around and was just telling him that I was going to pick up the needles and not pay for them and it was up to him to settle the whole thing. If they wanted money for them, I was perfectly willing and able to pay, but I wasn't going to see any more government officials, French or American. Well, he said, if that was the way I felt about it, that made it simple. 'Go ahead and take the needles.' I went and took and paid and told madame, 'C'est la guerre.' "

Though at the time this letter was written, July 28, 1943, the men and women of the 38th knew of no plans for moving the base from Tunis, they seemed to sense an impending transfer of the hospital even from Africa.

"When I woke up almost a year ago headed up the cold Atlantic," Captain Pickens wrote in the concluding paragraph, "I had no idea that the majority of my first year on foreign soil would be spent in Africa. I have the feeling that more has been spent here than will be spent now. I don't anticipate any immediate change, but you never can tell. In spite of our feeling that it would take too long to get organized, it still keeps grinding along and progress has been made. Benito's quitting has given us all encouragement that it will not take too long before this theatre will be cleared of the rats that have infested it. I am glad to hear Mr. Roosevelt say the leaders will be brought to trial and punished. I hope we don't begin to pussyfoot about this business and begin to feel sorry for those who caused this trouble, when things begin to go against them. It has not been pleasant to spend a year away from home and loved ones and there are too many gold stars appearing in the States. Someone must pay."

He expressed what was perhaps his fellow soldiers' opinions concerning the involvement of the United States on the ending of the war in the political affairs of that part of the world:

"I feel that we should keep our hand in what goes on in this section of the world. These Arabs should be given a chance to go to school and own land and have some medical attention. With all of our poor treatment of the Negroes in our section, they have at least had these few opportunities. They have not been slaves for a good many years and when they were it was open and above board. While we are going about the world liberating people we can do a little job thru this section. It won't be hard and it can be done. But," he hastened to add, "I must not get involved in these subjects. In the Army we are not supposed to think and certainly not supposed to speak our minds. Someone might say I sound like Billy Mitchell."

15

Within less than two weeks after Colonel White assumed temporary command of the 38th Evacuation Hospital and three weeks before the unit would be moved from its base at Tunis to follow the fighting front into Italy, the unit would receive further national recognition.

Time Magazine of August 9, 1943, in the leading article in its section devoted to medicine, would give a full-page discussion to what it titled *The Charlotte Evac*, and would illustrate the article with a two-column Associated Press photograph captioned *Charlotte Evac in Algeria*.

It happened that *Time's* correspondent in North Africa at that time was a young man named John Hersey. He would become famous both as a correspondent and an author. In fact, he had already published two best-selling volumes relating to the war in the Pacific, *Men on Bataan* and *Into the Valley*. Mr. Hersey had married a Charlotte girl, Frances Ann Cannon, and when his exhaustive schedule would permit it, he and his family would return to Charlotte for a visit.

"The term evacuation hospital may have a sound unpleasantly antiseptic to civilians," the *Time* report began. "To the badly wounded soldier it sounds like the difference between life and death. For the 'evac' hospital is the nearest place to gunfire where a wounded man can get more than emergency treatment. Until he gets there, a soldier keeps his boots on.

"Waiting last week on the African mainland to put the sick and wounded from Sicily to bed was the Charlotte, N. C., Evacuation Hospital, an all-tent, mobile affair, with over 1,000 cots and a big staff of doctors, nurses and enlisted men. Correspondent Ernie Pyle has told how this evac took in patients twelve hours after the U.S. landing near Algiers last November."

Time goes on to reveal the story of the 38th:

"*It's Different.* With over 9,000 patients and only 19 deaths behind it, the Charlotte Evac now has the honor of handling casualties from Sicily and routing them to other evacs or to station hospitals in the rear. Most such medical units are volunteer doctor groups backed by rich, big-city hospitals. This evac is different: its medical staff is composed of young doctors from Charlotte, N. C., and a sprinkling of other doctors, mainly Southerners. As Charlotte has no rich hospital, initial support for the unit came from the proceeds of a local show and from contributions around town."

The article says of the conception of the unit:

"The idea got started when blunt, handsome, 38-year-old Surgeon Paul Sanger confided to General Marshall at a cocktail party in 1940 that the Charlotte doctors wanted to form an Army unit. The unit was authorized in December, went on active duty at Fort Bragg in March, 1942, left for England Aug. 6, scrambled ashore in Africa Nov. 7, and was fully set up about ten miles from Oran a few days later. At Oran, the unit handled 2,027 patients."

It continues with other one-line descriptions of some of the officers in the 38th:

"Besides Surgeon Sanger, now a lieutenant colonel, there is medium-sized thin Lieut. Colonel Thomas Preston White, who heads the medical staff, Lieut. Colonel George T. Wood, executive officer, Dentist Vaiden Kendrick, Charlotte's ace tooth puller (there was a rush of dental procrastinators to his chair when he announced he was leaving Charlotte). Charlotte also contributed several other doctors, two businesss managers—Captain Stanton Pickens, who used to work for the Coca-Cola Co., and 'Buck' Medearis, manager of a laundry—and many of the nurses. Once when the Evac was stuck in a siding waiting to move nearer the front, the engineer of a train going the other way called: 'Anyone from Charlotte, N. C.?' The answering chorus nearly knocked him from his cab."

The *Time* account continues with mention of the commanding officer who had been transferred after the article was written:

"Though not from Charlotte, the commanding officer is one of the Evac's favorite characters: he is a non-medical Army man, Colonel Rollin L. Bauchspies of Nauch Chunk, Pa., who calls the hospitals venereal disease section 'Casanova.' The enlisted men of the unit are mostly New Englanders. They come in for a lot of Mason-Dixon Line ribbing.

"During the Mateur and Bizerte battles the Charlotte Evac was just behind the lines," the *Time* account continues. "The unit got so good at moving that in the final North African push it discharged patients in Beja and received some in Tunis (some 55 miles apart) on the same day."

The *Time* correspondent pictures the hospital in its Tunis location:

"Compared with those dynamic days, the tent hospital on its broad hill with gravel driveways now has a settled look. Italian prisoners have installed running water and some of the other comforts of home. The pharmacy hands out prescriptions and runs a blood bank (plasma is not enough for some cases with great blood loss, and Evac stores whole blood bled from its own personnel). The shock tents give transfusions, prepare men for operations; the operating tent can handle 16 cases an hour around the clock. The dentistry tent with only three chairs was for a long time the only place in North Africa where U.S. servicemen could get false teeth.

"As usual in war, there is much improvised equipment: sterilizers made from potato cans, shower baths made from gasoline drums, hinges from shell cases, an icebox from a Coca-Cola vending machine, can openers from any old thing (though 90 per cent of field rations come in cans, the hospital set out without a single can opener). The Evac's most elaborate contrivance is a 'Hawley' table, a device for holding a man's body suspended for the application of big casts, which some men from the Air Corps Ordnance Department made from spare parts."

The time reporter was impressed by the impartial treatment given the sick and wounded even though they may be of the enemy forces. He writes:

"Sicilian casualties (both Allied and Axis) are picked up by the U.S. Army Medical Corps in Sicily, get first aid, are then flown over the water in an air ambulance to a field near the Evac. A ground ambulance picks them up and deposits them at the hospital's receiving tent. There a casualty is treated much like a patient entering a ward at home. His field medical record is begun with entries describing his wound and how he got it—these entries are copied from the tag attached to his coverall. The record, stamped with the man's 'dog tag' and put in an envelope, goes with the patient until his hospital discharge, even if he goes to the United States to convalesce."

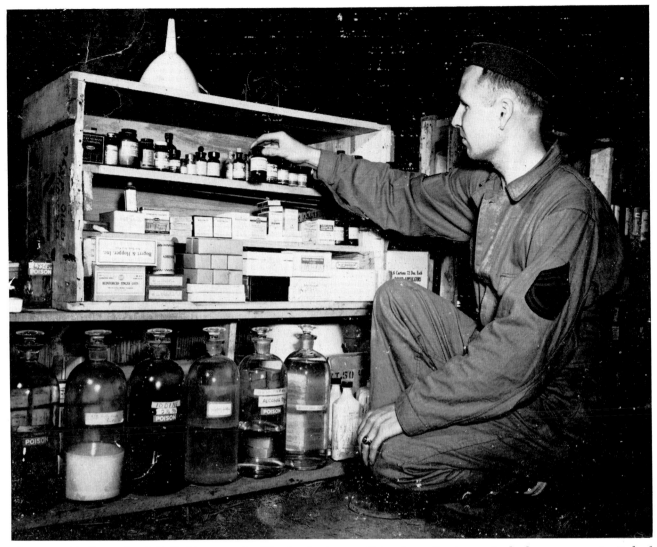

Pharmacist's aide Richard B. Robinson at St. Cloud selecting medicine from the improvised pharmacy constructed of wooden packing cases.

He goes on with his description of the hospital's routine:

"Patients are assigned to wards according to their injuries; there are orthopedic wards, head and spine wards, malaria, abdominal wound and dysentery wards. At his ward a patient is undressed, put in pajamas. His clothes, except for his shoes, helmet and gas mask, are stored away in a labeled bag. After that, he is X-rayed to find whatever metal he is carrying inside him, or the extent of his hurt. Then he is given what dressing and surgery he needs. As soon as a patient's condition warrants moving, he is sent to a hospital farther to the rear."

The *Time* account closes with a description of the photograph illustrating the article:

"The Charlotte Evac is a desperately efficient place these days, but its personnel still finds time for a little fun. Right now on the ground outside the surgical tent are two neat patches outlined in white pebbles and decorated with a heart-and-arrows design that says: 'Lieut. Perryman, Miss Guyett. Ward 28.' "

Seven weeks after John Hersey's article appeared in *Time*, Mr. Hersey came to Charlotte with his wife and two children for a short vacation before returning to his duties in New York. On Sunday morning, September 26, the *Charlotte Observer* carried an interview with the *Time* correspondent in which he related further details of his visit to the 38th in Africa. By that time, although he did not know it, the hospital had moved from North Africa to its location at Paestum in Italy.

"The best meal John Hersey had in Africa was the one he stumbled into one day when he came upon Charlotte's 38th Evacuation unit while searching along a back road in Tunis for a certain bombardment group," the lead paragraph in the *Observer* interview reported.

" 'Those fellows from Charlotte were doing all right,'

116

said Mr. Hersey yesterday," the article continued. " 'They were eating well. In fact'—he grinned—'I went back to see them several times. They had their bivouac all fixed up, too. They got some Italian prisoners over there and put in running water, and had even rigged themselves up a shower bath. If there is any such a thing as having a civilized war, they were having it then.' "

After an explanatory paragraph revealing Mr. Hersey's recent return from the African assignment for *Time*, the interview continued:

"The Charlotte unit, he thought, has likely moved up into Italy somewhere in the Naples area. He didn't know positively where it was. He knew quite a number of the Charlotte men before he ran into them that day in Africa and he was delighted to see them again, he said. 'We were out rambling along on a back road up in Tunis trying to find a bombardment group when I saw a sign on the side of the road, '38th Evacuation.' So I decided right then I didn't want to look for that bombardment group and I went down the road until I came upon the Charlotte crowd. We really had a good meal, too. They were looking fine, had the place all fixed up, and were living about as civilized a life as anybody I saw over there. I knew a bunch of them already and I met a lot of others. There were Paul Sanger, Buck Medearis, Stan Pickens, George Snyder, Stokes Munroe, Duncan Calder, Pres White and a lot of other fellows.'

"He even had some Coca-Colas with the Charlotte crowd, he said. You see American bottled drinks frequently. 'They even made Coca-Colas over there,' he said. 'But none of that for me. The syrup is real, all right, but they mix it with some sort of Algerian fizz-water that has lost its fizz. Well, it's worse than flat.' "

16

Three weeks after Colonel Bauchspies was transferred from the 38th, his adjutant, Captain A. J. Guenther, was transferred to another unit. His last signature on the Daily Bulletin was on August 20. That same day Captain Montgomery confided to his diary:

Capt. Guenther left today. Now all regular Army is out. We should have a good unit.

Four days later, August 24th, Captain Montgomery recorded:

The hospital closed officially at noon today. Packing has started.

It was on a Tuesday that the 38th closed its operation at Tunis. The Daily Bulletin for the following Saturday, August 28, announced:

By Special Order 166, Commanding General, Eastern Base Section, under the provisions of Circular No. 116, NATOUSA, the announcement is made of the appointment of Lt. Colonel George T. Wood, Jr., as Commanding Officer of the 38th Evacuation Hospital, effective 18 August 1943.

The next day, Sunday, one month and one day after he had written his last letter home, Captain Pickens wrote of the dullness of existence as the 38th's members awaited transfer to their next location:

"Our life has been so dull during the last few weeks," said he, "that there has been no inspiration for writing. Our hospital is closed and we await orders. We have been busy for awhile but now it has slowed down. We take time to get to the beach for a swim but seldom go into town. We have 'done' the town and have no reason for going in. We get used to staying in our tents and with our own crowd and it is hard to stir away. We have limited transportation and altho it is about a mile into the center of the city, we don't feel like walking. Calisthenics have started again in the morning and the extra exercise, plus the occasional trip to the beach, makes the cot feel mighty good when the day is finished. We are getting back into shape for some of the hardships that are sure to be ahead. The war news has been good these last few weeks and I fear we are prone to be too optimistic. The really rough sledding is before us. Our landing in Africa was hazardous enough, but I fear it was mild compared to what we may expect. The landing in Sicily was accomplished with small loss, but the coordination was almost perfect. I hope it continues."

A few days before he wrote that letter, Captain Pickens revealed, he and Colonel White had occasion to go down to Constantine on a mission for the hospital. His report of the trip reveals the difficulty at that time of obtaining seats on airplanes even when the missions

During one of the pauses between pulling or drilling teeth, Milo Hoffman catches some sunshine.

were on official Army assignments. He tells of that particular incident:

"It developed rather suddenly for me, although he had been planning it for some time. I appreciate his thinking of having me join him, since I had a pleasant experience. We arose early the other morning and had a driver take us to the nearest airport. There we made application for a seat to Telergma, the nearest airport to Constantine. We had some argument with the lieutenant in charge about the proper priority. Even here and in the Army you have to have a priority. We ended up with a No. 2, which we thought was very poor. At the time we received it the lieutenant said that the 8:30 plane had been cancelled and that our seats were on the 12:40 plane. A seat on one of these courier planes consists of a small space on a long aluminum bench that runs along the side of the plane. You squeeze in there among the mail bags and any important freight that must go thru. We were sorely disappointed in the delay and asked if there was a chance of getting other rides. The lieutenant said we might go to the neighboring field and see if the British had anything going down.

"Over we went and we had no luck, but there they said they would call Foch Field on the other side of the city and see if there were any freight planes going thru. The reply came back that they had four planes there waiting to get out and if we would hurry we might catch one. We drove thru the city like mad in the rattling jeep and got into the office of the other port in time. They booked us and said to go out and get into the second plane on the right. We checked and

asked to be sure if that plane was going to Telergma. Then the sergeant said no, the planes were all going to Palermo and that was what he had thought we had wanted when the telephone call came thru from the other field.

"So we were stymied again. I told the Colonel if he had no particular objection we might go on to Palermo, since it had been recommended so highly by my mother-in-law and since the enemy was no longer there. Of course, he said, we would have to get to Constantine. Then the thought hit us that possibly the photographing group might have a plane going in that direction, so over to that field we went. No, they said, the only plane they had going out was to take a general to Sicily and he wanted no company. We went back to the original field to wait for the midday courier. While standing around and watching the incoming and outgoing planes and hearing the conversation of the passengers, in came a general from London. He went to the nearest telephone and tried to call another general. He had been used to the conveniences of England and was slightly irritated with the poor communications in Africa. I overheard his trying to locate his associate and knew he was the one who was leaving for Sicily, so I walked up, and in my best military manner told him where he might find the general."

While the general was putting through this call, he talked with Captain Pickens, and the Charlotte officer learned that the general had met his brother Bob in London. After awhile their plane came in and he and Colonel White took off for the airfield near Constantine, where they arrived in about two hours. From the field they were provided transportation into Constantine.

"From the city proper we went out to a general hospital where Colonel White attended to his work and where we spent the night. The hospital is staffed by people from the University of Minnesota. They were very cordial and kind to us. We enjoyed the visit. The following afternoon we started back to our station. The priority No. 2 we thought was so poor turned out to be the highest one issued except by Mr. Roosevelt or Mr. Churchill or General Eisenhower. However, it did not get us on the last courier headed for the east by just a minute. We had to take a B-26 that was going east a few minutes later. Everyone says a B-26 is not safe and we boarded this one with plenty of misgivings. But, I must say, we made our trip back in one hour and with as comfortable a takeoff and landing as you could ask. We moved along at 10,000 feet and listened to the London radio thru the earphones used by the radio-navigator. The whole trip was most pleasant."

The 38th's Daily Bulletin of August 30, 1943, carried two congratulatory messages. The first was from the

President of the United States, the second from King George VI of England.

President Roosevelt's declared:

"All of us are thrilled over the Sicilian campaign now successfully concluded in accordance with the timing and planning of the Allies. This is especially true when we realize that the enemy forces in Sicily amounted to 405,000 men. The events of the past thirty-eight days show what can be done by teamwork based on preparation, training, timing, and above all on gallantry on land, on sea, and in the air. From the ancient Citadel of Quebec I send to you my warm congratulations, and to the officers and men under your command, British, Canadian, French and American, my thanks and enthusiastic approbation. Tell them 'well done.'"

King George's message to the Allied Forces was substantially the same:

"On the final accomplishment of the occupation of Sicily, I wish to send to you and to all members of the forces that you command with such distinction my heartfelt congratulations on a great achievement. Throughout the British Empire, we have watched with admiration the ordered progress of the campaign by sea, by land, and by air, and we rejoice at its successful conclusion. I should be grateful if you would convey to my British and Canadian troops a special assurance of my pride in their share in this victory."

That same day, August 30, 1943, General Clark wrote to Colonel Bauchspies, who two days before had been officially succeeded by Colonel Wood as commanding officer of the 38th, to express his satisfaction at the unit's having been assigned to the Fifth Army. The letter, marked RESTRICTED at that time, would remain in the records of the unit:

General Clark wrote:

"My dear Colonel Bauchspies:

"I want you and the personnel of your command to know that I am proud to have your organization assigned to the Fifth Army. In addition to the many U.S. organizations which belong to us, we are fortunate in also having British and French troops as a part of the Fifth Army. All of these Allied organizations will enter combat as an Army team, with but one thought in mind —the complete destruction of our despised enemy who for years has attempted to deprive us and our loved ones at home of the liberties and principles of freedom for which our country has always stood.

"I want you to explain personally to your men the necessity for being well disciplined and thoroughly trained, in order that they will outfight the German soldier who for years has been trained and disciplined for battle.

"Great opportunities lie ahead of our Fifth Army, opportunities which will lead to the complete liberation of Europe from its present rule of tyranny. It is a great privilege that we of the Fifth Army can be associated with such an enterprise. If your organization is alert, determined, disciplined and trained in the manner in which you are capable of being, we can and will defeat the enemy on the field of battle. It is absolutely essential that your organization do its part to win this victory.

"I am confident that the Fifth Army will be faithful to the American soldiers of the past and to the United States of America, whose glorious existence and development it is our privilege and duty to guarantee. With each man doing his duty to the exclusion of every other consideration, we shall be worthy of our trust. Our cause is a righteous one, and God will direct us in our undertaking.

"It is my desire that the contents of this letter be brought to the attention of every member of your command.

"Sincerely,
"Mark W. Clark,
Lieutenant General, USA,
Commanding"

On September 1, two days after General Clark wrote this letter, the Daily Bulletin temporarily suspended publication. The next day Captain Montgomery wrote in his diary the longest entry he had written since his landing in Africa on November 9 the year before. He lavished thirteen lines to record:

At nine this morning all our personal tents were struck and packed. Personal luggage was ready. I am to take the advance detail and go on the first train. Suppose to have left at noon. The train was ready at five.
Were loaded by 10 PM. 16 cars of equipment, two (40 and 8) for men. Men preferred the open cars. Bob with me. We have our cots, mattresses, sheets, etc., and half a car. Very comfortable. Finelli, Solomato, Zeilinski are with us. Pulled out of Tunis 10:45 PM.

His entry the following day, September 3, was much shorter:

Awoke after a good night's sleep at Medjez-El-Bab. 30 miles from Tunis. Engine is broken. Replaced it & left at noon. Elias & Riegan were A.W.O.L but caught up tonight.

September 4 he wrote but three lines:

During night 4 cars with 11 men taken from train to reduce load. Expect to be joined at Krubes.

Two days later, on September 6, he was again reckless with his supply of green ink and wrote:

Yesterday at Devivier was left with 3 men getting water. Said we would be an hour there. Left five minutes later. While there the 4 cars came in. Men had no rations. Rode to Krubes with them where I drew rations. Our train had gone. Last night I slept on a flat car. Was I filthy this morning. The engine broke this morning. Bummed a ride to Setif. Our train had gone. Continued on the truck for 100 miles. Met the train at Maillot. It was good to get back to my boxcar.

But they finally reached Oran. He wrote on September 7:

Arrived at Oran at 5:30 PM. At the staging area No. 1 near Fleurus at seven. In pyramidal tents.

His next day's recording was even briefer:

Sept. 8th. Went to Oran. Many changes since March. Italy surrendered today.

More than a score of years after it happened Dr. William Matthews recalled with keen delight their encountering their colleague, Jack Montgomery, that day in North Africa when he was attempting to hitch a ride after his train had left him stranded.

He tells the story with relish:

"The funniest thing that ever happened to us during the whole war, as I remember it now anyway, was Jack Montgomery's getting left and how he looked that day. We were taking the train from Tunis back to Oran so that we could be combat loaded. We came back in four or five groups, and I was in the last one breaking up camp. The truth of the matter is that we had a problem in breaking up the camp because of everything we had acquired in North Africa. For example, we had a generator that would light a town of 3,000 people. It was hard to get rid of it; you couldn't just leave it sitting out there in the field, and yet nobody wanted to sign for it. Or a water-purifying system that would take care of a town of 10,000; we weren't supposed to have had either one. We had picked up a lot of stuff for the hospital by the method of what we called moonlight requisition, like the way we sometimes ate.

"But, anyway, I was in the last group and with us was Bub Porter, I remember, and Bob Augustine. Bob wasn't a local fellow. He was an orthopedist, and a very good one. He happened to join our unit, I believe, because he had had a residency at Duke, maybe finished it here. But before he took medicine he had got a degree in engineering; for that reason he ended up being what you might call a planning officer. When we got into a new area, Bob would figure out the layout of the camp, tell where to set up the tents, that sort of thing.

"Well, this day we were ready to go, having got rid of our equipment in one way or another, and we were traveling in old 40-and-8 cars. We had fixed up our car for traveling in style. We had taken rugs and other things left from breaking camp, and we had two 55-gallon drums of water, and we bartered for eggs and other stuff along the way; so we were getting on fine. But Augustine had got in bad with the French engineer of the train; the fellow had wanted to pull out before Bob was ready and they'd had quite a tiff about it. But we'd got the thing straightened out and were going along down the road, when we looked out and there stood a bald-headed fellow with nothing on but a pair of shorts and GI shoes and a little bit of a pot in the middle. The fellow was waving desperately and shouting. We saw it was Jack Montgomery. Later we learned that he had got off to get something, some water I believe he said, or maybe boiled eggs.

"And speaking of boiled eggs," Dr. Matthews continues his recital of that North African experience, "I remember we had four Jewish boys on our train. They were good boys, and good traders. I recall we had some enlisted men, sixteen, I think, riding the cars to keep the Arabs from stealing from us. Of course, the Arabs got around this by stealing from the opposite sides of the cars from the sides on which the enlisted men happened to be sitting. It was always a job trying to protect things.

"This day while the train was stopped for a few minutes a man came up to the side of the train, an Arab, with a tremendously big woven basket of fresh eggs. He said they were fresh anyway, and they appeared to be edible. Well, one of these enlisted fellows, one of the four Jewish boys who prided themselves on being such sharp traders, looked at the basket of eggs and began trying to trade with the Arab. Our boy wanted to barter candy for the eggs. It was one of the big five-pound cans that we had been issued, but they had doctored it. They had taken out the candy, put some rocks and papers in the bottom to make the weight right, and then they'd covered this with about two layers of the candy.

"It was always the practice of our boys in bartering with the Arabs to haggle until just the last moment before the train got moving. So this day our fellow argued and haggled, though he was willing from the start to make the swap of candy for the eggs, until the train began moving. In fact, the Arab was running along the track by the time they agreed to trade. Our boy handed down the can of candy covered rocks and pulled the basket in the window, and with visions of all the good boiled eggs he and his buddies were going to have and delighted that he had worked such a clever trick on the Arab, he set the basket of eggs on the seat beside him and began to check on the bargain he'd made.

"Well, it didn't take him long to count his eggs. Two layers down he came to papers and under the papers neatly arranged a peck or so of North African rocks!"

During this period of Captain Montgomery's entries recording the movement of the hospital from Tunis a

120

considerably more detailed account of the transfer was being written by Captain Pickens in the longest and the last letter he would write home from Africa. The letter, dated September 2-7, 1943, gives the most complete available account recorded by any of the members of the 38th during this first week in September of 1943, one of the more eventful periods of the unit's action-crowded existence.

From North Africa he began writing:

"We leave our old station with a few things I would like to remember, things that might not interest you, but which will remain with me. Here are a few of them: the dust that covered everything in the tents; it sifted thru the clothes, it spread over the food before we could eat; the sirocco with its deadening heat from the southern desert; the selling of odd things we had accumulated during the last few days we were there; the Arabs and Jews had charged us exorbitant prices for meals and souvenirs, so we had to get it back; we charged and received 200 francs ($4) for a carton of stale cigarettes, 50 francs for wornout socks, old hand-kerchiefs brought 25 francs, underclothes that would stand very little strain brought as high as 100 francs; the comfort of having ice almost every day; the trips to the beaches with the sand cutting us on a windy day; trips into the Arabic section to trade and shop and visit; ice cream; the excitement when the Sicilian campaign started; the relief that came with the change in command; the buying of fresh vegetables, fruit, and melons (we never did find any corn); the neighboring Jews doing our laundry at high prices if we furnished the soap, and I am sure that over half of the soap is still there; the hiring of civilians for the first time to work in the hospitals; we tried a group that had been bombed out of their homes but they were very unsatisfactory as workers and carried off too many supplies; the Arabs that came into the hospital as patients when they had inadvertently stepped on a hidden mine; Mac Jackson's stop on his way back to Charlotte; John Hersey's and Raymond Clapper's visits to the hospital; the Arab boys selling the English newspaper the British published three times a week giving the news; the pleasant association with the Intelligence Group staying near us; the RAF descending on us to visit with the 'sisters;' watching the nearby air raids which lighted up the sky at night like a Fourth of July fireworks; the ground shaking with the big guns firing and the bombs dropping; the many visitors (we were at the crossroads and everyone stopped for the night, all ranks); the orderly packing and departure."

He went on to describe the unit's movement from the Tunis area:

"On the French trains operated by British transportation officers we spent five days to cover some

Drs. Calder, left, and Pennington pose during a moment's relaxing.

eight or nine hundred miles, an average of less than 200 miles per 24 hours. It was slow going, but we had learned from previous experience how to prepare for it and what to do. We had a kitchen car which allowed us two hot meals per day during the travel. The men used the 40 and 8's, the officers had compartment cars with wooden seats, the women had cushioned seats in their compartments. In my compartment I took the floor with my air mattress and spare blanket and slept quite comfortably. At the many stops we had to make we traded with the Arabs for melons, eggs, and ice. At one stop we were able to get a shower of good cold water. That always helps on a long trip, and more so when your car is attached too close to the locomotive. A part of the trip was covered with good American engineers operating the engine. It was a relief when we found them on the front, since we could make arrangements for the eating and know when to expect to pull out. When the French ran the train there was no telling when they would take off."

One of the "good American engineers" to whom Captain Pickens referred was a fellow Charlottean, the 38th group on that train happily discovered. He was Luther C. Clanton of the 761st Railway Transportation Company, Military Railway Service. Engineer Clanton, now retired and living in Charlotte, recalls well the assignment:

"We picked them up at St. Barbe about five miles from Oran. I had brought the engine out from Oran. There must have been about a dozen or so coaches in the Charlotte party. I remember when I got there I started back through the coaches. 'Anybody here from Charlotte, North Carolina?' I yelled out.

"'Everybody here's from Charlotte!' they hollered back. Pretty soon I was talking to the crowd and asking

121

Lieutenants Christine Wills, left, and Mary Blandford model the service coveralls that the hard working 38th nurses wore most of the time overseas.

Lieutenant Elva Wells, right, and Beth Killeen stand in front of the hospital's Receiving sign.

The X-ray service officers, Tyson, left, and Colin Munroe, chief and assistant chief, are dressed and shined and ready for a short rest leave.

about news from home. I surely was glad to run into that bunch. I remember Dr. Preston White introduced me to a fellow named Ernie Pyle.

" 'Ernie, you're one of these newspaper correspondents, aren't you?' I remember I asked him. Dr. White told me he had met Pyle at a hotel in Oran and while they were there, Dr. White said, Ernie helped him unstop the toilet in his bathroom. It's funny the things you remember after all these years."

The locomotive with which he shuttled troops and supplies from Oran to Algiers was a big one, he remembers. "It had sixteen wheels, and we burned briquettes compressed with creosote to provide the steam. We had two engine crews; one slept while the other was on duty, with three in the cab, the engineer and fireman, and a conductor. The Charlotte crowd was on a siding when we met them, as I recall. We pulled out late in the afternoon, went all night and about all the next day. We had no headlights, because of air raids, and had to feel our way—through tunnels, over bridges—not knowing just what was ahead. But we made it all right, though we had an air raid right after we got to Algiers."

Captain Pickens continues his account of this trip toward the embarkation port:

His account of the trip toward the embarkation port continued:

"Some of our group had traveled back in our own trucks. One officer had flown back a few days ahead of us. He was the lucky one of the crowd. He was Captain Medearis, and it took all of his persuasive powers to keep our allies from unloading the train about 20

miles from our destination in the middle of the night. He finally persuaded them that it would save truck wear and gasoline and since the train had to pull into the city anyway, why not let the personnel go in. That allowed us to get off of the train at a reasonable hour in the morning instead of 3 A.M. as they had planned. We were whisked out to our area about seven miles from the city. The nurses were sent to another area where all the females are kept, including the first contingent of WACs that are filing into Africa. Our area was a most temporary setup. We knew we had only a short stay there and the Army knew the same thing, so we both did little to add to the comfort of the place. The only thing the Army provided was a lot of pyramidal tents. We put in our own bedding and fortunately had our own kitchen with us. It was rough, but fair enough for a short stay. The wind blew and the dust sifted in. Everything was grimy until the last day we were there and then the rains came and great rivulets ran thru our tents and on down the hill. It settled the dust and also some of our enthusiasm."

Captain Pickens reveals opportunities they had for relaxation as they awaited embarkation:

"During our stay back near our original landing spot in Africa we had time to get into the city. There the Army had provided a comfortable officers' club with a snack bar with sandwiches and a drink bar and comfortable lounge chairs. The radio gave us the news on the hour, always from London. In the afternoon an orchestra played and there was dancing if there were any females. Some of the nurses came and a few of the WAC officers, but they were outnumbered 100 to 1.

There was a setup for showers, too. In another section of the city the Red Cross had set up a community spot for officers also. It was the first time that I had seen anything done for officers since I had been in the Army. Of course, all of this was done considerably back and away from any field work or any fighting. It was pleasant to get in town and get a bath, get some of that dust off and sit in comfortable chairs and read or listen to the radio and visit with the numerous officers that we knew and had not seen for some time. It was at the Officers' Club that I saw most of the Emory unit and visited with them. They were staying not far from us and had been in Africa for only a few days. They had about the same facilities, which amounted to nothing except a tent over their heads. It was a bit of a shock to them not to have all the comforts of home that can be found around most any Army camp in the United States. They were taking it in good graces but they did not like it. There was nothing they could do about it, however. We renewed our acquaintance with some French people we had known back last winter and some of us had a meal with them one evening. They all promised to come and see us in the States after the war, so you had better prepare for foreign visitors in droves when this mess is over."

Finally the day arrived for them to embark. He reviews the details of boarding ship:

"When the day came for us to board our transport, the rains came. We moved down to the docks in the long convoy and edged up right alongside the big ship which was to be our next home. Our equipment had been placed on a freighter except that housekeeping equipment that we always carry with us. Just as we were getting ready to board the ship, whistles blew and bells clanged and the gangplank was hoisted and the ship pulled out. I never thought a large ocean-going liner could move away from a pier so rapidly. In ten minutes it was almost out of sight and there we stood in the rain.

"I thought, well, this is the first time I had missed the boat. I have heard that expression all my life, but this was the first time it had ever happened to me. In spite of the rain and the drenched clothes, we all had to laugh at our predicament. We knew the nurses were on board and two of our officers, Lt. Col. White and Sanger. We all said, 'All right, we didn't want to go and fight a war anyway.' Let the blooming ship go wherever it wanted to go.

"It was not long before we learned that the ship had just pulled out to another part of the harbor and we could board it from another section of the city with the aid of barges. It had turned dark by this time and I was in a truck with my kitchen equipment and there is one thing you will learn in the Army, and that is, if you don't look after your own equipment, no one else will, so I was all set to stay with my stuff until it was loaded on that ship. The personnel got off on the personnel barges and disappeared in the rain. Buck and Augustine and Jimmy Dunn and I stayed behind to see that all the personal baggage got aboard. We finally located some barges and about midnight had all of our equipment loaded. Then the problem came up as to how to get the barges moved out to the big ship.

"I went to the Navy and asked their aid. They in turn gave me the French port authorities and they said they could not move us until after their workmen had had their midnight meal. That meant waiting until after one A.M. After I reported back to the crew we all thought that possibly we could find something to eat, too. I realized that I had not eaten anything since lunch and that was only a cold can of the famous 'C' rations, consisting of meat and vegetable stew with some crackers and some lemonade. Some Negro troops were having 'chow' down the wharf from us. We sent the men down to see what they could get. They found some very poor coffee and some applesauce. It tasted good in the rain.

"When I went back to the Navy down the row of docks, they were having a midnight snack and after I stood on one foot and then on the other for about ten minutes, one of their number offered me a cheese sandwich and a cup of coffee. Modestly I accepted it and nearly choked getting it down, I was so hungry and wet and cold.

"They called the French and they said they were ready to move us, but that they had no tugs available and would not have any for two hours. They were going to be busy getting some gasoline loaded on another ship. I felt like giving up and yet I knew it would not be safe to leave those two barges loaded with suitcases and bedding rolls and 'A' bags for the men sitting out there in that harbor. I pleaded with the Navy but they said they couldn't do anything for us. Finally a young corporal came in and overheard my plight. When I had given up and was prepared to spend the night on that barge in the rain and had started out of the Navy office, the corporal spoke up and said he knew how to run a barge; he was from New Orleans, and if we could find one he would see that we got our stuff to the ship. Out we went together to find a tug. We found one down the harbor all steamed up with the French still enjoying the midnight meal somewhere else. The Arab crew of two was aboard, so we just took it and started to move our stuff. The corporal knew how to maneuver a tug and it was not long before we were alongside the big ship.

"There, we could get no one to answer our calls.

Finally, the corporal cut loose on his whistle and then the English sailors began to stick their heads out of portholes. We got the gangplanks lowered and fastened the barges alongside and went aboard. I sent the crew of our men who had loaded the barges on to bed and decided to let the rest of the crew take over in the morning. Bob Miller had been along with us, too, and had been responsible for seeing that a lot of the equipment got on board. Buck and Jimmy had disappeared during the night around midnight, so it was Bob, Augustine and I that had the load. We found our quarters and fell into our bunks at a little after 3 A.M.

"The next morning the commanding officer sent word to us that we need not worry about the loading, that others would take over and see that everything was put on board. That was a relief. It had been a trying night and the rain had just kept coming down. It was not long before the big ship pulled up its two anchors and we were moving along the coast of Africa. For some time to come we had done our last walking on African soil. It was with a bit of relief that we watched it slip by us. We were tired of the dust and the rain and the mud. It was comfortable to stand on a ship where things were fairly clean and look at the blue water beneath and watch the coast slip along. What the future held was anyone's guess, but so far as Africa was concerned, we had done our duty and done it well. Charlotte's hospital had done a good job."

They had been on African soil ten months almost to the day, months filled with experiences none would ever forget. But Captain Pickens' letter continues with his description of the Mediterranean crossing:

"We picked up the rest of our convoy and left Africa behind and immediately began to see the islands of the Mediterranean. We guessed as to their names but didn't worry too much about it. There were eighteen officers in the large, or rather enlarged, stateroom where I was quartered. Fortunately none of them snored too loudly. We made the best of the crowded situation and, I think, lived together in good harmony. The water was turned on twice a day, in the morning from 6 to 6:30 and in the afternoon from 4 to 4:30. In the morning the early risers filled all available containers, including canteens and helmets. This allowed us to wash and shave in shifts at the two available basins. Across the hall the large bathtubs had plenty of hot and cold salt water for washing, but it was necessary to have a little fresh water to get the salt water off. It was good just to relax in those big tubs and soak. It had been so long since we had had a chance to do that."

He tells of the diversions aboard ship:

"In the lounge of the ship there was always a rummy game or a bridge game going on. Rummy took the place of chess on this move. At night it was crowded and the smoke was thick, since the blackout was strictly enforced. One night we had some entertainment put on by some of the personnel on board. There was a cry for the 38th and their glee club, but we had not practiced for some time, so we could not perform. During the day there were the usual boat drills and action stations. At boat drill you hurry to your appointed spot and wait. At action station you get off the deck and get under cover.

"The crossing was uneventful. I am satisfied with that, I am not interested in running into enemy action. On occasions we have come too near for comfort. It gets awfully personal at times. A big balloon floated along on the tail of the ship with us. They are placed there to keep a plane from coming in low and strafing the ship. Occasionally the gun crews would check their guns and fire a few rounds. The big cannon on board would shake the ship when they fired, but it was comfortable to know they were there."

He describes next the arrival on the shores of Italy:

"The landing was also uneventful, but the steady pounding of the artillery up the coast, or to the north of us could be plainly heard. We landed on almost every type of craft. From the big ship we took off on what is called an L.C.I. (landing craft Infantry) and when we were as near the shore as that boat could take us we moved on to what is called a duck. A duck is a most ingenious concoction. It is a 2½-ton truck with boat sides and a propeller. It is steered in the water with the steering wheel by just turning the front wheels. When the duck gets up to the beach, the gear is shifted from propeller to wheel drive and it takes off on the land like any truck. The wheels can be used in about five feet of water. We dashed along in the surf and then smoothly eased up on the shores of Italy. The only thing we did not ride or sail in was the amphibious jeep, but they were there and being put to good use."

He gives much credit for the smooth landing that day to the efficiency of the Engineers.

"One of our earlier instructors back at Bragg once said that 'the product of the battle is confusion,' and a beach landing with a war not ten miles away can prove that. The Engineers had cleared a part of the beach of barbed wire and marked the safe route over which there were no mines. All manner of units were unloading at the same time and all were moving in different directions. Signal, infantry, anti-aircraft with their guns, artillery, tanks and anti-tanks, quartermaster, medical and even AMGOT (Allied Military Government of Occupied Territory) all were pouring into Italy. Everyone moved swiftly to get off the beaches; it was not healthy to get caught there. Inland

This is another picture posed in North Africa. The "wounded" soldier about to enter the surgical tent, perhaps to have his "wound" dressed, is Ian (Scotty) MacLean; the soldier wearing cap is Robert C. Stahl; the nurse is Lieutenant Edith Guyett.

the dust was thick and settled on everything and everybody. Jaundice would be pale compared to the color of our troops; even the Negroes took on a dust color."

Just at nightfall they found their bivouac area and began to bed down, Captain Pickens records. "I had carried my air mattress and a blanket and these, coupled with my rain coat and field jacket, kept me fairly comfortable for the night. We were in a clover field and it smelled sweet as we lay there looking up at the stars. It was not too cold. We had some food given us before we left the boat and the British had made some cheese sandwiches also. I lay there and munched on a sandwich and looked for the Big Dipper, the North Star, Job's Coffin and any of the other constellations that I could recognize.

"The artillery up the way was booming along with monotonous regularity and the flares lighted up the

sky from time to time. You could feel the ground beneath quiver when the big boys fired. The excitement of the day kept us from sleeping immediately and the Italian loam would reach up and press into your hips when you tried to relax on the side. I was on my back and eventually I dropped off to sleep with thoughts of home in my dreams."

With the coming of morning, they were up and firing their little rock-made, individual stoves to heat water for coffee. For that morning's breakfast, he relates, hot coffee and some biscuits, which were actually hard crackers, never tasted better. After breakfast the mess officer then had to begin a search for food and water for the whole unit the next day.

"The same old grind began to set in," he says. "We sat this way for two days until we could get our housekeeping equipment off the boat. We set up our pup tents and began to get as comfortable as possible. Our hospital equipment did not get to us for several days, so we sat. About the fourth night a storm broke, the like of which I have never witnessed. The rains came and the winds blew. The wind blew with the ferocity of a whirlwind. It picked up pup tents like small scraps of paper. Some of them have never been seen since. I hung on to mine for a good two hours with the feeling that it was going to take off with the next blast. It seemed that the good Lord was determined that my tent should come down. It finally gave way but did not blow away as some did.

"The water just poured in. Everything I owned was soaked and I was not alone in my misery; nearly everyone had the same experience. Daylight the following morning was most welcomed. We were still able to laugh about it and no one was hurt and nothing of any great value was lost."

The day after the storm, with borrowed equipment, they set up the hospital and began work. The first day they had about 250 patients and by noon of the following day the patient list had grown to more than 800. "That was a real mushroom growth," he observes, "and if you don't think that taking care of a small community of a thousand with food and water and hospital treatment is a job, you are wrong. But that is what we came for and that is what we did. The mud was reminiscent of last winter in Africa, but we waded thru with little thought of the discomfort. We were busy."

Hardly had they got housekeeping arrangements made and their own equipment on the ground, however, before the war moved away from them. Naples fell and the fighting line moved on to the Volturno River. "Up we jerked and moved again, and so it goes."

His letter, begun in Africa, had been continued in Italy through late September. It would be November before he would have an opportunity to write again.

17

While the 38th's mess officer was recording in his long letter home the experiences of the unit as he observed them during the movement from North Africa to Italy and the settlement there, which embraced virtually all of September, 1943, Captain Montgomery was adding entries in his diary that served to supplement the information provided by Captain Pickens.

On September 8 he had recorded his arrival at Oran and his realization that many changes had been made there since his leaving it in March. His entry that day had noted, too, that "Italy surrendered today."

One week later he wrote:

Left Goat Hill at 5:00 PM after being ready all day. It rained off and on all day. Drove in open truck to Mes-El-Kabir & got there in time to see our boat—*Otranto*—pull out. Drove back to Oran and after much waiting around were taken by tender to the *Otranto* which was anchored. 18 in our cabin.

The next day, September 16, he wrote:

Still at anchor. Meds just fair.

The following day he recorded:

Pulled out of harbor this morning. Convoy pulled out about 5:30 PM. There are nine troopships. We have almost 5,000 aboard.

Four days later, on September 21, he recorded their arrival in Italy:

Arrived at our destination today, which is D 12. We are at Agropoli. Landed by LCI to Blue Beach & by duck from the LCI to the beach and up to one coordination field. Sat there amid much dust. Then by duck to our area, after going by the 16th. They are operating a few miles from us.

Three days later, he writes, they were still in tents. The date was September 24.

We are still living in our pup tents. There are many ingenious ways of putting them up. At noon today we had our first mess since landing. Up until now it has been C rations & tomatoes. Had a bath in the creek today.

Captain Montgomery's next entry dates the wind storm and heavy rain to which Captain Pickens referred to in his letter. The storm occurred on September 25, for Captain Montgomery's diary records on September 26:

Had a severe wind and rain storm last night. Blew down tents & the mess tent in which officers were quartered. Mine did not come down. The 16th Evac was leveled.

The last September entry, on the twenty-ninth, was terse:

Borrowing equipment from 56th. The hospital opened officially at 0800 today.

The 38th's Daily Bulletin, which had suspended publication on September 1, had resumed publishing the day before, Tuesday, September 28.

For that day, the Bulletin announced, Captain Snyder was officer of the day and Captain Pickens was alternate. The entire bulletin, written in capital letters, was devoted to a summary of the hospital's operations during the last five weeks:

HOSPITAL CLOSED IN TUNIS 24 AUGUST 1943
LEFT TUNIS BY TRAIN 0100 HOURS 3 SEPTEMBER 1943
ARRIVED ORAN 0300 HOURS 7 SEPTEMBER 1943
BY TRUCK TO STAGING AREA #1 MBS 7 SEPTEMBER 1943
LEFT STAGING AREA 15 SEPTEMBER 1943 AND BOARDED H.M.S. OTRANTO
LEFT ORAN HARBOR 1120 HOURS 17 SEPTEMBER 1943
ARRIVED BLUE BEACH NORTH OF PAESTUM ITALY AT 0800 HOURS 21 SEPTEMBER
DISEMBARKED AT 1500 HOURS 21 SEPTEMBER 1943
BIVOUAC AT N865-085 SHEET 198111 ITALY 1-50,000 FROM SEPTEMBER 21ST TO SEPTEMBER 28TH 1943
HOSPITAL WILL BE OPENED AT 0800 HOURS 29 SEPTEMBER 1943
THE DAILY BULLETIN RESUMES PUBLICATION. THE LAST EDITION WAS NUMBER 231 DATED 1 SEPTEMBER 1943.

By order of Lieutenant Colonel WOOD:
F. B. Pedrick,
WOJG, AUS.,
Asst. Adjutant

The Bulletin that day was marked at the bottom of the sheet SECRET, and the SECRET was underscored.

The next day's Bulletin announced:

The Hospital officially opened at 0830 Hours 29 September 1943.

The Bulletin had one other announcement:

PROMOTION OF OFFICERS

Since the Hospital closed in Tunis on August 24th the following officers have been promoted:

TO MAJOR

	DATE OF RANK
Capt. HENRY S. MUNROE, JR., M.C.	25 August 1943

TO CAPTAIN

1st Lt. CHARLES B. PORTER, M.C.	17 August 1943
1st Lt. ROBERT H. SCHIRMER, M.C.	24 August 1943
1st Lt. MILO J. HOFFMAN, D.C.	24 August 1943
1st Lt. CLAUD W. PERRY, JR., M.C.	29 August 1943
1st Lt. JAMES E. KIRKPATRICK, ChC.	9 September 1943

TO 1ST LIEUTENANT

2nd Lt. ROSAMOND S. SHIPP, ANC	24 August 1943

On the last day of September the Daily Bulletin in its Status of the Hospital report lists 197 patients, 201 admissions, four dispositions and 24 wards in operation.

The next day, October 1, a veritable flood of new patients arrived. The admissions that day were 598, with no dispositions. This brought the total to 795. Twenty-six wards were in operation. It was reminiscent of the hospital's busy days in North Africa.

The following day the patient list had climbed to 816, with only five dispositions. But 48 dispositions the next day lowered the patient load to 781.

That day, October 3, Captain Montgomery's entry explained the flood of patients:

Receiving many patients, but to date very few battle casualties. All are medical, mostly malaria.

The October Bulletin carried a suggestion to the personnel:

It is an old Army custom that personnel will be clean-shaven, with the exception of the upper lip—a suggestion to the wise should be sufficient.

This same issue carried congratulatory messages from the American Secretary of War Henry L. Stimson addressed to the Allied Forces and from King George VI addressed to Prime Minister Winston Churchill and Mr. Churchill's reply to the King.

The Secretary of War wrote:

"To you and your men, I extend my hearty congratulations and my admiration for the skill and fortitude with which you have carried through the conquest of Sicily. The power of your Army and its magnificent spirit gives assurance that it is poised to drive through to even greater successes."

The message from the King to the Prime Minister said:

"The invasion of Sicily has proved a model of planning and execution. Its success is, of course, largely due to the gallantry and efficiency of the sailors, soldiers, and airmen engaged in the actual operation. I feel that a very special tribute should be paid to those who, with their American colleagues and comrades, were responsible for its organization. They, for months past, have laboured devotedly and with a skill, of which the fruits of their labour are the most conclusive proof, to ensure that every man, every ship, every aircraft, and every item of equipment arrived at the right place, in the right order, and at the right time.

"I should therefore be grateful if you, as Minister of Defence, would convey to all who were engaged, directly or indirectly both at home and overseas on this immensely important task, my hearty congratulations on the manner in which they have discharged it and on the magnificent contribution that they have made towards the supreme end of winning the war.

"In saying this, I am, I feel, giving expression not only to my own gratitude, but to that of all in the British Empire."

To this message the Prime Minister replied:

"I shall be proud to convey Your Majesty's gracious message to all concerned both at home and overseas in the organization and planning of the invasion and conquest of Sicily.

"Your Majesty's congratulations will be received by those to whom they are addressed with the liveliest pleasure. They would, I know, wish me to convey to Your Majesty an expression of their gratitude for this gracious message and of their determination to undertake with all possible energy whatever tasks may lie ahead."

Soon other congratulatory messages would come to General Clark as commanding officer of the Fifth Army. The Daily Bulletin of October 9 carried the texts of the messages. The first was from Secretary of War Stimson:

"My dear General Clark:

"I have been following your Salerno operation with the keenest interest. I am delighted that you have now gotten your opponents pushed back into a position where they are no longer threatening, and I send to you and your brave men my heartiest congratulations on the successful accomplishment of one of the most difficult and hazardous operations in the history of warfare.

"I had intended to visit you at Oran on my recent trip to North Africa, but an emergency call shortened my stay and made it necessary for me to return to the United States earlier than I had expected. I shall always regret that I could not have seen you and given you in person my best wishes for the success of your Army in its coming adventure.

"With my most sincere good wishes for your continuing good fortune in the rest of this difficult Italian campaign, believe me

"Faithfully yours,

Henry L. Stimson"

Prime Minister Churchill wrote General Clark:

"On the hard-won successes of the Fifth Army, which have already inflicted grievous and largely irreparable injury on the Armed Forces of the enemy and have so far yielded the magnificent harbor and city of Naples, I send my congratulations."

To Mr. Churchill's message General Clark replied:

"Many thanks for your kind congratulatory message on the occasion of the capture of Naples. With the continued effective cooperation between British and American land, sea, and air forces the Fifth Army is confident that this is only the first of many victories. We are deeply grateful to you for your unwavering confidence in us."

That same issue of the 38th's Daily Bulletin confirmed and gave emphasis to Captain Montgomery's entry in his diary on October 3 recording the prevalence of malaria cases in the hospital. The first notice in the Bulletin warned that atabrine must be administered to the personnel daily:

Due to the high incidence of malaria in this locality, it is imperative that each member of this command and each patient in the hospital, not under malaria therapy, be given one atabrine tablet a day, six days a week.
It is the responsibility of the Detachment Commander to see that every enlisted man be given atabrine as directed, under the supervision of a non-commissioned officer.
It is the responsibility of the Chief of Service to see that each hospital patient receives prophylactic atabrine, in all cases which are not under malaria therapy.
Atabrine is available at all times in the Officers' and Nurses' Mess.
All members of this command who are sensitive to atabrine will take quinine as directed by the Chief of the Medical Service.
Failure to comply with this order will result in disciplinary action on the part of the individual concerned.

The day before this Bulletin was issued Captain Montgomery with some others in the 38th had taken a drive along the coast. He recorded it in three lines:

A group of us went to Amalfi this afternoon. Beautiful drive & had a nice time.

Three days later, on October 11, he made another trip:

Went to Sorrento today. Bought all my Christmas presents. Rained all the way home.

On October 15 he wrote in his little journal:

Hospital closed today.

But the next day's entry filled a page:

We left at 10:25 this morning by truck. Are in second echelon. First came yesterday. Drove thru Salerno, Pompeii, Naples, and on to Caserta.
The ruins of Pompeii were little damaged, but Naples has really taken a beating. The harbor was full of Allied ships, which was a good sight. The last few miles to Caserta was along a straight double lined road with sycamores. Lovely scene leading to the Palace.
We are installed in a brand new military barracks—beautiful, with terrazzo floors, high ceilings. The water mains were destroyed by the Germans. We hope it will be repaired in a few days. It is the best place we have ever had.

Arrived here at Caserta at about four p.m. We are on the second floor. Bob, T D, P B, & I in one room. At 5:30 battle casualties arrived & by 7:30 had completed four debridements.

First patients received 24 hrs. after last pt. left other location at Agropoli.

The Daily Bulletin of that day—Saturday, October 16—announced:

The Hospital located five miles North of Paestum, Italy, officially closed at 2400 hours 15 October 1943.

Number of patients, said the Bulletin, was zero, admissions zero, dispositions 384, vacant beds zero.

The next day the Bulletin announced:

The Hospital in its new site at Caserta, Italy, officially opened at 1630 hours 16 October 1943. Eight battle casualties were admitted. The first operation was performed at 1700 hours.

In capital letters underlined the Bulletin warned:

1. BLACKOUT
THERE WILL BE AN ABSOLUTE BLACKOUT REPEAT ABSOLUTE WHICH WILL BE ADHERED TO BY ALL MEMBERS OF THIS COMMAND. NO FLASHLIGHTS WILL BE USED OUT OF DOORS DURING BLACKOUT HOURS AND THE LIGHTING OR SMOKING OF CIGARETTES OUT OF DOORS DURING BLACKOUT HOURS IS STRICTLY PROHIBITED.
2. AIR RAID
During an air raid all personnel will seek shelter on the ground floor in whatever building they may happen to be in. All lights will be extinguished by cutting off the generator.

On Monday, October 18, 1943, Captain Montgomery noted the continued influx of patients:

Patients have been coming in rapidly, all battle casualties. We can hear the sound of artillery fire & the windows rattle with the vibration from the larger explosions.

Again the Daily Bulletin supported the captain's brief report. In the issue of that day it reported a total of 113 admissions to bring the patient total to 136, with no dispositions and 24 wards in operation, and 512 vacant beds. On this day Captain Hoffman was administrative officer of the day and Captain Medearis his alternate; Captain Matthews was medical officer of the day and Lieutenant Munroe alternate; Major Imes was surgical officer of the day and Captain Jones alternate. Captain Hoffman was also dental officer of the day and Captain Walker alternate. Lieutenant Mizelle was the nurse officer of the day and Lieutenant Fliedner was alternate.

The most significant entry in the Daily Bulletin of October 18, however, was a summary of the hospital's operation at Paestum:

The hospital was officially opened at 0830 hours 29 September 1943, five miles North of Paestum and was closed at 2400 hours 15 October 1943. The following figures show some of the experiences during the fifteen days of operation in the first phase of the Italian campaign:

TOTAL ADMISSIONS		1544
Disease	1371	
Injury	129	
Battle casualty	44	

DISPOSITIONS		1544
Duty	693	
Transfers	324	
Zone of interior	426	
AWOL	35	
Died	2	

LABORATORY EXAMINATIONS		1305
Malaria smears	680	
Total positive	199	
Tertian	194	
Estivo Autumnal	5	
Blood counts	428	
Urinalysis	166	
Stool	6	
Cross matching	7	
Sputum	2	
Gonococcus	14	
Chest fluid	2	

PATIENTS' MESS		
Total meals		27660
Ambulatory patients	13218	
Bed patients	14442	

From no patients listed for October 16 the patient load built up quickly during the approximately three weeks the hospital would be in operation at Caserta. The heaviest enrollment during the Caserta period was 604 on Sunday, October 24.

The Daily Bulletin of that day carried also the notice of promotion of four of the unit's officers, one of them a nurse. The announcement:

It is with pleasure the announcement is made of the promotion of the following named officers and nurse to the rank set opposite their name:

1st Lieutenant WILLIAM C. MATTHEWS, M.C.
RANK—Captain, DATE OF RANK—24 August 1943
1st Lieutenant ROBERT P. MILLER, M.C.
RANK—Captain, DATE OF RANK—24 August 1943
1st Lieutenant GEORGE A. SOTIRION, M.C.
RANK—Captain, DATE OF RANK—24 August 1943
2nd Lieutenant MARTHA G. FLIEDNER, ANC
RANK—1st Lt., DATE OF RANK—24 August 1943

From 604 patients on October 24 the total dropped the next day to 529, and from then on, as long as the hospital remained at Caserta, the total each day was less than five hundred.

On October 25 Captain Montgomery noted:

The push has slackened. It is the longest continuous busy time we ever had—from 5 AM until midnight the following day, with three hours (off) is my longest period.—40 hrs.—meals crowded in when possible. After that we made a new arrangement, I on during daytime, LaChance and Stokes at night. This worked better but I needed assistance from the Med service.

This same day, October 25, although Captain Montgomery did not record it in his diary, the 38th had two distinguished guests. They were Lieutenant General Mark W. Clark, commanding general of the Fifth Army, and Secretary of the Treasury Henry Morgenthau.

The two were photographed together standing beside the railway tracks at Caserta with a tangled mass of wrecked rail equipment in the background.

18

The official business of the 38th Evacuation Hospital day by day was reported by the Daily Bulletin and these reports, supplemented by the occasional and generally terse diary entries of Captain Montgomery, provide a factual chronology of the unit's service in Africa and Europe, but letters of Captain Pickens from Italy, as those he wrote from Africa had done, provide illuminating detail and frequently important additional data.

The first letter he wrote after landing in Italy, for example, provides color and evokes interest that the completely factual recording fails to achieve. In that way it brings home to Charlotte and North Carolina the phase of the war in which the 38th was involved. This letter followed by two months the last one he had written from North Africa. It was dated "2 November 1943" and the only identification of the place from which it was being written was simply "Italy."

He began:

"It has been said that all roads lead to Rome, but from our experience they are small and narrow when you get this close. What roads are here are well built and well marked, but it is impossible to have them running over some of the mountains that spread down this peninsula. Consequently, our progress must of necessity be slow. As I told you in one of my earlier letters from Africa, wars are fought on roads and for the control of roads. It is more true in this war than in any previous one since it moves, normally, very swiftly when it moves, and the roads are necessary for the moving of troops and their supplies.

"These roads remind me very much of the trip from Blowing Rock to Linville or from Clayton to Highlands. The Germans have placed their defense in strategic spots and it takes time to blast them out without making the cost too high. The cost in men and material so far has been most reasonable as far as I can see and we are in a position to see the cost in wounded men. You folks may become impatient, as we do over here, about the slowness of our progress, but it is better that way if the means justify the ends.

"The roads run along the valleys and each valley is dotted with small villages and small farms. The farms are highly cultivated and extensively irrigated. The villages are crowded and dirty but not as dirty as Africa. When the war has moved by, the villages are pockmarked and in a lot of cases are almost totally demolished. If there happens to be a railroad line thru the town, the town has been wiped out and the rail connections are ruined for great distances up and down the line. When I say ruined, I mean the rails are twisted and scattered and large holes mark the right of way, and boxcars are scattered up and down the tracks and the electric wiring is spread over the countryside. All of the trains are operated, or, I should say, were operated, by electricity. It will be many months before rail connections are made again in this section. This was all done by our Air Force to cut off the German supply line. The bridges across the streams and irrigation canals are all out. This might have been done by us or by the enemy as he moved up the peninsula, but in any case we move over temporary structures at slow speed. The engineers have done a remarkable job on this work and they work swiftly. Some of the bridges are forty or fifty feet high over the water."

More interestingly, he wrote also of the people in this war-torn region from below Salerno to Caserta:

"Where towns are demolished, the townspeople have been slow in coming back and trying to make any repairs. Occasionally you will see the natives cleaning up the rubbish and repairing the doors and putting on a temporary roof. Some of them open their shops for business. The barbers are all busy cutting soldiers' hair. The grocers have apples, nuts, small oranges and

This photograph, made by Margaret Bourke-White for *Life* during her visit to the encampment between Riardo and Vairano, shows the mud with which the 38th's personnel had to contend during the 1943–1944 winter. The nurse crossing the road is Lieutenant Violet Burgess.

some vegetables on crude tables. The pharmacies are open where their stocks have not been completely ruined. The photographers are busy taking pictures for the troops in the towns. Other than these, there is little business being transacted. The churches are open and mass is said regularly, and the little bells chime at regular intervals. The people merely stand around the streets and watch the big trucks and tanks go by. They are not too short of food except in certain lines. There is little beef available, and, surprising to me, practically no salt. There seems to be a reasonable amount of sugar. Cigarettes are in great demand. They have had little tobacco for some years and a package of cigarettes or a pound of salt go further in trade than any other two items. They have an animal called a water buffalo which seems to grow in quantity that might answer the meat need. Some of the Americans have purchased them for $25 to $30 a head and tried the steaks. I had a steak once with one of the Air Corps outfits, but it tasted like veal and was as tough as whet-leather. Of course, there is a shortage of wheat and consequently spaghetti, their main dish."

The members of the 38th were not long in discovering that the Italian soldiers with few exceptions, it appeared, were quite willing to be finished with the war.

"It appears that the farms were controlled by absentee landowners, that is, most of the farms. Some small farmers own their own land. Along the coast, these small owners have a tract of land running up from the sea, and with beautiful terracing, they grow grapes, fruit, and some vegetables. The big landowners apparently were close to the old government and many of them have not been seen since our landing. I don't know what the outcome will be after things are cleared up and we move on to the north. The children are no different from those in Africa when it comes to begging for candy, and are highly delighted when we give them a piece. It's hard to turn a youngster down when you think he had no part in this mess we are in. The older ones I waste little sympathy on, since they started this business and now want to stop when the going gets tough. The roads are lined with Italian soldiers walking southward, heading home. They all appear to think

131

the Americans are their best friends and try to be as chummy as possible.

"We have a difficult time in our particular unit because about one-third of our enlisted men are of Italian extraction and the majority of them speak the language or have relatives somewhere along the line. I think, on the whole, they are happy about being out of the war, in spite of the fact that Bagdolio has promised to raise an army and fight the Germans. I would not want that job. These folks don't want to fight anybody; they just want to go home. They have had all the fighting and glory and marching bands and parades, victories and defeats they want. The average one of them wants to get back to his little farm or vineyard or olive grove and be quiet for a while. It is bad that we have to fight this part of the war all over their country and leave so much devastation, but as I think back, I remember that they started it before we did. They will have to put up with it until we are finished in this section."

Captain Montgomery had noted on October 16 that they had been given quarters in a new military barracks, "beautiful, with terrazzo floors, high ceilings," from which the retreating Germans had torn out the plumbing.

In his letter Captain Pickens went on to describe the barracks to which his fellow officer had referred:

"In this last setup we have moved into some abandoned Italian officers' barracks. Our quarters are very comfortable, the first time we have had a roof over our heads that did not move with each gust of wind, since we left England. The first few days we were here our feet hurt from walking on the concrete floor. We are much more used to having a little mud or dust under our feet. The Germans took all the fixtures with them, including all the plumbing work. With typical American ingenuity, the men have brought the water in and we have showers, good and hot, and plenty of running water for washing. We still chlorinate our drinking water.

"There was enough scrap lumber around to build shutters for the windows; all the glass had been blown out from bombs. We have a good blackout and our own generators furnish the necessary light inside. Because of the unusual demand on our personnel, we were allowed to hire some civilian labor. We have four barbers who shave and cut hair for the patients and the rest of the command. We also have a number of women who keep our quarters clean and who clean up the hospital. By order of the mayor, in cooperation with Amgot, they are paid 40 lire per day, 40 cents. Buck and I have supplemented our maid by allowing her to do our laundry and keep our shoes shined and turn our beds down. We have added a couple of dollars a week to her income.

"Now you know the truth; we have become civilized again and we dread the day when we will have to pull up anchor and move on and back into tents. Buck is doing the hiring and today he had to do some firing. There were too many women, more than we needed, so we had to get rid of some. They have been crying all afternoon about their starving bambinos, but there was nothing he could do about the situation."

He wrote of the havoc the bombs had caused at Naples, particularly along its harbor area, and of the booby traps left by the withdrawing enemy:

"Naples is not the city it once was. The tourist hotels, located along the water front, have been almost completely demolished. The bombing of the dock area caused this, because some of the bombs reached over. What our Air Force did not do, the Germans did before they left. They also left time bombs, which went off until twenty-one days after their departure. This caused considerable damage and many casualties, casualties among our troops as well as the civilian population. The main post office building exploded about a week after the Germans got out. The Engineers had checked it thoroughly, but the Germans are smart about hiding their 'booby traps.' Only this week were the lights turned on. The whole city was evacuated for a day for fear the electric current would start other explosions. I don't know whether any came or not."

They were in a region that twenty centuries before had been the playground of the Roman Empire, but they had seen little of it except as they pushed through to their new base at Caserta. Roman Emperors and wealthy patricians had lived lavishly in their villas ringed about the hillsides above the bay of Naples and old Tiberius had sought the isolation of Capri in the company of his astrologers and philosophers during the

General Mud was the big enemy at the Vairano-Riardo site. This photograph of the entrance there further illustrates the fight the 38th had with this enemy.

132

last years of his reign, but though members of the 38th had seen Capri across the blue waters they had not had opportunity to visit the island. At least, wrote Captain Pickens, he hadn't:

"Capri is still across the bay, but there is no transportation across unless you know someone in Q.M. who runs a 'duck,' the amphibious truck. I have not been as yet, and don't know that I will get a chance. I have not seen Sorrento either. I think I will get there, however, since Fifth Army has taken over the Victoria Hotel for an officers' rest spot and we are allowed to go for two or three days when time permits. I think I shall be able to earn that much rest before long.

"The bay is filled with ships but there are no pleasure liners along the docks. The Neapolitan nights are strictly blackouts now. There is no singing, and no music. The restaurants along the hill overlooking the bay are open, but the food is poor. We tried one and had some dark brown spaghetti, fish that tasted like filet of cat, potatoes hot and cold, apples and grapes. This, with a poor grade of dago red wine, made the meal. Any other trips into the city will find us taking some good American corned beef and some hard crackers and a can of fruit juice.

"Vesuvius steams and smokes along in spite of the war around it. The American troops call it 'Smoky Joe.' With all the destruction, if you can get up on top of the hills overlooking the town, the sight is still impressive and inspiring. The shattered buildings and the sunken ships and the rubbish are forgotten for the moment."

They did have a closeup look, however, at one of the palaces that had escaped major damage, and he wrote about it:

"The King's castle is still intact and now used by the Army as it was used by the Germans. The old Duchess still lives in a part of it. It seemed funny to see Quartermaster troops working over requisitions in the main ballroom. G.I. shoes and O.D. uniforms seemed a little incongruous on that polished floor and under that magnificent chandelier, with the paintings of old masters looking on in disgust. The draperies of fine embroidered silk embellishing the windows blew in the wind and tangled with tommy guns and automatic rifles. On one beautifully carved recumbent statue of a maid a soldier had placed a little sign in one hand reading 'What is your telephone number?'

"But so it goes in time of war."

19

The day before the 38th's mess officer wrote this first letter home dated Italy, Captain Montgomery added two lines to his diary to record a trip he had taken. But he gave no details:

Nov. 1st. Went to Pompeii today. Then to Naples. Saw Victor Emmanuel.

But five days later, when on November 5 he made another entry, he was looking toward the imminent moving again of the hospital. He wrote:

All alerted. Back to tents, I expect. All patients to be out by noon tomorrow. Receiving closed yesterday.

That same day Captain Pickens wrote his second letter from Italy. In another three days the 38th Evacuation Hospital would have been on active duty overseas one year. On November 8 the year before the unit had landed at Arzew to begin its service in the African campaign.

The 38th's mess officer wrote of the arrival of a visitor from the States. He was Walter Nicholson of Charlotte. Nicholson was in the Merchant Marines and on his first trip his ship had met with some difficulty in the nearby harbor. While it was being repaired, he was sitting out the waiting period.

"What prompted this letter was the 'bull sessions' we have been having with him since his arrival," Captain Pickens explains. "He brings a fresh point of view to us and it was a bit of a shock to me to see how blasé we had become."

The letter reveals the change in attitude of the members of the hospital unit since their arrival in Africa, a change typical perhaps of the change that a year of warfare had brought to most of the nation's fighting men and women. Yet the members of the 38th were little more than a year and a half from the beginning days of their Fort Bragg training.

"The war came right close to him when he landed," he wrote of Nicholson, "and he was frankly scared.

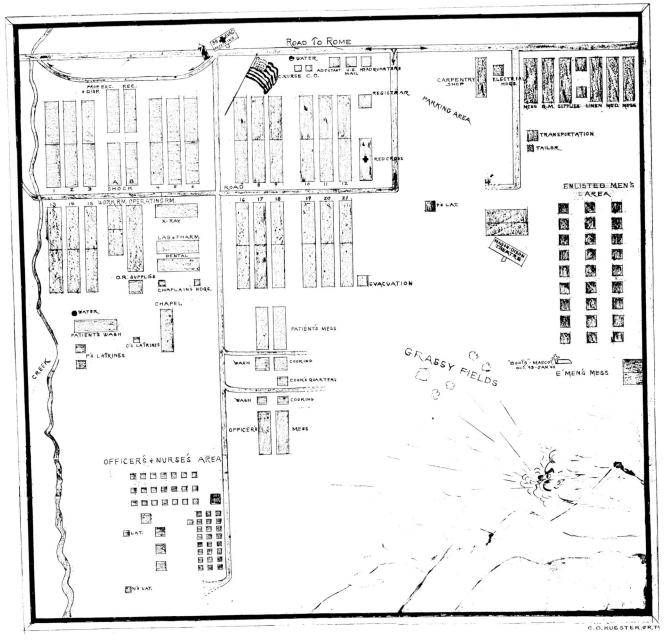

This drawing made during his service there by Sergeant Clarence O. Kuester, Jr., shows the general layout of the Vairano-Riardo encampment, with the hospital's treatment facilities concentrated in the top left quarter of the drawing.

He did not like the bombs dropping so near and seeing death and destruction around him. He was annoyed at our attitude of not getting excited when the air raids started. He spent a great deal of time telling us of the strategy that is being followed around the world, where the armies are being concentrated, where the next blow would fall, and above all how much the Navy was doing. We listened with politeness during the first two or three sessions and then it began to dawn on me that ordinarily we do not discuss the war when we go off duty, that our subjects were books, music, religion, philosophy, home, golf, fishing, and the like.

"Last year this time and a little later we were interested in what division was up front and which one in reserve and which one was resting," he went on. "We fell on every rumor about the Air Corps and what they were doing and where the parachute troops were located and what plans were in store for them. We talked excitedly about the air raids and gleaned every word from everyone who might know what happened. We drank in every word from any officer or man who had been in action.

"Now this is different. When the morning news broadcast comes on from London at seven o'clock there may be one, two, or three people listening. Six months ago our work could not start until we had heard the news in the morning and had a little discussion about what we had heard. Now we just ask if the Russians are still going and if there has been any material change on our own front, and the news from the Pacific has moved a million miles away. Last year we turned handsprings on the news from Guadalcanal, and now when Rabaul falls we will probably not think about it for a week."

Why this change in attitude, this seeming loss of interest in the broad range of the war, this weariness of satiation?

"All this change comes from some reason and I have been trying to figure it out," he observes. "It may be because we are tired and stale, altho we still rush out in good typical American style to watch the show when the air raid starts, unless it appears too close to us.

"Other than that, we have little interest. I am sure the Italian campaign is just as glamorous as the conquest of North Africa. We may have developed into seasoned campaigners and take it all in stride. It may be because during this phase we have moved closer behind the Army and feel more like we are a part of it, and our thinking is to get away from it. It is a bit of a puzzle to me and a source of annoyance to our visitor. Possibly some of you at home can explain it. You see the whole business from entirely another angle. I hate to think I am getting hard. I remember so many people who came back from the war 25 years ago and it was generally accepted that they would not talk about it. I have been determined not to be in that class. The only reason I can see why they wouldn't talk was because they didn't do much about it while they were overseas. So far, I have tried to store up any number of stories and happenings that I will be able to recite when I get back, about which I am unable to write because of security measures.

"But back to the causes of this change. It may be because we are bored with the slowness of the operations. It is amazing the time required to get a big movement under way, but when you see it on the ground, it is understandable. There are so many details that must be cared for and everything must be in order before the opening whistle can be blown. That isn't true in our operations because we move in and before we get the first tent up the patient can be admitted. We let him sleep on a litter, or, as we used to call it in civilian life, a stretcher, until we have some place for him to stay. It might be hours before we can give him anything to eat, but in the meantime he has had medical or surgical attention. As a matter of fact, we work exactly backwards from the rest of the Army. We start when we are most poorly prepared and work up, while the Army is fully prepared before the first attack is made. That, of course, must be true. Our attitude is a question mark still."

They had now been fifteen months, says he, without seeing bright lights. The only lights he had seen since leaving the United States were those of Tangiers when they passed that city on the African invasion. "I suppose we are developing into a sort of mole," he conjectures. "We have just read the directive that lights are being turned on in the streets in Africa, now that we have been away for some weeks. We missed that just like we did the rumored setting up of the Coca-Cola plants there. All of this will come to Italy just about the time we take off for other parts. . . ."

He turns to a discussion of what the American government might be planning to do at the end of the war. "From what I read there has not been any concrete planning done that has come to the surface," he asserts. "I have some definite ideas which I discussed in part in a recent letter to some of you. The reaction received from home indicated that I do not go fully into my premise. In spite of Washington's advice, I think we are going to have to tie in with some other government in order to keep the security which we may gain. What the individual countries do about their own problems should be left to them, but they should not be permitted to make plans to push their own ideas on others. In the same vein we should not try to push ours on them. Most of them can take care of themselves, economically and politically. What I want us to do is take care of ourselves, but at the same time be an example for other states. . . ."

The 38th's Daily Bulletin of November 6 listed 206 patients, two admissions, and 251 dispositions. The administrative officer of the day was Warrant Officer F. B. Pedrick and Captain Bernard Walker was his alternate. The medical officer of the day was Captain

The trucks at Riardo often were mired in mud, as this photo of one of the streets of the tented hospital unit discloses.

Evans and the alternate was Captain Stith. Captain Perry was surgical officer of the day and Captain Fleming alternate. Captain Walker doubled as dental officer of the day and Captain Hoffman was alternate. The nurse officer of the day was Lieutenant Jones and Lieutenant Bachoka was alternate.

They would be the last officers of the day at the base at Caserta. Captain Montgomery's forecast recorded the day before that the hospital would close the following day had been a correct one. The last item in the Bulletin that day announced:

HOSPITAL CLOSED 1200 HOURS 6 NOVEMBER 1943

The Bulletin of Sunday, November 7, was equally brief. Under Status of the Hospital it listed: Patients, zero; admissions, zero; dispositions, 206; vacant beds, zero; wards in operation, zero. Its only other announcement was:

UNIT MOVED TO NEW LOCATION ONE MILE SOUTH OF TAVERNANOUVA, ITALY, AND PROCEEDED TO SET UP THE HOSPITAL.

Monday's Bulletin had the single item:

THE HOSPITAL OFFICIALLY OPENED AT 1000 HOURS.

The next day 225 patients were admitted; no dispositions were made. The conservation of water was urged, "due to difficulty in transportation," and announcement was made that two buckets of coal a day would be permitted for use in each ward stove. This announcement was followed by one on November 10 giving to Captain Augustine "complete responsibility" for disposition of the limited supply of lumber.

The location of the hospital was noted by Captain Montgomery in his diary entry of November 7 as "a few miles N.E. of Teano. In the usual mud field," he added. "Tents got up just before the rain began this afternoon." And he recorded the next day: "Received first patients this afternoon and now they are pouring in."

Major H. Stokes Munroe, Jr., recording later the story of the 38th during these weeks of the late fall in 1943, would agree with Captain Montgomery in his description of the new site, which he called "a muddy field that soon was to become a sea of mud, near Riardo, Italy." Major Munroe, however, would locate the new base and describe it in considerable detail. "This field bordered the right side of the only main highway from Naples to Rome," said he. "It lay approximately 25 miles south of disastrous Cassino, Italy. On this movement, just north of Capua, we crossed the Volturno River, just above the demolished bridge of Highway 6 (Naples to Rome) on a temporary swaying pontoon bridge. The central arch of this large bridge was com-

pletely destroyed by the demolition experts of the retreating Germans. The U.S. Engineer Corps had not yet repaired this absent central portion of the bridge. We were traversing the Volturno plains and to the east could see the rising mountain ranges of the Apennines. These mountain ranges plagued the Fifth Army throughout its hard fought Italian campaign."

Major Munroe's account likewise substantiates Captain Montgomery's in referring to the early arrival of many battle casualties:

"We immediately set up our near-Riardo tent hospital upon our arrival on 7 November 1943 and officially opened the hospital at 1000 hours 8 November 1943. The battle casualties rapidly and continuously filled the shock tents to overflowing as the Army ambulances pulled from the highway into the muddy drive that fronted the receiving tent. The ambulance driver and his assistant deposited the litter-carried patients or ambulatory patients at our receiving tent, picked up exchange litters and dashed off for more casualties. Like the American jeep, the American Army ambulances and their drivers displayed marvelous performances in the deep, thick, Italian mud. We all had opportunities to see them go through mud, rocks, and hills, after preliminarily sizing up the desired route as impossible."

Interestingly, and important in the recording of the work of the 38th, Major Munroe proceeds to describe the tented hospital and its equipment and procedures as it sought to serve with all the efficiency its doctors, nurses, administrative officers and corpsmen could achieve. He goes on to record:

"Here we were, beginning to learn the more efficient use of tentage. Wards could be doubled in size by the simple end-to-end joining of two tents. To enter the muddy flap entrances, that were further complicated by blanket flaps to insure perfect blackouts, was no simple ordeal. With the lumber that we gradually accumulated, we constructed make-believe doors with intervening blanket flaps for the more frequently used receiving, shock, X-ray, laboratory and operating tents. In the distance at night no light was discernible from our busy hospital. We had obtained three big wall tents which when joined end to end made a large operation-room tent.

"The interior of the operation-room tent was almost completely covered with white sheets to enhance our lighting facilities. As one entered the front of the operating room, the long line of tables could be seen on the left side. Just beneath the line of electric bulbs down the center of the tent could be seen the wet X-ray films that hung on another wire at the foot of the operating tables. The uneven rough planking covered the floor of the tent and the many portable operating lights and gas machines bordered the tables. Each

The aerial photograph above pictures the Vairano-Riardo site covered in part by the Kuester drawing. The broad highway at the left of this photograph is the road to Rome shown at the top of the Kuester drawing.

team had two adjoining operating tables. While the operating team was finishing the surgical operation at one table, a patient, along with his record, X-rays and further necessary blood, was being placed on the other table in charge of the shock team. The sterile instruments and equipment were being set up for the next case. The short, concise field medical record was completed with the cigarette and then our next problem was met. The teams never knew what type of injuries the next case would present. We took what came. He was thoroughly reexamined and reevaluated by the responsible surgical team."

Major Munroe continues his recording of the early work at the new base with a revelation of "what happened to a patient from the time he entered the receiving tent until he was placed on our operating table." He writes:

"Upon his entering the receiving tent the following was done: A barracks bag was provided for the storage of the patient's clothing and accompanied him throughout his stay in our hospital. Personal property of value was checked with the receiving officer, placed in a safe, and a receipt was placed in the field medical jacket that was tied to his clothing. All conscious patients who did not wish to check valuables signed a statement to that effect. Unconscious patients were searched and valuables were collected for safekeeping. 'Valuables' or 'No Valuables' were written on the front of the flap of the field medical jacket. Civilian clothing was placed in a methylene bromide bag and was kept in property exchange. All ordinance equipment, as arms, hand grenades, and ammunition, was collected by the receiving officer and turned over to the Unit Supply. Litter bearers were always present in the receiving tent. The receiving officer examined and designated the patients' disposition. Battle casualties and

137

injuries were directly sent to shock tents. Medical cases were assigned and sent to medical ward tents."

His account traces in further detail the handling of casualties and other patients brought to the 38th's hospital:

"Those sent to the shock tents were cared for by the shock team, which was composed of a medical officer with nurses and enlisted personnel. The surgical officer of the day was always available. During these busy days and nights help was supplemented as needed and available. Captain Robert Stith was mainly in charge of the shock tents, but others helped fill in the 24 hours. Seriously wounded cases were left on the litters on the ground, or placed on either cot or shock horses. Blood pressure and pulse were immediately taken on admission to shock tents, and were recorded on his field record. A cursory examination was made to determine whether or not the patient was bleeding, had on a tourniquet, had a splint applied, etc. Shock treatment was instituted in all cases which manifested symptoms of shock or impending shock. Plasma and whole blood was given in adequate amounts. Intravenous saline and glucose were given in cases of severe dehydration. After reacting from shock, the patient was undressed and examined for location and number of wounds, signs of hemorrhage, wounds of entrance and exit, evidence of fracture, and evidence of nerve and blood vessel damage. All wounds of the head, face, chest, abdomen, pelvis and trunk were X-rayed after resuscitation.

"These cases that showed no response to shock therapy were seen by one of the surgical teams. Concealed intra-abdominal or intra-thoracic hemorrhage, marked intra-peritoneal soiling from perforated bowels, distorted mediastinal strictures from chest wounds, and prolonged irreversible shock frequently showed little or no response to shock therapy and surgical intervention of the shocked patient was too frequently necessary. All penetrating wounds, but not all perforating wounds were X-rayed. The path of the missile could be estimated rather accurately from the entry and exit wounds of perforating missiles. Unless bone fracture was suspected, X-ray was of no help, for the foreign body was gone. The surgical teams were kept informed of the number and types of cases awaiting surgery. Ordinarily, the more seriously wounded cases had first priority for surgery; however, an attempt was made to care for the less seriously wounded and the seriously wounded simultaneously."

After all this expert care, continues Major Munroe's review of the work of the hospital in this early phase of their Italian campaign participation, "the problem was dumped into the laps of the surgical teams. Every effort was made to keep the ball efficiently rolling, while carefully making decisions, for we knew that the shock tents were filling with casualties. Experience had already taught us many things, things that made us stay on the alert. The small benign appearing entry wounds frequently gave misleading evidence of the severe damage that the ebbing force of the missile left in its path. Knowledge of the likely anatomical structures that were traversed by the projection of the path of the missile from entry wound to exit wound or from entry wound to its final resting place, as shown by X-ray plates, came to our aid in our proposed surgery. We had many decisions to make promptly, such as the necessity of laporatomy (incision into abdominal cavity) when signs of perforated bowel or bowels were questionable; the type of incisional approach to the damage beneath; whether to enter the abdominal wall through the chest and diaphragm or directly through the abdominal wall, in wounds that involved both chest cavity and abdominal cavity.

"We learned that bullets and shell fragments could produce strange and bizarre wounds. The abdominal cavity could be injured by missiles that entered thighs, buttocks, back, chest, in addition to anterior and lateral abdominal wall. We learned that missiles could change their courses, when striking bone or tough fascia in their paths. We learned that some major vessels could be repaired by certain new methods that would save legs and feet. Such surgical technicalities could go to such length that they would prove tiresome in being related."

The Charlotte doctor summed up the medical and surgical activities: "Those were busy around-the-clock times at Riardo."

The Daily Bulletin figures of those weeks confirmed Major Munroe's observation. November 10 the patient load had increased to 387, including 216 admissions to the hospital. The list continued to mount as the last weeks of 1943 approached: 517 on November 11, Armistice Day; 633 on November 12. It had jumped to 695 the next day, but had dropped to 607 the day after. During the remainder of November the daily patient roll varied from more than 600 to less than 400. On Thanksgiving Day, November 25 that year, when the Bulletin carried a drawing of a steaming turkey and pumpkin pie, the patients numbered 462. This issue also carried President Roosevelt's Thanksgiving Day proclamation, the first paragraph of which declared:

"God's help to us has been great in this year of our march toward worldwide liberty. In brotherhood with the warriors of the other United Nations, our gallant men have won victories, freed our homes from fear, made tyranny tremble, and laid the foundation for freedom of life in a world which will be free."

During the 38th's location near Riardo, Major Mun-

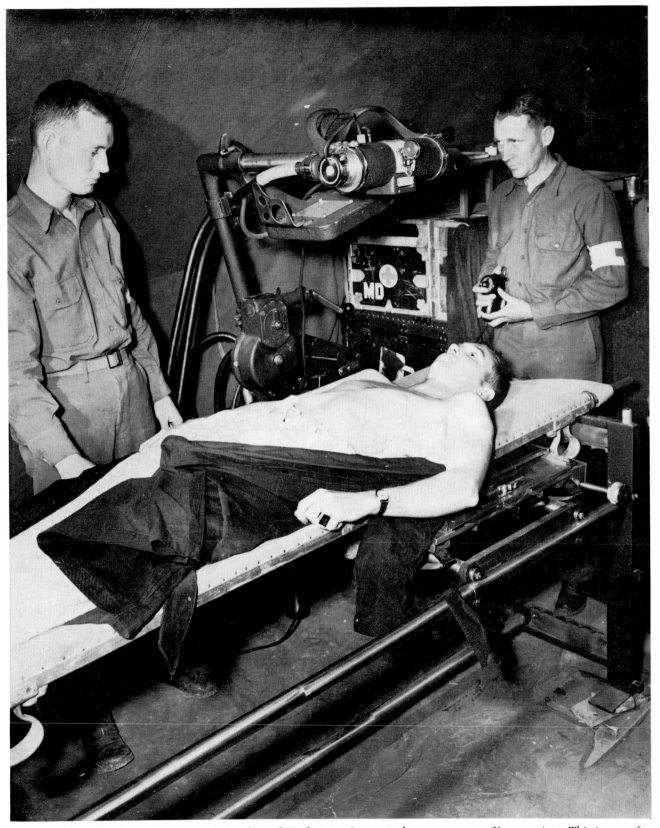

Sergeant Randall K. Davis (at patient's head) and Technician James Ambrose prepare to X-ray patient. This is one of a series of pictures of the 38th's operations by famed *Life* photographer Margaret Bourke-White.

roe points out in further reviewing that activity in the closing weeks of 1943, the hospital was close to the front and there was always grave danger that it might be overrun by the Axis forces. In fact, he reveals, plans had been made for the hurried evacuation of the 38th in event of a sudden sweep by the enemy might result in engulfing the hospital location.

"Times were harder for the Fifth Army troops at the Cassino front than the Axis forces realized," he writes for the record. "In mid-November there was fear that there would be some retrograde action, a fancy name for retreat. Our unit was the only forward hospital unit and we were just a short distance from the fighting front. We were briefed in the possibility, and plans were made for rapid evacuation to the rear if necessary. Members of the unit were given Medical Department Red Cross identification cards with photographs and fingerprints in accordance with Article II, Geneva Treaty, July 31, 1929. We knew that some of the officers and enlisted men would have to remain with patients that could not be transported. We did not know who were to remain and to this day do not know. The Red Cross identification cards were to offer us some protection during our capture. These cards were issued on November 22, 1943, during these tight days."

20

The doctors and nurses of the 38th Hospital occasionally had difficulty, because of language barriers, in communicating with patients brought in for treatment. One week after they had set up the hospital in the mud field at Vairano, near Riardo, for example, a soldier was brought in with a small leg wound who merely shook his head when the doctor began to question him.

The patient was very black and the doctor at first thought that he was a soldier from Alabama or Georgia, surely somewhere in the deep South. And when it was apparent to the doctor that the soldier did not understand what he was being asked, his examiner thought that perhaps the fellow was deaf. Then, he said to himself, perhaps the soldier is one of these Gouams from the French army. So he attempted to communicate in French, but that brought no response. Next, he sought to question him in German.

And then, evidently alarmed at hearing the German, the fellow jumped up from the cot and in his hospital garb tried to run away. He managed to get only a few feet from his cot, however, before he was caught and brought back. And the quizzing was resumed.

The doctor and nurse sought in every language with which they were at all familiar to explain to the man that they were Americans and he need not be alarmed. After a while, by using a mixture of phrases in many languages and much sign language, they made him understand that he was in the hands of friends who were trying to help him. And in a jargon of words and gestures he finally disclosed to them that he was a South African soldier and could not remember how or where he had been wounded. But when the doctor had said a few words in German he had become alarmed and thought he was in a German hospital. That is why, he said, he had tried to escape. He had managed to keep in his possession a dangerous knife with which, he explained, he had planned to slit as many German throats as he could in escaping.

The fellow showed he was pleased to discover he had fallen into friendly hands and then he cooperated with the doctor in treating his wounds.

This incident is related in the letter Captain Pickens wrote from Italy on November 15, ten days before Thanksgiving. "We have had all sorts of patients, but this was the first one no one could communicate with without the use of the old sign language. We never did figure out what language he spoke. We have men in our detachment who can speak French, English, German, Spanish, Portuguese, Italian, Greek, Russian, Arabic, Hebrew, Polish, Hungarian, Lithuanian, Estonian, Indian, Dutch, Welsh, and a good deal of Brooklynese. But with it all, no one could talk to this man. He must come from some tribe in South Africa which hasn't had a chance to hear other languages often."

In fact, the 38th's mess officer went on to reveal, he had been having difficulty himself with adjusting to use of the Italian language. "Just about the time I was getting able to find my way around with the French," he wrote, "I had to start over on Italian. Back in Africa I knew enough Arabic to run the urchins away from the

An Army—and particularly an army hospital—requires great quantities of water and often it is obtained with considerable difficulty. The water goes into this 38th tank through the pipeline over the top and comes out the pipe at the bottom.

camp or to trade with them for their eggs. I had heard enough French and with some lessons given to us by a French officer, I was able to move about quite freely. I have found that anywhere around the Mediterranean the use of the hands and the eyes is the best common language. If you were to tie the hands of a Frenchman or an Italian he would be almost speechless. With Arabs I used to use the 'evil eye' when I wanted them to move on. It worked."

But he was having a harder time with the Italians, said he. "It seems they have so many dialects and what one could understand to the south of Naples, the ones to the north would just say 'no capisco.' They pronounce every vowel and where words are the same as in English, the pronunciation is entirely changed. My main use of the language is with the great number of civilians and ex-soldiers who want to work for us. On occasions we make use of this additional labor.

They are willing to do anything for any price or just for their daily bread. During these latter days we have had to use them because we have been snowed under with work and the men have been worn out. They can just go so long under these trying conditions and then they must get some rest."

In this letter Captain Pickens revealed the methods they employed in setting up hurriedly their big tented hospital. This general plan had been followed in North Africa and Italy.

"It usually begins with an advance detail of two or three officers and some thirty to fifty men," he began. "These men pull away from the setup and move on to the proposed site. Their job is to get the skeleton setup in shape. They dig the latrines, dumps and drainage ditches. They put up the large water tanks, canvas, and sometimes these must be raised off the ground in order to get proper pressure. There are two or three of

141

these, depending on the size of the site and the number of patients expected and the availability of water.

"They set up enough tentage to start operating and house the personnel and then put in kitchens and eating spots. They mark off roads and if they can find the engineers, get the roads scraped. Sometimes they have to erect temporary bridges in order that the traffic flows freely. They put in telephone systems within the area. The Signal Corps will connect us with the outside world. Then comes the lighting system throughout the big area.

"It all looks like a big circus is moving in. When this is all done, the second echelon moves in. The first has done its work in a day or a day and a half. They must work swiftly and efficiently. We have done it so much now that it comes fairly easy, but the labor still has to be done. The second group is the main part of the hospital. The operating rooms, with flooring and under canvas, get set up with all the equipment. The x-ray comes in with its equipment, along with pharmacy with all its bottles and microscopes. The orthopedic section with its bone-setting apparatus comes next, and then the main part of the hospital, consisting of tents, cots, mattresses, and blankets. From there the receiving section, registrar, and many services are added. The Red Cross gets a tent, with chairs and tables, radio and other things for the patients. The chaplains have a small tent for consultation and a large one for services. The supply section, with laundry, extra clothing, medical supplies, and transportation with their few trucks have to be housed. Utilities with their tools, paint, lumber, etc., has a spot. Then the headquarters and the various offices go up.

"The last thing to rise is the morgue. By this time the last group has joined us, those who stayed behind to clean up and police the old area. In about three days

Three buddies of Russell Cotton, left, pose in front of his tent with a wooden door on which is the sign *Cotton's Dog House*. At right is Sergeant Vincent Elliott. It won prize given by Captain Pickens for most original. Others, left to right, Ogle, Santelli, Elliott.

142

the place is moving smoothly, but a lot of man hours has been used. When the setup is finished, then the men start their real work of moving patients in and out and waiting on them in the wards. They help the nurses. You can see why they deserve a rest occasionally. That is why we bring in the civilian labor, and that brings me back to the difficulty of talking with them. It becomes my part to direct them in some of their work. Of course, the many men we have of Italian extraction do most of the talking, but every once in a while it is necessary to talk directly to them. I'll learn if I stay here long enough and at the rate we are moving, I think I will have the time."

The hospital, he added, had been running day and night. The battle had been determined and no quarters had been asked on either side. "The terrain is worse for attack and easy to defend," he explained. "Hence, our lists have been full. Our doctors have done a marvelous job. Today at lunch with the rain pouring down, someone said what a pity we had to leave our last station, where for the first time we used some buildings. I asked whether the 25 miles we had moved up had meant anything in the saving of lives." The answer, said he, had come quickly that it had, "and materially and they were glad to put up with the discomforts in other to gain the end.

"So it goes in the war," he concluded, philosophically.

The Daily Bulletin's status of the hospital report confirmed his statement that the hospital had been busy. The day he wrote, November 15, the number of patients totaled 593. The day before, the total had been 607 and the day before that, 695. The admissions on those three days were 80, on November 15; on the fourteenth, 89, and on November 13, they totaled 130.

The hospital would continue to be busily engaged throughout the remainder of November and until the end of the year. On the last day of November, in fact, the patient load dropped to its lowest recording, 389, since November 10, three days after the hospital's establishment at Vairano. The surgeons, particularly, were busy, Captain Montgomery indicates in his entry of November 21:

It has been a hard two weeks. Anesthesia going 24 hrs. a day. I have been doing the night shift with Wright, Pomper, Hoffman & Gay assisting. Lola handled the day with Nowachi & Powers.

Captain Montgomery on this day added:

Geo. Snyder received his majority.

His next entry, November 30, checked with the Daily Bulletin's report for that day. He wrote:

Everything is quiet now. Very few cases for surgery. Medical admissions predominate today.

But despite the rush of patients southward to the hospital from the battle fronts, during these weeks at Vairano the members of the 38th had begun to settle into a dull sort of routine of timeless existence, according to the unit's mess officer. Three days before the end of November, with Thanksgiving of 1943 two days past, he sat down to his typewriter and wrote the homefolk of his feelings, doubtless shared by the majority of the unit.

He dated the letter "27 November 1943. Sunny (?) Italy."

"Time is of the essence, or so the saying goes in part in a lot of legal documents," he began. "We have been laughing about our measure of time in the Army overseas. The days of the week are not named and only on rare occasions are the months designated. We just move without any measure. After so long a time there is no interest in keeping up."

What had led him into such cogitating, he explained, had been the conversation he had had a few evenings before. His tentmate had asked him when some incident about which they were talking had happened and he had replied that it was in the period "from Telergma to Tunis." He went on to explain further:

"It was not from March 1943 to August 1943, but from one station thru another into a third. We measure long periods by the places we have set up our camp and operated our hospital. The shorter periods just fade. Tuesday is the same as Saturday. It is just a passage of time. We sometimes say that with the passing of a day it means that we are away from home just a little shorter time. It is an optimistic point of view, but

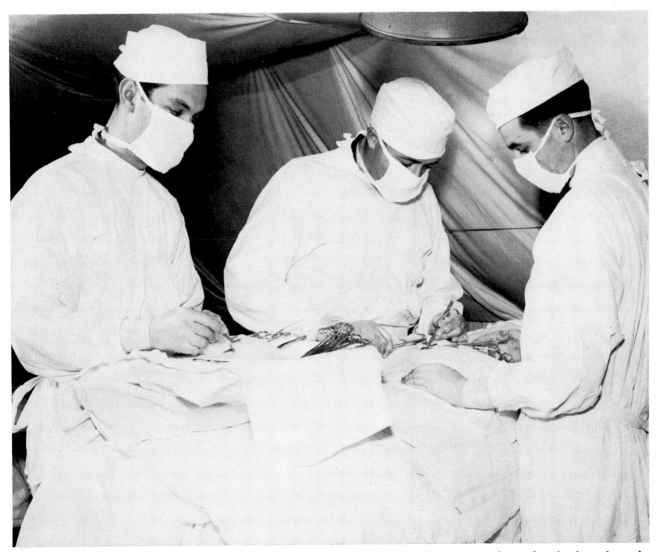

Operations were performed by the 38th's surgeons, with the aid of nurses and corpsmen, day and night throughout the period of service in North Africa and Italy. Natives in need of surgery, as well as hundreds of war prisoners, were treated by the medical men and surgeons of the evacuation along with wounded, many of them desperately, American and Allied soldiers. The operating surgeon here, center, is Captain Duncan Calder, Jr., of Charlotte.

Ambulatory patients were served their meals in the mess tents. These meals were occasions for the exchange of lively information, some of it factual.

keeps hope springing and that in a soldier's mind is paramount."

His letter provides a look-in on the 38th's observance of Thanksgiving:

"Thanksgiving came and we celebrated properly. The Chaplain had an appropriate service during the morning, which I was forced to miss. I got back to camp in the evening in time to enjoy a beautiful spread of food. The powers that be saw that a plentiful supply of good things to eat reached the front line troops and they were properly enjoyed. We had turkey and plenty of it. We actually had everything from soup to nuts, literally.

"It was a feast in spite of the rain. The fact that for days it had poured down buckets and tubs and whole lakes of water did not dampen our spirits when the food showed up. For that and a lot of other more important things we were thankful, properly so. But, as

time moves, it was just another day in doing our part and waiting for the time when we could start back home."

The reason he had missed the Thanksgiving service at the camp, he revealed, was his having made a trip to Naples to find a place where the members of the unit might spend time when off duty. "We have been running full tilt for a good many weeks and it becomes necessary for men to get away from their work and get some relaxation," he observed. "The Army had prepared a place at Sorrento for the officers. My turn comes some time in January, according to the drawing, so I have no hopes of getting there. The nurses were prepared for in Naples at the one remaining hotel that stands whole. Nothing had been done for the men. I found a pension that had about one-half of its rooms still usable. The manager said he could turn the water on so they could get a bath, altho he said there was no

144

way for him to heat any water. What we wanted was just a place where they could sleep on good comfortable beds, with some cover to keep off the rain. They could find some food if they failed to take any with them. We could use the Variety Club fund for the paying of the bills. That fund, as you may remember, was raised in Charlotte with a show by Bob Hope, Frances Langford, et al. The quarters for the men were worked out, altho they will have to climb a lot of debris to get to them.

"That is what kept me away from camp on that all-important day. I was thankful for a chance of doing something for someone else."

He refers to the frequent and heavy rains, and he expresses his wrath at the discovery of the latest dastardly scheme of the Germans in setting up booby-traps.

"The rains have kept the Fifth Army from making any progress to speak of," he reported. "You can't imagine what a mire they leave. General Mud has full control. I am more anxious than ever to see the enemy defeated since a visit from some members of the Engineer Corps. This particular group builds bridges and cleans up mine fields. We have had a lot of experience with mines in an indirect way, but recently I have heard of a new use of the oft used 'booby-trap.' The Germans have actually mined the bodies of dead soldiers, including their own. I think that is just about as low as a man can reach with his mind, and I don't mean any pun either. Chaplains going out on the battlefield to gather up the bodies of men have lost their lives thru this dastardly treachery. I think it is much worse than using gas. The Germans are past masters at planting these infernal machines."

He related some of the tricks the enemy used in setting these bombs.

"They are placed on the wheel of an overturned car or truck. You will find them adroitly planted in a tree laden with oranges. You will find them along the side of the road where you might pull off from the main traffic. They are never put in the middle of the road, because they will be seen too easily. I can't see what they gain by such tactics. They only kill a few people and cannot possibly stop a movement. They only delay and that for only a short period. I can understand the demolition work, where a road or a bridge or a building is blown up to hinder the progress of a large unit, but I can't see what is gained by this small-time, slimy murder. The mind that thinks these things up should be eliminated. An institution is too good for them."

He reported having seen old Charlotte friends among the Engineer group, which included some former members of the old 105th Engineers, of which his brother, Colonel Wiley Pickens, had been the commanding of-ficer. "They are doing a grand job in front of us," he revealed. "Incidentally, John Trescott, one of Wiley's old buddies, came by to see me. He is still in Sicily with his battalion, but flew up for a day to see how a real war is operated. He is fine and wanted to be remembered to Wiley and any of the old gang there."

It would be in the middle of December before he would write home again. And then also he would refer to the interminable raining and the frustrating mud at Vairano. Years later, when veterans of the 38th's members would happen to meet and begin reminiscing about the Italian campaign, they would invariably recall the mud of those last weeks of 1943.

Nor would they be exaggerating in their describing it. They have an abundance of photographic records proving the truthfulness of their stories. During that period one of World War II's most famous photographers visited the hospital and took a wealth of photographs, many of which were published in the February 21, 1944, issue of Life Magazine. These photographs show the deeply rutted, rain-filled sloughs that were the hospital's company streets and the mud-clogged boots of nurses and men busy in the routine of caring for ill and wounded soldiers.

The Life spread is headed: EVACUATION HOSPITAL—Nurses and Doctors Work in Italian Morass.

The lead paragraph of Life's story on the 38th says:

"Not all of the Americans fighting in Italy are in the firing line. Among the most valiant are the men and women of the American Medical Department, who fight their battle deeply echeloned from the Anzio beachhead back to North Africa. Shown on these pages is a small section of this battle, a mudbound evacuation hospital in Italy which was photographed last month by Life's Margaret Bourke-White."

Life's article continues:

"The evacuation hospital is an intermediate link in the medical chain which extends from the battlefield to general hospitals in the U.S. In Italy badly wounded men are treated in field hospitals close to the front but they begin actual recovery in the evacuation hospital, which is anywhere from five to 50 miles farther to the rear. Less serious casualties are sometimes sent directly to the evacuation hospital from front-line medical clearing stations. When patients who need additional treatment are strong enough to travel, they are sent back to bigger and more specialized hospitals far from the battle zone. Those who require more than 30 days to recover are evacuated to the hospitals in Sicily and North Africa, and those who require at least 120 days are sent to the U.S."

The article goes on to describe the evacuation hospital and its work:

"Although the evacuation hospital has none of the

tiled neatness of peacetime medicine, it is an efficient and complete medical unit. Many of its patients are discharged without further treatment. It is the first place where the sick and wounded have the luxury of warm baths, clean pajamas and soft bathrobes. It is also often the first place where they are attended by nurses.

"The wounds of the Italian campaign have made grisly work for surgeons in evacuation hospitals. A great many of American casualties have been caused by land mines, which the retreating Nazis have used in large numbers to slow the Allies. Land-mine wounds are a difficult surgical problem because the victim is often riddled with fragments of metal, stones, dirt and even grass. Men riding in trucks and tanks which have been blown up by mines suffer complex foot and leg fractures from the force of the blast. Another medical hazard of the Italian campaign has been the tendency of wounded men to develop gas gangrene infections, which medical men ascribe to the prevalence of gas-forming bacteria in manured Italian fields."

Three photographs on this first page of the Life spread on the Charlotte unit's hospital at Vairano show the tents sitting in a sea of oozing, clinging Italian mud, and a fourth shows a battle casualty being carried through the mud from an ambulance into the receiving tent. The cutline says: "Bringing in Casualty, litter bearers step carefully in mud. Hospital has taken in as many as 238 battle casualties in a single day. Tent at left is hospital receiving ward." The corpsmen carrying the wounded soldier are Gerard Albano, Helke Mc-Caughin, Vincent Mistkowski, and Jack Marcario. The nurses in the three other photographs are Violet Burgess, shown crossing a deeply rutted road alongside the tents, and Vera Neeley, Leah Rodstein, and Lillian LeBlanc.

"Nurses Quarters are small wall tents at edge of hospital camp," says the caption of one, and "Pajamaed nurses leave tent to which they refer euphemistically as 'the powder room,'" explains the caption on the other. The photograph shows a small board before the tent on which is the sign: NURSES' LATRINE.

The Life article on another four-photograph page continues with its description of an evacuation hospital, which is the 38th, although Life does not identify the hospital or its location:

"Unlike the simply equipped field hospital, the evacuation hospital does little dramatic medical improvisation. Its purpose is not to patch up casualties until they can be sent to bigger hospitals, but to heal as many of the wounded and to cure as many of the sick as possible. It is as well prepared for this as an excellent small civilian hospital. For diagnosis, the doctors of an evacuation hospital have a complete X-ray laboratory. For treatment, they have the latest in drugs and surgical equipment. Although the evacuation hospital is generally well supplied with blood plasma collected by the Red Cross, it still needs large quantities of whole blood. Because whole blood is rich in oxygen and contains vital red and white blood cells, it is essential in cases such as the soldier near death from bleeding who appears on the opposite page." The cut-lines under the full-page photographs referred to read: "Casualty Near Death is fortified by blood plasma in the shock ward. Critically wounded in the back by shell fragments, patient also needed transfusion of whole blood. As plasma is administered, patient's blood is typed because he has lost identification tag. Plasma is valuable in the treatment of shock, but whole blood is necessary in cases of great blood loss."

Another photograph by Margaret Bourke-White shows Major Richard Query and Corpsman William Davenport taking a pint of whole blood from Patient Donor. The cut-lines under the picture reveals that "Whole blood is usually obtained from service troops in area or from one of convalescent patients." Of this patient the observation is made: "Donor was given shot of whisky afterward."

One of the photographs on this page of Life shows a patient being X-rayed. In the picture are George Grant, Nichola Ierulli and Randall K. Davis of the 38th.

The picture beside it has the caption: "Technician rushes X-rays to the operating tent. Location by X-rays makes precise removal of foreign bodies possible, also prevents unnecessary probing." Shown in this picture are John Keough, Nichola Ierulli, and Captain Hallie E. Almond. Ierulli is sloshing his way with the X-rays through an ankle-deep slough of mud.

Another page of the spread in Life pictures in four photographs the problem of mud at Vairano. One shows Hallie Almond washing from her shoes under a spigot the mud caked on them; another shows convalescent patient Private Walter Bernard wading through the deep mud to the mess tent. "In his hand," the cut-lines say, "he holds a letter from home." Bernard was discharged a few days later. The third and fourth of the Bourke-White shots show views of the hospital street filled with thick, gummy mud. The captions say, however, that "Despite desolate appearance of camp, morale is high. Casualties which have been evacuated from front-line clearing stations here get their first baths and beds, see their first nurses. Number of patients in the hospital (about 750) remains the same because of balance between men arriving from front and men being evacuated to rear."

Four unidentified corpsmen in a half-page photograph are shown trudging through the mud with a convalescent soldier on a litter. "Wounded are evacuated from evacuation hospital in ambulances when they have recovered enough to travel," the cut-lines reveal. "They will be taken in ambulances to hospital trains and removed to bigger hospitals in the rear. Although a few will receive more surgery, most of them are returning as convalescents. Litter case shown above has suffered shattered arm and elbow, wears reinforced plaster cast. Litter bearers step carefully in slippery mud. These men told Miss Bourke-White they had never dropped a patient, even when they had fallen down themselves."

It was while the 38th was encamped here in the vicinity of Riardo that Sergeant Clarence O. Kuester, Jr., one of the few enlisted men in the unit from the Charlotte area, had an experience that after more than two decades remains for him one of the most memorable of the war.

Vividly he recalls it:

"We'd been having it pretty rough; the fighting in the mountains was heavy and casualties were streaming in. We were working day and night. I was a sort of handy man in the operating room, helping the doctors and nurses. I had been a misfit in the unit, and had never had a regular assignment. In fact, I was an enlisted man whose friends were officers I had grown up and gone to school with in Charlotte, while I knew few of the enlisted men, and that made it awkward for me and for them. But I had been helping around at various jobs, including drawing detailed maps and sketches of our encampments in various places in North Africa and Italy. One day I asked Major Sanger if I might help in the surgery tent and he said it would be o.k. if I didn't get in the way and mess up something. So I had been doing that, and I had seen some interesting and complicated operations.

"This time at Riardo I was working in the surgery tent when they brought in a young soldier who had been badly shot up; he appeared to be in desperate shape, and in spite of all the doctors were able to do for him, it looked to me like he wouldn't make it.

"He had been writing a letter to his sweetheart in Poughkeepsie, New York, before he was wounded, and after rallying from surgery he asked me to help him finish the letter. He told me what to write and I put it down.

" 'Will you mail this letter to her if anything happens to me so that I can't?' he asked me, and I told him I would. That seemed to relieve him, but pretty soon he was in a coma and I figured he wouldn't last much longer. I was staying with him while the others went to supper and when one of them returned, I went to the mess tent. I wasn't gone long, but when I got back, the boy, who was about twenty-one, was gone. I asked what they'd done with him.

" 'He died just after you went to eat,' he said.

" 'Where'd they take him?' I asked.

" 'To the morgue tent,' he said.

" 'What did they do with his things?' I asked the soldier. 'He had a letter in his pocket that I promised to mail to his girl at home. What did they do with it?'

" 'They didn't take anything off the body,' he told me. 'They just moved him like he was when he died.'

"I had promised that boy I would see that his letter to his sweetheart got mailed, and I felt like it was a sacred trust I had obligated myself to carry out. Yet I didn't like the idea of going into that morgue to search among the dead bodies for the boy and the letter that I felt was still in his pocket. But I got a flashlight and went over to the morgue tent. I didn't tell anybody I was going; I didn't get permission from anyone. In fact, I thought maybe if I asked about it they wouldn't let me go. So I just went over in the darkness—it was night now—and slipped into the dark morgue. I flashed my flashlight around and saw bodies stacked about the tent awaiting their being shipped back. I still remember the pairs of feet, toes pointing upward, and the long shadows on the tent wall of the stiffened feet as I turned the flashlight on those rows of dead boys.

"After awhile I found the boy. When I turned the flashlight on his face, I felt good that he seemed to be at peace; he evidently had died in the coma in which I had left him to go to the mess tent. I searched hurriedly and found the letter. And then quickly, more quickly than I had entered, I left. I took the letter to my tent and I remember I wrote a little note at the top in which I explained that the boy had been in the hospital and had asked me to help him finish the letter and then mail it to her. I didn't tell her that he was dead. Then I carried it to the sergeant in charge of getting out the mail and he sent the letter out. I'll never forget that experience, the young boy and his calm determination to get the letter finished and mailed even though, I suspect, he figured he wasn't going to make it. And I'll never forget those bare feet in the morgue tent and the shadows from my flashlight moving along the tent wall.

"That was one of my closest encounters with death. We didn't lose many in our hospital. Most of the desperately wounded died on the field or in the first aid stations before they got to us, and some of them in hospitals farther back. Our 38th doctors and nurses had a great record. The doctors were skillful, experienced medical men and surgeons, and they worked day and night with little rest during those times when casualties were heavy. Some of their operations were amazing. And the nurses, too, were experienced, efficient, and dedicated."

One operation at which Sergeant Kuester was one of the surgery tent helpers would be widely publicized in the American newspapers, and in an article in one of the national magazines some years after the war's ending the patient himself would speak of the skill of his surgeon and the dedicated work of the 38th's personnel.

"I was helping in the operating room when Major Bill Pitts operated on Richard Tregaskis," the former Sergeant Kuester remembers. "Tregaskis was one of the most famous of the war correspondents of that period, like Ernie Pyle and John Hersey and Margaret Bourke-White and some others who came to visit the 38th. He was the fellow who wrote *Guadalcanal Diary*. When they brought him in, few people thought he'd make it. His skull had been crushed by an exploding shell or mine, I heard, and they said parts of his brain were protruding from his skull, with skull splinters sticking into it. Dr. Pitts operated on him. It was a long and very tedious operation, as I remember. He had to remove portions of the damaged brain, they said. But, anyway, Dick Tregaskis recovered, and after a long period of recuperation went back to his correspondence duties, and later wrote a magazine story telling of that experience."

Many versions have been reported of this operation. But the two men most vitally involved, Tregaskis and Dr. Pitts, have recorded what happened, and their stories interestingly as well as authentically provide the details. After more than two decades Dr. Pitts recalls:

"We were just south of Cassino and the Germans were dug in heavily up there. At the time Tregaskis

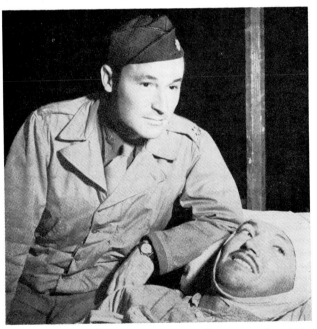

Major William R. Pitts of Charlotte in late November 1943 performed one of the most notable operations of the war. The patient, shown here shortly after the operation, was Richard Tregaskis, noted war correspondent. Tregaskis gives the story of the amazingly successful surgery in his book *Invasion Diary*, published by Random House.

148

came to the hospital we had had quite a flow of casualties from that area. On the particular night that he came in I had already performed two brain operations.

"His operation began about two or three o'clock in the morning. I remember when he came in he was virtually speechless. Occasionally he could get a word or two out; he was semi-conscious, and his right arm was helpless and his right leg was weak. He was a diabetic and he was trying to get through to us that he was a diabetic. That was very important to know and he wanted us to know it, but it was very difficult for him to get through to us. Finally, though, he did.

"At the time he was admitted and operated on we didn't know who he was at all; certainly I didn't know who he was; he was just another casualty, as far as I was concerned. I had never seen the fellow before; he was just another man with a brain wound. That, in fact, was true of most all my operations.

"His was the third one that night, and when I got through with his it was just before dawn. I went to my tent and went to bed and after two or three hours sleep I woke up and got up. I found that a number of newspaper people had come to the hospital and were wanting to know how Dick Tregaskis was. I said 'Who's Dick Tregaskis? What's wrong with him?' They said, 'Well, he had a brain operation.' Then they told me more about when he came in and so on and it was then I realized for the first time that the last patient I operated on was Dick Tregaskis. Dick, of course, was a very outstanding newspaper reporter and had a lot of friends in the news media, and every day he had several visits from the various reporters in that theatre, people there as representatives of the different news agencies and services."

Major Pitts saw him about nine o'clock that morning, some three hours after he had finished the long and extremely tedious operation. He was doing well and he continued steadily to recover. During the operation, Major Pitts had given him only local anesthesia.

"I did it under local anesthesia, with a little morphine," he recalls. "I did a majority of my brain operations in that way, because in the first place, it is a safe way, and number two, when the casualty load was heavy we didn't have anesthesiologists enough to give general anesthesia and those of us who could get along with local anesthesia had to do so. If you have a brain-injured patient, you want to test his state of consciousness, for that is your most important yardstick in knowing how he's getting along. If his state of consciousness diminishes, that's a bad sign.

"He got along very satisfactorily and about the second or third day he began to show some improvement in his speech and in the functions of his right-side extremities. When he came in to us he could not move his right hand at all, he had very little motion in his right arm, and he had weak motion in his leg."

Dr. Pitts revealed what had happened to the International News Service reporter:

"He had a shell fragment wound. He had brought his helmet along; this was his prized souvenir. In his book he tells about that, how he wanted to take it along with him. The shell fragment came in the front of his helmet and part of it hit his skull, part of it was embedded in his brain, and it had driven bone fragments into the brain, and another part of the shell fragment came out at the back of his helmet. Actually he had a gutter wound of the brain, a groove in it; his scalp wound was four or five inches long and an inch and half wide; the skull had been shattered over that distance and ten or twelve fragments of the bone had been driven into the brain. Part of the skull had been blown away, the brain was oozing out through the scalp wound. Of course in the operation all the shell fragments were removed, the in-driven bone fragments were removed, and the damaged brain was removed, the bone was smoothed up and the scalp wound was closed."

The hole in the skull, Dr. Pitts recalls, "was an oblong hole, approximately two inches or more long and an inch and a half wide. All that part of the skull, of course, was gone. Later on, after he had recovered and had come back to this country, he had a plate of inert metal put in at the Walter Reed Hospital by Dr. Barnes Woodall. From our hospital after about twelve or fourteen days he was transferred to a general hospital just north of Naples. This was a Wayne University unit and Jack Webster, a neuro-surgeon from Detroit, took care of him there, along with Captain Richard Schneider. From there he came on back to the States.

"After that, after he got his repair done, he went back into newspaper reporting, jumped with the paratroops in the invasion of France, and when the war ended he was in the Pacific on Saipan covering the big bombers."

Dr. Pitts continued to see his famous patient after the war; on trips to New York several times he had lunch and dinner with him. In his library he has a prized collection of books dealing in various phases with World War II. Two are Ernie Pyle's *Here Is Your War* and *Brave Men*. Both Pyle books give considerable attention to the 38th Evacuation Hospital's service. In *Brave Men* Pyle tells of visiting Dick Tregaskis a day or two after the operation, which he describes in characteristic Ernie Pyle manner:

"Late that night he arrived at the hospital, was put to sleep on morphine, and Major William Pitts performed the brain operation. It was Major Pitts' third head operation that night. He took more than a dozen

pieces of bone and steel out of Dick's brain, along with some of the brain itself. He and the other doctors were proud of pulling Dick through—as well they might be."

But there is another World War II book in the Pitts library, one even more highly valued. It is a first-printing copy of Tregaskis' *Invasion Diary*, written in the months between the operation and the author's return to duty. The biographical sketch of Tregaskis on the back of the book jacket tells of the operation and shows the author with his head swathed in bandages. And inside Tregaskis reveals in detail the incidents of his wounding on the afternoon of November 22, 1943, the operation in the early morning hours, his subsequent slow recovery of his lost speech and use of his right arm and right leg, and his day-to-day experiences in "Ward 13 of the 38th Evacuation Hospital" until his transfer December 10 to the General Hospital north of Naples.

But what for the Pitts family distinguishes this particular copy of *Invasion Diary* is the handwritten note on the first forepage:

To Bill Pitts,
who as far as I am
concerned is the hero
of this book —
and who made it
possible because he
saved my life —
Dick Tregaskis

This is the note written by Richard Tregaskis on the flyleaf of the copy of his *Invasion Diary* that he presented to Major Pitts. Within a few months after the operation Tregaskis returned to duty.

Of his operation and the period of recuperation as a patient of the 38th, Tregaskis in his book wrote, in part:

"I was propped up in a semi-sitting position. At the lower end of the operating table, white-masked at-

149

tendants were fiddling with bottles attached to a metal stand. They were giving me a transfusion of blood and plasma through veins in the foot. As the operation continued (it required four hours, all told) my legs grew stiff and I tried to move them. They were tied down at the ankles. Toward the end of the operation, I was more annoyed about my legs than by the operation on my head. My inability to move them irked and then infuriated me. At first I tried to hold them still, but, after a while, I gave up. I fidgeted."

But soon he was asleep. When he awoke, he relates, the "whole right side of my body was numb. In order to move my right arm I had to pick it up with my left. My right leg was a foreign body and the right side of my face was as thick and insensible as a layer of felt. My right eye refused to focus.

"The doctor who had operated on me came in to see me. He was a young, good-looking man with a smooth face and slick black hair. After many attempts, while he waited patiently for me to shape the words, I managed to convey the idea that I could not put my ideas into words. He smiled and seemed to apprehend my meaning. He explained why I could not speak, why I was paralyzed on the right side. I had been hit in the left side of the brain, in the region which controlled speech in a right-handed person. . ."

Tregaskis describes the surgery tent:

"The tent was a long, open corridor, with a peaked roof. Rows of cots lined both sides. I was not interested in any of the cases, although I knew when stretcher bearers passed my bed with a new load of humanity, inward bound.

"The first or second day, Margaret Bourke-White, the famed Life photographer, came in. She took some pictures, using two bright flash bulbs. She wanted me to smile and I tried several times, but the right side of the mouth resisted. Something like a grin resulted, but it felt lopsided, and the eyes were out of control. . .

"One or another of the nurses gave me pills several times a day; they were sulfadiazine tablets to prevent infection and aspirin to deaden headaches. One of the nurses, who had blonde hair and large blue eyes and a delicate face, like a child's, was on duty during the daylight hours. She had a sweet, piping voice, and smiled quickly. I called her 'Goldilocks,' when I could get the word out. She asked if I could pronounce her name—Miss McCain.

"The ward boy on duty during the day was Bob Trafford. I also learned the name of the doctor. He was a major and his name was Pitts: William Pitts, and he came from Charlotte, N. C. Some of the other doctors visited me. I could register their faces; there were three lieutenant colonels (Sanger, White and Wood). They all came from Charlotte—for this was a Charlotte medical unit, an evacuation hospital. The chaplain

(Captain Kirkpatrick, of Florence, Mass.) brought me a New Testament and several religious pamphlets. He asked me what denomination I belonged to and I could not say the word. I knew very well that it was 'Presbyterian,' but I had not the remotest idea how I could make the sound.

"Newspaper friends—Clark Lee, Mike Chinigo, Ernie Pyle, Bill Strand, Red Knickerbocker, John Lardner and others, dropped in and asked how I had been wounded. I stumbled incoherently over my words. All the details of my being wounded were fresh and clear in my memory, but I could not express them. In self-reproach I reviled myself as an imbecile. It was some comfort that at least I had brains enough left to recollect that word. . .

"Dr. Pitts came in one day and tried all my reflexes, using a rubber hammer and a pin. As usual, he preserved professional silence. I watched as he wrote a long report on the chart which was attached to my bed. I signaled for his attention. My words were confused, but determined, as I badgered him for information about my injury. . .

"He told me little: only that I would probably have to recuperate for at least six months; that later on, a surgeon would have to patch up my skull with a metal plate. The shell fragment had smashed the bone, driving fragments into the brain. These he had removed, and he had covered the hole only temporarily with fascia, or scalp muscle. Recovery, he emphasized, would be a slow process."

Tregaskis continues his account of his recovery—how he began to notice a returning feeling in the paralyzed areas and how his ability to speak normally was slowly restored.

"I came to know Bill Pitts, the surgeon who had operated on me. His brisk manner disappeared when we talked about good old times in the States, before the war. He showed me a folder full of pictures of his pretty wife and little son. That precipitated a general exhibition of photos of patients' wives and sweethearts. . .

"I remember distinctly the 8th of December. Then Dr. Pitts told me that I should get ready to leave the following day, or perhaps the day after. . . The day passed, uneventfully, and the next morning Maj. Pitts informed me that at last I was to have my trip to the rear. He dressed my head in an exceptionally sturdy casque of gauze and adhesive tape. Later in the day stretcher bearers came. I checked the belongings in my barracks bag to make sure that my notes, and my broken helmet, were there. Then I was carried down the corridor between the long lines of cots, and out into the sunlight." Few who had seen him brought in thought at the time that he would go out alive.

The Tregaskis case, though perhaps the most widely

publicized, was but one of hundreds handled by the 38th during the Italian campaign. Dr. Pitts remembers vividly how strenuous the work was, particularly during the Anzio period:

"We arrived at Anzio beachhead about sun-up on Easter morning. Before we had practically got to the grounds of the hospital, and while we were in the process of setting up, we received casualties from the bombing of the place exactly where we had disembarked. Those were our first casualties that we received in our hospital. And while we were there in Anzio we were all in a small area with hills surrounding us and the Germans were occupying the hills. We were crowded together. On one side of the hospital was the ammunition dump, on the other side was the airstrip. It was so hot from bombings that the planes from the airstrip went to Naples at night; they didn't stay there. And the Germans pulled an air raid every night, and they'd hit that ammunition dump and it would be like a Fourth of July celebration.

"And of course there was no such thing as clearing stations in forward areas there; the clearing station was right outside our admission tent. We got plenty of casualties that were brought to our hospital within fifteen, twenty, thirty, forty minutes from the time they were wounded—right from the front. Our hospital tents were dug in up to the level of the skirts, so that was about four feet below ground, and then sand bags were placed along the side.

"At Anzio," his report continues, "we had absolutely no goldbricking, because many a time the GIs would say, 'Doc, how about letting me go back to the front; I'm safer up there in my foxhole than I am here lying on your cot in this hospital.' It was a great rush all the time, with casualties pouring in, and you would try to get through before the night raid came so that you could get under your shelter. Our personnel tents were dug down below the ground just like the hospital tents, and we had what we called a flak shack built over our cots, which was a two-by-four frame with a layer of corrugated tin and about three layers of sandbags over it.

"When we were through at Anzio our tents were literally riddled with flak. One night, I remember, a shell fell on the X-ray tent and tore up an X-ray table. Fortunately, no one was wounded. There had been a unit there just preceding us, however, from Baylor, I believe, but anyway it was a Texas unit, and one night the head nurse was killed from bombing and the next night the assistant head nurse was killed, and several other personnel, from the bombing."

Fortunately, when the shell destroyed the X-ray table and riddled the tent, Technician Davis was in his small sandbagged retreat beside the X-ray tent hardly six feet from the place the shell struck.

"We had built up a little room at the end of our laboratory tent," he recalls. "But we had stacked the sandbags on only three sides; there were no bags at the open end of the X-ray tent. Things were pretty hot and one day the idea struck me, what if a shell hit inside the tent? There'd be no protection at that end. So we filled up some bags and stacked them at that open end of the X-ray tent, along the side of our dugout that we had walled up, too.

"That night I was back in our little place, lying on a cot. Nick Irulli, a young Italian boy who helped in the laboratory—he was an American citizen and in the 38th, but an Italian who often served also as interpreter for us—was sitting on the cot beside me. I don't know why I did it, whether it was intuition or what, but I said to him, 'Nick, you'd better lie down across me.' He did, and about that time, Whom-m-m! That shell hit right on the other side of that wall of sandbags. It riddled the bags and sand poured out and pieces of the shell shot over us. If Nick had been sitting up, I do believe they'd have got him. As it was, neither of us had a scratch. But it was close! The shell had been fired by our fellows, too, at invading planes. Three shells from their guns came down on us, but nobody, I heard, got hurt."

Dr. Pitts recalls vividly, too, the procedures of the hospital under the unusual stress of the Anzio experience during which casualties were streaming in from the heavy fighting nearby.

"In times like this, of course, everything becomes a surgical hospital. All efforts are bent toward surgically handling the wounds. The medical personnel were assigned to help in the treatment of shock, to administer anesthesia, and the surgeons worked night and day. I was the only neuro-surgeon in the hospital and when the push was on there were times I'd be on my feet and operating day and night for two or three days, and the only time I'd take out would be when I sat down to have a bite to eat. It was an ordeal and I must admit that my coefficient of efficiency diminished toward the end of that period. I'd been on my feet so much that actually my legs were swollen tight, the skin was tight, just from the effects of standing on my feet over such a long period of time. At other times—and this was true at Anzio—we had assigned personnel from the so-called auxiliary surgical unit and Dr. Charles Dowman of Atlanta was assigned to our unit. When he was with us, and he was with us a good bit of the time, we would take it on a twelve-hour basis, from seven to seven and seven to seven, and in that way I had an opportunity to help out with the problem of triage."

The designation "triage," Dr. Pitts explains, is given to the officer who goes through the shock tent where the acutely wounded people are and examines quickly each patient and as quickly makes a diagnosis of his case, decides what is to be done for him, gets the enlisted personnel started on the shock treatment, gives him the priority for the operating room, and actually designates him for a particular surgeon in the operating theater.

"This is a very important job, one of the most important," Dr. Pitts points out. "It is most important very quickly to find out what's wrong with the man, second, to get emergency treatment started on him, in the way of resuscitation, blood, plasma, fluid, medication. What is required for that is the surgeon who has had a lot of experience, is capable of coming to quick decisions, and knows his personnel in order to be able to make the proper assignments. So actually Dr. Sanger and I oftentimes in stress and strain when we had a lot of casualties to deal with would divide time being the triage. So when we had another neuro-surgeon assigned to us from one of the auxiliary units, that would leave me some free time to do this."

Major Pitts operated upon more than a hundred brain wounds during the Italian campaign alone, most of them, he reveals, received during the action around Anzio, Cassino, and the Rapido River crossing. On Anzio he did the neuro-surgery for the two British hospitals there. They had two casualty clearing stations, comparable to the American field hospitals, but no neuro-surgeon.

"So I did most of the neuro-surgery for the British on Anzio," he recalls, "and the only time I ever left my hospital area at Anzio was to go up there to one of their hospitals on consultation. They had a couple of patients who had multiple wounds as well as brain injuries and they felt that the patients were too sick to be moved. I got to be sort of a part of their unit, since I was taking care of their brain wounds, and their personnel officers would come down to visit the British patients that I had under my care there. So after the Anzio battle was over they had a hospital personnel farewell party up there for their personnel and they invited me to come up to their party because they felt I was a part of their personnel, since I'd been operating on their brain wounds."

The unit's work in the Anzio area quickly gained the attention of the Fifth Army's leadership, who spoke appreciatively not only of the great volume of cases it was handling but also of the excellence of the treatment being provided.

21

Sixteen officers—ten surgeons and six nurses—came into the 38th Evacuation Hospital's organization early in December from the Second Auxiliary Surgical Group.

The Daily Bulletin of December 4 listed them under "Item No. 2, Attached Personnel:

"The Commanding Officer takes pleasure in welcoming to the organization the following Officers and Nurses of the 2nd Auxiliary Surgical Group, who are attached to this unit for duty:

GENERAL SURGICAL TEAM NO. 18
Major Charles F. Chunn
Captain Charles L. Weston
2nd Lieutenant Anna B. Berret
2nd Lieutenant Mary V. Shearer

MAXILLO-FACIAL TEAM NO. 3
Captain John K. Nattinger
Captain Hubert H. Nall
1st Lieutenant Waldemar Hoeffding
2nd Lieutenant Marguerite Ruff

GENERAL SURGICAL TEAM NO. 2
Major Paul L. Dent
Captain James L. Koccour
2nd Lieutenant Anne K. Brix
2nd Lieutenant Catherine M. Rodman

THORACIC TEAM NO. 1
Major Reeve H. Betts
1st Lieutenant Aaron Himmelstein
Major Frederick W. Bowers
2nd Lieutenant Opal G. Davis

The transfer of Captain Irving Pomper, M.C., from the 38th Evacuation unit to the 45th Infantry Division was announced in the Daily Bulletin of December 10. There, the Bulletin revealed further, Captain Pomper would assume the duties of a psychiatrist in a newly formed medical unit.

The same issue of the Daily Bulletin carried instructions concerning the wearing of the uniform by personnel on pass:

"a. The dress for American troops is optional be-

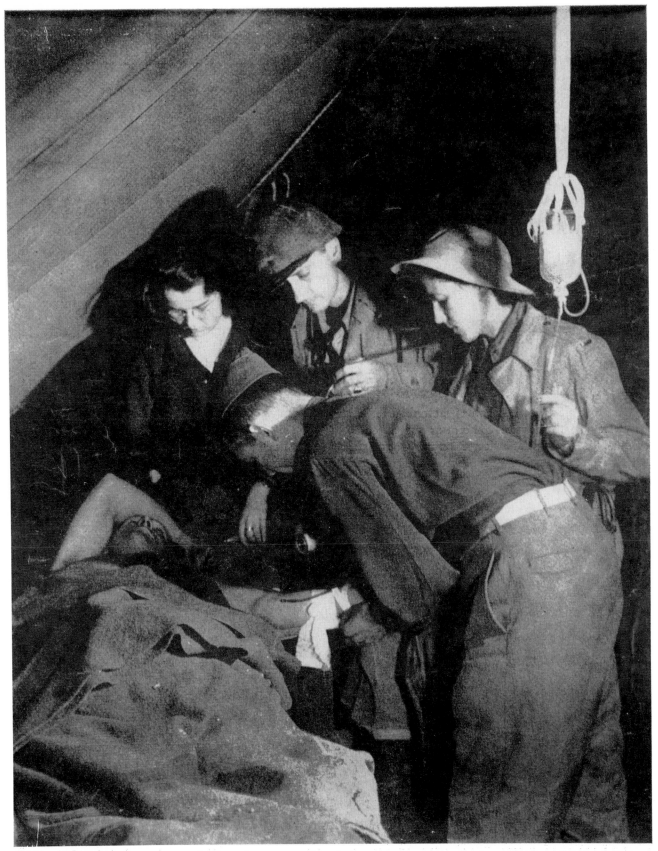

This badly wounded soldier, near death, is being given blood plasma in the 38th's shock ward. Wounded by shell fragments, he required also a transfusion of whole blood, since he had lost a considerable amount. The nurse in the fatigue hat is Lieutenant Hazel Simmons. This is another in the series of photographs made at Riardo by Margaret Bourke-White for *Life*.

Lieutenant Russell, right, with Lieutenant Rosamond Shipp, is drawing water from the Lister bag.

tween (1) the Service Uniform as prescribed for field duty and (2) the Service Uniform as prescribed for habitual wear when not in formation under arms.

(1) The Service Uniform as prescribed for field duty will be worn as follows:

(a) The shirt will be worn fully buttoned except when the necktie is not worn, in which case the collar will be left open. Sleeves will be down full length and buttoned.

(b) The field jacket will be worn fully zipped and buttoned. When combat jacket is worn in lieu of the field jacket it will be zipped as high as the first button from the collar of the shirt.

(c) The trousers will not be turned up at the cuff. Leggings may be worn when prescribed by unit commanders.

(2) The Service Uniform will be worn as prescribed for habitual wear when not in formation under arms.

(3) The knitted cap will not be worn as an outer garment.

(4) When the cap "Garrison" is not available, the helmet liner will be worn as an authorized substitute therefor.

(5) The Work Uniform will not be worn when on pass. When worn on duty, or when going to and from duty, the one-piece uniform will be buttoned throughout except that the collar may be left open. It will be fastened at the wrist and ankles. The two-piece suit will be worn with the jacket buttoned throughout ex-

cept that the collar button may be left unfastened. When the hat, herringbone twill, is worn, the brim will be turned down all around.

"b. Hands must be kept *out* of pockets."

The bulletin that day declared that "the Commanding Officer was well pleased with the condition of the hospital area on the general inspection this morning. Considerable improvement was noted over previously-tolerated conditions; however, every effort will be made to maintain the present good condition."

The Bulletin did not add that improvement in conditions in the camp had been ordered because distinguished visitors were momentarily expected. Nevertheless, on the following day the 38th was host to four generals, as noted in the Bulletin's announcement in its December 12 edition:

"The Hospital was honored yesterday by the visit of: General Arnold, Chief of the U.S. Army Air Forces; Lt. General Spaatz, N.W. African Air Forces; Lt. General Clark, Commanding Fifth Army; and Major General Cannon, N.W. African Tactical Air Forces."

But when three days later Captain Pickens wrote his next letter home he made no mention of the visit of the four officers of high rank. Instead, he wrote, more significantly and more dramatically, of the ministrations of the doctors and nurses and of the grievously wounded patients, privates and corporals and sergeants in the main, and of one young soldier in particular. He wrote of the very essence of war:

"15 December 1943
"Sunny (?) Italy

"Some time ago I was Officer of the Day and in making my nightly rounds to check the guards and the blackout and to see that our installation was in good shape, I stopped by the receiving tent and just back of it the shock tent. There the wounded come first from the battlefield just forward. Up there they have been given first aid and possibly a shot of morphine to ease their suffering and then as swiftly as possible, by ambulance, they are shuttled back to us. They sometimes stack up when the going is slow here and rapid there. They sit, if they are ambulatory, around a hot stove and dry their feet and get a cup of hot chocolate. If they are litter patients, they stretch on their litters across two wooden horses. They all await their turn to get to the X-ray tent and then thru the operating room to get their wounds treated.

"The operating tent is a busy place at night. Most of the patients come in at night. There, under bright lights, in a warm tent, skillful doctors and gifted nurses and able ward men do their work. The doctor probes for the foreign body, the bit of steel remaining in the arm or leg or chest. They sometimes have to take off a limb in order to save a life.

Frequently the 38th Evac was paid visits by the top brass of the nation's military service. In this photograph the 38th's Lieutenant Hallie Almond, left, and Lucy Brooke of the Red Cross stand between General H. H. (Hap) Arnold, head of the American air forces, left, and General Mark Clark, commanding general of the Fifth Army.

"On this particular night there was a young chap lying quietly on a litter in the shock tent. He was looking straight up at the ceiling of the tent. His eyes were fixed. The doctor said he was just coming out of shock and was fully conscious. His left leg was hanging on by a thread just below the knee. His belly had been riddled with bullets and the hurried dressing was in need of a change. He had a gaping wound on the left side of his head, which the doctor was examining when I stepped in. The others around on other litters were quiet and those around the tiny stove had stopped their talk about the day's fight. On the litter beside him were his few personal possessions, pocketbook, pictures from home, knife, and a little Italian money. In addition there were three packages with Christmas seals on them.

"I asked them what they were and they replied that

he had just received them that day and had insisted on bringing them along when his buddies had gently placed him in the ambulance to send him back. The doctor looked at me in a knowing way and said to him, 'Why don't you open your packages and see what the folks sent you?' He protested weakly and said he wanted to wait for Christmas. The doctor told him that it might be some time before he would be able to enjoy them and his advice was to enjoy them now.

"The lad slowly opened the first one. I helped him a little. Then the second came open, and the third. Such joy on that chap's face as we got the little things spread out before him. There were small paperbound books, candy, tooth brush, chewing gum, socks, a sweater with a note pinned to it from his mother saying she had knitted it for him for winter days and nights. There were other items too numerous to mention. He

155

handled each one slowly and gently and smiled each time we handed him one. Then he put them down and sighed and said in a voice almost inaudible, 'Wouldn't it be nice to be home for Christmas?'

"Then he closed his eyes and breathed his last."

Captain Pickens continued:

"The Red Cross worker in our midst wrote his family, acknowledging the receipt of the packages, and saying that he had enjoyed them. Of course, the War Department will send the actual message of his loss. But such is the drama of life and death around us every day. We don't lose many, but occasionally they come to us beyond hope of repair. This chap was quickly moved out and in a very little time those around the stove were talking again about what they had been doing that day when the shell broke a little too near them and caused them to be sent back for overhauling. So it goes in the war."

In this letter he revealed that he had been given a new assignment:

"I am no longer a kitchen knave but have the title of detachment commander, which primarily consists of seeing that three hundred Americans are fed, housed, and clothed and are on their jobs. This extra-curricular activity consists of writing letters for the few illiterates we have in the command. It is not the same as writing for a person who can speak English but who cannot write it but one who has had some education.

"This is different. It is hard to find out from them just what they want to say, and I steadfastly refuse to make up the letter myself. It is just another one of those duties that come in the Army that few people in civilian life ever think about. I doubt if any of you ever had an assignment of that sort. Try it sometime if you think it is easy."

It was beginning to appear likely that Christmas would be spent at the base, he reported. "We had hoped that we might see the midnight mass at St. Peter's, but the rain has just kept everything from moving on time. You have no idea how much mud can accumulate and there appears to be little sign of relief. However, we will make the most of it and continue to carry on. You folks at home have been doing a marvelous job. There appears to be a oneness of purpose that shows in your letters and in the public opinion that we are able to get. The headlines are still too optimistic, but that is typically American. We are beginning to get under way as a nation at war. . . ."

During the period of which Captain Pickens had written, Captain Montgomery, too, had been given a new assignment. He mentioned it, briefly, as was his characteristic manner of recording entries in his diary, in two lines:

Dec. 1st. I am officially chief of anes. Stan Nowacki added to service.

Captain Montgomery made no further entries until December 22, when he wrote of a visit he and Major Query had made to Naples:

Nothing startling since Nov. 30th except I had a three-day leave & Dick and I went to Naples. First we went to the Parco, but because of rank I couldn't stay. Then to the Touristico. Saw Billy Johnston. Also "La Traviata." Had a nice time. Tomorrow Bill Pennington, Paul and I going to Ravello.

The day after Christmas he reported a Christmas Day trip and the return to the base:

Went to Sorrento without orders & got back in O.K. at the Vittorio. Two nice rooms with balcony & bath. Good food, a grand rest. Arrived home Christmas evening in time for Buck & Stan's party.

Captain Montgomery's experience in being turned away from the Parco because of insufficient rank was not the only incident of that sort to be experienced by members of the 38th. Nor by Captain Montgomery. More than a year later he and Major Hunter Jones on their way back to the United States had to go to Naples and stay in the officers' pool until they could be assigned to a returning ship.

Dr. Jones records that experience:

"So while we were waiting to get a boat, Jack got the bright idea of trying to fly home. 'A lot of other folks are doing it,' Jack said. 'Why don't we go down and see the commanding officer and tell him we want to fly home?'

"'Well, Jack,' I said, 'I don't believe we can work it, but I'll go with you and we'll try.'

"So the next day we went down, and we got in to see the colonel, and we saluted, and the colonel said, 'How are you?' without seeming to be particularly impressed with us. Jack gave him a spiel, about how we'd been over a long time and working hard in the hospital and how we'd like to get a flight home, and so forth. The colonel, without raising his eyes from the paper we'd handed him, says, 'Captain, do you have any medals?'

"'Medals? Medals?' Jack repeated question. 'No, sir.'

"'Do you have any awards?'

"'No, sir, I don't.'

"'Have you the Legion of Merit?'

"'Don't have any of them, sir.'

"'Well, Captain,' the colonel said, 'we are saving these return flights for veterans who have honors and awards.'

"'I don't have a one, sir,' Jack told him.

"'That's all right, Captain. Don't think you'll make it, but thank you for coming.'

"So we walked out."

But these were not the only occasions when Captain Montgomery's plans had failed to materialize. And Colonel Sanger was also involved with him in another such incident. Captain Montgomery tells about it:

"This happened back when we were in North Africa. One day Paul said to me 'Would you like to go to Algiers?'

" 'Yes, I'll go,' I said. So we went to Algiers and to that big, old, fancy hotel, where everybody stayed—we thought. It was the Majestic, and was then being operated by the government. Paul said to me as we went in, 'I'll take care of this; I'll do the talking.' So we walked up to the desk, where there was a sergeant in charge whose creases in his pants would have cut your throat. 'We'd like to have a double room,' Paul said to the sergeant.

"This sergeant must have worked at the Waldorf or somewhere like that, because he just looked Paul up and down—and Paul was a lieutenant-colonel then—like he might have been the scum off the bottom of some ship, and he said, icily, 'Nobody below admirals and generals stay in this hotel.'

"We just crawled away."

22

The four high ranking generals had visited the 38th Evacuation Hospital on December 11. Two days later General Mark Clark wrote to Colonel J. I. Martin, the Fifth Army surgeon, commending the medical service for the excellent work its men and women had been accomplishing. Members of the 38th wondered if, and hoped that General Clark's visit to their hospital had occasioned the writing so quickly after his visit of the general letter of commendation.

General Clark's letter was transmitted to "all Fifth Army medical personnel, British and American," by Colonel Martin, and was published on Saturday, December 18, in the 38th's Daily Bulletin:

13 December 1943

Colonel J. I. Martin, M.C.,
Surgeon, Fifth Army,
Headquarters Fifth Army

Dear Colonel Martin:

Since our landing in Salerno Bay I have been continually impressed with the excellence of the medical service throughout the Fifth Army. Conditions in this campaign have, from the beginning, taxed all the services to the limit of their capacity, but none more than the Medical Department.

The removal of the wounded from the battlefields has required more than the ordinary amount of skill, fortitude and endurance on the part of the litter bearers, who carry their comrades by hand, over miles of treacherous mountain trails, through artillery and mortar fire, and in all kinds of weather. Truly they have earned their place among the unsung heroes of this campaign.

The skillful medical attention rendered each patient so willingly is indicative of a superior degree of singleness of purpose—to achieve the Medical Department's mission of conserving the fighting strength of the Army.

The many long hours spent each day, often in the face of danger, by enlisted men, nurses and officers in caring for the sick and wounded have not only contributed to the military achievements of the Fifth Army but have had a splendid effect on the morale of the entire force.

For this most willing sacrifice and outstanding service I wish to command all ranks of both the British and the U.S. medical contingents of the Fifth Army. It is my desire that you convey to them all my appreciation of their fine work and my confidence that the future will never present a problem that they will not meet with the same willing energy and skill that has been so evident to all.

Sincerely,
/s/ Mark W. Clark
/t/ MARK W. CLARK
Lieutenant General, USA
Commanding

To General Clark's letter Colonel Martin appended the message:

I wish to add, at this time, my personal appreciation of the splendid service rendered by all medical units of this command.

But a letter in further praise of the medical services, this one specifically in commendation of the 38th Evacuation Hospital, would be received within another few days from another general in the Medical Corps. This doctor, a personal friend of several of the officers in the 38th and first cousin of Charlotte's Dr. W. S. Rankin, was Brigadier General Fred W. Rankin of Lexington, Kentucky, a native North Carolinian and then attached to the Surgeon General's office in Washington. Dr.

Rankin had written Colonel Wood in high praise of the work of the hospital, which he had visited in North Africa.

In the Daily Bulletin of December 23 an excerpt of the letter was published:

The Commanding Officer takes pleasure in publishing an extract from a letter received yesterday from Brigadier General Fred W. Rankin, Surgeon General's Office, Washington:

"I was delighted to have your letter from 'Somewhere in Italy' and to know that the outfit is getting back into harness and is being kept busy. I think the greatest thing that can happen to our professional men is plenty of work and certainly nothing else keeps their morale at such a pitch. When I saw your hospital in Africa I was enormously pleased with all of you and with the things I had heard about you. I know that now that you have settled down and gotten some of the irritating factors ironed out that you will continue to do the splendid work that all of you are capable of. I think it should be a source of great satisfaction to the whole outfit that, despite unfavorable circumstances, you earned the commendation of two Surgeons General by the type of professional work you were putting out when they visited you. Certainly I found myself much elated at being an honorary member of your organization when I looked over your wards and interviewed your professional personnel.

That day's issue of the Bulletin carried three announcements in which members of the 38th were concerned. The first declared that "It is regretted that Captain William Evans and 2nd Lieutenant Martha Pegram have been separated from the organization, but we all share their pleasure in their return to the States." The second revealed that "word has just been received that Major Pat R. Imes was elected to the Southern Surgical Association at its last meeting." The other announcement was that "At the meeting of all Fifth Army medical officers, to be held at Caserta today, Major Pitts will present a paper on 'Penetrating Head Injuries.'"

On Christmas Day 1943 the Daily Bulletin was even more festive than it had been on Thanksgiving Day. Half the first sheet was given to a drawing of Santa Claus being pulled in his sleigh by two antlered reindeer above the rooftops of a village below. A tag attached to his sack of gifts had the notation: All for 38th Evac. Hosp.

The remainder of the first page carried the Christmas messages from President Franklin D. Roosevelt. The first was titled:

TO OUR ILL OR WOUNDED FIGHTERS

The President wrote:

"On behalf of a grateful nation, I welcome the privilege of sending you Christmas good wishes. The uncomplaining gallantry of our American soldier and sailor in his quiet, patient battle against illness and aching wound is no less epic than his uncompromising gallantry in his more widely heralded fight against the Axis. We cannot wish you a Merry Christmas. We can salute you—and we do. We can pray—and we do: May God speed your recovery."

The other message was directed:

TO THE MEN AND WOMEN OF THE ARMED FORCES

It said:

"Two years ago Americans observed Christmas in the first dark hours of a global war. By sacrifice and courage and stern devotion to duty, you accepted the challenge boldly. You have met and overcome a determined enemy on the land, on the sea, and in the air. Fighting with skill and bravery, you have already destroyed his dream of conquest. This Christmas, I feel a sense of deep humility before the great courage of the men and women of our Armed Forces. As your Commander-in-Chief, I send my greetings with pride in your heroic accomplishments. To you the Nation's prayers will be raised on Christmas Day. Through you at last the peace of Christmas will be restored to this land in our certain victory.

"(Signed) Franklin D. Roosevelt"

The remainder of the Bulletin was given almost entirely to Christmas messages from General Clark and Colonel Wood.

General Clark wrote:

"To an army in combat overseas, it is inevitable that Christmas is a very different occasion from the festival at home. We are deprived of the special happiness and inspiration which are found each year in the reunions of beloved families and friends during the holiday season. The loss of this phase of the great annual institution is part of the price paid for war.

"Nevertheless, during Christmas in the field we may derive encouragement and spiritual comfort in realizing that the principles, virtues and values which Christmas symbolizes still stand unshaken and that the preservation of freedom to cultivate them is the essence of our war aim.

"This Christmas of 1943 is in many ways the brightest one for us all since the beginning of the war. It marks the end of a year in which consistent progress has been made on land, on sea and in the air in the process of closing in on our determined but gradually weakening foe. We are determined that this process shall continue with such acceleration and crushing force that once victory is achieved there will be no more Christmases spent in overseas combat.

"It is my sincere hope that despite the circumstances of war each member of the Fifth Army will be able to feel the presence of Christmas and, inspired by the righteousness of our cause and the unity of this Allied team, will know that with God's help we shall make 1944 a decisively victorious year.

> "/s/ Mark W. Clark
> MARK W. CLARK
> Lieutenant General, USA,
> Commanding."

Colonel Wood's greeting was:

"Personally, and on behalf of my staff, I wish every member of our unit, all attached personnel, each hospital patient, and visitor—a very happy Christmas Day! Be as merry as you can, under the circumstances. And, God being willing, may you all be at home next year to celebrate Christmas by the fireside of your beloved ones.

> "G. T. Wood, Jr.
> Lt. Col., M. C.,
> Commanding."

On Christmas Day 1943 the hospital listed 646 patients, 116 of whom were admissions; twenty-two wards were in operation, 90 beds were vacant, and 105 dispositions were listed. The administrative officer of the day was Captain Walker and Major Snyder was alternate; medical officer of the day was Captain McGrath and Major Query was alternate; Major Pitts was surgical officer of the day and his alternate was Captain Calder; and dental officer of the day was Captain Hoffman and Captain Walker was alternate.

The observance of Christmas by the personnel of the 38th Evacuation Hospital is revealed in part and in a less formal way than the Bulletin reports it, however, in portions of the letter Captain Pickens wrote home three days after Christmas.

"The celebration of the birthday of Christ in our camp followed the routine as much as possible under the circumstances," he wrote. "We went to church, sang carols, listened to recordings of the Dickens story of old Scrooge, had guests by our tents for as much feasting as we could offer, and ate the best meal the Army has provided since we have been overseas. We all had many gifts from home and many delightful cards from friends. The Army did a grand job in getting these things over to us in plenty of time. It was all so much better than last year in Africa, but there is one thing that expresses the full feelings of us all and that was an expression of one of our number, 'It is difficult to be in two places at once, Charlotte and Italy.' There was another expression that tickled me, by one of the Scotch wags, to wit, 'Isn't it nice to have Christmas without the inevitable bills that come due at the first of the following month?' Probably the highlight of the celebration came with the playing of a recording from home in which several of the wives from Charlotte gave greetings."

There was one soldier in the 38th, however, for whom the Christmas season brought no happy thoughts of home, no looking with high hopes to the ending of the war and the returning to the States and resuming the life the fierce conflict had so dramatically interrupted. And this soldier's experience doubtless was being paralleled in many another American military unit overseas. Captain Pickens told about it in his December 28 letter:

"I have mentioned some of the things that I have inherited with the new job, such as seeing that three hundred young Americans get fed, clothed and have sufficient shelter and that they get properly paid at the beginning of each month no matter the amount allotted to each. I have told you that I must look after the maintenance of the hospital, a sort of glorified janitor. I write the letters of the illiterate.

"But recently I had my first assignment in domestic relations. One of our men reported that his wife had been unfaithful at home and he wanted to get a divorce and have the allotment of the pay being sent to her stopped. He was a pitiful sight as he talked, heartbroken about his plight and caught in a whirlpool over which he seemed to have no control. He had a letter from his wife back in Constantine in which she said that she no longer cared for him and was in love with another man. Constantine was last February or March. He said he just couldn't believe it and held on to hope against hope. Then the mail began to envelop him and he discovered that his wife had moved to a neighboring town with his best friend. She wrote him the facts. Still, he said, he could not believe it and drove the idea from his mind. Then just before Christmas he had a letter from her saying she was to become a mother in the early spring. That, he said, combined with Christmas, was just too much and he came to tell the whole story and ask how he could get relief. He said he had denied the facts and the truth from his mind as long as he could.

"I thought he was entitled to legal separation and set about to find what could be done. It is a long story that has just begun, but a tragic one for a good American soldier. I shall tell you the outcome when, as, and if we get it worked out. Such are the things that arise each day in an Army overseas that you don't think about at home."

During the Christmas season, Captain Pickens revealed, he had been reading a novel that would be one of the mostly widely read books of that decade.

"I am in the midst of reading the delightful book

called 'The Robe,' by Lloyd Douglas. The beginning of the story is based in this section in which I am living. It is the story of the robe that Christ wore at the time of His crucifixion. The Roman soldiers played dice for it, and the story follows the experience of the winner. With Douglas I have wandered over the Mediterranean from Rome to Naples to Capri, thru the Straits and into Athens and Joppa and then to Jerusalem and all over Galilee. What an effect one man has had on human living, but the lack of following His teachings has brought me here. It might be well that the soldiers at the front can sing Christmas carols to each other and across the line with the enemy, but the answer has not been found for the resumption of the artillery fire the following morning and the deadly earnestness with which they try to kill each other."

As 1943 was almost at its end he offered some trenchant observations, likely shared by most of the American service men and women serving overseas at that time, about the vast American aid program in the areas in which the 38th had been stationed and its effect upon the natives of those regions. His remarks, said he, had been provoked by his reading of newspaper clippings and magazines "about how people are starving over here or will be starving during this winter." He went on to elaborate:

"I read with a great deal of interest about the 400,000 yards of diaper material sent to North Africa. I have seen where thousands will die of hunger here in Italy before the winter is out. For the diaper deal, I never saw a diaper on an Arab the whole length of North Africa and I traveled from Ain-el-Turck, which is west of Oran, all the way to Tunis, a matter of nearly a thousand miles. I saw a lot of young Arabs during that tour which lasted just about a year. I saw them in the winter, spring, and fall, and in the summer, too. There must have been several thousand of them, but not one diaper was apparent. Now the French, who were in the minority, might use them, but they seemed to be as well clothed as our average folk at home. Possibly the need was there and I will be the first to say let's share with our needy neighbors, but from my observation, we could do more for those folks than try to inflict our sense of modesty on them in such a wasteful fashion.

"They would do a lot better with some good doctors, some teachers, and a lot of gasoline pumps for irrigation purposes and a few tractors and first-class plows," he suggested. "There was no shortage of food as far as I could see, of the vital necessities. Here in Italy they have been short of some things like salt and beef and flour, but as yet I have not seen anyone who was starving and I don't think there will be any. They still have enough flour for their beloved spaghetti, and there are plenty of fresh vegetables, fruits, nuts, and now, fish. If they are left alone, they will provide for themselves without becoming public charges.

"Over here when they get hungry they begin working rather than going to the government. Right here in our camp they plow right up to the edge of the tent and plant grain. They try to graze their cattle throughout our hospital area if we don't run them out. Back of our officers' row of tents there is a little shepherdess minding her small flock of sheep each day. She stays there in the driving rain each day and takes the mutton home with her at night. I hope we don't make another WPA out of these folks, but if we do, let's get the full credit for it ourselves. I can't see but a little of what goes on, but from Salerno on up I have had a chance to get a fair picture and it is not as bad as you are led to believe by those people who write long articles without having been here."

He continued to reveal his views in a paragraph commenting upon the news members of the unit had been receiving about strikes and industrial unrest in the United States:

"I don't know what to think of the strikes over there, but it is hard to fit them with our way of living and the sacrifices we make over here. I am reasonably sure I could be making more money at home than I am making here, and there are thousands of soldiers who could be better off financially if they were there. I realize our restriction is not entirely voluntary, but on the 30th of this month we do not plan to quit. We may not be doing so well, but we are not planning to walk out. It makes us wonder, as we sit in the rain and the mud, thousands of miles from home, living in the crudest fashion and subject to sudden annihilation, whether it is worth it when people at home squabble about their wages and hours. I thought for a while that the country was getting started so we could get this business over with, but I doubt if they realize fully just what is going on and what the price must be. The North African diapers should be kept at home."

The next year, 1944, would be a Presidental election year and in the spring the American people would be voting in the primaries. American soldiers abroad would be interested in the various political contests and hoped and expected to cast their ballots, as Captain Pickens observed in this last letter written home in 1943:

"The chance to vote in next year's election must be given to us. We are citizens worthy of the ballot. The issues should be given to us from both sides. I hope proper care will be taken to see that every man overseas gets his chance to express his opinion. This is particularly true in the local and state elections. I don't think many men over here will be interested in dema-

160

The operating room was lined on the inside of the tent's roof with sheets to help make it more sterile but also to increase the light from the overhead electric bulbs. In foreground is small space heater that provided some warmth.

goguery. The majority favor the bonus as it has been outlined, but the principal reason for this favor is because they feel they have not had a chance to earn that additional money during the time they have been in the Army. They are more interested in it and there is more talk of it when there are threatened strikes at home. . . ."

And as the year ran out rapidly toward its end he was still using all the ingenuity he could command to obtain for himself and his fellow members of the 38th what he had been trying to arrange with varying degrees of success since their arrival in North Africa more than a year before, adequate bathing facilities with ample supplies of hot water. He had written during the year many times of his efforts to get baths and to help provide the necessary facilities. In this last letter of the year his concluding paragraph would be a report on his most recent effort:

"In addition to other duties I spent a part of this day trying to wheedle a canvas water tank out of the Engineers. We have inherited a sterilizer and a hot water heater on wheels. It is of no use to us without water and water cannot be had without a tank. It is the first chance we have had to have hot water in the field for over a year now. The thought of a hot bath even in a cold tent spurred me on, but to no avail. I must have fifteen requisitions with at least six copies of each and a certificate of what the tank will be used for and a promise to take good care of it, as if I were going to run out and punch holes in it the first day, and all of this must 'go thru channels' to no telling where, possibly to the War Department. By next summer we may get the tank, if at that time the Engineers have any on hand which they are not using for their own benefit, which is highly unlikely. It was a noble try at least and altho I may not get any stars on my

Colonel Preston White takes to the open air for his morning's shave.

uniform for my efforts, I may get some stars in heaven on my crown, since cleanliness is said to be next to godliness. . . ."

The last few issues of the Daily Bulletin after Christmas were devoted largely to the publication of belated Christmas greetings that had failed to reach the 38th in time for publication on Christmas Day. The message from the Fifth Army's surgeon, Colonel J. I. Martin, was published the day after Christmas. Colonel Martin wrote:

"Although our holidays cannot be merry under these conditions, I want each one of you to get such consolation as you can in the knowledge that I am most deeply appreciative of your sterling work and loyalty. To me this knowledge is a real source of happiness.

"The record of the Medical Department to date in this campaign has been favorably commented upon by our Commanding General and in the press of the United States on numerous occasions.

"The credit for this belongs largely to you and your organization which from the beginning has shown a degree of fidelity to duty that is unsurpassed. We face the new year assured that we will not fail our responsibility.

"I pray that God may bless you all in the coming year and that we may all come through this trial safely to enjoy our next Christmas holidays with our dear ones at home.

"Will you please communicate these sentiments to every member of your organization.

"Sincerely yours,
/s/ J. I. Martin
Colonel, Medical Corps,
Surgeon."

Two days later, in its December 28 edition, the Daily Bulletin carried Christmas greetings from General George C. Marshall, Chief of Staff, whose visit to Charlotte two years earlier had signaled the organization of the 38th, and Secretary of War Henry L. Stimson.

General Marshall's was brief:

"In its training, in its landings against great odds, and in its fighting over the most difficult terrain in the worst possible fighting weather, the Fifth Army has exemplified the best traditions of our country's fighting forces. To you personally and to all members of your command I extend my highest admiration, my best wishes for Christmas and my firm confidence in even greater successes during 1944."

Secretary Stimson wrote:

"In the midst of war the coming of Christmas has a deep significance. Christmas becomes the symbol of our hope for peace and good will for our nation and throughout the world. Our thoughts turn to the men and women who will spend this Christmas day far from their home, many on the field of battle itself, striving to bring about the victories which will realize this Christmas hope of future peace. Those thoughts are in my mind as I send my greetings not only to our troops but to the thousands of civilians who are serving in the military establishments which provide arms and equipment for the front. Whatever and wherever your station, I know that you are performing with a soldierly devotion the duties to which you have been assigned and at this Christmas season I wish to express to you my deep appreciation. In the Theater of War our troops have accepted hardships and sacrifices with a fortitude which recognizes that these are the necessary prices of victory. Your deeds on the battlefield have been an inspiration to millions of your countrymen. To the love which your families and friends hold for you has been added the gratitude of the nation. On this day I send you my greetings. Throughout America the light of Christmas burns brightly in remembrance of you and in prayer for your return. God grant that your hand may be strengthened to hasten the day of final victory. Upon you and your comrades in arms, the world depends for the restoration of Christmas day as a symbol of peace on earth."

On that same day the Bulletin announced the promotion of Second Lieutenant Eugene M. Snell to the rank of first lieutenant.

The Daily Bulletin for the remaining days of December had no notices of general interest, except for one, from headquarters of the Fifth Army, and it was startling:

"1. Epidemic typhus fever has made its appearance in the population of the City of Naples. Existing conditions in the city are ideal for the development of a large scale epidemic of this serious disease. The occurrence of this disease in Army troops will have a very serious effect on our combat strength which must be maintained at all costs at its present high standard. Therefore until the effectiveness of measures now operative and others contemplated for the control of this disease in the Naples area is demonstrated, the City of Naples is, effective 0800 hours 26 December 1943, placed 'Off Limits' temporarily to Fifth Army troops, except for those units now situated in the metropolitan area of Naples and for individuals entering the area on official business of absolute necessity that cannot be transacted by any means other than their physical presence.

"2. All individuals having authority to visit Naples on official business will be required to have in their possession at all times a special pass, signed by the unit commander, stating the reason therefor.

"3. All organizations will immediately impress upon every member of their organizations the extreme seriousness of this situation and the severity of punishment to be given violators."

The warning, in substantially the same words but more detailed, was repeated in the Daily Bulletin of December 31. On this last day of 1943 Captain Pickens was administrative officer of the day and Captain Medearis was alternate. Captain Wright was medical officer of the day and Captain Nowacki alternate. Surgical officer of the day was Major Munroe and alternate was Major Betts. The dental officer of the day, Captain Mitchell, had as his alternate Captain Walker.

Number of patients in the hospital December 31 was 582, of which 165 were admissions. Seventy-nine dismissions were recorded, and there were 154 vacant beds, with 22 wards in operation.

Although the Daily Bulletin did not record it until the following day, the year ended with a furious blizzard that caused considerable damage and great inconvenience. Captain Montgomery in his entry of January 1, 1944, reported it:

A blizzard last night wrecked 34 ward tents & a few of officers & nurses small wall tents. Bob & I got up at five & repaired some broken ropes on ours. Evacuated 594 patients today. Hospital closed.

The Daily Bulletin of January 1, likewise, referred to the storm:

"The Surgeon, Fifth Army, is fully expecting the members of the 38th Evacuation Hospital to live up to their past reputation in being able to resume work without delay as a result of the storm last night. Your cooperation is expected and desired."

The year began clear and cold, with 596 patients in the hospital, 115 of which were admissions, the Daily Bulletin records, and Captain Montgomery noted in his diary of January 2, 1944:

Clear & cold. Wind has lessened. Wreckage being cleared.

The Bulletin of January 2 also referred to the storm:

"Various items of personal property were left in the wards by patients, due to the emergency evacuation yesterday. It is requested that every possible care be given this property. Collect it, keeping it separated; mark it, if possible; and turn same in to the Registrar for proper disposition.

The number of patients listed that day was but 29. A total of 595 had been evacuated because of the storm. But the hospital was reopened the next day, January 3, as recorded in Captain Montgomery's diary:

Hospital reopened last night. Half full now.

That day the hospital list, as shown in the Bulletin, numbered 187 patients and the next day it had climbed to 243. On January 5 it had 245 listed and 72 dispositions. And on that day the Bulletin published a letter written December 12 to the commanding officer of the 38th Evacuation Hospital by Major General Geoffrey Keyes of the II Corps and forwarded to the unit through General Mark Clark, who in sending it on to Colonel Wood wrote:

"It is with considerable pride that I forward this letter of commendation from the Commanding General, II Corps, as I am well aware of the fine work which prompted it."

General Keyes wrote:

"As a result of my personal visits combined with reports of visits of officers of my staff, I wish to commend you, your officers, nurses and enlisted men for the efficient manner in which you are caring for the sick and wounded soldiers, not only of the II Corps Command but of the entire Fifth Army Command. The wounded to whom I spoke were outspoken with praise for the attention they are receiving.

"In particular do I wish to extend my commendation to the nurses for their cheerfulness and attention to duty as they go about caring for the wounded under the most adverse conditions of weather.

"I am confident that your hospital is doing everything possible for the sick and wounded in such a manner that reflects credit to the high standards of the Medical Corps of the United States Army. Equally confident am I that this high standard will be upheld by each member of your organization in the battles to come!"

That same issue of the Daily Bulletin announced the promotion of Captain Duncan G. Calder, Jr., to the rank of major and Second Lieutenant Bertha Hough to the rank of first lieutenant.

On January 5, 1944, the Fifth Army marked its first anniversary. And in recognition of the day, General Clark sent a long message "To the Officers and Men of the Fifth Army," which was carried that day in the Daily Bulletin.

General Clark wrote:

"One year ago, on January 5, 1943, the Fifth Army was formed, and on this anniversary it seems fitting to look back over its first year. All of us can take personal pride in the achievements of our great Army.

"Most of you remember the long months of training which many of our units went through in Africa, months when our prospect of service in battle as an army seemed remote, and when our friends elsewhere were distinguishing themselves in action against the enemy. Through those months it was hard work and persistence in training which brought the Fifth Army to the splendid condition in which it landed at Salerno.

"The anxious weeks of preparation for invading the Italian mainland and the stirring events since September 9 are still so recent in memory that they call for no reminder. I can only say how proud I was of every member of my staff, and of all our units, British and American, at every moment of the critical Salerno landing operation and the operations subsequent thereto. I welcome our gallant French comrades in arms who have recently joined us.

"It is no more than just, at this time, that we reflect on the help in our operations which we have received from our comrades of the air and of the sea. Modern warfare demands that all forces work in a coordinated whole, and this has been splendidly achieved during our Italian campaign.

"On this occasion we pay warm tribute to those of us who have fallen, those gallant soldiers whose spirit will never die, whose will was to rid the world of the aggressor, whose indomitable spirit the Fifth Army will continue to hallow until, and after, victory.

"Ahead of us are critical days. They will call for all our fortitude, all our resolution, all our strength. We have a rough road to tread, but not one of us will hesitate until a lasting peace has been secured.

"To every officer and man in the Fifth Army I send my personal greetings, my thanks for work well done, and my wishes for every good thing during the coming year. And the best of these is a beaten enemy and a lasting peace.

"The peoples of the United Nations know what you have done. They know that you are the faithful heirs of the noble, brave and self-sacrificing traditions of their armies and of the soldiers who carried their standards through to victories in past years. You are the best soldiers in the world and no enemy can stand in your way. The Fifth Army can carry out any mission it is given. As Army Commander I salute you."

In this same issue of the Daily Bulletin Colonel Wood announced the promotion of Second Lieutenants A. Clementine Mills, ANC, and Margaret P. Bachoka, ANC, to the rank of first lieutenant.

That first full week in the new Year ended with 281 patients on the hospital rolls. The next day, Sunday, January 9, the number, with 222 admissions, jumped to 468. The following day the patient list was down to 374. Dispositions totaled 122.

That same day, January 10, Captain Pickens resumed his letter-writing. It was the first he had written in 1944, the first since December 28. His letter in large part would be a report on the terrific storm that struck the 38th's base as the year 1943 was ending. He wrote this time from "Cold, Muddy Italy." His letter provides a detailed account of the evacuation of the patients during this memorable experience.

His recital begins with New Year's Eve, 1943, and New Year's Day with, as he terms it, "an unforgettable experience." He was officer of the day on the last day of December, as the Daily Bulletin records, with Captain Medearis as alternate, and during the day he had to make a trip to the finance office to pick up the payroll for the 38th. He goes on with his account of that day:

"I made arrangements for the alternate to take over during my absence and started out. We had moved from one source of money to another. This last location was over across a ridge from us, a matter of ten miles as the crow flies, but a 35-mile trip by road. In a jeep or weapons carrier it takes about two hours to run 35 miles in a warring area, with one-way bridges, convoys, MPs and protests from the enemy of any movement.

"That particular trip was not important because nothing happened of great interest, except two stops, made hurriedly, and a quick search for cover. The four hours passed and with it came a driving rain, sometimes turning into snow as we crossed the ridge. As we returned, the weather got worse and by the time we were back in camp with our numb feet and wet clothes, the rain was coming in torrents and the wind had risen to a small gale. During the afternoon I paid the enlisted personnel and after supper I paid the nurses and officers. It was eight o'clock by the time the job was complete and we had counted our left over money and found we checked out exactly correct. The matter of dishing out something over $20,000 and not making a mistake is one for the books. It is the first time it has happened to me and I am particularly concerned about

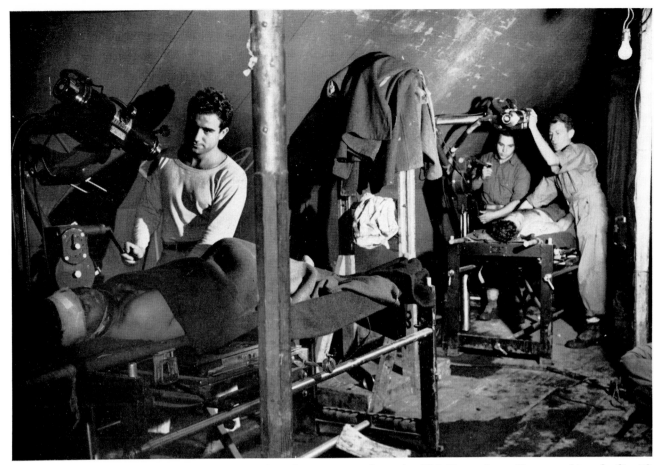

This photograph, another in the Margaret Bourke-White series made at the 38th Evac, shows X-ray machines built with racks to accommodate the patients' litters so that X-rays can be made without moving the patients from the litters in which they have been brought in. At the machine in foreground is Technician George Grant. In background Sergeant Randall K. Davis, right, has arm uplifted as he adjusts machine. The other soldier is Nick Ierulli.

it, since I have to sign a statement accepting pecuniary responsibility when I take the money from the finance office. I was feeling quite good about the whole business of finishing up the year with everything straight. The only thing I had to worry about was an investigation they were having about a water tank I had taken back in Tunis where some Frenchman had put in a claim saying the tank had been full of alcohol. He stated that I had overcome the protests of his guard and he wanted about $400 from my government. This had been answered properly, and even this did not worry me very much since I had gone thru the proper channels to get the equipment."

Captain Pickens goes on with his story:

"As the night began to wear on, the wind increased in velocity. The rains poured down. It developed into a night that was not too good for man or beast. I had to be out to see that the whole place was operating properly and that the guards were on their posts. By midnight the wind had gone too far and concern was felt about whether the tents would stand the pressure.

Here I was, on New Year's Eve, the time for celebration, wandering around tightening tent ropes and getting them to put on tent flies where the water was quitting the Methodists for the Baptists. At two o'clock in the morning I thought the worst of the blow had passed and we were safe and decided to get in my little trundle bed for forty winks. I checked my own tent and drove the pins in a little farther and tightened the ropes of the guys to keep the wind from blowing it down and then undressed and crawled in. About three-thirty I was almost pushed out of my flimsy cot by the wind and it seemed to me that the tent would come down on me any minute. The rain was pouring down. The lights had failed. I dressed hurriedly and waked up my tentmate and told him to try to save our tent, that I was going up in the hospital area. I had a feeling that we would not have a hospital for long.

"On the way out, and incidentally, I just put my uniform on over my pajamas, I saw one officer's tent blow down, but I did not stop and try to help. I was thinking about the patients who were helpless. When

Lieutenant Lorraine Benante, who died at Montecatini, was the only member of the 38th's nursing corps to die during its period of service.

I arrived in the area, none of the big ward tents had come down, but the wind had reached such gale proportions that it was merely a matter of minutes before they had to give somewhere. The night ward men were on duty along with the night nurses and as one tent gave away and began to fall, they hurriedly moved the patients to another tent that was more stable."

He continues with his account of this trying, challenging night:

"This went on for the better part of an hour and in the meantime the rain had changed to sleet, the most devastating, cutting ice I have ever felt. We had about six hundred patients"—the Daily Bulletin of December 31 listed 582—"and in the course of that hour about a third of them had been moved. Fortunately, only about a third of the total number were helpless; the others could at least walk the short distances between tents. But as time went on other tents gave way and there was no room to huddle together. The mess tents were down and there was no hot coffee or chocolate to be had. Then the latrine tents disappeared. It was pitch black. At about five o'clock in the morning the Commanding Officer got an ambulance company on the telephone and they sent us twenty vehicles. An Army ambualnce will hold four litter patients and with the motor going will keep them warm. We hurriedly took the very sick patients and moved them into the ambulances. Some of them had just been operated on that day and ordinarily it is very bad for them to be moved that soon, but better to be in a warm spot than

sitting out in the black with a cutting sleet beating you in the face and a bitter, cold wind whipping around your blankets.

"With these 75 or 80, some conscious and some unconscious, patients tucked away, we sent the ambulatory patients to a two-tent combination we had rigged up for a movie theatre. It is funny that the monstrosity that we thought would never weather any sort of storm stood thru the whole thing. We had a stove going in there and it was not too bad. Our emergency lighting equipment gave light for that section. There were about 200 in that group, sad looking, some in uniform, but most in pajamas with a couple of blankets held tightly around them. That left us with an equal number still in the wards that had not come down, but it looked like they would fall any minute."

About five-thirty in the morning—January 1, 1944—Captain Pickens continues his dramatic account of this memorable night, he telephoned Colonel John Trescott, who was set up down the road two or three miles from the 38th's base.

"I apologized for waking him up at that awful hour on New Year's Day, but begged for some trucks to evacuate our patients. He said they would be up in less than thirty minutes, and in that time exactly a young lieutenant reported that they were ready to help. I remember asking him if he had had any breakfast and he replied, no, that his kitchen had been blown down. I told him there was no chance getting any with us, but he said that did not matter.

"We loaded the remaining walking patients on the trucks and with the ambulances started the total evacuation of our patients to a permanent building some thirty miles to the rear, to a big general hospital. We could not get them on the telephone to warn them of this tremendous influx, but sent another officer along with the first vehicle to tell them. By the time it got light we had moved all of our patients to a safe place. The wind kept blowing and we just huddled in the tents that were still standing and waited, hoping the storm would abate. The morning wore on and there was little sign of any relief. We then began to talk of evacuating our personnel because some of the men's tents had come down and several of the nurses had been rained out and their personal belongings were catching the rain and sleet. About four or five of the officers' tents went down out of the twenty and it looked like there was no way of keeping anything up. Wherever there was a fire there was some individual cooking. In the headquarters tents we brewed up a little hot tea, which kept us warm for a little while. My clothes were soaking wet. Every time we got out to check a tent or help in moving a patient, the rain and sleet just beat so hard against us that everything got wet. My galoshes were holding water. I was foolish enough to keep my pants legs inside and the water just ran down the trousers into the boots. It was a mess. Everyone was wet by this time and there was little chance of drying, since the rain and sleet kept coming down. During the night I prayed as I have never prayed before. I had visions of those helpless soldiers on cots with no cover and that hammering sleet and that cutting wind tossing them about. I thought about the disciples who waked Him on the little Sea of Galilee to save their waterlogged fishing boat and how He came to their rescue in that storm. I asked Him to help us and I know He did, since no one was injured in the muddling and none of the patients was lost, as a later checkup showed. I was amazed at the gentle care shown by our men in the moving of sick men in that driving storm. I was thankful for the nurses on duty who stood out like solid rocks in that storm. They went about their duties as wet and afraid as I was with never a sign of a complaint. I will ever be an admirer of Army nurses because they came thru when the blue chips were down."

About noon that day, January 1, he continues his narrative of that frightful experience, the storm began to slacken.

"And we began to take stock of our damage," he goes on. "For the first time we were hungry. The army had provided turkey for New Year's Day. They had been cooked the night before, but now they were scattered over a two-acre field under canvas, in ditches, behind boxes and stoves. We gathered up as many as were salvagable and toward two o'clock in the afternoon the cooks had some turkey sandwiches with soggy bread and some hot coffee. This we took to our tents to eat, since we had no mess tents standing. Then we started to rebuild, since we had word that other patients were due in and we had to take care of them. By four o'clock we had beds for 300."

But their tremendous trial by weather was not yet ended, he goes on to relate:

"Just at nightfall the winds started again. The one redeeming feature was that the rain and sleet had stopped; but it was bitter cold. The patients from the front had begun to trickle in and we wondered if we were in for a duplication of the night before. All during the night I kept checking thru our area and keeping a watchful eye on our own little tent. By four o'clock it looked as if we would ride this one out without the loss of a tent, but on occasions the lights would fail when a line would break and every now and then a stovepipe would blow away and we would have to put the fire out hurriedly.

"It was a dreadful night. I dropped off to sleep at about four and got up at eight to keep up the vigilance.

During the second day the wind died down and the sun came out. That night I took off my clothes for the first time in three nights and discovered my pajamas still there.

"I never want that experience again. I'll take bombing or strafing or the constant artillery fire any time instead. There may be some help for these, but there was no help for that wind and that driving rain and sleet. At no time during the entire experience was there anything funny to relieve the situation. There was no relief."

He ends his report of the 38th's harrowing experience with a modest observation. "So much," his last line comments, "for an unusual few days in Army life overseas."

These same few days at the end of 1943 and the beginning of 1944 were dramatically recorded, too, by Major Stokes Munroe, Jr., who would write of that period:

"It was Christmas season, but wars don't stop for Christmas celebrations. The winter rains that followed the fall rains in late September were in full force. Creeks were transferred into raging torrents, and everything in our mountainous area of the Winter Line was deeply buried in mud. The fighting forces, after capturing one mountainous ridge, were always faced with another and another until each newly appearing one seemed more and more impossible. The enemy was always well fortified on his peaks that overlooked our advancing troops. The heavy casualties poured into our hospital. Christmas or no Christmas, the 38th Evacuation Hospital had a job to do, and it did it unsparingly.

"The New Year opened with disaster to our hospital. When the storm came on the evening of 31 December 1943, Captain Stanton W. Pickens was administrative officer of the day, Captain Harold S. Wright was medical officer of the day, Major Henry Stokes Munroe, Jr., was surgical officer of the day, and Captain Charles F. Mitchell was dental officer of the day. The cold, powerful sleet-carrying wind from the northwest began to shake the tents with its angry gusts. As tent pins began to pull from the mud-softened ground, everyone was running about driving tent pins and making every attempt to save our hospital. The wind seemed to be angered by our efforts. As tents began to collapse and large tent poles crash and splinter, Lieutenant Colonel George Wood and Executive Officer Major William Pennington, along with the rest of us were running about evaluating damage and impending damage. Communications to Fifth Army headquarters were impossible, due to destruction of telephone lines. It was finally decided that the safety of our wounded demanded immediate evacuation to the rear. The falling sharp-splintered tent poles with canvas filled with

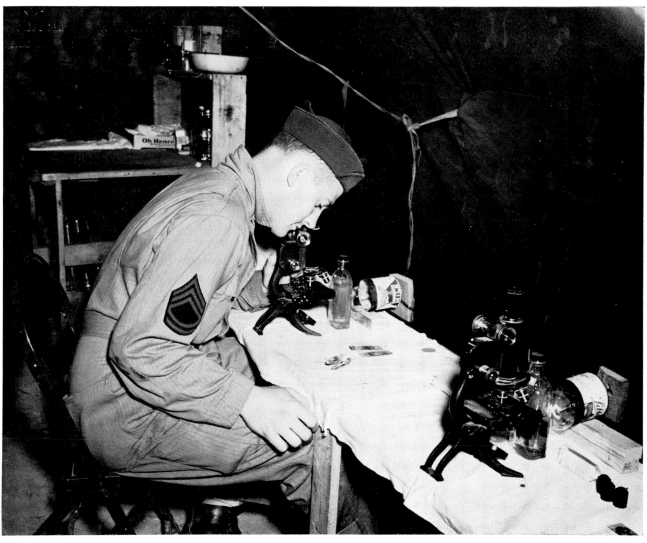

Shown in the 38th's laboratory studying a slide under the microscope is Sergeant Robert W. (Skin Head) Dahn.

the powerful gale drove far into the ground among the cots of the wounded patients. Before dawn, and with many hands on deck, over six hundred patients were loaded into ambulances for their travel to housed hospital units in the rear. How so many patients in the fury of the sleet and rainstorm were quickly and efficiently ambulanced and taken to rear hospitals still seems miraculous to us. The powerful wind and sleet continued almost to New Year's midday. Our tent hospital and personnel tents were in a wreck. Equipment, canvas, papers and tents were so strewn about the area that our hospital appeared beyond repair. Many of our ready cooked turkeys lay in the mud about the mess tents and kitchens.

"New Year's Day was spent in rapidly repairing our damage and readying our hospital for resumption of hospital duties. . . . The hospital was repaired sufficiently for admission of patients by New Year's night. We all enjoyed our 'turkey with trimmings' dinner New

Year's evening and were glad to learn that, after washing, the mud had done little damage to the turkeys. We shared the pleasure of the promotions of Second Lieutenants Lela O. Russell, Hazel A. Simmons, Ruth I. Barbee, and Lorraine M. Benante to first lieutenants."

Colonel Wood in the January 1, 1944, issue of the Daily Bulletin, illustrated in recognition of the day with a drawing of bearded Father Time and cherubic 1944, in wishing everybody a happy New Year referred to the storm recalled by Major Munroe and described in detail by Captain Pickens.

"The Surgeon, Fifth Army, is fully expecting the members of the 38th Evacuation Hospital," said Colonel Wood, "to live up to their past reputation in being able to resume work without delay as a result of the storm last night. Your cooperation is expected and desired."

The Bulletin during January was devoted mainly to routine reports and announcements, including the

168

daily recording of the status of the hospital, but it continued to list an unusual number of promotions, principally of nurses. After announcing the promotions of Captain Calder to major and Second Lieutenants Hough, Mills, and Bachoka to first lieutenant, the Bulletin in the last half of January recorded:

On January 15: Katherine Conturso, Sara Moran, and Violet Burgess from second lieutenant to first lieutenant.

On January 16: Deborah Doskow and Edith Guyett from second lieutenant to first lieutenant.

On January 21: Mary Blandford and Christine Wills, from second lieutenant to first lieutenant.

On January 22: Carolyn Haltiwanger, from second lieutenant to first lieutenant.

On January 24: First Lieutenant James R. Felts, Jr., to captain, effective January 16.

On January 25: Vera H. Dexheimer and Nelia C. Shields, from second lieutenant to first lieutenant.

On January 28: Margaret B. Mizelle, Charlotte J. Webber and Ruby E. McCain, from second lieutenant to first lieutenant.

On January 30: Gladys Pilger from second lieutenant to first lieutenant.

On the last day of January the Bulletin extended the congratuations of Colonel Wood and the 38th to Colonel J. I. Martin, Surgeon of the Fifth Army, on his promotion to brigadier general.

Two transfers to the 38th of officers from other units were announced during January. On the nineteenth the Bulletin recorded:

"Major Kenneth B. Boyd, recently commanding officer of the 93rd Station Hospital in West Africa, has reported for duty with the 38th Evacuation Hospital and is assigned to the Medical Service. Major Boyd's home is in Baltimore, Maryland. The Commanding Officer takes this opportunity of welcoming Major Boyd to the unit."

The January 22 Bulletin reveals that "The Commanding Officer takes pleasure in announcing the assignment to duty with this hospital of Captain John M. Crawford, M.C., formerly of the 36th Infantry Division. Captain Crawford is a graduate of the University of Texas, Class of 1928."

During this first month of 1944, however, several of the officers had an opportunity to enjoy short leaves in an Italian region that for more than two thousand years had been a famous playground of the wealthy and privileged, including the Roman emperors from the days of Augustus and Tiberius. Among those of the 38th who spent some time at a tourist hotel at Sorrento taken over for officers were Colonel Wood and Captain Pickens.

The captain in a letter home, written on January 30 from what he identifies as "Same Place" as the one from which he had written on January 10, tells in considerable detail of their experiences at Sorrento.

"The Army finally got wise enough to find what the headquarters like to call a rest camp for officers," he begins his letter. "They established one last summer on the shores of the Mediterranean in Tunisia for officers and men combined. It consisted of some barracks and the beach. I never went because the first to go reported that it was no different from being in our own camp. But, here in Italy, the Fifth Army does it a little differently. For the officers they have taken over a tourist hotel in Sorrento with all accommodations. The only difficulty is the fact that the place will hold about a hundred people and fifty places must be held open for brass hats, so about fifty of the working class can get there for three or four days out of thousands in this theatre.

"Each unit is allotted space. Ours was about four officers per month. My chance of getting there on the regular schedule was slim and that would have been next August at the present rate. By that time I hope to be too far away from this part of Italy to be interested.

"The CO and I decided to take the bull by the horns and go right to the head man and ask for the favor of using one of the sacred rooms being saved for the chance visitor from the upper crust. This we did, and to our surprise the permission came back immediately. We could go and it would not interfere with the regular schedule for the others of our command."

He describes the ancient, still famous playground of international society:

"Sorrento, as you know, sits on the opposite side of the Bay of Naples and overlooks the sea. The hotel taken over by the Army sits on a commanding bluff and from my balcony I could look down two hundred feet into the sea. The fishermen were at work with their nets in the waters just off shore. I don't know what they were catching, but the native population was happy that the sea food was coming in again. We ate only GI food supplemented with just a few of the local products, such as oranges and cauliflower, but no sea food. It was a grand place to rest and I got the most from it. It was most remarkable to me how quickly we returned to the civilized state. Only the second sitting got me back into pulling the chain and my second bath found me staying in the tub only ten minutes. The third day I began putting my cigarette ashes in the ash trays and the third meal I discovered the napkins and found what they were used for. The beds were long and the first night I found how nice it feels to sleep between sheets. I don't believe it will

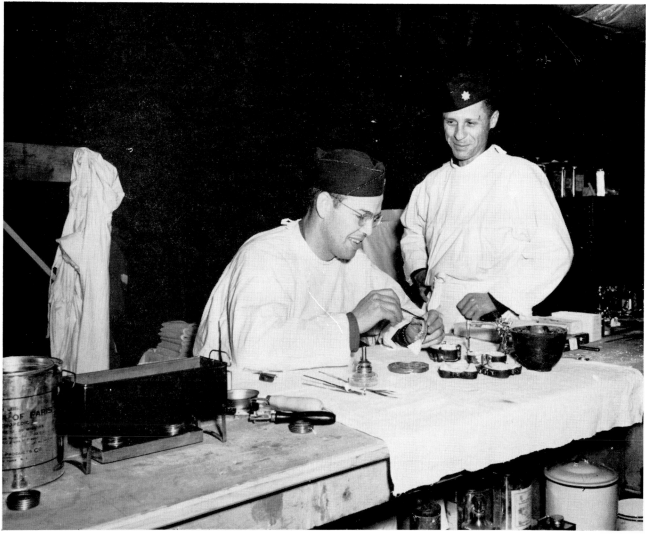

Assistant Dental Officer Milo Hoffman, seated, is examining a newly completed dental plate. With him is Major Vaiden Kendrick, dental oral surgeon of the 38th.

take me long to get back in the groove of living like gentle folk when this mess is over."

The coming of the American troops to the area, he reveals, had a great effect on the prices charged for various items in the Sorrento area:

"The principal excuse for Sorrento, outside of the fishing and the scrubby oranges and lemons, is the production of linen tablecloths and napkins and fine handkerchiefs. The women do the work and they are skillful with their needles. Of course, since the war began there has been little raw material coming in, so their production has been limited. When the Americans came they must have clapped their hands with glee and raised their prices 100%. The shops had plenty of choice, but the prices were outrageous. Two hundred lire or $2 was the cheapest priced handkerchief for either man or woman. The tablecloths and

accompanying napkins started at $90 and went on up. From this you can see that my shopping was limited, although I spent a good deal of time looking. I bought a few things which I have sent on to Mary. The wooden box business is good, too. They make cigarette boxes, jewel boxes, canes, umbrella handles, and card boxes. The prices were just as bad on these. I bought a few nuts and sent them on home, which I hope pass the censorship. I also picked up a few ash trays made from olive wood that may be useful to some of my friends and be fair mementos of Italy. The shopping was interesting in spite of the high prices. The sales people all spoke English, French, German, Spanish. I say they all spoke all of these languages. I wouldn't be sure, but they said they did, and since they spoke English, I assumed they could speak the other languages as well. Their advertising was not

170

along the typical American lines; there were no screaming signs in front of any of the shops and there were no loudspeakers playing 'Funiculi, Funicula' or 'Return to Sorrento.' There were a few people along the streets who would stop you in a furtive sort of way, like they were going to sell you some questionable post cards, and ask if you wanted to buy some boxes or linen very cheap and then hand you a card giving an address that you had already visited several times. The sales people were enthusiastic about their wares and were surprised when we said we did not have the money to buy at their prices. In one shop I asked the man in charge if he would be interested in trading some cigarettes and some candy and chewing gum, which I had accumulated, for some of his handkerchiefs and boxes. He said he would trade, so I swapped him Twenty Grand, Chelsea, Wings and Old Golds at the rate of 400 lire or $4 per carton. I also worked in some multi-flavored Life Savers and some chewing gum. These things we have issued to us at regular intervals and we accumulate them, since no one likes them in spite of the Army thinking we do. This was the best way of disposing of them. We occasionally trade a package of cigarettes for an egg when they can be found or for a dozen sour little oranges. I think I came out all right with this merchant and we were both satisfied that we had beat the other in the trade."

He continues the account of his visit:

"As I said, Sorrento is a quiet place and an ideal place to rest. It is inaccessible except by boat or a very bad road. From there it is customary to go to Capri, the little island which lies just a few miles off shore. The Army had arranged for us to go each Monday, Wednesday, or Friday. We got there too late on Monday and had our reservations for Wednesday, but on that particular day the weather was so rough that the little boat could not make the crossing, so I missed the chance. I am sorry not to have seen the Blue Grotto, although I have a feeling that going there is a little like going to Silver Springs in Florida. What I did want to see was some of the handiwork of the old Tiberius Caesar who was not too bad an architect in his day. Possibly I will get another chance.

"In this hotel there was a young singer who performed during the dinner hour," he recalls. "She was very attractive and had an unusually good voice. She made the meal time more pleasant with her selections from the Italian operas and the folk songs. The orchestra consisted of several string instruments and one brass horn and the piano. . . . Once during the evening meal they brought in a native folk dance-tarantella performed by local talent in native costumes. It was quite close kin to the Hungarian folk dances, but with

the men using the castanets. To have a floor show during a war and that near the fighting was just too much, but it helped to make the vacation more pleasant."

He defends the program of a rest hotel for Army officers:

". . . I tell you it is worthwhile after living in the mud and dirt in a canvas tent for a year and a half," he says. "They even had our shoes shined if we could remember to leave them outside our room door at night. I forgot the first two nights, but the third and fourth nights the shine was on the house. They had 48-hour laundry service. I had heard about that before going down, so I went with all the dirty clothes I possessed. They apparently used hot water, because all my clothes seemed cleaner when they came back, and I know the local senorinas here around the camp don't bother to heat the water before trying to do the wash. Sometimes I send the things back for a second scrubbing and that helps a little."

Captain Pickens sums up the time-out period from the mud and dreariness of life in the 38th's tent city:

"All in all, it was a pleasant interlude in this rather dull existence. I came back much refreshed and somewhat cleaner."

But as in all his other letters, he cannot avoid entirely referring to the war as the members of the 38th were seeing it in the early days of the new year of 1944:

"The war has taken on new life in this theatre with the advent of almost two weeks of clear weather. Some of the Bulldogs slipped out on an end run and it appears to have caught the enemy by surprise. The pressure has been great in front, too. Possibly we will get somewhere with our phrase before the spring thaw allows bigger things to come from other directions. I hope so. We are anxious to get the whole business over with and start toward home. The sinking of the hospital ships off the new beachhead, a deliberate assault, has made everyone more determined. That is not propaganda. Some of our friends were lost trying to save some of the helpless patients."

Major Munroe summarized the activities of the Fifth Army during the three months preceding the middle of January and wrote appreciatively of the 38th's experiences in that period:

"During this period Lieutenant Colonel Thomas P. White, Major R. Z. Query, Jr., and twenty-two enlisted men were transferred from the unit. Most of them were going immediately to the good old U.S.A.—from Spain to home.

"Toward the latter days in Riardo," he continues his account, "many visited Capri, Naples (when the typhus epidemic was over) and other nearby spots. For a while weekly Fifth Army medical meetings were held in the opera house at Caserta, but were transferred and held in our unit's 'Mason-Dixon Theatre.' At these meetings everyone's experience and opinions in the care of the wounded and the sick were aired. Some members returned to Sorrento to revisit the Hotel Vittoria that was taken over by Fifth Army for a rest camp.

"During the three-month period from October 12, 1943, to January 15, 1944 the Fifth Army push consisted of three phases: the Volturno River crossing and the advance to the Winter Line (12 October-15 November); regrouping (15-30 November); and the push through the Winter Line toward Cassino (2 December-15 January 1944)," he wrote.

"Many of us visited the more forward zones, where after 15 January 1944 we could view the Liri Valley. We could see Highway 6 as it coursed across the plain below to German-held Cassino, bent around the lower edge of Monastery Hill, and disappeared in the haze of the valley on its ninety-mile path to Rome. The plain of the Liri Valley was cut up by the Rapido River, which entered the Gari River. This latter river then wandered two and one-half miles to its junction with the Liri River, which drains the Liri Valley to its junction with the Gari to form the Garigliano River, a sizable stream that entered the sea fifteen miles away.

"These continuous water barriers in the Liri Valley confronted the Fifth Army forces. Beyond the valley could be seen the mountain ranges and the little village of Cassino near the foot of Monastery Hill. Behind these rivers lay the strongly fortified Gustav Line. Cassino was more strongly fortified than any other city that the Fifth Army had encountered. The rivers were diverted in such manner that the mud and mire of the Liri Valley were almost impassable for heavy armor. Mines were lavishly placed. One has to see the Liri Valley from the distance to more clearly visualize the difficulty of breaking the strongly fortified Gustav Line."

Many members of the 38th, Major Munroe reveals, witnessed the initial bombardment of the monastery atop the mountain. "On February 15 the hallowed Benedictine monastery, the Abbey of Monte Cassino, was heavily bombed and this was subsequently followed by thousands of tons of bombs and shells."

During the first half of February several members of the 38th, through arrangements made by the Special Service section of the Army, enjoyed some experiences removed about as far as possible from the usual routine of operating an Army hospital.

They went to the opera.

"What a far cry from the war to be sitting listening to one of the world's favorite operas!" Captain Pickens wrote the homefolk on February 10, 1944. "But that is the way I spent the other evening."

He went on in his letter to relate in considerable detail his evening at the San Carlo Opera Company's production of *La Boheme*. And six days later, on February 16, he tells of his second visit, this time to see *Lucia di Lammermoor*. Both evenings, he declared, were pleasant interludes in the grim business of war. His accounts, as many of his previous letters provided, add color, atmosphere, and details to the picture of the 38th's strenuous months overseas.

"It is always funny when Mimi in *La Boheme*, being sung to and made love to by Rudolph, turns out to be a buxom filly with plenty of health, altho she is supposed to be passing away with consumption," he begins his first letter. "Her full bosom, rising and falling with emotion, belies the presence of the heartless little bugs within her broad frame. Such was the case with Gilda in *Rigoletto*, which I saw the other night. She was bigger than Ponselle and her father had plenty of trouble carrying his sack in which her nearly lifeless body was placed."

The San Carlo Opera Company, "which was either caught or escaped to our side of the lines," he said, was in charge and did a good job. "They have been running a series for the headquarters group," he went on. "Common field troops get in by knowing someone among the brass hats. I happen to know Alec Schenck from Charlotte, who made the arrangements, and he was exceedingly kind to do it. They have the opera series on an average of three times a week, but this was the first time I had had a chance to hear one. The little opera house is in the castle built many years ago. It seats about 200 in the orchestra and another fifty or seventy-five in the boxes which tier up around the wall up to a high ceiling. It was the royal opera house in reality and while I sat there between acts I thought about the scenes that must have been enacted there in the years past when knighthood was in flower. The royal box was just two sections away from me and occupied by an American general and two British generals. There were no civilians to be seen, except in the orchestra pit and on the stage. The audience was entirely GI with a generous sprinkling of our allies scattered about.

"It was an appreciative audience," he reported, "and sounded considerably more genuine in its applause than that heard in the Diamond Horseshoe. When they like a particular aria they do not hesitate to whistle and stomp their feet as loudly as they would cheer Glenn Miller or Kay Kiser. Only the enlisted men were in the orchestra seats and the officers used the boxes. The appreciation came equally from both sections. The unusual part of the applause was the fact that the company would repeat the aria as many times as the crowd wanted it and they did not hesitate bringing the singers back for more. They sang the famous quartet three times before going on with the rest of the performance, and the age-old 'la donna e mobile' was called back three times also. If I were writing a review or criticism of the whole performance I would say the main weakness was the orchestra's drowning the singers. They apparently keyed their voices to the smaller house, but the director of the instruments kept them at full tilt. On the whole, the performance was not up to anywhere near what the Met puts out, but it was pleasant relief from the dullness of the war drag."

His letter went on to reveal the arrangement of the orchestra, whose members, said he, must have been cold, since there was no heat in the house. Then he returned to a description of Gilda:

"She was a tall, buxom woman with a fairly good voice. As I said before, it might have been better if the orchestra had not outplayed her. The one time she came thru nobly was in the quartet and then they all did, but she particularly. Rigoletto, the old hunchbacked jester, did his part the best of the lot. He was dramatic in his presentation but did not overplay the part. He had a good voice and carried the whole show. The Duke who did the tenor was not the match of Martinelli, whom I heard last in Boston many years ago. He failed to have the fullness of voice, but his principal aria about all women being fickle was much appreciated and he sang it three times."

Of the staging that had been arranged for the American servicemen he wrote:

"The small stage was filled with old used scenery. There was too much of it, but I suppose they were making the best show possible. It is a far cry from the elaborate settings staged by the Metropolitan and the costumes had seen better days. Italians either don't believe in washing too much or there has been a prolonged shortage of soap. The costumes would have looked better with a washing."

But, said he, "it was a welcome relief to hear good music a safe distance from the war. Getting inside the huge castle, fourth largest in the world, if that means anything, and then into the intimate little theatre was like slipping into another world. The imagination could run rife on what went on in that little room a hundred years ago when command performances were held. Even that night I could look with hazy eye and see lovely gowns and white tie and tails instead of dull olive drab. The one thing that would shock you out of your pleasant reverie between the acts would be the sight of the singers and the musicians alike moving around the audience giving autographs in exchange for cigarettes. Every surrounding and every art has its price, I suppose."

After the performance, his letter reveals in closing, they "hurried back across more than 30 miles and an hour and a half's travel to get to the mud and canvas and the sordid scenes of our part of this war. For a little while we had had something better."

Three other officers and a nurse from the 38th accompanied Captain Pickens on his next trip to the opera. He began his letter of February 16 with an apology for taking time out from a war to attend this performance.

"It seems a bit of a shame when the war is going on so tough up at the front to be chasing off for an evening, but the opportunity comes so seldom that I went to the opera again," he wrote. "There is little I could do about the pushing around being done up there and over on the beachhead, so I didn't feel too guilty. After over eighteen months overseas you take any relief you can get."

On this particular evening, he reported, the San Carlo company was producing *Lucia di Lammermoor*, and though he had heard the sextette many times, he had never heard the full performance. "This was the chance and I took it. The chance was well worth it, because the performance was far superior to that of *Rigoletto*, about which I wrote not so long ago. Everything seemed to work out properly.

"Alec Schenck again had made arrangements for the tickets. . . . He had six seats, but as luck would have it, only five of us could get away, and he was away up on the next landing. Four officers—Bill Matthews, Ed McCall, Mitch Mitchell and I, along with one nurse, Miss Polly Bell from Iredell County, made the trip. Upon arrival at the source of brass hats in this area, Alec had persuaded another officer to act as host, Lt. Col. Luther. . . . He did a grand job in showing the country folks around. We had dinner and he arranged for us to eat in the Colonel's mess, which was not a mean accomplishment. The only difference between the upper mess and the lowly company grade mess is that they have backs in their chairs and they all look tired and bored with each other. We did not have to sit on the stools, altho the food was the same, and I think we added a little life to an otherwise dull gathering. . . . After dinner we went directly to the little opera house in another section of the castle. When crossing the courtyard you dodge bomb craters and use a flashlight sparingly. Into the house we hurried, since we were running late. They start at 7:30 PM, which is somewhat earlier than the Metropolitan. Our box was partially filled when we arrived. The host did not like the seats to which we were relegated and made no bones about it. Before the performance got underway

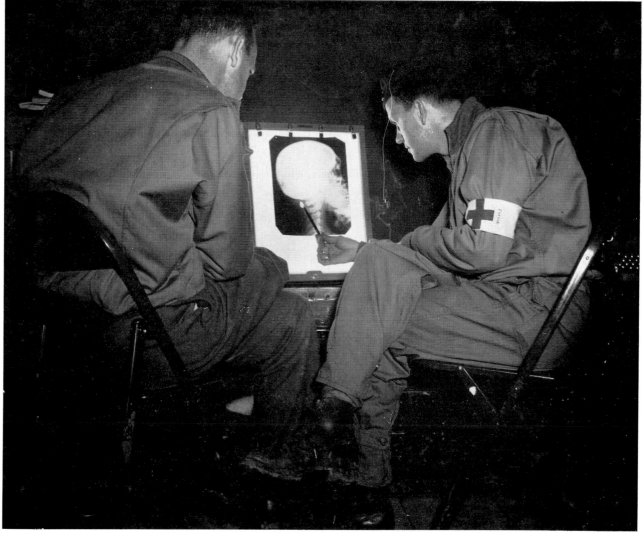

Captain Thomas D. Tyson, chief of X-ray service, left, and First Lieutenant Colin A. Munroe, X-ray service assistant, are studying X-ray of a war casualty showing shell fragment lodged at the base of the brain.

he moved out and made a reconnaissance and came back with the information that they should move, presto, as the Italians say, into the General's box. It was the royal box and was the choice box in the house. We took over with befitting modesty and made the most of the extra privilege. The accoustics were obviously designed for that spot; we heard everything at its best. The British generals from the Royal Air Corps occupied a part of the box, but they were non-communicative, so we wasted no glowing personality on them. I'm not certain they enjoyed the opera at all. We did."

Lucia, he went on to say, was less buxom than Mimi had been. "But, nevertheless, she could sing, and she did. Without her the whole show would have fallen flat, since she carries the business until the last act. She had a grand voice and did not spare. When she hit a note it was like a ski jumper when he takes off after the preliminary slide is covered. She hit it exactly,

solid, true, and her voice was as clear as a bell. It was invigorating to listen to and I revelled in it. The supporting cast was good, too, and the chorus was as good as any I have heard."

He described the scene of the opera, the costumes, which were fresh, since this had been the first performance of this selection during the series. "The swarthy looking Italians looked a little incongruous with their skirts on and their actions were not as natural in them as I have seen with some of the Scottish troops with us, but they did all right. The dark-complected ladies did not resemble too closely those fair-haired females I saw in Edinburgh, but they could sing and that was what mattered. The individual arias were well executed, but the familiar sextette was the piece de resistance. The whole group pitched into that number in such a way that it brought the house down. Even the whole orchestra personnel arose and turned and

174

applauded. It was a real ovation. We were reticent in our box to turn on the heat too much but we let them know we appreciated their efforts and approved their talents. Different from the rendition of *Rigoletto*, the performers did not give an encore. . . ."

So another pleasant evening away from the tented city of the 38th's hospital came to an end. "After being in another world for a little while," he ended this letter almost in the words he had ended the one of the week before, "we hurried back over bumpy roads in the cold to our tents in the field." And there they were back in the routine of the war. "The wounded keep coming in a steady stream. We are busy as usual."

Captain Montgomery made no entry in his diary from January 24, 1944, when he wrote that the hospital had "just completed another batch of 190 battle casualties," until February 19. On that date the entry was characteristically brief:

Am going to 300th Gen. today to see about my cough.

But soon he would be leaving on a much longer journey and one long anticipated. In preparing to start the trip, he would be one of the actors in an amusing small drama that after two decades remains memorable and revealing.

"In February of 1944 I received orders to return home on a 30-day leave," he recalls. "So I had to go up to Fifth Army headquarters to check out the officers' mess fund, which I'd been handling. We had it set up so that every month I turned in the account to Colonel Pennington and it was verified and the money was counted, and then we just threw the records away. So I went up to the Fifth Army to check it out before going on leave, and this colonel at headquarters said, 'Captain, you can't do that. You'll have to bring me every record from the time you left Fort Bragg.'

"'But we don't have any such records,' I said, and I explained how we'd been doing.

"'Well, you can't go back home until you've brought the records accounting for every penny.'

"'But our executive officer has signed out everything as being all right,' I told him again. 'And there just aren't any records now.'

"'He's got nothing to do with it,' he said. 'We can't have that.'

"So I went back to the base and told Paul Sanger what had happened.

"'I'll go back up there with you and see what I can do about it,' said Paul.

"So we went, and we were sitting there talking, this Fifth headquarters colonel, and Paul and I, and Paul said to him, 'Colonel, this was just a little private fund among the officers.'

"'I can't help that, Colonel,' he said to Paul. 'The

Captain's got to—huh-uh-huh-h'—he started coughing—'account for this money by producing—uh-huh-huh-uh-huh—all the records before he can leave. He's got to —huh-huh-huh-uh-huh—do that.'

"'That cough you've got there, Colonel,' said Paul. 'Why're you coughing so much?'

"'I've had this little cough in my chest—' he began.

"'Sounds pretty bad, Colonel,' Paul told him. I think you'd better come out to the hospital and let us x-ray you. I think maybe you'd better go back to the States.'

"'You think, Colonel, I could go back to the States with this?'

"'Well, I don't know, Colonel, but it sounds bad. You come out and let us x-ray your chest and we'll see. I have an idea you ought to go back for a while. But you just go ahead and sign these orders for Captain Montgomery to go back to the States, and you come out tomorrow and let us check you over.'

"He signed the papers right there and then, and I left two or three days later. I don't know whether he ever got home or not. But Paul was really smooth that day."

Captain Montgomery's next entry in his diary was dated March 12. He wrote:

Returned today. Feel better. Have a chronic bronchitis. Geo Wood got his chickens today.

The Daily Bulletin of March 14 would report the promotion of Lieutenant Colonel Wood to full colonel in more formal phraseology:

"It is with pleasure that we learn that the Commanding Officer, Lieutenant Colonel George T. Wood, Jr., has been promoted to the rank of Colonel."

The Bulletin was issued that day under the signature of Captain Medearis as adjutant.

Two days before Captain Montgomery recorded Colonel Wood's promotion, Captain Pickens wrote a long news-filled and anecdotal letter home. It would be his last from the base at Vairano. It was datelined simply "Italy."

At the outset he tells of an incident illustrating his theme that "Even the bigwigs sometimes remember that the war is fought by a lot of little people and they have human feelings like anyone else. It gives you added faith in the leadership that we depend upon so much. It was a little thing, but it made everyone feel a little happier who had anything to do with it and most of all the general and the corporal."

He had related this anecdote:

"Most generals appear to move with a great deal of fanfare. We see them pass with big escorts of MPs on motorcycles and jeeps with radio equipment and weapons carriers with anti-aircraft guns. They have sirens screaming their coming and going. They have red spotlights which blink a warning at night. It is quite a show when they go by.

"But we have one general who prefers to travel with as little of this as possible. He gets in a jeep with a driver and looks like any other soldier except for the three stars that show where the license plate is on a civilian car. He likes to move swiftly and consequently uses a siren occasionally. Recently this story was told about him by one who was his guest for dinner.

"There had been much traveling and the general thought he needed two drivers, since it was both wearing and tearing on one. He ordered his GI section of the Army to search thru its files of all personnel who had experience in driving and get him a good driver. His only qualifications were that the man be able to drive swiftly and safely. GI, as you know, is the personnel section. They keep all records of all members of the Army. The search was made and a driver produced. In civilian life he had been a dirt track racer. He had driven many miles without an accident and had won many races. He was the answer to the general's order.

"When he reported, the general made a trip with him and he took him there in less time than it was thought possible. The general said he had to hold his breath at times, but the corporal drove with assurance and confidence. He was not conscious of driving for a general and the general liked that.

"He performed his work well for some weeks. One day the general said to him that he had done a good job and asked him if there was anything he, the general, could do for him. The corporal replied that there was, but that he could not think of asking one of his rank for such a favor. The general told him to speak up, so the corporal stated that he had been overseas for some seven months and because of constant moving had not heard from home in about three months. He was due to become a papa about a month previous and he had been worried, not having heard anything from home. The general said that he would make the proper inquiry for him and for the corporal to quit worrying.

"The general told his aide to send a radiogram to Washington with the man's name and the other information necessary and ask for an immediate reply. He knew it was wrong to use the Army service for personal matters but this one time he thought he would try. Within a very few hours came the reply radiogram. It read something like this:

" 'General —————, Italy, re: Cpl. Robert Jones stop Robert Jones, Jr., arrived 7th February stop mother baby well stop baby sends this message "hurry up win war and come home" stop signed Marshall, Chief of Staff.' "

Captain Pickens went on with his letter to report the routine of the 38th's activities during the last few weeks:

"We are being spoiled in our present setup because of the added service given by what is commonly called a striker. The British have another name for him, a batman. Here our striker is an Italian who turned up a few days after we set up at this camp. He was ill-clad and very dirty, but he smiled and asked if he could work for us. He kept on smiling and seemed so sincere that my tentmate and I decided to hire him. Back in our last stand we had a woman who cleaned up for us and did other chores. She had two teeth and scared us in the morning when she came, she was so ugly. But she worked.

"This new helper is named Gino Madzucci and he works, too. He was in the Italian army and when it disintegrated he found himself in the southern part of the country. He made his way up as far as he thought it safe, since the Germans don't treat them too well. That's how he came to us. His home is a few miles west of Pisa and he is counting on us getting him home. He has invited us to come and stay at his humble casa. We can have his primo da letto, his first bedroom. We will probably never get that far south (? north?) but I would like to see where he lives. He has not been home in four years and has not heard from his wife in over a year. With it all he is cheerful and has a winsome smile. He is either not very bright or doesn't understand how Americans live and act. But we are patient with him since he is so willing. He comes in the morning and wakes us as he lights the oil stove and puts on a No. 10 can filled with water. Then he makes a trip to the mess and picks up some bread and butter and salt if we need it. He has scoured the countryside and collected some fresh eggs for us and we have developed the habit of cooking our own breakfast in our own tent. He brings us fresh oranges each day. He trades cigarettes, candy and anything we want to get rid of for these things. If we have nothing to trade he just brings them in anyway. He sits and watches us as we shave and dress. He has been fascinated with my electric razor. He empties the wash basin for us and then sits smilingly by while we cook our breakfast. We have an orange and then fix the eggs either with canned milk scrambled or 'sunnyside up' or occasionally we soft-boil them."

His letter goes on further to describe the breakfast:

"The toast is brown and buttered. Gino has brought coffee from the mess. We have a little marmalade or jam to go with the rest. It's a good breakfast and it's warm in the tent. As soon as we get out, Gino gets the bedding outside, if it isn't raining, and lets it air out. He sweeps the floor we have installed with a vengeance and the dust spreads everywhere. We have never gotten it through his head that he should sprinkle a little water around before sweeping. The Italians don't mind a little dirt and dust on everything.

"He takes our dirty clothes off and two or three days later returns them washed and ironed. He keeps a laundry list and nothing is ever missing. The socks have been darned and all holes patched. The shoes are always shined regardless of all the rain and mud outside. The galoshes are always washed each day. When we want some English walnuts or almonds, he is sent out to find them and turns up with them. Then he sits down and cracks them for us. We had a time keeping him from cracking them with his teeth. We have furnished him with old clothing, a razor and a toothbrush. He has built himself a little lean-to at the edge of the camp and has fixed himself up quite comfortably. He enjoys most when we try to learn the language and he can talk with us. He makes no effort to learn English. So far his only word of English is 'OK.' At first we paid him at the rate of 10 cents per day, but then he hired himself out to some of the others, since he wanted to keep busy, and he accumulated so much money that he doesn't want any pay now. He can't buy anything or has no wants other than an occasional bottle of vino. While I was a patient in the hospital recently with a mild case of flu, he was a constant companion, running errands, doing anything to make me more comfortable. At the same time he was keeping the tent in good shape. I don't know what we will do without him if we should move in such a way that he could not follow. We are very dependent upon him."

The Daily Bulletin of Monday, March 6, had this "Notice to all Enlisted Personnel" that "A party will be held tomorrow night for Enlisted Men. Full details are given in the notices posted on the Bulletin Boards in Enlisted Men's Mess and Enlisted Men's Recreation Tent."

The next day the Bulletin had this further notice to enlisted personnel:

"Trucks will depart for the Enlisted Men's Dance at 1830 hours. Enlisted Men attending the Dance will assemble in front of Detachment Headquarters at 1815 hours."

And in his letter of March 10 Captain Pickens describes in considerable detail this dance. He writes of it in the concluding section of his long letter:

"Until a few days ago," he says, "I had never seen a WAC. That branch of the Army was being organized just about the time we left the States. The first part of this week, we, not being very busy, decided to organize a dance for the enlisted men.

"That is where the WACs entered the picture. I said that we decided to organize a dance when I mean that one of our Red Cross workers thought it would be a good idea and promised to work on it. She did a beautiful job, too. She went to the neighboring town and got the Red Cross club there to let us have their building for the night. Of course, we could not have a dance out here in this mud or in any of these little tents. The men had not enjoyed anything like that since we left England a long time ago.

"With the club room and the orchestra from John Trescot's Engineers and with plenty of food, Coca-Cola and coffee, all we needed was some girls. That was the snag. The Italians won't let their daughters go out after dark unless mama goes along, and usually two-thirds of the family with her. That usually means about fourteen in all to get one girl who is the dance age. That stumped us. The Red Cross worker rounded up all her cronies for miles around. They came from the airfields where they dish out doughnuts and personality to the incoming fliers. They came from neighboring hospitals and they even left the headquarters comfort to help us. But in all only about ten of them were available and that number with a bunch of young jitterbugs, 130, to be exact, was not a drop in the bucket. We needed more females.

"We learned that a platoon of WACs was stationed about thirty miles from us and about six miles from the Red Cross club. The worker took some of our more attractive men down to see if they could line up some partners. They turned on the heat and as a result of their enthusiasm, they got the promise of several to come and also try to get others. I followed up the next day with a trip to see their captain and ask her aid. She was not in at the time, so I left my message and asked her to come as my guest.

"To my surprise, many of the girls came and when I arrived at the party the WAC captain was there, too. I was going as a sort of patron or chaperone, but I found I had to work, too. There were plenty of girls and the men had a good time. It was a change for them, altho I never looked forward to lumbering 25 miles in the back of a 2½-ton truck. They didn't mind and the girls didn't seem to mind bundling up in the big truck either. We started at seven-thirty and quit at eleven P.M. The last truck came in at one-thirty because of some trouble in getting started. I was sitting up like an old hen with a lot of biddies until the last one came in safely. I enjoyed seeing them have a good time. I think it was worth the trouble because the mud gets awfully tiresome after all these months."

On March 15, 1944, one month after the opening bombardment of Monte Cassino, another intensive air and heavy artillery assault was carried out with the dumping of tons and tons of bombs and shells on Cassino and Monastery Hill. "This was to precede the New Zealand drive," Major Munroe's recording of that late winter period explains. "The city of Cassino and the Abbey were in ruins, but the Germans received few casualties in their deep dugouts, concrete-and-steel pillboxes, and strong fortifications. The New Zealand troops advanced a few miles into the valley, but little was gained. The Cassino effort, in fact, led to a critical reexamination of the use of air power in direct support of ground forces. The Gustav Line battle was on the verge of a stalemate, although casualties were still suffered by Allied troops."

On March 1 the Daily Bulletin had listed 392 patients, including 79 admissions. On March 9 the patient roll had increased to 426, with an even 100 admissions. Six days later, when the intensive bombing of Monte Cassino was resumed, the hospital had 232 patients. Two days later the patient load was down to 200 and to the end of the month it continued to decline.

The Bulletin of March 21 announced the promotion of Second Lieutenant Odessa M. Lindsey to first lieutenant and the welcoming to the hospital of Second Lieutenant Ruth Dierker, formerly of the 52th Station Hospital. Four days earlier Colonel Wood had welcomed Captain Henry Doubilet and Captain Harold Grosselfinger.

One week after the announcement of the arrival of Captains Doubilet and Grosselfinger, on March 24, the Bulletin carried the announcement:

"THE HOSPITAL OFFICIALLY CLOSED 1200 HOURS 24 MARCH 1944"

The announcement added that "All Passes and Leaves will terminate at 2300 hours, 25 March—no passes after that time, until further notice."

On March 24 the hospital had on its rolls 53 patients. The following day no patients were listed. Dispositions had been made of all patients. A notice to officers and nurses revealed that "Trucks will be ready at 0800 hours for those Officers and Nurses moving Sunday. Hand luggage will be carried on personal trucks."

The Sunday March 26, Bulletin carried the single notice:

"Approximately one-half of the personnel and organizational equipment moved to new location, 1 mile north of Nocelletto, Italy."

The Monday, March 27, Bulletin was equally brief. It announced:

"Completed movement of Personnel and Organization Equipment to new Hospital location, 1 mile north of Nocelletto, Italy."

Major Munroe summarized the work of the hospital

from the beginning of its operations at the Riardo site near Vairano, beginning November 7, 1943, and continuing until its closing March 24:

"The hospital was officially opened for a total of 138 days, during which time we admitted and cared for 9,793, almost ten thousand, patients, with a mortality rate of 0.77." That was one death in 130.

His account of the moving to the new site is more detailed than the Daily Bulletin's. It reveals:

"On 26 March 1944 approximately one-half of the unit personnel and organizational equipment were moved by trucks to a new location, two miles southeast of Carinola. To reach our new site, the trucks went south toward Naples and then turned west on Highway 7 toward the coast of the Tyrrhean Sea. We turned off Highway 7 to a smaller route to the south that after a few miles emptied us into a field that was to be our home. The remainder of the unit was transported on 27 March 1944. The hospital was set up and officially opened at 0800 hours on 29 March 1944."

March 28 Colonel Wood announced that Captain Earl Rasmussen had joined the 38th.

The following day the Daily Bulletin reported:

"THE HOSPITAL OFFICIALLY OPENED AS OF 0800 HOURS 29 MARCH 1944."

The next day the Bulletin listed four patients and 636 vacant beds. It also announced the meeting that afternoon at 2:30 o'clock in the Mason-Dixon Theatre of the medical officers of the Fifth Army for a conference on the subject, "Epidemiological and Clinical Aspects of Infectious Hepatitis." Happily, for all personnel, it also announced that enlisted men, officers and nurses would be paid at Detachment Headquarters.

"Blood Transfusions" was the subject of another Fifth Army medical conference, held April 6.

Operation of the 38th at the new location was short-lived. The April 7 Bulletin carried the announcement:

"THE HOSPITAL OFFICIALLY CLOSES AT 1200 HOURS 7 APRIL 1944."

The number of patients on that day was 255.

During the period from the official closing March 24 of the hospital in the vicinity of Vairano and near Riardo until its closing April 7 near Carinola, Captain Jack Montgomery had been making several entries in his diary and one of them had been extended to ten lines. On March 25, 1944, he had recorded:

Hospital closed today.

His ten-line entry was written two days later:

Left location near Riardo this morning. Arrived near Carinola in about an hour. This is the best location we have had in Italy. Green fields with trees. The engineers have done a good job with drainage & roads. Bob & I have a good tent. We were all settled by supper time. Anteo came with us.

His next two entries:

March 29th. Hospital opened noon today.
April 5th. Buck got his orders to go home today. We are leaving this nice location. 2nd. Lt. Clarke & 2nd Lt. Johnson arrived to enlarge anes. dept.

He was referring to the transfer of Captain Medearis to the states, and to the stories going the rounds of the hospital that the unit itself would soon be moving.

"We knew that the unit was slated for Anzio," Major Munroe's account continues, "but we did not know when. We knew that the Carinola site was really a staging area for our Anzio takeoff. We were off the beaten path, so, of course, had very little hospital work. To keep mind and body occupied, all efforts were directed toward making our camp site a show place. The neatly arranged hospital and personnel tents, the crushed stone roadways, the whitewashed stones that lined the walkways and roadways, the abundant grass of the area, all these things added to the neatness of our area. The Fifth Army weekly medical meeting met at our 'Dixie Theatre.' Our time was spent twiddling thumbs, playing checkers or chess, bridge or poker, writing letters, and speculating on what was to come. Due to our uncertainty as to when we were to leave, everyone was closely kept on or near the area. We walked about the surrounding terrain but were always fearful of mines."

During the short stay there, from March 26 to April 8, Major Munroe revealed, the hospital admitted and cared for 311 patients.

The Charlotte surgeon continues his account:

"In the early afternoon of 7 April 1944 we were briefed on the facts of our ordered Anzio venture. On 8 April we were transported by trucks to the reconditioned harbor of Naples, where we embarked on two relatively small, but rugged, fast and compact L.C.T.'s. The trucks containing our hospital equipment were run into the L.C.T.'s, from where they could rapidly disembark on their own power upon our Anzio arrival. The officers, nurses and enlisted men were equally divided in the two L.C.T.'s. The night was moonless and black as we rather smoothly sailed toward our destination."

Captain Montgomery, too, recorded the unit's moving from the Carinola area. The entry was made in his diary on April 8:

We left the location near Carinola at 9:30 A.M. Arrived at Nedisa (near Naples) at 11:30. In a few minutes were on board LST 327. It is a remarkable boat. Bow opens for tanks & trucks to drive in. We are divided into two groups. Weighed anchor at 1930 hours. A full moon at nine o'clock.

The next day, April 9, 1944, Captain Montgomery continued his report of the 38th's move to a new location:

Arrived at Anzio 0730 hrs. It has been shelled & bombed but not so damaged as Battapaglia. We went as rapidly as possible to our truck & out to the 56th area. One shell landed near us on the way. Quite a noise, but not visible.
The 56th personnel has gone. Our tents are all dug in & sandbagged on all sides. Shell fire is intermittent & we can hear them whistle overhead. Saw one explode across the road today. "The lonesome polecat" has been busy. This has been a busy Easter Sunday.

Two decades after that Anzio experience, several former officers of the 38th, including Major Montgomery, were reminiscing about those lively days on the Italian seacoast just south of Rome and "the lonesome polecat" to which Jack Montgomery had referred in his diary notation. What did he mean by "lonesome polecat," one of them wanted to know.

Dr. Hunter Jones recalled that it was also referred to by the soldiers as "the Anzio Express." He explained:

"We had been called up because one of the hospitals there had been bombed and they were sent back to rest; we were asked to replace them. As soon as we arrived in the harbor these shells started coming over. I got into a two-and-a-half-ton truck with some fellows and we started out, and the shells were coming over, but we finally made it into our camp. Then we saw tremendous holes on the ground right beside our tents, and somebody asked, 'What's that hole doing there?' and another fellow said, 'Oh, that. That's what the Anzio Express did.' Others called it 'the lonesome polecat.'

"We were right down on the coast," George Snyder added in further explanation, "and there was a mountain right behind us, and it had a tunnel cut into it in which they had placed a sixteen-inch gun—I saw it later on a train up around Rome. From time to time the enemy would pull it out of the tunnel and fire it, and the shell coming over us sounded like a freight train flying over your head. The shells were going over the airport and some houses down on the beach and they sounded just like a long freight train rolling by. That's why they called it 'the Anzio Express.' Others spoke of it as 'the lonesome polecat.' I never did exactly get the connection, but both terms, I was told, were used in speaking of the great gun firing down from the mountainside."

So warm had been their reception at Anzio, members of the 38th recall vividly two decades afterwards, that at the first opportunity they had to do so they began

179

This picture, made at Anzio, shows a member of the 38th emerging from the dugout shelter against the enemy shelling and bombing raids.

strengthening their defenses against the murderous fire being poured down upon them.

"At first we were down on the beach not far from the water," Dr. Milo Hoffman remembers. "When we got off the ship at Anzio, I'll never forget, regular Army men were there telling us to "Step lively! Step lively. Shells landed right here yesterday morning and killed four men, and right over there a bomb fell and killed ten people. Step lively!' So we were pretty nervous right at the beginning.

"We were, too, and that's a fact," Dr. Hoffman adds. "We were taking over this hospital filled with equipment and they were taking over ours we had left farther back from the fighting. Now we were right close to the water. George Snyder, I recall, and Bill Matthews were tentmates. The first night it was ack-ack all night, everything coming over. So the next morning early, George and Bill start digging their hole —there were foxholes all around the area and one was right beside George's and Bill's tent, and they were digging it deeper—when, so help me, they struck water. It wasn't much of a place to jump into for protection. It was pretty rough around there about that time, probably the roughest time we had."

The day after the arrival at Anzio Major Montgomery added an entry. It was dated April 10, 1944:

Artillery fire awoke me last night many times. None near us though.

The Daily Bulletin of that same date, April 10, announced:

"THE HOSPITAL OFFICIALLY OPENED AT 1200 HOURS 9 APRIL 1944."

It announced further that Captain James W. Dunn,

QMC, had been appointed unit supply officer and First Lieutenant Eugene M. Snell, MAC, had been named adjutant.

On this date the hospital listed 193 patients, all of whom were that day's admissions, and it counted 723 vacant beds, with 16 wards in operation. Captain Hoffman was administrative officer of the day and Captain Pickens alternate. Captain Crawford was medical officer of the day and Captain Munroe alternate. Surgical officer of the day was Major Leonard, with Captain Sotirion alternate. Major Walker and Captain Mitchell were dental officer of the day and alternate. Lieutenant Fruth and Lieutenant Dierker were nurse officer of the day and alternate.

"General Notices to Personnel" that day indicated the fact that the 38th in its new location was not far from the fighting:

"All personnel are reminded that helmets will be worn at all times.

"During an air raid, all personnel, not on duty in wards, will take cover. Personnel on duty in wards will remain in their respective wards.

"Our 'APO' number remains '464.'

"'Anzio Beachhead' will not be mentioned in any correspondence.

"All personnel are restricted to the Area of the 38th Evacuation Hospital."

It warned the "Blackout must be strictly enforced. Every individual will be held responsible for his quarters. Flashlights will not be used outdoors by any member of this command."

The next day's Bulletin gave more explicit warning against lights during blackout hours, which were set from "1930 to 0630," and gave instructions to personnel on what to do in case of air raids and the suffering of casualties.

"Strict blackout will be maintained at all times during blackout hours," the Bulletin declared. "Each individual will check the blackout of his or her own quarters. Flashlights will not be used outdoors at any time. Smoking outdoors is prohibited during blackout hours. During an air raid, each individual is held responsible for having the lights out in his or her quarters. Violations of blackout regulations by any member of this command will be followed by rigid disciplinary action."

Under "AIR RAID" the Bulletin posted these instructions:

"ALARMS: Air raids will be announced by 3 sharp blasts on whistles or horns or by three blinkings of the electric lights.

"Every member of the command will take cover.

"Personnel on duty with patients will remain at

their stations and use every means to protect the patients and themselves from falling flak or bombs. All unnecessary lights in wards and operating rooms will be extinguished.

"Disciplinary action will be taken against any member of this command who is reported as having been outdoors during an air raid.

"The ALL CLEAR will be announced by long blasts on whistles or horns and turning on of the lights."

The Bulletin of April 13 gave the information that the Award of the Legion of Merit had been made to Colonel Rollin L. Bauchspies, the 36th's former commander, "for meritorious service rendered during the period September 9 to 26 in the Salerno area."

The number of patients in the hospital swelled that day to 352 from 231 the day before. And on the next day the total climbed to 532. That was the day—April 15—that Colonel Wood welcomed to the unit Chaplain Cecil P. Sansom, who assumed the duties of the 38th's Protestant chaplain.

That, too, was the day that Captain Pickens sat down at his typewriter to write a letter home, his first since March 10. Because the announcement had been made on April 11 that the words "Anzio Beachhead" might be used as a headline in personal correspondence, the captain datelined the letter "15th April 1944, Anzio Beachhead."

He begins with a description of the place near Carinola which Captain Montgomery had called "the best location we have had in Italy. Green field with trees." But Captain Pickens elaborates:

"It was such a beautiful camp. We had spent plenty of time planning it and moved rather leisurely. The Engineers had been there ahead of us and put in the roads and water lines. The place looked like a well-manicured country club when we finally put the finishing touches on. The tents were properly spaced, there were fine gravel walks, the grass was green and flourishing and almond trees were just beginning to bloom. We sat on a hill facing north and a beautiful range of mountains, and to the back and southwest was the sea. Of course, we might have been eaten by mosquitoes

At Anzio the tents were set above dugouts to provide more protection from enemy shelling than they would have offered if they had been entirely above the surface. This is an enlargement of a small snapshot of the enlisted men's sector of the camp.

during the summer, but that did not concern us too much at the time. The last of the main projects had been completed and we were beginning to take things a little easier on some of the comforts, when, presto, came the order to move up here.

"We were sad and glad at the same time, sad at the thought of leaving our best setup just when it was beginning to be lived in and glad of the chance to keep up with the war and do our part where we were obviously needed most. Back to the south things were running very slowly and we had developed a bit of complacency. Up here things are never certain and the war is very personal."

He continues with a description of the actual moving:

"We were exchanging with another unit which saved the packing of all equipment. It was a question of getting personnel moved. We packed our few personal belongings and loaded into trucks and trundled for what seemed like hours thru the densest dust to get to the port. Everyone turned a sort of jaundice color. Very orderly, and more swiftly than ever before, we moved on to one of the small Navy craft, two of them, in fact. This was in case something happened to one boat there were enough people in the other to carry on. Cheerful little idea this, but the Army has a way.

"The boats were not too uncomfortable for an overnight run. I certainly wouldn't care to cross the Atlantic in one of them, as some people have had to do. Sleep was at a premium because of our crowded conditions and the general excitement. We were up early to see the most famous beach since Dunkirk. It was a drab looking sight. The town was in ruins, the comfortable villas enjoyed by the Romans during the summer season were just so much rubble. The Engineers were hauling the place off systematically to have rock for their roads along the marshy plain. I have never seen a more orderly or swift disembarkation. The enemy has a habit of shelling the town more often than somewhat. It took less than twenty minutes to get everything we owned and ourselves into trucks and out of the place. It was a ghost city with only MPs to hurry the traffic along. Fortunately, everything was quiet during the move. It stayed that way for several hours and we thought this whole business was no worse than our experiences in Beja, Oran, Paestum, Caserta, and some other stands. But we were wrong. During our first afternoon and the first night it seemed that all hell had broken loose. We had moved up the beach and inland a little where all of the hospitals are located. As you know, there is not a great deal of room on the socalled bridgehead. We are not too far from the enemy in any direction except toward the sea. Our own guns and those of the enemy seemed to move right into the next hole from me and the ground shook most of the

time from the explosions. The noise was terrific and steady nerves were a necessity."

He goes on to relate the 38th's experiences as the unit took up its new position:

"Again the Engineers had been here ahead of us and dug in and countersunk our tents, so that my little tent is about five feet below the ground and around the edge outside are piles of sandbags. All in all, I can stand up and have a thick layer of protection all around me. They went a step further and over each cot they have placed a corrugated tin roof supported by 2 by 4s on top of which is an additional layer of sandbags. Now when everything starts, we just retreat to our cots and stretch out. That is the safest place. The whole place looks just like the pictures of the last war when trenches were in vogue."

Captain Pickens speaks of the 38th's present greater hazard from enemy air raids and the anti-aircraft fire of the Americans:

"An air raid is no fun, as we know from past experience from England thru Africa and into Italy, unless it is far enough away so that you can get out and watch the show. Here it is entirely too close for any comfort and the din created by the anti-aircraft guns is something for Hollywood. The hazard is much greater, apparently, from falling flak than from anything the enemy may drop. There must be a million guns and they all fire at once. What a Fourth of July celebration it would make at a county fair. The people wouldn't believe it until they heard it. Sometimes it goes on for hours and gets very tiresome. Nearly always it comes at night and sleep is just about impossible. I am thankful for my one deaf ear, for at least I can eliminate some of it.

"You wear your helmet all of the time except in bed and sometimes there if a system is worked out whereby it is comfortable. It gets heavy and bundlesome and hot, but it has saved people, so we keep it on. No one wastes time in open spaces. Any time wasted is in tents under good cover. Fortunately, the ground is sandy, but you can't dig too deep without running into water. Sea level is not too far down. I have dug a little farther down in my own tent in order to gain head room. Then we pick up a few scrap pieces of lumber or parts of ration boxes and put in a bit of flooring. When there is no air raid we have electric lights. I brought my little oil stove along, so it stays warm under ground. It's not a bad existence if it would not get so noisy all of the time. We are reasonably busy with patients and that keeps the whole crowd in a better frame of mind."

He and his tentmate back in Vairano had been unable to take along their Italian man of all work when they moved to Anzio. He tells of it:

"We lost our strikers and the added burden of getting my own water and making my own bed (when I get around to it) and filling the oil stove and taking out the trash is tiresome. We have been spoiled and I most of all. My striker cried when we left, partially because my tentmate was going to the States and partly because we were all leaving. He said he would make his way up here within a short time, and I wouldn't be surprised, but the hazard of traveling between two lines is great. I hope nothing happens to him. He was a good servant and did his work well. The civilians have moved out of this area en masse, so there is no hope of finding another. I will have to get back to washing my own clothes again, too, and that is still worse. I never did a very good job of it in Africa and I'm less inclined to it now. C'est la guerre."

During the last two weeks of April the hospital remained busy. The Daily Bulletin showed for that period an average of more than 600 patients each day, ranging up to 703 on April 23. Daily admissions continued high also. On April 22, the report discloses, admissions totaled 128 and number of patients 681.

Brigadier General Blesse paid his last visit to the 38th before leaving for the United States to be Army Ground Forces Surgeon, War College, Washington, the Bulletin of April 18 announced. "He expressed his appreciation for the work done by the personnel of this Unit," the Bulletin added, "and regretted that he could not say good-bye to each of you personally."

On that same date the Bulletin announced also the promotion of Major William H. Pennington to the rank of lieutenant colonel as of April 11.

Blackout regulations and censoring of mail continued rigid. Interestingly, the Daily Bulletin of April 20 observed that "United States troops in this theatre may relate in letters to their homes that they have witnessed the eruption of Vesuvius." But, it went on to warn, "Personal accounts will contain no direct statement or inference as to dates of observation, relative distance of writer's or any other military unit. For example, statements such as 'near to,' 'far from,' 'last week,' or 'day before yesterday' are prohibited."

But when on April 24, 1944, Captain Pickens wrote a long letter to a Charlotte friend, the Reverend C. Alfred Cole, rector of St. Martin's Episcopal Church, from Anzio Beachhead, as he had datelined the letter of April 15, he gave no further identification of the 38th's location. He wrote, however, of the frequent air raids and of the measures they had taken for defense against enemy bombings and the flak from their own weapons, as he had revealed to the homefolk in the earlier letter.

The primary value of his letter, however, is its revealing what its writer insists is a representative feeling of an American World War II soldier about religion as his own beliefs are tested in the rigorous experiences of war. It provides, therefore, an intimate close-up of a soldier's inmost thoughts as far from his homeland he looks ahead with faith to the victory of his cherished way of living.

"Dear Al," he began the letter to his clergyman friend. "Your letter of March 14th reached me only a few days ago because we seem never to be static. Being the son of a Methodist minister has stood me in good stead in the Army because I am used to moving at regular intervals. In spite of the fact that the Italian front seems to the general public to be standing still, there is considerable movement going on and plenty of hard fighting.

"The article by the Reverend Bernard Bell which you wrote about was most thought provoking. Although I am not a member of St. Martin's, I want to reply because I can claim at least pseudo relationship, since my wife is a loyal member. What might apply to St. Martin's would be the same in any church. I am tired of too much denominational feeling. It appears that we waste time in quibbling about minor creeds. But I must not get into that now. It is so easy to throw rocks at the church for one reason or another. I had the feeling that Dr. Bell was doing that without offering too much of a plan in answer. Self-criticism is always healthy if it is backed by a personal reformation. But I get a little weary of the constant calling of wolf when the danger in not too real. There is no great change apparent from my point of view in the men in the armed services unless it is for the better. Anyone who says that men in foxholes don't get nearer God without begging is totally misinformed. The author of your article seems to back the contention of some chaplains who intimate that we beg for life when the going gets rough. That may be true to some extent, but I vouchsafe that the majority of our supplications ask for strength to face whatever is before us, and strength alone. We fight for the dignity and sanctity of the individual and we ask no quarter. Our strength must come from above. Where else can we turn?"

To the minister he describes his Anzio Beachhead tent home:

"I write now from a hole dug six feet underground and almost daily we are subjected to air raids and artillery fire and the nights are a continuous nightmare. We never know where the next shell or bomb will land. The hospitals appear to be no exception in this war. We are afraid, yes," he concedes, "but I don't think we beg God for life alone. In spite of our fear I don't think we are groveling or crawling. The faith of our fathers is truly living still."

He tells Reverend Mr. Cole that he disagrees further

"with the assertion of the writer that whatever we were before coming into the Army is the way we will come out, just exaggerated.

"I have seen men," he goes on, "who were selfish and self-centered learn with intimate living and mutual hardships to give and share. That is the rule rather than the exception. Further, in spite of the fact that chaplains, so far as my experience has been, have not been too profound and too inspiring, the interest in religion as exemplified by interest in religious services has been on the increase."

This has been true, he testifies, in the 38th Evacuation Hospital unit certainly, and he has heard discussions concerning it in other groups. "Last night at our Sunday evening service a most interesting example of this occurred. We had teased our chaplain about not having any 'terminal facilities.' His services sometimes stretched out a little long as all ministers' are prone to do. He had announced that this was to be a very short service because of the hazard of having too many people congregated in one spot. After an unusually good songfest, when he was about to conclude, he asked if some of the group (there were well over a hundred) would stand up and recite their favorite verse from the Bible. Without a moment's delay they started, soldiers from the front who were back a few miles for a few days' rest, long-bearded men who man the nearby anti-aircraft guns, ambulance drivers who would be off in a few minutes to bring back more wounded, patients who were able to walk or whose buddies carried them to the service, our own personnel. It went like a forest fire and it was thirty minutes later before the chaplain could give his benediction. There was no indication of interest in religion dying. On the other hand, it appeared to be a thirsty crowd getting their fill of an abiding substance."

Further to support his contention, the captain points to the types of periodicals and books he has observed the men and women of the 38th reading.

"The reading material, outside of our Army newspaper and a few of the weekly magazines from home, is interesting to observe," Captain Pickens writes. "In nearly every dugout you can find an 'Upper Room' or 'Forward' or one of the many church publications. 'The Robe,' that most interesting novel about the cloak which Christ wore at the crucifixion, has prompted no end of discussion. I have had two or three of my friends, to whom I had loaned my copy, come and talk about it with me, and, to a man, they said the arguments in favor of 'the faith' were most convincing. I don't know of any book which has provoked as much interest as that one since I have been overseas.

"Sholem Asch's 'The Apostle' has been a widely read sequel. I saw it first on the desk of a corporal in the Finance section of the Army; then my father sent me a copy. That story of Paul and his own struggle and the struggle of the early church has made a profound dent on our thinking. We have had many discussions on it and it has helped us to answer the question of 'From whence cometh *this* help?' Cronin's 'Keys of the Kingdom' has also made the rounds. More soldiers have read these books than you would imagine. Is that a trend away from religion?"

His letter thus far, he continues, brings him to a consideration of "what we may want upon return. I am not interested in returning to the camp meeting days of twenty-five years ago, although there was plenty of religion felt and seen in those gatherings," he concedes. "We do want an inspiration from our leadership. I would like to come back to join a mighty surge, a reaffirmation of faith, a rededication all moving, so strong and swift that no small eddy would stop the current. I am frank to say that the spark must come from the pulpit. We must be led, we must be inspired, we must be taught. . . . I want sermons like my father preached, like Bishop Gribbin preached at St. Philips, like Bishop Mouzon gave in his day. When you heard them, you welled up inside and went out knowing that you had been nearer God. You had heard His disciple speak and you wanted to follow his teachings, knowing that you had found the truth."

He goes on in an attempt, which he says may not be successful, to explain his feeling that "In our religious education, to me, there has always been something lacking. There is a stiltedness about it; we have always been dressed up too much," he writes. "Why should it be any different from our secular schools? There seems to be a hush-hush about it that is not healthy. It's moldy. It's always been too churchy. I don't know whether I get my idea across or not, but it's too routine. I wish I were able to write some of the texts or guides for study. In any case, I think more laymen should be used in preparing these studies in order to get a new point of view. The study of the Bible is one of the most interesting in all literature, but the average layman, from the early ages on up to maturity, does it with an apologetic tone. I know that is true because of my own shyness in discussing it with friends even here in the Army when inhibitions are at a premium. I sometimes think it would be best to study the life of Jesus purely from the historical angle as we would the life of Napoleon or Lee or Benjamin Franklin or Leonardo da Vinci. Then let the power of the story grow, see the effect one man's life has left in the world over the centuries. The question of faith or the things that are sometimes beyond the mind of the average would not necessarily be argued. The facts would see the truth. Then we could go beyond and see the value of a Christian soul.

"Just before coming into the Army," his letter to the minister continues, "I taught a small Sunday school class. My tenure of office was short, but I remember one day asking this question of my associates: What difference would it have made if Jesus had been able to use the radio? After some weeks of discussion on this subject I threw at them the same question using Paul. What would Paul have done with his personality, sincerity, and logic had he been able to broadcast to his fast-growing following? These sorts of ideas might be foolish, but I thought they brought the questions up to date. Of course, we had to go back and find out what each of these men propounded. We studied in a cursory sort of way, but I think we learned something and without the old bugaboo. Call it unorthodox if you like, but it created interest and the results were satisfactory. We need some sort of change in our approach. You and the other leaders must find it if the appeal is to be attractive. We can continue to go to Sunday school because mama makes us, but that is not the answer when the control is gone. I don't know the answer, but there is one.

"I hope I haven't tired you with too much talk," he concludes the unusual letter from the war front in Italy. "I just wanted to visit a while in answer to your gracious letter."

When the 38th Evacuation Hospital unit sailed from the United States for England in midsummer of 1942, the members had specific and rigid instructions about what they could and could not take with them. One thing they could not carry, for example, was a camera. They had to remove the unit number, too, from every record and every piece of correspondence. No one in England was to know who or what they were.

But now, less than two years later, the situation had changed greatly. Captain Pickens in his letter home, written April 28, 1944, speaks of the change:

"Now, of course, the 38th is almost everywhere, on every piece of mail, in a lot of magazines, in the newspapers and sometimes over the radio. In addition, we hurry out as soon as we set up our camp and put up road signs directing traffic to us. At every crossroads you will find a big Red Cross and a 38th Evac painted on an arrow pointing toward our setup. We advertise to the world that we are here."

Another item they were forbidden to bring along to England was a radio.

"Now, as the war progresses, there are many radios in our camp," Captain Pickens writes. "I don't have one myself but I hear those put out by the Special Service section of the Army or those of my friends. They are on all sides of me and one which bellows loudly at the mess. We tell our time and set our watches when BBC comes on with Double British Summer Time. We hear the broadcasts from the States when they are relayed from London, rarely when they come direct. We even have a broadcasting station here on the beachhead. Just the other day they broadcast from here to the States. One of my friends, Carey Dowd, with the Signal Corps, helped in setting it up. He was amused, after having heard conversation with New York all morning, to hear the announcer there say that 'Now, if we are able, we will take you to Anzio.' No shells landed during the broadcast, so it was not as real as it could have been."

It was in the spring of 1944, too, that Axis Sally was being widely heard and written about in the Allied press. In his April 28 letter Captain Pickens gives an overseas view of the Axis propagandist, a picture of Axis Sally as she was envisioned by the American soldiers in the battle regions:

"One of the more amusing broadcasts to which we listen is one put on by the Germans. They are still putting out propaganda and to the average American soldier it sometimes measures up to Bob Hope. The particular program which interests us is put on by one who calls herself Sally. Sally has a nice, sweet voice, rather intimate sounding, typically American. She has a collection of the latest dance records from the States and intersperses her conversation with snappy tunes. She also has a small orchestra which is slightly better than mediocre. I think the program comes from Rome, the reception is so good here. She tells stories, puts on little dramas, gives the names and messages of prisoners.

"A typical prisoner report sounds like this: 'Private Joe Doakes, service number 35592784, whose mother lives at 921 Maple Street, Oakville, Michigan, sends this message to her: "I am well and happy as a prisoner of war. Don't worry about me. Hope to see you soon. Love." Then Sally will say, 'Now, boys, some of you take that down and send the message on to Joe's mother, some of you in his old outfit.' She is very chummy and chatty. Then will come a hot tune from Glenn Miller's orchestra. When that is finished, she will say in her most visiting manner, 'Boys, wouldn't it be nice to be home again and hear some good music like that and go to a dance again?' Her two associates, two men, obviously read their script. It couldn't be that ragged otherwise. One speaks with a decided accent and very guttural. They add the fun to the programs with their attempt to sound like the soap operas. By the way, do they still have soap operas back home? No one ever mentions those sorts of things."

The Daily Bulletin of April 20 discloses that Captain Pickens was administrative officer of the day on that date. In his letter he refers to Axis Sally's broadcasts early the next morning:

"The other morning at six, after a very harassing night as OD, I listened to one of Sally's Little Dramas. We had three air raids, which took up the greater part of the night, and I had not bothered to go to bed. Sally said she was going to interview an American general from the Engineer Corps. The general was imported, since he didn't sound like her usual associates. He had a voice which reminded me of Andy in Amos and Andy when he used to say 'hol' de phone.' Sally said she had heard he was working on a new project and would he tell her about it. In his big bass voice he said he was designing a bridge that would reach from the beachhead to Staten Island.

" 'What is the purpose of the bridge?' asked Sally.

" 'So the boys can walk home on their furloughs,' said the general.

" 'You know that won't work,' said Sally. And the general, in a surprised tone, said, 'You think not?'

" 'Well,' said he, 'men, just cancel that order I just gave you for the bridge.' "

In another broadcast, he related, Sally announced that she was celebrating the first quarter of a year spent by the American forces on the beachhead.

"She had a cake which she cut and then said she would save the remaining three-fourths for us and we could have a quarter each time she celebrated. She has often said that the beachhead was the largest German prison camp in the world. It was self-supporting, got its own food and gasoline, ran its own hospitals and generally took care of itself. All they had to do was keep a small patrol around the outer edge and occasionally smack us once in awhile with a few shells to keep us quiet.

"If she keeps that sort of junk up she will make this crowd mad and they will cut loose and run on up to Rome. I hope she keeps it up. She gives us the news and continuously cautions us against taking the Russian reports too seriously. She says they have dropped back, yes, and the Russians have come forward, but when they get ready to stop, it will be just like they stopped at Cassino and at the beachhead. She says they have to get ready for the boys coming across the channel. It is all very entertaining and amusing. I'm sorry you can't hear it. And to think, no one puts in an advertising plug each fifteen minutes. What a good spot going to waste."

He explained that the din around him had contributed to the poor typing of the letter. "The artillery duel is on and the typewriter shakes with each shell that takes off or lands. Too, it is not conducive to regular thinking. Our big boys are at it heavy and they make an awful noise and the earth rocks with each explosion. It has a certain amount of comfort with it, however," he concludes his report, "in spite of the shakes it produces."

The day the letter was written, April 28, the Daily Bulletin announced the welcoming to the 38th of Lieutenant Colonel Granberry D. Boyd, Jr., to the organization. That day the hospital had 666 patients. The Bulletin listed 67 admissions and 63 dispositions, with 334 vacant beds. Two days later, as April ended, the hospital roll numbered 536. Sixty-two patients were admitted, but 207 dispositions were recorded, so that May began with 571 patients—85 admitted, 50 dispositions.

The Daily Bulletin of Wednesday, May 17, announced that the Standard Operating Procedure of the 38th Evacuation Hospital "has been completed and will be distributed today. All key personnel are held responsible for reading, absorbing its instructions, and compliance with same. Section Chiefs and Section Leaders are expected to make personnel in their departments familiar with the contents of this SOP."

The Bulletin that day repeated the warning often made before, particularly since the unit's arrival in Italy, against lights at night:

It is again called to the attention of all personnel that each individual is responsible for the blackout of his or her quarters. There have been repeated violations, and in the future drastic action will be taken against offenders.

The use of flashlights in the area is a flagrant violation of blackout regulations. Violators will be subject to disciplinary action.

How stringent these blackout regulations were and how blacked-out the hospital was during this period at Anzio is revealed in a letter written the Sunday after the Bulletin notice was carried. The date was May 21, 1944, and the letter, written by Captain Pickens, located the unit at "Anzio Beachhead."

"It has been a long time since I remember being in the complete black" he began. "Even in Cornelius, I remember we had oil lamps and electricity from there on. That was before the second war, I mean. Since leaving the States there has been little light shown at night around where I have been living. I recall the bright lights of Tangiers when we passed thru the Straits of Gibraltar. That was the last time I saw any lights outdoors. In England they have small green lights to move traffic and an occasional blue light to show the entrance to a building, but nothing else. All thru Africa we were kept in the dark. Even in Tunis

Movement from one camp site to the next was made easier for the hospital's pharmacy by transporting the drugs and medicines in packing cases that could be set up to serve as shelves. "I'd throw a blanket in the case to serve as packing during the moving," Pharmacist Joe Neil reveals, "and when we set up in the new place I'd take out the blanket and be in business."

after the defeat of the Axis, all lights were out at night. In Italy, everything has been kept dark."

He goes on to explain:

"But the blackest place on earth is the beachhead. Here there is no question because the enemy can see any light that shows if the smoke screen has been blown away by a shifting wind. The guards challenge you if you inadvertently go out of a tent with a cigarette lighted. They sometimes shoot to make their warning more emphatic. Trucks and jeeps and tanks move along the road with a wee single light in front and a red tail light, neither visible for more than a hundred yards. We have built blackout entrances to our tents and hung canvas or blankets to hide the light. We patch up the holes made from the small flak every morning after an air raid so the light won't shine thru at night.

"When the moon is out and it is clear, it is fairly easy to move around the camp without stumbling over a tent rope or falling into a drain ditch. But when the moon is gone and the smoke screen heavy, there is not even the small silhouette of a tent or a trash can or anything to guide you. We walk slowly or from memory or just feel our way along inch by inch.

"In the middle of our camp there is a wide road in the sand and we walk there with ease. The other night I was walking along with the corporal of the guard just after midnight. A group of our enlisted men was coming from the operating room and making their way to their midnight supper at the mess. They could hear us talking and we could hear them, but neither of us could see the other. There was not a shadow of a shadow. It was pitch black. Then out of the inkiness came a resounding shout from the other group, 'FORE!' We headed to one side and passed without bumping, like the proverbial ships in the night."

Sometimes during artillery bombardments members of the 38th were able to get about by moving in the flashes from the firing. "The other night," his letter went on, "I climbed out of my hole to watch a thirty-minute barrage by our guns at a forward position. They flashed around the whole perimeter of the beachhead, a huge semicircle of white and reddish flares, a terrifying sight when combined with the rumblings and sounds of heavy doors slamming. Fortunately, they were headed the other way. You don't watch it when its headed this way, and you can tell by the sound which way it's going. There is a sickening whine or whistle to those headed toward the sea and the explosions are like a thousand blastings.

"There is a story about two Negroes, working down at the ration depot, who talked at great length about the shells headed in this direction. One of them said

to the other, 'Joe, eve' time I hears one of them shells comin' in my direction, it jes' talks to me.'

" 'Zat so?' Joe said. 'What does she say?'

" 'She says, "Joe, youooooooooooooc ain't goin' to git to Ala-BAM!" '

"That is about as graphic a description of the sound as you could get, and it leaves you tight inside," he adds. "Fortunately, it doesn't go on all the time, otherwise it might result in more psychopathic cases. We have a number of them pass thru our hospital. There were some among the personnel of the hospital we relieved here. The shelling has been a little too close for comfort."

He tells of one of the men who after a heavy shelling got out his clarinet and proceeded to go through the motions of a concert rendition, except that no sound came from his instrument. The next day he did the same thing, and the next. When on the third day his buddies were about to tie him up in a strait jacket, he explained to them that he didn't have a reed in his clarinet and while he was waiting to receive one from home was simply practicing his fingering.

The Daily Bulletin the next day after the captain wrote his letter home—Monday, May 22, 1944—announced that the commanding officer "takes pleasure in welcoming Captain Francis G. Genin to the organization. Captain Genin has been assigned to the EENT Clinic of the Surgical Service."

This day marked the end of a four-month period evaluated by another member of the 38th on his return home. Major Munroe in summarizing the work of the American evacuation hospitals in the area northeast of Nettuno from January 22 to May 22, 1944, revealed that despite the difficulties of the situation, they participated in the successful evacuation by sea of 23,860 American casualties and 9,203 British casualties.

Major Munroe's account of the Anzio beachhead experiences of the Charlotte unit provides an interesting and important view paralleling those offered by other members of the 38th.

"Due to the tremendous difficulties of the Fifth Army against a wiry, strong enemy force in the face of such difficult terrain and inclement weather, its northward progress in the Italy campaign was slow," he observed. The launching of the Anzio Beachhead Operation Shingle was planned to coincide with the attack on the Winter Line, but the proposed progress toward the Winter Line had not reached anticipated plans. This area, in fact, would be one of the most bitterly contested sectors of the Italian campaign. Operation

Shingle had reached an eventual strength of over 100,000 men when at 0500, 22 January, 1944, on a black night the Allied assault convoy of 50,000 men dropped anchor."

He went on to describe the subsequent action:

"The assault crafts headed toward the beach. Promptly at H hours, 0200, the first crafts reached the beach and collected themselves for battle. The beachhead landing surprised the enemy and there was no enemy to meet them. Much air support was supplied. Though the enemy had completely failed to foresee our landing at Anzio and had apparently expected it either at Gaeta or Leghorn, he quickly recovered and directed to Anzio larger portions of the reserve he was moving from the Rome area, the Adriatic, and North Italy to bolster the sagging Gustav Line. By 24 January the pattern of enemy reaction had taken powerful shape about the Anzio beachhead. Instead of removing any of the enemy troops from the Gustav Line, the enemy fortified his Anzio forces by troops from the north. The failure of the main Fifth Army to pierce the Gustav Line," the major continues his appraisal, "quickly reduced the prospect of early linking of the southern front with the beachhead and of thus forcing a general retreat of the enemy toward Rome.

"It was immediately apparent that the Anzio beachhead was a small island surrounded by sea and a determined enemy force, that used every attempt to force the beachhead into the sea. The beachhead was the largest that could be held with the limited number of troops, but it was so small that any part could be easily reached by enemy artillery and there was little room for defense in depth. A breakthrough at any point would bring the Germans almost to the sea. Mines and other defensive preparations were immediately taken by the Allied forces."

Major Munroe's account continues the narrative of the Anzio fighting:

"The attacks and counterattacks of Allied forces and of German forces soon became remindful of the trench warfare of World War I. It was soon apparent that the Allies were unable to broaden the beachhead and the German troops were unable to push us into the sea. It was a slugging effort of shells and bombs.

"It was a new experience for the Fifth Army to play the defensive role that the VI Corps was forced to assume at Anzio beachhead," says Major Munroe's appraisal. "The Fifth Army had always been in the offensive role. The flat level land of the beachhead was under the constant observation of the surrounding enemy-held hills.

"The confined area of the beachhead and the lack of distinction between the front line and rear areas were nowhere more evident than in the district northeast of the Nettuno air strip where the American evacuation hospitals were located. This was the area where for almost seventeen weeks medical personnel gave aid and comfort to the sick and wounded in an area only a few miles from the enemy's artillery and so close to the harbor and other military targets that it was constantly subject to air bombardment as well as to shelling. At the end of March, when the ground began to dry out, the hospitals were placed three and one-half feet below the surface to protect the patients. As far as possible the wounded were evacuated to the Naples area. Air evacuation, however, could not be used until our breakthrough in May because the dust raised by the planes in landing or taking off from the air strips invited German shelling. Evacuation by sea was complicated by shallow beaches, stormy weather, and constant enemy shelling. Since the hospital ships could not dock at the wharf, they received casualties from the shore by means of L.C.T.'s. Storms and high seas frequently interrupted this method of evacuation, and L.S.T.'s were necessarily often used, despite the resultant 30-hour trip to the base hospitals." Nevertheless, Major Munroe records, the 33,063 casualties—23,860 Americans and 9,203 British—were evacuated by sea.

The obstacles that had slowed progress of the campaign in Italy, of which Major Munroe would write in some detail, were referred to by General Clark in a letter directed in May to the officers and men of the Fifth Army. But the General, nevertheless, expressed his optimism as well as his appreciation of the Fifth Army's accomplishments since it invaded Italy, and forecast an early resumption of a strong and determined offensive.

"During the eight months that have passed since your invasion of the Italian mainland you have accomplished results of major strategic and tactical importance to the United Nations," General Clark wrote. "The entire world, including the Axis, knows the success and significance of your Salerno landing against bitter opposition, and of your subsequent capture of Naples in the face of the enemy's determination to deny to us the port which was indispensable to support our further operations in Italy. After the fall of Naples you pressed your attack relentlessly and without delay, forcing the Germans to continue their retreat until they had reached carefully prepared lines, where the exceedingly difficult mountainous terrain provided extreme advantages to the defender. Notwithstanding the obstacles of mountains, lack of roads, bitter weather and concrete defensive fortifications, you have in your various well-executed attacks forced the enemy to reinforce heavily his advantageous positions at the expense of other commitments and have harassed him continuously."

He referred to the area in which the 38th Evacuation Hospital was at that time operating:

"At the same time you have established firmly a strong beachhead in the Anzio-Nettuno area, where you have provided a serious threat on his lines of communication which he is attempting to meet by the diversion of a large force from other operations.

"It may appear to you, since the Fifth Army's progress in terms of territory gained during the past few months has been slow, that our campaign is no longer a major one or that it is not having significant success in the war as a whole. Nothing could be further from the truth. You have made a conspicuously successful invasion of the continental fortress which the Germans boasted was impregnable. You have required the Germans to devote more than twenty divisions to the costly and losing task of retarding the Allied progress to the north. You have inflicted heavy losses upon their troops and have taken more than 13,000 prisoners. You have placed the enemy in his present distressing position of trying hopelessly to hold back the Allied forces, which he knows will eventually overrun him from two directions.

"I have direct personal knowledge that the accomplishments of the Fifth Army are understood and appreciated by the governments and peoples of the United Nations. They appreciate not only that you have accomplished as much as was possible with the strength of your force, but also that you have contained in this campaign many thousands of German soldiers whom the Nazis have needed desperately in their attempts to stem the Russian advance and to prepare themselves against invasion in other parts of Europe."

In the offensive that would be resumed soon, the General predicted the Fifth Army would have "what you need to strike smashing blows and to follow them through to completion: thorough training, superior equipment, heroic courage and the knowledge that we can and will destroy the German armies.

"I have full confidence," he concluded the message, "that, as in the past, the men of the Fifth Army will meet the tests to come as true soldiers and that with God's guidance and help you will press on to great and decisive victories."

General H. R. Alexander, Commander-in-Chief of the Allied Armies in Italy, writing also in May to "Soldiers of the Allied Armies in Italy," expressed confidence, too, that "the bad times are behind us" and that the Allied forces "now assembling for the final battles" will "crush the enemy once and for all."

The Commander-in-Chief wrote:

"Throughout the past winter you have fought hard and valiantly and killed many Germans. Perhaps you are disappointed that we have not been able to advance faster and farther, but I and those who know realize full well how magnificently you have fought amongst these almost insurmountable obstacles of rocky, trackless mountains, deep in snow, and in valleys blocked by rivers and mud, against a stubborn foe.

"The results of these past months may not appear spectacular, but you have drawn into Italy and mauled many of the enemy's best divisions which he badly needed to stem the advance of the Russian Armies in the East. Hitler has admitted that his defeats in the East were largely due to the bitterness of the fighting and his losses in Italy. This, in itself, is a great achievement and you may well be as proud of yourselves as I am of you. You have gained the admiration of the world and the gratitude of our Russian Allies.

"Today the bad times are behind us and tomorrow we can see victory ahead," the optimistic message continued. "Under the ever increasing blows of the air forces of the United Nations, which are mounting every day in intensity, the German war machine is beginning to crumble. The Allied armed forces are now assembling for the final battles on sea, on land, and in the air to crush the enemy once and for all. . . blows are about to fall which will result in the final destruction of the Nazis and bring freedom once again to Europe, and hasten peace for us all. To us in Italy has been given the honour to strike the first blow.

"We are going to destroy the German Armies in Italy," General Alexander assured his forces. "The fighting will be hard, bitter, and perhaps long, but you are warriors and soldiers of the highest order, who for more than a year have known only victory. You have courage, determination and skill. You will be supported by overwhelming air forces, and in guns and tanks we far outnumber the Germans. No Armies have ever entered battle before with a more just and righteous cause.

"So with God's help and blessing, we take the field— confident of victory."

The members of the 38th, reading the letters of General Clark and General Alexander, had no comprehension at the time of how quickly the general's promises of impending bitter action would begin to materialize. It was still a week from the end of the May in which the letters were written that the 38th's faithfully kept Daily Bulletin attached to its file the Daily News sheet from the headquarters of the Third Infantry Division, dated Thursday, May 25, 1944, and marked Italy Edition Vol. III No. 124, at the head of which was the warning: "This news bulletin contains information valuable to the enemy and should not be circulated outside military channels. It will be read to front-line units as soon as possible after distribution and then destroyed by burning." Under these instructions, in bold letters, was the further injunction: READ AND BURN.

Then under the heading TODAY'S SITUATION, the sheet revealed:

"The Anzio beachhead ceased to be a beachhead at daylight this morning, according to a British liaison plane pilot, who reported landing and talking to a British recon force as it joined hands with a Fifth Army Southern Front patrol that had headed up the coast from Terracina even before that town was rid of German troops.

"Meanwhile, the Third Division continued to battle fiercely for Cisterna while the Armored troops cut Highway 7 northwest of the town, and were reported at least a quarter of the way to Velletri. While the 'Friscans' moved around Cisterna from the left to reach the Cori-Cisterna road, the 'Dragons' battled north from the railroad to circle the town from the right.

"The Germans were holding Cisterna with everything they had, making every house a pillbox. The 'Cotton Balers,' whose task it was to occupy the town, were moving in from the northwest and south; and one company was reported in the center of the town late this morning.

"Close to 700 prisoners have been taken since H hour by the Third, and the Armored troops have captured that many or more. Units of the Specialists reached Highway 7 where it crosses the Mussolini Canal, and the 'Thunderbirds' last night repulsed the only German counterattack of considerable size."

The principal news story of that day, however, as reported from Third Infantry Division headquarters, carried a page-wide two-line headline:

ANZIO BEACHHEAD BECOMES HISTORY AS CONTACT IS MADE WITH FIFTH ARMY FORCES DRIVING NORTH FROM TERRACINA; CANADIAN TANKS SMASH CENTER OF HITLER LINE

The story began:

" 'We are no longer a beachhead!' "

"With these dramatic words, Allied headquarters on the Anzio front announced today the juncture made at 0900 hours this morning between British reconnaissance patrols and American forces driving up the west coast.

"The juncture took place midway between Anzio and Terracina, 25 miles to the south.

"A sizable German force is believed trapped between the joining Allied forces and the coast.

"Thus the entire western hinge of the Adolf Hitler Line has been rolled back from the west coast like a rug.

"Meanwhile, Canadian tanks north of Pontecorvo, most southern stronghold of the Hitler Line, have torn large gaps in the German defenses."

Canadian infantry, the article continued, had reached the Melfa River, north of Pico. Other Canadian forces, together with French troops, had closed in on Pontecorvo and were battling for possession of the town.

"The Americans to the west, who have completely retaken Terracina," it went on, "are pouring more troops inland over the mountains to drive deeper the wedge which has contacted the Anzio forces.

"With most of the Liri Valley in Allied hands, the Hitler Line has disintegrated into a series of nearly isolated strong points."

The day before, the Daily News says in still another story, Prime Minister Churchill said to Parliament: "The Germans will be completely driven out of Italy."

Captain Montgomery made but one short entry in his diary during May. On May 1, 1944, he wrote:

The bombings at night continue. The noise of the ack-ack is the worst part of it. The 90 mm guns shake the tents.

But his tempo of recording, like the tempo of the war, would gain speed in June, though his entries would continue terse. On June 1 he wrote:

The push continues. It has been going day & night in the OR. The casualties continue.

Then on June 4 his three-word entry would be even for him a classic in understatement, rivaling, indeed, Julius Caesar's "Veni, vidi, vici." Captain Montgomery recorded:

Rome has fallen.

The Stars and Stripes, however, had much more to say of that historic event. In its issue of June 5, 1944, labeled "Vol. 1 - No. 1 Published in Rome" and datelined "Rome, June 5 1944," it emblazoned the news under a screaming top line in one-inch high black letters:

WE'RE IN ROME

The story was written by Sgt. Paul Green of the service newspaper's staff. A subhead proclaimed: NO LETUP AS ALLIED FORCES CHASE FLEEING GERMANS NORTHWARD. Sergeant Green wrote:

Rome, June 5 —The kraut was fleeing today along the roads that lead north from Rome as 5th Army troops poured through the Italian capital in relentless pursuit of the decimated enemy forces. Exactly 24 days after the first guns boomed from Minturno to Cassino, the Eternal City was completely in Allied hands.
There was no letup in the crushing offensive as American, British and French soldiers—taking in stride their magnificent victory in liberating Rome—kept on going with a good chance of cutting off and annihilating many thousands

of Jerries before they could reach some stable line of defense.

The world rang with praises of the campaign that has been climaxed with the capture of the city. Rome has fallen many times to military conquerors, but this is the first time that it has been taken from the south. That was something for the GI to talk about at his next bull session.

But GI Joe was a little too tired today to realize the full importance of what he had done. It's been a tough fight all along the line, and the dogfaces are plenty weary. You could see it as they walked through the streets of Rome. You could feel it from the tired nods as they answered the cheering of the people.

The GI's who passed through the city could relax their trigger fingers for a while. The city was theirs—completely. It was especially the pretty signorinas who caught the eye of appreciative Yanks. Ear-seeing ones scrawled down a few addresses for reference later on when they come back to Rome on leave. Others took a little time out to get a quick look at the famous ruins.

But to most of them, Rome is just another stop—although a main one—on the road that leads home. The GI who saw Africa last year or Sicily has marched on a long trail since then. Others have joined him. The trek that led through the toughest, most grueling days of the Mediterranean campaign opened up for its last chapter at Salerno and went from Naples up the never-to-be-forgotten hills of Italy. Now the trail is nearing its end in a burst of welcome from the people of Rome.

Sergeant Green's report of the fall of Rome continued to relate details of the Fifth Army's entrance, its reactions and the reactions of the welcoming Italians. Other articles developed the many phases of the capture of the ancient city. The entire edition of June 5, in fact, was devoted to the great victory announced in Captain Montgomery's three-word entry.

The next day, June 6, would be recorded in history as one of the most significant dates during World War II. The Stars and Stripes had a single word, this one in letters two inches high, headlining the story:

INVASION

And in smaller letters, but spread in a streamer across the page, the subhead proclaimed:

SECOND FRONT IN FRANCE

The news story, datelined London, June 6, revealed:

Allied forces landed this morning on the northern coast of France, it was announced at 0945 hours from General Dwight Eisenhower's Supreme Headquarters of the Allied Expeditionary Force in England. The German official news agency said that Allied airborne and seaborne troops which landed on the coast of the Seine Bay early this morning had been reinforced. The agency added that Allied airborne landings in Normandy were made in great depth. Allied naval forces, supported by strong air forces, began landing armies early this morning and reinforcements followed the initial sea and airborne assault waves. It was announced that General Sir Bernard Law Montgomery, former chief of the Eighth Army, is in command of the com-

bined American, British and Canadian army group carrying out the assault.

Giving the latest news of the landings, Prime Minister Winston Churchill disclosed this afternoon that 4,000 ships crossed the Channel and that up to 11,000 aircraft are taking part in the operation.

It continued for several columns to give sensational details of the mighty assault, and interviews with GI's in Rome and other stories supplemented it.

The 38th's Captain Montgomery recorded it, too, and in his characteristic manner:

June 6th. D-day. We heard at 8:30 that the invasion had begun by assaults on the Cherbourgh peninsula.

In this first week of June, 1944, the 38th's Daily Bulletin, too, was making entries—both denying receipt of information concerning possible movement of the unit and posting instructions in preparation for such a movement. On June 5, the day the Fifth Army entered Rome, the Bulletin, under the heading IDLE RUMORS, declared:

"Information has *not* been received concerning unit movement. Any rumors pertaining thereto *will be stopped* immediately."

Yet the Bulletin continued:

"POLICE OF AREA. A letter from the Army Surgeon pertaining to the condition of bivouac areas calls attention to the fact that it is the responsibility of each unit to leave occupied areas in good condition, when departing. Each section and each individual will immediately dispose of all non-transportable, unnecessary equipment that would constitute trash, and place at a disposal point.

"PREPARATIONS FOR MOVEMENT. Each section chief will be responsible for making an immediate survey of equipment in the possession of his section and will complete arrangements for proper packing so that, in case of movement, there will be no delay."

The next day, June 6, the Bulletin made no mention of a projected movement of the unit. The following day there was no Bulletin. But Major Montgomery recorded in his diary:

June 7th. Hospital closed today

And June 8 he wrote:

Arrived in Rome. Are setting up in a beautiful park— "Pamphilli."

Publication of the 38's Daily Bulletin was resumed on Saturday, June 10. Captain Pickens was administrative officer of the day and Warrant Officer Pedrick was alternate. Medical officer of the day was Captain Gay and Captain Schirmer was alternate. Major Calder and Captain Denning were surgical officers of the day

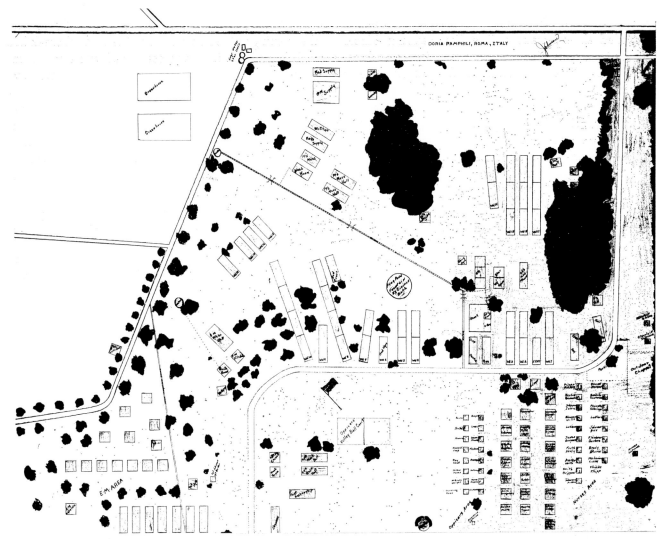

The layout of the encampment in Rome's suburban Doria Pamphilli is shown in this drawing. The 38th's stay there, however, was short. The hospital opened on June 9, 1944, and closed on June 30 to move to Massa Marittima.

and alternate, respectively. Major Walker was dental officer of the day and Captain Hoffman was alternate. Nurse officer of the day and alternate, respectively, were Lieutenants Webber and Wells.

The first announcement in the day's Bulletin was:

"THE HOSPITAL WAS CLOSED AT NETTUNO AT 1200 HOURS, 7 JUNE 1944.

"THE HOSPITAL OPENED AT DORIA PAM-PHILLI, ROME, AT 1100 HOURS, 9 JUNE, 1944."

On the opening day the number of patients was 292 and 368 beds were vacant.

The June 12 Bulletin listed 700 patients and no vacant beds. It published a directive from Fifth Army headquarters:

"This headquarters has been advised that troops may mention in private correspondence that they have visited Rome, provided that:

"(a) The writers' units or headquarters are not linked

in any way with their personal accounts other than by the correct use of proper return address. For example, it is forbidden for a writer to state that his unit or headquarters is in or near Rome.

"(b) No dates will be mentioned."

The 38th was hardly settled down and operating at Doria Pamphilli, however, before at the end of June it was closed. The next day's Bulletin announced:

"THE HOSPITAL OFFICIALLY CLOSED AT 1630 HOURS, 30 JUNE 1944.

"HOSPITAL MOVED FROM DORIA PAMPHIL-LI, ROME, ITALY, TO A SITE FOUR KILOME-TERS NORTH OF MASSA MARITTIMA, ITALY."

Next day's Bulletin announced the opening of the hospital at Massa Marittima "at 0900 hours, this date."

The Bulletin carried, too, Colonel Wood's commen-dation of the unit:

"The work accomplished by members of the unit

in the movement from Rome to the present site has exceeded all expectations. The Commanding Officer wishes to express his sincere appreciation to each individual for his and her commendable performance of duty."

The July 3 Daily Bulletin announced the promotion of Captain John K. Nattinger to major.

On the day the hospital opened at Doria Pamphilli, June 9, Captain Montgomery recorded in his diary that he had had an audience that day with the Pope. He made no further entry until June 30 when he recorded:

Hospital closed today.

The next day, July 1, he wrote in his little journal:

Left Rome at 8:30 A.M. Came up Highway No. 1 to Massa Marittima. Arrived at 5:30 P.M. A large alfalfa field in the mountains.

July 2 he wrote that the hospital opened at nine that morning.

"Casualties are slowing down since the rush of the first night," he recorded on July 7.

Three days later the unit's chief anesthetist noted "Lt. Doskow added to anes. service," and observed with evident satisfaction:

I have a real dept. now.

He listed his department's personnel:

Capt. John C. Montgomery, chief
Capt. Stanley Nowacki, asst. chief
1st Lt. Lola LaChance
1st Lt. Deborah Doskow
2nd Lt. Clarke
2nd Lt. Helen Johnson

Captain Montgomery's diary and the Daily Bulletin issues during the last three weeks in June and the first two weeks in July when the 38th was arriving and getting established in the Rome area provide little information about the day-to-day activities of the unit's personnel. Fortunately, however, a letter written home in mid July by Captain Pickens provides an intimate and illuminating picture of the Italian capital in the days immediately after it was cleared of the German invaders. The principal value of the long letter is its revelation of Rome in this significant period as seen by an American soldier in World War II. On July 15, 1944, Captain Pickens wrote from Italy:

"For two thousand years people have been trying to describe Rome. So far as I know, no one has done it adequately. I have hesitated for too long now to try, but I must give you some of my impressions. Before getting into my visits to the Eternal City, I want to give you one picture of our setup before seeing the Roman capital.

"From the news, our battles on this front have been relegated to second-class, which is as it should be with the opening of the new front. But the original breakthru and the starting from the beachhead was a major engagement if I know anything about war, and we have seen our share. The enemy was on the hills looking down at us with perfect observation and the price we had to pay for those early days was high. Our hospital was running over; everyone was working at fever pitch. The job done by all the hospitals in that area will go down in history, so far as the Medical Corps is concerned, as simply magnificent. But a lot of our boys never got back to the hospitals; they never had a chance. It was a part of the price. When we left that area, to follow behind the advancing army, I had the occasion to pass the American cemetery. There, neatly set out, were the inevitable white crosses, thousands of them. But the battle had been so furious that the bodies of American soldiers were still coming in and the efficient graves registration section had long gotten behind in their work."

His description of what he saw there, after more than a score of years since his visit, is shocking:

"There were huge piles of our dead awaiting identification and proper burial. Some of them had been dead for days and days and had been caught in the see-saw of the battle raging around them. They did not know the sacrifices made to try and rescue them, but their sacrifices had been the most. Here they were in all stages of decomposition, some swelled so large as to break out of their uniforms, some turned a midnight blue, some with only parts of a body left. As you neared the scene, there was a buzz in the air that rose to a crescendo as the big bluebottle flies swarmed in and out of the section. Death was in the air. The faint, sweet odor of death permeated the countryside. Here was the picture of the price of glory. Of course, that section of the Army quickly caught up with their work and followed behind us. They do a grand job with identification and there can be no error. Of all the Americans they had there, there was only one who could not be identified. He will be one unknown soldier for the politicians to lay wreaths at his feet. Of course there were Germans there and many of the Allies, all getting the same treatment. I pray this time that our soldiers will not have died in vain."

Having offered this arresting introduction, he went on to provide a detailed account of the Eternal City as seen by a member of the Charlotte hospital unit in midsummer of 1944:

"But, on to Rome, and all roads in Italy still lead to Rome. What a magnificent city! What a paradox! Here was the combination of the old and the new. Modern doubledeck buses moving along well paved streets and passing the prodding oxen bringing produce to

Much effort was directed toward keeping the surgery tents sterile. This sign—SURGERY—CLEAN—OPERATING—was moved with the tent from one hospital campsite to the next.

the city. Here were ultra-modern apartment houses overlooking the ruins of the pre-Christian era. Here was the home of the Christian religion and the foster father of paganism. I went one Sunday afternoon to St. Peter's for the vesper services. What a picture with the entrance of the Cardinal in his flaming red and the colorfully attired assistants. It was the celebration of St. Peter's Day, a feast day for all Rome, and the people were there by the thousands. The magnificent choirs sang to each other and then combined in a grand finale. It was inspiring. But alongside this display was a line of people, twelve wide and reaching back outside beyond the Egyptian obelisk called Cleopatra's Needle, all lined up to kiss the toe of the statue of St. Peter.

"St. Peter's statue is in bronze. On this particular day they had dressed him with fine, regal clothes and on his head was a crown with many priceless jewels. Around his neck hung other jewels, beautiful stones

gathered from the four corners of the world. And people stood in line to kiss his toe."

"Here was one of the first cities where the plebeians contested with the aristocracy and eventually gained citizenship. That was the strength of early Rome. And in the modern times they had fallen again upon evil days and followed Il Duce to an ignominious state. He may have made the trains run on time and cleaned up the city and cleared some slum areas and paved some streets, but he has left the minds of the people in a muddle that two generations will not clear. They are wrangling among themselves even now about the temporary government.

"I stood in the Piazza Venezia and looked at the balcony where Mussolini used to carry on his tirades against the decadent democracies and wondered what might have happened had he used his talents in the right direction. I had a friend, a priest from America,

195

who lived on the square just opposite. He told me of the spectacles produced there. We stood at the window at a simple American Army retreat when Secretary Stimson was here and we spoke of the contrast. I almost found myself being ashamed because we did not put on a better show, but I guess it was enough."

He spoke of his visit with his friend the priest to the famous Colosseum:

"From the Piazza Venezia it is an easy walk to the Flavian Amphitheatre, commonly called the Colosseum. It was the Madison Square Garden from 80 A.D. on for several centuries. The circuses were brought in by Caesar's legions or the gladiators fought or the Christians were fed to the beasts. Fifty thousand could push in for a show. Sometimes they flooded the arena and the navy took over to show their wares. Now it is used for a sort of latrine for those Romans who are not housebroken and the upper tiers show couples courting for lack of other rooms in the crowded city. Benito had cut a street thru from his quarters to the Colosseum, right thru the old Roman Forum. They uncovered many things of interest and preserved them for future tourists. I asked why all the structures were below street level and Monsignor Hemmick gave me this answer: in the old days they pitched their garbage out of the windows; there was no other way to dispose of it. Then when the street was filled up they either left the house and built another or they added another story. It sounded plausible to me after looking at some of the excavations. Many of the Romans still dispose of their garbage in the same way even in these modern times and if you are not careful when you are walking down a street, you may be buried with debris."

Rome, members of the 38th found, had been little damaged by the Allies' bombing, Captain Pickens revealed, except for the marshaling yards. "There has been no damage by the war in Rome save the marshaling yards, where the Allies literally tore the place up. It is a good example of precision bombing. The stray bombs hit a cemetery nearby. I say there has been no damage; I mean to any of the old relics. The Germans systematically blew up all of the substations and the power plants and gas works. It would not be good to leave electricity or gas for the Allies. That helped keep the place blacked out until they had moved a comfortable distance to the north."

He further pictures the modern Rome almost three thousand years after its legendary founding in 753 B.C. as seen by personnel of Charlotte's evacuation hospital group:

"The old Tiber meanders along thru the city about the same as it did a thousand years ago. I was surprised at its small size. The many bridges, almost one at the end of every street, with their statues and ornate decorations, and the small boats and swimming beaches in the river make the scene picturesque. The wide streets that flank the river on each side with their large elm trees interspersed with oleanders give room for Romans to walk and they love to get out with all the family and wander up and down. They block military traffic and run the chance of being run down at every turn, but they don't seem to mind. They are obviously not accustomed to the fast moving traffic of American GI's.

"St. Peter's and the Vatican across the river from the main part of the city are a sight never to be forgotten. The Vatican was closed to the public except for audience with the Pope and a hurried visit to the Sistine Chapel. I went to see the Pope and carried some rosaries and a crucifix to be blessed. . . . The Pope spoke to us in English and appeared to be in a hurry . . . he hurried away to do the same thing with a group of French in the next hall. But just outside the hall of the meeting and next to it was the Sistine Chapel. That is worth a visit to Rome if nothing else is seen. I wouldn't attempt to describe it. St. Peter's is the same. The size of the place is most impressive, including the markers in the floor showing that it is larger than St. Paul's in London and Notre Dame in Paris. Monsignor Hemmick had a most healthy attitude in his descriptions and placed emphasis where it was due and laughed at the funny things. We had a good time looking at the statue of some Queen of Sweden who had ridden horseback over all Europe and ended up in Rome to die. Because she was generous with her worldly possessions, she gained a marked place in the church. Veronica's Veil came in for her share of interest. She was the one who covered the face of Christ on his way to Calvary and left the imprint of his countenance on her veil. She rated a tremendous statue and once a year they bring out the veil from a high balcony in the church and show it to the people with proper pomp and display. Of course, many of the Popes rate prominent spots, and there have been 260 of them.

"The constant mixture of church and state is in evidence. Until 1929, when Mussolini signed an agreement giving the church 100 acres of free land and a free state, there apparently were those who thought the Pope should be the temporal ruler of Rome and Italy and most of the world as well as looking after our spiritual well being. I was impressed with a lot of the things which had been taken from other countries and other peoples and brought to Rome as a result of conquest. We cannot criticize Hitler too much for carting off the spoils when it has been a practice of warring nations for centuries. We Americans are the only suckers who capture territory and things and then glibly give them back to their owners. If it were possible, I would crate

196

Lieutenant Lela Russell, the hospital's dietitian, kept an alert eye on the kitchen and the cooks. Here she is about to put soup into a container for delivery to the patients in the wards. Left is Sergeant William Vaughn; right, Leonard Weinheimer.

up one of these monoliths from ancient Egypt and put it in my back yard and a marker showing my tour with the Army thru Italy. I might be the low man on the totem pole but at least I'd have more than gray hair and flat feet for my conquests and my two years overseas."

The 38th's members visiting Rome found the city after four years of war "with only bare necessities and very few of these," the letter revealed. "No manufacturing has been done except for the war. There is nothing in the shops except the fabulous things for the collectors, or junk. Shoes are made of wood with a small canvas binding; there are little textiles to be seen and food is just wherever you can find it. The black market controls most of it. I almost made a trade for some draperies with a marchesa for a few pounds of butter. Butter is priced at $20 per kilo at present. My hurried

departure kept me from disobeying all rules and working it out."

One of the places of principal interest to visiting members of the 38th was the famous Catacombs. Captain Pickens referred to an atrocity committed in the St. Agnes catacomb by the occupying Germans. "During their occupation of the city one of their soldiers was killed by some civilians. In retribution, they took all of the political prisoners out of the city, some 350 of them, and escorted them to the Catacombs and finished them with machine guns and left the bodies without any other burial. They denied the families the opportunity of collecting their loved ones. There was an awful stench at the place, and the atrocity was the principal subject of conversation among the Romans. Their former allies had not treated them right."

Perhaps the most memorable occasion for the per-

197

sonnel of the 38th during these weeks in the vicinity of Rome was a dance arranged, as others had been at various bases on the movement across northern Africa into southern Italy, primarily for the enlisted men of the unit. Captain Pickens, who had promoted the previous dances, wrote of the one at Rome:

"We wanted to have a dance for our enlisted men while in that vicinity. The Red Cross worker who is connected with our hospital went with me to find a spot. We had the orchestra from John Trescot's Engineers; all we needed was suitable space. We combed the section near us asking the help of the local padre. He was no help at all, but some ladies at the church heard our questions and offered to help. We went then to the American Academy, but it was closed to such frivolity. The manager told us of four villas that might be available. We tried them all and it was the last one that turned out to be available. The Villa Abamalik overlooks St. Peter's, with beautiful gardens and what was once a nice house. The owner, an Arab, was living in Florence. Out and away from the main house was a ballroom complete in every detail, a large dining room, which could seat forty people easily, a powder room on the second floor, and a kitchen in the basement. The place was built for just such purpose as we had in mind. The caretaker was delighted to have us use it.

"The Germans had been there and broken some of the statuary and had stolen some of the magnificent draperies and oil paintings. They had used the spot for a mess. There were no lights, so our electrician rigged up one of the small generators and gave light thru the beautiful chandeliers. The ballroom was a dream, just the right size and none better to be found anywhere either in Italy or the U. S. With all the necessary equipment on hand, all we needed was females. Here we enlisted the aid of some American women who had married Italians and who lived in Rome. They invited their friends' daughters and we bundled them all in our big two-ton trucks with their mamas and carted them out to the villa. Most of them had never seen the inside of one of Rome's grand houses. They came in droves, more girls than men for the first time since we had been overseas.

"The party started at 6:30 and finished at 9:30. The Romans have to be off the streets by 10 o'clock at night. At 8:30 we announced that food and other refreshments were available and the ladies would be served first. By the time the men started to get cheese or chicken or spam sandwiches, all the food had disappeared. The young Romans had made away with it in fast style. They stuffed sandwiches in their pocketbooks, they put cheese in their handkerchiefs, they even put slices of bread down their bosoms and con-

tinued to dance in a most buxom manner. The party was a huge success, particularly for the young ladies. Where neither could speak the other's language, they made up one of their own."

His letter spoke of other experiences in Rome he and comrades of the 38th shared and historic places visited, most of them, it added, "on foot, and the city spreads out considerably."

But now the jaunts in and about Rome were behind them, "and there are other spots of interest. It is a changing scene and with the rapid progress of the Army, I have little time other than for work. Possibly the opportunity will come to see the Leaning Tower or some of the beauties of Florence. Time will tell. There should be some compensation for the drudgery that comes with these many months following an Army."

Two days after he wrote the letter, the 38th was closing its operations at Masa Marittima to set up its base at St. Luce. The next day, July 18, 1944, the Daily Bulletin recorded:

"THE HOSPITAL CLOSED AT MASSA MARITTIMA, ITALY, AT 1000 HOURS 17 JULY 1944.

"THE HOSPITAL RE-OPENED AT 1300 HOURS 17 JULY 1944, WHEN NO. 1 DETAIL ASSUMED CHARGE OF 18 PATIENTS FROM 15th EVACUATION HOSPITAL AT CECINA, ITALY.

"THE HOSPITAL PROPER WAS MOVED FROM MASSA MARITTIMA, ITALY, TO A SITE APPROXIMATELY 1½ KM NORTHEAST OF ST. LUCE, ITALY."

The Daily Bulletin of Wednesday, July 19, recorded further:

"THE HOSPITAL OFFICIALLY OPENED IN THIS LOCATION AT 1200 HOURS, 19 JULY 1944."

Blackout warning declared that "This area is under direct observation of the enemy, and strict Blackout will be maintained. For the time being, only those tents which are essential for hospital operation will be wired for electricity." Number of patients that day totaled 14.

Captain Montgomery's diary also refers to the 38th's detail assigned to take charge of a group of patients from the 15th Evacuation Hospital. On July 16 he wrote:

Today Bill Pennington & I went to Pomerance, Saline & Cecina. Bill Leonard, Hunter & I are to take over the setup of the 15th Evac at Cecina tomorrow.

The following day he added the entry:

We arrived at noon. Made a property exchange with the 15th. We have 15 patients.

Two days later, July 19, he noted:

The unit opened 9 miles north of here today. We are having a nice rest. Went swimming today.

On the twenty-first he wrote that they "Discharged all out-patients today." The next day he recorded:

Closed our little unit. Arrived at 38th at noon. We are near Santa Luce. This is a barren hot place.

Meanwhile, two personnel changes were being noted in the Daily Bulletin. In the issue of July 20 it was announced that Captain Robert P. Miller left that day for temporary duty in the United States and congratulations were "extended to Howard J. Seesel, 550th Ambulance Company, attached, on his promotion to First Lieutenant."

Three days later the Bulletin noted other personnel changes:

"Major Duncan G. Calder, Jr., Team Captain, with the following members of his team have been placed on temporary duty with the 33rd Field Hospital as an auxiliary surgical unit: Captain George A. Hawes, Captain Stanley M. Nowacki, 1st Lieutenant A. Clementine Mills, T/5 Harold R. Carter and Pfc Carl V. Neff.

"An auxiliary surgical unit of the 300th General Hospital is welcomed to this organization on temporary duty. Team Captain is Captain Wilbur K. Brubaker. Other team members are: Captain Robert C. Benson, Captain John P. Hand, Jr., 2nd Lieutenant Margaret I. Davies, T/4 Wick V. Ballettine, and T/4 Joseph C. Shaeffer."

One week after the hospital opened at its new base the patient load had grown to 463.

The Bulletin of July 30 recorded the welcoming by Colonel Wood of Captain Carlo Natalini to the 38th as replacement for Captain Medearis and his assignment as assistant unit supply officer.

In the United States the Presidential race between President Roosevelt, seeking a third term, and Thomas E. Dewey, the Republican nominee, was nearing the home stretch, and the excitement at home was being reflected in varying degrees among the men and women in the service overseas. The Daily Bulletin, taking notice of the campaign, on July 31 inserted this notice:

"Any personnel who are interested in voting in the November elections and who have not as yet forwarded their ballot requests, contact Captain Pickens in detachment headquarters, tomorrow, 1 August."

The Fifth Army held a swimming meet in Rome on July 30. The August 1 Bulletin announced the 38th's representatives and the results of their competing:

"T/5 Sigismund Patronik, Pfc. Kenneth Ackerman, Pfc. John Melnyk, Pvt. Ian MacLean, Pvt. Michael Angarano, and Pvt. Mike Pollo.

"Private MacLean placed third in the one-meter board dive, and fourth in the three-meter board dive. Private Angarano placed second in the 100-meter swim. Both these enlisted men will remain in Rome, training

for the Theater finals to be held on August 18 or 19, and will participate as members of the Fifth Army team."

Captain Montgomery that same day recorded:

No work much. Everyone is getting a rest.

The Bulletin for August 1, however, reported 392 patients being treated in fourteen wards, with 608 vacant beds. The patient load continued to decrease through the first week in August. On August 7 the commanding officer welcomed Lieutenant Colonel Robert O. Y. Warren, MC, into the 38th as chief of medical service. His home, Colonel Wood revealed, was in Wilmington, Delaware. The new chief of medical service was a graduate of Johns Hopkins medical school. From August 19, 1942, until his transfer to the 38th he was chief of medical service of the 32nd Station Hospital.

The Daily Bulletin called attention to a significant anniversary:

"Today we begin our third year in overseas service. Since the hospital opened in Africa, approximately 40,000 patients have been treated by you," Colonel Wood revealed, "and I wish to commend each member of the unit for his and her efforts in the excellent care which these patients received. The termination of the European campaign is in sight, but we must not relax and become passively interested. During future operations, in all that you do, a high degree of efficiency will be required. It is desired, that by performance of duty, better discipline, and a higher standard of military courtesy on the part of each individual, the organization be in a position to receive the recognition for the work it will perform in the future."

During the weeks the 38th was based in the vicinity of Rome the members of the unit visited the capital whenever they had opportunities. Captain Montgomery recorded on August 12 that he had returned that day from a four-day leave in Rome. He used only a line and a half.

But when Captain Pickens twelve days later wrote another letter home, he again reported in considerable detail. On this visit to Rome he had been accompanied by three fellow officers, including Colonel Wood, the 38th's commander. He wrote:

"A Roman holiday, modern war style, is different from any other. But it is worth it after weeks and months of the same grind and the same boredom of wait. This was the first time I had been away overnight from our camp since last January, when I spent three days in Sorrento. Bernard Walker, Pat Imes, George Wood and I took off from camp at five in the morning. It takes about six hours to drive to Rome and we wanted to miss as much of the heavy military traffic as possible.

With the 38th, as with the other units of the military service, wash day wasn't limited to Mondays. For the nurses it came, as a usual thing, every day. Here Lieutenants Madeline Jensen and Margaret Bachoka are hanging up clothing they have just done.

"We stopped about midway at a general hospital for breakfast. We took our own eggs, which are fairly plentiful at this time of year in Tuscany. That made us a little more welcome. We arrived in Rome and got settled in our hotel, the Excelsior, at a little before noon. The Fifth Army had taken the hotel over for a rest camp for Army troops. Of course, it is now located back in the supply area and socalled Army troops are never very welcome back where they are strictly GI. There is always a friendly rivalry between the service troops and those who work in the forward areas. They all want to get up in the battle and all those in the forward area want to get back and forget about it. The hotel is one of the modern ones of Rome, plenty of room and excellent service. There are many conveniences, Turkish baths, ping pong and pool tables, barber shops,

photograph shops, gift shops but with nothing in them, snack bars, finance office where you can get paid in advance if you run short of money, post office for regular mail and for wrapping packages, theatre tickets and sightseeing tours, and many others. The Army has done a good job in getting it set up properly. The food is GI but with enough of the local produce added to give it flavor. Even dehydrated eggs had a spot of garlic in them and tasted good. The bakers knew how to handle our flour and the rolls and pastries were excellent."

He and Bernard Walker had a room together with a sitting room adjoining. "We felt like kings," he said. "The beds were long enough for me and the bath room was just right. I think we washed three times a day because of the luxury. The maid service was good and there was a valet on call at all times to get your clothes pressed or to get ice or to help in any way possible. We just had to press a button. The cost for all this was $1.50 per day, real American Plan. It was hot and we were supposed to keep the place blacked out at night but that did not matter. It was too good to complain about a few inconveniences."

On this trip to Rome Major Imes wanted to visit St. Peter's. Captain Pickens accompanied him. "I witnessed another audience," he reported. "This time the Pope was carried in in his great chair and down the long corridor he put his hands on people and their rosaries and charms. There were about a thousand people there, mostly French and British, with a sprinkling of Brazilians and Poles. The Pope spoke first in English, then in French and then in Italian. It was about the same speech I had heard before . . . . We hurried up to the Sistine Chapel and looked around, then spent the rest of the morning going thru the museum and a part of the Vatican gardens . . . .

"One morning we went out to the Villa D'Este to see the gardens. The villa is located some fifteen miles from the city at Tivoli. The story goes that the father divine told three of the cardinals that the one who could construct the most beautiful summer residence within riding distance of Rome would be given a prize. Cardinal D'Este won the prize. I did not see the other two villas and gardens but I can readily understand how this one in its prime could win a prize. At present the old villa has been shot all to pieces. Shells landed in many parts of the building, including the attached church. They landed in all parts of the garden, but with all the destruction, it is one of the garden spots on the earth. The fountains were not playing, but it was still a spot of beauty. The D'Este family died off and the place was left to the state as a sort of park and the state has been busy waging war and has left the beautiful things to grow in weeds. Now that the war is over in this part of Italy, I hope they get to work and repair this lovely spot. On the way back from Tivoli we stopped at the sulphur pools and had a swim. The water is cold and surprisingly invigorating in spite of the awful smell. We were there on Sunday and many Romans had come out for the holiday. They came the five or six miles on their bicycles and brought their lunch and a bottle of wine."

Once again he enjoyed an evening of music. "There was a special arrangement for the opera, a sort of combination, one evening. We heard the second act of *Madame Butterfly*, then followed a concert with full orchestra. After this there was a ballet. It was the piece de resistance. The opera house was built by Mussolini and it is magnificent. I don't know whether it was the surroundings or what, but I enjoyed the performance so much better than I did last winter down at Caserta. There, of course, we had ridden in the rain and cold and we had to go back to those cold tents. Here we were comfortable and went back to a grand hotel. *One Fine Day* is one of my favorite arias and it was well done. The scenery was better than it had been last winter, too. The concert was equally good. They played a series depicting the fountains of Rome and, as you know, there are plenty of them. It was modern, but not like we hear in the states. The strings were predominant all thru and I favor them. We had to leave before the ballet was finished, since we had to get back to our hotel in time for supper. The opera starts at 6 p.m. and our dining room closed at 9 p.m. We had been out all day and it was necessary to get back. I hated to miss the ballet."

The group from the 38th had the good fortune, too, of seeing the finals of the swimming competition in Rome in which Private Ian MacLean and Private Michael Angarano competed after having scored in the preliminary meet on July 30. He reported:

"In this theatre of war they have sponsored a series of sports, the finals of which took place while we were here. They made use of the stadium and pools and track sets built by Mussolini for the Olympic Games in '39 and '40. The games never took place, but the Allies made use of the equipment to run a series of games that were as good as the Olympics. We had two of our men in the swimming meet. One man is a diver and the other is a hundred-meter swimmer. Both men came to the finals, did not win, but placed creditably. The Hawaiians from Fifth Army took most of the swimming medals. The Fifth, in competition with the Air Corps, and the service sections and the Eighth Army and the French and other allies took off the majority of the places. We watched the finals of the swimming in addition to all the other running around we did. You can see that we kept busy all the time."

During the quartet's visit to Rome in August, 1944, Captain Pickens further revealed, he and Major Walker entertained in their rooms at a party attended by about thirty persons, including friends from the 38th and some they had met in Rome, among them Charlie Wasden of Macon and Monsignor Hemmick, the American priest. "In all there were some thirty people," he wrote. "We had brought some eggs and Mary had sent me some sandwich spread. The chef combined these, added some local color and touches, and our food was excellent. He had fresh lemons for juice and lemonade and we combined to produce a fair martini. I think the folks had a good time. I did."

One night, he said, he visited Monsignor Hemmick for supper. "I furnished the bread and butter and he had everything else. He had a British friend and a count in to join the gathering. I can never think of the count's name. He was a nice young fellow, about thirty, who talked about 'my people.' The British captain, named Utley, had lived in Rome for eighteen years before the war and knew most of the people there. He and the monsignor had known each other before the war. I enjoyed this get-together as much as anything I did while in Rome. I hope to see them all again after the war."

Shopping in Rome continued unsatisfactory, he reported. "There is nothing available within a reasonable price. Inflation has really hit this part of the world. Leather shoes, like the type made in Florence, sell for $30 to $40. There are no textiles except for some cheap rayon. I bought two pieces of Sevres china, two vases for Mary. That was the sum total of my purchases except for some Christmas cards."

They had the good fortune as they were returning to the base to have a lavish meal at the home of an American woman who had married an Italian. She had a farm half way between Rome and the 38th's base and they had given her a ride from Rome home. She was trying to get to the farm to get some food, Captain Pickens wrote. "She was a friend of Pat's. She asked us to be her guests for supper and we agreed. We stopped on the way at a general hospital and picked up some bread, coffee, salt and pepper, and some sugar. She said she had everything else. We asked her if we could have fried chicken for supper and she replied that if we could catch the chickens, we could have all we wanted. The farm turned out to be 3,000 acres with plenty of chickens, guineas and turkeys. Pat caught the chickens and cut them southern style. The peasants cooked them, under his directions, with olive oil. It was just plain good eating. We had fresh corn on the cob, too. After that good meal and visit on an Italian farm, we hurried back to camp. The Roman holiday was a success."

Late in August of 1944 a group of medical personnel of the Brazilian Expeditionary Forces was attached to the 38th Evacuation Hospital to aid in caring for the Brazilian personnel of the Fifth Army.

In the Daily Bulletin of August 27 announcement was made of the arrival of the Brazilians and their names were listed. "The Commanding Officer takes pleasure in welcoming the following members of the Brazilian Expeditionary Forces to this organization," the notice began. The 21 men and women named were:

    Major Ernestino G. de Oliveira
    Major Ari D. Nunes
    Captain Mirandolino J. de Caldas
    First Lieut. Djalma C. Contreiras
    First Lieut. Renato D. Batista
    First Lieut. Waldemar D. dos Santos
    Second Lieut. Ari A. Soares

    Second Lieut. Jose C. Amado
    Nurse Virginia N. Portocarrero
    Nurse Antonieta Ferriera
    Nurse Carmen Bebiano
    Nurse Lucia Osorio
    Nurse Maria de Carmo e Castro
    Nurse Berta Morais
    Nurse Olga Mendes
    Nurse Altanira Valadares
    Sgt. Alfredo A. de Farias
    Sgt. Osvaldo M. Farias
    Sgt. Dimas S. de Silva
    Sgt. Renato S. Bahia
    Sgt. Sebastiao R. dos Santos

On August 28, 1944, the day after the Brazilians were welcomed, Captain Cecil P. Sansom, the Protestant chaplain of the 38th, received orders from Fifth Army headquarters placing him on temporary duty in Palestine. "Thus was realized another of my lifelong dreams," the chaplain would write on his return to duty with the hospital unit. His report, dated September 27 and filed with the papers of the 38th, provides a 2,000-word summary of his visit by air to the Holy Land.

Chaplain Sansom left while the unit was at St. Luce; when he rejoined the organiation it had moved to Pisa.

On August 1, 1944, the official report listed 392 patients under the care of the 38th's doctors and nurses; on the last day of the month the total was 324. On August 9, the total dropped to 229. September began with 301 patients; by September 14, when the unit moved its base again, but 59 were on the rolls. The Daily Bulletin of that date recorded:

"The hospital moved from the location at 1½ Km NE St. Luce Station, Italy, to a point approximately I Km N of Pisa, Italy."

The next day, September 15, the Bulletin carried this notice:

THE HOSPITAL IN ITS PRESENT LOCATION OFFICIALLY OPENED AT 0930 HOURS.

Fifty-three patients were on the rolls the day the hospital opened at Pisa. There were no admissions that day and but six dispositions. Vacant beds numbered 244.

Blackout hours were posted: 1945 to 0615 and a notice in the Daily Bulletin that day—September 15, 1944—warned:

"Blackout will be rigidly enforced in this area, in accordance with the schedule of blackout hours as published daily. All personnel are cautioned against the indiscriminate use of lights."

The Bulletin warned also that "Until further notice, the city of Pisa is off limits to all enlisted personnel. Any enlisted man entering Pisa without proper authority will be subject to disciplinary action."

Two days later, however, the Bulletin announced that "Pisa is now 'On Limits'. Enlisted men not on duty may obtain passes at detachment headquarters." Officers and nurses were required to have permission of their section chiefs and to sign out and in to leave the camp area.

One week after the base was set up at Pisa the patient load had increased to 315. Officers of the day—September 22—were: Administrative, Captain Felts; medical, Captain Crawford; surgical, Captain Sotirion, day, and Captain Doubilet, night; dental, Captain Hoffman.

Ballots for voting in the November Presidential election became available October 3 for distribution to all military personnel and attached civilians eligible in their home states for voting under absentee ballot acts. North Carolina was one of the twenty states permitting such voting.

On the day that distribution of the ballots began, Captain Pickens wrote home. "There is little to write about from the front, because things have settled to such a dull stage for us," he observed, and his appraisal is confirmed by the official record as reflected in the issues of the Daily Bulletin of that period. "We are holding the bag. I wish it were possible to describe it properly, but for security reasons and fear of the censor, I pass it by."

He had been to Rome twice since his last letter home, he disclosed. "The first trip to Rome I went with Bill Leonard from Talbottom, Georgia. We went down in a weapons carrier. A weapons carrier is a creation of the devil, capable of carrying one and a quarter tons of discomfort. We sat in the back under a flapping bit of canvas which wore all the braid off my cap and, I think, most of my fast graying hair. There is no way to get comfortable in the back end of a weapons carrier and whoever made the outrage never heard of shock absorbers. My behind was as bad off as my head. But we got there, and that was the main thing. Our rooms were comfortable and we washed every few hours just to stretch in a big tub of hot water. I had some flowers sent to my room, gladioli and tuberoses. They made it feel more homelike."

They went to the opera and this time *Il Trovatore* was performed. But most of the time, he said, they "just wandered around the city from the Pantheon to the Forum and rubbernecked at the new and the old."

On the return trip he flew in a little artillery observation plane piloted by a friend, Stanley Williamson of Aiken, South Carolina. "Where it had taken us six hours of back-breaking riding to get there, I returned in an hour and a half," he related. "Stanley put his little ship down just across the road from our camp, within easy walking distance. We landed between two rows of grape vines. Leaving Rome, we went down to the Lido to see who was swimming. We swooped down the beach and saw no bathing beauties, so we took off up

the coast. After moving along for about half an hour, we went inland to find a less bumpy lane. I covered up with my field jacket because it got cold at about 5,000 feet. With the hum of the motor I dozed off to sleep and must have inadvertently put my feet on some of the dual controls, because I awoke with a start as we started to drop very rapidly. Stanley called back to me not to touch any of the protruding things less we land too hard. From then on I spent my time examining the countryside. We saw where gun emplacements had been and looked at the anti-aircraft installations, saw how thoroughly the Germans had knocked out each bridge in their retreat. Village after village was just one mass of rubbish. You have no idea how completely Italy has been destroyed. I suppose it looks the same over on the east side where the Eighth Army has been slowly following up."

The second trip to Rome in these weeks was made after the 38th had moved up to Pisa. "I got back in camp in time to take part in a move farther up," he revealed, though apparently because of censorship regulations he did not mention the Pisa location. "With that completed and very little else to do for some days, I had another chance to get back to the city. This time there was no transportation available, but I had the leave and I would make the most of it. I thumbed my way down. It is supposed to be beneath the dignity of an officer in the United States Army to get out on the road and thumb a ride, but with that precedent also came plenty of Army transportation. Here we had none, so I rode in eight different vehicles, but I got there. This one was to rest and do nothing. I seldom left the hotel, just slept, read and went to meals. I did get out once to see *Aida* at the opera house, a grand performance. I went one day and spent a morning at the Keats-Shelley house, the house where Keats died. I just browsed around and had a good time by myself. Incidentally, the trip down was alone. I returned in a jeep, seven hours, all in the one vehicle. I finished reading *A Yankee from Olympus*, reread *The Robe* and worked thru the latest Omnibook."

The most famous landmark in the 38th's new location, of course, was the Leaning Tower. One day after his return from Rome, Captain Pickens went to see it. His description reveals the famous tower as it was seen by thousands of service men during World War II. He wrote:

"It has not been damaged; one shell hit it but made little imprint. I walked up the 160 feet and looked out over the great Arno River valley. There is no doubt but that it really leans. . . . The south side of Pisa is as much rubble as any Italian city but the north side is fairly well preserved. At present the city is a ghost city. The people have not returned in any number and the place is heavily mined. We lost one of our enlisted men when he went into a shop and picked up a musical instrument and with that the whole building exploded. We fished him out the following day. The Germans are past masters at booby traps and mines. So we have been very careful about where we walk and have stayed away from vacant buildings. No doubt our experience with this one man will discourage the remaining from attempting any looting or souvenir gathering again. This was our first casualty with about as long a period of combat zone as any unit in any Army. I sometimes have the feeling that we are now living on borrowed time. I thought that particularly the other night when some of the German 280 mm. shells were coming in over our heads. This is the same gun which harassed us so long at Anzio. They have left us alone now for several nights, so we have hopes that they have been forced to move back out of range."

The soldier killed that day was Private Stanley C. Surowitz. In the 38th's roster of personnel he is listed as having joined the 38th on April 15, 1942, at Fort Bragg, and "Date departure, Sep. 18/44, killed in action, 1800 hrs. Pisa, Italy."

Dr. Charles H. Gay remembers well Private Surowitz and the account given him of the soldier's tragic death.

"Surowitz had prided himself on being the first fellow in our unit into any new town we came to. When we got outside Pisa we were told that a lot of mines had been laid in the town and we were warned not to attempt to enter the place until it had been cleared by the engineers. But either the night or the next day before we had been given clearance, Surowitz and two of his buddies, according to the story I was told, saw this music store. Surowitz played the piano; in fact, he was quite a musician. So he walked boldly into the store and when he saw a piano, he went over and sat down to play, even though there were warning signs MINED all over the place, put there by our engineers.

"And the first time he touched a key, the whole place blew up. He was killed, of course, one of his buddies standing in the doorway was blown out into the street, and the other, still in the street, was knocked down.

"Surowitz was the only enlisted man in our unit who was lost during our entire service. We had one nurse, Lieutenant Benante, to die overseas. She was a victim of hepatitis."

But at least one surviving member of the 38th was on the scene that day in Pisa.

Pharmacist Joe Neil, now of Huntersville, North Carolina, who was then in charge of the 38th's pharmacy, after more than a score of years remembers vividly the death of Private Surowitz.

"We were moving into Pisa in a convoy. When we got into the middle of the town, the Germans up at the head of these big streets started shooting right straight down the streets with 88s. We stopped there and these boys got off the truck and ran into this store; the door was open, and it was a music store, had instruments hanging up. One of them picked up something, and WOOM! That building was leveled! We had been warned not even to get off the trucks. I was two or three trucks behind; I saw the whole thing. The store just caved in. It was just about dark. The only thing I saw come out of there was Surowitz's little dog. Surowitz was killed right then; we didn't know what had happened to the others, but later we heard he was the only one killed. He was the one, they said, who picked up a musical instrument that the Jerries had mined."

Afterward the trucks moved through Pisa and stopped in a field, where the enemy continued to fire upon them, the unit's pharmacist recalls. "After we knocked out those guns at the heads of the streets," he continues his recital of their reception that day, "we moved on through Pisa beyond the Leaning Tower and pulled into this field, and, boys, the Jerries were throwing that stuff into us. We didn't know where it was coming from; we stayed under our trucks over in this field until daylight; we couldn't work out there that night."

23

The story of the 38th Evacuation Hospital's stay at the base at Pisa can be summarized, certainly for those members of the unit who look back more than two decades to those memorable days, with the one word: flood.

In many pictures and thousands of words the story of that flood has been recorded and in countless sessions of reminiscing about the war days the veterans of the 38th have recounted their personal experiences. News services correspondents sent out detailed dispatches relating dramatically stories of the inundation of the hospital, members of the unit wrote lively letters home in which they told of their own involvements, and Colonel Wood put down a chronological record of the flood, that Sergeant Jack Foisie, a staff correspondent with the Fifth Army described as "believed to be the greatest single disaster ever to overtake a hospital in this theater."

"Noah was forewarned and built his ark, but this Evacuation Hospital was not and had to hurriedly remove 516 patients from the rapidly rising waters, so as a result virtually all organizational and personal equipment had to be left to the flood," Sergeant Foisie's lead paragraph recorded.

"That was on Nov. 2, when the Arno River broke through the dikes in the Pisa area and inundated both the city and the adjacent hospital area with a sea of water as high as six feet, it can now be revealed.

"Today that hospital, set up in a new location, is a going concern again, with much of its equipment salvaged and most of the rest replaced. But it will be a long time before they forget the night of the flood, just as the same hospital has never forgotten the night of the great wind last New Year's Eve."

Rita Hume, International News Service correspondent with the Fifth Army, provided a dramatic report of the ravaging Arno. "As ward men worked frantically to rescue the last patient from the 38th Evacuation Hospital, they could hear the radio in the receiving tent. It was playing 'River, Stay 'Way from My Door.' A wry joke for a front line hospital about to be flooded."

Her report continued:

"At 7:31 that evening the 38th's veteran commander,

Col. George Wood of High Point, North Carolina, ordered the evacuation of litter patients. It was only a precaution. No one expected the Arno River, then coursing over its banks into the streets of Pisa, to get that far.

"Another Carolinian and the region's chief engineer, Col. John Trescot of Charlotte, figured that even if the water did get to the hospital's field it couldn't possibly rise more than a foot or two in the tents. No one then knew that the Arno was rising to inundate Tuscany in its worst flood since Nov. 8, 1844, almost 100 years ago to the day.

"By 10 o'clock the flood was running through the enlisted men's quarters. By midnight the hospital tents and the equipment in them were five feet deep in muddy water.

"The 38th—otherwise known as the 'Charlotte Evac'—is a veteran of two and a half years overseas. Its personnel landed under fire in North Africa. They have lived through wind, mud, heat, cold and shelling. Tunisia, Anzio, and Cassino are merely chapters in the 38th's book.

"The flood was their worst catastrophe. It wiped out the hospital equipment as well as all the personal possessions of its staff. Partners in the disaster were the hospital's Brazilian complement—including a staff of 80 doctors, nurses and wardmen."

Miss Hume's dispatch continued:

Water everywhere was the story at Pisa. The tents of the 38th appeared to have been set up in a veritable sea.

Pisa in northern Italy during a part of the 38th's encampment there in the fall of 1944—September 14–November 9—was a quagmire from the overflowing Arno River. The famous Leaning Tower is shown in the distance, left.

"A cloudburst in the mountains caused the Arno, choked with blasted bridges and sunken ships at its mouth, to spill over with unexpected swiftness. It was nearly 9 o'clock when Chief Nurse Hallie Almond of Charlotte stuck her head in our tent.

"'Pack up your bed rolls, girls. The nurses are going to spend the night in a building in town.' Lucy Brooke and I started to pile Lucy's belongings on tops of tables and cots. Lucy, of 100 East Palisade Avenue, Englewood, New Jersey, was worried about the supplies in her Red Cross tent. But we still had that 'it can't happen here' feeling. The hospital was a scene of activity. In the tent next door five Brazilian nurses were in a mad scramble of putting their possessions on anything high in sight."

She went on with her on-the-scene reporting:

"You don't move a 500-bed hospital in a couple of hours. We found out how rapidly a flood can rise as we were stalled in a slow moving line of hospital trucks. The water rose steadily around the wheels, glimmering murkishly in the headlights. Trucks were no longer able to get to the hospital.

"The litter patients were safely evacuated to the warehouse building of the 12th Medical Depot in Pisa. But some of the ambulatory patients had to walk for it. A straggling line of men sloshed by, the convalescent patients still wearing their wine bathrobes and blue pajamas. You could quickly identify the Brazilians from the Americans. The former had adopted the Italian technique of carrying their bed rolls on their heads.

"At midnight our convoy line had finally progressed to the building where the nurses were to spread their bed rolls for the night. The water there was only two feet deep in the street. A driving rain added to our flood scene the next morning."

She pictured the newly improvised facility:

"In the drafty warehouse of the 12th Medical Depot, Captain Richard P. Gilbert of Robinsdale, Minnesota, somehow managed to make room for their emergency invasion of an evacuating hospital. Walking patients, ward men, nurses, and doctors crowded through narrow aisles between floors covered with litters. The scene was drab with the monotony of army blankets. More blankets hung hastily tacked to gaping windows. In one ward patients were tossing a baseball from bed to bed—laughing. Some were sitting quietly, propped up in their litters, or playing cards. Beside them, brown rubber tubes poured plasma into deathly still forms. The frightened screams of a 6-year-old Italian boy punctuated the din of one ward.

"'Mama! Mama!'

"Lieutenant Marie Tetzloff of Dayton pushed through to comfort this little casualty. A doctor wearing the green shield of Brazil stopped to stroke the tear-stained face, hushing him in Italian.

"Enlisted men, the unsung heroes of any hospital emergency, were busy sandbagging the door against flood waters. Hospital Clerk Howard S. Simpson, West Englewood, New Jersey, moaned over the thought of hospital files drenched in water.

"'So, you're a war correspondent.' A thin and bitter face challenged me from a litter. 'Why don't you tell them about this. The forgotten front. God, another winter in Italy!'"

Correspondent Foisie reported, too, incidents in which personnel of the 38th were involved during the Arno's flooding of the 38th's Pisa base. "The hospital staff—officers, nurses, and men—spent most of their time wading hip-high about the area attempting to catch up with their belongings. None of the wading uniforms could be described as GI. Nurses favored barrack bag pants, sheets draped diaper style, and nightgowns, flattering some but not others.

"Upon wading into their still standing tents, the occupants were greeted by weird scenes." For example, he related, "Lieutenant Nellie Gross of Manchester, Pennsylvania, reached into her value pack and ran across a snake. Lieutenant Ann Brady of Holyoke, Massachusetts, reached into her bedroll and the 'Christmas bottle' she had been saving for four months was still there. Cradling it like a baby, she carried it back to dry land and later placed it under her bed. 'Then someone with feet as big as mine came along and kicked it,' moaned the jolly nurse. 'No more Christmas bottle.'"

He told of Private Charles "Butch" Neubauer's dog Skippy. "Skippy did his own scavenging and found morphine tablets floating around the area. He liked them, ate them—and slept for three days.

"The Brazilian nurses attached to the hospital adopted their native land's custom of carrying bundles on their heads. 'Some of the nurses aren't very tall and it looked from a distance like barracks bags floating across the water,' chuckled Corporal Harry Roberts of New Bedford, Massachusetts. Cases of beer also were seen to float away, but whether by human hand or just the current is not known," Correspondent Foisie added.

He told of Captain Cecil P. Sansom's stepping into his tent—he was Protestant chaplain of the 38th at the time—"to find the field organ floating like a marshmallow and his Bible and other books ruined. But still flying, although water lapped at its fringes, was the chaplain's flag."

He reported the incident of Captain Harney's shined shoes:

"Capt. James N. Harney of New York City had a couple of pairs of nicely-shined shoes on his foot locker.

Rescuing trucks managed to save the day for the 38th at Pisa when the sudden flood inundated the camp.

But this heavily loaded truck fell into a ditch hidden under the Pisa flood waters.

When he waded into his tent the sight that met his eyes was the foot locker floating about, with the shoes on top, still neatly shined."

Many other possessions of the 38th's personnel were floating in the swollen Arno's rampaging waters. One of the Charlotte officers had the framed picture of his wife on an improvised table in his tent. The flood carried it away. Days later he happened to be in the tent of one of the enlisted men of the outfit. There, displayed with other pictures in the soldier's gallery of pinup girls, was his wife's photograph.

"Where in the dickens did you get my wife's picture?" the officer demanded.

"It was floating in the water the night of the flood," the soldier replied. "I saw she was a good looking woman, so I put her up there with the others."

Another of the Charlotte officers greatly concerned was Captain Felts. "I was officer of the day and mess officer," he recalls. "I had gone to town to get a haircut. When I came out of the barbershop water was coming up the street." He rushed back to the camp and worked furiously to rescue the unit's food and other supplies. "We had just brought in a shipment of $2,500 worth of stuff for the PX," he remembers. "We lost the whole works."

"But most of it wasn't really lost," Pharmacist Joe Neil comments. "It just got distributed free. I remember for a while Jimmy was worried greatly about whether he'd have to pay for all that stuff. But of course the flood wasn't his fault and it was marked off. But the stuff, all but a little candy and chewing gum and other odds and ends in that shipment was beer, cases after cases of beer in bottles. It just floated off, and boys pulled it in, good and cold. Some of us, I remember, were about as high on that beer as the water was high in our tents."

As the flood waters at Pisa began to rise relentlessly in the tents of the 38th's hospital area, however, Phar-

This nurse has decided it's time to move—with her water-logged belongings. Many nurses and men lost much of their personal property during the Pisa flood.

208

macist Neil's immediate concern was for the saving of the pharmaceutical supplies.

"We had about fifty gallons of good whiskey and a large quantity of grain alcohol that we were mighty anxious to save. But, more important, we had narcotics always desperately needed in the operation of a hospital. We didn't want to lose them, of course, and we didn't want any of that stuff floating around where they might be picked up and maybe used."

But everything of considerable value, and particularly the supply of narcotics, was moved to higher ground and saved, the unit's pharmacist recalls.

On November 7, 1944, Captain J. W. Perkins, flood control officer of the Toscana region, published his report:

SUBJECT: *Flooding at Pisa*

1. The times given in this report are approximate only, as I did not make a particular note of times on the day in question.
2. The river ARNO started to rise unusually rapidly on the morning of November 2, and by 1100 hours was level with the ground at Pisa. Emergency repairs to damaged walls were started. This flood came from the river ERA, and therefore no warning was received from Florence.
3. After visiting various sites along the north bank of the bank of the river, I came to the conclusion that there was a risk of flooding, unless the river ceased rising very soon. I therefore warned C.O. 38 Gen. Hospital that it might possibly have to evacuate at short notice. This would be between 1600 and 1630 hours.
4. About 1800 hours I received a verbal message that Florence warned us to expect the river to start rising at 2200 hours and to be at maximum height at 0900 hours on Nov. 3. At about 1830 hours I communicated this information to C.O. 38 Gen. Hospital.
5. This message was confirmed at 1915 hours from A.M.G. 5 Army, and after inspecting the water on the roads in the Hospital area, I visited the C.O. again, with the Provincial Commissioner. This would be about 1930 hours, and we advised the C.O. to evacuate the site.
6. I then left to see the Report Centre which had been established on the ARNO bridge Route 1, intending to get the latest news and keep the Hospital informed. It must have been about this time that one of the temporary dams put up in the city was washed out, and the flood increased so rapidly that I had the greatest difficulty both in going and returning, and on my return sometime after 2200 hours found that the hospital was already under water and personnel evacuating.
7. The flooding was due to an unfortunate combination (a) the ERA flood, which arrived early in the day without warning owing to the enemy destruction of flood observation points and communications. (b) The second flood from Florence area which arose with a rapidity unequaled in the last 100 years.

But the most revealing account of the 38th's involvement in the disastrous flooding of the Arno at Pisa is provided in a letter written two weeks later by Captain Pickens, who was serving as adjutant of the unit at the time of the flood.

This reveals graphically the extent of the flooding during the Pisa period. In some places the water was five or six feet deep inside the 38th's tents.

On Saturday, November 18, he sat down to report to the homefolk the 38th's experiences during those days of ordeal.

"We thought we had seen every experience but torpedoing and snow banks when we had had rain, wind, sleet, desert dust storms, shelling and bombing, but the answer was no," he began. "We had not been completely flooded out. That has been our latest experience and we have not fully recovered as yet.

"The hospital had been set up on some flat grazing land about a half-mile from the river but with the city between us. There were numerous drainage or irrigation ditches and canals running over the area and moving to the sea. The river was shut in by high levees on each side, since the land is only nine feet above sea level and the slightest rise would flood the whole countryside. The numerous breaks in the levees caused by shelling and bombing had been repaired to a great extent.

"The October rains set in and they fell harder and more constantly. The old Arno began to bulge with the strain but she held her burden pretty well. In Florence the water just lapped over the wall, a great stone wall

many feet above the normal level of the river. The Vecchio Bridge, the only one left by the Germans, looked like it would go, but held on. The hastily erected temporary bridges strained at their bases but held. Down the river numerous tributaries poured in and added to the old Arno's cross. We were down toward the mouth."

His narration moved quickly to the day of the breakthrough, Thursday, November 2:

"On the afternoon of the break, I had taken five nurses and two new officers into town to get them paid. The nurses had reported from the quiet station hospitals back in Africa, Casablanca and Algiers, where they had lived in relative comfort for the past eighteen months. The finance officer said there was talk of the river getting out of its banks. I paid no attention to him.

"About the middle of the afternoon Jimmy Felts came into headquarters, where I now have my office as adjutant, and said the water was pouring thru the streets of the city. He had gone to a barber shop in town and when he came out he had to wade across the street. I still doubted him but thought it wise to

209

drive in and see for myself. This was about 4:30. As I approached the city the MP stopped me at the north gate and said no traffic was allowed in town, the water was too high. While I talked, water began to pour thru the gate but took off down the street to the west. There was a 20-foot canal running to the sea between the city and the hospital area. The canal had room for about four feet of water. I hurried back and reported to the Colonel. While I was talking, a British captain from Allied Military Government came in and said that flood conditions were possible but danger was not imminent. That was typical British conservatism. He said he was the flood control engineer for the province and would warn us of any danger. I persuaded the Colonel to go with me and look at the situation, and we made plans for finding higher ground if it got too bad. No water was in our area at that time but it was coming. We had supper and all the officers and nurses were warned of possible evacuation to nearby buildings and villas. The men were notified of all possibilities."

But about eight that evening, he continued his report, the British captain came in and was noticeably agitated. He reported that information had come from Florence that the high water was to be expected at nine o'clock the next morning. "He thought we had better get out. I had thought that for about four hours but no one would agree with me. I had gone down to George Snyder's tent and told him what the situation looked like to me and advised him to get his equipment and get over to the building we had picked out to use. He replied that I was just an old alarmist and come on in and sit down, that he had some late mail from home. I left him hurriedly and sometime after midnight when I saw him again, he said he wished he had listened to me."

A few minutes after eight o'clock, his letter went on to reveal, orders were put out to evacuate. "There still was no water in the area outside of the small ditches. The moon had come out, full and bright. That was a great help. The loudspeaker system was working and all directions came from there. The ambulance company, which normally supports us, was on hand with their nine vehicles and we had our own trucks and trusty John Trescot sent us several of his trucks. There were over 500 patients and many of them could not walk."

He described the evacuation:

"The evacuation was slow, because the ambulances could pull into the old bombed-out building where we were moving to only one at a time. At about nine o'clock the water started into our area, and in thirty minutes there was two feet of water over everything and it was flowing fast. The current picked up the little bridges we had constructed across drain ditches

and not being able to feel them, people fell into the ditches. The ambulatory patients were ordered to get their bedding, cots and any personal belongings and march to the new spot. My particular job was to get the nurses, who were not on duty in the hospital, over to a nearby villa. They were slow to get under way because they had not seen the water and thought it all foolish. When they got to the villa about three or four blocks away they had to crawl out of the trucks into three feet of water. We had enough notice to get an emergency operating room set up in the old building and Jim Felts had moved two trucks loaded with food, stoves, gasoline and messing equipment over. We dragged one generator over and the electrician hastily hooked up some wire and bulbs. There were lights in the new hospital. The patients piled in and were packed in like sardines, but they were dry and warm. Four battle casualties were operated on during the night under conditions that most doctors would have laughed at, but the patients lived and that was what counted. Some 18 or 19 patients, who had been ordered back to their units during the day, turned up to stay with us and further crowd us. They had been washed back to us by high water on all the roads."

After he had settled the nurses in the new quarters, he returned to the base they were evacuating. "Everything was moving as well as possible in four feet of water," he found. "Fortunately, the trucks built for the army are high and they kept plying back and forth. We marked our roads with white bandage material and tall poles so we could stay on them. In spite of this one truck got into a deep ditch and could not recover. It was still there three days later. I hurried down to my own tent and tied my bedding roll and fiddle to the ridge pole. The water was up to the cot when I left it. I then, paradoxically, filled my canteen with good water. The spigot was still above the river water. I put a few hard biscuits in my pocket, my breast pocket, and started out again. By midnight everyone was out of the area and the Colonel ordered the last generator turned off. We walked on up to the new area together with water sloshing against our chests and a fairly swift current running. I was thankful to get out alive. The hospital, except for a little equipment, was ruined. It was a ghostly sight there in the moonlight with not a soul in sight and very quiet except for the swishing of the water as it flowed by. No lives were lost, but it was a close shave. There was no panic but there could easily have been."

But while the water was flooding the tented hospital they had abandoned, Captain Pickens went on to relate, it was rising also in the half-ruined buildings to which they had fled. "Sandbags were placed at the entrance to hold it out as long as possible," he continued his story of the memorable night at Pisa. "The next morning found water just seeping thru but not enough to make us move again. The crest came about the middle of the morning, but it was slow in receding. Three days later we were still wading around in water three and four feet deep. But it went down enough to get ambulances in and we sent our patients on to safer and drier places. Most of our personnel was scattered around to other units. A few of us stayed behind to help with the salvage details. I made my way back to my tent and found my clothes dry and the fiddle in good shape. All of the little things that I owned were still under water, such as pictures, books, shoe polish, bedroom slippers, toilet articles, mousetrap, flyswatter, dirty laundry, helmet, messkit, maps, and a lot of similar articles. There was nothing of great value lost, but I will have a time drying it all out or washing the mud and slime and silt out of it."

"Such is the story of the flood in Italy," Captain Pickens concluded his account. "It adds to our various experiences just one more story, and if we are living on borrowed time, we are still enjoying it. Not one person caught cold."

Major Montgomery also recorded, in his characteristically brief diary entries, the experiences at Pisa. On October 30 he wrote:

We were told that it looked like we were to be here in Pisa for the winter. Bob and I bought us a radio last week. Now we have a white ceiling of sheets in the tent. It is warmer and we are set for the winter.

But a week later, on November 6, he recorded:

Everything has been changed. On the night of the second the hospital was destroyed by flood. The 3rd was spent at 12th Med Depot but all patients evac. that night. On 4th a group of us—8 officers, 9 nurses, 17 men came to Lucca. We are nicely situated in a brick bldg. that had been a children's hospital. Have no work yet.

November 8 he added the entry:

One Jeep accident case last night. An explos. cap. Have made one salvage trip back to area. We were issued new clothes.

The entry was made as the 38th was preparing to leave Pisa for its new location at Montecatini. A week earlier, on November 1, the Daily Bulletin announced that six officers from other hospital groups had been welcomed into the unit. The six were:

Captain Clayton A. Blake, Jr., DC, formerly of the 1st Armd. Div.
2nd Lieut. Julia E. Victor, ANC, formerly of the 56th Station Hospital
2nd Lieut. Adrienne J. Ellison, ANC, and
2nd Lieut. Angeline M. Long, ANC, also of the 56th
2nd Lieut. Elsie I. Gilliam, ANC, and
2nd Lieut. Mary E. Townsend, ANC, formerly of the 57th Station Hospital

The 38th would remain at Montecatini until late in April and from that base would provide treatment for thousands of soldiers, American and foreign, civilians and prisoners of war. For a short period between Pisa and Montecatini, too, it would operate a branch hospital at Lucca, Italy, with a small force of doctors, nurses and enlisted personnel serving emergency cases. The main hospital opened the middle of November— the Daily Bulletin of November 16, 1944, says "The Hospital in its present location officially opened at 0800 hours"—at Montecatini.

The same issue of the Bulletin—Volume III, Number 311, Thursday, November 16, 1944—carried also the announcement:

"The Commanding Officer, George T. Wood, Jr., Colonel, M.C., was awarded the Legion of Merit, today, at a ceremony in Montecatini. Details of the award will be published later." Surviving in the records of the 38th also is an interesting photograph of the period immediately following Pisa. It shows General Mark W. Clark pinning the Legion of Merit on Colonel Wood at this ceremony.

The Daily Bulletin of the next day carried the citation:

"George W. Wood, Jr., 04455228, Colonel, Medical Corps, 38th Evacuation Hospital, for exceptionally meritorious conduct in the performance of outstanding service in Italy from 28 September 1943 to 5 June 1944. As Commanding Officer, 38th Evacuation Hospital, Colonel Wood displayed marked abilities in directing the operations of his command under combat conditions. When directed to effect a rapid movement of the personnel in his command from the Cassino front to replace the entire personnel of a beachhead hospital, his untiring efforts and sound employment of the facilities at his disposal proved equal to the difficult problem in hospital movement and administration with which he was confronted. Under his able guidance, the personnel of the 38th Evacuation Hospital were prepared for transport without delay, and on landing at Anzio, quickly familiarized themselves with both the utilities of the hospital they occupied and with the medical requirements of the patients whose care they assumed. As a result of this action, numerous casualties were safeguarded from harm which would inevitably have followed a break in the schedule of medical treatment. Throughout the period in which the 38th Evacuation Hospital functioned at Anzio, the installation, its personnel, and patients were subjected to constant enemy fire. Despite the hazards and the heavy burden of work arising from his many responsibilities, Colonel Wood frequently exposed himself to enemy fire in order to bolster the morale of his command and to guarantee that the professional work of his unit be

At Montecatini on November 16, 1944, General Mark Clark, commanding the Fifth Army, pinned upon Colonel George T. Wood, Jr., the Legion of Merit, and the 38th's Daily Bulletin the next day carried the citation summarizing Colonel Wood's "exceptionally meritorious conduct" that led to the bestowal of the award on the 38th's commanding officer.

kept at a consistently high level of performance. Colonel Wood has reflected the highest credit upon himself and the Medical Department of the United States Army. Entered service from Charlotte, North Carolina."

One week later was Thanksgiving. The hospital was again operating on a normal schedule. Within five days the number of patients had advanced from four on November 18 to 367 on the twenty-third. Fourteen wards were in operation, 508 beds were vacant. Officers of the day were: Administrative, Captain Dunn, Captain Pickens, alternate; medical, Captain Harney, Captain Munroe, alternate; day surgical, Captain Sotirion, Captain Porter, alternate; night surgical, Captain Porter, Captain Sotirion, alternate; dental, Captain Crotts, Captain Hoffman, alternate.

The Daily Bulletin was enlivened with the drawing of a steaming turkey and a pumpkin pie, and the

only announcement was Colonel Wood's Thanksgiving greetings:

"I take this means of wishing each of you—officer, nurse, enlisted man, patient, attached personnel, and visitor—a Happy Thanksgiving.

"I am particularly thankful for the splendid and unselfish spirit shown by each member of the command during the recent misfortune when the hospital was flooded. Your devotion to duty permitted the safe evacuation of all the patients and saved a large amount of government property from irreparable damage and loss. And your interest in our present setup assures me of your desire to make this the best we have had.

"As we continue to carry on with our duty let us be thankful that we can be of service to our country and to the men 'up front' who are so gallantly fighting our fight. And let us all look forward to, and work

212

harder than ever for, our biggest Thanksgiving of all—when we can return to our homes and loved ones."

In mid-December General Mark W. Clark was assigned from command of the Fifth Army to the 15th Army Group in Italy and Lieutenant General L. K. Truscott, Jr., was given command of the Fifth Army. On December 16, 1944, the Daily Bulletin carried General Clark's farewell message to his comrades of the Fifth Army. General Clark wrote:

"When I assumed command of the Fifth Army two years ago upon its activation in North Africa on January 5, 1943, it was with pride and confidence. I was proud of the organization I had been appointed to lead, and I had confidence in its ability to accomplish the great mission assigned to it. Subsequent events have fully justified my feelings. Much has been demanded of you in this difficult campaign. No commander could have received a more gratifying response.

"In assuming command of the 15th Army Group in Italy, I do so with those same feelings. Side by side, through the bitterest fighting and against the most difficult obstacles in the history of warfare, the Fifth and Eighth Armies have driven a strong, resourceful and fanatical enemy from the extreme south of Italy to the Valley of the Po.

"Your contribution to an Allied victory does not rest upon the mere liberation of an Axis-dominated land. Far more destruction has been your effect upon the enemy's forces and your destruction of thousands upon thousands of his troops and their equipment. It is our campaign that holds in this theater many of the enemy's best divisions which could otherwise be used against the Eastern or Western fronts. We shall continue to defeat them and eventually shall destroy them. Never underestimate the vital and continuing importance of your role in the Italian campaign.

"I can wish my successor, General Truscott, no finer heritage than the loyalty, courage, determination, and combat skill you have always shown me. We shall continue to form a powerful Allied force of ground, sea, and air power, dedicated to the defeat of our enemies."

One day shortly before Christmas of 1944, Major Hunter Jones decided to have a party in his tent. It would be memorable because of the attendance of one guest. Years later Dr. Jones and his Charlotte companions of the 38th who were there that evening would recall it.

"It was up at Montecatini and that was the last stand before Jack Montgomery and I came home. We had been having it pretty rough, with the flooding at Pisa, the fighting and the long hours in the hospital, and we

were pretty tired. I thought it would help our spirits to have a little party. And I wanted to try out one scheme I had in mind. So I decided to invite our chaplain.

"I had noticed that our Catholic chaplains generally were more liberal about things, like drinking, for example, than our Protestants, more broadminded about having a little drink now and then. You got a day off every week or ten days or so in town, and if you went to town with the Baptist chaplain, I noticed, you soon lost him, especially if you headed toward a bar. But the Catholic chaplain would go along with you and he'd have a drink with you and you could sit and talk. But not the Baptist chaplain; he would just disappear soon after you got to town.

"That worried me a great deal. I was Baptist, born in the town of Wake Forest; I grew up there and went to school there. So I figured I'd see if I couldn't do something about it. I'd have a party in my tent and I'd invite the Protestant chaplain, my Baptist preacher friend. And I did. I invited eight or ten officers and eight or ten nurses, and I went to the chaplain and told him what I had done.

"'And Chappie,' I said to him, 'I want you to come to my party tomorrow night.'

"'You know,' he said, 'I don't drink.'

"'Yes, I know that,' I said. 'That's why I'm asking you. If you come, we'll give you a Coca-Cola. George Snyder has got in some cokes, and we'll give you one, and the rest of us will be drinking a little cognac and lemon juice. And we'll all have a good time, Chappie, and it will do you good, and help us, your being there with us.'

"He considered my invitation a moment. 'Let me think it over until tomorrow,' he said.

"The next morning Chappie came to me. 'I've been thinking over what you said,' he told me. 'I've decided to come to your party.'

"He did, too.

"I hadn't told any of the others that the chaplain was coming. And when he came, I said to them, 'Now I know you all are surprised to see the chaplain here.' A quiet had suddenly come over the crowd. 'You know he doesn't drink. But he's a good sport and he wants to be a part of us, and I urged him to join us. Chappie, you are welcome; we're glad you came.'

"So we had a little cocktail party before dinner, and we had some cognac and juice—the usual stuff in those days—and George had brought some cokes and we gave Chappie a coke, and after half an hour or forty-five minutes everybody was feeling fine, doing nothing wrong, just having a good time, and so was Chappie. The nurses and officers were drinking cognac and lemon juice and feeling no pain and Chappie was drinking Coca-Cola and also in fine spirits, and then we had a wonderful dinner.

"The next day I saw Chappie. 'You know, Major,' he said to me. 'I've been doing a lot of thinking since last night. Maybe I've been wrong about this thing. Maybe I should have been meeting with the officers and nurses more and seeing them as they really are.'

" 'Chappie,' I said, 'I think you should have. This is a good group. They aren't bad. And you just can't stand off from them and preach hellfire and damnation. These folks are all going to take a drink now and then. But they have a tremendous respect for you, and the fact that last night you came to the party and mixed with them and were a part of us did us all a lot of good.'

"So the next day I went around among the group. 'You all go to prayer meeting next Wednesday night,' I told them. We had prayer meeting once a week. 'Chappie came to our party; now you go to his prayer meeting.'

"The next Wednesday night you never saw such a crowd. They turned out in droves. And they sang and they listened to Chappie's talk and they took a great interest in the service and enjoyed it. After it was over, Chappie came to me. 'You know,' he said, 'I'm glad I went to your party. I've never before seen so many folks out to prayer meeting. I think we understand one another better now.' I'm sure we did, too. I'm sure his going to our little party opened his eyes. He said so some time later. 'You know, I guess I've just been wrong about this thing,' he repeated his earlier expressed opinion. 'Here were men and women a long way from home, and lonesome, and they were just wanting to have a little fun. And that's all they were doing, just having some fun. Major, I'm glad you invited me to the party and that I went.' "

One of the biggest social occasions in which members of the 38th were involved was the wedding of one of the 38th's most popular nurses during the encampment of the hospital at Massa Marittima in midsummer of 1944.

The bride was Lieutenant Jean Webber from Cynthiana, Kentucky, and the groom, Lieutenant Harold Lewis, was a member of a tank company. Dr. Jones recalls the wedding:

"That was our first wedding. It took place while we were at Massa Marittima in July of 1944. Jean Webber made her own wedding gown—and it was a beautiful one—out of a parachute that some fellow had brought to the hospital. Our camp was out in an old field and the ceremony was on a late afternoon. It was held in the mess tent. The night before, we had a rehearsal and a big party, and the Colonel authorized Jimmy Felts to take some alcohol from the laboratory and mix it with grapefruit juice and that sort of thing for the drinks. Colonel John Trescot from Charlotte, commander of the 105th Engineers, had sent a group of his men over to build a wooden floor in the mess hall, and that night after the wedding his Engineers' band played for the big dance we held to honor the bridal couple. We had a wonderful time; it was, no doubt, our biggest social affair of the 38th's service overseas."

The 38th's biggest social event of its overseas service was the wedding of Lieutenant Charlotte Jean Webber and Lieutenant Harold Lewis of a tank company located nearby. It was during the stay at Massa Marittima in July, 1944. Left to right, Captain Hunter Jones of Charlotte, Lieutenant Lewis, his bride, and Lieutenant Elva Wells, the maid of honor.

The bride and groom cut their wedding cake. Lieutenant Harold Lewis and the former Lieutenant Charlotte Jean Webber, one of the 38th's popular nurses.

214

24

Christmas 1944 came on a Monday with the 38th Evacuation Hospital still based at Montecatini and 424 patients under treatment in fifteen wards. The returning season brought again a series of greetings from the unit's various commanding officers from Colonel George T. Wood, Jr., to the President of the United States.

The Daily Bulletin of Sunday, December 24, carried the greetings of the Fifth Army's new commander, Lieutenant General L. K. Truscott, Jr. The General wrote:

"I am particularly pleased that my first greeting to you should come at the time of the year when people throughout the Christian world are drawn together closest in the spirit of the season.

"I have known the Fifth Army since its beginnings and am familiar with its great achievements. I am proud of my former service with it—from the beaches at Salerno beyond the fall of Rome. I left it for a time to participate in the operations in Southern France but when I went off I carried with me a feeling of deep attachment for the organization of which I had been so long a part and have followed all of its operations since with close personal interest.

"I am honored to be returning as its commander and feel that I am coming back to friends with whom I have broad common interests and whose problems I understand. It is as a friend—as well as commander—that I extend to you my sincere good wishes at this Christmastime.

"Unfortunately the conditions of war have separated us from homes and loved ones and have once again denied us the blessing of being with them at this season of traditional family reunion. The forces that have compelled our presence here—those which have challenged the world and engulfed it in unprecedented struggle—must be destroyed and eradicated so that with the end of fighting there will remain no shadow to cloud any future Christmas.

"I hope that each and everyone of you here in Italy will have the best possible Christmas under the circumstances in which you find yourselves and I pledge you that I will do all in my power to lead you to the future successes in this theater which can contribute so much to the final allied victory—with which will come happy, lasting reunions and the restoration of an enduring peace in the hearts and minds of all mankind."

Brigadier General J. I. Martin, Fifth Army surgeon, four days earlier, on December 20, had addressed his greetings to "Officers and Men, 38th Evacuation Hospital:"

"Dear Friends:

"As medical troops in war you have been guided every day by the ideals of human action the first Christmas brought to the world. In various ways and in various stations you have healed the sick, revived the wounded, strengthened the weary and brought peace and comfort to the minds and bodies of thousands of our fellow men.

"I know the poignant feelings a Christmas celebration away from home arouses in your own minds; how you, who daily see the shattering consequences of war, long to know once again the spirit with which you and your families approached the Christmas season. I join you in the earnest hope that beyond this year the state of the world's affairs will no longer isolate any of us from the desires closest to our hearts.

"But please know this Christmas that countless thousands of families who are strangers to you—in addition to those with whom you are tied by kinship—embrace you in their thoughts. By your valor, skill, and wholehearted devotion to the welfare of the men they love, you have become an indivisible part of those families. Through your own sacrifices in fortifying the health of others you have created the preconditions for the celebration of future Christmas Days in homes throughout the nation.

"To the nation's thanks," he concluded his greetings, "let me add my own voice in prayer for your continued well-being. I am very proud of each and everyone of you and cherish the friendship and fealty so manifest in the past year. May God bless you all."

The Christmas Day Daily Bulletin of the 38th carried the greetings from Colonel Wood, President Roosevelt, General George C. Marshall, Army Chief of Staff, and Secretary of War Henry L. Stimson.

The President wrote:

"To Our Ill and Wounded Fighters

"With a deep personal sense of obligation I welcome the privilege of sending to you this Christmas Day a message of admiration and affection. You have given of your blood and health to restore to Christmas its meaning and to make the spirit of Christmas genuinely prevail throughout the world. It takes courage to fight on a battle front and it takes courage to fight from a hospital bed. We would not cheapen your hours of heroism by wishing you a 'Merry Christmas' but we wish you to know that we are with you in spirit, in comradeship and in faith.

"To the Men and Women of the Armed Forces

"On behalf of a grateful nation, I send to the men and women of our Armed Forces everywhere warm and confident good wishes this 4th Christmas of War. On Christmas Day more than any other day we remember you with pride and with humility, with anguish and with joy. We shall keep on remembering you all the days of our lives.

"It is, therefore, with solemn pride that I salute those who stand in the forefront of the struggle to bring back to a suffering world the way of life symbolized by the spirit of Christmas."

General Marshall's message emphasized the improvement in the war situation in the year since he sent his 1943 greetings:

"Since my Christmas message a year ago a great change has come over the Army," he wrote. "In Europe

Red Cross worker Lucy Brooke, left, and Lieutenant Sara Moran are flanked by officers from Charlotte, left to right, Milo Hoffman, Buck Medearis, Colin Munroe, and Jack Montgomery.

216

our troops with the British are attacking the enemy along a thousand-mile front. American bombers and fighters are covering all of Germany. In the Pacific more and more troops and planes are being deployed against the enemy, and with the tremendous blows of the Navy, the liberation of the Philippines is now well within our reach. In Burma and China, American planes are punishing the Japs with the vigorous support of our grand echelons. The nation is thankful for the victories of recent months, for the magnificent work and sacrifices of the men in the field. The people are very proud of the Army and they have great confidence in its ability to crush the enemy's final resistance.

"This Christmas message goes to every man and woman in the service," General Marshall's greetings continued, "with my personal thanks for what each of you is doing for the honor and security of AMERICA and for the liberation of oppressed people throughout the world. I am aware of the hardships and the hazards that are your daily portion and I am conscious of the price you pay for every victory. May the Lord watch over you and may you find, wherever you are, some cheer in this Christmas season."

The Secretary of War's message was similar in expressing the nation's appreciation:

"At this Christmas season the thoughts of an entire nation are with the troops. The candles which burn in the windows are beamed straight from the heart of AMERICA to the men and women in uniform. Wherever you are stationed it is your Christmas that we hope to share.

"I have a very personal knowledge of your service and your sacrifices. I have been with you on distant fronts where your courage has overcome the fiercest resistance of the enemy. The pride I feel in your valor has been deepened by the evidence of your humanity and your dignity in foreign lands. In liberated areas I have seen the gratitude of people whom you have rescued from the oppression and misery engendered by a savage foe. This year, because of you, the meaning of Christmas has been restored to them.

"From millions of homes the spirit of Christmas flows out to the posts and bases and battle lines where Americans serve throughout the world. From thousands of altars the nation offers up its prayers for you in the midst of war. In sending you my warmest greetings I express the admiration of a grateful nation for your courage and fortitude. Through you the joy of Christmas will return once more to a world at peace."

Colonel Wood's message was addressed, of course, to the members of the 38th. On the front page of the Daily Bulletin, beneath a drawing of the nativity scene and the dateline: VOLUME III NUMBER 350 MONDAY 25 DECEMBER 1944, it said:

CHRISTMAS GREETINGS

"Merry Christmas" from one who is just as lonely for his home and family as you are, has a hollow sound, but I sincerely hope that this will be a happy day for each of you and that you know how deeply appreciated is every effort you have exerted during the year in performance of your duties, and particularly thank you for doing so much to provide our patients with the atmosphere of Christmas.

On behalf of my staff I extend greetings to everyone and may God grant your wish that next year you will be by your own fireside and "Peace on Earth" will be a reality.

G. T. WOOD, JR.
Colonel, M.C.,
Commanding.

At the bottom of the page an inked ribbon proclaimed:

Merry Christmas and Happy New Year.

For the men and women of the 38th Evacuation Hospital, with few exceptions, it would be the last Christmas overseas.

On Christmas Day 1944 at Montecatini, the Daily Bulletin of that date further discloses, the number of patients in the hospital was 424 and there were 487 vacant beds.

During the next six days the patient load increased daily— 443; 613; 624; 722; and on December 30, to 810. On that day the Bulletin announced the welcoming to the 38th of two surgical teams to temporary duty from the 2nd Auxiliary Surgical Group. They were:

General Surgical Team No. 37-1:

Major Edward M. Phifer, M.C.; Captain David S. Fetters, M.C.; 2nd Lieutenant Carol F. Sleezer, ANC; 2nd Lieutenant Sophie T. Cowin, ANC; Tec 4 Robert L. Myers, MD; and Tec 4 Richard J. Tysarczyk, MD.

Shock Team No. 105-1

Captain Hermann L. Hegner, MC; 2nd Lieutenant Elaine C. Hatchew, ANC; 2nd Lieutenant Winifred E. Cochran, ANC; Tec 4 Walter H. Cotner, MD; Tec 5 Anthony Serino, MD; and Pfc Elwood D. Heirominus, MD.

December 30 the Bulletin listed service newspapers approved for mailing home: Union Jack, Eighth Army News, Crusader, Parade, Stars and Stripes (Italy edition), Stars and Stripes (Sicily edition), Stars and Stripes (Mediterranean edition), Maple Leaf, NZEF Times, APW (Polish), Yank, and Basic News (compiled by PWB.)

On the last day of 1944 the patient roll dropped to 714.

25

As the year 1945 opened, with the 38th still based at Montecatini, Lieutenant General Joseph T. McNarney, from MTOUSA headquarters, sent to the service men and women a New Year's message urging them to exert superhuman effort to insure victory and peace within the forthcoming year.

The message was reproduced in the Daily Bulletin by order of Colonel Wood on January 2. General McNarney wrote:

"Never before has the vital importance of the Italian Front been so obvious as in this crisis of the great counter-offensive which the Germans have launched against our forces in Luxembourg and Belgium.

"The great number of men and vast amount of supply needed by the Germans to pursue the Italian campaign is costing him dearly now in his all-out, desperate counter-attack on the Western Front.

"Anything short of a superhuman effort on our part, any slackening in our effort, means a longer and more difficult war. It is not enough for us merely to hold and engage the enemy force. We must carry the fight to him and destroy him. We must force him to pour more and more men and supplies into Italy.

"As we enter the New Year I call on every one of you, in every branch of the Service, to drive yourselves to the utmost, to give your last ounce of courage and determination, and to destroy the enemy ruthlessly wherever you find him. Only by putting all that we have into this final battle for victory can we be assured that the New Year will bring us the peace and the reunion with our own that we all so much desire. May good fortune attend your efforts."

On Sunday, January 7, the Bulletin carried a congratulatory message from General Mark W. Clark, the

Surgeon Stokes Munroe is caught in his usual genial mood.

Fifth Army's former commander then commanding the Fifteenth Army Group:

"Heartiest congratulations to Fifth Army and yourself on second anniversary of Fifth Army today, January 5. By skill, courage and will to win, the Fifth Army will make a great contribution to the success of Allied arms in 1945, which we hope will be a year of complete victory against our German enemy. May God continue to guide and bless the Fifth Army and its teammate, the Eighth Army, in coming operations."

In the first week of 1945, Captain Pickens, who at intervals during the fall months had served as the unit's adjutant, was transferred from the 38th to the 170th Evacuation Hospital. The Daily Bulletin of January 9 carried Colonel Wood's announcement of the transfer:

"Captain Pickens has received orders transferring him to the 170th Evacuation Hospital, where he will serve as executive officer. I personally appreciate the recognition accorded Captain Pickens by the Army Surgeon, but regret very much that he will no longer be with this organization. I know each of you joins me in this regret, but too, wish him the greatest success in his new position, where fuller use can be made of his ability. Good luck, Stan, and be assured that the latch string will be hanging on the outside whenever you return."

That same Bulletin announced the promotion of Mary Alyce Culley from second lieutenant to first lieutenant. The following day the commanding officer welcomed First Lieutenant Harold J. Brelsford, transferred from the 94th Evacuation Hospital.

The Bulletin of January 21 revealed the promotion of Captain Milo J. Hoffman to major and Second Lieu-

tenants Elva E. Wells and Barbara L. Wingo to first lieutenant.

At the beginning of February two officers were welcomed to the 38th. The February 3 Bulletin made the announcement:

Major William B. Crawford, Jr., from the 15th Field Hospital, and Major Byford F. Heskett, a member of the 12th General Hospital, on a temporary duty exchange basis, in place of Major Pat R. Imes.

February 7 notice was given of the arrival at the 38th of First Lieutenant Charles Victorine, Dental Corps, as a replacement for Captain Blake. Three days later two promotions were announced: Second Lieutenants Madeline I. Jensen and Helen E. Johnson to be first lieutenants.

The new commander of the Fifth Army, as revealed in the Daily Bulletin of February 12, awarded commendations to a group of the personnel of the 38th for their services during the emergency resulting from the flooding in early November of the hospital at Pisa.

General Truscott's commendation declared:

"The above named personnel of the 38th Evacuation Hospital are commended for meritorious service near Pisa, Italy, on 2 and 3 November 1944. When the Arno River overflowed its banks, the hospital site was flooded with water three to six feet in depth. By displaying exceptional initiative, and with complete disregard for personal safety, these members of the hospital staff directed and aided in the safe and expeditious evacuation of all patients to a place of safety, recovered equipment and immediately established an emergency hospital in order to maintain the necessary treatment and care of the wounded. As a result of the quick thinking and able leadership displayed by these individuals, all treatments were continued without interruption and operations were performed with a minimum of discomfort to the patients. The actions of these officers and enlisted men are in accord with the highest traditions of the Medical Corps of the United States Army."

Those members of the 38th to whom the commendations were made "for outstanding services rendered during the flooding of the hospital on 2 November 1944" were:

Lieutenant Colonel William H. Pennington
Lieutenant Colonel Paul W. Sanger
Lieutenant Colonel Robert O. Y. Warren
Captain Hallie E. Almond
Captain James R. Felts, Jr.
Captain Stanton W. Pickens
Captain George E. Pugh
Captain Rosamond S. Shipp
First Lieutenant Martha G. Fliedner
First Lieutenant Annette M. Heaton
First Lieutenant Lela O. Russell
Master Sergeant Herbert L. Johnson
Staff Sergeant William F. MacDonough

Staff Sergeant James J. O'Donnell
Staff Sergeant Adam J. Piperato
Technician Third Grade Paul H. Kugler
Technician Third Grade William E. Smith
Sergeant John A. Boulier
Sergeant Wilbur H. Knapp

Further honor came to the 38th in the award of the Bronze Star Medal to Private First Class George R. Porter, "for meritorious service in combat on 18 August 1944, in Italy. Entered the service from Hancock, New York." The award was announced in the Daily Bulletin of February 20, 1945.

One week later, on February 27, announcement was made of the promotion of Technical Sergeant William E. Vaughn to second lieutenant and his assignment to the 15th Field Hospital.

February ended with the visit to the hospital of Major General Stayer, Surgeon, MTOUSA, to inspect the facility. The next day Colonel Wood reported:

"To All Personnel:

"Major General Stayer, Surgeon, MTOUSA, seemed favorably impressed by the appearance of the hospital during his inspection yesterday, and gratified with the professional care the patients were receiving. Each member of the organization may feel a just pride in his or her contribution to the efficient operation of this small unit of the Army Medical Service."

On the day of the General's visit, the 38th listed 355 patients being cared for in 15 wards, with 555 beds vacant.

Interestingly reflecting the changing political situation in Italy at that time was the directive issued by the commanding general of the Fifth Army and published in the day's Bulletin:

"Personnel of the Fifth Army will refrain from direct, indirect or individual participation in Italian politics. Strict compliance with this principle will become even more important as the Italian Government assumes an increasing measure of political responsibility over a more extensive area of Italy. Casual attendance by Fifth Army personnel at political meetings, and even private conversation with Italians on political subjects, may lead to misunderstandings and will be avoided on all occasions."

First Lieutenant Eugene M. Snell, who had served frequently and at length as adjutant of the 38th, was promoted on February 27 to captain, and on that day Second Lieutenant Christine Fruth was advanced to first lieutenant. Notice of the promotions was carried in the Daily Bulletin of March 3. The Bulletin three days later announced that the 38th was extending its "welcome" to six of its members "who have just returned after an 'extended rest' in the states." The six were: Major George C. Snyder, Captain Robert B. Stith, Jr., Captain Charles H. Gay, Sr., Captain George E. Pugh,

Lieutenant Hallie Almond and Captain Robert Augustine are getting a little off-duty sunshine.

First Lieutenant Annette M. Heaton, and First Lieutenant Deborah R. Doskow.

Considerable change in the personnel marked the remaining weeks the 38th was based at Montecatini. Promotions, transfers, receptions from other units were frequently recorded. The most notable change was reported in the Daily Bulletin of March 11:

"Colonel George T. Wood, Jr., Commanding Officer, is being transferred to the United States to a new assignment, as yet unannounced. We are all happy to learn that his leadership, ability and wisdom are recognized by higher authorities and feel that our loss is a distinct gain to some other organization.

"The sincere good wishes of all members of the 38th Evacuation Hospital go with you, Colonel, and we hope you will be happy in your new assignment."

The same day announcement was made of the promotion of Pearl M. Satre from second lieutenant to first lieutenant.

Lieutenant Colonel William H. Pennington succeeded Colonel Wood as commanding officer of the 38th. On this last day of Colonel Wood's commanding the unit the hospital had 369 patients enrolled and 541 vacant beds.

On March 18 Miss Janet Seelye, Red Cross worker attached to the 17th General Hospital, was transferred to the 38th. Two days later the promotion of Second

Lieutenant Adrienne J. Ellison to first lieutenant, effective March 17, was revealed. On March 22 official announcement was made of the appointment of Colonel Pennington to command the unit, effective March 19.

Captain Spiros P. Sarris, who had been attached to the 38th from the Sixth General Hospital, was promoted to major. The announcement was made March 23.

A page of *News in Brief* in the March 27 Bulletin listed an item that reminded 38th members old enough to recall it that almost three decades earlier the world had ended another great holocaust that their fathers had hoped would bring a lasting era of peace. It noted the death of one of the great leaders of the Allied forces in World War I:

"Earl Lloyd George died last night at his home in Wales. He was 82."

On March 30 Lieutenant Charlotte McVeigh was welcomed into the 38th as a replacement for Lieutenant Leah Rodstein. Her home was Cleveland, Ohio. She came to the 38th from the 37th General Hospital.

The next day two other officers were received: Major Benjamin Rawles, Jr., and First Lieutenant David Speer. Major Rawles came from the 45th General Hospital; he was assigned to the 38th for six weeks as replacement for Major Calder. Lieutenant Speer, from Bronxville, New York, a graduate of Harvard Medical School, was assigned as replacement for Captain Crawley. The same day announcement was made of the promotion of three nurses, Ida P. Bell, Elizabeth E. Killeen, and Billie Wittler from second lieutenant to

The 38th's routine wasn't all work all the time. Occasionally the men—and the nurses—had time for sports. George Waide, left, shown with two buddies, judging by his shoes, had been in some sort of game at Montecatini. The others are William Minovich and Edmond Coviello.

first lieutenant. A week later four other second lieutenants received their silver bars. They were Vera M. Neely, Pauline B. Pisinsky, Frances L. Robbins, and Mary E. Townsend.

April 11 Colonel Pennington welcomed Captain Walter A. Russell of Somersworth, New Hampshire, to duty with the 38th. Two days later the commanding officer welcomed a group of officers, nurses, and enlisted men:

Captain Jean N. Le Clerc, from Manchester, New Hampshire, assigned to the 38th from the 329 Field Artillery Battalion for duty with the Surgical Service, replacing Captain Claud Perry.

First Lieutenant Robert A. Brower, of Cincinnati, Ohio, assigned to the 38th from the 171st Evacuation Hospital as replacement for First Lieutenant Brelsford, transferred to the 12th General Hospital.

From 182nd Station Hospital (Surgical Team)
Major James K. Gibson, MC
Captain Herbert B. Gaston, MC
First Lieutenant Carrie V. Exum, ANC
First Lieutenant Marguriete Ocheltree, ANC
First Lieutenant Loretta P. Spears, ANC
Tec 4 Leonard A. Canarile, MD
Tec 5 Merle E. Loux, MD

From 2nd Auxilliary Surgical Group (Surgical Team 45-2)
Captain Beverley B. Clary, MC
Captain Harvey W. Carter, MC
Second Lieutenant Gertrude L. Barbour, ANC
First Lieutenant Nellie R. Beagans, ANC
Tec 5 Gerard J. Robinson, MD
Pfc John Krane, MD

On the overleaf of this sheet under the heading *News in Brief*, set in a square of double-spaced type with a black border, was an announcement already heard around the world:

President Roosevelt died suddenly yesterday afternoon at his summer cottage in Warm Springs, Georgia, from cerebral hemorrhage. He was 63. The funeral services will be held in the White House tomorrow and the interment will be on Sunday at Hyde Park, the President's New York home. Vice-President Truman was yesterday sworn in as President for the remainder of Mr. Roosevelt's term. In a message of sympathy to Mrs. Roosevelt, Mr. Churchill says, "The President's death is a loss to the British Nation and the cause of freedom in every land." Marshal Stalin has also expressed his personal sorrow and the sympathy of his government.

But in the 38th Evacuation Hospital, as throughout the embattled area of the world, the business of war went on without pause. On the next day, April 14, two days after the President's death, another group was assigned for service with the 38th. In this group were:

Captain Martin Stein, MC, and Captain Joseph L. Pisani, MC, from the 161st Medical Battalion.

Major Newton C. Mead, MC; Captain Benjamin F. Lounsbury, MC; First Lieutenants Olive A. McCuen,

The rolling mountains of Italy that in Rome's golden era sheltered fabulous villas of the Empire's patrician families in this photograph can be seen beyond the 38th's encampment at Montecatini.

ANC, and Cora B. Kelso, ANC; Tec 5 John P. Jerling, MD, and Pfc William P. Sidell, MD, from the 2nd Auxiliary Surgical Group (Surgical Team 12-1).

Three promotions were announced April 20. Second Lieutenants Sara J. Green, HD, and Marie A. Tetzlaff, ANC, were given their silver bars, and Captain Stanton W. Pickens, transferred early in January from the 38th to the 170th Evacuation Hospital, was advanced to major.

Major Pickens had been serving in the new assignment a month when he wrote home on February 10 to tell about the new location and his latest responsibilities.

"It has been many weeks since I last wrote," he began. "The reasons have been fairly obvious. In this area things have been static while we watched with more than usual interest the developments in the east and west. I know now what a veteran is; he watches with interest what the young do. With the exception of the abortive push the Germans made down the Serchio valley a few weeks ago, nothing has happened here for many weeks. Our colored troops took the burden of that push until the Indians came to their rescue. The BRRR had a time of it, which proved more conclusively to those of us who have seen it first-hand that they had no business there in the first place. In addition, our Yankee friends here have concluded that

we know best how to handle the problem, that they are inexperienced. The Indians came in with their British officers, had a spot of tea, and then busied themselves tidying up the battlefield. Tidying up the battlefield consisted of gathering up equipment our troops had hurriedly left behind. After they had done this, they set about and took back most of the territory the Germans had taken from us. Then Eleanor's favorites were given the job of holding it again."

The comparative inactivity of recent weeks had caused them to develop "a softness that is not becoming," he wrote. "The social and rest periods have increased. We have thought more of entertainment and comfort than of winning the war quickly. We cannot take all the blame for this, since we do what we are told to do."

Then he revealed he had left the 38th:

"To offset this for my own part, I have accepted a transfer to another outfit. I don't know that I had any choice in the matter, but was led to believe that I did. The surgeon presented the matter in the most complimentary terms. Possibly this was his method of snaring me into more work. Anyway, it worked, and here I am the executive officer of a new hospital, set up about 20 miles from the old outfit."

He wrote of the new group:

"I have not yet decided whether this new organiza-

221

tion is an accumulation of a lot of excellent people or the castoffs from many units. Sometimes I think we might be good and then at other times I am sure we are the dregs. The fact is that most of the personnel came from a station hospital which remained in Africa until last fall. They still think and work from that angle, but it will not take long, when we get busy, to get away from the former methods and get down to rock bottom. The nearer you are to the front, the more corners are cut."

The Charlottean wrote of several of the staff:

"The Commanding Officer is from Atlanta, not regular Army. His name is Benjamin S. Read. His father was with the telephone company there for many years, as president, I believe. We have found many people and things in common, although he is a few years my junior. He went to Dartmouth, undergraduate, and studied medicine at Harvard. The chief of medicine is Major John O. McNeel from West Virginia. The chief of surgery, Lt. Col. Shakelford, studied at Princeton and took his medicine at Johns Hopkins. He is a Virginian, although he was teaching at Hopkins when the war started. He went to the Pacific for some 18 months in the Figi Islands and Bougainville. After recuperating in the States for three months, he asked foreign duty again and was headed for the China-Burma-India theatre, but for some reason was taken off the boat in this theatre. It happened about the time Uncle Joe Stillwell was leaving China to the Chinese. It strikes me as an unusually strong team. The other doctors stack up in the same manner. The medical administrative officers are all young, freshly commissioned officers. They appear to be well chosen and efficient."

He gave his view of the new assignment he had been given:

"The job of executive officer as expressed in the SOP (Standard Operating Procedure) reads like this: 'the

Major George Snyder hangs up his wash to dry. The place? Where else but Pisa!

principal assistant of the commanding officer and supervises the workings of the remainder of the staff. He enjoys the confidence of the C.O. and possesses a thorough knowledge of his policies and plans. He performs such routine administration of the unit and the hospital as does not require the personal action of the C.O. In the absence of the C.O. he makes such decisions as he thinks the C.O. would have made in like circumstances and notifies him of such decisions at the earliest opportunity. In addition to his regular duties, the executive officer also acts as intelligence officer, summary court officer, and possibly president of the special court. He will have general supervision over headquarters.' It looks like a job of taking the dirty linen out to wash. The exec takes all the blame for the bad and makes the good look like the C.O. thought about it. So far, I have done very little, because I did not know the people with whom I was dealing. I thought it wise to move slowly. From point of overseas service, I am the oldest officer here, and from point of age I am among the oldest. I am outranked on all sides but that has promise of being equaled to some extent, and the grey hair and experience help. This month I draw what the Army calls a 'foggy.' For every three years service you get a five per cent increase in pay. Since I accepted my commission in February 1942, I am now eligible to draw the additional five per cent. This is on the base pay of a captain, which is $200 per month, so the foggy will amount to $10 per month."

The 170th Evacuation Hospital, he revealed further, had a capacity of 400 beds, smaller than the 38th but, said he, more mobile. "We have a few more trucks. In this way, when the war gets under way again, we should be able to move often and faster. This might bring us a little nearer the front, but I can't see how that will be, since we have more often than somewhat been sitting in front of the division artillery. Any moves further forward will put us in the battalion CPs or possibly alongside the frontline patrols. I am frankly a little weary of getting that far ahead without some sort of weapon in my hands."

He wrote again of the severity of the winter from which they had not yet emerged:

"The winter has been long and dull and cold. The snow has come and gone regularly, but we have been fortunate in getting flooring in our tents and since I have been in the new place, I have aided in constructing a Rube Goldberg type of oil heater. We have plenty of diesel oil and with a small valve or spigot taken from a wrecked jeep, and some copper tubing, we rigged up a creditable stove which warms the tent. Of course, we are covered with soot whenever the wind blows from the wrong direction, but being dirty is one of the prerequisites of war. We get our stovepipe by robbing the gutters and drain installations from fascist homes in the neighborhood. The owners usually disappear before the Army moves in. We have to be fast in our stealing before the native population returns because that is the first place they go for their pillaging. The bigshot racketeer has stolen from them for so long, they feel they are entitled to anything they can find. Of course, we still feel a little like the conquering army and take what we need, although many people are getting soft about the Italians and think we should go easy on them. I don't forget that just a little over a year ago they were shooting at us with an aim to kill."

26

Five months after the 38th set up its tents at Montecatini the hospital was entering its final days at that location. It had arrived there November 10; it would close its operations officially, the Daily Bulletin of April 20, 1945, would record, "at 0930 hours." Major Snyder was administrative officer of the day and Captain Harney was medical officer of the day. Alternates were Lieutenant Brower and Captain Payne.

During the last day of operation, the Bulletin would further disclose, sixteen patients were admitted and 361 dispositions were made to clear completely the roster of patients.

The Bulletin that day was a short one. It listed only the promotions of three officers and summarized in one paragraph news of the action on the Eastern Front. Two nurses, Second Lieutenants Sara J. Green and Marie A. Tetzlaff, three days earlier had been promoted to first lieutenant. "Announcement is also made," said the Bulletin, "of the promotion to Major of Captain Stanton W. Pickens, 170th Evacuation Hospital, a former member of this command."

The *News in Brief* summary revealed:

"Moscow has finally announced the opening of the great Russian offensive across the Oder and reports that the Red Army are pushing the Germans back in a mighty drive toward Berlin. The Germans say that the Russians are advancing on a 40-mile front and have made a crossing of the river where they are getting non-stop reinforcements across the Oder. At several points the Russians are reported a little more than 18 miles from the outskirts of Berlin. The Russians who crossed the Neiser River have captured three towns, one about 50 miles from Dresden."

Next day's Bulletin—of Saturday, April 21, 1945—had but the one announcement:

"THE HOSPITAL WAS MOVED FROM ITS LO-CATION AT MONTECATINI TERME, ITALY, TO A NEW SITE APPROXIMATELY 1 KILOMETER SOUTH OF MARZABOTTO, ITALY—COORDI-NATES, L772311.

"DISTANCE TRAVELED FROM OLD LOCA-TION: APPROXIMATELY 55 MILES.

"THE HOSPITAL WAS ERECTED IN THE NEW LOCATION AND READY TO RECEIVE PATIENTS BY 2400 HOURS."

The Bulletin of April 22 also was terse. It reported:

"THE HOSPITAL OFFICIALLY OPENED AT 0100 HOURS.

One other announcement warned:

"All personnel are instructed to remain within the camp limits, as the areas immediately adjacent to the hospital have not been checked for mines. The area between the eastern border of the camp and the creek is expected to be heavily mined."

The warning was emphasized in the Bulletin of Monday, April 22:

"The surrounding area is heavily mined and information from G-2 is that there are many booby traps scattered about. All personnel are again warned!! Until further notice, the area east of the east water tower is out of bounds."

Lieutenant Colonel W. H. Pennington in that Bulletin declared that "it is very gratifying to see the results of hard work and interest on the part of all members of the command during the move and erection of the hospital. The Commanding Officer takes this means of thanking each and every one who has labored to make the rapid move possible."

Colonel Pennington announced that he had welcomed into the 38th the following officers, nurses, and enlisted men:

Captain John C. Todd, assigned to the 38th from the

A portion of the Montecatini race track provides a street between the 38th's tents. The hospital was stationed at Montecatini following the period at Pisa. It moved from here on April 21, 1945, to Marzabotto.

168th Infantry Regiment. Captain Todd, from Pittsburgh, Pennsylvania, was assigned to the Dental Service as a replacement for Captain Jack Raymer.

The following personnel were attached for temporary duty from the Second Auxiliary Surgical Group:

General Surgical Team 21-1
Captain Edgar H. Keys, MC
Captain Francis W. Chamberlain, MC
1st Lt. Eunishis H. Sorenger, ANC
2nd Lt. Madelyn N. Parks, ANC
Tec 4 Dale J. Clayton, MD
Tec 3 Tavner E. Henry, MD

Neuro-Surgical Team (15th Evac)
Captain Donald Wrork, MC
Captain Gourand, MC
1st Lt. Blanche Bird, ANC
2nd Lt. Dorothy Coveny, ANC
Tec David Morrison, MD

General Surgical Team 37-3
Major Arthur A. Weinberg, MC
Captain Morris J. Bloom, MC
2nd Lt. Eva L. Ross, ANC
2nd. Lt. Marcia N. Webb, ANC
Tec 4 John J. Gunn, MD
Tec 5 Vernon Johnson, MD

The newly located hospital on this day listed 92 patients under treatment and 670 vacant beds. The next day the patient roll had almost doubled, to 175. The next two days it went to 277 and 318. Items in the Daily Bulletin's *News in Brief* that day—April 26—in concise form revealed:

"Marshals Zhukov and Koniev have joined up to the northwest of Berlin and the city is now completely surrounded. This dramatic news came swiftly behind the Moscow announcement that a link-up had been made south of the city earlier in the day, trapping thousands of Germans between the rivers Spree and Oder. Reports from within Berlin by correspondents say that the fires inside the city are so intense that the heavy rains that have been falling for the last couple of days are hardly noticeable to the troops bitterly fighting inside the capital. The Nazis continue to say that Hitler is still in the capital but hourly his chances of escape lessen. . . . In Bavaria, American Third Army troops were last reported within 18 miles of the Austrian frontier. Other American forces driving down the Danube are about 55 miles from Munich. In the north, British troops are fighting in Bremen and to the west, Canadian troops were last reported within 4 miles of the naval base of Emden. . . . RAF Lancasters yesterday dropped 6-ton bombs in Hitler's Berchtesgaden home. They also bombed Hitler's mountain refuge some 5 miles away. American bombers attacked rail targets near Berchtesgaden and more than 300 other American

224

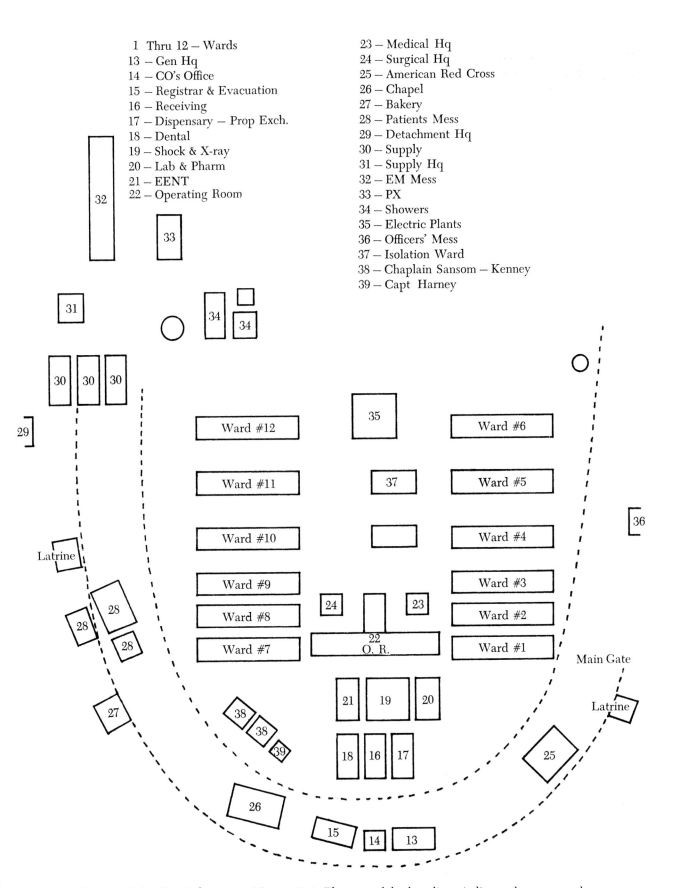

1 Thru 12 — Wards
13 — Gen Hq
14 — CO's Office
15 — Registrar & Evacuation
16 — Receiving
17 — Dispensary — Prop Exch.
18 — Dental
19 — Shock & X-ray
20 — Lab & Pharm
21 — EENT
22 — Operating Room
23 — Medical Hq
24 — Surgical Hq
25 — American Red Cross
26 — Chapel
27 — Bakery
28 — Patients Mess
29 — Detachment Hq
30 — Supply
31 — Supply Hq
32 — EM Mess
33 — PX
34 — Showers
35 — Electric Plants
36 — Officers' Mess
37 — Isolation Ward
38 — Chaplain Sansom — Kenney
39 — Capt Harney

Layout of the Hospital Area at Montecatini. The curved broken lines indicate the race track.

225

heavies bombed the Skoda arms plant in Czechoslovakia. Last night, RAF bombers attacked Kiel and an oil storage depot in Norway. . . . Both Fifth and Eighth Army troops are sweeping north beyond the river Po. Fifth Army troops are near Mantur, 10 miles beyond the river. Thousands of more prisoners have been taken. . . . About 250 Super-Forts today bombed airfields in Japan. In Burma, British and Indian troops advancing down from Meiktila have captured the important base of Toungoo. Their advance continues. The capture of Toungoo follows an advance thru the jungles of more than 160 miles in 21 days during which these troops have killed nearly 5,000 Japanese. . . . The announcement has been made in Washington of the promotion of General George Patton to 4-star rank for his brilliant offensive operations in Germany."

On the last day of April, a little more than a week after it had been established at Marzabotto, the hospital was again on the move. The Daily Bulletin of April 30, 1945, reported:

"THE HOSPITAL WAS MOVED FROM ITS LOCATION AT APPROXIMATELY 1 KILOMETER SOUTH OF MARZABOTTO, ITALY, TO A NEW SITE APPROXIMATELY 3 KILOMETERS SOUTHEAST OF FIDENZA, ITALY —COORDINATES, P918923.

"DISTANCE TRAVELED FROM OLD LOCATION: APPROXIMATELY 95 MILES.

"THE HOSPITAL WAS ERECTED IN THE NEW LOCATION AND READY TO RECEIVE PATIENTS BY 2000 HOURS."

The next day, May 1, the Bulletin reported: Number of patients, 1; admissions, 1; vacant beds, 199. *News in Brief*, in the May 2 Bulletin, included: "The German Radio announced last night that Hitler died yesterday in his Chancellory in Berlin. It said that Hitler had appointed as his successor, Grand Admiral Doenitz, Commander and Chief of the German Navy since 1943. Doenitz then broadcast a message revealing that Germany would fight on. . . . The Russians have cleared two districts in the center of Berlin as well as another hundred blocks of buildings. They are nearing the Tiergarten."

The principal announcement in the Daily Bulletin of May 3 reported the presentation of the Bronze Star Medal "to Major William R. Pitts, a member of this command." The citation declared:

WILLIAM R. PITTS, (0468119), Major, Medical Corps, United States Army. For meritorious services in support of combat operations, from November 1942 to March 1945, in North Africa and Italy. Serving as Assistant Chief of the Surgical Service and as neurological surgeon for an evacuation hospital, Major PITTS, in addition to performing a large number of

In boots, sweater, and scarf knotted turbanlike, Lieutenant Sara Moran stands in tent doorway.

general surgical operations, has operated on more than 118 patients with brain injuries. The extremely low mortality rate incident to these operations was achieved as a result of his professional skill, attention to detail and close supervision of all cases. Normally the only neurological surgeon in the hospital, Major PITTS worked long hours without relief in a manner which provided an inspiration to his associates and reflects the finest traditions of the Medical Corps. Entered military service from Charlotte, North Carolina."

The big news of that day's *News in Brief* in the Bulletin, however, was the announcement under "FINALE:"

"All enemy land, sea and air forces in Italy have surrendered unconditionally to Field Marshal Alexander. Nearly a million men are involved. The terms signed on Sunday at the Royal Palace in Caserta in the presence of Alexander and his staff with a representative of the Russian government present, called for the cessation of hostilities at 12 noon GMT yesterday in Northern Italy and in Western Austria. President Truman has sent a special message to the troops of the Allied Armies in Italy in which he praised the gallant forces and said that this will be very interesting news to the Japanese, interesting indeed. Mr. Churchill, giving the news to the Commons last night, said this surrender brought to a conclusion the work of as gallant an Allied Army as ever marched."

The news from the Eastern Front, as reported in the same issue of the Bulletin, was equally cheering:

"German resistance in Berlin ended yesterday afternoon after a house-to-house battle lasting just over a week. The Commander of the garrison was among the 70,000 Germans taken prisoner yesterday. Another 80,000 Germans have been killed and more than 120,-000 captured southeast of Berlin where the enemy pocket has been wiped out."

The final item in the day's *News in Brief* was dramatic:

"Moscow says one of the prisoners taken in Berlin was the German radio commentator Fritsche. They say Fritsche declared that both Hitler and Goebbels had died by their own hands."

By May 7 the number of patients in the hospital, which was then ending its first week at Fidenza, had increased to 368, of which 31 were new admissions. Ten wards were in operation. No hospital news of general interest was reported. But on the over-page the *News in Brief* continued to be lively and of significance. Among the items:

"Admiral Doenitz has issued an order to U-Boats to cease hostilities and return to base. He told U-boat men that the continuation of the struggle is impossible.

"A broadcast declaration by Mr. Churchill announcing the end of the war in Europe is likely to begin the next few days. It is expected to give the news of Germany's unconditional surrender to Great Britain, the United States and Russia. There will be similar announcements from Washington and Moscow at the same time. On the night of V-E Day, the King will broadcast at 1900 hours G.M.T."

And the next day, May 8, the Daily Bulletin on its first page carried the single announcement, under "Chaplain's Notice," that "A service, giving thanks to God for V-E Day, will be held in the chapel at 1600 hours today."

But the over-page was devoted to a tremendously significant announcement. Set in double-spaced lines across the page in a square framed top, sides, and bottom with the words "V-E DAY," was the welcomed message:

"Today is Victory in Europe Day. The official announcement will be broadcast by the leaders of all the major powers today at 1300 hours GMT. The King of England will broadcast to his people at 1900 hours. The King has sent his congratulations to General Eisenhower on the success of the Allied Armies. First news of Germany's capitulation came from an agency correspondent yesterday afternoon. It said the surrender was made at 0241 hours GMT yesterday in the school-house at Rheims, General Eisenhower's Headquarters. The surrender was signed for Germany by Col. General Gustav Jodl, new chief of staff of the German Army. Lt. General Smith signed for General Eisenhower and Major General Susladatov signed for Russia. The Germans were repeatedly asked if they understood the significance of the terms. They replied, 'Yes,' and said they would be carried out by Germany. The Germans in Prague and Norway have also agreed to the terms of unconditional surrender."

Below this announcement, under "FAR EAST," was the four-line report:

"American Super-Fortresses have made their 18th attack on the southern island of Japan. American carrier-planes have again attacked airfields on an island off Okinawa. In Borneo, Allied warplanes are operating from the airfield captured by Australian troops on Tarikan Island."

The next day, Wednesday, May 9, the Daily Bulletin in the *News in Brief* summary reported:

"The end of the war in Europe was celebrated thruout the Allied Nations yesterday with great rejoicing, tempered only by the statements of the Allied leaders that Japan still remained to be subdued. Although the official end of the war was timed to take place at one minute past midnight last night, an earlier announcement had been made by Supreme Headquarters that a cease-fire had been given early on Monday. It has now been confirmed that the final terms of surrender were signed early Monday morning at General Eisenhower's Headquarters in Rheims.

"At home there was no let-up in the war production and no holiday was declared in any of the cities. Many of the larger cities report that the celebration was confined to a short period on Monday night when the news was first released in the States. New York reports that the streets around Times Square were jammed thruout Monday night with the celebrators but that the curfew which was not lifted limited the hour of the celebration and sent most pleasure-seekers home early in the evening."

On May 26, less than a month after it had been established at Fidenza on the last day of April, the 38th moved again. The Daily Bulletin recorded the change in location:

THE HOSPITAL LOCATED 3 KILOMETERS SE OF FIDENZA, ITALY, CLOSED AT 0800 HOURS AND OPENED AT 0800 HOURS AT SALSOMAG-GIORE, ITALY.

On the day of the moving the hospital listed 154 patients, 14 admissions, 40 dispositions, 206 vacant beds and seven wards in operation. The largest group of patients during the stay at Fidenza had been 507 on May 11.

27

On May 31 and June 1, 1945, forty enlisted personnel were transferred from the 38th and twenty-two were received from other units of the medical service in anticipation of the forthcoming disposition of the organization.

The Daily Bulletin of Friday, June 1, listed 135 patients, with 13 admissions, 17 dispositions, 140 vacant beds, and 31 wards in operation.

"Within the next few days," the Bulletin noted, "there will be several showdown inspections for all officers, nurses and enlisted men. The purpose of these inspections is to check for all shortages and overages of G.I. clothing and equipment, preparatory to any future movement of the unit. Complete cooperation of all individuals is expected and any instances of evasion or disobedience of these instructions will be dealt with promptly and severely."

That same day the transfers were announced:

"The following enlisted men were transferred yesterday to the 171st Evacuation Hospital:

"Tec 5 William C. Bercaw, Tec 5 Harry D. Coder, Pfc William Elkin, Tec 5 Edward L. Evenson, Tec 4 Frederick Federspiel, Tec 5 Delbert P. Jones, Pfc John L. McMahon, Pfc Joseph E. Mederos, Cpl Joseph Pajak, Pvt Steve J. Pardikes, Cpl John J. Piwowarski, Tec 5 George R. Porter, Tec 5 Walter A. Rex, Tec 4 Gardner C. Sellers, Pfc Milton J. Smoliar, Pfc Melvin R. Smith, Tec 5 Howard J. Spry, Tec 5 Theodore Stack, Tec 5 John A. Stefanchik, Pfc Roman B. Golankiewicz, and Tec 5 George W. Brannon.

"The following enlisted man was transferred yesterday to the 163rd Medical Battalion:

"Pvt Tracy G. Akers.

"The following enlisted men are transferred to the 38th Evacuation Hospital from the 171st Evacuation Hospital:

"Tec 3 Louis A. Anderson, Pfc Robert R. Beamer, Jr., Tec 4 Alfred L. Blackler, Pfc H. H. Brandenstein, Pfc Patrick Camderlengo, Tec 5 Ivan W. Fuoua, Jr., Tec 5 Leonard C. Kimble, Pfc Ferinin Martinez, Tec 4 Eugene McClain, Tec 5 Dewey J. Nunez, Cpl Irenio M. Ortego, Sgt. Anthony C. Pisa, Tec 5 Noah W. Ragsdale, Pfc Herman W. Ripkoski, Tec 5 Henry S. Roy, S/Sgt Maurice J. Rosen, S/Sgt Simon Schultz, Tec 4 Frank

N. Semeraro, Pfc Jasper Sexton, Pfc Gordon C. Swenson, and Tec 5 William Young.

"The following enlisted man is transferred to the 38th Evacuation Hospital from the 163rd Medical Battalion:

"Pfc Marcus B. King, Jr.

"The following enlisted men are transferred to the 7th Replacement Depot and will leave tomorrow, 2 June, 1945:

"Pfc Charles L. Ogle, Pfc Harry W. Coats, Pvt Willard G. Riano, Pfc Daniel J. Trivison, Tec 5 James L. Ambrose, Pvt Paul E. J. Cook, Pfc Charles L. Neubauer, Tec 5 Michael Angarano, Tec 5 Joseph D. Dubendorfer, Tec 5 Paul W. Edger, Cpl Robert G. Folmar, Pfc Harold L. Galusha, Tec 4 Leroy M. Goodyear, Tec 5 William E. Griswold, Tec 5 Alfred G. Hafner, Pfc Helke A. McCoughin, Pvt Jack L. Shobert, and Pvt Donald E. Waring."

Closing down operations began June 1. The Bulletin announced:

"Within the next few days, there will be several show-down inspections for all officers, nurses and enlisted men. The purpose of these inspections is to check for all shortages of G.I. clothing and equipment, preparatory to any future movement of the unit. Complete cooperation of all individuals is expected and any instances of evasion or disobedience of these instructions will be dealt with promptly and severely.

"Officers', nurses', and enlisted men's lists, which will be distributed, are to be checked by all personnel to see that they are correct. *All* equipment and clothing listed *will be* in the possession of each individual, and any excess will be turned in."

The June 4 Bulletin had the announcement:

"Any individual *not* desiring to be returned to the United States will report to the adjutant today."

Three days later, further reflecting the preparations for closing, the Bulletin announced:

"There will be an 'odds-and-ends' clearance sale in the PX at 1300 hours today, for unit personnel. First come, first served!"

The next day there was another:

"All kerosene stoves will be turned in at Supply Headquarters, regardless of where or how obtained."

June 10 the Bulletin revealed plans for the subsequent preparation of a history of the unit. "Pictures of the hospital are needed for the annual history," it declared. "The Commanding Officer would be grateful for any pictures of the hospital installations at Montecatini, Marzabotto, Fidenza, or Salsomaggiore. Anyone having pictures and wishing to donate them please leave them with adjutant."

In the Bulletin two days later a more insistent notice ordered the turning in of GI equipment:

"When this unit moves to a redeployment area, all hospital equipment must be turned in. In order to assess our shortages and overages, a *final* count of all GI equipment must be determined. From time to time, announcements will be made that certain items will be turned in. This means that *all* items of this class, whatever the source or the method of procurement, will be turned in to the supply department. No *variation of this order will be tolerated.* Any officer or nurse retaining GI equipment after it is ordered turned in will be subject to disciplinary action and NCO's will be automatically reduced to privates. Individuals will be held responsible for equipment in their rooms."

This notice, word for word, was repeated in the next two issues of the Bulletin and on June 14 the first list of items to be turned in was carried. June 15 the Bulletin announced further:

"Effective this date, all enlisted men will carry a permanent pass which will be good in Salsomaggiore only. Curfew in Salsomaggiore is 2400 hours and all enlisted personnel will be off the streets at that time. While on pass all members of this organization will be in proper uniform. Passes will be issued in Detachment Headquarters this afternoon."

Colonel Pennington announced in the June 17 Bulletin:

"General Martin will be here at 1600 hours today. All departments of the hospital will be thoroughly policed and military courtesy will be strictly observed."

Warning not to discuss future movements of the 38th with civilians or personnel unauthorized to possess such information was published in the Bulletin of June 23, nor, said the announcement, could mention of any future movements be made "in any correspondence to friends and relatives in the United States or elsewhere."

The June 29 issue of the Daily Bulletin announced:
THE HOSPITAL OFFICIALLY CLOSED AT 1200 HOURS, 28 JUNE 1945.

The final Status of the Hospital report that day, with Captain Todd as officer of the day and Lieutenant Brower as alternate, revealed:

"Number of patients, 0; admissions, 1; dispositions 20; vacant beds, 0; wards in operation, 0."

The Daily Bulletin during the following weeks was

This snapshot of Major George Snyder armed with his shooting iron explains why he was called by his 38th comrades "the sheriff."

devoted in the main to notices concerned with the turning in of various types of Army equipment. On July 1 the Bulletin emphasized the necessity of compliance:

"These instructions are repeated for all concerned. Government property which is not authorized for issue to individuals will be turned in to Supply immediately. GI clothing or equipment which is privately owned by officers and nurses may be taken away or turned in. Under no circumstances will it be left or discarded. Individuals occupying rooms are responsible that no property is left in them. This is an official order and will be obeyed by all personnel."

The order for moving from Salsomaggiore was posted July 2. Under MOVEMENT SCHEDULE it said:

"All personnel will move from this location tomorrow morning, 3 July.

"Transportation for movement will be here by 0700 hours, 3 July.

"Immediately after breakfast, enlisted men will deposit their baggage at the main entrance to the building. The Detachment Commander will designate the vehicles in which the enlisted men will ride.

"Officers and nurses will leave in 4 buses from the vicinity of the side gate at 0800 hours. Major Crawford will be in charge of the officers' bus; Major Boyd, Major Calder and Captain Wright will be in charge of the 3 nurses' buses. Rosters will be on the officers' bulletin board indicating which bus the officers and nurses will ride. It is necessary that you ride in the bus to which you are assigned. Hand luggage may be carried on the bus with you.

"A luggage detail will go to the officers' and nurses'

Moving day again. Lieutenant Lela Russell, awaiting her transportation, is seated behind Lieutenant Bessie Full-bright's luggage, ready for the departure of the 38th to a new location.

quarters between 1800 and 1900 hours this evening to carry down any luggage which may be ready at that time. Other luggage will be carried down by the owners tomorrow morning before 0730 hours. All officers' and nurses' luggage will be loaded on one truck at the side entrance of the floor beneath the officer-nurse quarters. Nurses' luggage will be loaded *first* since it is to be unloaded last at a separate point.

"Officer-nurse buses will not travel in the main convoy and must take off by 0800 hours.

" 'C' rations will be aboard the vehicles. No water will be available except from your own canteens.

"Breakfast tomorrow morning will be served as follows:

"Enlisted men: 0545
Officers and nurses: 0630."

On July 5 that day's issue of the Official Bulletin of the Florence Redeployment Training Area appeared in the records of the 38th. That was Number 30 of that publication and the items published in it, its masthead proclaimed, were "Official Orders of this Headquarters." It was signed by George W. Fair, AGD, adjutant general, "by command of Brigadier General George W. Fair."

Interestingly, and further anticipating the imminent disbanding of the unit, the Official Bulletin of the Florence Redeployment Training Area of the Fifth

Army noted on July 5 that the Area's new telephone number, effective the day before, was LIQUIDATE 1811.

July 6 the 38th's Daily Bulletin announced that the regular professional and administrative officer of the day rosters were being discontinued. It added:

"An 'Officer of the Day' roster is hereby placed in effect. The tour of duty will be from 1100 hours to 1100 hours. The Officer of the Day will be responsible for handling cases of illness at other than regular Dispensary hours, and will handle such administrative matters as may arise in the absence of the Commanding Officer and his Staff. He will inspect the Guard at intervals during his tour of duty. The Officer of the Day will remain in the camp area during his tour of duty."

The single item in the Daily Bulletin of July 10, signed by Captain Snell by order of Lieutenant Colonel Pennington, announced that "All Coke bottles will be returned to the empty tent near the showers as soon as possible."

On July 12 the 38th headquarters received from the Fifth Army headquarters, office of the Surgeon, a letter dated July 10 from Brigadier General J. I. Martin, Fifth Army surgeon. It was addressed to members of the Fifth Army Medical Service. General Martin wrote:

"Two months have gone swiftly by since the resounding victory of our armed might over the enemy in Europe. In that brief interval, the military destinies of all of you have been reshaped and the part you will take in our nation's continuing battle against the forces of evil aggression has become clear. Some of you will carry the fight to the enemy in the Pacific; some will support the effort from the continental United States; some will be separated from the service and deservedly return to your homes and families.

"Now also, I have been ordered from Fifth Army for a new assignment. It is difficult to put into words the emotions which I feel upon this leavetaking. For anyone who has watched this medical service of ours develop from its formative stages in the early planned days of North Africa, and has seen it mature into the magnificent organization that functioned so well throughout the twenty hard months of the Italian campaign, such a leavetaking necessarily must fill the heart with sadness.

"But I go secure in the knowledge that those of you I leave behind will continue to carry high the standards of medical service established under such duress in the past, and that those of you who will accompany me toward our new goal will let Fifth Army's record serve you, as it will me, as a guiding light toward future accomplishment. For the superb spirit of cooperation and devotion to duty you have evidenced, I offer you my deeply heartfelt thanks. I shall be everlastingly proud of you. Good-bye, good luck, and may God bless you all."

That same day, July 10, the 38th's Daily Bulletin, listing Major Crawford and Major Rogers as officer of the day and alternate, respectively, had but one notation:

"All Coke bottles will be returned to the empty tent near the showers as soon as possible."

The Daily Bulletin of July 13, however, contained detailed instructions relating to the return of military personnel to the United States. "The objective of return to the U.S." was stated:

"a. There are two principal purposes for moving units to the United States for redeployment: first, to permit the major command to which the unit will be assigned in the United States an opportunity to prepare and recondition the unit for futher service; and second, to permit the recuperation, rehabilitation and recovery of personnel of the unit.

"b. It is essential, particularly in overseas commands, that unit commanders and personnel be fully informed regarding both purposes. In this connection all personnel of such units must be informed that:

"(1) The War Department will authorize their being ordered, at Government expense, to travel to their homes or other designated place in the United States for a period of recuperation (not to exceed thirty [30] days), except when such action is precluded by military necessity.

"(2) Movement of individuals (except personnel in AAF flight and air echelons moving by air) to their homes, or other points chosen for period of recuperation, will be made through reception stations in order that transportation may be planned and utilized in such manner as to secure proper rail accommodations for all personnel."

Further recognition of the work of the 38th Evacuation Hospital was reported in the Daily Bulletin's issue of July 20, 1945—Volume IV Number 201—in an extract of General Orders No. 89 Headquarters Fifth Army 17 July, which revealed:

"The 38th Evacuation Hospital has been awarded the 'Meritorious Service Unit Plaque' for superior performance of duty in the accomplishment of exceptionally difficult tasks from 1 March to 30 April 1945, in Italy.

"All personnel in the unit are entitled to wear the Meritorious Service Unit Insignia as long as they are assigned or attached to the unit.

"The Insignia, a two-inch square of olive drab cloth with a yellow laurel wreath, will be worn centered on the outside half of the right sleeve of the service coat and shirt, with the points of the laurel wreath up, the lower edge of the insignia 4 inches above the end of the sleeve. Insignia will be obtained and distributed as soon as possible."

Not a word was in the Daily Bulletin of July 24 signed by Captain Snell as adjutant by order of Lieu-

Lieutenant Hallie Almond of Charlotte caught laughing, with Captain Perry, evidently because she appears to be posing as the unit's chief nurse.

tenant Colonel Pennington, except the listing of Captain Wright as officer of the day and Captain Collins as alternate. The same was true of next day's Bulletin, except that Captain Collins was officer of the day and Captain Gay was alternate and announcement was made of a Protestant service that evening at seven o'clock at the Baptist Church in Florence. The next day the Bulletin announced the "promotion of Mr. Walter H. King to chief warrant officer, effective 18 July." That same day Captain Gay was the last of the 38th's officers from Charlotte to serve as officer of the day. Captain Bard was alternate. Three days later the Bulletin announced the promotion of Second Lieutenant Elizabeth Gloser to be first lieutenant, effective July 25. August 1 the Bulletin again was blank. Major Crawford was officer of the day and Major Rogers was alternate. The August 3 Bulletin also reported nothing happening in the unit. Captain Letterese and Major Yankauer were officer of the day and alternate. The next day's Bulletin was the same, except that Major Yankauer was the officer of the day and Captain Pugh was alternate. Sunday, August 5, with Captain Pugh and Captain Doubilet on duty as officer of the day and alternate, and Monday, with Captain Doubilet and Captain Nowacki in those roles, passed with no activity reported. The last issue of the 38th's Daily Bulletin to be preserved in the unit's collection of materials from which its members hoped to evolve its history was that of Tuesday, August 7, 1945. It was Volume IV, Number 218. It offers no eloquent valedictory. It contains only the OD roster, "By order of Lieutenant Colonel Pennington" and signed by Captain E. M. Snell, adjutant, with Captain Nowacki officer of the day and Captain McGrath alternate.

28

A casual examination of the 38th Hospital's admissions and dispositions records, which survive fortunately in detail, will reveal readily that the award of the Meritorious Service plaque to the unit was deserved.

An analysis of the work done by the hospital, for instance, during its stay at Beau Site, Tunis, Tunisia, prepared and released November 4, 1943, by Captain George C. Snyder, the registrar, and covering the period from the opening of the hospital there on June 21, 1943, to the closing on the following August 24, reveals:

TOTAL ADMISSIONS   2940

Status:

Disease (American)	1963
Injuries and wounds (American)	826
Others (Dis., inj. and wounds)	102
P.O.W. (Dis., inj. and wounds)	49

The 2940 admissions consisted of:

American	2789
British	59
French	7
Civilian	36
P.O.W.	49

Battle Casualties:

American	346
British	2
French	5
P.O.W. (German, Italian)	14

Total patients transferred to other hospitals	1251
Total patients discharged to duty	1671
Total AWOL	7
Total deaths	11
Total number of diagnoses	3328

An analysis of the period from the opening of the hospital five miles north of Paestum, Italy, on September 29 to its closing October 15 discloses continued activity in the opening phase of the service in Italy:

TOTAL ADMISSIONS   1544

Status:

Disease (American)	1336
Injuries and wounds (American)	144
Other units (Dis., inj., wounds)	64
P.O.W. (Dis., inj., wounds)	0

The 1544 admissions consisted of:

American	1480
British	24
French	0
Civilian	40
P.O.W.	0

Forty-three Americans and one British were listed as battle casualties; total patients transferred to other hospitals, 746; total patients discharged to duty, 761; total deaths, 2; total AWOL, 35.

From Paestum the hospital moved to Caserta, where it was stationed from October 16 to November 6. During this three-week period, Captain Snyder's analysis of the detailed records of the unit reveals, the hospital admitted 1,389 patients, classified as: disease, 541 Americans; injuries, 262 Americans; battle casualties, 551 Americans; other units, diseases, injuries, and wounds, 23; and P.O.W., 12. Patients transferred to other hospitals numbered 1,073; discharged to duty, 286; deaths, 17; AWOLs, 13; total diagnoses, 1,798.

The bitterness of the enemy resistance during the four months after the 38th transferred from the Caserta station is quickly revealed in the hospital records from its opening three miles south of Vairano, Italy, to its closing on March 24, 1944, after 137 days of operation. Some of the more important figures of the analysis provided by Major Snyder include:

Total admissions, 9,793; total diagnoses, 11,657; admissions for disease, 5,642; injury, 1,046; for battle casualties, 3,105. Of the 9,793 admitted, 9,527 were Americans, 69 were British, 8 were Canadian, 22 French, 60 Italian, and 43 were war prisoners. The battle casualty figures showed: 3,016 American; 7 British, 1 Canadian; 15 French, 7 Italian, and 38 were prisoners of war. Only 63 patients died during the Vairano period, and 111 were listed as AWOL.

Only 311 admissions to the hospital were recorded during its short stay, from March 29 through April 7, two miles southeast of Carinola. Of these patients, 301 were Americans and only 10 were battle casualties. There were no deaths.

It was a far different story, however, at Nettuno. During the two-month operation there, following the Anzio landings, admissions to the hospital numbered

Chaplain Kirkpatrick, right, greets incoming Chaplain Sansom, who succeeded Chaplain Jones.

Major Snyder's next analysis, dated October 20, 1944, revealed:

"The 38th Evacuation Hospital officially opened at 1300 hours, 17 July 1944 at Cecina, Italy, when a detail took over 18 patients from the 33rd Field Hospital. The main hospital opened at 1200 hours, 19 July 1944, 8 miles North of Cecina (Route 168). The hospital was closed at 0700 hours, 13 September, 1944. Forty-five patients were moved to the new hospital location at Pisa."

Of the 2,390 patients admitted during this period of almost two months, 440 were battle casualties, 417 were injured otherwise, and 1,533 were listed under disease. Of the 440 battle casualties, 362 were American soldiers, 24 were British soldiers, 11 were Brazilian, 24 were civilians, and 19 were war prisoners. 25 deaths were recorded.

On December 2, 1944, Warrant Officer Frank B. Pedrick, acting registrar, provided the analysis of the Pisa operation:

"The 38th Evacuation Hospital officially opened at 0900 hours, 15 September 1944 at Pisa, Italy. On opening day 27 patients were admitted thru Receiving and 45 patients were transferred from Ward 602, 8 miles North of Cecina, Italy, to the new hospital wards. The hospital closed 1700 hours, 3 November 1944 after being flooded out and 529 patients evacuated."

Total admissions were 2,853. Injuries were 424 and battle casualties 704. Of the 2,853 admissions, American Army personnel totaled 2,091, British 386, and Brazilian 263; 27 were war prisoners. In the battle casualties category, 524 were American, 32 British, 73

7,979. Battle casualties and injuries exceeded other illnesses. The totals from April 9 through June 7 were: disease, 3,733; injury, 789; battle casualties, 3,457. Of the 7,979 admissions, 6,943 were Americans. The largest group not American was composed of prisoners of war, 767, all of them battle casualties.

Of these almost 8,000 admissions, dispositions included 1,398 returned to duty, 6,230 evacuated to bases, 35 AWOL, and 104 died. Battle casualties generally were not severe, as indicated by the average stay of 1.2 days in the hospital of those in that category.

From Nettuno the hospital moved to Doria Pamphilia, Rome, for a stay of three weeks—from June 9, 1944, to June 30. Total admissions there were 2,470 patients. Ten deaths occurred. Disease accounted for three-fourths of the admissions. Half the patients were returned to duty after an average stay in the hospital of 5.4 days.

The same general level of work by the hospital was recorded at the next station, Major Snyder's analysis reveals. The hospital opened "officially at 0900 hours, 2 July, 1944, 4 miles North of Massa Marittima, Italy, and closed 1000 hours, 17 July, 1944, after 16 days of operation," and during that period admitted 1,860 patients, of whom 598 were listed under disease, 229 injury, and 1,033 battle casualties. Of the 1,860 admitted, 1,797 were Americans, and 36 were war prisoners. 10 died during the period there.

The 38th Evacuation Hospital unit sailed from New York on August 6, 1942. That date marked the beginning of its overseas service. The dance at Montecatini, as the ticket reveals, celebrated two and a half years away from American soil, during which it had achieved an enviable record of caring for many thousands of ill or wounded American and Allied service men and women, war prisoners, and natives of the sectors in which it had been located during those thirty months.

This picture of Lieutenant Russell was
made the day she said goodbye to Italy
and her overseas service.

Brazilian, 5 Italian, and 25 prisoners of war. 23 deaths
were recorded, 1,161 soldiers were returned to duty,
and 19 were reported AWOL.

The next analysis provides a summary of the hospital's operation at Montecatini, a period covering more
than five months. Introducing this report, the continuing analysis reveals:

"The hospital opened at 1530 hours, 4 November
1944 at Lucca, Italy, when 7 officers, 7 nurses, and 10
enlisted men set up 15 beds for emergency cases only.
The main hospital opened at 0800 hours, 17 November
1944 at Montecatini. The installation at Lucca closed
1000 hours, 15 November 1944. The hospital at Montecatini closed 0930 hours, 20 April 1945 after having
been in operation 157 days."

During the Montecatini operation, the summary discloses, more than 9,000 patients were admitted, of
whom 8,705 were American service personnel, 170
were British, 16 were Brazilian, 1 was French Army
and 24 were Italian Army and 1 Italian Navy, 73
were civilians and 39 were prisoners of war. Battle
casualties totaled 1,813, of which 1,758 were American
soldiers, and 39 were war prisoners. Amazingly, only
10 deaths occurred. Almost eight times that many, 79,
were reported AWOL. Diagnoses, reported in detail
in the complete analysis, totaled 10,163.

From Montecatini the hospital moved for one week
to Marzabotto. The continuing analysis records:

"The hospital opened 0100 hours, 20 April 1945,
when Platoon 'A' with 2 officers, 6 nurses, and 15 men
took over 27 patients from 'B' Platoon, 32nd Field
Hospital, 2 miles South of Paretta, Italy. Main hospital
opened 0100 hours, 22 April 1945, at Marzabotto, Italy.
The hospital was closed 1500 hours, 29 April 1945."

Battle casualties and injuries accounted for all but
90 admissions during the brief stay at Marzabotto.
Here the battle casualties were proportionately heavier
by far than at the other locations. Of the 948 admissions that week, 820 were casualties. But more than
half of all admissions were prisoner of war patients—
581. American casualties totaled 183. Brazilian casualties were next heaviest, 37. Deaths numbered 11.

After Marzabotto the hospital was set up at Fidenza.
Of this period of service the continuing analysis of
admissions and dispositions reveals:

"The hospital opened at 2000 hours, 30 April 1945,
two (2) miles South of Fidenza, Italy, and closed at
0800 hours, 26 May 1945. 136 patients remaining were
transferred to the new location at Salsomaggiore, Italy."

Total admissions during the almost one month at
the Fidenza location were 1,165, of which a little more
than one-half, 651, were listed in the disease category.
Injured patients totaled 279 and battle casualties 235.
But at Fidenza considerably more than one-third of
the patients, or 479, were war prisoners, and almost
one-half these prisoner patients, 215, were casualties of
the fighting. Ten deaths were recorded and 42 AWOLs.

A report of the surgical service of the 38th Evacuation Hospital during the five months preceding June 1,
1945, as compiled from dispositions of patients, survives
among the records of the unit to provide interesting
statistical information.

The report, summarized to reveal quickly totals in
the various categories, shows that during the January
1—May 31, 1945, period, the Charlotte unit handled
4,697 cases, of which 3,724 involved American personnel, 721 were war prisoners, 181 were Brazilian, and
the remaining 71 included Italian, British, South African, Russian, and French.

Of the 4,697 patients treated, the figures further
show, 1,032 were returned to duty, 736 were sent to
convalescent hospitals, and 2,911 were transferred to
hospitals in the rear. Eighteen deaths occurred during
the five-month period.

The figures relating to American personnel reveal
that of the 3,724 cases, 1,561 were battle casualties,
939 were injuries, 1,160 were disease, and 64 were
self-inflicted wounds. Only five Americans died.

The great majority of the prisoner of war cases were
battle casualties, 636 of the 721. The other 85 cases
were in the disease category. Seven deaths were recorded in this grouping.

Of the other foreign patients, Italian civilians, 29
in all, made up the largest group. Forty-nine Italians

were treated. Nineteen British composed the next largest non-American group.

A study of the detailed report shows the 38th's surgeons performed operations of numerous kinds, the largest single type of which included debridements, the removal of foreign substances of many kinds—bullets, shell fragments, metal pieces, dirt, and grass from exploding mines—numbering 1,758. In general surgery, the report further reveals, the largest category was hemorrhoidectomies, 46; next largest, appendectomies, 39.

The records of the 38th include, too, for that same period, with the exception of an interval of less than three weeks—January 1, 1945, through May 12, 1945—an analysis of admissions that gives additional important figures indicating the extent of the unit's work in this closing period of the war.

Total admissions during those four and a half months, including 705 patients remaining January 1, 1945, numbered 8,987, of which 2,727 were listed as battle casualties. More than half the total, however, were classified under diseases—4,820. The remaining, 1,440, were admitted for the treatment of injuries.

More than four-fifths of the patients were Americans —7,393, or 82.2 per cent. The next largest group, 1,044 or 11.6 per cent, were prisoners of war. Sixty-eight point six of the battle casualties, 1,871 of the 2,727, were personnel of the American Army; almost all the remainder, 770, or 28.2 per cent, were prisoners of war. Almost nine-tenths, 89.4 per cent, of those treated in the disease category were Americans. Almost five per cent of the total, 234, were war prisoners. The comparatively few other patients in the various categories were British, Brazilian, Italian, and French military personnel and civilians.

In the final weeks of the 38th's hospital operations and contemporaneously with the encampment at Salsomaggiore, Major L. E. Fleming had been serving at a little substation hospital at Alessandria, a few miles southwest of Milan. Shortly before the unit left Salsomaggiore he returned to it, and when at the Florence Redeployment Training Area in the late summer Lieutenant Colonel Pennington was transferred, Major Fleming succeeded him and served as the 38th's last commanding officer.

"The hospital, of course, had been closed since late June, about a week before we left Salsomaggiore," Dr. Fleming recalls, "and at Florence our activities in the main were connected with the transfer of our personnel. Some were being sent home for discharge and some were slated to go to other units for further service, probably in the war in the Pacific. But the war with Japan was over, of course, in late August and so in late September we were pretty well deactivated. The enlisted men were the first to go. I remember at the last we were quartered in an old tobacco factory at Florence and I think that the Catholic chaplain, Captain Natalini and I were the last ones out." He got home, he remembers, on October 10.

"The 38th had ended a notable career of service," Dr. Fleming summarizes the more than three years of experience since the unit's beginning training with activation at Fort Bragg. "I wonder if people today realize that we handled some 50,000 patients."

Pharmacist Joe Neil believes he was the last of the 38th's enlisted personnel to leave Florence. "I got orders to go to Naples where I'd catch the ship home," he remembers. "I had been staying in a tent near the University of Florence and I hadn't had any duties to amount to anything since the closing of the hospital about a week before we left Salsomaggiore. It must have been about the middle of August when I left Florence, the last enlisted man of the 38th, as far as I knew, to leave.

"At Naples I hung around about ten days waiting for the boat on which I was to go home. While I was in Naples I was billeted in a stable down at the race track. About the end of August I got my ship and we started for home. We were going through the Strait of Gibraltar on September 1, I remember, when we heard on the radio that the Japanese had formally surrendered to General MacArthur on board the Missouri."

Sergeant Neil was separated from the service at Fort Bragg on September 15.

POSTSCRIPT

Twenty-three years after his operation performed by Major William R. Pitts of Charlotte, Richard Tregaskis was still covering the wars. In a letter written in Honolulu on October 31, 1966, in reply to a request for permission to quote passages from *Invasion Diary*, Mr. Tregaskis granted permission and expressed his delight that the history of the 38th Evacuation Hospital unit was to be published.

"It was a fine outfit and their innumerable good works deserve all possible notice," Mr. Tregaskis wrote.

"You certainly are welcome to quote what you need from *Invasion Diary*. Among many other Americans, I owe at least my life to the 38th Evac.

"I say 'at *least* my life' because Bill Pitts did such a good job with my bit of neuro-surgery that I've been able to go on walking, talking and writing just about as before.

"There were some residual effects, it is true, but I was able to go back to the wars as correspondent, first for International News Service and then the *Saturday Evening Post*.

"I went to the Normandy Beachhead, then across France, Belgium, Holland, and into Germany with the First Army, then back to the Pacific to fly with the B-29's and a torpedo squadron from the *USS Ticonderoga* making bombing strikes into Japan. When the war ended I went into Japan with the Military Government, to write about them.

"Subsequently, I was involved as a correspondent in many of the small wars which broke out at the conclusion of the WW II hostilities. This Leninistic Cycle started right after World War II and still confronts us in Vietnam and elsewhere.

"I was involved as a Correspondent in China, Indo-China, Malaya, Indonesia, Korea, the Formosa Straits and most recently, in Vietnam.

"I also found time to be involved in writing screenplays and teleplays, mostly concerned with these wars. In case you have been watching the TV late shows, I should point out I had author's credit for *Guadalcanal Diary, Force of Arms, Mission Over Korea, Wild Blue Yonder*, and *Fair Wind to Java*. I also wrote scripts for the television series called *Winston Churchill, Flight, Steve Canyon* and *Blue Angels*. And I've had a series of books too—most of them the eye-witness, non-fiction kind: *Seven Leagues to Paradise, X-15 Diary, John F. Kennedy and PT-109*; two novels, *Stronger Than Fear* and *Last Plane to Shanghai*; most recently *Vietnam*

Captain John S. Anderson, of Wadena, Minnesota, a Green Beret officer, at Dak To, a Special Forces outpost in the mountains of South Vietnam near the Laotian border. Richard Tregaskis at right. Note camp in background.

Diary. Because of *Vietnam Diary*, I was awarded the CBS George Polk Award for hazardous reporting in 1964.

"For the last couple of years I've been working on my third novel, *China Bomb*. It has to do with the Asian war situation, and in the course of research for the book my wife and I travelled as far as Ladakh, on India's Northwest Frontier with China. At the time of China's detonation of the first A-bomb in 1964, we were as close to their nuclear testing ground in Sinkiang as you could be without actually being in China.

"That was up in the Indian Karakoram, a collection of horrific mountains, the roof of the world. In the course of that trip, and amidst those very primitive Tibetan surroundings, I injured a foot in a riding accident and nearly lost it to gangrene.

"But the doc saved the extremity, I've managed to finish the book and it is scheduled for publication next year."

ROSTER OF OFFICERS

[List gives name, serial number, rank on date assigned to unit, branch of service, date assigned to unit.]

Whittier, Raymond W.	O-4098	Colonel	M.C.	Apr. 15, 1942
Angen, Willard F.	O-23596	Captain	M.C.	Apr. 15, 1942
Yankauer, Alfred, Jr.	O-420765	1st Lt.	Med. Res.	Apr. 15, 1942
Burwell, Lewis C., Jr.	O-460893	Captain	M.A.C.	Apr. 20, 1942
Augustine, Robert W.	O-464167	Captain	M.C.	Apr. 28, 1942
Calder, Duncan G., Jr.	O-345368	Captain	M.C.	Apr. 15, 1942
Felts, James R., Jr.	O-429484	2nd. Lt.	M.A.C.	Apr. 15, 1942
Fleming, Laurence E.	O-427967	Major	M.C.	Apr. 15, 1942
Gay, Charles H., Sr.	O-468098	Captain	M.C.	May 8, 1942
Hawes, George A.	O-266113	Captain	M.C.	Apr. 15, 1942
Hoffman, Milo J.	O-356321	1st Lt.	D.C.	Apr. 15, 1942
Imes, Pat R.	O-469603	Major	M.C.	May 11, 1942
Jones, Otis	O-402856	Captain	CHAP	Apr. 15, 1942
Jones, Otis H.	O-415623	Captain	M.C.	Apr. 15, 1942
Kavanagh, William P.	O-402444	Captain	M.C.	Apr. 15, 1942
Kendrick, Vaiden B.	O-415628	Major	D.C.	Apr. 15, 1942
Leonard, William P., Jr.	O-356437	Captain	M.C.	Apr. 15, 1942
McCall, Robert E., Jr.	O-301748	Captain	M.C.	Apr. 15, 1942
Matthews, William C.	O-415603	1st Lt.	M.C.	Apr. 15, 1942
Medearis, William F.	O-461017	Captain	M.A.C.	May 2, 1942
Miller, Robert P.	O-463455	1st Lt.	M.C.	Apr. 27, 1942
Montgomery, John C.	O-415606	Captain	M.C.	May 1, 1942
Montgomery, John C.	O-281845	Captain	M.C.	Apr. 15, 1942
Munroe, Colin A.	O-463046	1st Lt.	M.C.	Apr. 27, 1942
Arnold, Lowndes W.	O-174131	Captain	Q.M.C.	Apr. 18, 1942
Munroe, Henry S., Jr.	O-418220	Captain	M.C.	Apr. 15, 1942
Pennington, William H.	O-460894	Major	M.C.	May 2, 1942
Perry, Claud W., Jr.	O-464778	1st Lt.	M.C.	May 1, 1942
Perry, Glenn G.	O-441331	Captain	M.C.	Apr. 15, 1942
Perryman, Olin C.	O-460894	1st Lt.	M.C.	Apr. 27, 1942
Pickens, Stanton W.	O-436406	Captain	M.A.C.	Apr. 15, 1942
Pitts, William R.	O-468119	Major	M.C.	May 6, 1942
Porter, Charles B.	O-448880	1st Lt.	M.C.	Apr. 15, 1942
Query, Richard Z., Jr.	O-403448	Major	M.C.	May 1, 1942
Rowe, George C.	O-446490	1st Lt.	M.C.	Apr. 15, 1942
Sanger, Paul W.	O-335946	Major	M.C.	Apr. 15, 1942
Schirmer, Robert H.	O-419555	1st Lt.	M.C.	Apr. 15, 1942
Snyder, George C.	O-430356	Captain	M.A.C.	Apr. 15, 1942
Sotirion, George A.	O-445223	1st Lt.	M.C.	Apr. 15, 1942
Stith, Robert B.	O-432226	Captain	M.C.	Apr. 15, 1942
Tyson, Thomas D., Jr.	O-475912	Captain	M.C.	June 3, 1942
Walker, Bernard N.	O-300485	Captain	D.C.	Apr. 15, 1942
White, Thomas P.	O-246499	Lt. Colonel	M.C.	Apr. 15, 1942
Williams, McChord	O-441324	Captain	M.C.	Apr. 15, 1942

Wood, George T., Jr.	O-445228	Major	M.C.	Apr. 15, 1942
McGrath, Frank B.	O-322566	1st Lt.	M.C.	July 21, 1942
Dunn, James W.	O-321129	1st Lt.	Q.M.C.	July 14, 1942
Powers, John S.	O-1696547	1st Lt.	M.C.	July 14, 1942
Pugh, George E.	O-368304	1st Lt.	M.C.	July 14, 1942
Evans, William Jr.	O-1696410	Captain	M.C.	July 22, 1942
Nowacki, Stanley M.	O-1696171	1st Lt.	M.C.	July 25, 1942
Bauchspies, Rollin L.	O-17819	Lt. Colonel	M.C.	Oct. 15, 1942
Guenther, Augustus J. D.	O-422216	1st Lt.	M.A.C.	Dec. 15, 1942
Kirkpatrick, James E.	O-489038	1st Lt.	Ch.C.	May 28, 1943
Snell, Eugene M.	W-2108356	WO(jg)	AUS	Apr. 19, 1943
Pedrick, Frank B.	W-2108369	WO(jg)	AUS	July 1, 1943
Clune, James Patrick	O-477335	Captain	Ch.C.	Sept. 8, 1943
Denning, Walter S.	O-262688	Captain	M.C.	Oct. 9, 1943
Pomper, Irving	O-360277	Captain	M.C.	Oct. 23, 1943
Wright, Harold S.	O-1690564	1st Lt.	M.C.	Oct. 29, 1943
Harney, James N.	O-449572	Captain	M.C.	Nov. 19, 1943
Mitchell, Charles F.	O-302623	Captain	D.C.	Nov. 24, 1943
Boyd, Kenneth B.	O-485804	Major	M.C.	Jan. 18, 1944
Crawford, John M.	O-335591	Captain	M.C.	Jan. 21, 1944
Jacobson, Wyman E.	O-404322	Captain	M.C.	Feb. 18, 1944
Carmouche, Ernest N.	O-414229	Captain	M.C.	Mar. 8, 1944
Grosselfinger, Harold W.	O-468659	Captain	M.C.	Mar. 16, 1944
Doubilet, Henry	O-439406	Captain	M.C.	Mar. 16, 1944
Rasmussen, Earl	O-441328	Captain	M.C.	Mar. 26, 1944
Sansom, Cecil P.	O-476514	Captain	Ch.C.	Apr. 15, 1944
Boyd, Granberry D., Jr.	O-249297	Lt. Colonel	M.C.	Apr. 27, 1944
Genin, Francis G.	O-493707	Captain	M.C.	May 20, 1944
Crawley, Walter G., Jr.	O-359694	Captain	M.C.	June 22, 1944
Stone, Walter V.	O-361743	Captain	M.C.	June 24, 1944
Raymer, Jack L.	O-368095	Captain	D.C.	July 11, 1944
Purdy, Charles I.	O-1691737	2nd Lt.	M.A.C.	July 12, 1944
Kenny, John L.	O-480101	Captain	Ch.C.	July 14, 1944
Natalini, Carlo A.	O-1534581	Captain	M.A.C.	July 29, 1944
Warren, Robert O. Y.	O-475486	Lt. Colonel	M.C.	Aug. 6, 1944
Crotts, Hylton K.	O-296270	Captain	D.C.	Oct. 23, 1944
Blake, Clayton A., Jr.	O-347363	Captain	D.C.	Oct. 27, 1944
Brelsford, Harold J.	O-1546917	1st Lt.	M.A.C.	Jan. 9, 1945
Crawford, William B.	O-1684058	Major	M.C.	Feb. 1, 1945
Victorine, Charles	O-544423	1st Lt.	D.C.	Feb. 6, 1945
Monteleone, Joseph	O-367945	Captain	M.C.	Feb. 20, 1945
Bard, Eli	O-347704	Captain	M.C.	Mar. 4, 1945
Speer, David S.	O-444474	1st Lt.	M.C.	Mar. 30, 1945
Payne, Joseph T.	O-462502	Captain	M.C.	Apr. 6, 1945
Russell, Walter A.	O-470914	Captain	M.C.	Apr. 10, 1945
LeClerc, Jean N.	O-462199	Captain	M.C.	Apr. 12, 1945
Brower, Robert A.	O-1541382	1st Lt.	M.A.C.	Apr. 12, 1945
Todd, John C.	O-1694300	Captain	D.C.	Apr. 20, 1945

ROSTER OF NURSES

[List gives name, serial number, rank on date assigned to unit,
branch of service, date assigned to unit.]

Almond, Hallie E.	N-741920	2nd Lt.	A.N.C.	Apr. 30, 1942
Barbee, Ruth I.	N-742318	2nd Lt.	A.N.C.	Apr. 30, 1942
Bell, Ida P.	N-741921	2nd Lt.	A.N.C.	Apr. 30, 1942
Bivens, Wilma G.	N-742319	2nd Lt.	A.N.C.	Apr. 30, 1942
Blandford, Mary F.	N-742320	2nd Lt.	A.N.C.	Apr. 30, 1942
Burgess, Violet O.	N-741923	2nd Lt.	A.N.C.	Apr. 30, 1942
Calton, F.	N-742380	2nd Lt.	A.N.C.	Apr. 30, 1942
Camenisch, Helen J.	N-742321	2nd Lt.	A.N.C.	May 3, 1942
Coggins, C.	N-742322	2nd Lt.	A.N.C.	Apr. 30, 1942
Fliedner, Martha G.	N-741926	2nd Lt.	A.N.C.	Apr. 30, 1942
Frye, L.	N-741972	2nd Lt.	A.N.C.	Apr. 30, 1942
Fullbright, Bessie V.	N-741927	2nd Lt.	A.N.C.	Apr. 30, 1942
Greene, M. K.	N-742324	2nd Lt.	A.N.C.	Apr. 30, 1942
Haltiwanger, Carolyn T.	N-742325	2nd Lt.	A.N.C.	Apr. 30, 1942
Harman, Josephine Lee	N-741928	2nd Lt.	A.N.C.	Apr. 30, 1942
Hough, Bertha E.	N-741929	2nd Lt.	A.N.C.	Apr. 30, 1942
Johnson, Beatrice E.	N-742326	2nd Lt.	A.N.C.	Apr. 30, 1942
LaChance, Lola J.	N-742548	2nd Lt.	A.N.C.	May 18, 1942
Martin, Winnie Rae	N-742327	2nd Lt.	A.N.C.	Apr. 30, 1942
McCain, Ruby E.	N-741930	2nd Lt.	A.N.C.	Apr. 30, 1942
McElwee, R. G.	N-741931	2nd Lt.	A.N.C.	Apr. 30, 1942
Mills, Clementine A.	N-742328	2nd Lt.	A.N.C.	Apr. 30, 1942
Mizelle, Margaret B.	N-742338	2nd Lt.	A.N.C.	Apr. 30, 1942
Moran, Sara Marion	N-742329	2nd Lt.	A.N.C.	Apr. 30, 1942
Neely, Vera Mae	N-742330	2nd Lt.	A.N.C.	Apr. 30, 1942
Neil, M. A.	N-727061	2nd Lt.	A.N.C.	May 13, 1942
Payne, Minnie T.	N-742330	2nd Lt.	A.N.C.	Apr. 30, 1942
Pegram, Martha	N-742382	2nd Lt.	A.N.C.	Apr. 30, 1942
Russell, Lela O.	N-742558	2nd Lt.	A.N.C.	May 10, 1942
Shields, Nelia C.	N-742333	2nd Lt.	A.N.C.	Apr. 30, 1942
Shipp, Rosamond S.	N-742334	2nd Lt.	A.N.C.	Apr. 30, 1942
Schronce, J. B.	N-742339	2nd Lt.	A.N.C.	Apr. 30, 1942
Simmons, Hazel Ann	N-741933	2nd Lt.	A.N.C.	Apr. 30, 1942
Thompson, Margaret L.	N-741934	2nd Lt.	A.N.C.	Apr. 30, 1942
Webber, Charlotte Jean	N-742335	2nd Lt.	A.N.C.	May 3, 1942
Wells, Elva Earle	N-741935	2nd Lt.	A.N.C.	Apr. 30, 1942
Wills, Christine	N-742559	2nd Lt.	A.N.C.	Apr. 30, 1942
Wingo, Barbara L.	N-742336	2nd Lt.	A.N.C.	May 14, 1942
York, J. O.	N-742560	2nd Lt.	A.N.C.	Apr. 30, 1942
Bachoka, Margaret P.	N-725056	2nd Lt.	A.N.C.	Aug. 5, 1942
Benante, Lorraine M.	N-730749	2nd Lt.	A.N.C.	Aug. 5, 1942
Brice, Nina V.	N-725659	2nd Lt.	A.N.C.	Aug. 5, 1942
Burnham, Audrey J.	N-730741	2nd Lt.	A.N.C.	Aug. 5, 1942
Carroll, Bernice	N-730801	2nd Lt.	A.N.C.	Aug. 5, 1942

Conturso, Katherine	N-723069	2nd Lt.	A.N.C.	Aug. 5, 1942
Cox, Marion J.	N-725691	2nd Lt.	A.N.C.	Aug. 5, 1942
Culley, Mary A.	N-730682	2nd Lt.	A.N.C.	Aug. 5, 1942
Doskow, Deborah L.	N-723053	2nd Lt.	A.N.C.	Aug. 5, 1942
Dexheimer, Vera H.	N-730663	2nd Lt.	A.N.C.	Aug. 5, 1942
Gaynor, Helen A.	N-723143	2nd Lt.	A.N.C.	Aug. 5, 1942
Guyett, Edith E.	N-723054	2nd Lt.	A.N.C.	Aug. 5, 1942
Heaton, Annette M.	N-730622	2nd Lt.	A.N.C.	Aug. 5, 1942
Hirtz, Rosalie D.	N-723055	2nd Lt.	A.N.C.	Aug. 5, 1942
Hustak, Mildred	N-723071	2nd Lt.	A.N.C.	Aug. 5, 1942
Killeen, Elizabeth E.	N-723067	2nd Lt.	A.N.C.	Aug. 5, 1942
Logan, Ruth O.	N-725735	2nd Lt.	A.N.C.	Aug. 5, 1942
Meyers, Claire S.	N-725732	2nd Lt.	A.N.C.	Aug. 5, 1942
Pilger, Gladys P.	N-723047	2nd Lt.	A.N.C.	Aug. 5, 1942
Pisinsky, Pauline B.	N-723118	2nd Lt.	A.N.C.	Aug. 5, 1942
Radigan, Cathaleen	N-723052	2nd Lt.	A.N.C.	Aug. 5, 1942
Robbins, Frances L.	N-725661	2nd Lt.	A.N.C.	Aug. 5, 1942
Monson, Jeannette A.	N-741551	2nd Lt.	A.N.C.	Feb. 12, 1943
Brady, Ann K.	N-722895	2nd Lt.	A.N.C.	Feb. 28, 1943
D'Auria, Clara R.	N-723179	2nd Lt.	A.N.C.	Feb. 28, 1943
Jensen, Madeline L.	N-730829	2nd Lt.	A.N.C.	Mar. 1, 1943
Gloser, Elizabeth	N-730831	2nd Lt.	A.N.C.	Mar. 1, 1943
Jones, Juanita	N-729263	2nd Lt.	A.N.C.	Aug. 20, 1943
Choate, Faye	N-725513	2nd Lt.	A.N.C.	Aug. 26, 1943
LeBlanc, Lillian I.	N-721836	2nd Lt.	A.N.C.	Sept. 2, 1943
Steffee, Janet L.	N-725228	2nd Lt.	A.N.C.	Sept. 4, 1943
Rodstein, Leah	N-759140	2nd Lt.	A.N.C.	Sept. 4, 1943
Cornish, Gene F.	N-731472	2nd Lt.	A.N.C.	Sept. 8, 1943
Green, Sara J.	R-495	2nd Lt.	H.D.	Sept. 25, 1943
Satre, Pearl M.	N-731251	2nd Lt.	A.N.C.	Dec. 17, 1943
Griffen, Mary E.	N-721252	2nd Lt.	A.N.C.	Dec. 19, 1943
Fruth, Christine	N-743467	2nd Lt.	A.N.C.	Jan. 9, 1944
Smith, Edna E.	N-720540	2nd Lt.	A.N.C.	Feb. 25, 1944
Dierker, Ruth	N-730288	2nd Lt.	A.N.C.	Mar. 20, 1944
Clarke, Lula A.	N-742460	2nd Lt.	A.N.C.	Apr. 1, 1944
Tetzlaff, Marie A.	N-728712	2nd Lt.	A.N.C.	Apr. 6, 1944
Johnson, Helen A.	N-742145	2nd Lt.	A.N.C.	Apr. 20, 1944
McMahon, Lillian A.	N-721794	1st Lt.	A.N.C.	Apr. 20, 1944
Gross, Nellie R.	N-760269	2nd Lt.	A.N.C.	June 22, 1944
Bertrand, Lucille B.	N-726172	2nd Lt.	A.N.C.	Sept. 22, 1944
Victor, Julia E.	N-730242	2nd Lt.	A.N.C.	Oct. 29, 1944
Gilliam, Elsie I.	N-726914	2nd Lt.	A.N.C.	Oct. 30, 1944
Ellison, Adrienne J.	N-727531	2nd Lt.	A.N.C.	Oct. 30, 1944
Long, Angeline M.	N-724729	2nd Lt.	A.N.C.	Oct. 30, 1944
Townsend, Mary E.	N-720660	2nd Lt.	A.N.C.	Oct. 30, 1944
King, Marguerite M.	N-742965	1st Lt.	A.N.C.	Nov. 6, 1944
Wittler, Billie	N-741541	2nd Lt.	A.N.C.	Jan. 3, 1945
Swanson, Elizabeth A.	N-741617	1st Lt.	A.N.C.	Jan. 3, 1945
Robicheaux, Mabel M.	N-745299	1st Lt.	A.N.C.	Jan. 5, 1945
Miller, Lexie W.	N-721908	2nd Lt.	A.N.C.	Jan. 13, 1945
Perry, Catherine A.	N-753252	2nd Lt.	A.N.C.	Feb. 9, 1945
McVeigh, Charlotte R.	N-729192	2nd Lt.	A.N.C.	Mar. 29, 1945
Alexich, Darinka	N-741462	1st Lt.	A.N.C.	June 4, 1945
Jackson, Marion G.	N-720999	1st Lt.	A.N.C.	June 4, 1945
Knicely, Helena K.	N-724066	1st Lt.	A.N.C.	June 4, 1945

ROSTER OF ENLISTED MEN

[List gives name, serial number, rank on date assigned to unit,
branch of service, date assigned to unit.]

Johnson, Herbert L.	32035245	Staff Sergeant	M.D.	Apr. 15, 1942
Pedrick, Frank B.	33026855	Staff Sergeant	M.D.	Apr. 15, 1942
Reeves, Hurschel S.	6912228	Staff Sergeant	M.D.	Apr. 15, 1942
Snell, Eugene M.	33010965	Staff Sergeant	M.D.	Apr. 15, 1942
Elliott, Vincent J.	33021538	Sergeant	M.D.	Apr. 15, 1942
Pricskett, William J.	33027190	Sergeant	M.D.	Apr. 15, 1942
Schmidt, Edward F.	33026625	Sergeant	M.D.	Apr. 15, 1942
Simpson, Howard S.	33027357	Sergeant	M.D.	Apr. 15, 1942
Fenocchi, Amelio R.	32031893	Corporal	M.D.	Apr. 15, 1942
Auberger, Raymond W.	32032145	Private First Class	M.D.	Apr. 15, 1942
Behre, Stanley C.	33027502	Private First Class	M.D.	Apr. 15, 1942
Baker, Alex	36152277	Private First Class	M.D.	Apr. 15, 1942
Cook, Paul E. J.	6129481	Private First Class	M.D.	Apr. 15, 1942
Cox, Virgil H.	35121237	Private First Class	M.D.	Apr. 15, 1942
Cologgi, Louis F.	32035152	Private First Class	M.D.	Apr. 15, 1942
Comisar, Allen	36120865	Private First Class	M.D.	Apr. 15, 1942
Citron, Manuel	32032155	Private First Class	M.D.	Apr. 15, 1942
Cooper, Floyd M.	35121279	Private First Class	M.D.	Apr. 15, 1942
Darrow, Seymour E.	32069372	Private First Class	M.D.	Apr. 15, 1942
Dunkle, Clarence O.	33021532	Private First Class	M.D.	Apr. 15, 1942
Evans, Robert L.	32031984	Private First Class	M.D.	Apr. 15, 1942
Fluck, David E.	33021284	Private First Class	M.D.	Apr. 15, 1942
Foldie, George T.	36152493	Private First Class	M.D.	Apr. 15, 1942
Fairbrother, Warren L.	32035177	Private First Class	M.D.	Apr. 15, 1942
Groff, Jacob S.	32035038	Private First Class	M.D.	Apr. 15, 1942
Gleba, Joseph S.	33026412	Private First Class	M.D.	Apr. 15, 1942
Houghton, Frank H.	32032119	Private First Class	M.D.	Apr. 15, 1942
Hulse, Ernest B.	32032087	Private First Class	M.D.	Apr. 15, 1942
Hamashin, Lloyd J.	33032386	Private First Class	M.D.	Apr. 15, 1942
Jones, Gwynfryn T.	33020955	Private First Class	M.D.	Apr. 15, 1942
Jackson, Edward A.	33037506	Private First Class	M.D.	Apr. 15, 1942
Jacob, Meier	32035221	Private First Class	M.D.	Apr. 15, 1942
Laubengayer, Robert E.	32032177	Private First Class	M.D.	Apr. 15, 1942
Mitchell, John T.	32035103	Private First Class	M.D.	Apr. 15, 1942
Miccinelli, John	32031979	Private First Class	M.D.	Apr. 15, 1942
Pierson, Arthur W.	32035014	Private First Class	M.D.	Apr. 15, 1942
Purcel, Eugene J.	32031980	Private First Class	M.D.	Apr. 15, 1942
Piperato, Adam J.	33032500	Private First Class	M.D.	Apr. 15, 1942
Pekorosky, Joseph B.	33021002	Private First Class	M.D.	Apr. 15, 1942
Rarrick, Richard F.	32035003	Private First Class	M.D.	Apr. 15, 1942
Rau, Waldo J.	36152348	Private First Class	M.D.	Apr. 15, 1942
Rausch, Harry W.	32035114	Private First Class	M.D.	Apr. 15, 1942
Robinson, Richard B.	33031910	Private First Class	M.D.	Apr. 15, 1942
Saide, Abraham C. L.	32035148	Private First Class	M.D.	Apr. 15, 1942

Schueler, Herbert P.	32035230	Private First Class	M.D.	Apr. 15, 1942
Smith, William E.	32034950	Private First Class	M.D.	Apr. 15, 1942
Solomon, Charles A.	32004058	Private First Class	M.D.	Apr. 15, 1942
Savino, Dominic J.	32035109	Private First Class	M.D.	Apr. 15, 1942
Talbot, William F.	32032099	Private First Class	M.D.	Apr. 15, 1942
Tracy, Edward V.	32032126	Private First Class	M.D.	Apr. 15, 1942
Wollke, Charles	32032133	Private First Class	M.D.	Apr. 15, 1942
Waldron, Carl R.	32032100	Private First Class	M.D.	Apr. 15, 1942
Zielinski, Herman J.	32035151	Private First Class	M.D.	Apr. 15, 1942
Buchanan, James E.	32035110	Private	M.D.	Apr. 15, 1942
Bates, Willard F.	36152320	Private	M.D.	Apr. 15, 1942
Bittner, Theodore P.	36152368	Private	M.D.	Apr. 15, 1942
Bucher, Ralph C.	36152517	Private	M.D.	Apr. 15, 1942
Cotton, Russell B.	33040593	Private	M.D.	Apr. 15, 1942
Campione, Joseph J.	32032151	Private	M.D.	Apr. 15, 1942
Cieslinski, Martin T.	36152329	Private	M.D.	Apr. 15, 1942
Darling, Leslie R.	32032134	Private	M.D.	Apr. 15, 1942
Donnelly, Eugene R.	33032737	Private	M.D.	Apr. 15, 1942
Dunkel, Ezra W.	36152433	Private	M.D.	Apr. 15, 1942
Foote, George W.	32032030	Private	M.D.	Apr. 15, 1942
Fantacone, Carmine G.	32011603	Private	M.D.	Apr. 15, 1942
Fink, Louis O.	36152421	Private	M.D.	Apr. 15, 1942
Grant, George J.	35154815	Private	M.D.	Apr. 15, 1942
Hepkins, Donald E.	32035228	Private	M.D.	Apr. 15, 1942
Jackson, Richard A.	33033628	Private	M.D.	Apr. 15, 1942
Kener, George C.	32035123	Private	M.D.	Apr. 15, 1942
Maurath, Gerard A.	33037490	Private	M.D.	Apr. 15, 1942
Melnyk, John B.	32032153	Private	M.D.	Apr. 15, 1942
MacLean, Ian	32035113	Private	M.D.	Apr. 15, 1942
Meaney, Alphonsus J.	33027594	Private	M.D.	Apr. 15, 1942
Marticello, Victor	32032022	Private	M.D.	Apr. 15, 1942
Matison, Lynn S.	32034991	Private	M.D.	Apr. 15, 1942
Nellis, Leo P.	32032098	Private	M.D.	Apr. 15, 1942
O'Connell, John	32035120	Private	M.D.	Apr. 15, 1942
Ogle, Charles L.	34143475	Private	M.D.	Apr. 15, 1942
O'Donnell, James J.	32035106	Private	M.D.	Apr. 15, 1942
Patronik, Sigismund	32035149	Private	M.D.	Apr. 15, 1942
Piotrowski, Stephen	32032091	Private	M.D.	Apr. 15, 1942
Pollino, Frank S.	32035078	Private	M.D.	Apr. 15, 1942
Pierleoni, Ennius F.	32032046	Private	M.D.	Apr. 15, 1942
Parker, Paul R.	32034989	Private	M.D.	Apr. 15, 1942
Rich, Frank C., Jr.	32032054	Private	M.D.	Apr. 15, 1942
Renwick, Wilbur D.	36152370	Private	M.D.	Apr. 15, 1942
Reynolds, Norman S.	32225798	Private	M.D.	Apr. 15, 1942
Reinbold, Edwin	36152347	Private	M.D.	Apr. 15, 1942
Stewart, Harry L.	12071771	Private	M.D.	Apr. 15, 1942
Surowicz, Stanley C.	32032185	Private	M.D.	Apr. 15, 1942
Scardamaglia, Carl	32035070	Private	M.D.	Apr. 15, 1942
Soeder, Harlan D.	33021193	Private	M.D.	Apr. 15, 1942
Schillace, John A.	32032109	Private	M.D.	Apr. 15, 1942
Santelli, Lawrence J.	32026218	Private	M.D.	Apr. 15, 1942
Schulenburg, Carl J.	32032042	Private	M.D.	Apr. 15, 1942
Silsby, Alfred L.	32035001	Private	M.D.	Apr. 15, 1942
Stoddard, Owen C.	32035048	Private	M.D.	Apr. 15, 1942
Siedlecki, Caesar J.	33021452	Private	M.D.	Apr. 15, 1942

Smith, Frank L.	32226051	Private	M.D.	Apr. 15, 1942
Tipton, Joseph H.	15044989	Private	M.D.	Apr. 15, 1942
Tubiolo, Anthony R.	32032047	Private	M.D.	Apr. 15, 1942
Tanyi, Paul	32035141	Private	M.D.	Apr. 15, 1942
Virginski, Stanley C.	36152438	Private	M.D.	Apr. 15, 1942
Vosburgh, Rexford L.	32032265	Private	M.D.	Apr. 15, 1942
Freedburg, Myer A.	6136054	Private First Class	M.D.	Apr. 15, 1942
Welbourne, Paul A.	32032259	Private	M.D.	Apr. 15, 1942
Waid, George W.	32035094	Private	M.D.	Apr. 15, 1942
Chiswell, Alfred G.	14068509	Private	M.D.	Apr. 15, 1942
Davis, Randall K.	14068510	Private	M.D.	Apr. 15, 1942
Kuester, Clarence O., Jr.	14068512	Private	M.D.	Apr. 15, 1942
Masten, William F., Jr.	14068513	Private	M.D.	Apr. 15, 1942
Neil, Joseph W.	14068511	Private	M.D.	Apr. 15, 1942
Bastin, Charles L.	17056242	Private	M.D.	June 2, 1942
Elias, Micheal	34155697	Private	M.D.	June 2, 1942
Carter, Harold R.	14062455	Private	M.D.	June 2, 1942
Graves, Altman L.	34186906	Private	M.D.	June 2, 1942
Purdy, Lloyd D.	15098550	Private	M.D.	June 2, 1942
Molta, Charles J.	20282285	Private	M.D.	July 30, 1942
Angarano, Michael	20282261	Private	M.D.	July 30, 1942
Allen, Robert J.	32225968	Private	M.D.	July 24, 1942
Henry, Jack T.	32088871	Private First Class	M.D.	July 24, 1942
DeCoursey, John J.	20282335	Private First Class	M.D.	July 24, 1942
Credno, Joseph J.	20282317	Private	M.D.	July 24, 1942
Franklin, John L.	32226416	Private	M.D.	July 24, 1942
Galusha, Harold L.	20281979	Private First Class	M.D.	July 24, 1942
Muleskey, Stanley J.	13005000	Private	M.D.	July 24, 1942
Sherman, Harry	32194532	Private	M.D.	July 24, 1942
Bednarski, Stanley J.	32088847	Private	M.D.	July 24, 1942
Riano, Willard G.	20282346	Private First Class	M.D.	July 24, 1942
Edger, Paul W.	20281977	Private First Class	M.D.	July 24, 1942
DeBarbieri, John P.	20282334	Private First Class	M.D.	July 24, 1942
Waring, Donald E.	20282360	Private First Class	M.D.	July 24, 1942
McCormack, Joseph P.	32116619	Private	M.D.	July 24, 1942
Coats, Harry W.	20282007	Private First Class	M.D.	July 24, 1942
Kertis, Michael	32116760	Private First Class	M.D.	July 24, 1942
Shobert, Jack L.	20282000	Private First Class	M.D.	July 24, 1942
Mapes, Gelbert R.	20281964	Private	M.D.	July 24, 1942
Benick, Joseph L.	32225966	Private	M.D.	July 24, 1942
Button, Richard H.	20281991	Private First Class	M.D.	July 24, 1942
DiNapoli, Joseph	32116606	Private	M.D.	July 24, 1942
Fernandez, Januario	32116814	Private First Class	M.D.	July 24, 1942
Morse, James E.	32047545	Private First Class	M.D.	July 24, 1942
Carney, John R.	32116733	Private First Class	M.D.	July 24, 1942
O'Malley, Michael F.	32109676	Private First Class	M.D.	July 24, 1942
Schmitt, Charles P.	32116943	Private First Class	M.D.	July 24, 1942
Durand, George H.	20282172	Private	M.D.	July 24, 1942
MacDougal, Richard S.	20282215	Private	M.D.	July 24, 1942
Dellapolla, Joseph	32226175	Private	M.D.	July 24, 1942
Mistkowski, Vincent E.	32226191	Private	M.D.	July 24, 1942
Sharkey, Hugh J.	32116880	Private	M.D.	July 24, 1942
Stepnoski, Edward S.	32225965	Private	M.D.	July 24, 1942
Gromko, Peter	32088884	Private First Class	M.D.	July 24, 1942
Pello, Mike	32088882	Private	M.D.	July 24, 1942

Antoniello, Louis F.	32088854	Private First Class	M.D.	July 24, 1942
Jackson, William W.	32116489	Technician 5	M.D.	July 24, 1942
McKeon, Walter	32047556	Technician 5	M.D.	July 24, 1942
Chakalos, Sam G.	32109262	Private	M.D.	July 24, 1942
DeBono, Anthony J.	32116645	Private	M.D.	July 24, 1942
Brownstein, Robert S.	32226490	Private	M.D.	July 24, 1942
Tisdell, Leroy K.	20282291	Private	M.D.	July 24, 1942
Elder, John H.	32116538	Private First Class	M.D.	July 24, 1942
McKenna, John T.	20282280	Private First Class	M.D.	July 24, 1942
Marinelli, Dominick	32116281	Private	M.D.	July 24, 1942
Eckart, Wilson P.	32225964	Private	M.D.	July 24, 1942
Doucett, William H.	32225958	Private	M.D.	July 24, 1942
Losito, Carmine N.	32116903	Private	M.D.	July 24, 1942
Sokol, Joseph	32088820	Private	M.D.	July 24, 1942
Minovich, William	32116478	Private	M.D.	July 24, 1942
Kricki, Mike	32088855	Private	M.D.	July 24, 1942
Smith, John J.	32226104	Private	M.D.	July 24, 1942
Dubendorfer, Joseph D.	20281976	Private	M.D.	July 24, 1942
Beers, Donald H.	20281882	Technician 5	M.D.	July 24, 1942
Vaughn, William E.	20281875	Technician 4	M.D.	July 24, 1942
Camarata, Andrew	32116584	Private	M.D.	July 24, 1942
Fleischman, George H.	32225981	Private	M.D.	July 24, 1942
Giragosan, Martin M.	32226528	Private	M.D.	July 24, 1942
Kopcha, Andrew	32088805	Private	M.D.	July 24, 1942
Szelwian, Frank J.	20281917	Private	M.D.	July 24, 1942
Davenport, William B.	32047514	Private	M.D.	July 24, 1942
Loerke, Bruce W.	20282009	Private First Class	M.D.	July 24, 1942
Scarola, Vito J.	32088803	Private	M.D.	July 24, 1942
Lucy, Joseph B.	32047573	Private	M.D.	July 24, 1942
Link, Frank C.	32116625	Private First Class	M.D.	July 24, 1942
Duerr, Richard	32116786	Private First Class	M.D.	July 24, 1942
Intintoli, John	32116613	Private	M.D.	July 24, 1942
Spear, John	32116949	Private	M.D.	July 24, 1942
Perri, Gerardo	32116710	Private	M.D.	July 24, 1942
Seeley, Berlen	32225392	Private	M.D.	July 24, 1942
Danko, Michael	32225618	Private	M.D.	July 24, 1942
Montrose, James V.	32116646	Technician 5	M.D.	July 24, 1942
Husowec, John	32088875	Private	M.D.	July 24, 1942
White, Henry J.	20281926	Private	M.D.	July 24, 1942
Glatkowski, Walter	32088864	Private	M.D.	July 24, 1942
Sears, Kenneth R.	20281913	Private First Class	M.D.	July 24, 1942
Picone, James A.	32116779	Technician 5	M.D.	July 24, 1942
Rowan, Joseph E.	32116635	Private	M.D.	July 24, 1942
Grugan, Donald B.	20281921	Private	M.D.	July 24, 1942
Kugler, Paul H.	32116774	Technician 5	M.D.	July 24, 1942
Remillard, Louis D.	20281912	Private First Class	M.D.	July 24, 1942
Merksamer, Norman M.	32225836	Private	M.D.	July 24, 1942
Ackerman, Kenneth E.	20282326	Private	M.D.	July 24, 1942
Fredericks, Charles A.	32047522	Private	M.D.	July 24, 1942
Haynes, Robert E.	20281983	Private First Class	M.D.	July 24, 1942
Kutil, Henry J.	32116594	Private	M.D.	July 24, 1942
Lavin, Louis L.	32088801	Private	M.D.	July 24, 1942
Mastrangelo, Tony J.	32116843	Private	M.D.	July 24, 1942
Solomito, Christopher	32116088	Private	M.D.	July 24, 1942
Zimmer, Herbert L.	20282351	Private First Class	M.D.	July 24, 1942

Harmatz, Murray	32088826	Private	M.D.	July 24, 1942
Brown, Thomas F.	20282122	Private	M.D.	July 24, 1942
Boulier, John A.	20282320	Sergeant	M.D.	July 24, 1942
Weinheimer, Leonard	20282322	Private First Class	M.D.	July 24, 1942
Button, William S.	20281972	Private First Class	M.D.	July 24, 1942
Griswold, William E.	20281980	Private	M.D.	July 24, 1942
Corrigan, Thomas K.	32116799	Private	M.D.	July 24, 1942
Folmar, Robert G.	20282074	Private First Class	M.D.	July 24, 1942
Coley, Dominic A.	20282159	Technician 5	M.D.	July 24, 1942
Leo, Daniel A.	20282273	Private	M.D.	July 24, 1942
McCaughin, Helke A.	20282216	Private	M.D.	July 24, 1942
Coley, James	20282160	Technician 4	M.D.	July 24, 1942
Whitford, Cecil B.	20282202	Private	M.D.	July 24, 1942
Suddard, Harold E.	20282193	Private First Class	M.D.	July 24, 1942
MacDonough, William F.	20282218	Corporal	M.D.	July 24, 1942
Bopp, John C.	32047457	Private	M.D.	July 24, 1942
Greene, Harold W.	32226404	Private	M.D.	July 24, 1942
Mattison, Duane A.	20282162	Private First Class	M.D.	July 24, 1942
Trombley, John I.	20282198	Private	M.D.	July 24, 1942
Nicholas, William J.	32088868	Private	M.D.	July 24, 1942
Janesko, Joseph	32226188	Private	M.D.	July 24, 1942
Mandarino, Dominic J.	20282297	Private First Class	M.D.	July 24, 1942
Presutto, Eugene J.	20282286	Private	M.D.	July 24, 1942
Westbrook, Paul L.	20282090	Private	M.D.	July 24, 1942
Ireland, Kenneth S.	32116817	Private First Class	M.D.	July 24, 1942
Beauter, Frederick M.	20282066	Technician 4	M.D.	July 24, 1942
Youmans, Arnold E.	20282101	Private First Class	M.D.	July 24, 1942
Leisenfelder, Joseph J.	32047515	Private	M.D.	July 24, 1942
Mainero, Nicholas L.	32116856	Private First Class	M.D.	July 24, 1942
Bradle, Russell J.	32047465	Private	M.D.	July 24, 1942
Goodyear, Leroy M.	20282125	Technician 5	M.D.	July 24, 1942
Chasky, Hyman	32088846	Private	M.D.	July 24, 1942
Goldsmith, Eugene	32088798	Private	M.D.	July 24, 1942
Nober, Kenneth P.	32047594	Private	M.D.	July 24, 1942
Youschzak, Stephen	32088865	Private	M.D.	July 24, 1942
Waynas, John P.	32088881	Private	M.D.	July 24, 1942
Rose, Howard W.	20282131	Private First Class	M.D.	July 24, 1942
Klemens, John P.	32225603	Private	M.D.	July 24, 1942
Ierulli, Nicola A.	32116436	Private	M.D.	July 24, 1942
Failla, Salvatore J.	32116745	Private	M.D.	July 24, 1942
Constantinople, Louis W.	32116628	Private First Class	M.D.	July 24, 1942
Briggs, Stuart C.	32047404	Private	M.D.	July 24, 1942
Hershkowitz, Jack	32088808	Private	M.D.	July 24, 1942
Perugini, Oswald	32116784	Private First Class	M.D.	July 24, 1942
Finelli, Frank	32047433	Private First Class	M.D.	July 24, 1942
Boiko, William	32116680	Private First Class	M.D.	July 24, 1942
Coviello, Edmund T.	32088853	Private	M.D.	July 24, 1942
Naznitsky, Peter	32088806	Private First Class	M.D.	July 24, 1942
Albano, Gerard L.	32088830	Private First Class	M.D.	July 24, 1942
Horvath, John J.	32225834	Private First Class	M.D.	July 24, 1942
VanNostrand, Walter R.	20282109	Technician 5	M.D.	July 24, 1942
Lorber, Robert L.	20282276	Staff Sergeant	M.D.	July 24, 1942
Waldron, Edward J.	20282349	Private	M.D.	July 24, 1942
Murphy, Robert G.	20282344	Private	M.D.	July 24, 1942
Fisk, George T.	20281826	Private First Class	M.D.	July 24, 1942

Knapp, Wilbur H.	32047552	Private First Class	M.D.	July 24, 1942
Hafner, Alfred G.	20281828	Private First Class	M.D.	July 24, 1942
Krisak, Michael J.	20282272	Corporal	M.D.	July 24, 1942
Noonan, William J.	32088860	Private	M.D.	July 24, 1942
Pisano, Almerindo J.	32116172	Private First Class	M.D.	July 24, 1942
Boebeck, Jacob	32325442	Private	M.D.	July 10, 1942
Kieffer, Fred W.	32296163	Private	M.D.	July 10, 1942
Davis, Edward, Jr.	32321429	Private	M.D.	July 10, 1942
Snider, Randolf G.	33310977	Private	M.D.	July 10, 1942
Stahl, Robert C.	31101708	Private	M.D.	July 10, 1942
Zmijewski, Edward W.	32281876	Private	M.D.	July 10, 1942
Little, Henry R.	31060521	Private	M.D.	July 10, 1942
Lowney, Francis J.	31112820	Private	M.D.	July 10, 1942
Musiel, Thadeus T.	32279878	Private	M.D.	July 10, 1942
Sylvester, Raphael	11066364	Private	M.D.	July 10, 1942
Sirois, Come E.	31060551	Private	M.D.	July 10, 1942
Allen, Marion K.	32314467	Private	M.D.	July 15, 1942
Purdy, Charles I.	12062674	Private	M.D.	July 15, 1942
Cleary, Dennis P.	32334385	Private	M.D.	July 15, 1942
Dale, Kenneth M.	32298018	Private	M.D.	July 15, 1942
Davis, Benjamin	32324638	Private	M.D.	July 15, 1942
Irwin, Thomas S.	32312762	Private	M.D.	July 15, 1942
Thomason, Lester	33189574	Private	M.D.	July 15, 1942
Voss, Rudolph A.	32326737	Private	M.D.	July 15, 1942
Pollack, Charles	32325746	Private	M.D.	July 15, 1942
Hawks, Everett M.	32315836	Private	M.D.	July 15, 1942
Kaplan, Isadore	33054887	Private	M.D.	July 15, 1942
McDaniel, Charles A.	33189421	Private	M.D.	July 15, 1942
Musmeci, Dominick	32310668	Private	M.D.	July 15, 1942
Niciu, George J.	32312740	Private	M.D.	July 15, 1942
Towler, John N.	32312805	Private	M.D.	July 15, 1942
Wood, George B.	32298844	Private	M.D.	July 15, 1942
Dionne, Francis X.	31075270	Private	M.D.	July 15, 1942
Keough, John P.	32315269	Private	M.D.	July 15, 1942
Kroeger, Louis F.	32314433	Private	M.D.	July 15, 1942
Narducci, Adelchi A.	31113201	Private	M.D.	July 15, 1942
Trodden, James	32297763	Private	M.D.	July 15, 1942
Beraduce, Donald F.	31121790	Private	M.D.	July 15, 1942
Blotsky, Anthony	31106163	Private	M.D.	July 15, 1942
Czyzewski, John A.	32316080	Private	M.D.	July 15, 1942
Denega, George W.	33265168	Private	M.D.	July 15, 1942
Marcario, Jack J.	32335359	Private	M.D.	July 15, 1942
Smith, Paul R.	32298203	Private	M.D.	July 15, 1942
St. Peter, Oren L.	31060519	Private	M.D.	July 15, 1942
Tabi, Israel	32295529	Private	M.D.	July 15, 1942
Schwartz, Ben	32324799	Private	M.D.	July 20, 1942
Edwards, James M.	33001072	Private	M.D.	July 24, 1942
McCaffrey, Edward F.	32116861	Private	M.D.	July 30, 1942
White, Paul G.	6968714	Staff Sergeant	M.D.	July 24, 1942
Nienhaus, Elmer L.	32035216	Sergeant	M.D.	July 24, 1942
Dahn, Robert W.	32032210	Technician 5	M.D.	July 24, 1942
Morrison, Roy H.	32035159	Technician 5	M.D.	July 24, 1942
Ambrose, James L.	14000037	Technician 5	M.D.	July 24, 1942
Miloshevsky, Joseph G.	33027121	Private First Class	M.D.	July 24, 1942
VanderWoude, Andrew	36152158	Private First Class	M.D.	July 24, 1942

George, Robert W.	11062173	Private First Class	M.D.	July 24, 1942
Zeiser, Lester L.	31102925	Private	M.D.	July 24, 1942
Roberts, Harry H.	11051163	Private	M.D.	July 24, 1942
Berman, Nathan	32311684	Private	M.D.	July 24, 1942
Campbell, Sedley F.	31108242	Private	M.D.	July 24, 1942
Demchuk, Peter	32298729	Private	M.D.	July 24, 1942
Lubrano, Louis A.	32222196	Private	M.D.	July 24, 1942
Perry, Arthur J.	31070186	Private	M.D.	July 24, 1942
Hodgson, Albert	31087011	Private	M.D.	July 24, 1942
Bakelaar, Louis J.	32263227	Private	M.D.	July 24, 1942
Tabor, Samuel B.	31070292	Private	M.D.	July 24, 1942
Kogucky, William	32322385	Private	M.D.	July 24, 1942
Janbaz, Edward H.	32266123	Private	M.D.	July 24, 1942
Zaleckas, Stanley P.	31073876	Private	M.D.	July 24, 1942
Trainovech, William T.	31107090	Private	M.D.	July 24, 1942
Reynolds, John J.	31075904	Private	M.D.	July 24, 1942
Downey, Richard J.	32313727	Private	M.D.	July 24, 1942
Trivison, Daniel J.	20282292	Private First Class	M.D.	July 30, 1942
DeVerso, John A.	20282267	Private First Class	M.D.	July 30, 1942
Maletz, Raymond H.	33146334	Private First Class	M.D.	Jan. 22, 1943
Stead, William T.	12047872	Private	M.D.	Jan. 27, 1943
Samson, Carl A.	37071692	Private	M.D.	Feb. 15, 1943
Allison, Guy J.	36125285	Private First Class	M.D.	Apr. 27, 1943
Hager, Sidney H.	35210318	Private	M.D.	Apr. 27, 1943
Ferrantino, Samuel S.	33130373	Private	M.D.	Apr. 27, 1943
McKenzie, Jack D.	35308155	Private	M.D.	Apr. 27, 1943
Neubauer, Charles L.	12001037	Private	M.D.	Apr. 27, 1943
Jomisko, Charles	12006532	Private	M.D.	Apr. 14, 1943
Nelson, Grant E.	39227667	Private First Class	M.D.	Apr. 18, 1943
Watson, Cecil G.	34312492	Private	M.D.	Apr. 19, 1943
Stewart, James A.	11013569	Private	M.D.	Apr. 19, 1943
Doyle, Thomas C.	11024518	Private	M.D.	Apr. 8, 1943
Trafford, Aubrey C.	6149472	Private	M.D.	Apr. 8, 1943
Brannon, George W.	38292822	Private	M.D.	Apr. 6, 1943
McGarrity, Elmer E.	34214558	Private	M.D.	Apr. 6, 1943
Barnes, Charles R.	33227599	Private	M.D.	Apr. 6, 1943
Hotz, Irvin W.	38158558	Private First Class	M.D.	Apr. 6, 1943
Garman, Robert C.	33242295	Private	M.D.	Apr. 6, 1943
Melton, Roy (NMI)	35038809	Private First Class	M.D.	Apr. 6, 1943
Maldonado, Sabino M.	38158542	Private First Class	M.D.	Apr. 6, 1943
Regan, Marvin D.	14073620	Private	M.D.	June 5, 1943
Gagnon, Philippe	11048728	Private	M.D.	Apr. 12, 1943
Pittigher, Aldo	32610843	Private First Class	M.D.	Oct. 27, 1943
Lindeman, Raymond	32618182	Private	M.D.	Oct. 27, 1943
Neff, Carl V.	7024016	Private	M.D.	Oct. 27, 1943
Tirocchi, Angelo	31181682	Private	M.D.	Oct. 27, 1943
Hebron, Clarence	33345881	Private	M.D.	Oct. 27, 1943
Elkin, William	32361679	Private First Class	M.D.	Oct. 28, 1943
Rickard, Edward H.	11047871	Private First Class	M.D.	Nov. 6, 1943
Smith, Melvin R.	34771398	Private	M.D.	Nov. 25, 1943
Smolier, Milton J.	32882700	Private	M.D.	Nov. 25, 1943
Speranza, James A.	32880036	Private	M.D.	Nov. 25, 1943
Spry, Howard J.	34670373	Private	M.D.	Nov. 25, 1943
Stack, Theadore (NMI)	32855525	Private	M.D.	Nov. 25, 1943
Stefanchik, John A.	32882252	Private	M.D.	Nov. 25, 1943

Sherman, Harry	32194532	Private	M.D.	Dec. 9, 1943
MacDougal, Richard S.	20282215	Technician 5	M.D.	Dec. 16, 1943
Shobert, Jack L.	20282000	Private	M.D.	Dec. 23, 1943
Evenson, Edward L.	17037021	Technician 5	M.D.	Apr. 25, 1944
Lambert, Virgil	35751689	Private	M.D.	Apr. 29, 1944
Phillips, Paul A.	37460270	Private First Class	M.D.	May 4, 1944
Pajak, Joseph	31215117	Private First Class	M.D.	May 4, 1944
Federspiel, Frederick	19062982	Technician 4	M.D.	May 4, 1944
Blass, Robert L.	39678037	Sergeant	M.D.	June 1, 1944
Berger, Thomas C.	13096852	Technician 4	M.D.	June 3, 1944
Rex, Walter A.	35574032	Private First Class	M.D.	June 19, 1944
Record, Samuel A.	38175182	Technician 4	M.D.	June 19, 1944
Malott, Chester P.	35790208	Private	M.D.	Aug. 16, 1944
Leppert, Charles W.	36049265	Technician 4	M.D.	Aug. 20, 1944
Zieja, Stephen J.	32130319	Private	M.D.	Aug. 22, 1944
Upton, Raymond F.	12008178	Sergeant	M.D.	Aug. 16, 1944
Coder, Chester P.	38583809	Private	M.D.	Aug. 16, 1944
Gagnon, Philippe	11048728	Private	M.D.	Mar. 5, 1944
Rendl, John	36352891	Corporal	M.D.	Nov. 17, 1944
Sanfilippo, Joseph	32148850	Technician 5	M.D.	Jan. 13, 1945
Ludwig, Warren C.	37236934	Private First Class	M.D.	Jan. 27, 1945
Porter, George R.	32940841	Private First Class	M.D.	Jan. 27, 1945
Wass, Lloyd I.	36536179	Private First Class	M.D.	Jan. 27, 1945
Golankiewicz, Roman B.	42134765	Private	M.D.	Feb. 13, 1945
Lewis, Floyd Y.	34771435	Private	M.D.	Feb. 28, 1945
Jones, Delbert P.	37285757	Technician 5	M.D.	Dec. 24, 1944
Davis, Leslie	37448827	Private	M.D.	Apr. 7, 1945
Sellers, Gardner C.	37204913	Technician 4	M.D.	Apr. 16, 1945
Piwowarski, John J.	36352874	Corporal	M.D.	Apr. 26, 1945
McMahon, John L.	32752303	Private First Class	M.D.	Apr. 26, 1945
Mederos, Joseph E.	39390234	Private First Class	M.D.	Apr. 26, 1945
Csyczka, Harry	32296755	Private	M.D.	Apr. 26, 1945
Pardikes, Steve J.	36170286	Private	M.D.	Apr. 26, 1945
Simons, Charles F.	32513069	Private	M.D.	Apr. 26, 1945
Sposato, Ralph A.	35331574	Private First Class	M.D.	Apr. 26, 1945
Starbird, Walter R.	31188182	Private	M.D.	Apr. 26, 1945
Stronczewski, Joseph T.	33336724	Private	M.D.	Apr. 26, 1945
Tabor, Walter J.	36357614	Private	M.D.	Apr. 26, 1945
Akers, Tracy G.	35449360	Private	M.D.	Apr. 26, 1945
Blodgett, Donald R.	37442293	Private	M.D.	Apr. 26, 1945
Fradenburgh, Raymond G.	37323393	Private First Class	M.D.	Apr. 26, 1945
McDaniel, James D.	15099216	Private	M.D.	Apr. 26, 1945
Bishop, Robert E.	34240207	Private First Class	M.D.	Apr. 26, 1945
Bercaw, William G.	36421295	Technician 5	M.D.	May 5, 1945
Stowe, Wilbur W.	34663517	Private First Class	M.D.	May 5, 1945
King, Marcus B., Jr.	11012145	Private First Class	M.D.	June 1, 1945
Anderson, Louis A.	36216010	Technician 3	M.D.	June 1, 1945
Beamer, Robert R., Jr.	37084718	Private First Class	M.D.	June 1, 1945
Blakler, Alfred F.	11054251	Technician 4	M.D.	June 1, 1945
Brandenstein, H. H.	36292792	Private First Class	M.D.	June 1, 1945
Camderlengo, Patrick	32202276	Private First Class	M.D.	June 1, 1945
Fuoua, Ivan W., Jr.	14097874	Technician 5	M.D.	June 1, 1945
Kimble, Leonard C.	33246925	Technician 5	M.D.	June 1, 1945
Martinez, Ferinin	38011016	Private First Class	M.D.	June 1, 1945
McClain, Eugene	38121529	Technician 4	M.D.	June 1, 1945

Nunez, Dewey J.	34005286	Technician 5	M.D.	June	1, 1945
Ortego, Irenio M.	38010312	Corporal	M.D.	June	1, 1945
Pisa, Anthony C.	32109574	Sergeant	M.D.	June	1, 1945
Ragsdale, Noah W.	37066378	Technician 5	M.D.	June	1, 1945
Ripkoski, Herman W.	6298918	Private First Class	M.D.	June	1, 1945
Roy, Henry S.	31034380	Technician 3	M.D.	June	1, 1945
Rosen, Maurice J.	39161658	Staff Sergeant	M.D.	June	1, 1945
Schultz, Simon	37130833	Staff Sergeant	M.D.	June	1, 1945
Semeraro, Frank N.	31046286	Technician 4	M.D.	June	1, 1945
Sexton, Jasper	34193799	Private First Class	M.D.	June	1, 1945
Swenson, Gordon C.	37177624	Private First Class	M.D.	June	1, 1945
Young, William	36016786	Technician 5	M.D.	June	1, 1945
Cathey, Ben A.	34071722	Technician 5	M.D.	June	5, 1945
Davies, Sylvester T.	20644012	Private First Class	M.D.	June	5, 1945
Petty, Edgar R.	35001225	Private First Class	M.D.	June	5, 1945
Walton, William R.	34353533	Private First Class	M.D.	June	5, 1945
Barton, George F.	32355371	Private	M.D.	June	5, 1945
Carvey, Philip H.	36179270	Private	M.D.	June	5, 1945
Alsteen, Raymond W.	36201938	Technician 4	M.D.	June	5, 1945
Cothron, Oscar G.	20428040	Staff Sergeant	M.D.	June	5, 1945
Middleton, Ellsworth T.	20318720	Sergeant	M.D.	June	6, 1945
Duke, Linwood A.	6941867	Private First Class	M.D.	June	6, 1945

INDEX

Index of illustrations begins on page 260.

Abbey of Monte Cassino, 172, 178
Abduk, 70-71, 74
Abraham, 100, 112
Ackerman, Pfc. Kenneth, 199
Adams, Gen. E. S., 3
Adriatic, 189
Affaires de Ration, 113
Africa, 31-33, 36, 40-41, 43, 45-49, 52, 55, 58-60, 65, 68-70, 72-73, 75-80, 86, 89, 91, 95-96, 99, 104, 106, 109-110, 114-119, 121-124, 126, 130-131, 133, 135, 140, 158-159, 164, 182-183, 186, 192, 199, 209, 222. *See also* North Africa.
Africa Korps, 96, 102
Agropoli, 126, 129
Aiken, S. C., 203
Ain-el-Turck, 160
Air Raids, 22, 24, 29, 129, 134-135, 151, 180-183, 186
Airborne Infantry, 14
Airplanes, 32, 34, 49, 106, 108-109, 117-118; B-26, 118; DC-3, 110; P-25, 106, 108; P-38, 106
Akers, Pvt. Tracy G., 228
Alabama, 140, 188
Albano, Gerard, 146
Alcohol, 165, 208, 214
Alessandria, 235
Alexander, Gen. H. R., 103, 190, 226
Alexandria, Egypt, 50
Algeria, 33, 40, 45-46, 71, 76, 105, 117
Algiers, 62, 69, 78, 98, 115, 122, 157, 209
Allen, Gen. Terry, 59
Allied Expeditionary Force in England, 192
Allied Military Government, 210
Allies, 32, 98, 103-104, 115, 119, 122, 127, 143, 146, 172, 178, 185, 189-192, 194, 196, 201, 213, 215, 218, 220, 227, 233
Almond, Capt. Hallie E., 6, 25, 146, 155, 206, 218-219, 231
Alps, 101
Alsace, 100
Amado, 2nd Lt. Jose C., 202
Amalfi, 128
Ambrose, T/5 James L., 139, 228
Ambulances, 49, 115, 136, 146-147, 155, 166, 184, 199, 210-211
American Academy, 198
American Aid Program, 160
American Consul, 113-114
American Hospital, 26
American Legion Memorial Stadium, 1
AMGOT, 124, 132
Anderson, Gen., 103
Anderson, T/3 Louis A., 228
Anesthesia, 142, 148, 151
Anesthesiologists, 148

Angarano, Pvt. Michael, 199, 201, 228
Angen, Capt. Willard F., 5
Anzio, 91, 145, 151-152, 179-183, 185-186, 188-191, 204-205, 211, 232
Anzio Beachhead, 188-191
"Anzio Express, The," 179
Apennines, 136
Appendicitis, 50, 54, 62
Arabia, 50, 100
Arabs, 33-34, 41-42, 48-50, 55, 58, 60, 62-63, 68-73, 76-79, 84, 89, 91, 95, 97-98, 101, 113-114, 120-121, 123, 141, 160, 198; Home life, 73; Marriage, 72
Armistice Day, 138
Arnest, Col. Richard T., 90
Arno River, 205-209, 218
Arno River Valley, 203
Arnold, Gen. H. H. (Hap), 154-155
Aryans, 101
Arzew, Algeria, 31-36, 46, 50, 60, 62, 75-76, 94, 133
Asch, Sholem, 184
Asia, 101
Associated Press, 114
Astrackon, Pvt. Raymond, 44
Atabrine, 88, 128
Athens, 160
Atlanta, Ga., 3, 5, 6, 66, 151, 222
Atlantic Ocean, 20-21, 114
Atlas Mountains, 69
Augustine, Capt. Robert W., 19, 111, 120, 123-124, 136, 219
Augustus, 169
Australians, 227
Austria, 224, 226
Austrians, 96
Avenue Jules Ferry, 113
Avonmouth, England, 26, 62
Axis, 40, 49, 103-104, 115, 140, 158, 188-189, 213
Axis Sally, 185-186
Azores, 31

Bab-Saddoun, 98
Bachoka, 1st Lt. Margaret P., 26, 75, 136, 164, 169, 200
Bagdolio, 132
Bahia, Sgt. Renato S., 202
Bakelaar, Tech. 4th Grade Louise J., 111
Baker, Sgt., 53
Baker, Tech. 3rd Gr. Alex, 104
Baker, Dr. Thomas W., 3
Ballettine, T/4 Wick V., 199
Baltimore, Md., 169
Bank of Algiers, 98
Bank of England, 27
Bank of France, 100
Baptist Church, 7, 165, 213, 231
Barbee, 1st Lt. Ruth I., 25, 75, 168

Barbour, 2nd Lt. Gertrude L., 220
Bard, Capt., 231
Batista, 1st Lt. Renato D., 202
Battapaglia, 179
Bauchspies, Lt. Col. Rollin L., 25-26, 28, 31, 34, 38, 47-48, 50, 58-60, 62, 64, 71, 79, 90-91, 110-111, 115, 117, 119, 181
Bavaria, 224
Baylor University, 151
BBC, 185
Beagans, 1st Lt. Nellie R., 220
Beamer, Pfc. Robert R. (Jr.), 228
Beau Site, 105, 232
Bebiano, Carmen, 202
Beer, 207
Beggars, 98
Beja, Tunisia, 89-90, 97, 101-103, 105, 110-111, 115, 182
Belgium, 217
Belk, Ensign Henry, 63
Bell, Rev. Bernard, 183
Bell, 1st Lt. Ida Pauline, 6, 26, 173, 220
Benante, 1st Lt. Lorraine M., 26, 166, 204
Benedictine Monastery, 172
Benny, Jack, 79
Benson, Capt. Robert C., 199
Berbers, 84, 91
Bercaw, T/5 William C., 228
Berchtesgaden, 224
Berlin, 223-224, 226-227
Bernard, Pvt. Walter, 146
Berret, 2nd Lt. Anna B., 152
Betts, Maj. Reeve H., 152, 163
Bird, 1st Lt. Blanche, 224
Bizerte, Tunisia, 91, 96, 104, 115; Bizerte Battle, 115
Black Market, 197
Blackford, Staige, 70
Blackler, T/4 Alfred L., 228
Blake, Capt. Clayton A. (Jr.), 211, 218
Blandford, 1st Lt. Mary F., 21, 25, 82, 122, 169
Blesse, Brig. Gen. Fred W., 90, 110-111, 183
Blizzard, 163
Blood, 137-138, 146, 150, 152-153, 178
Blood Bank, 115
Blood Plasma, 88, 115, 138, 146, 150, 152-153, 207
Bloom, Capt. Morris J., 224
Blowing Rock, N. C., 130
Blue Beach, 126-127
Blue Grotto, 171
Blythe, Ga., 95
Boggs, Second Lieut. Mary I., 6
Bone, 89
Borneo, 227
Bosche, 97
Boston, Mass., 65, 68, 95, 173

Bougainville, 222
Boulier, Sgt. John A., 111, 219
Bourke-White, Margaret, 131, 139, 145-148, 150, 153, 165
Bowers, Maj. Frederick, 152
Boxes, 170-171
Boy Scouts, 9, 93
Boyd, Lt. Col. Granberry D. (Jr.), 186
Boyd, Maj. Kenneth B., 169, 229
Brackett, Fred, 79
Brady, 2nd Lt. Ann K., 207
Brandenstein, Pfc. H. H., 228
Brandon, Barbara, 103
Brannon, T/5 George W., 228
Brass, 100
Brave Men (Pyle), 149
Brazilian Expeditionary Forces, 202, 205, 207
Brazilians, 233-235
Brelsford, 1st Lt. Harold J., 218, 220
Bremen, 224
Brenizer, Dr. Addison, 5
Brice, 2nd Lt. Nina V., 26
Bridges, 130, 136, 142, 145, 164, 186, 203, 206, 208-210
Briquettes, 122
British, 22, 24, 26-30, 34, 36-37, 62, 67-68, 79, 91, 94-99, 102, 110, 118-119, 121, 124-125, 157, 164, 172, 174, 189, 197-192, 201-202, 210, 216, 220-221, 224, 226, 232-235
British Eighth Army, 52
British Empire, 119
British Museum, 27
British Navy, 37
Bristol, England, 24, 28, 31
Bristol Channel, 31
Brix, 2nd Lt. Anne K., 152
Bronxville, N. Y., 220
Bronze Star Medal, 219, 226
Brooke, Mrs., 86
Brooke, Lucy, 155, 206, 216
Brooklyn, N. Y., 13, 17, 100
Brower, 1st Lt. Robert A., 220, 223, 229
Brubaker, Capt. Wilbur K., 199
Bryden, Gen., 1
Bryn Mawr, 68
Buckingham Palace, 27
Bude, Mississippi, 7, 48
Buffalo, N. Y., 50
Burgess, 1st Lt. Violet O. B., 6, 25, 131, 146, 169
Burma, 110, 216, 222, 226
Burnham, 2nd Lt. Audrey J., 26
Burns, 88
Burwell, Capt. Lewis, 9

Caesar, 82, 84, 191, 196
Calder, Maj. Duncan G. (Jr.), 5-6, 8, 15-16, 19, 25, 28, 53, 79, 117, 121, 143, 159, 164, 169, 192, 199, 220, 229
Calhoun, Kentucky, 6
Calhoun, W. G., 6
Camderlengo, Pfc. Patrick, 228
Camenisch, 2nd Lt. Helen J., 25
Camp Barkeley, Texas, 4
Camp Grant, Illinois, 4, 5
Camp Lee, Virginia, 4
Canadians, 119, 191-192, 224, 232
Canarile, T/4 Leonard A., 220
Cancer, 70
Candler, Mr., 64

Cannon, Maj. Gen., 154
Cannon, Frances Ann, 114
Cannon, Martin L., 1
Cape Bon, 53, 99
Capri, 132-133, 160, 171
Capua, 136
Carinola, 178-179, 181, 232
"Carolina Avenue," 35, 49, 54, 58
Carroll, 2nd Lt. Bernice, 26
Carter, T/5 Harold R., 199
Carter, Capt. Harvey W., 220
Carthage, 99-101, 105
Casablanca, 31, 111, 209
"Casanova Park," 50, 64, 115
Caserta, 45, 128-130, 132, 136, 158, 172, 182, 201, 226, 232
Cashatt, Second Lieut. Mary Louise, 6
Cassino, Italy, 136, 140, 148, 152, 172, 178, 186, 191, 205, 211
Cavanaugh, Capt. William T., 5
Cecina, Italy, 198, 233
Chamberlain, Capt. Francis W., 224
Chaplains, 142, 144-145, 150, 184, 202, 213-214, 235
Charleston, S. C., 14
Charlotte, N. C., 1-7, 9, 11-14, 17, 21, 27, 40, 47-49, 53, 59, 63, 66-67, 69-70, 79-80, 84, 86-87, 104-105, 111, 114-115, 117, 121-122, 124, 130, 133, 138, 143, 145-148, 150, 157, 159, 172, 179, 183, 188, 194, 196, 205-206, 208, 212-214, 216, 226, 231
"Charlotte Evac, The" (*Time*, Aug. 9, 1943), 114
"Charlotte Evac in Algeria" (*Time*, Aug. 9, 1943), 114
Charlotte Variety Club, 10, 145
Cherbourgh Peninsula, 192
Chiningo, Mike, 150
Chiswell, Alfred G., 6
Chlorinating Tablets, 96, 132
Chlorine, 104
Christmas, 55, 60, 78, 128, 155-156, 158, 160, 162, 167, 202, 207, 213, 215-217; President's Message, 158
Chunn, Maj. Charles F., 152
Church services, 91, 142, 159, 184, 214, 231
Churchill, Col., 75
Churchill, Sir Winston, 7, 118, 127, 191-192, 220, 226-227
Cincinnati, Ohio, 68, 220
Cisterna, 191
Citadel, The, 14
Citadel of Quebec, 119
Clanton, Mr., 79
Clanton, Luther C., 121-122
Clapper, Raymond, 121
Clark, Gen. Mark W., 28, 52, 119, 130, 154-155, 157-159, 163-164, 189-190, 211-213, 217
Clarke, 2nd Lt. Lula A., 179, 194
Clary, Capt. Beverley B., 220
Clayton, T/4 Dale J., 224
Clayton, N. C., 130
Cleveland, Ohio, 220
Clyde, Firth of (Scotland), 31, 62
Coats, Pfc. Harry W., 228
Cochran, 2nd Lt. Winifred E., 217
Coder, T/5 Harry D., 228
Cold Stream Guards, 96
Cole, Rev. C. Alfred, 183
Coles, E. P., 1

Collins, Capt., 231
Cologgi, Louis F., 56
Colonna, Jerry, 9
Colosseum (Rome), 196
Columbia, S. C., 11
Comité du Textile, 113
Concord, N. C., 5, 6
Constantine, 74-76, 84, 89, 94, 98, 117-118, 159
Contourso, 1st Lt. Katherine, 25, 169
Contreiras, 1st Lt. Djalma C., 202
Cook, Col., 16
Cook, Pvt. Paul E. J., 228
Cooleemee, N. C., 5
Cori-Cisterna Road, 191
Cornelius, N. C., 186
Cotner, T/4 Walter H., 217
Cotton, Pvt. Russell B., 142
"Cotton Balers," 191
"Cotton's Dog House," 142
Coveny, 2nd Lt. Dorothy, 224
Coviello, Edmond, 220
Coward, Noel, 27
Cowin, 2nd Lt. Sophie T., 217
Cox, 2nd Lt. Marion J., 26
Cox, Corporal Virgil H., 111
Crawford, Capt. John M., 169, 180, 203
Crawford, Maj. William B. (Jr.), 218, 229, 231
Crawley, Capt. Walter G. (Jr.), 220
Creosote, 94, 122
Cronin, A. J., 184
Crotts, Capt. Hylton K., 212
Crusaders' Cross, 98
Culley, 1st Lt. Mary Alyce, 25, 218
Cumberland Hotel, 26, 29
Cunningham, Admiral, 103
Cynthiana, Kentucky, 43, 214

D Day, 62
Dahn, Sgt. Robert W. (Skin Head), 168
Dale, Tech. 4th Grade Kenneth M., 111
Dartmouth College, 222
Davenport, William, 146
Davidson, N. C., 5
Davidson College, 1
Davies, 2nd Lt. Margaret I., 199
Davis, 2nd Lt. Opal G., 152
Davis, Gen., 29
Davis, T/4 Randall K., 6, 52-53, 62-63, 104, 139, 146, 151, 165
Davison, Mrs., 68
Dayton, Ohio, 207
de Caldas, Capt. Mirandolino J., 202
de Carmo e Castro, Maria, 202
de Farias, Sgt. Alfredo A., 202
Dehydration, 138
Denning, Capt. Walter S., 192
Dennison, Mr. & Mrs. Louie, 58-59, 71-73
Dent, Maj. Paul L., 152
Dentists, 3, 4, 6, 49, 54, 59, 81, 115, 170, 203
de Oliveira, Maj. Ernestino, 202
D'Este, Cardinal, 201
de Silva, Sgt. Dimas S., 202
Detroit, 149
Devivier, 119
Dewey, Thomas E., 199
Dexheimer, 1st Lt. Vera H., 26, 169
Diamond Horseshoe, 172
Diarrhea, 105
Dickens, Charles, 159

254

Dickson, R. S., 2, 5
Dierker, 2nd Lt. Ruth, 178, 180
"Ditty Bags," 88
"Dixie Theatre," 179
"Doctor's Dilemma, The" 27
Doenitz, Grand Admiral, 226-227
Doolittle, Gen., 108, 110
Doolittle, Mr., 114
Doria Pamphilli, 192-194, 233
dos Santos, Sgt. Sebastiao R., 202
dos Santos, 1st Lt. Waldemar D., 202
Doskow, 1st Lt. Deborah R., 26, 169, 194, 219
Doubilet, Capt. Henry, 178, 203, 231
Douglas, Lloyd, 160
Dowd, Carey, 185
Dowman, Dr. Charles, 151
"Dragons," 191
Dresden, 223
Dubendorfer, T/5 Joseph D., 228
Duce, Il, 93, 195
"Duck," 124, 126, 133
Duerr, Pvt. 1 cl. Richard (NMN), 111
Duke Hospital, 54, 120
Duke University, 68
Dunbar, Col. C. E., 5
Dunkirk, 104, 182
Dunn, Capt. James W., 19, 123-124, 180, 212
Durham, N. C., 6
Dysentery, 50, 104, 116

Easter, 151, 179
Eastern Task Force, 31-32
Eddy, Mary Baker, 82
Edger, T/5 Paul W., 228
Edinburgh, 26, 174
Eggler, 2nd Lt. Evelyn Kohler, 6
Egypt, 50, 197
Eisenhower, Gen. Dwight D., 104, 118, 192, 227
El Guerrah, Algeria, 74
Electricity, 36, 54, 60, 78, 98, 130, 132, 136, 142, 161, 165, 167, 182, 186, 196, 198
Elkin, Pfc. William, 228
Elliott, Sgt. Vincent J., 111, 142
Ellison, 1st Lt. Adrienne J., 211, 220
Emden, 224
Emory, 123
Engineers, 14, 49, 54, 60, 62, 120, 124, 130, 132, 142, 161, 177-178, 181-182, 204
England, 21-33, 36, 38, 45, 47-48, 55, 60, 62, 65, 70, 78, 86, 94, 108, 110, 115, 118, 132, 177, 182, 185-186, 192, 227
Englewood, N. J., 86, 206
Ennis, Skinnay, 9
Ethiopia, 93
Ethiopians, 91
Europe, 17, 30, 96, 101, 119, 130, 190, 196, 216, 227
European Theater of War, 17
"Evacuation Hospital—Nurses and Doctors work in Italian Morass" (Life, Feb. 21, 1944), 145
Evacuation hospital setup, 136-138, 141-142; Work of, 145-146; Method of handling entering patients, 137-138
Evans, Capt. William (Jr.), 19, 31, 35, 79, 135, 158
Evenson, T/5 Edward L., 228

Excelsior Hotel, 200
Exum, 1st Lt. Carrie V., 220

Fair, George W., 230
Far East, 227
Farias, Sgt. Osvaldo M., 202
Fayetteville, 11, 17
Federspiel, T/4 Frederick, 228
Felts, Capt. James R. (Jr.), 6, 19, 28, 75, 79, 169, 203, 208-210, 214, 218
Fenocchi, Staff Sgt. Amelio R., 104
Ferriera, Antonieta, 202
Fes-Meknes, 104
Fetters, Capt. David S., 217
Fidenza, Italy, 226-227, 229, 234
Figi Islands, 222
Finelli, Frank, 119
Fink, Tech. 4th Grade Louis A., 111
First Medical Laboratory in Salisbury (England), 2
"First Street," 35, 54
Fitts, Lieut. Col. Francis M., 2, 3
Flavian Amphitheatre, 196
Fleming, Maj. Laurence E., 5, 19, 28, 65, 90, 136, 235
Fleurus, 120
Fliedner, 1st Lt. Martha G., 6, 25, 129, 218
Flood at Pisa, 205-213, 218
Florence, Italy, 198, 202, 208-210, 231, 235; University, 235
Florence, Mass., 150
Florence, S. C., 5
Florence Redeployment Training Area, 235
Flu, 50, 177
Fluck, Sgt. David E., 104
Fluoroscope, 49
Foch Field, 118
Foisie, Sgt. Jack, 205, 207-208
Folmar, Cpl. Robert G., 228
Fort Bragg, N. C., 2, 4-9, 11-18, 25, 31, 60, 74, 86, 115, 124, 133, 175, 204, 235
Fort Dix, 11
Fort Sill, Oklahoma, 60
"Forward," 184
France, 68-69, 96, 112, 149, 192; Invasion of, 149, 192
Francis, Mary, 95
Fredendall, Maj. Gen., 50
Freedburg, Tech. 4th Grade Myer J., 111
French, 31-34, 40-41, 45-46, 49-50, 74
French, 31-34, 40-41, 45-46, 49-50, 55, 57, 60, 62, 67-69, 74, 76-86, 91-93, 95, 98, 100-102, 112-121, 123, 140-141, 160, 164-165, 191, 196, 201, 232, 234-235
French Morocco, 31
"Friscans," 191
Fritsche, Mr., 227
Fritz, Mrs. Ben C., 75
Fruth, 1st Lt. Christine, 180, 219
Frye, 2nd Lt. Lucille, 6
Fullbright, Lieut. Bessie Viola, 4, 6, 25, 49, 51, 230
Fuoua, T/5 Ivan W., 228

Gaeta, 189
Galusha, Pfc. Harold L., 228
Gari River, 172
Garigliano River, 172

Gas gangrene, 146
Gas mask, 8, 28, 96, 116
Gaston, Capt. Herbert B., 220
Gastonia, N. C., 5
Gay, Capt. Charles H. (Sr.), 16, 19, 28, 64, 75, 82, 142, 192, 204, 219, 231
Gaynor, 2nd Lt. Helen A., 25
Geneva Treaty, 140
Genin, Capt. Francis G., 188
George, Earl Lloyd, 220
George VI, King of England, 103-104, 119, 127-128
Georgia, 140
Germans, 7, 13, 32, 34, 40-41, 73, 76-77, 82, 86, 89, 91-93, 95-100, 102-103, 108, 110, 119, 128, 130, 132-133, 136, 140, 145, 148, 151, 172, 176, 178, 185-186, 189-192, 194, 197-198, 203-204, 209, 217-218, 221, 223-224
Germany, 24, 68, 88, 95-96, 98, 216, 226-227
Gibraltar, Rock of, 31, 32
Gibraltar, Straits of, 31, 62, 160, 186, 235
Gibson, Maj. James K., 220
Gilbert, Capt. Richard P., 206
Gilliam, 2nd Lt. Elsie I., 211
Gleba, Sgt. Joseph, 42
Gloser, 1st Lt. Elizabeth, 231
Glucose, 138
Goat Hill, 126
Goebbels, 227
Goering, Hermann Wilhelm, 24
Golankiewicz, Pfc. Roman B., 228
Good Conduct Medal, 104, 111
Goodyear, T/4 Leroy M., 228
Gouams, 91-92, 98, 100, 140
Gourand, Capt., 224
Gourock, 62
Gower, Sgt. Ralph, 44
Grant, George, 146, 165
Green, Sgt. Paul, 191-192
Green, 1st Lt. Sara J., 221, 223
Greenock, Scotland, 31, 62
Gribbon, Bishop, 184
Griswold, T/5 William E., 228
Groff, Jacob, 43
Gross, 2nd Lt. Nellie R, 207
Grosselfinger, Capt. Harold, 178
Guadalcanal, 135
Guenther, Capt. A. J., 90, 117
Guerlain perfume, 98
Gunn, T/4 John K., 223
Gunners, 106, 108
Gustav Line, 172, 178, 189
Guyett, 1st Lt. Edith E., 26, 116, 125, 169

Hafner, T/5 Alfred G., 228
Halifax, Nova Scotia, 20
Haltiwanger, 1st Lt. Carolyn T., 26, 169
Hancock, N. Y., 219
Hand, Capt. John P., Jr., 199
Harmon, 2nd Lt. Josephine Lee, 6, 26
Harney, Capt. James N., 207, 212, 223
Harvard, 109, 220, 222
Hatchew, 2nd Lt. Elaine C., 217
Hawes, Capt. George Aubrey, 5, 14-16, 19, 36, 74-75, 199
"Hawley" table, 115
Heaton, 1st Lt. Annette M., 26, 41, 44, 218-219

Hegner, Capt. Hermann L., 217
Heirominus, Pfc. Elwood D., 217
Hemmick, Monsignor, 195-196, 201-202
Henry, T/3 Tavner E., 224
Henry, Thomas R., 102-103
Hepatitis, 178, 204
Here Is Your War (Pyle), 46, 48, 149
Hersey, John, 114-117, 121, 148
Heskett, Maj. Byford F., 218
High Point, N. C., 5, 205
Highland Blackwatch, 96
Highlands, N. C., 130
Himmelstein, 1st Lt. Aaron, 152
Hirtz, 2nd Lt. Rosalie D., 26
Hitler, Adolf, 24, 95-97, 190-191, 196,
    224, 226-227
Hoeffding, 1st Lt. Waldemar, 152
Hoffman, Maj. Milo Johnson, 6, 8, 19,
    38, 74-75, 90, 118, 127, 129, 136,
    142, 159, 170, 180, 193, 203, 212,
    216, 218
Holdings, Mr. & Mrs., 59
Holland, 108
Holyoke, Mass., 207
Home Service, 87-88
Hope, Bob, 9-10, 38, 79, 145, 185
Hospitals:
    British 95 General Hospital, 111
    Camp Sutton Hospital, 5
    Charlotte Memorial Hospital, 2, 3,
        5, 47, 54
    Presbyterian Hospital, 21, 65
    Roosevelt Hospital, 94
    St. Cloud Hospital, 34-39, 41-48, 52-
        53, 56, 58, 61, 63-65, 70, 76, 80,
        85, 96, 109
    Telergma hospital encampment, 87,
        107
    Walter Reed Hospital, 149
    3rd Provisional Hospital, 89
    6th General Hospital, 220
    12th General Hospital, 218, 220
    15th Field Hospital, 218, 219
    16th Evacuation Hospital Unit, 126
    17th General Hospital, 219
    32nd Station Hospital, 199
    33rd Field Hospital, 199, 233
    37th General Hospital, 220
    41st Evacuation Hospital, 5
    45th General Hospital, 220
    52nd Station Hospital, 178
    56th Station Hospital, 211
    57th Station Hospital, 211
    61st Station Hospital, 74
    77th Evacuation Hospital, 75, 89
    93rd Station Hospital, 169
    94th Evacuation Hospital, 218
    170th Evacuation Hospital, 218, 221-
        223
    171st Evacuation Hospital, 220, 228
    182nd Station Hospital, 220
    300th General Hospital, 199
Hough, 1st Lt. Bertha Elizabeth, 6, 21,
    25, 164, 169
Houston, Texas, 95
Hume, Rita, 205-207
Huntersville, N. C., 6, 204
Hustac, 2nd Lt. Mildred, 25
Huyton, England, 22, 26
Hyde Park (London), 27
Hyde Park, N. Y., 220

Iceland, 110
Ierulli, Nichola, 146, 151, 165

Imes, Maj. Pat R., 19, 34, 70, 112, 129,
    158, 199, 201-202, 218
India, 31, 222, 226
"Indiana Ave.," 35, 54
Indianapolis, 103
Indiantown Gap, Pa., 18, 20
Indiantown Gap Military Reservation,
    17
International News Service, 149, 205
Invasion Diary (Tregaskis), 148-150
Iredell County, 173
Ireland, 48
Irish Sea, 31
Iron Cross, 98
Italians, 73, 76-77, 81-82, 93, 95, 97-98,
    100, 112, 115, 117, 125, 131, 132,
    135-136, 138, 141, 151, 173-174, 176-
    177, 179, 182, 192, 194, 206-207, 217,
    219, 223, 232, 234-235
Italy, 95, 101, 106, 108, 114, 116-117,
    124, 126-127, 130, 133, 140-141, 143,
    145, 147, 158-160, 164, 169-170, 175,
    178, 182, 186, 188-192, 193, 196-198,
    203-215, 218, 219, 221, 226, 234

Jackson, T/5 Edward A., 111
Jackson, Mac, 121
Jacksonville, 5
Japan, 108-110, 226-227, 235
Japan, Sea of, 108
Japanese, 13, 216
Jensen, 1st Lt. Madeline L., 200, 218
Jerling, T/5 John P., 221
Jersey City, N. J., 20
Jerusalem, 98, 160
Jews, 95, 100-101, 112, 120-121
Jodl, Col. Gen. Gustav, 227
Johns Hopkins Medical School, 199, 222
Johnson, 2nd Lt. Beatrice E., 21, 26, 179
Johnson, 1st Lt. Helen E., 194, 218
Johnson, Master Sgt. Herbert L., 104,
    218
Johnson, Gen. Otto, 4
Johnson, T/5 Vernon, 224
Johnston, Billy, 156
Jones, T/5 Delbert P., 228
Jones, T/4 Gwynfryn T., 111
Jones, 2nd Lt. Juanita, 136
Jones, Capt. Otis (Chaplain), 7, 19, 48,
    79, 233
Jones, Maj. Otis Hunter, 5, 7-8, 15, 19,
    21, 48, 52, 79, 129, 156-157, 179, 198,
    213-214
Jones, Cpl. Robert, 176
Jones, Robert (Jr.), 176
Junior League, 87

Kavanagh, Capt. William P., 16, 19, 31,
    74, 84, 94, 96, 109
Keelin, Mildred, 95
Kelso, 1st Lt. Cora B., 221
Kemp, T. D. (Jr.), 53
Kendrick, Maj. Vaiden B., 6, 8, 16, 19,
    25, 28, 38, 49, 57, 59, 71, 73-75, 115,
    170
"Kentucky Ave.," 35, 43, 54
Keough, John, 146
Kew Gardens, 29
Keys, Capt. Edgar H., 224
Keyes, Maj. Gen. Geoffrey, 163
Kiel, 226
Killeen, 1st Lt. Elizabeth E., 25, 122,
    220
Kimble, T/5 Leonard C., 228

King, Pfc. Marcus B. (Jr.), 228
King, Mr. Walter H., 231
Kirk, Maj. Norman T., 90
Kirkpatrick, Capt. James E., 127, 150,
    233
Kiser, Kay, 172
Knapp, Sgt. Wilbur H., 219
Knickerbocker, H. R., 59-60
Knickerbocker, Red, 150
Knopp, Wilbur, 40
Knox, John, 26
Koccour, Capt. James L., 152
Koniev, Marshal, 224
Krane, Pfc. John, 220
Krubes, 119
Kuester, Clarence O., 60, 87
Kuester, T/4 Clarence O. (Jr.), 6, 37,
    59-60, 83, 99, 103, 134, 137, 147-148
Kugler, T/3 Paul H., 104, 219

Laboratory, 54, 64, 136, 168
Laboratory Technician, 6, 12
LaChance, 2nd Lt. Lola J., 25, 130, 194
La Goulette, 101
Lake McArthur, 11
La Massa, 105
Landing Craft Infantry, 124, 126
Langford, Frances, 9, 40, 145
Lardner, John, 150
La Senig, Algeria, 33
Laubengayer, Tech. Sgt. Robert E., 111
Laundry Association, 48
Lear, Gen. Ben, 13, 16-17
LeBlanc, 2nd Lt. Lillian I., 146
Le Clerc, Capt. Jean N., 220
Lee, Gen., 78
Lee, Clark, 150
Leghorn, 189
Legion of Merit, 156, 181, 211-212
Leigh, Vivien, 27
Leonard, Bill, 203
Leonard, Maj. William P. (Jr.), 5, 19,
    60, 62, 64, 75, 79, 180, 198
Les Andalouses, 32-33
Letterese, Capt., 231
Lewis, Lt. Harold, 214
Lexington, Kentucky, 5, 33, 70, 75, 157
Lido, 203
Life Magazine, 131, 139, 145-146, 150,
    153
Lincolnton, N. C., 6, 80, 100
Lindsey, 1st Lt. Odessa M., 178
Link, T/4 Frank C., 111
Linville, N. C., 130
Liri Valley, 172, 191
Lister bags, 105, 154
Liverpool, England, 20, 22, 26
Logan, 2nd Lt. Ruth O., 25
London, 21-22, 24, 26-31, 42, 48, 78-
    79, 94, 118, 122, 134, 185, 192, 196
"Lonesome Polecat, The," 179
Long, 2nd Lt. Angeline M., 211
Long Stop Hill, 97
Louisville, Kentucky, 6, 95
Lounsbury, Capt. Benjamin F., 220
Loux, T/5 Merle E., 220
Lucca, Italy, 211, 234
Lucy, T/4 Joseph B., 111
Luxembourg, 217

Macario, Jack, 40
MacArthur, Gen. Douglas, 11, 235
McCain, 1st Lt. Ruby Elnora, 6, 25, 82,
    150, 169

McCall, Capt. Robert E. (Jr.), 5, 19, 79, 173
McCaughin, Helke A., 40, 146, 228
McClain, T/4 Eugene, 228
McCuen, 1st Lt. Olive A., 220
MacDonald, Maj. J. Kingsley, 5
MacDonough, Staff Sgt. William F., 104, 218
McElwee, Second Lieut. Ruby G., 6
McGrath, Capt. Frank S. (Shorty), 19, 35, 75, 79, 104, 159, 231
MacKay, Lt. Col. W. G., 110-111
McKenzie, Jack D., 56
MacLean, Pvt. Ian (Scotty), 77, 125, 199, 201
McMahon, Pfc. John L., 228
McNarney, Lt. Gen. Joseph T., 217
McNeel, Maj. John O., 222
McVeigh, Lt. Charlotte, 220
Macon, Georgia, 201
Madzucci, Gino, 176
Maillot, 120
Maison Prunier, 27
Malaria, 50, 89, 105, 116, 127-129
Malta, 32
Manchester, N. H., 220
Manchester, Pa., 207
Mantur, 226
Marcario, Jack, 146
Marseilles, 101
Marshall, Gen. George C., 1, 2, 115, 162, 216
Marshall, Mrs. George C., 1
Martin, Brig. Gen. Joseph I., 90-91, 157, 162, 169, 215, 229-230
Martin, 2nd Lt. Winnie R., 21, 25, 54
Martinelli, Giovanni, 173
Martinez, Pfc. Ferinin, 228
Marzabotto, Italy, 223-224, 226, 229, 234
"Mason-Dixon line," 35, 37, 49, 115
"Mason-Dixon Theatre," 172, 178
Massa Marittima, 193-194, 198, 214, 233
Masten, William F. (Jr.), 6
Mateur-Ain Rhelal Road, 105
Mateur Battle, 115
Matthews, Mr., 63
Matthews, Capt. William C., 5, 19, 28, 79, 120, 129, 173, 180
Mauch Chunk, Pa., 59
Mead, Maj. Newton C., 220
Mecklenburg County Medical Society, 4
Medearis, Capt. William P. (Buck), 19, 21-22, 25-26, 28, 38, 48, 69, 74, 80, 93, 101, 115, 117, 122-124, 129, 132, 156, 163-164, 175, 179, 199, 216
Mederos, Pfc. Joseph E., 228
Medical Inspectors, 12
Medical Replacement Center, 4
Mediterranean Sea, 31, 58, 69, 77, 79, 89, 124, 141, 160, 169, 192
Medjez-el-Bab, 97, 100-101, 119
Meiktila, 226
Melfa River, 191
Mellon's Store, 65
Melnyk, Pfc. John, 199
Mendes, Olga, 202
Meritorious Service Unit Plaque, 231-232
Mers-El-Kebir, 32, 32-33, 126
Mersey River, 20
Methodist Church, 26, 100, 165, 183
Miami, 110
Middle East, 110

Milan, 235
Miller, Glenn, 172, 185
Miller, Dr. O. L., 5
Miller, Capt. Robert P., 6, 19, 54, 68, 80, 84, 94-95, 100, 105, 110, 124, 129, 199
Mills, 1st Lt. Clementine A., 21, 25, 164, 169, 199
Mines, 145-146, 172, 179, 204, 223, 235
Minnesota, University of, 118
Minovich, William, 220
Minturno, 191
Mistkowski, Vincent, 146
Mitchell, Billy, 114
Mitchell, Capt. Charles F., 163, 167, 180
Mitchell, Mitch, 173
Mizelle, 1st Lt. Margaret B., 26, 129, 169
Mohammed, 97
Mohammedans, 92
Monastery Hill, 172, 178
Monroe, N. C., 5
Monte Cassino, 177-178
Montecatini, 166, 211-213, 215, 217, 219-221, 223-225, 229, 233-234
Montgomery, Gen. Sir Bernard Law, 103, 192
Montgomery, Maj. John C., 5-8, 15, 19, 24, 38, 54, 62, 65, 74-75, 86, 89-91, 95, 105, 110-111, 117, 132-133, 136, 142, 156-157, 163, 175, 178-181, 191-192, 194, 198-199, 211, 213, 216
Montgomery, John Crowson, 6-7
Montgomery, Mildred, 62
Moody, Stowe, 26
Moore, Dr. Robert, 5
Mooresville, N. C., 6
Morais, Berta, 202
Moran, 1st Lt. Sara M., 21, 25, 169, 226
Morgenthau, Henry, 130
Morgue, 142, 147
Morphine, 46, 148-149, 154, 207
Morris, 89
Morris Field, 5, 7
Morrison, Tec. David, 224
Morrison, Roy, 42
Moscow, 223-224, 227
Moslem religion, 38, 41, 69
Mosquitoes, 49, 88-89, 181
Mother's Day, 90-91, 93
Mouzon, Bishop, 184
MTOUSA, 217, 219
Munich, 224
Munroe, Capt. Colin A., 6, 8, 19, 31, 67, 95-96, 104, 122, 129, 174, 212, 216
Munroe, Maj. Henry Stokes (Jr.), 2, 4-5, 17-22, 24, 26, 31-36, 38, 40, 42, 53-54, 63, 65, 74, 89, 96, 105, 117, 127, 130, 136-138, 140, 163, 167-168, 171-172, 176, 179-180, 188-189, 218
Murray, Sidney H., 6
Musette Bags, 102, 109
Musgrove Military Park Hospital, 24, 26, 28
Mussolini, Benito, 114, 195-196, 201
Mussolini Canal, 191
Myers, 2nd Lt. Claire S., 26
Myers, Dr. John Q., 5
Myers, T/4 Robert L., 217
Myers Park Country Club, 2, 5

Nall, Capt. Hubert H., 152
Nalle, Dr. Brodie C., 2, 3, 5

Naples, 117, 126, 128, 132-133, 136, 141, 144, 149, 151, 156, 160, 163, 169, 171, 179, 189, 192, 235
Napoleon, 55, 184
Narcotics, 208
Natalini, Capt. Carlo, 199, 235
"Native Surgery," 49
NATOUSA, 90, 104, 110-111, 117
Nattinger, Maj. John K., 152, 194
Nauch Chunk, Pa., 115
Nazis, 71, 96, 102-103, 146, 190, 224
Neal, Joseph Walton, 6
Nedisa, 179
Neely, 1st Lt. Vera M., 26, 146, 220
Neff, Pfc. Carl V., 199
Negro, 13, 29, 49, 78, 82, 89, 114, 125, 188, 121
Neil, Second Lieut. Angeline, 6
Neil, T/4 Joseph W., 52, 78, 111, 187, 204, 208, 235
Neinhouser, Elmer, 84
Neiser River, 223
Nettuno, 188-190, 193, 232-233
Neubauer, Pvt. Charles L. (Butch), 207, 228
Neuro-surgery, 148-152, 226
New Bedford, Mass., 207
New England, 49, 115
New Jersey, 20
New Orleans, 123
New Year's Day, 164, 166-168, 205, 217
"New York Avenue," 35, 54
New York City, 20, 22, 49-50, 63, 68, 94, 112, 116, 149, 185, 207, 233
"New York Hotel," 43
New York Port of Embarkation, 17, 20
New Zealand, 31, 178
Newspapers:
    Charlotte News, 25, 55, 59-60
    Charlotte Observer, 2, 46, 55, 59, 65, 67, 97, 116-117
    The Chicago Sun, 59
Newspapers, Service:
    APW (Polish) 217
    Basic News (Compiled by PWB), 217
    Crusader, 217
    Daily Bulletin, 75, 80-81, 89-91, 103-105, 110-111, 117-119, 127-130, 135-136, 138, 142, 152, 154, 157-159, 162-169, 175, 177-178, 180-181, 183, 186, 188-190, 192, 194, 198-199, 202-203, 211-213, 215-220, 223-224, 226-231
    Daily News, 190-191
    Eighth Army News, 217
    Maple Leaf, 217
    NZEF Times, 217
    Parade, 217
    Stars and Stripes, 191-192, 217
    Union Jack, 217
    Yank, 217
Nichols, Amy, 95
Nicholson, Walter, 133
Niemeyer, Lt., 90
Nocelletto, Italy, 178
Normandy, 192
North Africa, 33-37, 42, 47, 49, 60, 62, 67-68, 77-78, 84-89, 92-99, 101, 103-105, 111-116, 120-121, 125-126, 128, 130, 135, 141, 143, 145, 147, 157-158, 160-161, 205, 213, 226, 230.
North American Newspaper Alliance, 102

North Carolina, 18, 50, 59-60, 70, 78, 86, 130, 157, 203, 212
Northcentral Africa, 79
Northwest Africa, 43, 62-63, 67, 71, 86
Norton, Lt. Col. Roy, 78
Norton Manor Camp, 25-26, 28, 31, 62
Norway, 96, 226-227
Notre Dame, 196
Nowacki, Capt. Stanley M., 19, 80, 142, 156, 163, 194, 199, 231
Nunes, Maj. Ari D., 202
Nunez, T/5 Dewey J., 228
Nurses, 4, 6, 9, 12-17, 18, 21-22, 24, 26, 33-35, 43, 45-50, 52, 54, 59-60, 62, 66-71, 74-76, 78-79, 82, 86, 89-95, 102, 105, 111-112, 115, 122-123, 125, 128, 131, 136, 140, 142-146, 150-153, 163-164, 166-167, 173, 178-179, 193, 200, 202, 204, 206-214, 220, 223, 229-230, 234

Ocheltree, 1st Lt. Marguriete, 220
Oder River, 223-224
O'Donnell, Staff Sgt. James J., 219
Ogle, Pvt. Charles L., 142, 228
Okinawa, 227
Olympic Games, 201
Omnibook, 203
Operas, 156, 171-175, 201, 203
Operation Shingle, 188-189
Oran, Algeria, 31-34, 36, 45-46, 57, 59, 62-63, 74-76, 78, 98, 112, 115, 120-122, 127-128, 160, 182
Ortego, Cpl. Irenio M., 228
Osorio, Lucia, 202

Pacific, 108, 114, 135, 149, 216, 222, 235
Paddington Station, 27, 29
Paestum, Italy, 35, 116, 127, 129, 182, 232
Pajak, Cpl. Joseph, 228
Palermo, 118
Pamphilli, see Doria Pamphilli
Pantelleria, 106
Pantheon, 203
"Parade, The," 35, 54
Parco, 156
Pardiker, Pvt. Steve J., 228
Paretta, Italy, 234
Paris, France, 196
Paris, Kentucky, 76
Parks, 2nd Lt. Madelyn N., 224
Patronik, T/5 Sigismund, 199
Patton, Gen. George, 226
Payne, Capt. Joseph T., 223
Pearl Harbor, 4
Pedrick, Master Sgt. Frank B., 104, 127, 135, 192, 233
Pegram, 2nd Lt. Martha, 21, 25, 158
Pennington, Lt. Col. William H., 5, 19, 33-34, 59, 62, 65, 70, 74, 121, 156, 167, 175, 183, 198, 218-220, 223, 229-231, 235
Pennington, Mrs. William H., 33
Pennsylvania, 13, 48
"Pennsylvania Ave.," 35, 54
Perkins, Capt. J. W., 208
Perry, Capt. Claud Walter (Jr.), 5-6, 19, 31, 74, 127, 136, 220
Perry, Capt. Glenn G., 5, 19, 31
Perryman, 1st Lt. Olin C., 19, 31, 116
Pharmacist, 6, 12, 52, 73, 78, 116, 187, 204, 208, 235

Pharmacy, 115-116, 142, 187, 204
Phifer, Maj. Edward M., 217
Philadelphia, Pa., 20, 86, 95, 100
Piazza Venezia, 195-196
Pickens, Robert, 27, 29, 38, 42, 48, 78, 118
Pickens, Maj. Stanton W., 6-7, 9, 11-14, 16-17, 19, 21-23, 25-26, 28-30, 36-38, 40-43, 48, 55-60, 63-73, 75, 77-79, 81-102, 105-110, 112-115, 117-118, 121-127, 130-135, 140-142, 154-156, 159-177, 180-186, 188, 192, 194-203, 208, 212, 218, 221
Pickens, Mrs. Stanton W. (Mary), 9-11, 17, 26, 59, 66, 170, 201-202
Pickens, Col. Wiley, 145
Pico, 191
Pilger, 1st Lt. Gladys P., 26, 169
Piperato, Staff Sgt. Adam J., 219
Pisa, Sgt. Anthony C., 228
Pisa, Italy, 176, 198, 202-211, 213, 218, 222, 224, 233
Pisa, Leaning Tower of, 203-204, 206
Pisani, Capt. Joseph L., 220
Pisinsky, 1st Lt. Pauline P., 26, 220
Pitts, Maj. William R., 19, 27, 53, 62, 69, 74, 112, 148-152, 158-159, 226
Pittsburgh, Pa., 65, 224
Pittsburgh, University of, 12
Pius XII, Pope, 194, 196, 201
Piwowarski, Cpl. John J., 228
Plain, Lt. Col. Louis, 46
Po River, 226
Po Valley, 213
Poland, 95
Polish, 109
Pollo, Pvt. Mike, 199
Pomerance, 198
Pompeii, 128, 133
Pomper, Capt. Irving, 142, 152
Pontecorvo, 191
Port of Algiers, 31
Porte de Bab-el-Kadra, 98
Porte de France, 98
Porter, Capt. Charles Bryant, 6, 19, 120, 127, 212
Porter, Pfc. George R., 219, 228
Portocarrero, Virginia N., 202
Potash, 104
Poughkeepsie, N. Y., 147
Powers, 1st Lt. John S. (Jr.), 19, 28, 77, 142
Prague, 227
Presbyterian Church, 150
Presidential election, 199, 203
Presque Isle, 57, 110
Pricskett, Tech. Sgt. William J., 61, 111
Princeton University, 222
Prisoner of war camp, 97
Prisoners, 95-97, 100, 102-103, 115, 117, 143, 186, 190, 197, 211, 226-227, 232-235
Psychiatrist, 152
Psychopathic cases, 188
Pugh, Capt. George E., 19, 218-219, 231
Purdy, T/3 Charles L., 111
Purple Heart, 57, 59, 110
PX, 208, 228
Pyle, Ernie, 44-50, 52-53, 67, 78, 94, 115, 122, 148, 150

Quebec, 119
Query, Maj. Richard Z. (Jr.), 2, 5, 16,

19, 34, 53, 62, 74, 105, 146, 156, 159, 171
Quinine, 89, 128

Rabaul, 135
Radigan, 2nd Lt. Cathaleen V., 25
Raeford, N. C., 6
RAF, 37, 121, 174, 224, 226
Ragsdale, T/5 Noah W., 228
Rangers, 33, 62
Rankin, Brig. Gen. Fred W., 70, 157-158
Rankin, Dr. W. S., 70, 157
Rapido River, 152, 172
Rasmussen, Capt. Earl, 178
Ravello, 156
Rawles, Maj. Benjamin (Jr.), 220
Raymer, Capt. Jack L., 224
Read, Benjamin S., 222
"Rebel Street," 49, 58
Rebels, 35, 37, 48
Red Cross, 21, 29, 39, 42, 49, 80, 86-88, 93, 97, 102-103, 106, 123, 140, 142, 146, 155-156, 177, 185, 198, 206, 216, 219
Regan, Pvt. Marvin, 110
Republican Party, 199
Rex, T/5 Walter A., 77, 228
Reynolds, Norman S., 40
Rheims, 227
Riano, Pvt. William G., 228
Riardo, Italy, 131-132, 136-138, 140, 153, 171, 178
Riardo-Vairano encampment, 131-132, 134-135, 137, 138, 140, 147
Richardson, Stanley, 27
Ripkoski, Pfc. Herman W., 228
Robbins, 1st Lt. Frances L., 26, 220
Roberts, Cpl. Harry, 207
Robinsdale, Minnesota, 206
Robinson, T/5 Gerard J., 220
Robinson, Richard B., 116
Rodgers, Kate, 95
Rodman, 2nd Lt. Catherine M., 152
Rodstein, Lt. Leah, 45, 146, 220
Rogers, Maj., 231
Roman Forum, 196, 203
Romans, 69, 84-85, 98-99, 101, 106, 132, 160, 169, 182, 197
Rome, 40-41, 84, 130, 136-137, 160, 172, 179, 185-186, 189, 191-202, 221, 233
Roosevelt, Pres. Franklin D., 4, 45, 55, 90, 103, 109, 114, 118-119, 138, 158, 199, 216, 220
Roosevelt, Mrs. Franklin D., 220
Roosevelt, Gen. Theodore (Jr.), 42, 59, 78
Roosevelt, Mrs. Theodore (Jr.), 42
Rosalie, 71-72
Rosen, S/Sgt. Maurice J., 228
Ross, 2nd Lt. Eva L., 224
Rowe, 1st Lt. George C., 6, 8, 19, 28, 38
Roy, T/5 Henry S., 228
Royal Rensselaers, 96
Rue d'Algers, 113
Rue Es Sadikia, 113
Ruff, 2nd Lt. Marguerite, 152
Russell, 1st Lt. Lela O., 4, 21-22, 25, 61, 65, 154, 168, 197, 218, 230, 234
Russell, Capt. Walter A., 220
Russia, 95-96, 108-110, 223, 227
Russians, 97, 135, 186, 190, 226, 234

Sacks, Eva, 95
Saide, Pvt. Abraham Casper Leon, 50, 52
Sailors, 100, 109, 124, 127, 158
St. Agnes Catacomb, 197
St. Barbe, 121
St. Cloud, Algeria, 32, 34-39, 41, 51, 53, 55, 62-63, 67, 71, 73-76, 80, 89
St. George's Church, 84
St. Giles Cathedral, 26
St. James Palace, 27
St. Louis, Missouri, 103
St. Luce, 52, 198-199, 202
St. Martin-in-the-Fields, 27
St. Martin's Episcopal Church, 183
St. Paul's Cathedral, 24, 27, 196
Saint Peter's, 156, 195-196, 198, 201
Saipan, 149
Salerno, 128, 130, 157, 160, 164, 181, 189, 192
Saline, 138
Saline, Italy, 198
Salisbury, England, 22, 26, 30
Salisbury, N. C., 9
Salsomaggiore, Italy, 227, 229, 234-235
San Carlo Opera Company, 172-173
San Francisco, Calif., 60
Sanger, Lt. Col. Paul W., 1-5, 8, 18-19, 27, 33-34, 38, 48, 59-60, 64-65, 68, 70-71, 74, 78, 93, 101, 105, 115, 117, 123, 147, 150, 152, 157, 175, 218
Sansom, Capt. Cecil P. (Chaplain), 181, 202, 207, 233
Santa Lucia, Africa, 67
Santelli, Pvt. Lawrence J., 142
Sardinia, 106
Sarris, Maj. Spiros P., 220
Satre, 1st Lt. Pearl M., 219
Schenck, Alec, 172-173
Schirmer, Capt. Robert H., 5, 19, 28, 69, 80, 90, 94, 127, 192
Schmidt, Sgt. Edward F., 104
Schneider, Capt. Richard, 149
Schultz, S/Sgt. Simon, 228
Scipio Africanus the Elder, 101
Scripps-Howard Newspapers, 45
Sears, Corp. Kenneth R., 111
Second Auxiliary Surgical Group, 152, 220-221, 224
"Second Street," 35, 43, 54
Seelye, Janet, 219
Seesel, 1st Lt. Howard J., 199
Seine Bay, 192
Sellers, T/4 Gardner C., 228
Semeraro, T/4 Frank N., 228
Senegalese, 98, 100
Serchio Valley, 221
Serino, T/5 Anthony, 217
Setif, 120
Sexton, Pfc. Jasper, 228
Shaeffer, T/4 Joseph C., 199
Shakelford, Lt. Col., 222
Shearer, 2nd Lt. Mary V., 152
Shelby, N. C., 6
Shields, 1st Lt. Nellie C. (Nelia), 21, 26, 169
Shipp, Capt. Rosamond S., 25, 35, 54, 127, 154, 218
Ships:
    H.M.S. Andes, 20-21
    U.S.S. Arkansas, 20
    H.M.S. Malta, 28, 31
    U.S.S. Missouri, 235

D.S.S. Nieuw Zeeland, 26, 62
H.M.S. Otranto, 126-127
Shobert, Pvt. Jack L., 228
Sicily, 101, 106, 110, 115, 117, 119, 121, 128, 145, 192
Sidell, Pfc. William P., 221
Sidi-Bou-Said, 101
Silver, 100
Silver Springs, Florida, 171
Simmons, 1st Lt. Hazel Ann, 6, 21, 25, 153, 168
Simpson, Staff Sgt. Howard S., 104, 207
Sirocco, 121
Sistine Chapel, 196, 201
Skoda arms plant, 226
Sleezer, 2nd Lt. Carol F., 217
Smith, Lt. Gen., 227
Smith, Pfc. Melvin R., 228
Smith, T/3 William E., 104, 219
Smoliar, Pfc. Milton J., 228
Snell, Capt. Eugene M., 162, 180, 219, 230-231
Snyder, Maj. George C., 6, 8, 16, 19, 23, 25, 28, 35, 38, 48, 60, 63, 65, 68, 78-80, 90, 104-105, 117, 127, 142, 159, 179-180, 210, 213, 219, 222-223, 229, 232-233
Soares, 2nd Lt. Ari A., 202
Somerset, England, 24, 26, 28
Somersworth, New Hampshire, 220
Sorenger, 1st Lt. Eunishis H., 224
Sorrento, 128, 133, 144, 156, 169-172, 199
Sotirion, Capt. George A., 5, 19, 129, 180, 203, 212
Souks, 100
South Africa, 140, 234
South Carolina, 50, 59-60, 78
South Pacific, 17
Southern Surgical Association, 158
Spaatz, Lt. Gen., 154
Spain, 31-32, 55, 101, 171
Spanish Morocco, 31-32
Sparrow, Dr. Thomas D., 3
Spears, 1st Lt. Loretta P., 220
Speer, 1st Lt. David, 220
Spree River, 224
Spring Lake (N. C.), 5, 7
Spry, T/5 Howard J., 228
Stack, T/5 Theodore, 228
Stahl, Robert G., 125
Stalin, Marshal, 220
"Standard Operating Procedure," 186, 222
Staten Island, 186
Stayer, Maj. Gen., 219
Stefanchik, T/5 John A., 228
Stein, Capt. Martin, 220
Stillwell, Joe, 222
Stimson, Henry L., 1, 127-128, 162, 196, 216
Stimson, Mrs. Henry L., 1
Stith, Capt. Robert B., 5, 16, 19, 25, 28, 53, 62, 74, 136, 138, 219
Strand, Bill, 150
Striker, 176, 183
Submarines, 32, 108
Sulfa drugs, 88
Sulfadiazine, 150
Sulfanilamide, 45, 60
Sullivan, Mary Ann, 95
Sulphur pools, 201
Summerville, Dr. W. M., 5

Surowitz, Pvt. Stanley C., 204
Susladatov, Maj. Gen., 227
Swastika, 96
Sweden, Queen of, 196
Swenson, Pfc. Gordon C., 228
Switzerland, 58-59
Syria, 68

Taake, Edith, 103
Tabi, Pvt. Israel, 50, 85
Tafaraoui, Algeria, 33
Talbottom, Georgia, 203
Tangiers, 31, 135, 186
Tarikan Island, 227
Taunton, Somerset, England, 24, 26, 28
Tavernanouva, Italy, 136
Teano, 136
Tedder, Air Marshal, 103
Telergma, Algeria, 74, 80-82, 86-89, 118, 143
Terracina, 191
Tetzlaff, 1st Lt. Marie, 207, 221, 223
Texas, 7, 151
Texas, Univ. of, 169
Thanksgiving Day, 41, 138, 140, 143-144, 158, 212-213
Thibar, 104
Thompson, 2nd Lt. Mary Lahome, 6
Thompson, Dr. Raymond, 2, 5
"Thunderbirds," 191
Tiber River, 196
Tiberius, 132, 169, 171
Tidworth, England, 22, 26
Tidworth Park, 22, 24, 26, 30
Tiergarten, 226
Time magazine, 114-117
Timgad, 84-86
Tivoli, Italy, 201
Todd, Capt. John C., 223-224, 229
Tokyo, 108-110
Toscana, 208
Toungoo, 226
Touristico, 156
Townsend, 1st Lt. Mary E., 211, 220
Toy Town Salvage Corps, 29
Trafford, Bob, 150
Trainor, Lt., 90
Tregaskis, Richard, 148-150
Trescott, Col. John, 145, 166, 177, 198, 205, 210, 214
Triage, 151
Trivison, Pfc. Daniel J., 228
Troy, 99
Truman, Pres. Harry S., 220, 226
Truscott, Lt. Gen. L. K. (Jr), 213, 215, 218
Tuggle, Dr. Allan, 5
Tunis, 52-53, 76, 83, 89, 91, 97-101, 104-105, 108, 113-117, 119-121, 143, 160, 165, 186, 232
Tunisia, 76, 91-92, 94-98, 102-103, 105-106, 112-113, 169, 232
Tunisian Palace Hotel, 105
Tuscany, 200, 205
Typhoid, 82, 85
Typhus, 17, 93, 100, 163, 171
Tyrrhean Sea, 178
Tysarczyk, T/4 Richard J., 217
Tyson, Capt. Thomas D., 16, 19, 67-68, 90, 104, 122, 174

"Ulio, Washington, D. C.," 5
United Nations, 138, 164, 189-190

U. S. Adjutant General, 4
U. S. Air Corps, 9, 76, 106, 108-109, 112, 115, 130, 131, 132, 134, 154-155, 201; Ordnance Dept., 115; Parachute troops, 134
U. S. Army, 11-14, 18, 54, 59, 65-66, 69-70, 80, 86-88, 91-93, 97, 114-115, 118, 122-123, 135, 143-144, 156, 159, 163, 167, 169, 176, 182, 184-185, 194-198, 200, 204, 223
 First Army, 98
 Second Army, 11-14, 17
 Third Army, 224
 Fifth Army, 31, 74, 90-91, 119, 128, 130, 133, 136, 140, 152, 155, 157-158, 162-164, 167-169, 171-172, 175, 178-179, 188-193, 199-202, 205, 212-213, 215, 218-219, 226, 230-231
 Eighth Army, 98, 192, 201, 203, 213, 218, 226
 15th Army, 213, 218
U. S. Army Medical Corps, 5, 3, 45, 102, 194, 212, 218, 226
U. S. Army, Quartermaster Corps, 13
U. S. Engineer Corps, 35-36, 62, 136, 145, 186, 198
U. S. Marine Corps, 46, 100
U. S. Merchant Marines, 133
U. S. Navy, 14, 20, 60, 123, 134, 216
U. S. Secretary of Treasury, 130
U. S. Secretary of War, 3, 4, 127-128, 162, 196, 216
U. S. Signal Corps, 142, 185
U. S. Surgeon General of the Army, 2, 3, 4, 62, 70, 74, 90-91, 157-158
U. S. War Dept., 1, 2, 3, 4, 55, 156, 161
Utley, Capt., 202

V-E Day, 227
Vairano, Italy, 131-132, 134, 137, 140, 142-143, 145-146, 175, 178, 182, 232
Valadares, Altanira, 202
Valentine's Day, 79
Van Buren, Maine, 57, 93
Vatican, 196, 201
Vaughn, 2nd Lt. William E., 56, 104, 197, 219
Vecchio Bridge, 209
Velletri, 191
Venereal disease, 50, 64, 115

Veronica's Veil, 196
Vesuvius, 133, 183
Victor, 2nd Lt. Julia E., 211
Victor Emmanuel, 133
Victoria, Queen, 27
Victoria Hotel, 133
Victorine, 1st Lt. Charles, 218
Villa Abamalik, 198
Villa D'Este, 201
Virginia, 13, 18, 222
Virginia, Univ. of, 70
Virginia Military Institute, 1
Vittorio Hotel, 156, 172
Volturno River, 126, 136, 172

WACs, 122, 177
Waide, George, 220
Wake Forest, N. C., 213
Waldorf Hotel, 157
Waldrop, Col., 5
Wales, 220
Walker, Maj. Bernard N., 6, 19, 25, 28, 38, 79, 81, 90, 129, 135, 136, 159, 163, 180, 193, 199-201
War College, 183
"Ward 13," 149
Waring, Pvt. Donald E., 228
Warm Springs, Ga., 220
Warren, Lt. Col. Robert O. Y., 199, 218
Wasden, Charlie, 201
Washington D. C., 1, 4, 5, 7, 9, 49, 56, 62, 66, 70, 135, 157-158, 176, 183, 226-227
Water supply, 54, 60, 78-80, 85, 91-92, 98-99, 105, 115, 117, 119-121, 124-125, 128, 132, 141-142, 144-145, 154, 161, 165, 167, 176, 181, 183
Waterloo Station, 27
Wayne University, 149
Waynesville, N. C., 95
Webb, 2nd Lt. Marcia N., 224
Webber, 1st Lt. Charlotte Jean, 26, 33, 43, 45, 75-77, 88, 169, 193, 214
Webster, Jack, 149
Weinberg, Maj. Arthur A., 224
Weinheimer, Tech. 4th Grade Leonard (NMN), 111, 197
Wells, 1st Lt. Elva Earle, 6, 21, 25, 33, 45, 67, 82, 88, 122, 193, 214, 218
Welsh, 37
West Africa, 169

West Englewood, N. J., 207
West Virginia, 222
Western Task Force, 31
Westminster Abbey, 27, 29
Weston, Capt. Charles L., 152
Whatley, Bob, 57
Whisnant, Albert, 80
White, Sgt. Paul, 77
White, Lt. Col. Thomas Preston, 2, 4, 5, 8-9, 16, 18-19, 27, 48, 64-65, 69, 74, 85, 111-112, 114-115, 117-118, 122-123, 150, 162, 171
Whittier, Col. Raymond W., 5, 8, 10, 15, 17, 19, 22, 24-27, 62
Williams, Capt. McChord, 5, 19, 79, 90, 104
Williamson, Stanley, 203
Wills, 1st Lt. Christine, 21, 26, 122, 169
Wilmington, Delaware, 199
Wilts County, 22, 26
Wingo, 1st Lt. Barbara L., 26, 67, 218
Winston-Salem, N. C., 27
Winter Line, 172, 188
Wittler, 1st Lt. Billie, 220
Wood, Col. George Thomas (Jr.), 2, 5-6, 38, 51, 64, 68, 70-71, 73, 78, 115, 117, 119, 127, 150, 158-159, 163-164, 167-169, 175, 178, 181, 193-194, 199, 205, 211-213, 215-218
Woodall, Dr. Barnes, 149
World War I, 4, 5, 69
Wright, Mrs., 86
Wright, Capt. Harold S., 142, 163, 167, 229, 231
Wrork, Capt. Donald, 224

X-ray room, 49, 54, 136, 142, 146, 151, 154, 165
X-ray technician, 6, 12, 52, 62, 81
X-rays, 111, 116, 122, 137-139, 146, 174-175

Yankauer, Maj. Alfred (Jr.), 5, 8, 16, 19, 231
Yellow fever, 17
Yellow Sea, 108
Yemen, 50
Young, T/5 William, 228

Zhukov, Marshal, 224
Zies, Lt. Col. F. W., 28

INDEX OF ILLUSTRATIONS

Almond, Capt. Hallie E., 155, 219, 231
Ambrose, Technician James, 139
Anzio, 91, 180-181
Arnold, Gen. H. H. (Hap), 155
Astrackon, Pvt. Raymond, 44
Augustine, Capt. Robert W., 219

Bachoka, 1st Lt. Margaret P., 200
Bauchspies, Lt. Col. Rollin L., 38
Beja Hospital encampment, 103
Benante, 1st Lt. Lorraine M., 166
Blandford, 1st Lt. Mary F., 21, 82, 122
Brooke, Lucy, 155, 216

Burgess, 2nd Lt. Violet O. B., 131

Calder, Capt. Duncan G. (Jr.), 8, 25, 28, 53, 121, 143
Casanova Park, 64
Clark, Gen. Mark W., 52, 155, 212
Cologgi, Louis F., 56
Cotton, Pvt. Russell B., 142
"Cotton's Dog House," 142
Coviello, Edmond, 220

Dahn, Sgt. Robert W. (Skin Head), 168
Davis, Sgt. Randall K., 139, 165

Dickson, R. S., 2
Doria Pamphilli encampment, 193

Elliott, Sgt. Vincent J., 142
Evans, Capt. William (Jr), 35

Felts, Capt. James R. (Jr.), 28
Fullbright, 1st Lt. Bessie Viola, 4, 51

Gleba, Sgt. Joseph, 42
Gower, Sgt. Ralph, 44
Grant, Technician George, 165
Groff, Jacob, 43

Guyett, 2nd Lt. Edith E., 125

Heaton, 1st Lt. Annette M., 41, 44
Hoffman, 1st Lt. Milo Johnson, 8, 118, 170, 216
Hope, Bob, 10
Hough, 1st Lt. Bertha Elizabeth, 21

Ierulli, Nichola, 165
Imes, Maj. Pat. R., 34

Jensen, 2nd Lt. Madeline L., 200
Johnson, 2nd Lt. Beatrice E., 21
Jones, Capt. Hunter, 214

Kavanagh, Capt. William P., 96, 109
Kendrick, Maj. Vaiden B., 8, 25, 28, 57, 170
Killeen, 2nd Lt. Elizabeth E., 122
Kirkpatrick, Capt. James E., 233
Knopp, Wilbur, 40

Lewis, Lt. Harold, 214
Lister Bag, 154

Macario, Jack, 40
McCain, 2nd Lt. Ruby Elnora, 82
McCaughin, Helke A., 40
McGrath, Capt. Frank S. (Shorty), 35, 104
McKenzie, Jack D., 56
MacLean, Pvt. Ian (Scotty), 77, 125
Martin, 2nd Lt. Winnie R., 21
Matthews, Capt. William C., 28
Medearis, Capt. William P. (Buck), 25, 28, 101, 215
Miller, 1st Lt. Robert P., 95
Mills, 1st Lt. Clementine A., 21
Minovich, William, 220
Montecatini encampment, 221, 224-225
Montgomery, Maj. John C., 216

Moran, 1st Lt. Sara M., 21, 216, 226
Morrison, Roy, 42
Munroe, Capt. Colin A., 8, 67, 95-96, 104, 122, 174, 216
Munroe, Maj. Henry Stokes, (Jr.), 2, 96, 218

Neil, Joe, 78
North Africa, map showing operation "Torch," 32

Officers and Nurses of the 38th Evacuation Hospital, 14-15
Ogle, Pvt. Charles L., 142

Pegram, 2nd Lt. Martha, 21
Pennington, Lt. Col. William H., 34, 59, 121
Pickens, Maj. Stanton W., 23, 25, 28
Pisa flood, 205-209
Pitts, Maj. William R., 148
Powers, 1st Lt. John S. (Jr.), 77
Pricskett, Sgt. William J., 61
Pyle, Ernie, 44

Query, Maj. Richard Z., 2, 34

Rex, Pvt. Walter, 77
Reynolds, Norman S., 40
Riardo-Vairano encampment, 131-132, 134-135, 137
Robinson, Richard B., 116
Rodstein, Lt. Leah, 45
Rowe, 1st Lt. George C., 8
Russell, Lt. Lela O., 4, 61, 154, 197, 230, 234

St. Cloud Hospital, 37, 39, 46, 47, 51, 56, 58, 61, 64, 85, 92, 96, 109
Sanger, Lt. Col. Paul W., 2, 18, 34, 38, 101

Sansom, Capt. Cecil P., 233
Santa Lucia, Africa, 67
Santelli, Pvt. Lawrence J., 142
Shields, 1st Lt. Nellie C. (Nelia), 21
Shipp, 1st Lt. Rosamond S., 154
Simmons, 1st Lt. Hazel Ann, 21, 153
Snyder, Maj. George C., 8, 23, 25, 28, 35, 104, 222, 229
Stahl, Robert G., 125
Stith, Capt. Robert B., 25, 28, 53

Tabi, Pvt. Israel, 85
Telergma, Algeria hospital encampment, 87, 107
Thompson, Dr. Raymond, 2
Tidworth Park encampment, 30
Tunis encampment, 83, 99, 113
Tyson, Capt. Thomas D., 67, 104, 122, 174

Vaughn, Sgt. William E., 56, 197

Waide, George, 220
Walker, Maj. Bernard N., 25, 28
Webber, 2nd Lt. Charlotte Jean, 33, 45, 88, 214
Weinheimer, Leonard, 197
Wells, 1st Lt. Elva Earle, 21, 33, 45, 67, 82, 88, 122, 214
White, Sgt. Paul, 77
White, Lt. Col. Thomas Preston, 2, 18, 85, 162
Whittier, Col. Raymond W., 6, 10, 15
Williams, Capt. McChord, 104
Wills, 1st Lt. Christine, 21, 122
Wingo, 2nd Lt. Barbara L., 67
Wood, Col. George Thomas (Jr.), 2, 6, 51, 212

Yankauer, Maj. Alfred (Jr.), 8